KB250728

2011 청주국제공예비엔날레
Cheongju International Craft Biennale 2011

2011년 9월 21일 - 2011년 10월 30일

21 September 2011 - 30 October 2011

2011 청주국제공예비엔날레

2011년 9월 21일 - 10월 30일

인쇄일 2011년 9월 15일
발행일 2011년 9월 20일

지은이 2011 청주국제공예비엔날레 조직위원회

펴낸이 이상만
펴낸곳 마로니에북스
주소 413-756 경기도 파주시 교하읍 문발리 파주출판도시 521-2
전화 02)741-9191(대표) 031)955-4919(편집부)
전송 031)955-4921
홈페이지 www.maroniebooks.com
출판등록 2003년 4월 14일
등록번호 제 2003-71호
ISBN 978-89-6053-215-1

이 도록의 저작권은 2011 청주국제공예비엔날레에 있습니다.
출판이나 사진사용, 영상물 복제등 일체의 행위는 본 비엔날레의 허락을 얻어야 가능합니다.

2011 Cheongju International Craft Biennale

21 September 2011 - 30 October 2011

©2011 Cheongju International Craft Biennale
Published Maroniebooks Co.
413-756
521-2 PajuBookCity Munbal-ri Gyoha-eup Paju-si Gyeonggi-do, KOREA
Tel 02)741-9191
Fax 031)955-4921
Home Page www.maroniebooks.com

All materials contained on this book are protected by KOREA copyright law and may not be reproduced, distributed, transmitted, displayed, published or broadcast without the prior written permission of 2011 CHEONGJU International Craft Biennale

Copyright in all countries.

Printed in Korea

ISBN 978-89-6053-215-1

의자, 걷다

Chairs, Flow

마로니에북스

Exhibition
전시

주최 청주시
Host Cheongju City

총감독 Director
정준모 Chung, Joon Mo

총괄큐레이터 Chief Curator
박남희 Park, Nam Hee

큐레이터 Associate Curator
윤효진 Yoon, Hyo Jin

전시디자인 Exhibition Design
이상철 Lee, Sang Chul

전시장 시공 Production
휴먼_C Human_C

장 관 Jang, Gwan
백지영 Back, Ji Young
박수현 Park, Su Hyun
이재웅 Lee, Jae Ung
신대철 Shin, Dae Cheol
김대형 Kim, Dae Hyoung

Acknowledgement
감사의 말씀

2011 청주국제공예비엔날레를 위하여 기꺼이 작품을 대여해 주신 국내외 미술관, 화랑, 개인 소장가 그리고 기관과 단체에 마음으로부터 고맙다는 말씀을 드립니다. 이 분들은 청주국제공예비엔날레가 세계 공예의 중심이 되도록 물심양면으로 도와주시고 조언을 아끼지 않았습니다.
아울러 기꺼이 작품을 출품해주신 작가와 그 어시스턴트 분들께도 감사의 말씀을 올립니다.

2011 Cheongju International Craft Biennale would like to thank
museum, galleries and private collectors for generously lending their art works.
A Special thanks to the exhibiting artists and theirs assistants.

강익중	이세섭	전문인력사업단
김미정	이영배	_croft
김방은/예화랑	이옥경/가나아트갤러리	UNICEF
김복기	이 일	ZIG
김승민/국제갤러리	이지미	Anna Jackson
김수경	이지영	Anna Rikkinen
김언정	이호숙	David Revere McFadden
김영호	이호재/가나아트갤러리	Dmitry Shevchenko
김인혜	이현숙/국제갤러리	Dominique Forest
김진영	이현희/서울옥션	Huuhtanen Riitta
김진하	임일균	Judy Kim
김태철	임용섭	Jukka Savolainen
노경조	준초이	Junichi Shibata
도형태/갤러리 현대	정연진	Kaisa Leidy
류민자	정영산	Kaori Tabata
류소영	정우진	Klaus Klemp
류지연	정윤지/가나아트갤러리	Kozo Kumamoto
류태희	정종효	Maarten Bertheux
마영범	정창수	Madeleine Hoffmann
맹완호	정 현	Pekka Wuoristo
박경미/PKM갤러리	조영하	Rebecca Kong
박경희	조희경	Ria Hawthorn
박동은	최윤석/서울옥션	Rupert Faulkner
박명자/갤러리 현대	최인경/가나아트갤러리	Sarah Davies
박영주	국립국악원	Satu Iivarinen-Roth
박필재	고양문화재단	Stefan Lee
박혜경	대지를 위한 바느질	Stephan von der Schulenburg
소육영/서울옥션	마로니에북스	Tohru Matsumoto
송향선/가람화랑	명보랑	Tomoko Ogawa
서지형	순천제일대학	Artware Edition NY
성동제	우리들 체어	Brain Trust Inc.
신경숙	이가스퀘어	Copenhagen Design Center
양성진	이건산업	Design Museo, Helsinki
오유정	이랜드 문화재단	Embassy of Finland, Seoul
우찬규/학고재	임옥미술관	Galerie Pierre-Alain Challier
운지원/예화랑	주영 한국문화원	HAKONE Open-air Museum
유재응/진화랑	청주시 새마을 부녀회	Judd Foundation
유진환	코스모 양행	Kauniste
윤명로	풀집박물관	LAPPONIA JEWELRY OY
윤애영	한국공예관	Les Arts Decoratifs, Paris
원용기	한국문화재 보호재단	Möbel Museum Wien
이규현	한국미술품 감정가협회	London Design Museum
이동준	한국아트체인	Museum für Angewandte Kunst, Frankfurt
이병혜	한국주요무형문화재 기능보존협회	Museum of Arts and Design, NY
이상만	한국화랑협회	Osaka City Museum of Modern Art,
이상철	한향림 세라믹 뮤지엄	Planning Office
이성춘	홍익대학교 BK21 메타디자인센터	Ornamo

Books
도록

편집장 | Chief Editor
정준모 Chung, Joon Mo

편집 | Editing
윤효진 Yoon, Hyo Jin

디자인 | Design
최우정 Choi, Woo Jung
이종훈 Lee, Jong Hoon

번역 | Translation
김애림 Kim, Ae Lim
김정혜 Kim, Jung Hae
이경애 Lee, Kyoung Aea
이현경 Lee, Hyun Kyung
장   원 Chang, Won

제작 | Publisher
이상만 Lee, Sang Man

Contents 목차

Chair, an Art of Everyday Life

Chung, Joon Mo
Director, Cheongju International Craft Biennale 2011

Why a Chair again?

A chair has various meanings. It represents the user's social position and honor, and can provide efficiency and rest, while at the same time exhibiting beauty and regulation. Through the diverse aspects, a chair has become indispensable for human's relaxation in particular and long-time labors. Today, it has transformed to be a part of the human body, used in everyday life, as one hardly notices that a chair is barely 'there.'

In order to understand how the chair has become a part of 'nature,' we need to comprehend how it has changes over time; how it has developed into an object of craft. In the book, *The Chair: Rethinking Culture, Body and Design*, architect Galen Cranz traces back to the meaning, symbols, lives, culture, and the social significance of chairs, that has been taken for granted due to its mundane character. According to her essay, the emotional sense we would get from a chair results from nothing other than its shape and symbolism. In this case, a chair is not merely an extension of the human body, but a cultural product, meaning, as a cultural mirror which reflects its time. Therefore, a chair is a personal and microscopic being when it represents its user's status, authority, and personality, whereas it becomes a macroscopic being which contains a great epochal and social discussion.

During the ancient period, in mythical ideology, a chair was of a supernatural symbol that only gods sat on. Later, during the Ontological era of scientific, rational criteria with an absolute value, a chair was a symbol of human's political power, owned only by male gender; it replaced the position of the gods. Seeing that only men could be seated on a chair during the thirteenth century, a chair represented political authority and power. After the nineteenth century, an era of functionality emerged under the influence of Modernism, and a chair became something personal exposing relative values and individual tastes.

In spite of its long history, it has only been a whort period of time since the chair has been seen to function like today. For thousands of years, its role was limited merely as a means of authority's ostentation or as supplementary for dignities display rather that its practical use. In fact, a chair was regarded as a precious object until the sixteenth-century when the Renaissance closed its era. The tradition still lingers today in cases where the president of a group is called a "chairman" in the Western culture and the premier of a communist party is the "main seat" in China. A chair in such cases is usually large and grand in scale, decorative and authoritative in expression, compared to regular chairs that serve for practical purpose of comfort, convenience or aesthetic values. The splendor and magnificence of grandeur is often accompanied by ridiculous scenes where the sitter's feet did not reach the floor in uncomfortable poses, as they put up with this inconvenience to show off their authority and power. In this case, a chair is for a single person. This kind of symbolic meaning still exists. In a hit TV drama's song, "Swivel chair" sung by Kim Yongman in the 1960's in Korea, a periodical symbolism of a chair is well articulated in the lyrics:

의자, 일상의 예술

정준모 | 2011 청주국제공예비엔날레 총감독

새삼 의자인 까닭은?

의자는 우리에게 다양한 의미로 다가온다. 신분이나 명예를 의미하기도 하고, 아름다움이나
능률, 규칙이라든가 휴식이라는 뜻으로 새겨지기도 하는 의자의 다양한 면모는 인간이 두발로
걷기시작하면서 특히 휴식을 위해서 그리고 장시간 노동을 위해서 꼭 필요한 물건이 되었다.
시간이 흐를수록 당연하게 그리고 절실하게 인간의 신체의 일부처럼 무의식적으로 인식되었
고 오늘날에는 의자가 '거기'에 있다는 사실조차 인식하지 못할 만큼 일상이 되어버렸다.
이처럼 우리에게 '자연'이 된 의자를 이해하기 위해서는 시대를 이어오며 변모한 그것
의 역사를 이해할 필요가 있다. 이에 더하여 의자가 공예의 대상물로서 발전해 온 사실 역
시 주목해야 한다. 건축가인 갤런 크렌츠(Galen Cranz)는 그녀의 저서 『의자(The Chair:
Rethinking Culture, Body and Design)』를 통해 우리가 너무나 일상적인 나머지 당연
한 것으로 받아들이는 의자의 의미와 상징 그리고 문화적 사회적 의미를 살펴보고 있다.
그의 글에 의하면 의자로부터 어떤 정서적 느낌을 갖느냐의 문제는 결국 의자의 모양과 의자
의 상징성에서 비롯된다고 한다. 이럴 경우 의자는 단순하게 우리 신체의 연장선상에 있는 것
이 아니라 문화적인 산물이라는 것이다. 결국 의자는 시대를 반영하는 문명의 거울인 셈이다.
그래서 의자는 신분과 권력이나 인품을 상징하는 동시에 시대를 상징한다. 때로는 매우 개인적
이고 미시적인 대상이지만 때로는 시대적 사회적 담론을 담지한 거시적인 존재이기도 하다.
선사시대를 풍미했던 신화적 사고의 시대에 의자는 신만이 앉을 수 있는 초자연적인 의미의
것이었다. 그 후 과학적, 이성적, 절대가치, 규범이 중심이 되는 존재론적 시대에 의자는 상징
이자 권력이었으며 신을 대신하는 권좌의 의미로 대체되었다. 또한 의자는 남자들의 것이기도
했다. 13세기까지 의자에 앉을 수 있었던 것은 남성들에 국한 된 권리였다. 이렇듯 의자는 권력
과 힘의 상징이기도 했지만 18세기 말 프랑스혁명을 거치면서 귀족과 신흥 부르주아 계급에
게까지 그리고 산업혁명과 자유, 평등, 인권사상이 일반화되면서 의자는 일반시민들에게까지
자리를 내 주었다. 그리고 19세기 이후 모더니즘이 세상을 풍미하는 기능적 시대에 들어서면서
의자는 종래의 가치에 상대적인 가치와 개인의 취미와 취향을 보태어 드러내는 것이 되었다.
의자는 아주 오랜 역사를 갖고 있지만 오늘날의 의자처럼 기능하기 시작한 것은 그리 오래전
일은 아니다. 따라서 의자는 수 천년동안 실용적인 의미보다 존엄과 위엄을 과시하기위한 수
단이자 권력을 대체하는 보조재였다. 사실 르네상스시대가 막을 내리는 16세기까지도 의자는
귀한 것으로 취급되었다. 오늘날 회장을 체어맨이라 부르고 중국에서도 주석(主席)이라고
부르는 것도 의자의 이런 상징성과 무관하지 않다. 이런 경우 의자는 편안함이나 안락함이라
는 실용적인 목적에 봉사하거나 아름답다는 심미적인 부분을 충족시켜주는 일반적인 의자에
비해 대개는 매우 크고 장대하며 장식적이고 권위적이다. 의자의 크기와 화려함은 그 자리
에 앉을 사람의 힘과 권력을 대신하는 것이었기 때문에 불편하고 발이 바닥에 닿지 않아 다소
우스꽝스러운 모습으로 앉아있어야 했어도 기꺼이 그 불편을 감수하고 권좌(?)를 애용해야만
했다. 이 경우의 의자는 한 사람만을 위한 것이었다. 이렇게 상징적인 의자의 의미는 여전하
다. 1960년대 연속극 주제가로 크게 히트했던 가수 김용만이 부른 '회전의자' 라는 노래가사를
보면 당시 의자의 시대적 상징성이 잘 드러난다. '빙글빙글 도는 의자, 회전의자에/ 임자가 따
로 있나, 앉으면 주인인데/ 사람 없어 비워둔 의자는 없더라/ 사랑도 젊음도 마음까지도/ 가는

Curatorial Essay
기획의 글

"For a chair turning round and round/ for a swivel chair/ there's no owner/ You can be its owner/ when you sit on it/ There's no chair vacant/ Your love, your youth, and even your heart/ are crushed in your rough future/ Alas, if you feel it unfair, rise in the world, achieve your success."

Like this, a swivel chair is a symbol of social success, an object of ordinary people's hopes and desires, and sometimes the chair itself was an object of respect. Therefore, a fact that one has their own chair among others in workplace represents that they are a permanent employee, and if is one that is quite large, swivels, and made of leather, you can identify its owner's social position.

Until the Renaissance period, people utilized storage closets, benches, and stools without armrests or backing as a symbolic use for a chair. An epoch-making change of the chair resulted from the freedom and the equality newly acquired by French and Industrial Revolution. Still, a chair represented its position of the user. It became too mundane, as a chair sometimes stands by its owner and sometimes gets personified as the owner himself/ herself. From our observations, a chair's diversity and many facets have various meanings as circumstances change. I would say that a chair holds a thousand meanings with its hundred faces.

The concept of the equality acquired from a chair, began to develop because of the various shapes in accordance with a desire to have a distinguished looking chair. As chairs accessible to everyone, people began to be selective. Human beings have always strived for equality, but at the same time they wish to be served ahead of others. This became apparent no sooner than its acquisition due to their autonomous nature. Human beings craving for such differentiation consequently resulted in the extension of the true symbol of a chair's authority.

On the other hand, chairs are not only mere 'objects,' but also bears an artistic value. In particular, sculptors and architects have shown interest in chairs. It probably attributes to its complex functions composed with various techniques in science, ergonomics, biology, mechanical engineering, and so on, in spite of its simplicity in shape and ease in production. In this respect, I would say that "a chair is science." It is another type of architecture for the architects who have needed firm, solid chairs produced in regards to their structure and dynamics. In other words, a chair was of a more architectural style. The masters of architecture, used the latest materials, were the most creative and designed cutting-edge buildings, dedicated themselves to making chairs during the early twentieth-century, due their attraction to chairs.

As a chair cares about the qualification of those who will sit on it, the qualification for a chair is also required. First of all, it must be strong and solid as well as comfortable for the sitter. In addition, a chair should be artistic as an aesthetical being. Moreover, it is required to consider medical aspects for the sitter to avoid strains while sitting. To summarize, a chair's quality is evaluated like "composite arts." In this point of a view, it was not easy to find something other than a "chair" in order to embody "Yuyongjimul: not just new, but necessary," which is the subject of the 2011 Cheongju International Craft Biennale. Frankly, nothing was more appropriate as the subject than a chair because it has been already a

길이 험하다고 밟아버렸다/ 아아~ 억울하면 출세를 하라, 출세를 하라.' 따라서 회전의자는 출세의 상징이자 소시민들의 소망이자 욕망의 대상이었고 의자 그 자체가 존경의 대상이기도 했다. 따라서 여러 사람이 일하는 직장에 자신의 의자가 있다는 것은 온전한 직업을 가진 정규직을 의미하며 그 의자가 제법 크고 회전의자인 동시에 가죽의자라면 그 주인이 도달한 사회적 지위가 높다는 것을 가늠할 수 있다.

이런 상징적인 의자가 르네상스 시대에는 수납장, 벤치 등과 같이 팔걸이와 등받이가 없는 스툴로 사용되기도 했다. 이런 의자가 획기적인 변화를 가져온 것은 프랑스 대혁명과 산업혁명을 거치면서 인간이 얻게 된 자유와 평등에의 외침의 결과이다. 하지만 여전히 의자는 신분을 상징한다. 그리고 너무나 일상화한 나머지 의자는 그 의자의 주인을 대신 하기도 하며 때로는 의인화하여 그 사람자체가 되기도 한다. 이렇게 의자는 다양한 면모와 얼굴을 지니고 있으며 경우에 따라 그 의미를 달리한다. 즉 천의 얼굴을 갖고 만의 의미를 지닌 셈이다.

하지만 의자를 통해 이룩한 평등의 개념은 곧 남다른 의자를 갖고 앉고 싶은 욕망으로 이어지면서 각각 특정한 모양을 얻기 시작했다. 누구나 의자를 갖게 됨에 따라 사람들은 나만의 의자를 소망하였다. 인간은 누구나 남과 같아져야 한다고 생각하고 그것을 얻기 위해 투쟁한다. 하지만 그것을 얻어 남과 같아지면 그 사람들과는 다른 좀 더 나은 대접을 받기를 원하는 이율배반적인 속성 때문에 다른 사람들과는 차별화 된 의자를 갈망하면서 다시 의자가 지니는 권력의 의미는 배가된다.

한편으로 의자는 오브제인 동시에 공예품으로서의 가치를 지닌 것이기도 하다. 특히 조각가와 건축가들은 항상 의자에 대해 관심을 가져왔다. 그것은 아마도 의자가 매우 단순하고 간단하지만 인간의 삶의 공간에 구조적이고 공학적인 요소로 작용하고 있는 까닭에서 일 것이다.

따라서 구조와 역학을 고려해서 넘어지지 않고 삐걱거리지 않는 견고한 의자를 필요로 했던 건축가들에게 의자는 또 다른 건축이기도 했다. 즉 의자는 또 다른 건축양식이었던 셈이다. 20세기 초 새로운 재료로 인류역사상 가장 독창적이고 획기적인 건축물들을 설계했던 건축의 대가들이 새로운 의자 만들기에 몰입했던 것도 이러한 의자의 매력 때문이었다.

의자는 자리에 따라 앉을 사람의 자격을 따지지만 의자 또한 의자가 되기 위해서는 갖추어야 할 자격이 있다. 우선 튼튼하고 견고한 한편 앉는 사람의 몸에 맞는 편안한 것이어야 한다. 여기에 아름다움을 갖춘 예술적인 동시에 미학의 구체적인 실존적 존재이어야 하며 몸 특히 척추에 무리를 주지 않아야 하는 의학적인 면까지 고려해야 하는 소위 '종합예술'인 것이다.

그런 점에서 2011 청주국제공예비엔날레의 주제인 '유용지물'(有用之物, not just new, but necessary)의 실체를 구현하기에 '의자' 이상의 것을 찾기란 쉽지 않았다. 아니 솔직히 말하자면 적격이라는 생각을 하지 않을 수 없었다. 의자는 손과 기계, 예술과 산업, 그리고 공예와 디자인, 생산과 소비라는 대척점에 있는 등가의 가치를 충실하게 반영하고 있는 사물로 이미 인간에게는 자연이자 환경이었기 때문이다. 또 이미 전 세계에 보편화된 일상으로서의 '의자'는 과학적이고 물리적인 조건을 충족시키는 한편 심미적이며 감성적인 부분까지 책임을 져야 한다는 점에서 특히 더욱 그러했다.

예술 또는 공예로서의 의자

오늘날 일상적이면서도 심미적인 요소가 강조된 의자의 시발점은 아마도 수공예운동을 시작한 윌리엄 모리스(William Morris, 1834~96)가 1870년대 자신의 별장을 위해 만들었던 의자로부터 비롯되었다 해도 과언이 아닐 것이다. 그와 함께 19세기말 비엔나 분리파(Secession) 멤버로 공예와 순수미술의 경계를 넘는 아르누보 운동의 핵심이었던 오스트리아의 건축가 요제프

nature and an environment for human beings, made by the most fully reflecting the equal values between two antipodes; hand and machine; art and industry; craft and design; production and consumption. It is adequate to say that looking at a chair, as a generalized item in everyday life, fulfills scientific and physical conditions and takes responsibilities in aesthetic as well as emotional parts.

A Chair as Art or Craft

The starting point of a chair emphasized with its mundane and aesthetic elements was perhaps one made by William Morris (1834-96), an advocate of the Arts and Crafts Movement, from his summer house in the 1870s. I also want to point out, Joseph Hoffmann (1870~1956), an Austrian architect who surpassed the boundaries between craft and fine arts as a key figure of Viennese Secession during the late nineteenth-century and of Art Nouveau. Instead of a chair being a symbol of a plain, simple article of daily use, or of an artistic object, they created chairs to satisfy both "beauty" and "utility" which were embodied in the spirit of pragmatism.

Following the previous achievements, numerous architects, sculptors, painters, and designers have come to produce creative chairs. These successors have built a new history of chairs with their commercial successes in mass-productivity. While there is no systematic study which traces back to the entire range of such works and meanings, I recollect Charles Rennie Mackintosh (1868~1928) who achieved his own aesthetics with chairs by making people comfortable in their lives. As an heir of British Arts and Crafts Movement, Mackintosh influenced the Viennese Secession and French Art Nouveau with his chairs, architecture, and design which spread all over the Europe. His chairs, however, kept a strong inclination toward decoration rather than function, and gave a feeling of authoritative in stiffness. It later developed in definite forms with Modernism's aesthetics through the combination of German Bauhaus' style and Netherlands' De Stijl in order to reach its substantiality by obliterating unnecessary ornamentation.

A chair is a furniture that resembles the human body, an instrument and a symbol to help relax those who stand erect by allowing us the most frequent body contacts. For this reason, countless architects and designers have chosen the chair as a means to represent their design philosophy and to express their artistic languages.

1. The Embodiment of Modernism

Ludwig Mies van der Rohe (1886 ~1969), called a "father of Modernism architecture," has a deep connection with chairs reminding him of his *Barcelona Chair*. Saying, "Designing a chair successfully is as difficult as designing a building," van der Rohe created a chair in a simple, monotonous yet with balanced and restrained expression. As a representative of Modern architecture, he created the stereotype of modern design by pursuing utmost simplicity and neatness. In the 1929 World Expo in Barcelona, He designed the German Pavilion and needed chairs to fit the building. The *Barcelona Chair* is what he designed at that time, and it is still recognized as a monumental piece.

호프만(Joseph Hoffmann, 1870~1956)도 빼 놓을 수 없는 인물이다. 이들은 단순한 상징으로서의 의자뿐 아니라 일상의 가구와 같이 폭넓게 의자를 다루었다. 단지 조형적인 도구나 대상인 예술적 오브제가 아닌 '아름다움'과 '쓸모'를 동시에 충족시키는 의자를 만들었다는 점에서 예술의 실사구시(實事求是)를 구현하고 삶에서 예술을 실천에 옮겼던 이들이다.

이후 수많은 건축가, 조각가, 화가, 디자이너들에 의해 다양하고 독창적인 의자들이 제작되어 세상에 나왔다. 하지만 그 모든 것을 이 글에서 언급하고 의미를 되새길 여력은 없다. 다만 의자의 역사와 기능 그리고 시대적 요구였던 대량생산과 상업적인 성공도 의자의 긴 역사의 일부로 더해졌던 것은 사실이다. 그런 점에서 의자를 통해 자신의 미학을 실현하는 동시에 사람들을 편안하고 행복하게 해 준 이들을 시대적으로 살펴보자면, 먼저 찰스 레니 매킨토시(Charles Rennie Mackintosh, 1868~1928)를 들 수 있다. 영국의 미술공예운동의 맥을 잇는 그의 의자와 건축, 디자인 등은 빈의 분리파와 프랑스의 아르누보에 영향을 주면서 급속도로 유럽전역으로 퍼져 나갔다. 하지만 이들 의자는 기능보다 장식을 우선시하는 경향이 짙었고 다소 권위적이며 딱딱한 느낌을 주는 것이었다. 이후 독일의 바우하우스운동과 네덜란드의 데스틸 운동등과 결합하면서 장식을 제거하고 본질에 충실한 이념과 결합하여 모더니즘 미학을 실천하는 구체적인 형태로 진화하여 오늘에 이르고 있다.

의자는 인체를 닮은 동시에 직립한 인간들의 휴식을 위한 도구이자 상징이다. 또한 가장 신체접촉이 많은 가구이다. 이런 이유 때문에 20세기에 들어서면서 수많은 건축가와 디자이너들은 자신의 디자인 철학과 조형언어를 상징하고 압축하여 표현하는 대상으로 의자를 선택했다.

1. 모더니즘의 구현

모더니즘 건축의 아버지라 불리는 미스 반 데어 로에(Ludwig Mies van der Rohe, 1886 ~1969)하면 *바르셀로나 의자(Barcelona Chair)*가 생각날 만큼 의자와 인연이 깊다. "의자를 성공적으로 디자인 하는 것은 건물을 디자인하는 것만큼 어려운 일이다."라고 말했던 그는 매우 간결하고 단조롭지만 절제미가 균질하게 표현된 의자를 만들었다. 현대 건축물의 전형을 창조한 그는 극도의 단순함과 깔끔함을 추구하는 모더니즘을 대표하는 건축가이다. 1929년 바르셀로나에서 열린 세계박람회에서 독일관을 설계한 그에게 필요한 것은 그 건축에 걸 맞는 의자였다. 그리하여 만든 것이 바로 의자의 역사에서 기념비적인 작품으로 대접받는 *바르셀로나 의자*이다.

당시 그의 건축은 기존의 건물들과는 전혀 다른 거의 모든 장식을 모두 제거한 재료와 구조 그 자체만의 극한의 아름다움을 가졌다. 즉 그의 지론인 "Less is More"를 구현한 순수주의 그 자체인 건축이었다. 예를 들어, 건물과 얕은 물이 깔리는 연못에 반영된 건물은 조경과 건물이 하나가 되어 무척이나 정적이면서 은은한 건물을 연출했다. 대개의 박람회 파빌리온은 일회용 건물이지만 미스 반데어 로에의 걸작인 독일 파빌리온은 1986년 복원되어 지금까지 건축학도들의 성지가 되기도 하였다. "몬드리안" 의자로 유명한 리트벨트(Gerrit Thomas Rietveld, 1888~1964)의 *지그재그 의자*도 모더니즘의 원리를 그대로 적용시킨 예이다. 그는 의자의 기능을 생각하기 전에 형태의 짜임새를 확실하게 하고자 면과 면, 선과 선으로 공간을 명확하게 분할했다. 이렇게 모더니즘은 미학적, 공학적인 변화와 함께 왔고 어찌 보면 시대의 흐름이었던 셈이다.

2. 자연의 기하학

의자의 걸작 중 걸작은 덴마크 가구 디자인의 명장 인 건축가 아르네 야콥슨(Arne

Unlike other buildings, his architecture embodies his belief, "Less is More," and is of utmost purity of itself. He used materials in which most decorative elements were eliminated to acquire the sole beauty of the building's structure. Van der Rohe achieved such an effect by the surroundings of a shallow pond that has a still and subdued sensibility. While pavilions from most expos are disposed of, van der Rohe's German Pavilion was restored in 1986 and has become a sacred place for students studying architecture.

Widely known as "Mondrian Chair," the *Zigzag Chair* by Gerrit Thomas Rietveld (1888~1964) is another example that applied Modernist principles. Before considering a chair's function, he clearly divided its space with face to face, line to line, in order to secure the structure of its shape.

2. Geography of Nature

A chair's masterpiece among masterpieces was born by a great architect Arne Jacobsen (1902~71), a Danish master of furniture design. His major works are the *Egg Chair* and the *Ant Chair*, which were inspired by nature. Educated in plastering and engineering in Copenhagen, Jacobsen was influenced by Bauhaus, functionalism, Le Corbusier, and De Stijl. He was not only satisfied with architecture but also meticulously designed the interior and furniture for his work. It was in 1952 when his famous *Ant Chair* was first shown to the world. With great dexterity he made organic forms by curving plywood, and adopted ergonomics to a chair with a technique influenced by Eames in the United States (Charles Eames, 1907-78; Ray Eames, 1912-88). The personified *Ant Chair* by Jacobsen who laid stress on the process of the materials and their uses, made great commercial success selling millions of pieces and altered the direction of the Danish design industry. Based on its success, he listed his name as a furniture designer in art history by producing *Egg Chair* in 1957, the *Swan Chair* in 1958, and the *Waterdrop Chair* in 1959 in relays. Regarding architecture and its interior objects as a single thing, he sought for a "Gesamtdesign" and harmonized leather and fabric with interior design.

Following Jacobsen, the chairs made of teakwood, oakwood, and rattan by Hans J. Wegner (1914~2007) represented the characteristics of Danish designs and the *Pelican Chair* with simple but beautiful organic curving lines by Finn Juhl (1921~89) created an Oriental sensibility. George Nakashima (1905~90) brought Danish design to perfection by supplementing its artificial aspects by his natural design with the emphasis on the grains and lines of hardwood. It was a Finnish designer, Alvar Aalto (1898~ 1976), however, who opened a new prospect in the field of design by using wood's natural property and the elegance of composition as decorative motifs.

3. A tool as an object

As a matter of fact, the success of such an experiment attributes to Le Corbusier (1887~1965), who "defined objects as human limbs." By designing his illustrated furniture in real appeared in his book, *L'Art Décoratif d'aujourd'hui (Today's Decorative Art)* published in 1925, Le Corbusier expresses creative opinions and helps us understand today's chairs.

Jacobsen,1902~71)의해 탄생했다. 자연에서 영감을 얻은 그는 *에그 의자(Egg Chair)*와 *개미 의자(Ant Chair)*를 제작했다. 코펜하겐에서 미장 수업과 엔지니어 교육을 받은 그는 바우하우스와 기능주의, 르 코르뷔지에, 데 스틸 운동의 영향을 받았다. 그는 건축에 만족하지 않고 자신의 건물내부는 물론 그 안에 사용될 가구까지 디자인하는 치밀함을 보여주었다.

그의 유명한 *개미 의자*가 세상에 나온 것은 1952년이다. 그는 합판을 휘어서 유기적인 형태를 만드는 기술이 뛰어났는데, 미국의 임스 부부(Charles Eames, 1907~78), Ray Eames, 1912~88)의 영향으로 합판을 자유자재로 성형하는 기술과 의자에 인체공학을 도입했다. *개미 의자*는 엉덩이가 닿는 부분은 넓은 원형으로, 등받이 부분도 원형 만들고 그 사이를 허리처럼 잘록하게 만들어 개미를 연상시키지만 자세히 보면 사람이 의자에 앉았을 때 모습을 그대로 재현한 듯 보이기도 한다. 결국 의자를 의인화 한 셈이다. 소재의 제작과정 용도를 중시했던 야콥센의 *개미 의자*는 수백 만 개가 팔릴 정도로 상업적으로도 대 성공을 거두면서 덴마크 디자인 산업의 방향을 바꾸어 놓았다. 그는 이 의자의 성공에 힘입어 1957년 *에그 의자(egg chair)*를, 1958년 *백조 의자(swan chair)*, 그리고 1959년에는 *물방울 의자*를 연거푸 내놓으면서 가구 디자이너로서도 미술사에 이름을 올렸다. 건축과 그 안의 것을 하나로 보았던 그는 총제적인(Gesamtkunst)디자인을 추구했으며, 특히 가죽과 천을 인테리어에 훌륭하게 조합시킨 것으로도 유명하다.

이후 등장한 한스 베그너(Hans J. Wegner, 1914~2007)는 정교한 곡선으로 된 티크, 오크, 등나무로 의자를 만들었다. 또한 핀 율(Finn Juhl, 1921~89)은 *펠리칸 체어*를 비롯한 단순하면서도 유기적인 곡선이 아름다운 의자를 통해 동양적인 느낌까지 드러내는 덴마크 스타일을 완성시켰다.

그런 점에서는 조지 나카시마(George Nakashima, 1905~90)는 원목의 결과 선을 최대한 살린 자연적인 디자인으로 덴마크 디자인의 인공적인 면을 보완했다. 하지만 나무의 천연적인 속성과 구성의 우아함을 장식적인 소재로 활용하여 디자인의 새로운 지평을 연 것은 다름 아닌 핀란드의 알바 알토(Alvar Aalto, 1898~ 1976)였다.

3. 사물로서의 도구

사실 이러한 실험이 가능했던 것은 "인간의 수족으로 사물을 정의"한 르 코르뷔지에(Le Corbusier, 1887~1965)가 있어서 가능했다. 그는 1925년 발간한 자신의 책 『오늘날의 장식예술(L'Art Décoratif d'aujourd'hui)』에서 매우 독창적인 견해를 피력하여 오늘날의 의자를 이해할 수 있도록 해주었다. 그는 "그것은 우리의 팔다리의 연장이며 인간의 기능들에 적합한 것이다. 유형으로서의 요구, 유형으로서의 기능이며 그러므로 유형으로서의 사물이면서 유형으로서의 가구이다. 선택, 섬세함, 비례, 조화에 의해 명시된 영속하는 좋은 취향이다."라고 주장하면서 인간의 수족으로서의 사물과 가구의 유형을 정의했다.

이와 함께 그는 모듈에 모듈러(Modulor)라는 이름을 붙여 자신의 건축과 모든 디자인에 그 개념을 적용시켰다. 그의 모듈러 개념은 아름다움의 근원인 인간 신체의 척도와 비율을 기초로 한 황금분할을 바탕으로 무한한 수학적 비례 시리즈를 만들어 디자인의 새로운 길을 제시했다. 이와 함께 뒤샹(Henri Robert Marcel Duchamp, 1887~1968)가 발견한 '발견된 오브제'의 개념 이후 등장한 오브제 개념은 일상적인 기능이나 역할을 초월해서, 또 다른 의미를 미술에 부여했던 것처럼 의자도 일상의 의자가 아닌 예술로서의 의자 또는 작품으로서의 오브제가 될 가능성을 열어주었다.

He defines the types of objects and furniture as the limbs of the human body in the book, saying, "it is an extension of our limbs and appropriate for the human body's operations. It is a demand as a type, a function as a type; thus, an object as a type and a furniture as a type. It is of a good taste lasting which is specified by choice, delicacy, proportion, and harmony."

In addition to it, he entitled his module a "Modulor" and applied its conception to all of his architecture and design. Le Corbusier's "Modulor" concept proposed a new path of design by making a series of mathematical proportions on the basis of the gold sections of the human body's criterion and proportions as a root of beauty.

4. A Chair in changeable forms and definite forms

The most important development of design and the chair in the twentieth-century is the application of new materials. The growth of science and industry was linked to the change of the materials that developed in traditional chairs. An enormous change occurred by the emergence of steel in the early twentieth-century, and of fiber-glass and plastic in the latter half of the century. Steel brought a fundamental change in the structures of chair's legs. The hallowed steel pipes being very flexible enabled free alteration despite its intense solidity. It also allowed a cantilever structure to withstand the heavy weight with less volume. A new structure was created where a loose part of a chair together with other parts that support the weight, led to the principles of the four legs to disappear. Jean Prouve (1901~84) produced a cutting-edge chair that had the strong properties of steel, saying "do not even think of a design if you cannot make a product from it." As the use of glass-fiber and plastics in chairs emerged, competitive price was secured through mass production by injection molding which resulted in a true artistic democratization by the supply of beautiful craft works with low prices.

What is more important here is the enormous range of artistic freedom was given to designers. As individual expressions become possible without obstacles, a chair meets another development as a walking chair and as a running chair. *La Chaise* by Charles & Ray Eames is a chair made of glass fiber, recollecting the image of Henry Moore's sculpture. Their *LCW Chair* released in 1945 expresses an organic line's sensibility by using veneers, which became possible by the invention of a new technique of wood manufacturing. Besides, the *Wassily Chair* initially produced in 1925 by Marcel Breuer (1902~81) was the first chair that utilized steel and leather, and its popularity still holds till today. Another designer Verner Panton (1926~98) produced the *Panton Chair* out of plastic and has changed the users' outlook on plastics which were light and cheap. Since the 1950s, plastic with its low prices has contributed to new designers with their creative works. The use of plastics has also attributed to the power of Italy, the relative newcomer, positioning itself as the center of furniture industry.

4. 의자, 성형하다

20세기 디자인과 의자의 발달에서 가장 중요한 것은 새로운 소재의 적용이다. 과학과 산업의 발달은 전통적인 의자의 재료의 변화로 이어졌고 20세기 초에는 강철이, 중반 이후에 유리섬유와 플라스틱이 등장하면서 엄청난 변화를 가져왔다. 강철은 의자다리의 구조에 근본적인 변화를 가져왔다. 속이 빈 강철파이프는 강도가 뛰어나남에도 불구하고 유연해서 자유자재로 변형이 가능하다. 또 부피는 작아도 커다란 하중을 견디며 무엇보다 외팔보 즉 캔틸레버(cantilever) 구조가 가능해졌다. 따라서 고정된 한 쪽에 무게가 실리면서 다른 한쪽은 자유스러운 혁신적인 기능이 가능하게 되었고 의자의 다리가 4개여야 한다는 원칙도 사라졌다. "만들어 낼 수 없는 디자인은 생각하지도 말라."던 쟝 푸르베(Jean Prouvé , 1901 ~84)는 이런 강철의 속성을 살려 획기적이면서도 튼실한 의자를 제작했다. 여기에 유리섬유와 플라스틱이 의자의 소재로 등장하면서 금형을 만들면 한 번에 사출 성형된다는 점에서 대량생산을 통한 가격 경쟁력을 확보할 수 있게 되었다.

이리하여 저렴하면서도 아름다운 공예품의 공급이 이루어졌고 이로 인해 진정한 예술의 민주화를 이룩할 수 있게 되었다. 여기에 더 중요한 것은 디자이너에게 엄청난 조형의 자유를 부여했다는 것이다. 자유자재로 자신의 생각을 표현 할 수 있게 되면서 의자는 이제 걷고 뛰는 의자로 발전하게 된다. 찰스와 레이 임스의 *라 셰즈(La Chaise)*는 유리섬유로 제작된 대표적인 의자로 마치 헨리무어의 조각을 연상시킨다. 또 그들이 1945년 발표한 *LCW 의자*는 얇은 목재를 여러 겹 붙인 합판을 사용해서 유기적인 선의 느낌을 표현한 의자이다. 이는 새로운 목재가공법이 등장하면서 가능해진 일이었다. 또 마르셀 브로이어(Marcel Breuer, 1902~81)의 *바실리 체어(Wassily Chair*, 1925년)는 처음으로 강철과 가죽을 이용한 의자로 90여년이 지난 지금도 그 인기가 여전하다. 특히 베르너 팬톤(Verner Panton, 1926~98)은 플라스틱을 통째로 구부려 만든 듯한 *팬톤 의자(Panton Chair)*를 디자인해서 가볍고 저렴한 재료였던 플라스틱에 대한 인식을 바꾸어 놓았다. 이후 1950년데 이후의 신진디자이너들에게 플라스틱은 자신의 독창적인 작품을 위한 값싼 재료로서 기여했다. 또 비교적 후발주자인 이탈리아가 가구산업의 중심에 설 수 있었던 것도 실은 플라스틱의 힘이었다.

걷고 뛰는 의자들

이렇게 끊임없이 변화하고 발전해 온 의자들은 모더니즘의 상징이자 현대적인 삶의 형식을 결정짓는 그릇인 동시에 도구였다. 이제 의자는 장식을 거부하면서 그 자체로 하나의 대상물이 되었다. 그리고 새롭게 등장한 새로운 재료들은 19세기로 돌아가려는 복고풍의 의자를 경멸하는 수단이기도 했다. 구부린 목재(Bentwood)나 쇠파이프, 심지어 판지에 이르는 다양한 재료는 의자의 새로운 변신을 이끌었다. 또한 실용적이고 인체공학적인 척추 뼈를 지지해주는 의자도 생물학적인 의자도 속속 등장했다. 여기에 건강과 환경문제가 대두되면서 의자의 기능이 예술적인 측면도 중요하지만 인체와 조화를 이루는 효율성이 강조되기 시작하였다. 여기에 종래의 의자의 개념을 뛰어넘는 의자이상의 의자가 등장하기 시작했다. 의자로서의 기능을 넘어 사물로서 기능하기 시작한 의자가 하나의 예술형식으로 때로는 예술적 제재로 등장한다. 이제 의자는 더 이상의 의자가 아닌 예술이 되었다.

Chairs Walking and Running

Chairs with incessant changes and developments have been symbols of Modernism and instruments that have made an impact on modern lifestyles. Now a chair becomes an object by itself by refusing decoration. And new materials were means of disdaining other chairs in retro style toward the nineteenth-century. Diverse materials like bentwood, steel pipe, and even cardboard have led to the transformation of chairs into pragmatic, ergonomic, and biological states. But chairs have stayed between mid-twentieth-century's anti-aesthetics and early designers' audacious experiments. The emphasis on the functionality in harmony with the human body along with the artistic aspects is, however, a recent trend with the emergence of health and environmental problems.

1. Chairs of Artists

Van Gogh's chair in his painting symbolizes the suffering and poverty during his Arles days. For artists, a chair becomes a motif of social criticism or interpretation as well as an instrument for the expression of visual humor. The experience of Modernism has trained our eyes to observe artistic forms carefully, and a chair has become one of visual art. To an artist, a chair is both a single object and artwork. On the other hand, it is a means for the expression of their own aesthetics. The reason that a chair could be a mundane tool as well as an art form and a means of social reformation was because of the support of the artists' wanderlust by furniture companies such as Herman Miller, Vitra, Fritz Hansen, Cassina, Kartell, and so forth.

In Phanton's *Living Tower* (1969) also known as "Pantower" it shows a good example where furniture is elevated into an artistic position by altering the concept of its wall and floor to perfection. An Italian designer of an electronic typewriter (1978) of Olivetti Company, Cassina Company's leather chair, and Flos Company's lighting apparatus, Mario Bellini (1935~) dressed a chair through his *Figura* (1992). Its cloth is washable, changeable, and can be accentuated by wearing a belt in its waist. In addition to this interesting chair, he exhibited his wide steps between art and utility by his ergonomic chair, *Ypsilon Chair* in 2004, claiming it as the most convenient chair.

Those who appeared in the late twentieth-century such as Philippe Patrick Starck (1949~), Ron Arad (1951~), and Jasper Morrison (1959~), could have built their own artistic world by embracing new materials. In Ron Arad's case, his unconventional deformation with flowing but powerful lines using metals enlisted him as a representative of today's design. Practicing the unique French style of humorous and luxurious quality, Philippe Patrick Starck has shown his talents in various fields like architecture, furniture, and tiny items for living. Jasper Morrison exhibits a new minimalist style to maximize the users' convenience by excluding decorative elements on the basis of a proposition, "super normal." His Basel Chair is simple but sticks to its function. Visually it looks as if the entire piece is made of wood; the chair is wittily combined with plastics in the seat and back. The plastic created to mimic wood sometimes looks more realistic than wood itself making viewers stunned with disbelief, but they soon come to appreciate the humor behind it.

고흐의 그림에 나오는 의자는 그의 아를시절의 고통과 가난을 상징한다. 이렇듯 예술가들에게 의자는 사회비판적인 소재가 되기도 하고 신분을 비롯한 사회체제에 대한 해석이나 시각적인 유머를 표현하는 장치나 수단이기도 했다. 모더니즘의 경험은 우리에게 형식을 주의 깊게 보도록 하는 눈을 부여함으로서 의자는 이제 조각의 영역처럼 조형예술의 하나가 되었다. 예술가들에게 의자는 하나의 오브제인 동시에 그것 자체가 작품이기도 했지만 한편으로는 자신의 미학을 드러내는 표현수단이기도 했다. 이렇게 의자가 일상의 도구이자 예술로서 그리고 사회를 변혁시키는 수단이 될 수 있었던 것은 허먼 밀러(Herman Miller)나 비트라(Vitra), 프리츠 한센(Fritz Hansen), 카시나(Cassina), 카르텔(Kartell) 같은 가구회사들이 그들의 예술적 방랑벽을 지원해 주었기 때문이다.

사실 일명 "팬 타워(Pantower)"라고 불리는 팬톤의 *리빙타워*(1969년)는 가구의 벽과 바닥의 개념을 완전히 뒤바꾸어 놓음으로서 가구를 예술로 승격시킨 경우이다. 물론 이런 시도는 회화와 조각의 경계를 넘나드는 도널드 저드(Donald Judd, 1928~94)에서 비롯된 것으로 미니멀리즘의 구체적인 실현이자 '기능적인 미술'(Functional art)로서의 전환을 예고한 것이었다. 이것은 형태와 기능, 조각과 순수미술이 만난 것이라 할 수 있다. 의자 디자이너에서 미술가로 전향한 리차드 아츠슈와거(Richard Ernst Artschwager, 1923~)의 경우 의자를 대상으로 그것을 분해하고 재조립하는 과정을 통해 3차원적인 공간 속의 의자를 철저하게 평면화 함으로서 의자와 미술을 하나로 통합시켰다는 점에서 의자의 미술로서의 소재의 가능성을 열어놓았다.

20세기 초 예술 또는 미술로부터 영감을 받았던 아방가르드 시대의 디자인은 20세기 말에 이르면서 디자인이 예술을 결정짓도록 전세를 역전시켰다. 예술의 세계에도 영원한 승자는 없는 셈이다. 1990년대부터 호세 파르도(Jorge Pardo, 1963~)나 토비아스 레베르거(Tobias Rehberger, 1966~)등의 작업에서 이러한 현상은 두드러지는데 이들의 작업은 생활과 예술, 가구와 작품, 미술과 일상의 범주를 넘나들거나 그 두 가지를 모두 포함하는 것으로 유명하다. 이들의 작업은 예술과 기술의 세계를 정교하게 구분했던 19세기 중반부터 형성된 개념의 통합을 이룬 것으로 과학적이고 정량적인 '딱딱한'(hard)한 이성적 개념과 미학적인 가치를 평가하는 '부드러운'(soft) 감성적 개념으로 구분되었던 종래의 문화를 실용과 개념 그리고 설치라는 미술형식을 통해 통합을 이루면서 또 다른 의미의 토탈 아트를 실천에 옮겼다. 브루노 무나리(Bruno Munari, 1907~98)는 *짧은 방문을 위한 의자*(1945년)를 발표했다. 모양은 의자지만 제대로 앉을 수 없는 의자로 아츠슈와거의 예고편에 해당되는 의자였다. 요셉 보이스(Joseph Beuys, 1921~86)의 의자 위에 올려놓은 비계 덩어리나 중국의 아이 웨이 웨이(艾未未, Ai Weiwei, 1957~)는 2007 카셀도큐멘타에 출품한 *동화-1001개의 의자*라는 작품을 통해 의자의 현대미술로서의 가능성을 실험했다.

디자이너들은 새로운 전통이 되어버린 모더니즘에 대항하여 1960년대부터 세를 불린 반디자인(Anti-Design)운동은 1980년대 에토레 소트사스 (Ettore Sottsass, 1917~2007)를 중심으로 한 멤피스(Memphis)그룹이나 스튜디오 알키미아(Studio Alchymia)로 이어지면서 급진적인 변화를 추구했고 그 결과 예술과 기술 그리고 디자인과 순수미술 또 공예와의 간극은 거의 사라지게 되었다.

모더니즘이라는 교조주의적 고삐가 풀리면서 새로운 아티스트들이 등장하기 시작했고 아연 활기를 띠기 시작했다. *허니 팝(Honey Pop)*이나 *빵 의자(Pane Chair)* 또는 인공 크리스털이 자라나 의자모양을 이루는 *수정의자(Venus Chair)*로 유명한 젊은 다자이너 토쿠진 요시카와(Tokujin Yoshioka, 1967~)나 폐목재를 재활용해서 의자나 책상 또는 가구를 만드는 네덜란드

2. Chair=Body

Until now, artists have used a chair in order to express their abstract interests by and large, meaning social, psychological, or cultural utterance. Therefore, artists focused on the material such as plastic, steel, and wood instead of the chair itself, or the impacts the chair made to the structure of the human body. Consequently, the human body has actually existed within a remote place outside of a chair's purpose. Recently, however, chairs started to pay its close attention to the human body again.

While Bellini's *Ypsilon Chair* was faithful to the true character of a chair to support waste and back with his "Y"-shaped frame, the *T-Chair* by Antonio Citterio (1950~) has a casual shape with a cover on the back that is as interchangeable as a t-shirt. In that note, we should not ignore a Norwegian designer Peter Opsvik (1939~). Opsvik was discovered like a sudden comet through his *Tripp Trapp* in the 1970s. His chair, a type of elevator chair has the ability to grows, much like a child would grow, and such a Copernican design developed into another amazing idea in his *Gravity Balance Chair* (1983). Being able to bend down and lay back in this chair, the cutting-edge design challenged the concept of traditional chairs. This chair overwhelmed people's common sense and achieved a conspicuous commercial success.

Alberto Meda (1945~) still follows the Modernist doctrine, "Form follows function," as shown in his *Light Light Chair* (1987). Meda believed that "The more intricate the technique, the more appropriate to make a single organic body simple." He embodied his idea through a small, light chair made of carbon fiber. His simple and weightless chair is an expression of his physical and psychological feelings through its weight and brightness. At first, upon evaluations, tests shown that its appearance seemed too light and far too high-tech for the public despite its solid build. Building a career at a plastic chair manufacturer, Kartell, Meda adopted an organic method to develop from his imagination through the combination of design, engineering, technology, and the experimental process.

A Brazil-born front-runner of Spanish design, Jorge Pensi (1949~), accomplished a balance between form and function by his elegant design and by using the quality from materials. His major piece *Toledo* (1988) is an organic and minimalistic chair cast from aluminum. In his *Orfilia Thonet* (1989), a chair with an aluminum cast frame and lacquer-varnished seat and back, Pensi exhibited the image of traditional Spain through the eyes of modern viewpoint.

Aeron, a chair which is equal to all, began its first production in 1994 at Herman Miller by Don Chadwick (1936~) and Bill Stumpf (1936~2006). This chair is designed to control its height and width on the basis of ergonomics in pursuit of users' comfort to fit the body that's in it. It is *Aeron*'s peculiarity with a typical "over-cushioning" design that the chair's seat and back are covered with translucent mesh fabric to protect the health of users' waste by supporting their lumbar vertebra.

디자이너 피트 하인 이크(Piet Hein Eek, 1967~), *넝마의자(Rag Chair)*로 유명한 테요 레미(Tejo Remy, 1960~), 일본의 신예 넨도(Nendo Oki Sato, 1977~)등의 수많은 예술가들이 나이의 고하와 국적, 인종을 망라해서 예술과 의자, 의자와 디자인사이를 넘나들며 작업하고 있다.

2. 신소재와 의자

합판을 자유자재로 성형하는 벤트우드(Bentwood)기법이 의자의 모양과 가능 그리고 생산성의 증대를 통한 가격혁명을 이루면서 '아름다운 것들의 일반화'를 이룩한 이래 과학의 발달로 인한 신소재의 발달은 종래의 의자가 지녔던 기능을 변화시켰다. 그중 하나는 패션으로서의 의자이다. 올리베티(Olivetti)사의 전자 타자기(1978)를 디자인하고 카시나(Cassina)의 가죽 의자와 플로스(Flos)의 조명 기구 등을 디자인한 이탈리아의 디자이너 마리오 벨리니(Mario Bellini, 1935~)는 *피구라(Figura*, 1992년)를 통해 의자에게 옷을 입혔다. 그리고 그 옷은 빨아 입을수도 있고, 갈아입을 수도 있는 옷으로 벨트를 매어 허리를 강조할 수도 있다. 그는 이런다소 재미있는 의자를 만들었지만 2004년에는 최고로 편한 인체공학적 의자라는 *입실론 의자(Ypsilon Chair)* 발표해서 예술과 실용사이를 넘나드는 자신의 보폭의 넓이를 보여주었다.
또 20세기 후반 등장한 필립 스탁(Philippe Patrick Starck, 1949~), 론 아라드(Ron Arad, 1951~), 재스퍼 모리슨(Jasper Morrison, 1959~) 같은 이들은 새로운 소재를 적극적으로 수용함으로서 자신의 독창적인 예술세계를 구축할 수 있었다. 론 아라드 경우 금속을 사용하면서 유려하면서도 힘이 넘치는 곡선미와 형태를 없애는 파격성으로 오늘을 대표하는 작가의 반열에 오르게되었다. 프랑스 특유의 유머러스하고 고급스러운 디자인을 실천해 온 필립 스탁은 건축, 가구, 생활 소품 등 모든 영역에서 기량을 발휘하였다.
재스퍼 모리슨은 슈퍼 노말(Super Nomal)이라는 명제를 기본으로 장식적인 요소를 과감히제거하고 사용자의 편의를 극대화하는 뉴 미니멀리즘적 경향의 디자인을 내 놓았다. 그의 *바젤체어(Basel Chair)*는 간결하면서도 기능에 충실한 의자이다. 특히 모두 나무로 만든 것처럼 보이지만 시트와 등받이 부분은 플라스틱을 사용한 위트가 넘치는 의자이다. 나무보다 더 나무처럼보이는 플라스틱은 가끔 사람들을 망연자실하게 만들기도 하지만 그의 유머에 이내 풀어지고만다.

3. 의자=몸

지금까지 예술가들은 대체로 추상적인 관심사를 표현하기 위해, 즉 사회적 심리적 또는 문화적 발언을 위해 의자를 표현수단이나 제재로 사용해 왔다. 따라서 의자자체 또는 의자와 의자의 구조가 인체와 인체의 구조에 미치는 영향이 아니라 다양하게 사용되는 플라스틱이나 금속, 목재 등의 의자의 재료에 집중했던 것이다. 따라서 정작 몸은 의자의 목적과는 동떨어진 곳에존재했다. 하지만 최근 들어 의자는 다시 사람들의 몸에 주목하기 시작했다.
벨리니의 *입실론 의자*가 Y자 프레임을 통해 허리와 등을 지지하는 의자 본연의 기능에 충실한 의자라면 안토니오 치테리오(Antonio Citterio, 1950~)의 *티 체어*(T-Chair)는 티셔츠처럼 등받이 부분의 커버를 입혔다 벗겼다 할 수 있는 캐주얼한 형태를 지니고 있다.
노르웨이의 디자이너 페터 옵스틱(Peter Opsvik, 1939~)은 정말 상상을 넘어서는 그런 독창적인 의자로 사람들의 의자에 댈한 인식을 바꾸어 놓았다. 1970년대 그는 어린아이가 자라나는 것과 같이 의자도 함께 자라나는 의자 *트립 트랩(Tripp Trapp)*을 발표하면서 혜성처럼 등장했다. 즉 키 높이 의자인 셈이다. 자라나는 의자라는 획기적인 생각은 다시 놀라운 아이디어로

Conclusion

The main reason of the Cheongju International Craft Biennale is to look into the transformation of the designs of chairs from the late nineteenth-century to present days and to examine the true nature of Modernism and Post-modernism through chairs which covers the whole range of the evolutions of modern architecture, aesthetics of craft, and design philosophy. No one can deny that the experience of Modernism for Koreans is more like being led by periodical demand than by leading it. Due to the absence of Modernism in Korea, the culture has been stunned, much like a technician who lacks basic skills who suddenly discovers a new technique which sends them in a tizzy. In this sense, 430 chairs including London Design Museum's representative 70 pieces provides us with a vivid experience of distinctive and innovative Modernism.

A chair has always kept its nature and yet has also adopted itself to a new epoch by transforming at will. In the past, the traditional and basic materials for chairs were wood and textiles. In the early twentieth-century, however, steel was introduced to architecture and then to the chair, and later glass fiber and plastics emerged as an innovative way of using different materials after the mid-century. Particularly, the flexibility of steel combined with its solid quality allowed for fundamental changes in the structure of a chair's legs. The emergence of glass fiber and plastics enabled mass production through new techniques using inject molding, which resulted in the acceleration of the institutionalization of craft and design allowing lower prices to the public. The development of new materials endowed artistic freedom especially to many artists, architects, and designers who wanted to invent new chairs. The *Phanton Chair* of 1959 by Verner Panton (1926~98) exhibited its peculiar lines by bending whole plastics and achieved practicality with a simple design. As the world changed craft and design, at the same time, craft and design also change the way humans live.

In this context, craft and design should be more a method, an instrument, and a goal of life rather than a means of poor taste with pretentious brand-names or labels. A cultural and artistic democratization in a well balanced development should be achieved through the popularization of chairs with luxurious brands. It is very encouraging to see that the chairs, known as "It Item" amongst select designers and/or of those related to the art field, are currently getting recognized.

The chair is one of the most familiar items through the history for mankind that has influenced society and the most important cultural criterion that have been evaluate over time. Nevertheless, our lack of cultural refinement and of the experience in Modernism has resulted in the low level of design functionality, being blinded by the flamboyance of a chair's appearance. This year's Special Exhibition of "Chairs, Flow" in the Cheongju International Craft Biennale will provide an opportunity to increase the values and quality of life of contemporary Koreans who are dissatisfied with the quality of their lives in spite of their thickened wallets. Now let's hit the road with chairs.

이어졌는데 *그래비티 밸런스 체어*(Gravity Balans chair, 1983년)라고 하는 '중력 균형 의자'이다. 이 의자는 앞으로 숙인 자세로부터 뒤로 눕는 자세까지 취 할 수 있는 종래의 의자의 개념을 흔드는 독특한 구조를 가졌다. 이와 같이 그의 상식을 넘는 의자는 사람들을 놀라게 했고 이를 상품화해서 상업적인 면에서도 괄목할 만한 성공을 이룩했다. 알베르타 메다(Alberto Meda, 1945~)는 이름 그대로 *정말 가벼운 의자*(Light Light Chair, 1987년)>를 통해 '형태는 기능을 따른다.'는 모더니즘의 강령을 지금껏 따르고 있다. 메다는 "복잡한 기술일수록 하나의 유기체를 단순하고 간단하게 만드는데 적합하다"고 믿는다. 그는 탄소섬유를 가지고 만든 일련의 작은 가벼운 의자를 통해 그의 아이디어를 실현해 보였었다. 그의 단순하고 심플하며 가벼운 의자는 무게와 밝기를 통한 신체적, 심리적 표현이기도 하다. 처음 만든 모형의 사용자 테스트에서 의자는 튼튼하지만 대중들이 보기에는 외양이 너무 가볍고 하이테크 하다는 평을 받기도 했다. 그는 플라스틱의자 제조업체인 카르텔에서 재직하면서 자신의 경력을 쌓기 시작해서 디자인 뿐 만 아니라 엔지니어링과 기술과 설계, 실험 과정의 융합을 익혔다. 즉 복합적인 통합 기술 및 설계, 실험을 통해 그의 상상력을 구현하는 유기적인 방법론을 택했다. 또한 브라질 출신의 스페인 디자인의 선두주자인 호르헤 펜시(Jorge Pensi, 1949~)는 우아한 디자인과 재료의 특성을 살린 형태와 기능의 균형을 달성했다. 그의 대표적인 의자 *톨레도*(Toledo, 1988년)는 알루미늄 주조를 통해 만든 유기적이면서도 미니멀 한 의자이다. 그는 1989년 알루미늄 캐스팅을 한 프레임에 의자의 좌석과 등받이를 옻칠로 마감한 의자 *오필리아 토넷 (Orfilia Thonet)*을 선보이면서 스페인의 이미지와 전통을 오늘이라는 시점을 통해 드러낸다.

여기에 모두에게 평등한 의자인 *에어론(Aeron)*은 돈 채드윅(Don Chadwick, 1936~)과 빌 스텀프(Bill Stumpf, 1936~2006)에 의해 허먼 밀러에서 1994년 생산되기 시작하였다. 의자를 사용하는 사람의 몸에 맞추어 높이와 폭의 조절이 가능한 *에어론*은 매우 편안한 인체 공학을 바탕으로 한 의자이다. 이 의자는 전형적인 오버 큐셔닝(Over cushioning) 디자인으로 좌석과 등받이에는 유연한 반투명 메쉬 천을 사용해서 요추를 받쳐주어 허리건강을 지켜준다는 점이 큰 특징이다. 이렇게 의자는 결국 의자 본연의 모습으로 되돌아오기도 하고 때로는 아주 멀리 떠나버리기도 하지만 의자로서의 기본적인 개념은 우리에게 여전이 인간의 4발을 대신해주는 대용물이라는 것이다.

예술의 민주화를 기대하며

청주국제공예비엔날레에서 19세기 말부터 20세기를 거쳐 오늘에 이르는 의자들의 변화를 살펴보고자 하는 이유는 현대 건축과 공예미학, 디자인 철학과 기술의 진화까지를 망라하는 의자를 통해 모더니즘과 포스트모더니즘의 실체를 살펴보고자 하는 것이다. 사실 우리에게 부재한 모더니즘적 체험은 항상 기본기를 익히지 않은 기능공처럼 가끔 어리둥절해 하거나 어딘지 부족하고 새로운 것을 만나면 허둥대게 하곤 하였다. 즉 그로인해 시대적 요구를 이끌어 가기보다는 끌려간다는 느낌을 주어온 것이 사실이다. 그런 점에서 이번에 선보이는 영국 런던의 디자인미술관이 소장한 20세기를 대표하는 의자 70여점을 비롯해서 약 430여점의 의자들은 우리들에게 분명하고 새로운 모더니즘을 생생하게 체험할 수 있도록 해 줄 것이다.

의자는 언제나 새로운 시대에 적응하면서 자신들의 모습을 지켜나가는 동시에 변모시켜나 갔다. 의자의 가장 기본적인 재료는 나무와 천이었다. 하지만 20세기 전반에 건축에 도입된 철강재는 의자에 자연스럽게 도입되었다. 이후 강철관의 등장과 함께 섬유유리와 플라스틱이 도입이라는 엄청난 혁신이 이루어졌다. 특히 유연하면서도 강도가 뛰어난 강철은 의자 다리의

구조에 근본적인 변화로 작용했다. 섬유유리와 플라스틱의 등장은 금형을 통해 한 번에 사출 성형된다는 점에서 대량생산이 가능해졌고 그 만큼 단가가 낮아지면서 시민들에게는 '같은 값이면 다홍치마'로 공예와 디자인의 일상화는 가속화하기 시작했다.

특히 이런 새로운 소재의 개발과 발달은 의자를 고안하고자 했던 많은 예술가, 건축가, 디자이너들에게 조형적인 해방을 부여했다. 베르너 팬톤 (Verner Panton, 1926~98)의 1959년 작 *팬톤 체어*도 당시로서는 신소재였던 플라스틱을 통째로 구부려 곡선을 살린 것으로 단순한 디자인과 실용성이 돋보이는 디자인이다. 이렇게 세상은 공예와 디자인을 바꾸지만 공예와 디자인 또한 사람들의 삶을 바꾸어 놓는다.

그런 점에서 우리에게 공예와 디자인은 더 이상 사치품이나 명품이라는 왜곡된 이름으로 저급한 취미나 기호를 충족시키는 수단이 아니라 삶의 방식이자 도구인 동시에 목적이어야 한다. 또 소위 명품이라고 불리는 의자의 대중화를 통해 문화와 예술의 민주화, 균형발전을 이루어야 한다. 최근 들어 과거 소수의 디자이너나 예술분야에 종사하는 사람들에게만 잇 아이템(It Item)으로 알려졌던 의자들이 점점 대중화하기 시작한 것은 매우 고무적이다.

의자는 우리가 생활하면서 가장 오랫동안 함께 하는 익숙한 물건이자 우리 삶을 이루는 큰 환경인 동시에 우리의 시대를 평가할 수 있는 가장 중요한 문화적 척도이기도 하다. 하지만 우리의 빈곤한 문화적 소양과 모더니즘에 대한 경험부족은 의자를 바라볼 때도 외양의 화려함에 현혹되어 이면의 디자인과 기능성을 소홀히 해왔다. 그런 점에서 이번 청주국제공예 비엔날레의 <의자, 걷다(Chairs, Flow)>전은 지갑은 두꺼워졌지만 여전히 삶의 질에 만족하지 못하는 동시대 한국인들의 삶의 가치와 질을 업그레이드할 수 있는 기회를 제공 할 것이다. 이제 의자와 함께 진정으로 잘사는 아름다운 삶이 기다리는 길을 떠나보도록 하자.

MORDERN

Michael Thonet 미하엘 토네트

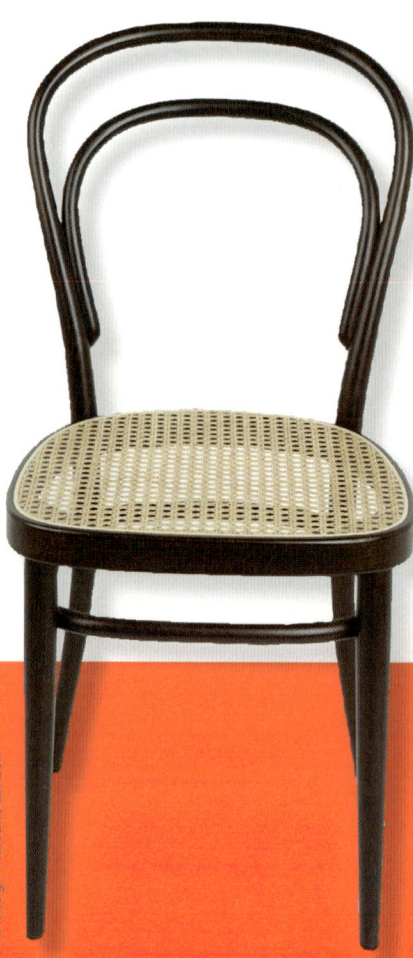

© Design Museum, London

Bentwood Chair
벤트우드 체어
85x41.5x50cm
Bent, solid and laminated beech with woven cane seat
너도밤나무, 등나무
Gebrüder Thonet, Austria 게브뤼더 토넷, 오스트리아
1860

Determined to produce high-quality furniture at an affordable price, the Austrian furniture maker Michael Thonet experimented for years with different techniques. In 1842, he was granted a patent for his process of bending wood laminates and by the late 1850s had developed Chair *No.14*, the bentwood dining chair, which was to achieve sales of 50 million by 1930. This is a variation on Thonet's design of Chair *No.14*.

오스트리아 가구 장인인 미하엘 토네트는 적당한 가격에 질 좋은 가구를 생산하기 위해 수년 동안 여러 가지 기술들을 실험했다. 그 결과 1842년에 그는 얇은 나무를 구부리는 공정으로 특허를 취득했는데, 이 작품 *No.14*는 목재를 금속 틀에 넣어 모양을 잡는 공법으로 1850년대 말 제작되었으며, 1930년까지 전세계적으로 5000만개 이상 판매되었다. 이것이 바로 토네트 디자인에서 *No.14*의 변화된 지점이다.

Gebrüder Thonet 게브뤼더 토네트

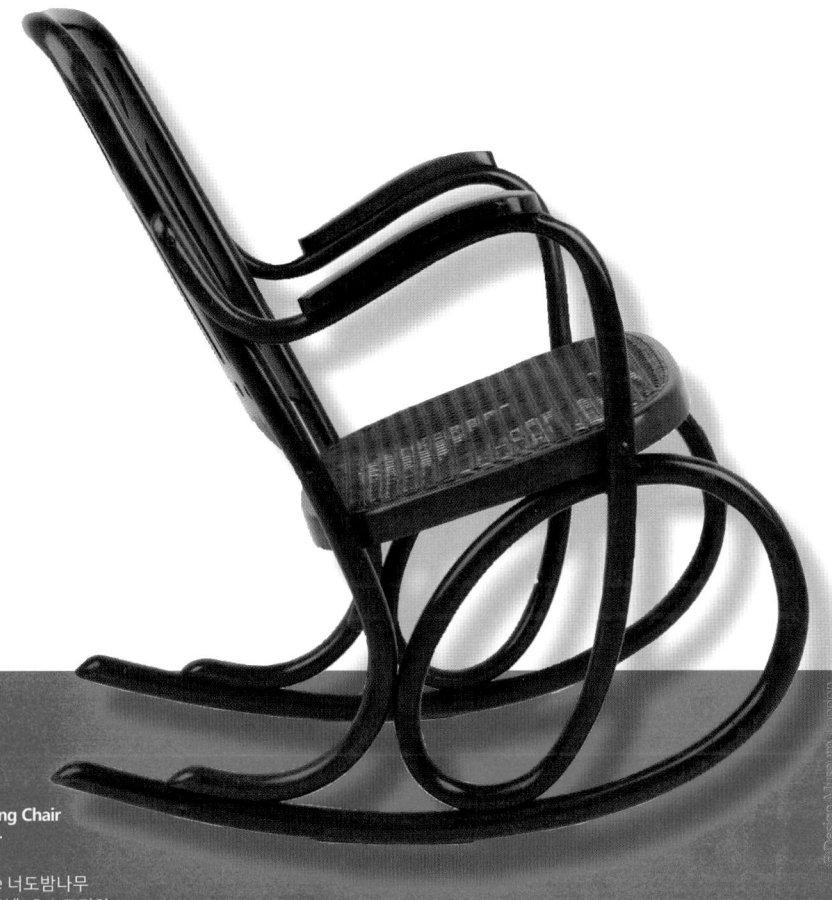

Thonet 14 Rocking Chair
토넷 14 흔들의자
85x61x60cm
Bent beech frame 너도밤나무
Thonet, Austria 토넷, 오스트리아
1888

The popularity of the Arts and Crafts movement encouraged the middle and upper classes to regard rocking chairs and other rustic styles of furniture with a new affection during the late 1800s. Despite its industrial ethos, Thonet drew inspiration from Arts and Crafts design in the styling of its products. The company developed its first rocking chair, Rocking Chair No. 1, in 1860. Subsequent rockers steadily gained popularity and by 1913, one in every twenty chairs sold by Thonet was a rocking chair.

1800년대 후반 미술공예운동의 대중성은 상류층과 중산층의 사람들이 흔들의자를 비롯하여 소박한 양식의 가구들에 대해 새로운 호감을 갖게 했다. 이 운동이 가지고 있는 산업 정신에도 불구하고 토네트는 미술공예운동이 내놓은 제품들의 디자인으로부터 영감을 얻었다. 이 회사는 1860년에 흔들의자 No. 1이라는 첫 번째 흔들의자를 내놓았다. 뒤이은 의자들은 꾸준히 대중성을 얻었고, 1913년까지 이 회사에서 판매된 스무 가지 의자들 중에 하나가 바로 이 흔들의자였다.

Charles Rennie Mackintosh 찰스 레니 매킨토시

Mackintosh, one of gifted creative architects, built a bridge at a turning point of the century. Completely different from previous chairs by others, Mackintoshi's chair expressed the most creative and personal British furniture. Each piece was produced with a design to create an atmosphere of a particular background, and designed to solve an 'artistic' problem to ornament interior space with the most attractive way.

매킨토시는 세기의 전환점에 다리를 놓은, 창조적 재능을 지닌 건축가 중의 한 사람이다. 매킨토시의 의자 디자인은 이전의 의자들과는 완전히 다른 것으로, 가장 창의적이고 개인적인 영국의 가구를 표현했다. 각 작품은 독특한 배경의 분위기를 창조하는 디자인으로 제작되었고, 가장 매력적인 방식으로 인테리어 공간을 장식하는 '예술적인' 문제를 해결할 수 있도록 디자인되었다.

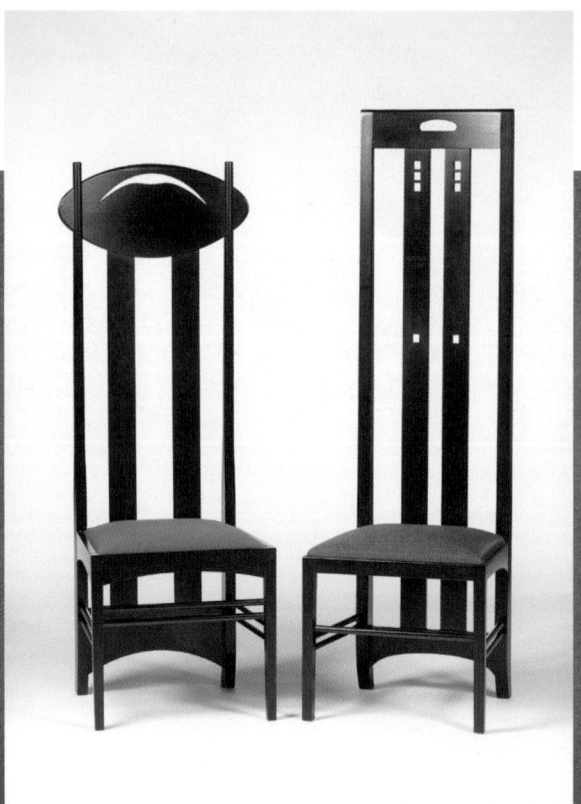

Argyle Chair
아가일 체어
136x48x46cm
Ash wood frame stained black, upholstered seat
물푸레나무, 천
Reissued by Cassina, Italy 카시나, 이탈리아
1897

High-Backed Chair for Ingram Street Tea Rooms
잉그램가 티룸을 위한 높은 등받이 의자
115x47x42cm
Dark stained oak 오크 나무
Reissued by Cassina, Italy 카시나, 이탈리아
1900

High-Backed Chair for Ingram Street Tea Rooms

An ebonized oak tree chair with horsehair fabric seat, arranged with center table in the tea room at Argayle Street, Cranston. It was exhibited at the Vienna Secession, which was actually an artistic movement that took place in Vienna, 1897. This was Mackintosh's first chair and designed with a high back of which the shape is oval and was inscribed with swallow patterns.

잉그램가 티룸을 위한 높은 등받이 의자

크랜스턴의 아가일 가 티룸의 중앙 테이블에 놓여진 말털(horsehair fabric) 시트의 흑단색 참나무 의자로, 1990년 비엔나에서 일어난 예술 운동인 비엔나 시세션(Vienna Secession)에 전시되었다. 이것은 등받이를 높게 디자인한 매킨토시의 첫번째 의자이다. 머리를 받치는 부분을 타원형으로 만들었으며, 제비 무늬를 새겨놓았다.

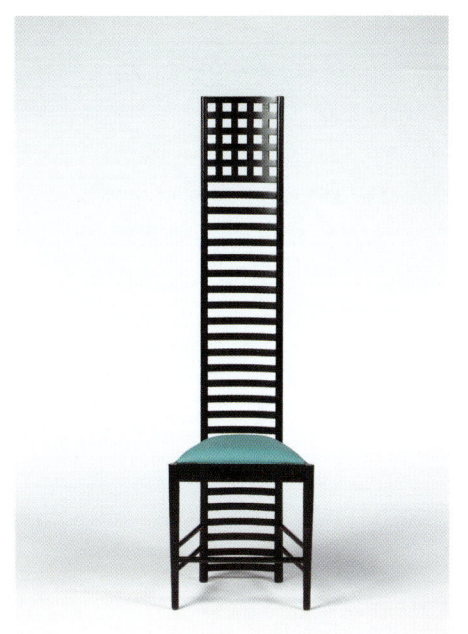

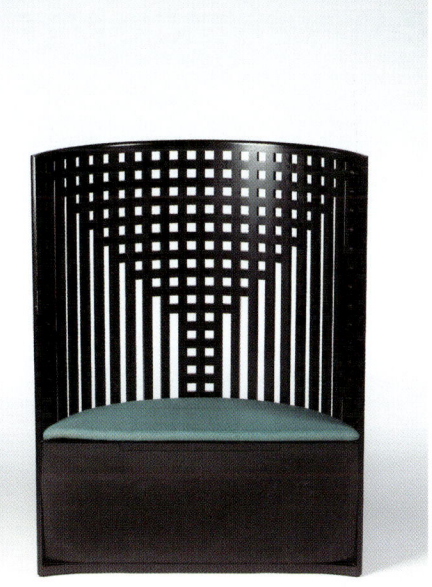

Ladder Back Chair
사다리 등받이 의자
141x41x39cm
Ash wood frame stained black, upholstered seat
물푸레나무, 천
Reissued by Cassina, Italy 카시나, 이탈리아
1902

Curved Lattice Back Chair for Willow Tearooms
윌로우 티룸을 위한 곡선모양의 격자무늬 등받이 의자
120x93x43cm
Ebonized ash wood frame, upholstered seat 물푸레나무, 천
Reissued by Cassina, Italy 카시나, 이탈리아
1904(1973)

Having commissioned Mackintosh to design the furniture for her small chain of Glasgow tea rooms, Miss Cranston then asked him to work on the interior of the Ingram Street tea room. Mackintosh devised this high-backed chair to contrast boldly against the white walls of the ladies' luncheon room.

It was designed for the Willow Tearooms ground-floor, particularly to function as the manager's seat.
The back, dropping like a shawl around the seat, defines and enclosed a specific, self-contained space in relation to the surrounding space, while establishing a choice-level in the constant status of the other chairs in the room.

글래스고에 있는 작은 티룸들을 위한 가구 디자인을 매킨 토시에게 의뢰했던 크랜스턴은 또다시 잉그램가의 티룸 인테리어를 의뢰했다. 매킨토시는 숙녀들을 위한 오찬 객 실의 하얀 벽과 뚜렷한 대비를 보여주고자 이 같이 높은 등받이의 의자를 고안했다.

이 작품은 '윌로우 티룸'의 매니저를 위해 특별히 디자인 한 의자이다. 같은 방의 다른 의자들과 동질성을 가짐과 동시에 숄처럼 늘어뜨린 듯 좌석을 감싸고 있는 등받이로 인해 주변 공간과 분리된 자신만의 독립된 공간을 만들 수 있다.

Koloman Moser 콜로만 모저

Intended for the Josef Hoffmann-designed sanatorium in Purkersdorf, this armchair is typical of the Viennese Secessionist style in its geometric form and monochrome palette. A painter and craftsman as well as a designer of glass, textiles and furniture, Koloman Moser co-founded the Wiener Werkstätte craft workshop with Hoffmann in 1903.

요제프 호프만이 설계한 이 팔걸이 의자는 푸르커스도르프의 요양원을 위해 제작된 것으로 기하학적인 형태와 흑백 무채색에서 볼 수 있듯이 전형적인 비엔나 분리파 양식을 띠고 있다. 화가이자 공예가일 뿐만 아니라 유리, 섬유, 가구 디자이너인 콜로만 모저는 1903년 호프만과 함께 비엔나 공방을 공동 설립했다.

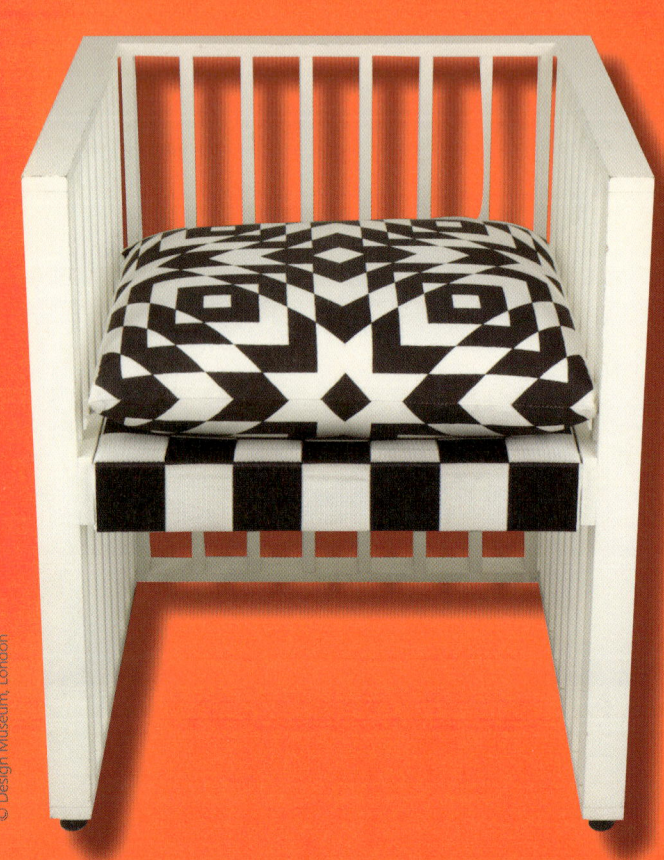

© Design Museum, London

Armchair for the Purkersdorf Sanatorium
푸르커스도르프 요양원을 위한 팔걸이 의자
70x61x61cm
Painted beech frame with wicker seat
너도밤나무, 고리버들
Reissued by Wittmann, Austria 비트만, 오스트리아
1902

Josef Hoffmann 요제프 호프만

Inspired by the Arts & Crafts Movement's belief in craft's importance over industry, Josef Hoffmann visited England in 1902. During his visit he befriended the Scottish architect Charles Rennie Mackintosh whose influence is visible in this elegant, geometric chair designed for a cabaret in Vienna. Hoffmann conceived the cabaret's design as 'a total work of art.'

산업전반에 걸친 공예의 중요성을 강조하는 미술공예(아트&크래프트)운동으로부터 영감을 얻은 요제프 호프만은 1902년 영국을 방문했다. 이 시기에 요제프 호프만은 스코틀랜드 건축가 찰스 레니 매킨토시와 친분을 쌓게 되는데, 매킨토시는 비엔나의 카바레를 위해 디자인된 이 우아하고 기하학적인 의자에 영향을 주었음이 분명하다. 호프만은 이 작품, 카바레 플레더마우스의 카페의자를 '총체적인 예술작품'이라고 생각했다.

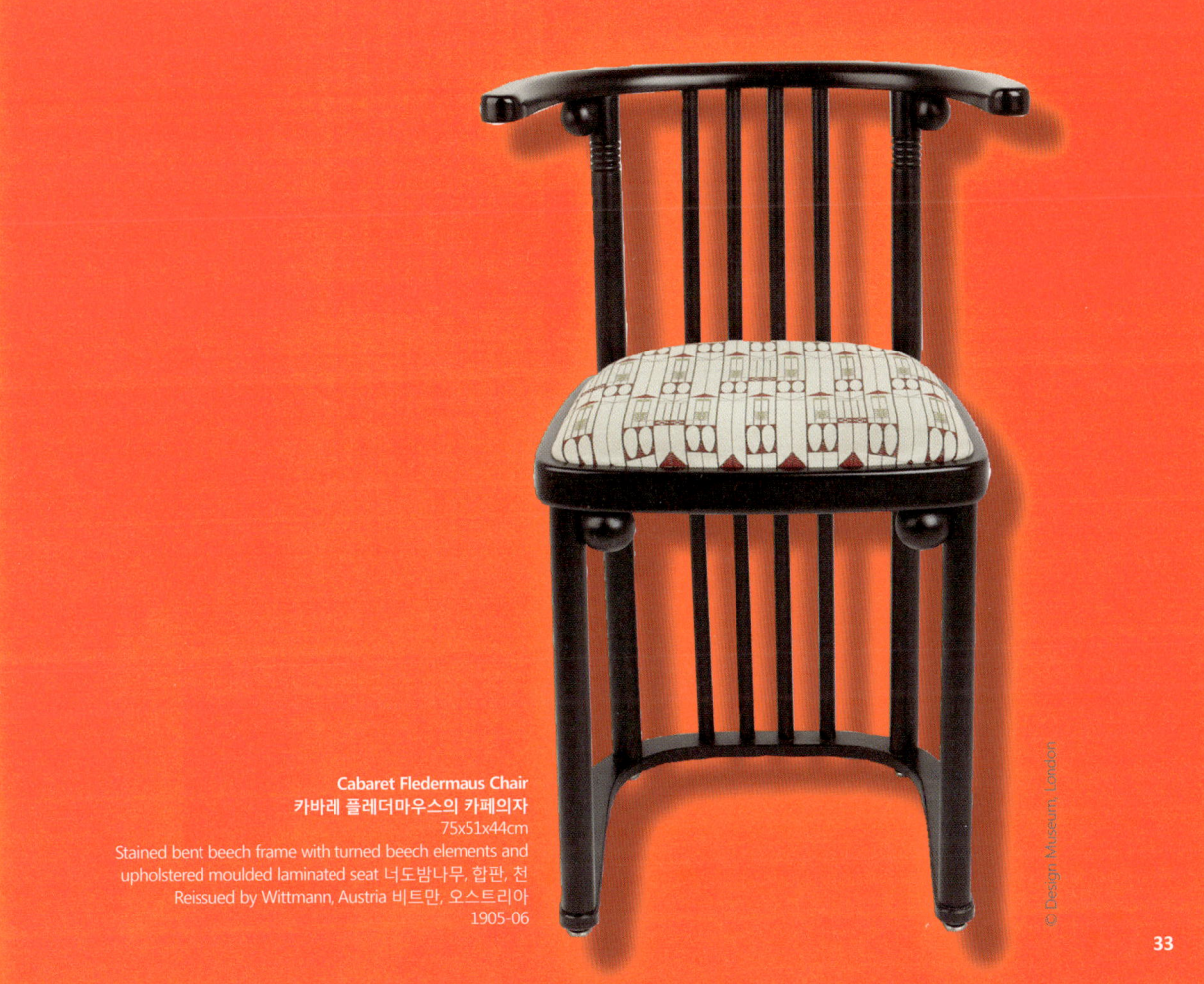

Cabaret Fledermaus Chair
카바레 플레더마우스의 카페의자
75x51x44cm
Stained bent beech frame with turned beech elements and upholstered moulded laminated seat 너도밤나무, 합판, 천
Reissued by Wittmann, Austria 비트만, 오스트리아
1905-06

© Design Museum, London

Frank Lloyd Wright 프랭크 로이드 라이트

"Machines can be valuable tools for a better society when used synthetically."
The characteristic of Wright's design is adoption of natural elements, cubist thought, and the influence of Japanese style architecture. In other words, Wright sought for the life of his work in nature and adopted natural materials to it so as to express organic property by eliminating the boundary between the exterior and the interior of architecture. As a member of Prairie School, he is a designer who found a design element from nature, cubic, and something Oriental, and pursued simplicity in his design through his entire life.

"기계는 종합적으로 사용된다면 보다 나은 사회를 위해 유용한 도구가 될 수 있다."
라이트 디자인의 특징으로 자연적 요소의 도입, 큐비즘적 사고 그리고 일본식 건축의 영향을 들 수 있다. 즉 작품의 생명을 자연으로부터 얻고자 자연재를 작품에 도입했으며, 건축 내·외부 공간의 경계를 없앰으로써 유기적 특성을 표현하였다. 그는 프레리 학파로서 기계에 긍정적인 태도를 보이면서도 자연과 큐빅 그리고 동양적인 것으로부터 디자인적 요소를 발견하여, 전 생애에 걸쳐 간결한 작품세계를 추구한 작가이다.

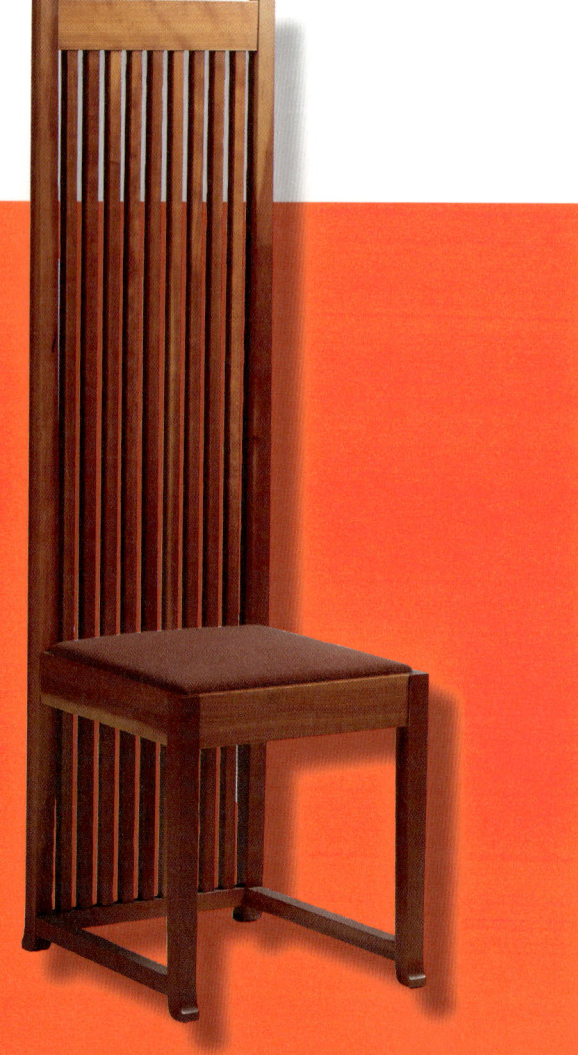

Robie Chair
로비 의자
133x40x45.5cm
Natural cherry wood, seat upholstery in polyurethane foam, fabric
체리나무, 폴리우레탄 폼, 천
Reissued by Cassina, Italy 카시나, 이탈리아
1908

The Chair, which was never actually made at the time, has been produced by developing design sketches for interiors within the Midway Gardens. In the certainty that it effectively includes the aesthetic intentions of the architect, the chair is based on hexagonal forms deriving from Wright's creative skill with a set-square within a framework of straight lines and horizontal plains. In his eyes, shapes are visually pleasing forms, and, in actual fact, the gardens were to be a comment on the art of building, particularly through the furnishings. In this context, the design of the surround of the chair is remarkable. The side wings bring together the functions of arm-rest, but, however, the chair is no way out of place at a table. Moreover, the basic hexagonal aesthetic shape was to be used by Wright again in the interior of the Imperial Hotel in Tokyo and late still it was to become a basic feature of his work.

그 당시에는 실제로 제작되지 않았던 이 의자는 '미드웨이 가든'의 인테리어를 위한 스케치로 고안된 디자인이었다. 확실히 그것은 건축의 심미적 의도를 포함하고 있다. 육각형을 기본으로 한 이 의자는 직선적이고 수평적인 구조를 특징으로 하는 라이트의 창의적 틀에서 기인했다. 그의 시선에서 이 형태는 시각적 즐거움을 주는 도형이었다. 사실 가구를 배치하고 선택하는 작업은 정원을 관리하는 것만큼이나 건축의 예술성에서 중요한 요인이다. 이와 관련해서 의자의 가장자리 디자인은 주목 할만 하다. 팔걸이의 기능을 하는 양쪽 날개는 테이블과 함께 놓았을 때, 어떤 공간도 차지하지 않는다. 라이트는 또한 이와 같은 육각형의 미적 형태를 도쿄 '임페리얼 호텔'의 인테리어에도 사용했다. 따라서 이 형태는 그의 작업에 있어 기본적인 특성으로 자리잡았다.

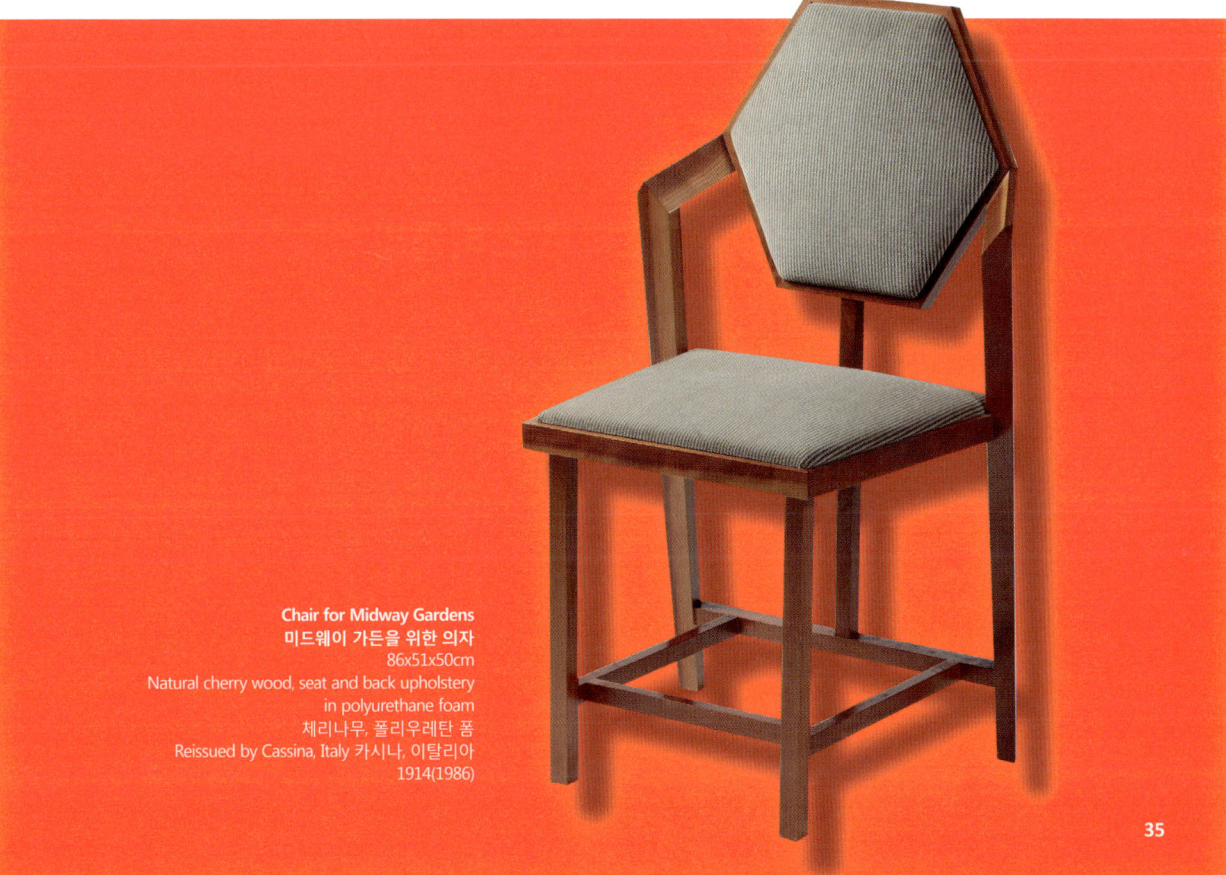

Chair for Midway Gardens
미드웨이 가든을 위한 의자
86x51x50cm
Natural cherry wood, seat and back upholstery
in polyurethane foam
체리나무, 폴리우레탄 폼
Reissued by Cassina, Italy 카시나, 이탈리아
1914(1986)

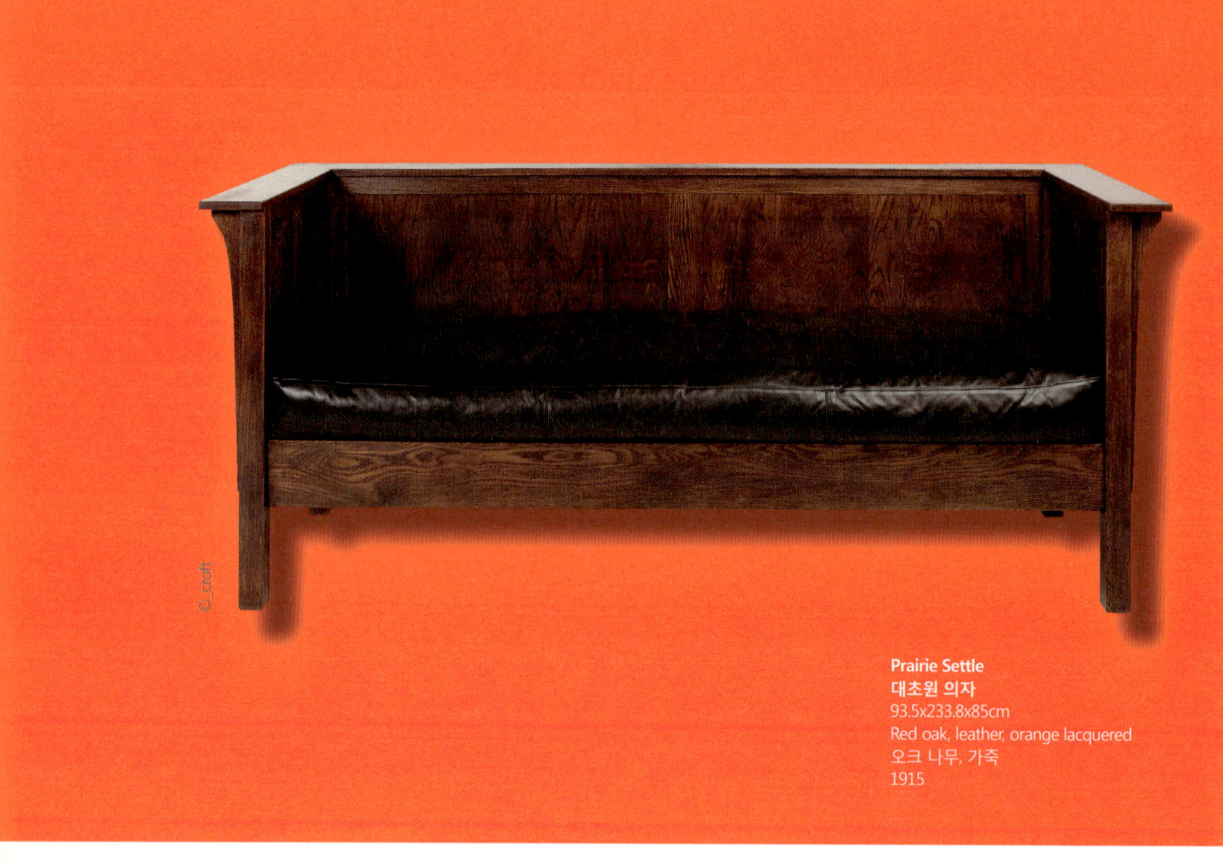

©_croft

Prairie Settle
대초원 의자
93.5x233.8x85cm
Red oak, leather, orange lacquered
오크 나무, 가죽
1915

USA | 미국

Gustav Stickley 구스타브 스티클리

About his aesthetic principles, Stickley briefly states, "A prominent concept on structure means to display intentions straightforwardly that an object intends, but to impair or hide its structural property so as to strictly exhibit no decorative aspect applied in all works equally". His firm and simple design of chairs, made of rushes, leather seats, and oak trees almost without ornaments, completely represents his viewpoint. His works exhibit the influences by his uncle who produced plain chairs in unique ways with oak tree cane as well as by the apprentices by Morris.

스티클리는 "탁월한 구조 개념은 하나의 대상이 의도한 목적을 솔직하게 나타내는 것을 의미하며 구조적인 특색을 손상시켜버리거나 감추어 버리는 응용장식이 없는 것과 완성된 것을 모든 작품에 엄격하게 적용시키는 것"으로 자신의 미학적 원리를 약술했다. 골풀이나 가죽시트, 그리고 장식이 없는 참나무에 거의 변화를 가하지 않고 만든, 그의 견고하고 단순한 의자 디자인은 이러한 생각들을 완전히 구현하고 있다. 이는 등나무 줄기 시트로 단순한 의자들을 특색 있게 만들었던 캐비닛 제조업자인 그의 삼촌과 더불어 모리스와 스티클리의 도제들의 영향을 받았음을 보여준다.

Sources | Frank Russell, *A Century of Chair Design*,
        trans. kim, Kyung Sook, Gimundang, 1991.

출처 | 프랭크 러셀, 김경숙 역, *현대 의자디자인의 역사*, 기문당, 1991.

Pierre Chareau 피에르 샤로

Chareau's furniture was produced mostly by orders. His chairs in the early 1920's were produced with thick seats, using mahoganies, walnut and oak trees, poplars and maple trees as wooden materials polished in round shapes with few decorations.

For ten years after on, Chareau received orders for furniture from commercial spaces like bars, hotels, and clubs, and used metal frames for them. His contemporary presses highly applauded his works made of wood or metal because his designs achieved a harmony in combination of aesthetical elegance and technical dexterity as well as their functions in chairs, stools, tables, and cupboards designs.

Sources | Frank Russell, *A Century of Chair Design*, trans. Kim, Kyung Sook, Gimundang, 1991.

샤로의 가구는 대부분 주문 디자인이었다. 1920년대 초반의 그의 의자 디자인들은 장식이 많지 않은 둥그런 형태로 광택을 낸 나무-마호가니, 호두나무, 참나무, 사시나무, 단풍나무-등을 사용하고, 두꺼운 시트로 만들었다.
그 뒤 10년 동안 샤로는 바, 호텔, 클럽들과 같은 상업적 공간을 위한 가구 주문을 받았고, 금속 뼈대를 사용했다. 동시대의 출판물에서는 나무나 금속으로 만든 그의 의자, 스툴, 테이블과 찬장 디자인 등을 대단히 격찬했는데, 그 이유는 그의 디자인들이 우아함과 기술적인 문제를 기능적으로 잘 결합시킨 것이었기 때문이다.

출처 | 프랭크 러셀, 김경숙 역, *현대 의자디자인의 역사*, 기문당, 1991.

Chair
의자
66x54x65cm
1920'

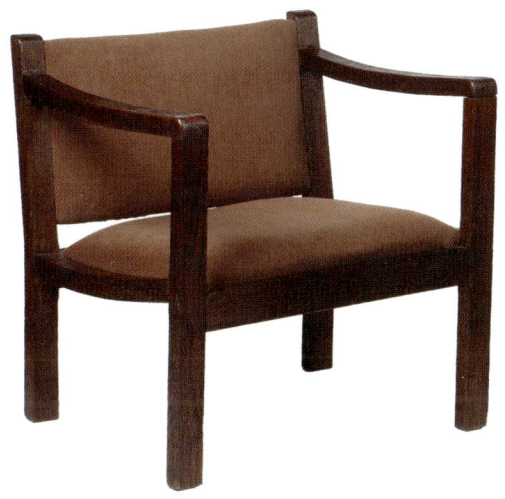
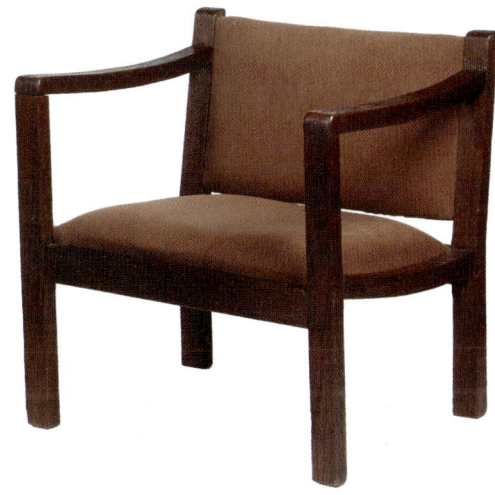

Gerrit Thomas Rietveld 헤릿 토마스 리트벨트

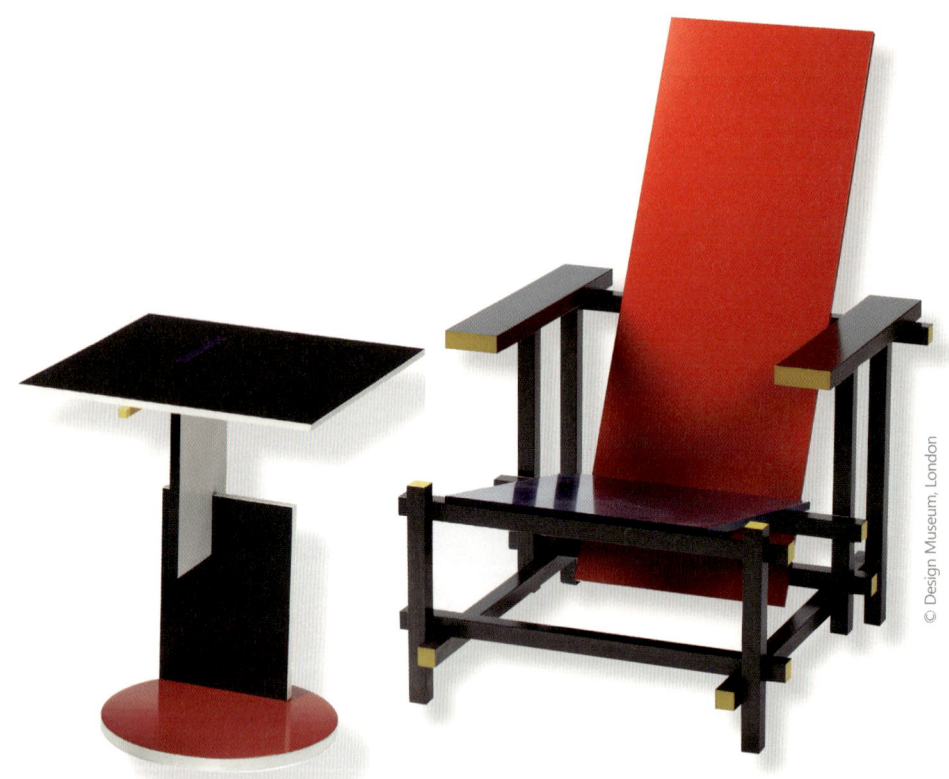

© Design Museum, London

Red Blue Chair
레드 블루 의자
90x66x80cm
Painted solid beech and plywood 너도밤나무, 합판
Reissued by Cassina, Italy 카시나, 이탈리아
1918

Table
테이블
60x50x50cm
Painted solid beech and plywood 너도밤나무, 합판
1917-19

Conceived as an abstract composition of surfaces and lines in space, this chair resembles a three-dimensional Mondrian painting, yet Rietveld always intended it for mass-production. Made from standard lengths of wood, it requires little skill to construct. Originally finished in natural wood, the *Red Blue Chair* was painted by Rietveld in 1921.

공간 속에서 면과 선의 추상적 구성을 보여주고 있는 이 의자는 3차원의 몬드리안 그림과 유사하지만, 리트벨트는 늘 대량 생산을 염두에 두었다. 표준 규격의 나무로 만들어진 이 의자는 조립하는데 약간의 기술만이 필요하다. 원래는 자연색의 나무로 제작되었다가, 1921년 리트벨트가 색을 입혔다.

The son of a Utrecht cabinetmaker, Gerrit Thomas Rietveld worked in his father's workshop as an apprentice craftsman from the age of eleven. Rietveld's early work with wood reinforced his later role as a radical designer, architect and member of the avant-garde De Stijl movement. It gave him the technical expertise to put some of De Stijl's principles into practice, notably by realising its zest for oblique diagonal lines in this cantilevered *Zig-Zag* chair.

위트레흐트의 가구제작자의 아들인 헤릿 토마스 리트벌트는 11살 때부터 도제장인으로 그의 아버지 작업장에서 일했다. 나무로 만든 리트벌트의 초기 작품들은 진보적 디자이너, 건축가이자 아방가르드 데 스틸 운동의 구성원으로서 리트벌트의 역할을 강화시켰다. 켄틸레버 *지그-재그* 의자는 경사진 각에 대한 그의 흥미를 뚜렷이 보여주고 있는데, 이와 같은 리트벌트의 기술적 전문성은 데 스틸 운동의 원칙들을 잘 실현할 수 있게끔 했다.

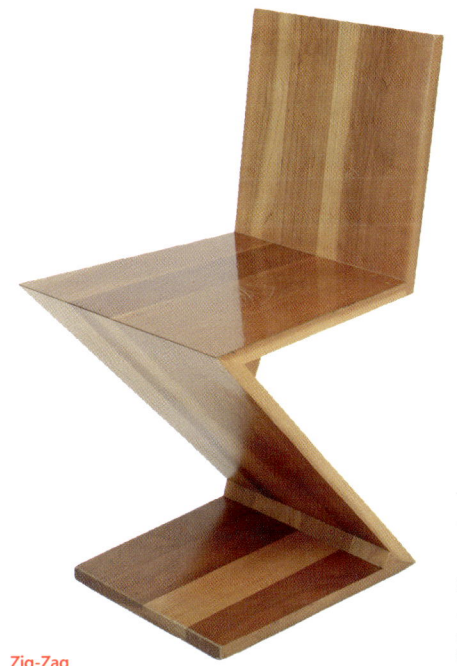

© Design Museum, London

Zig-Zag
지그-재그
74x38x42cm
Oak and brass 오크나무, 황동
Cassina, Italy 카시나, 이탈리아
1932-34

Intended for use in holiday homes, the *Crate* reflects the growing enthusiasm of its designer, the visionary architect Gerrit Rietveld for rudimentary construction. Like its predecessor, the *Zig-Zag* Chair, the *Crate* was simply constructed from inexpensive planks of wood with visible flaws. For Rietveld, the uncompromising simplicity of the *Crate* was an honest response to the harsh economic climate during the early 1930s.

휴일에 가정에서 사용하기 위해 만든 크레이트 의자는 기본 구조에 있어서 공상적인 건축가 헤릿 리트벌트의 초창기 열정을 보여준다. 이전 모델인 *지/그-재그* 의자처럼 크레이트 의자 역시 흠집들이 그대로 보이는 값싼 나무 판자로 간단히 만들어 졌다. 리트벌트의 크레이트는 타협 없는 단순함으로 1930년대 초 혹독한 경제난을 숨김없이 반영하고 있다.

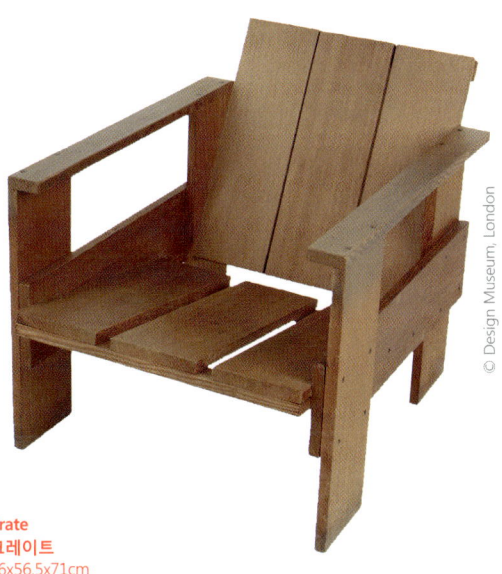

© Design Museum, London

Crate
크레이트
56x56.5x71cm
Red spruce 빨간 가문비나무
Cassina, Italy 카시나, 이탈리아
1934

Marcel Breuer 마르셀 브로이어

Wassily, Model No. B3
바실리, 모델 No. B3
74x79x70cm
Frame is seamless tubular steel with a polished
chrome finish 크롬도금 강철튜브
1925

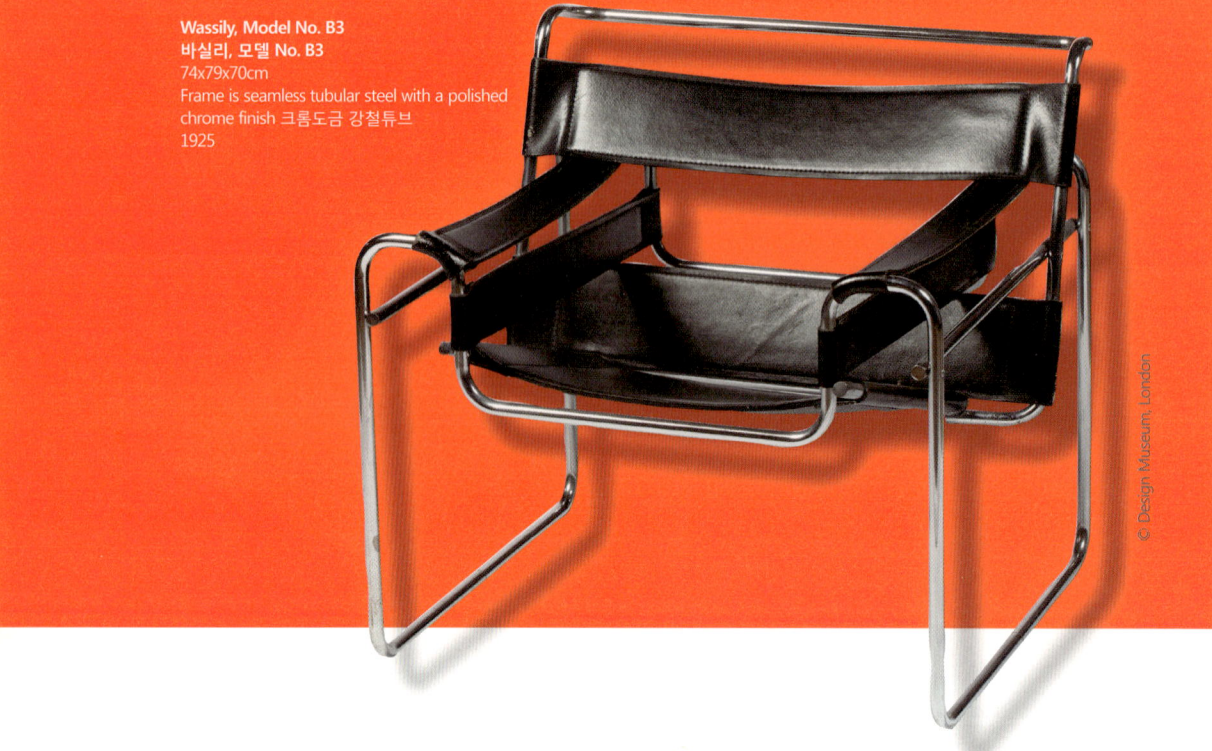

© Design Museum, London

If one asks who, of the Second Generation in Europe, captured the essence of his period in furniture, the answer must be Marcel Breuer. When the Eames were at their start point, Marcel Breuer was in America. In the same way as when one sees the drawings of the Beard House one says, "the Eames' House starts here", on sight of a photograph of Breuer´s aluminium lounge chair one says: "the Aluminium group starts here"; for line is in the eye of a single generation and fabrication and process are tied to what is uniquely available to that generation.

Sources | From "The Eames Within their Generation" 1985 (P.S.) a fragment published in *Changing the Art of Inhabitation*.

어떤 사람이 만일 유럽의 제 2세대 중 당대 가구의 본질을 보여준 사람이 누구냐고 묻는다면, 그 대답은 아마 마르셀 브로이어가 될 것이다. 임스 부부가 처음 작업을 시작할 때 마르셀 브로이어는 미국에 있었다. 마치 누군가가 비어드 하우스를 그린 드로잉을 보고 "임스의 집이 여기에서 시작되었군."이라고 말하는 것처럼, 브로이어의 알루미늄 안락 의자를 본다면 "알루미늄 작업은 여기서 시작된거였군." 이렇게 말할 것이다. 왜냐하면 눈에 비친 라인들은 단일한 덩어리의 산출이며, 그 조작 방법과 진행 방식은 이 산출에서만 가능한 방식이기 때문이다.

출처 | *주거의 예술을 바꾸다* 중 "자신들의 세대 속에서의 임스 부부"에서 발췌, 1985.

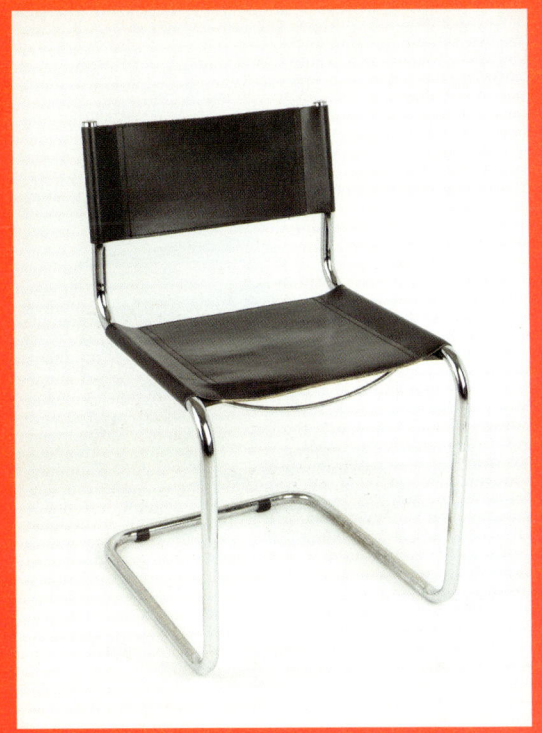

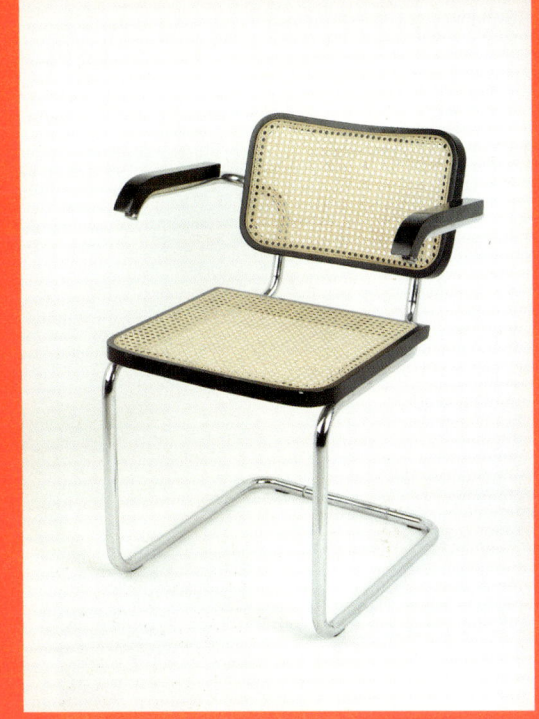

Model No. B33
모델 No. B.33
80x48x52cm
Chrome-plated tubular steel, leather 크롬도금 강철튜브, 가죽
Gebrüder Thonet, Austria 게브뤼더 토네트, 오스트리아
1927-28

Model No. B64
모델 No. B64
80x60x60cm
Chrome-plated tubular steel, cane 크롬도금 강철튜브, 등나무
Gebrüder Thonet, Austria 게브뤼더 토네트, 오스트리아
1928

When the *B33* chair went on sale, the spectacle of such a slender chair without conventional legs or arms was so unusual that many people were frightened to sit on it. The *B33* was a bittersweet project for Breuer. He started work on it knowing that he had lost the race to develop the first cantilevered chair to the Dutch architect Mart Stam, who had completed the his *MS33* side chair in 1926. Made of non-reinforced tubular steel Breuer's chair was more resilient and more comfortable.

*B33*의자가 판매되기 시작됐을 때, 다리와 팔걸이가 없는 매우 슬림한 의자의 모양새가 너무 특이해서 많은 사람들은 여기에 앉는 것조차 꺼려했다. *B33*의자는 브로이어에게 있어 괴롭고도 즐거운 프로젝트였다. 최초의 '켄틸레버 의자'를 누가 먼저 개발하는가 하는 분위기 속에 독일 건축가 마트 스탐이 1926년 *MS33* 사이드 의자를 먼저 발표하면서 브로이어는 이 프로젝트에 공을 들이기 시작했다. 비강화 강철튜브로 만들어진 브로이어의 의자들은 더 탄력적이고 더욱 더 편안했다.

Like the earlier *B33*, Breuer's *B32* is made of non-reinforced tubular steel. The *B32* marries the use of the modern aesthetic of the tubular steel with the more traditional woven cane seat.

이전의 *B33* 모델처럼, *B32*는 비강화 강철튜브로 만들어졌다. B32는 전통적인 재료인 등나무 줄기로 엮은 시트와 강철튜브를 함께 사용함으로써 현대판 심미적 만남을 잘 구현하고 있다.

* The chair appears to have no rear legs but supported by 'ㄷ' shaped steel tubes.
  뒤쪽 다리 없이 외형적으로 하나의 구부러진 강철 튜브 ('ㄷ'자 모양의 다리)가 의자를 받치는 형태

Ludwig Mies van der Rohe
루드비히 미스 반 데어 로에

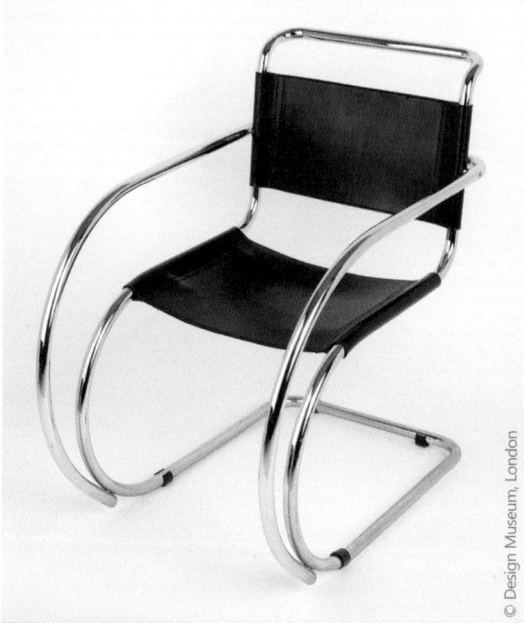

© Design Museum, London

MR20
86x55x80cm
Chromium-plated tubular steel and leather
크롬도금 강철튜브, 가죽
Reissued by Knoll International, US 놀 인터내셔널, 미국
1927

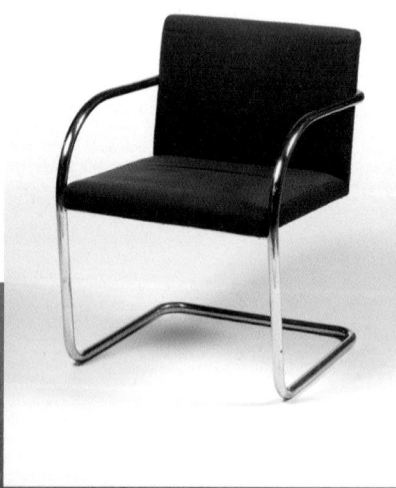

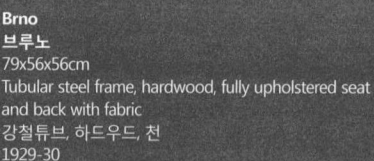

Brno
브루노
79x56x56cm
Tubular steel frame, hardwood, fully upholstered seat
and back with fabric
강철튜브, 하드우드, 천
1929-30

During his collaboration with the interior designer Lilly Reich, Mies developed a series of seminal pieces of furniture. One was the *MR20*, a cantilevered chair intended to offer the comfort of a conventional armchair without the bourgeois associations of upholstery. The *MR20* was exhibited at the 1927 Die Wohnung exhibition of modern living at the Weissenhof Settlement in Stuttgart.

미스는 인테리어 디자이너인 릴리 라이히와 협력해 중요한 가구 시리즈들을 개발했다. 그 중 하나가 부르주아를 연상시키는 쿠션을 쓰지 않으면서 기존 안락의자의 편안함을 제공할 수 있게끔 디자인된 켄틸레버 의자 *MR20*이다. 이 *MR20*은 1927년 스투트가르트의 뷔센호프에서 열린 디 뷔농 모던 리빙 전시회에서 소개되었다.

Barcelona Chair, Model No. MR90
바르셀로나 체어, 모델 No. MR90
73x75x75cm
Bent chromed flat steel frame with leather straps and leather upholstered cushions
강철, 가죽
Reissue by Knoll International, US 놀 인터내셔널, 미국
1929

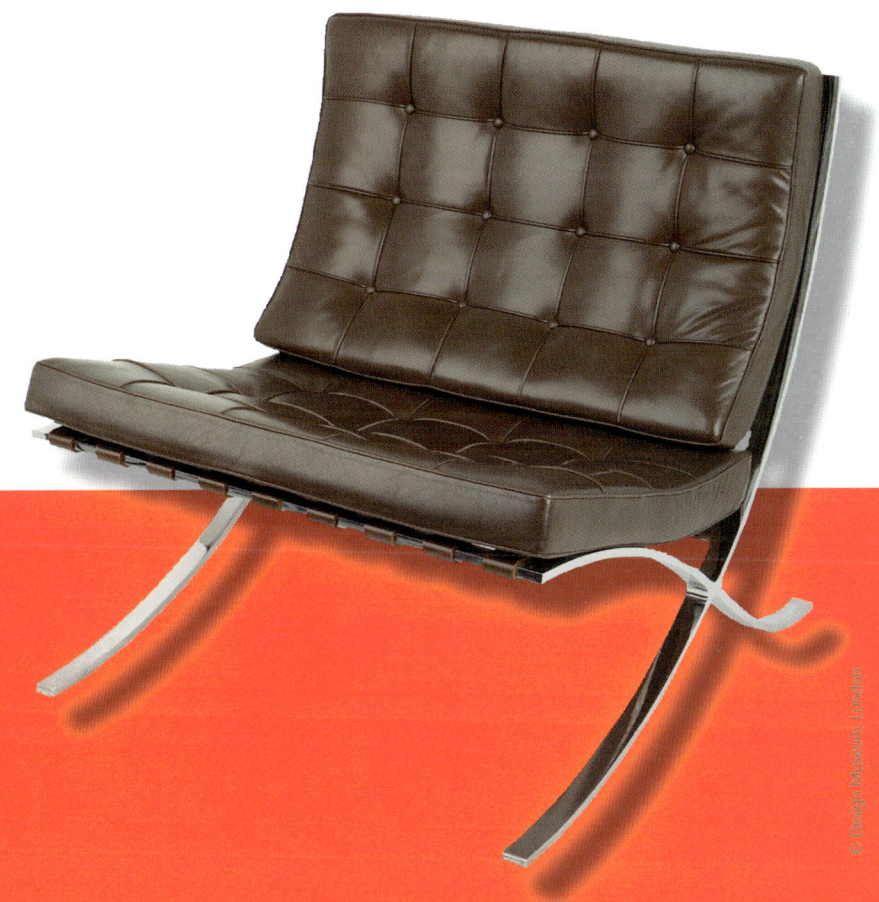

© Design Museum, London

In 1929, Mies was commissioned to design the German Pavilion for the International Exhibition in Barcelona and its contents. As the pavilion was to be the setting for the official opening ceremony, Mies chose a throne-like form for its chairs. His *Barcelona Chair* was inspired by the *sella curulis*, an ancient stool used by Roman magistrates.

1929년, 미스는 바르셀로나에서 열리는 만국박람회의 독일 전시관(Pavilion) 설계와 내부 구성을 맡게 되었다. 전시관은 공식적인 오프닝 행사를 위해 구성되어야 했기 때문에, 미스는 옥좌와 같은 형태의 의자를 선택했다. *바르셀로나 의자*는 로마 치안대에서 사용된 고대 스툴인 *셀라 쿠룰리스*에서 영감을 받았다.

© Design Museum, London

Grand Confort Model No. LC2 Club Chair
그랑 콩포르 모델 No. LC2 클럽 체어
62x98x72cm
Chromed bent tubular steel, leather 크롬도금 강철튜브, 가죽
Thonet Frères, Austria 토네트 프헤예스, 오스트리아
1928

France, Switzerland | 프랑스, 스위스

Le Corbusier, Charlotte Perriand, Pierre Jeanneret
르 코르뷔지에, 샬롯 페리앙, 피에르 잔느레

Until the arrival of Charlotte Perriand, Le Corbusier had furnished his residential projects and exhibition sets with chairs by Thonet and Maples. With Perriand, Le Corbusier's studio started to develop furniture in the angular forms and industrial materials of the modernist movement. Originally designed for Maison La Roche in Paris, this chair was inspired by Le Corbusier's favourite Maples club chair.

샬롯 페리앙을 초청하기 전, 르 코르뷔지에는 주택 프로젝트와 전시회 등에 쓰이는 의자를 토네트와 메이플스에 주문하곤 했다. 페리앙이 합류하면서 르 코르뷔지에의 스튜디오는 모던디자인의 움직임으로 등장한 산업소재들을 가지고 각이 진 형태의 가구를 개발하기 시작했다. 원래는 파리의 라 로쉐 주택을 위해 디자인된 이 의자는 르 코르뷔지에가 좋아하는 메이플스 클럽 의자에서 영감을 받았다.

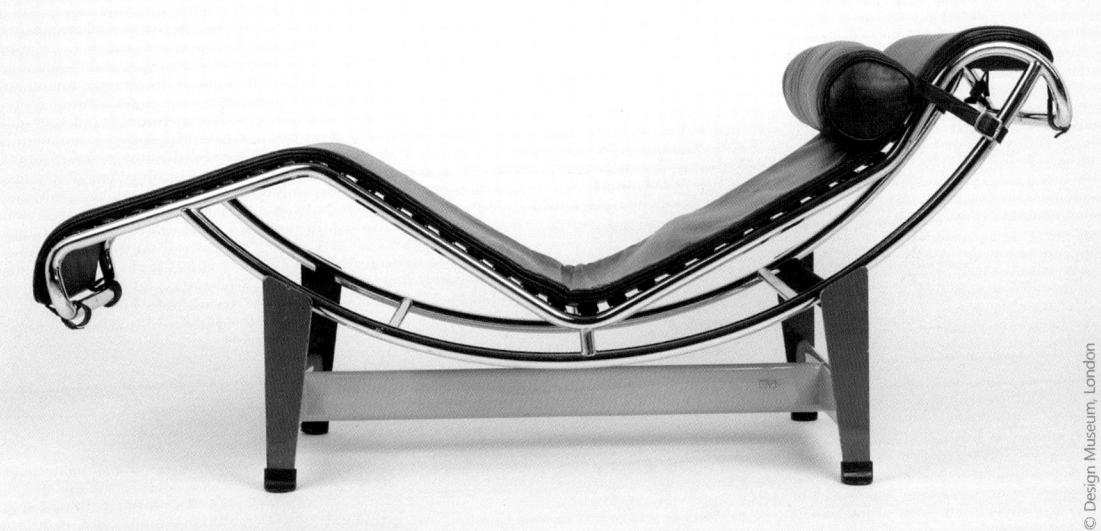

© Design Museum, London

Chaise Longue Model No. B306
쉐즈 롱 모델 No. B306
64x163x55cm
Chromed bent tubular steel, leather 크롬도금 강철튜브, 가죽
Thonet Fréres, Austria 토네트 프헤예스, 오스트리아
1928

Inspired by the graceful curves of 18th century French daybeds, the *chaise longue* combined the utility of tubular steel with the decadence of pony skin and leather. "I thought of the cowboy from the Wild West smoking his pipe, feet in the air higher than his head, against the chimney-piece: complete rest," recalled Le Corbusier. Charlotte Perriand posed for the publicity shots of the *B306* with bobbed hair, a daringly short skirt and a necklace of industrial ball bearings.

18세기 프랑스 침대겸용소파의 우아한 곡선으로부터 영감을 받은 디자인 쉐즈 롱(긴 안락의자)은, 조랑말 가죽의 데카당스한 이미지와 강철튜브의 유용함을 결합했다. 르 코르뷔지에는 "나는 완벽한 휴식에 반하여 파이프 담배를 피우며 발을 머리보다 높은 곳에 둔 서부의 카우보이를 생각했다."고 회상했다. 샬롯 페리앙은 B306의 홍보 촬영을 위해 단발머리에 대담한 미니 스커트, 그리고 산업용 볼 베어링으로 된 목걸이를 착용하고 포즈를 취했다.

Alvar Aalto 알바 알토

As one of the most important Scandinavian architects and designers, Alvar Aalto presented Finland, his homeland an honor in the field of architecture and furniture design. Being recognized as a master of Modern Movement, Aalto is the only designer, among his contemporaries, who has produced works paying regard to warmness, naturalness and human emotions. His working method was to contrast functionalism and didacticism of main currents in modernism. Observing furniture as 'a belonging of architecture,' Aalto explains that his purpose is 'creation of organic volumes made of multi-dimensional and sculpture-like looking wood's forms...neither artificially cut nor sculpted.'

Sources | Frank Russell, *A Century of Chair Design*, trans. Kim, Kyung Sook, Gimundang, 1991.

알바 알토는 20세기 가장 중요한, 스칸디나비아의 건축가이자 디자이너이고, 그의 조국 핀란드 건축과 가구 디자인 분야에 명성을 가져다 준 장본인이었다. 모던 운동(Modern Movement)의 거장으로 인정받고 있는 알토는 그의 동시대인들 중에서도 따뜻함과 자연스러움, 그리고 인간의 감정을 고려한 작품을 디자인했던 유일한 사람이다. – 그는 모더니즘의 주류인 기능주의와 교훈적 특성을 대조시켜 작품을 제작했다. 알토는 가구를 '건축에 따르는 부속물'로 보았으며, '다차원적이고 조각 같은 나무 형태들... 자르거나 조각하지 않은 나무가 만들어내는 유기적인 부피의 창조'가 그의 목적이라고 말했다.

출처 | 프랭크 러셀, 김경숙 역, 현대 의자디자인의 역사, 기문당, 1991.

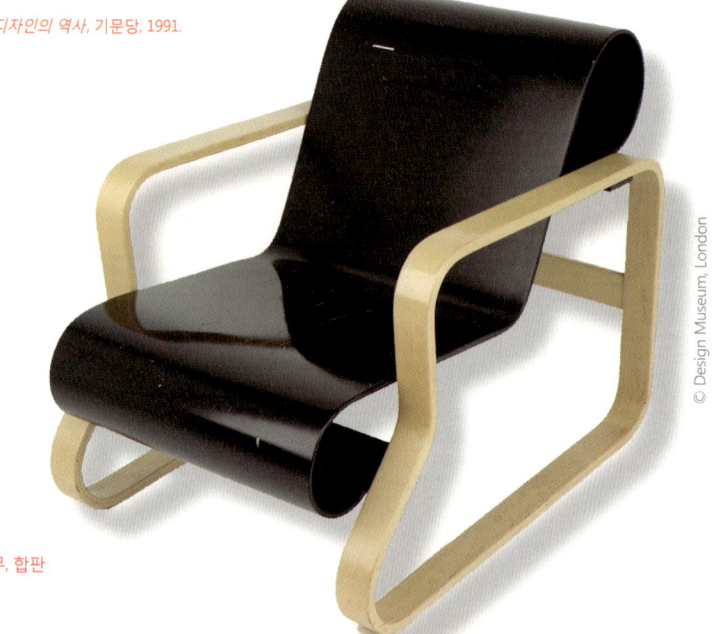

© Design Museum, London

Paimio Lounge Chair 41
파이미오 라운지 체어 41
66x60x83cm
Laminated birch and plywood 자작나무, 합판
Artek, Finland 아르텍, 핀란드
1930-31

When Alvar Aalto won the commission to design the Paimio Sanatorium in the late 1920s, he approached the project as if he was a patient. No detail escaped him: from the cheerful canary yellow paint on the stairs, to the strong, comfortable furniture. Aalto experimented with plywood for three years to develop a chair which would ease the breathing of tuberculosis patients. This was the first pliant chair to be built without a rigid framework.

알바 알토가 1920년대 후반 파이미오 요양원 설계의 권한을 위임 받았을 때, 그는 마치 환자가 된 듯 프로젝트에 임했다. 밝은 카나리아 노란색의 계단부터 튼튼하고 편안한 가구까지, 어떤 사소한 것 하나라도 놓치지 않았다. 알토는 결핵환자의 호흡을 편안하게 해줄 수 있는 의자를 개발하기 위해 3년 동안 합판을 가지고 실험했다. 이 작품은 최초로 단단한 뼈대 없이 만들어진 탄성이 있는 의자였다.

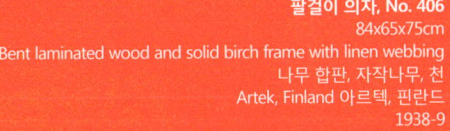

Arm Chair, No. 406
팔걸이 의자, No. 406
84x65x75cm
Bent laminated wood and solid birch frame with linen webbing
나무 합판, 자작나무, 천
Artek, Finland 아르텍, 핀란드
1938-9

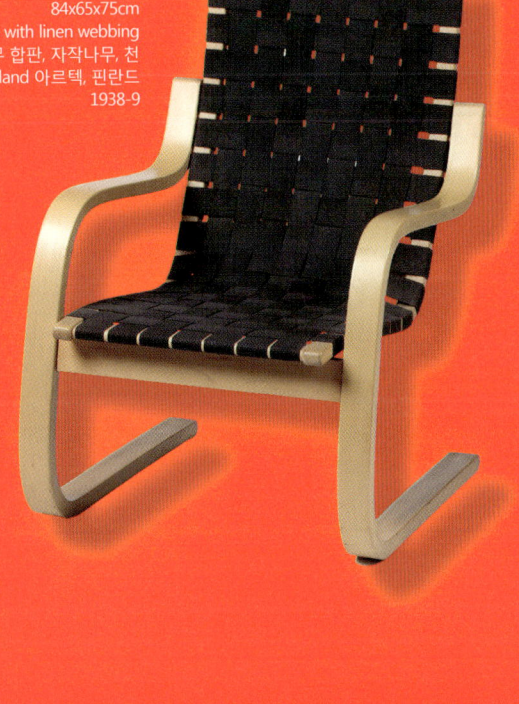

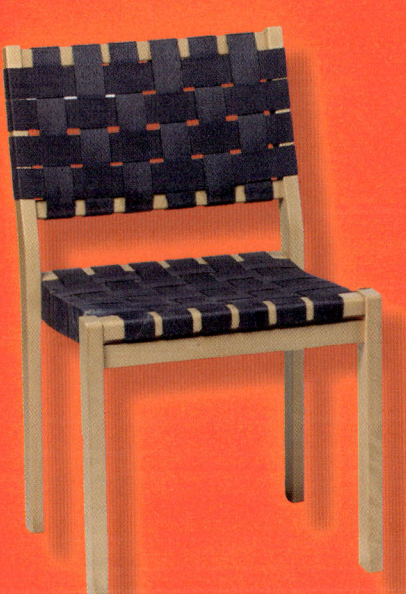

No. 611
80x49x48.5cm
Solid birch frame with linen webbing 자작나무, 천
Artek, Finland 아르텍, 핀란드
1929

Stacking Stools Model No. 60
스태킹 스툴 모델 No. 60
44x38x38cm
Bent laminated birch 자작나무 합판
Artek, Finland 아르텍, 핀란드
1932

Stacking Stools Model No. 60

Throughout the 1920s and 1930s Alvar Aalto's work was influenced by that of the International Style designers he had admired on trips to France and Germany, but he was determined to interpret it in a distinctive style, notably by using native Finnish woods. Originally designed for the Viipuri Library, these stools caused a sensation when they were exhibited in 1933 with Aalto's *Paimio Chair* at Fortnum & Mason department store in London.

스태킹 스툴 모델 No. 60

1920년대와 1930년대 전반에 걸친 알바 알토의 작품은 그가 프랑스와 독일을 여행하면서, 경의를 표했던 국제 양식 디자이너들의 영향을 받았다. 그는 특히 핀란드 본토의 나무들을 이용하여 독특한 스타일로 작품을 해석하고자 했다. 원래 비이프리 도서관을 위해 디자인된 이 의자들은 1933년 제작된 *파이미오 체어*와 함께 런던의 포트넘 & 메이슨 백화점에서 전시되었을 때 센세이션을 일으켰다.

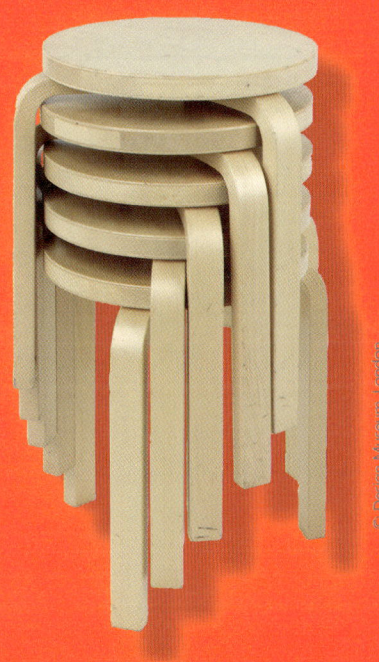

© Design Museum, London

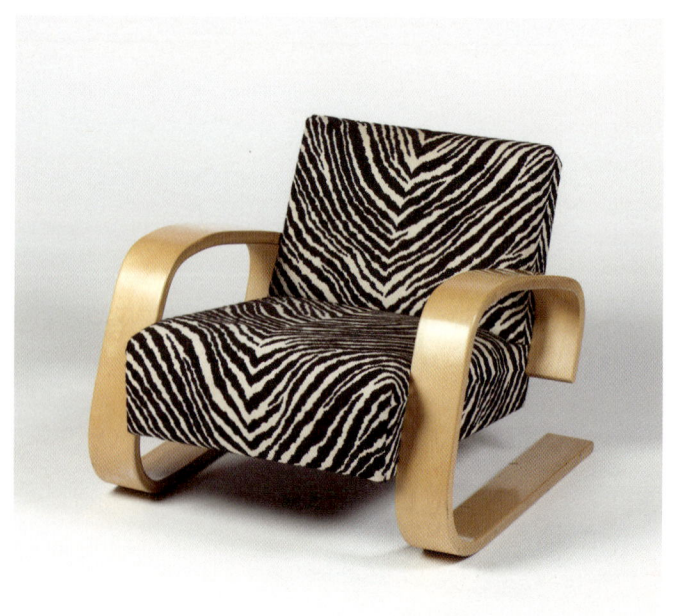

Arm Chair, No. 37
팔걸이 의자, No. 37
87x72x60cm
Laminated birch, wool and cotton
upholstery 자작나무 합판, 울, 면
Artek, Finland 아르텍, 핀란드
1935-36

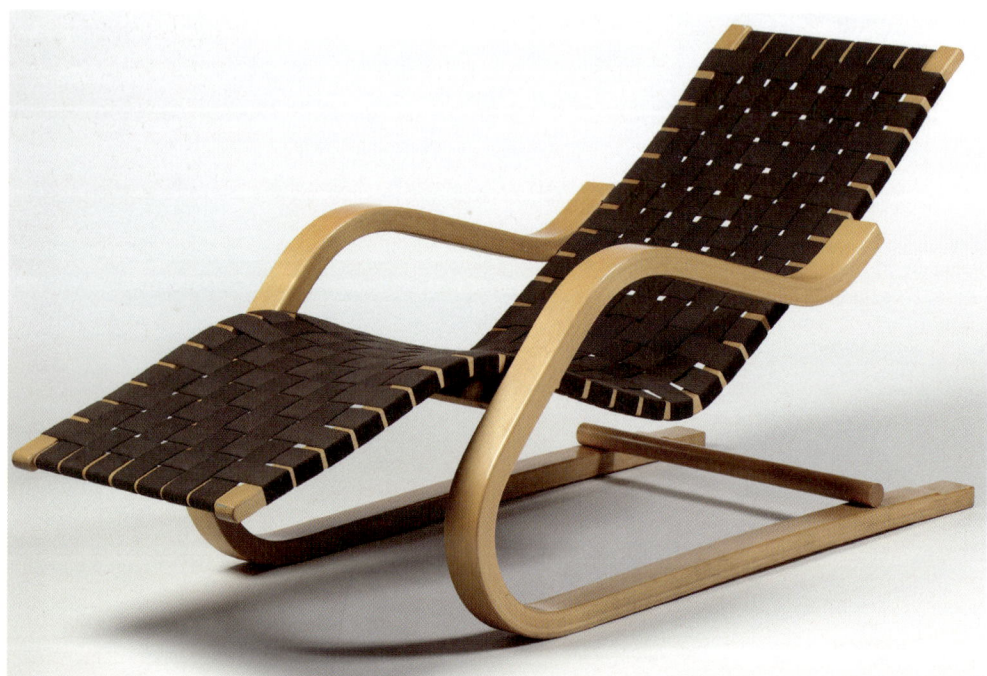

Chaise Lounge
체이스 라운지
270x110x100cm
Bent laminated wood and solid birch frame with linen webbing
합판, 자작나무, 천
Artek, Finland 아르텍, 핀란드
1936

Bruno Mathsson 브루노 마트손

As an apprentice at Karl Mathsson, his father's woodworking company in the early 1930s, Bruno Mathsson experimented with bentwood. By combining these experiments with detailed anatomical studies, he developed new methods of bending and laminating wood to make furniture intended to give greater comfort to the sitter. In the *T 102* chair the laminated beech and stretched hemp webbing allows for greater mobility and elasticity.

1930년대 초 브루노 마트손은 아버지의 목공회사인 칼 마트손에서 견습생으로 있으며 목재를 금속 틀에 넣어 모양을 잡는 공법을 실험했다. 그는 이러한 실험들과 상세한 인체해부학적 연구를 결합하고, 앉는 사람에게 더욱더 큰 편안함을 줄 수 있는 가구를 만들기 위해 나무를 구부리고 얇은 판으로 만드는 새로운 방법을 개발했다. *T102 체어*와 같이 얇게 만든 너도밤나무와 신축성 있는 마(천)를 짜는 방법은 더 나은 이동성과 탄력성을 제공한다.

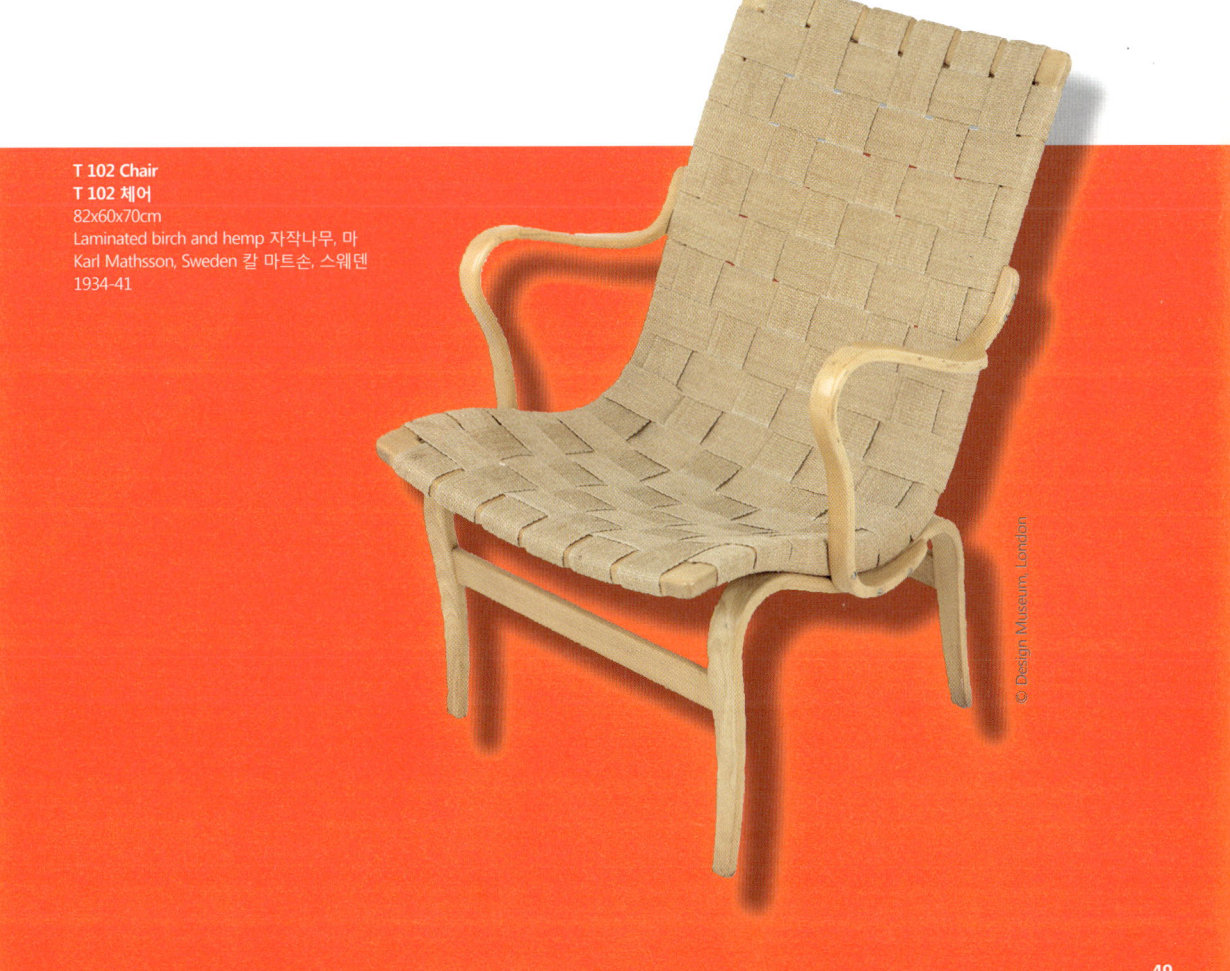

T 102 Chair
T 102 체어
82x60x70cm
Laminated birch and hemp 자작나무, 마
Karl Mathsson, Sweden 칼 마트손, 스웨덴
1934-41

© Design Museum, London

Salvador Dali 살바도르 달리

During the 1930's, Dali continued his creative search for new ways to express himself artistically, by developing a friendship with Jean-Michel Frank, a renowned Parisian furniture-maker and decorator of the time. Dali's focus was on the surrealistic transformation of everyday practical objects into ones of indeterminate use. Together they collaborated on several ideas, the culmination of which was a Surreal Room which was originally laid out in the London home of Dali's great patron, Edward James.

The Surreal Room has as its focal point the famous *Mae West Lips Sofa*, a sensuous piece of furniture that reflects the great actress' phenomenal fame. She was renowned more for her voluptuous figure and her risqué one liners that for her acting skills, and Dali, with his great skill for publicity and maintain his place in the public eye, paid homage to her with this inspired and original sofa.

1930년대에 달리는 그 당시 파리의 가구 제작자이자 실내장식업자였던 쟝 미쉘 프랭크와 친분을 쌓으면서 자신을 예술적으로 표현할 새로운 창조적 방법을 모색하고 있었다. 달리는 일상생활의 실용적인 물건들을 사용목적이 불확실한 것으로 바꾸는 초현실적 변형에 관심이 있었다. 그들은 몇 가지 작업을 함께 했으며 그 작업의 절정은 달리의 큰 후원자였던 에드워드 제임스의 런던 저택에 있던 초현실주의 방이었다.

그 초현실주의 방의 중심에 있었던 감각적인 가구 *메이 웨스트 입술 소파*는 유명 여배우의 경이로운 명성을 반영하고 있다. 그녀는 연기 실력보다 관능적인 외모로 유명했고 홍보에 능하고 대중들의 관심을 유지하는 법을 알았던 달리는 그녀에게는 영감을 받은 이 오리지널 소파를 통해 그녀에 대한 경의를 표했다.

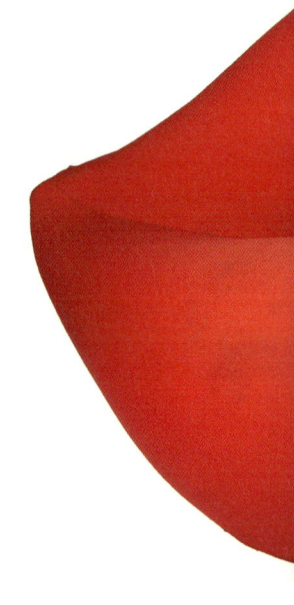

Mae West Lips Sofa
메이 웨스트 입술 쇼파
86.5183x81.5cm
Felt-covered upholstered wood frame 펠트 천, 나무
1936

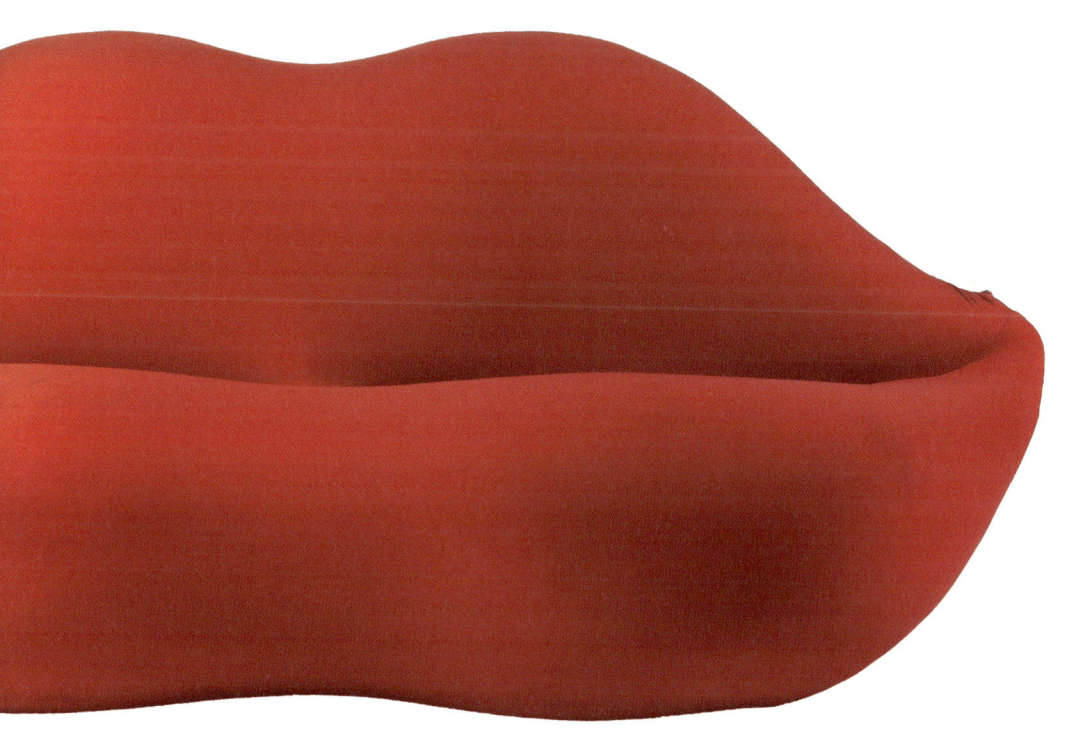

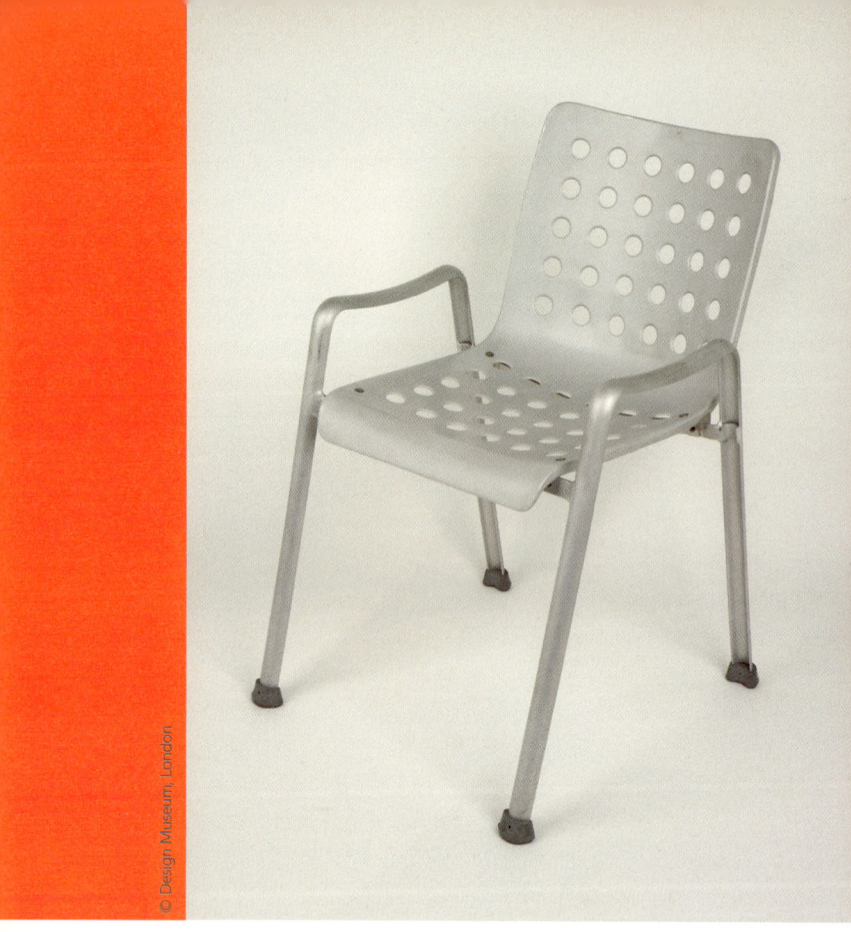

© Design Museum, London

Landi
랜디
76.5x51x65cm
Aluminium alloy frame 알루미늄
Reissued by Zanotta, Italy 자노타, 이탈리아
1938

Switzerland | 스위스

Hans Coray 한스 코레이

When Hans Fischli, the architect of the 1939 Swiss National Exhibition in Zurich, organised a competition to design the official chair used in the parks and gardens, it was won by a literature student Hans Coray. Although he continued to dabble in design, Coray did not take it up full time until 1950, but the *Landi* – named after the nickname for the exhibition – was an instant success and remained in production for 50 years.

건축가 한스 피슐리가 1939년 스위스 취리히에서 개최된 국립 전람회의 공원과 정원에서 사용될 공식 의자 디자인을 공모했을 때, 문학도였던 한스 코레이가 당선되었다. 그는 디자인에서 계속 손을 떼지는 않았지만, 1950년까지는 디자인에 매진하지 않았었다. 하지만 "전람회(Landesausstellung)"라는 단어에서 따온 이름인 *랜디*가 즉각적인 성공을 거두게 됨으로써, 이 의자는 50년간 생산이 지속되었다.

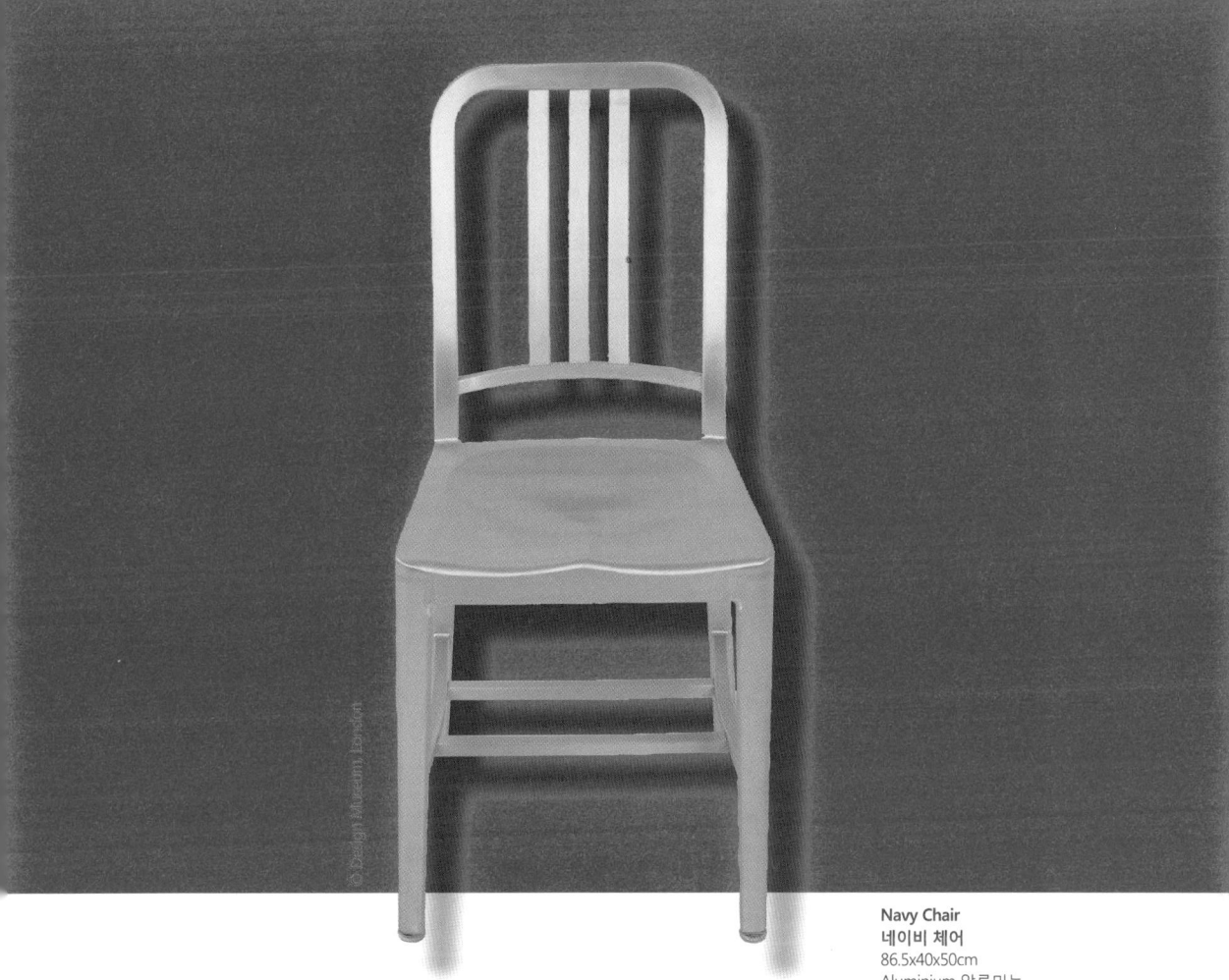

© Design Museum London

Navy Chair
네이비 체어
86.5x40x50cm
Aluminium 알루미늄
Emeco, US 에메코, 미국
1944

USA | 미국

Emeco 에메코

The *Navy Chair* was designed specifically for use at sea by the Electric Machine and Equipment Company – known as Emeco – and the Alcoa aluminium group. Emeco's founder, Wilson 'Bud' Dinges, was a master tool and die maker and a skilled engineer. He worked with Alcoa's scientists and naval engineers to develop and test the *Navy Chair*. Emeco put it into production at its manufacturing plant in Hanover, Pennsylvania where the *Navy Chair* is still made today. Each chair is constructed by a small number of skilled craftsmen, each of whom is entrusted with a designated task.

*네이비 체어*는 바다에서 사용하도록 특별히 디자인 된 의자로, 에메코로 알려진 전기 기계 및 장비 회사인 알코아 알루미늄 그룹에 의해 만들어졌다. 에메코의 설립자 윌슨 '버드' 딘지스는 도구 마스터이며 금형 제조자이자 숙련된 엔지니어였다. 그는 *네이비 체어*를 개발하고 테스트하기 위해 알코아의 과학자, 해군 기술자들과 협력하였다. 에메코는 오늘날까지도 *네이비 체어*를 만들고 있는 하노버와 펜실베니아에 있는 제조공장에서 생산을 시작했다. 각각의 의자는 각자 지정된 작업을 수행하는 숙련된 장인에 의해서 만들어 진다.

Hans J. Wegner 한스 J. 베그너

Wegner was called as "a chair maker among chair makers," and produced design works of which the property was not so different but could be accorded with other designers' pieces. His chairs were made by an adequate use of minute structure, imagination, and wood as his favorite material. The peculiarity of his works is a very simple design with light and pure forms so as to be appropriate for mass production

Sources | Korean Institute of Interior Design, *Chair Design in the 20th Century*, 2003.
Frank Russell, *A Century of Chair Design*, trans. Kim, Kyung Sook, Gimundang, 1991.

베그너는 "의자를 만드는 사람들 중에서 의자를 만드는 사람"이라 불렸고, 다른 디자이너들과 적절한 조화를 이루는 디자인을 제작했다. 그의 의자들은 정밀한 구조와 상상력, 그리고 그가 좋아했던 재료인 나무를 적절하게 사용했다. 베그너 디자인의 특징은 대량 생산에 적합하도록 가볍고 순수한 형태로 매우 단순하게 설계했다는 것이다.

출처 | 한국실내디자인학회, *20C 의자 디자인*, 기문당, 2003.
프랭크 러셀, *김경숙 역, 현대 의자디자인의 역사*, 기문당, 1991.

CH-24
73.5x54.5x52cm
Beech, paper 너도밤나무, 종이
Carl Hansen, Denmark 칼 한센, 덴마크
1949

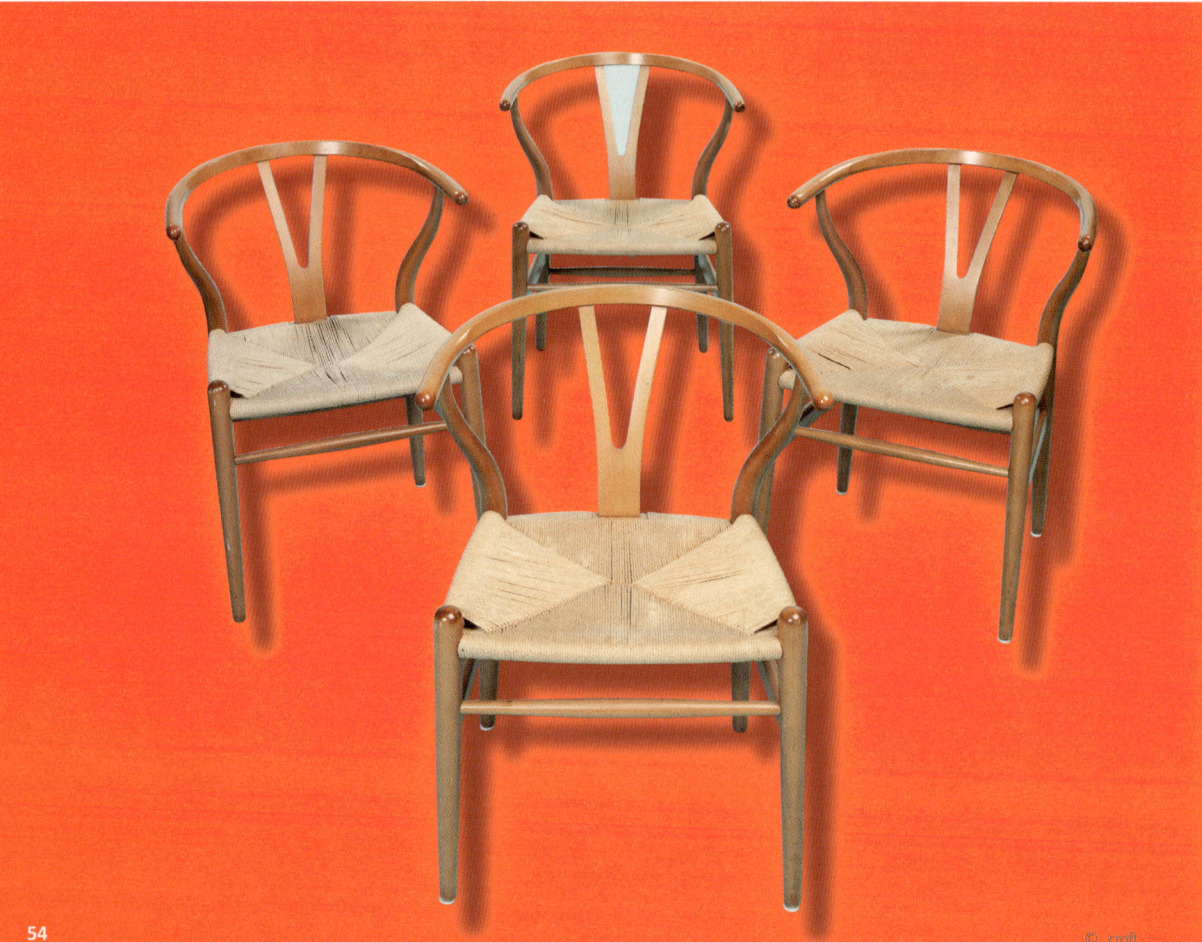

China Chair
차이나 체어
81x59x54cm
Oak, woven paper 오크 나무, 엮은 종이
Fritz Hansen, Denmark 프리츠 한센, 덴마크
1945

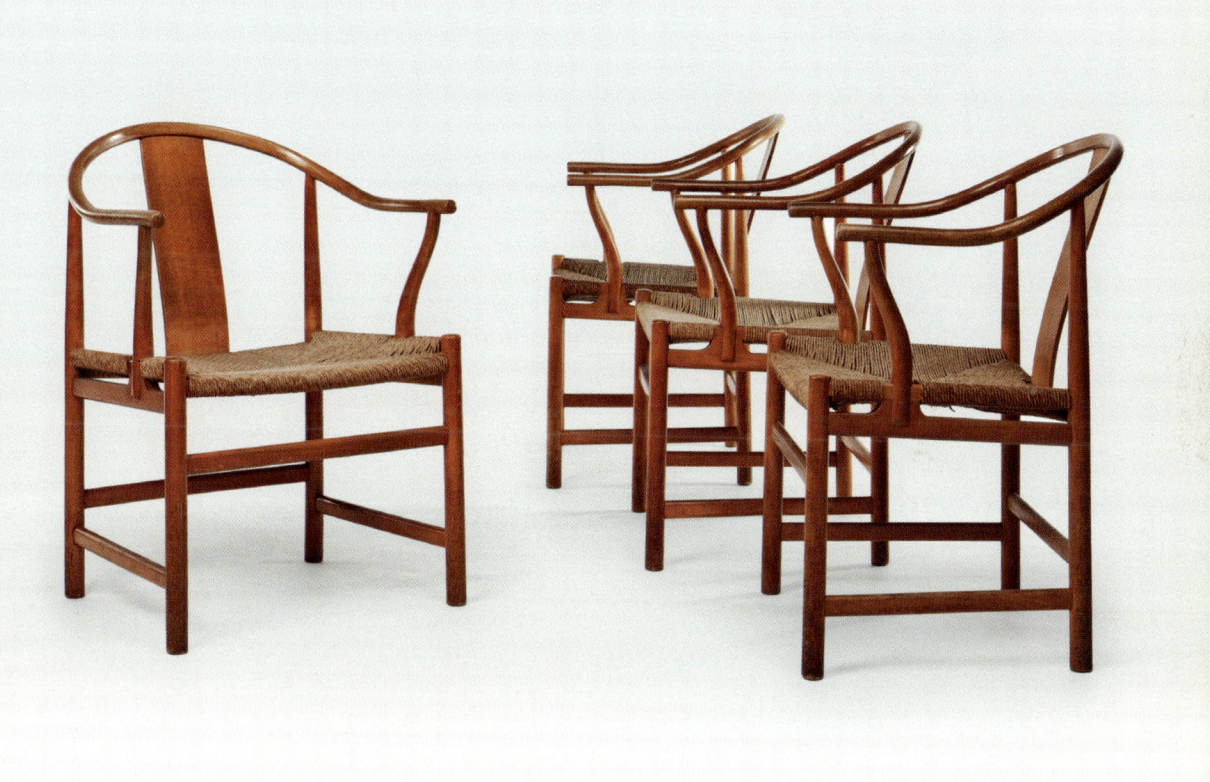

© _croft

55

©_croft

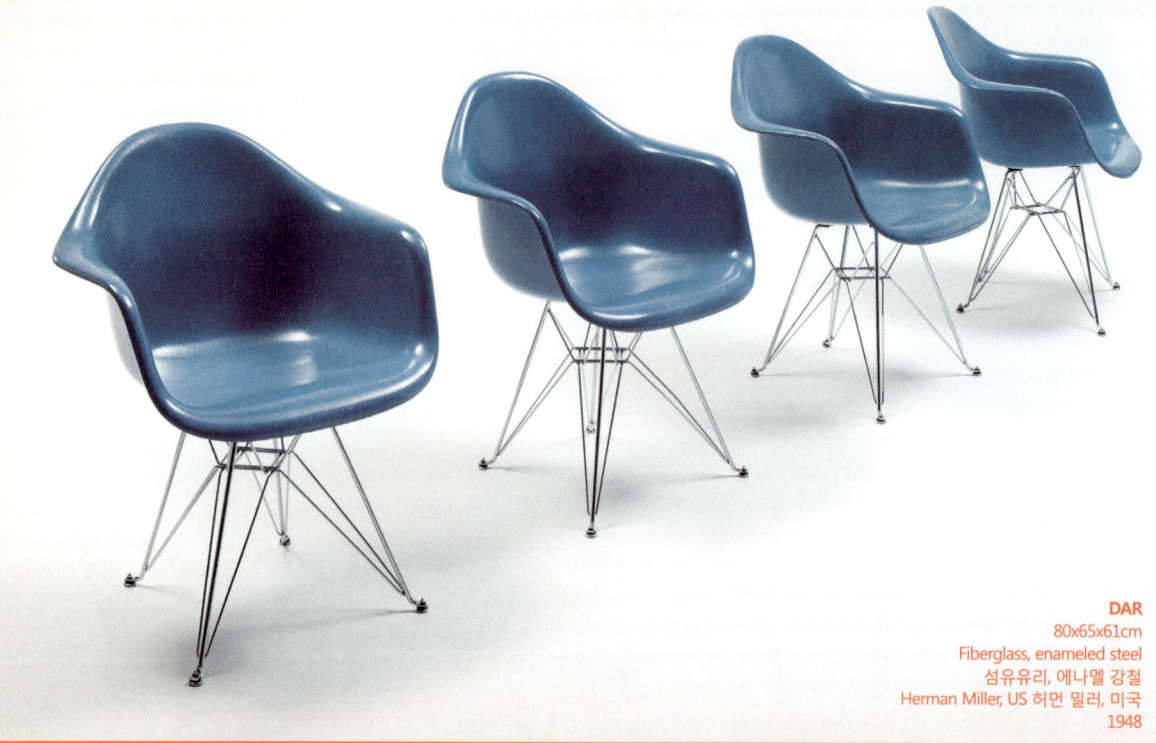

DAR
80x65x61cm
Fiberglass, enameled steel
섬유유리, 에나멜 강철
Herman Miller, US 허먼 밀러, 미국
1948

USA | 미국

Charles Eames and Ray Eames 찰스 & 레이 임스

Since the chairs by Eames have a variety of colors and are light in weight, they could be available for any place inside of an empty bar. This means that their chairs provide a familiarity to residents, not to a building itself. Charles Eames made his design possible to utilize mass production in highly industrial system in which machines can be controlled. Under such circumstances, Eames aimed to produce comfortable and light chairs in reasonable prices to fit human bodies with flexibility as the body moves. The designers stressed that chairs must be comfortable to use. In other words, all chair users must feel comfortable when sitting on them. Charles & Ray Eames held a faith that a chair should be able to experiment human body's dimension according to architectural concepts.

임스의 의자는 다양한 컬러와 가벼운 무게로 인해 빈 바의 어떤 장소에든지 조화롭게 어울릴 수 있고, 건물이 아니라 거주자에게 친밀함을 느끼게 했다. 그는 고도의 산업 생산이 가능하고, 기계로 조절할 수 있으며, 그것들을 사용하여 디자인된 세계를 창출할 수 있게 한 것이다. 임스의 디자인은 인체 유형에 적합하고, 앉는 동작에 따라 융통성이 있으면서 가격이 적당한 동시에 튼튼하고, 안락한 가벼운 의자를 제작하는데 그 목적이 있었다. 그는 의자는 편해야만 한다고 강조하였다. 즉 의자를 사용하는 모든 사람이 편안해야 한다는 것이다. 의자 디자이너로서 그는 건축적인 개념에 따라 인체치수의 기능적 용어로 직접 실험할 수 있어야 한다는 것을 신념으로 하였다.

출처 | 한국실내디자인학회, *20C 의자 디자인*, 기문당, 2003.

Sources | Korean Institute of Interior Design, *Chair Design in the 20th Century*, Gimundang, 2003.

An extension of the *Aluminum Group* chairs designed in 1958 for the Irwin Miller home, the *Soft Pad Group* repeats the structure of the earlier chairs, adding cushions to the seat and back. Covered in leather or fabric, these cushions transformed the spare character of the *Aluminum Group* into a luxurious version for homes and offices.

The seat-back suspension was a major technical achievement and represented a departure from the concept of the chair as a solid shell. The *soft pad group* is wonderfully comfortable, strong, yet lightweight.

알루미늄 그룹 체어는 1958년 아르윈 밀러의 집을 위해 디자인 되었는데, 소프트 패드 그룹은 이 초기 디자인 구조에 부드러운 쿠션을 등받이에 추가 했다. 가죽 또는 천으로 덮은 쿠션은 알루미늄 그룹 체어를 사무실과 집에서 사용하는 고급스런 의자로 탈바꿈시켰다. 의자 뒷부분의 서스펜션은 중요한 기술적 업적으로, 이전에는 딱딱한 소재로만 제작되던 의자에 대한 고정관념을 타파시켰다. 부드러운 패드가 더해짐으로 인해서 의자는 놀라울 정도로 편하고 튼튼하며 가벼워졌다.

Soft Pad Group
소프트 패드 그룹
88x55x57cm
Aluminum, leather upholstery 알루미늄, 가죽
1969

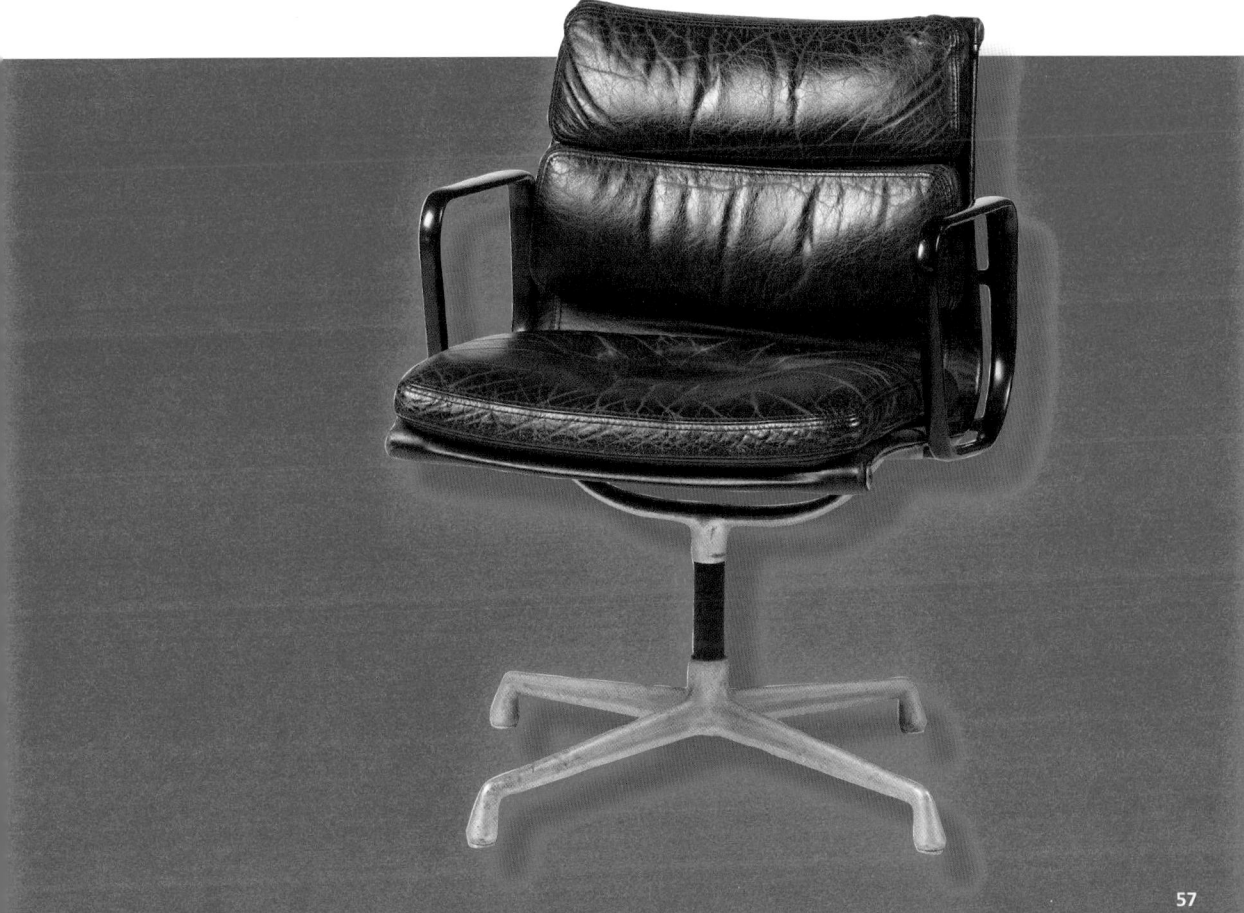

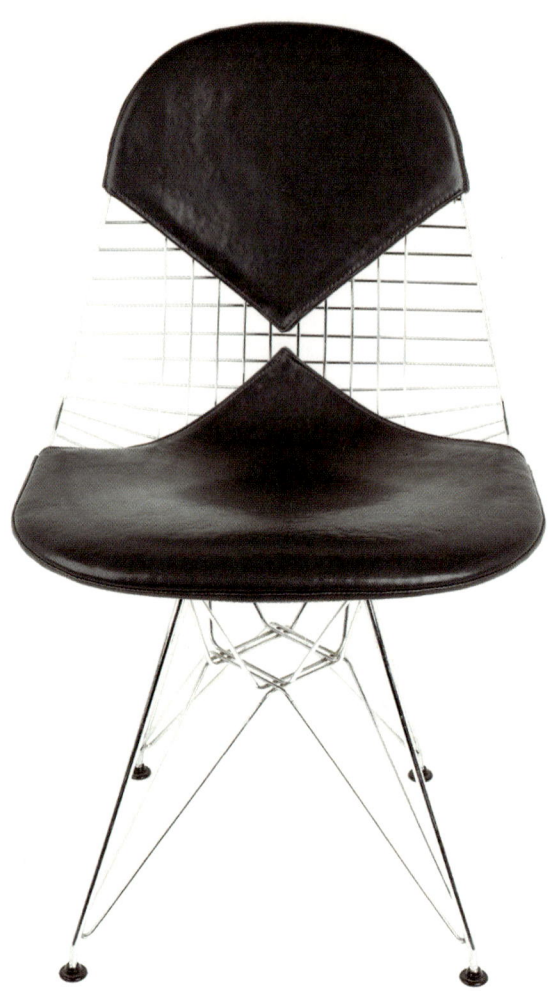

© Design Museum, London

DKR-2(Dining Bikini Rod)
DKR-2(다이닝 비키니 로드)
81x50x52cm
Bent and welded steel rod shell, metal rod base
and leather upholstery
강철, 금속, 가죽
Herman Miller, US 허먼 밀러, 미국
1951

Having considered producing wire-mesh chairs when developing their revolutionary Plastic Shell seating system in the late 1940s, the Eames revived the idea for the *DKR-2* and wooden-legged *DKW-2* chairs in the early 1950s. The legs were inspired by the Eiffel Tower and the two-piece upholstery was dubbed the 'bikini'.

찰스 임스와 레이 임스는 1940년대 후반 혁신적인 플라스틱 쉘 좌석 시스템을 개발할 때 와이어 메쉬 의자를 생산했던 것을 떠올려, 1950년대 초 *DKR-2*와 목조다리로 된 *DKW-2*의자를 만들었다. 의자의 다리 부분은 에펠탑에서 영감을 얻었고, 위-아래 가죽으로 덮인 부분은 '비키니'라 명명되었다.

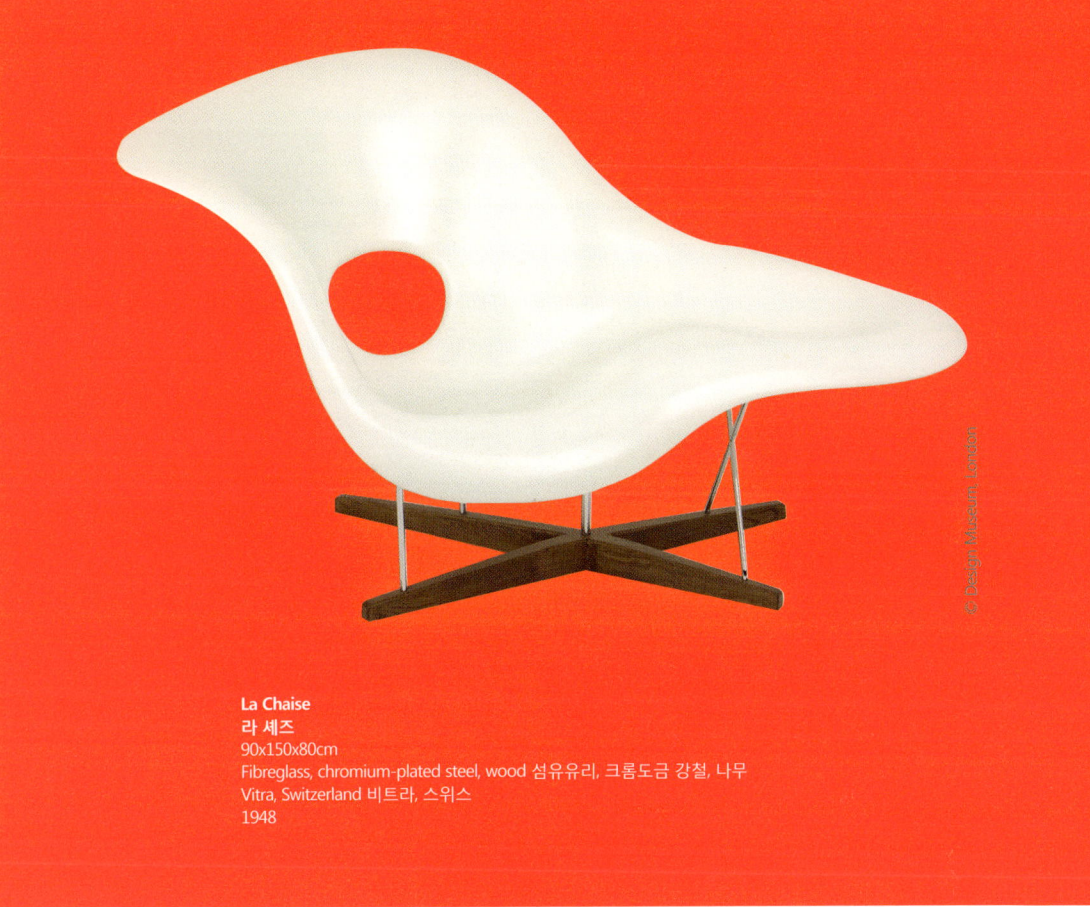

La Chaise
라 셰즈
90x150x80cm
Fibreglass, chromium-plated steel, wood 섬유유리, 크롬도금 강철, 나무
Vitra, Switzerland 비트라, 스위스
1948

© Design Museum, London

An icon of the Atomic Age, the abstract form of *La Chaise* resembles a reclining human figure. The chair was named after the French sculptor Gaston Lachaise (1882-1935). Made from two fibreglass shells which have been glued together, filled with styrene and separated by a rubber disc, *La Chaise* was designed by the Eames as a lightweight chair. Even its appearance evokes lightness: emphasised by the hole at the back. Too costly to mass-produce when it was first designed, it finally went into production in 1990.

원자력 시대의 아이콘 같은 *라 셰즈*의 추상적 형태는 비스듬히 누운 인간의 모습과 유사하다. 이 의자는 프랑스 조각가 갸스통 라셰즈(1882-1935)의 이름에서 따왔다. 이어 붙인 두 개의 섬유유리 껍데기에 합성수지를 채운 후 고무 디스크로 분리하여 만들어진 *라 셰즈*는 임스에 의해 디자인 된 경량의자이다. 특히 등받이 부분의 구멍으로 강조된 그 모양은 가벼움을 더욱 강조시킨다. 이 의자가 처음 디자인 되었을 당시에는 대량생산하기에 돈이 너무 많이 들었던 탓에 1990년이 되어서야 마침내 생산에 들어갔다.

Jens Risom 옌스 리솜

On becoming the first designer commissioned by Hans Knoll, Risom created The *Lounge Arm Chair 652W* as part of a series using discarded parachute straps. This irregular material choice was influenced by the scarcity of usual fabrics and upholstery material during wartime. The chair is still available in an updated format.

리솜은 한스 놀로부터 디자인을 의뢰 받은 첫 번째 디자이너가 되면서, 버려진 낙하산용 줄을 이용해 *라운지용 팔걸이 의자 652W* 시리즈를 제작하였다. 이 범상치 않은 재료의 선택은 전쟁 기간 중 일반 섬유나 소파 덮개 등의 재료가 부족하기 때문이었다. 이 의자는 지금까지도 계속 업데이트된 형태로 생산되고 있다.

Lounge Arm Chair 652W
라운지 팔걸이 의자 652W
75x61x70cm
Spruce frame and woven canvas seat 가문비나무, 등나무
Knoll International, Germany 놀 인터내셔널, 독일
1941

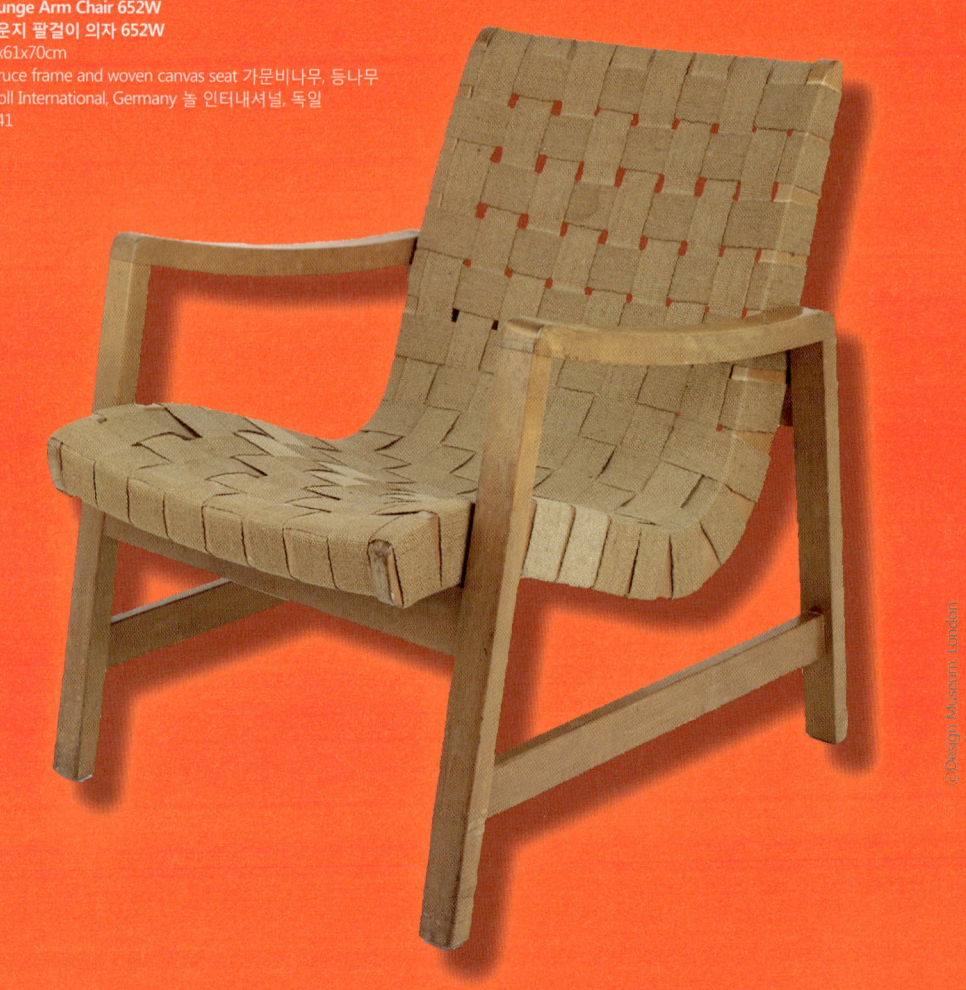

©Design Museum London

Pierre Jeanneret 피에르 잔느레

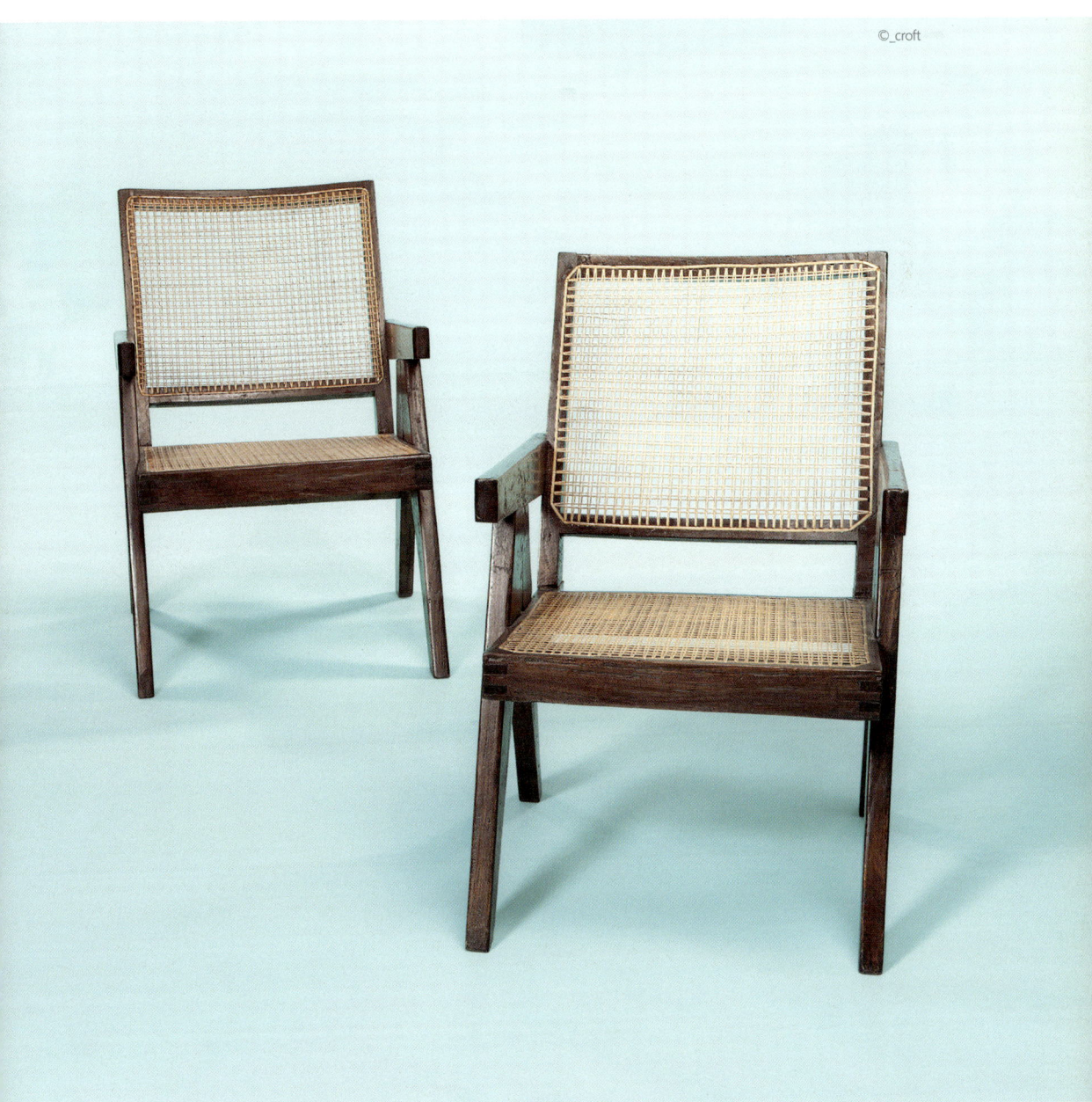

©_croft

©_croft

Easy Chair
이지 체어
76.5x52.3x75cm
Teak, cane 티크 나무, 등나무
1950

Ernest Race 어니스트 레이스

Light, compact, and made with minimum material, the *Antelope* chair by Ernest Race embraced all the practical requirements of post-war furniture. The jaunty curves, spindly legs and comical ball feet evoked the growing optimism of the British as they entered the 1950s convinced that science and technology would create a better future. The *Antelope* was commissioned to furnish the outdoor terraces of the newly built Royal Festival Hall for the 1951 Festival of Britain.

가볍고 콤팩트하며 최소한의 재료로 만들어진 어니스트 레이스의 *앤텔로프*는 전쟁 후 가구에 필요한 모든 실질적인 요구사항들을 수용하고 있다. 경쾌한 곡선, 가늘고 긴 다리 그리고 우스꽝스러운 공모양의 발은 1950년대에 들어서면서 과학과 기술이 더 나은 미래를 만들 것 이라는 영국인들의 낙관적인 발전적 전망을 떠올리게 한다. *앤텔로프*는 1951년 영국의 축제를 위해 새롭게 지어진 로얄페스티벌 홀의 야외 테라스에 비치되었다.

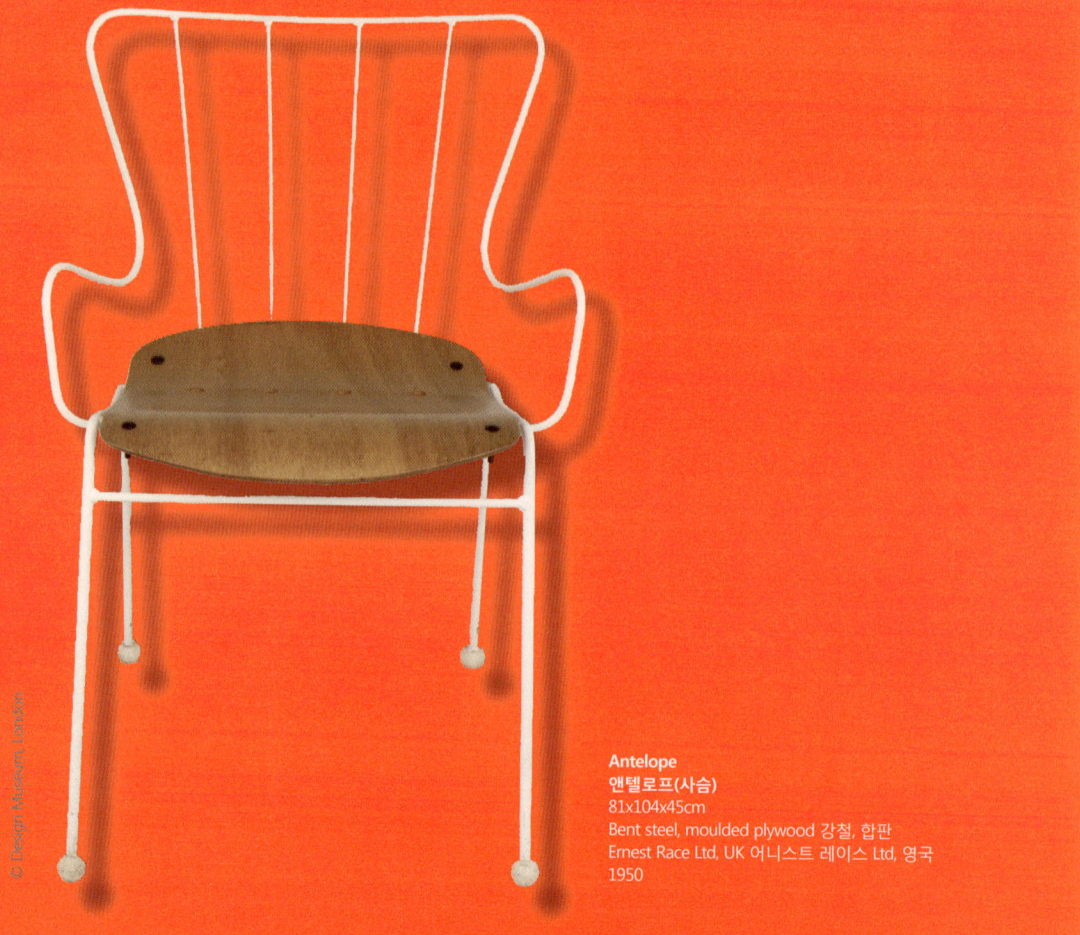

© Design Museum, London

Antelope
앤텔로프(사슴)
81x104x45cm
Bent steel, moulded plywood 강철, 합판
Ernest Race Ltd, UK 어니스트 레이스 Ltd, 영국
1950

Harry Bertoia 해리 버토이아

'If you look at these chairs, you will see that they are mainly made of air, just like light sculptures,' said Bertoia. 'Space goes clean through them.' While studying at the Cranbrook Academy, Michigan with Eero Saarinen and Florence Knoll, Bertoia developed ideas for mass-produced iron wire furniture with the manufacturer Knoll Associates. Many of those pieces, including the *Diamond*, are still in production today.

버토이아가 말했다. '당신이 이 의자를 본다면, 마치 빛의 조각들처럼, 그것들은 공기로 만들어졌다는 것을 알 수 있을 거예요. 의자들을 관통해 뒤에 있는 공간이 훤히 보이죠.'
버토이아는 에로 사리넨, 플로렌스 놀과 함께 미시간에 있는 크랜브룩 아카데미에서 공부하던 중, 디자인 회사인 놀과 함께 대량생산이 가능한 강철 와이어 가구에 대한 아이디어를 개발했다. *다이아몬드 의자*를 포함한 그 당시 작품들의 대부분은 현재도 여전히 생산되고 있다.

Diamond Chair
다이아몬드 의자
75x85x72cm
Steel wire 강철 와이어
Knoll International, US 놀 인터내셔널, 미국
1952-53

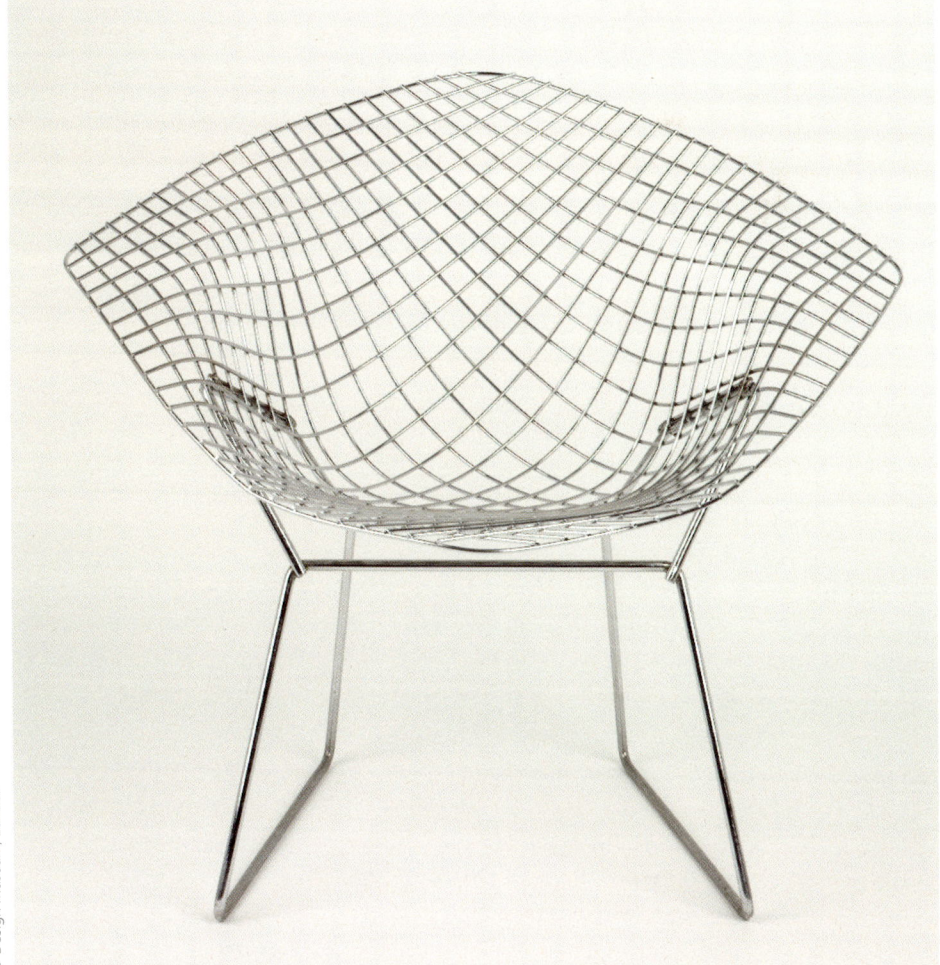

© Design Museum, London

©_croft

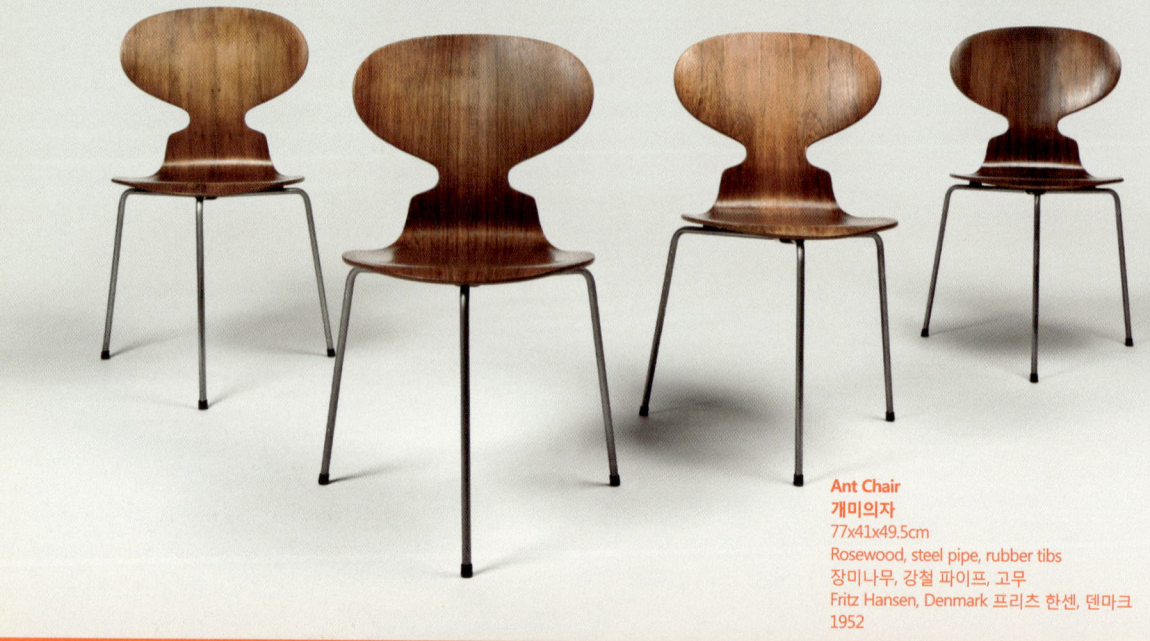

Ant Chair
개미의자
77x41x49.5cm
Rosewood, steel pipe, rubber tibs
장미나무, 강철 파이프, 고무
Fritz Hansen, Denmark 프리츠 한센, 덴마크
1952

Denmark | 덴마크

Arne Jacobsen 아르네 야콥슨

As an architect, Arne Jacobsen was renowned for combining the rationalist principles of modernism with a Nordic love of organic forms and materials. He also insisted on designing every element in his buildings including the furniture. Inspired by Charles and Ray Eames' plywood experiments, the *Series 7* sports a sleeker silhouette than Jacobsen's earlier *Ant Chair*.

건축가로서 아르네 야콥슨은 모더니즘의 합리주의 원칙들을 북유럽인들이 사랑하는 유기적인 양식과 소재에 결합한 것으로 유명해졌다. 그는 또한 가구를 포함하여 그의 건물의 모든 요소들을 직접 디자인해야 한다고 주장했다. 찰스와 레이 임스의 합판 실험들에서 영감을 받은 *Series 7*은 야콥슨이 이전에 만든 *개미 의자*보다 더 매끄러운 실루엣을 자랑한다.

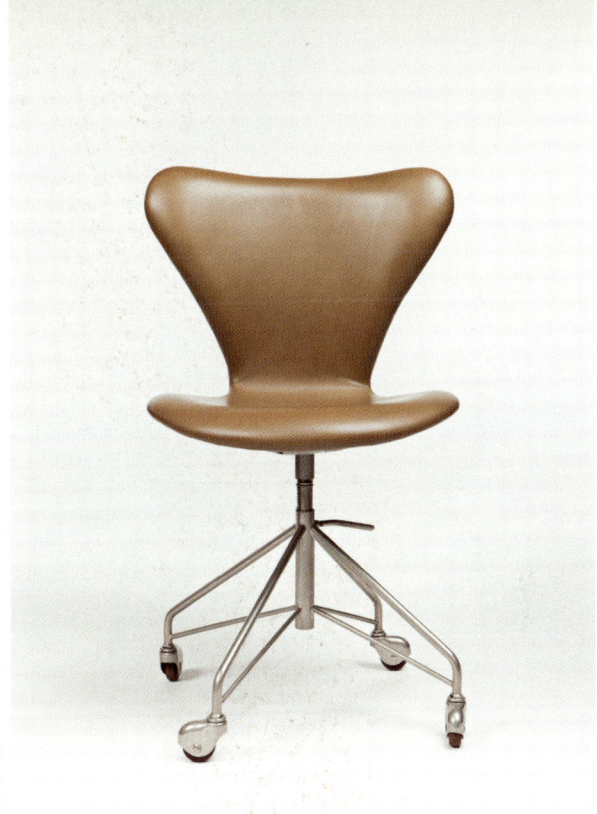

© _croft

Swivel
스위블
77x50x47cm
Ochre leather, chromed steel 가죽, 크롬도금 강철
Fritz Hansen, Denmark 프리츠 한센, 덴마크
1955

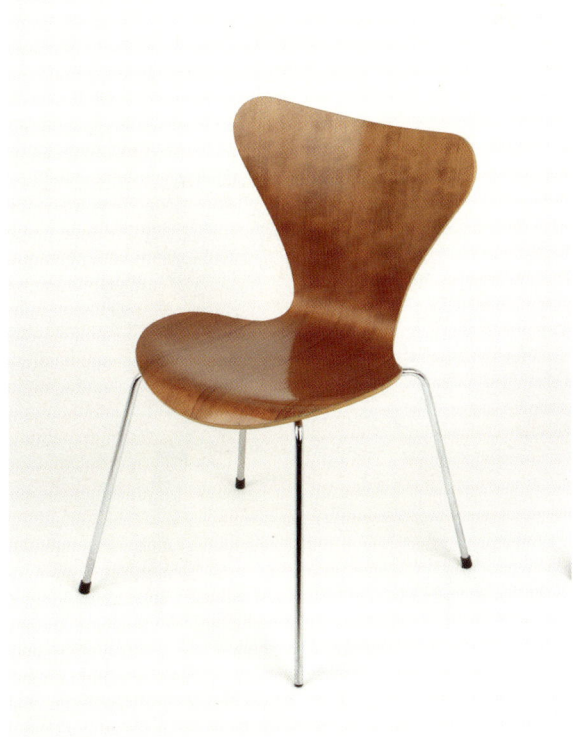

Series 7 Model No. 3017
시리즈 7, No. 3017
67x49.5x47cm
Teak-faced moulded plywood seat and bent tubular
steel base 합판, 강철튜브
Fritz Hansen, Denmark 프리츠 한센, 덴마크
1955

© Design Museum, London

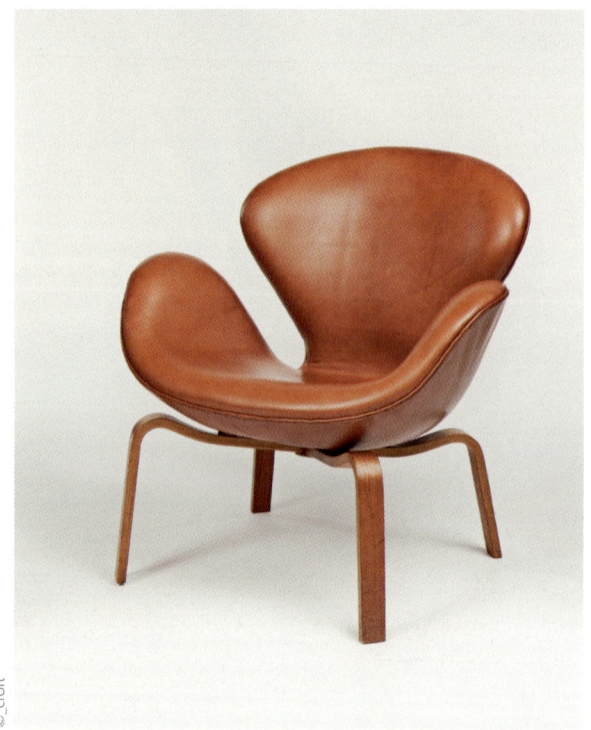

© _croft

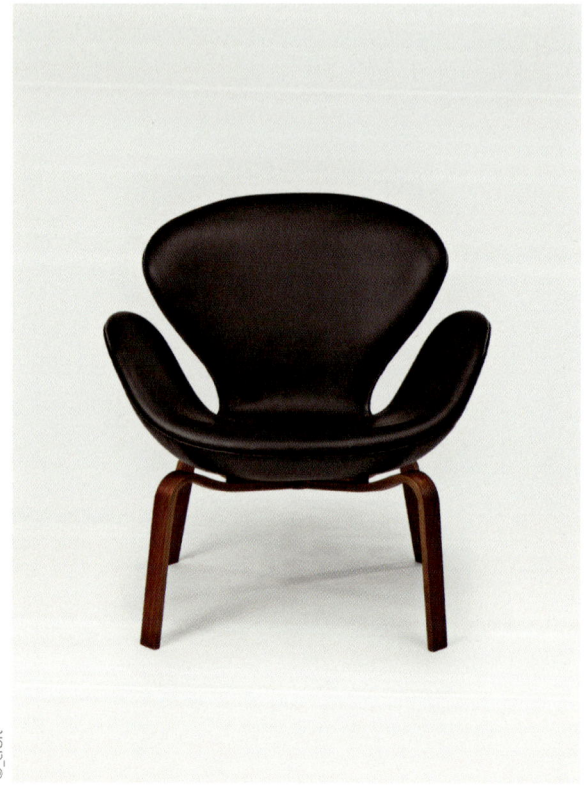

© _croft

Swan Chair
백조 의자
76x76x66cm
Leather, wood 가죽, 나무
Fritz Hansen, Demark 프리츠 한센, 덴마크
1958

Finn Juhl 핀 율

Dining Chair
식탁 의자
79x49x53cm
Teak, fabric 티크 나무, 천
Bovirke, Denmark 보비르케, 덴마크
1952

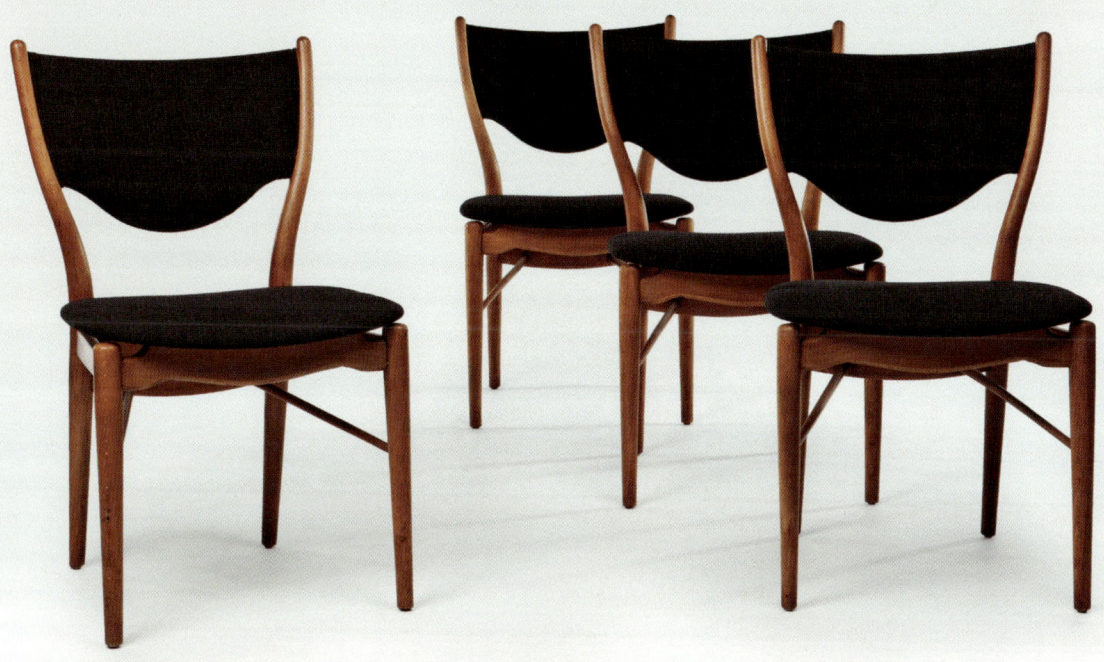

© _croft

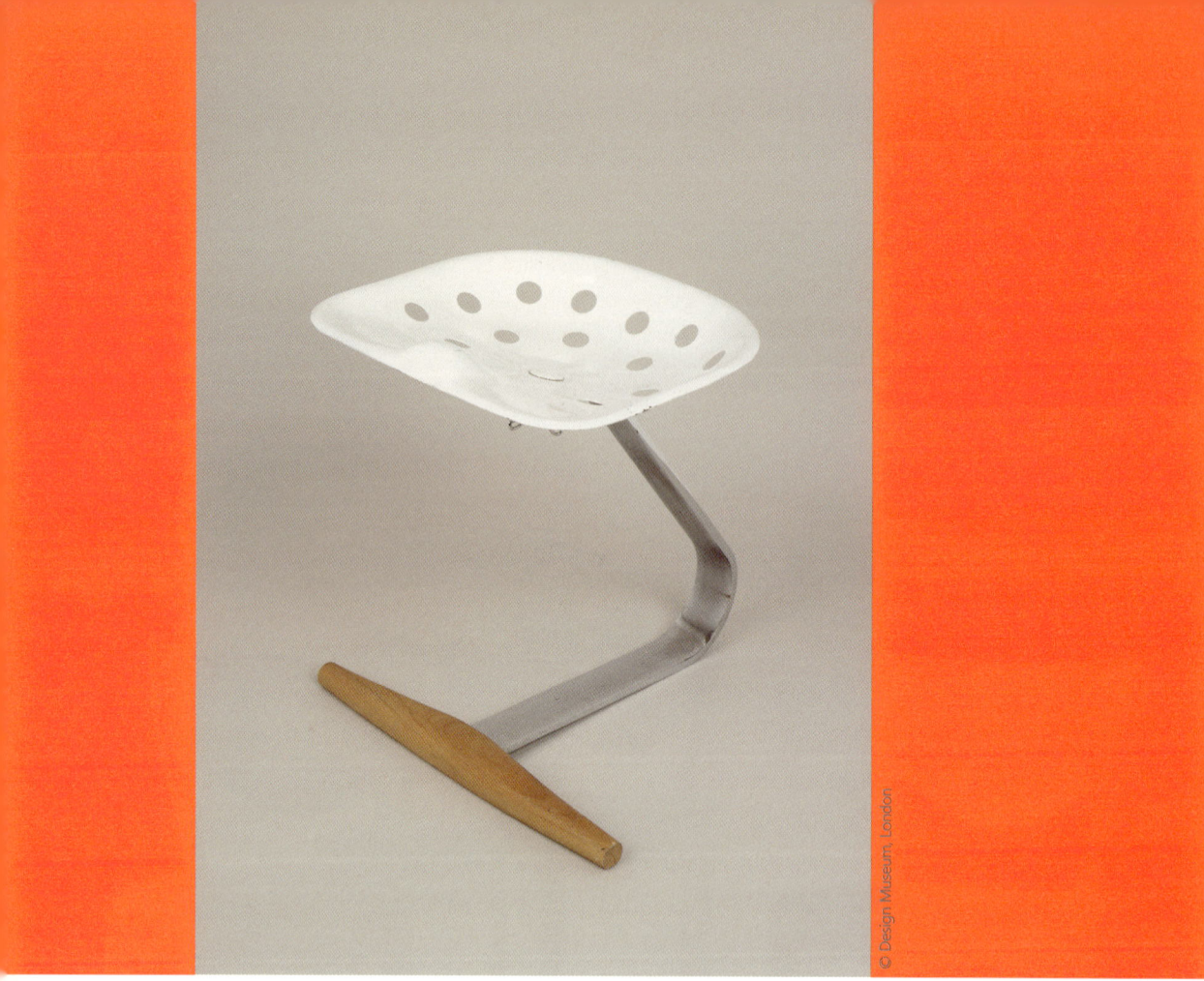

© Design Museum, London

Mezzadro
메차드로
50.5x49.5x52cm
Sheet steel tractor seat, beech wood and steel 철제 트랙터 의자, 너도밤나무, 강철
Reissued by Zanotta, Italy 자노타, 이탈리아
1954-7

Italy | 이탈리아

Achille Castiglioni and Pier Giacomo Castiglioni
아킬레 & 피에르 자코모 카스틸리오니

The Castiglioni brothers presented their first prototype for the Mezzadro, or 'sharecropper', at the Tenth Milan Triennial in 1954. It was not exhibited in its current form until a 1957 exhibition at Villa Olmo in Como. This is one of a series of Duchamp-inspired ready-mades in which the brothers incorporated found industrial objects – such as a tractor seat and a cycle wing nut – in their designs. Radical for its time, the Mezzadro was not put into production until 1970.

카스틸리오니 형제는 1954년 10번째로 열린 밀라노 트리엔날레에서 *메차드로* 혹은 '소작인' 이라고 불리는 이 의자의 첫 프로토타입을 발표했다. 그것은 1957년 코모의 빌라 올모에서 열린 전시회의 디자인들과는 달랐다. *메차드로*는 뒤샹에 영감을 받은 레디메이드 시리즈 중 하나로, 카스틸리오니 형제는 트랙터 의자와 자전거의 윙너트 같은 산업제품의 레디메이드(기성제품)를 그들의 디자인에 포함시켰다. 하지만 이러한 방법이 그 당시로서는 너무나 급진적이었기 때문에 *메차드로*는 1970년까지 생산에 들어가지 못했다.

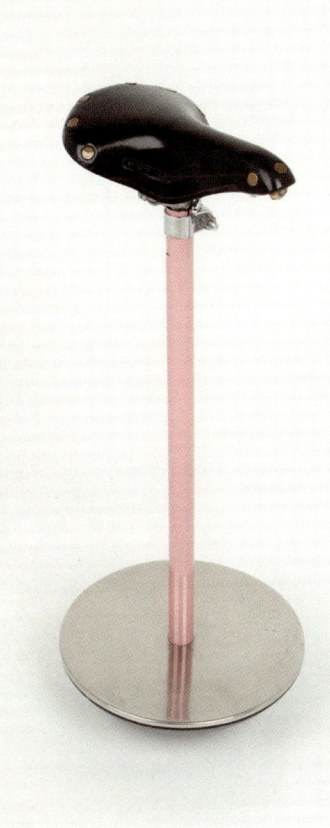

© Design Museum, London

Sella
셀라
69x30x28cm
Racing bicycle saddle, tubular steel and cast-iron
경주용 자전거 안장, 강철튜브, 주철
Reissued by Zanotta, Italy 자노타, 이탈리아
1957

Like the *Mezzadro* tractor seat stool, the *Sella* appropriates a ready-made industrial object by transforming the saddle of a racing bicycle into a telephone stool. Although reduced to their essential elements both stools are full of playfulness and wit. The Castiglioni brothers' ready-mades have remained inspirational for younger designers – from Jasper Morrison to Juergen Bey – who have also used found industrial objects in furniture and product designs.

트랙터 의자 스툴 *메차드로*와 마찬가지로, *셀라*는 경주용 자전거 안장을 텔레폰 스툴로 탈바꿈 시키면서 레디메이드(기성제품)를 디자인에 가져다 썼다. 의자의 본질적인 요소들은 축소되었지만, 두 의자는 장난기와 재치로 가득하다. 카스틸리오니 형제의 레디메이드 디자인은 재스퍼 모리슨부터 위르겐 베이까지, 가구와 제품디자인에 레디메이드 오브제를 사용하는 젊은 디자이너들에게 여전히 영감의 원천이 되고 있다.

Roland Rainer 롤란트 라이너

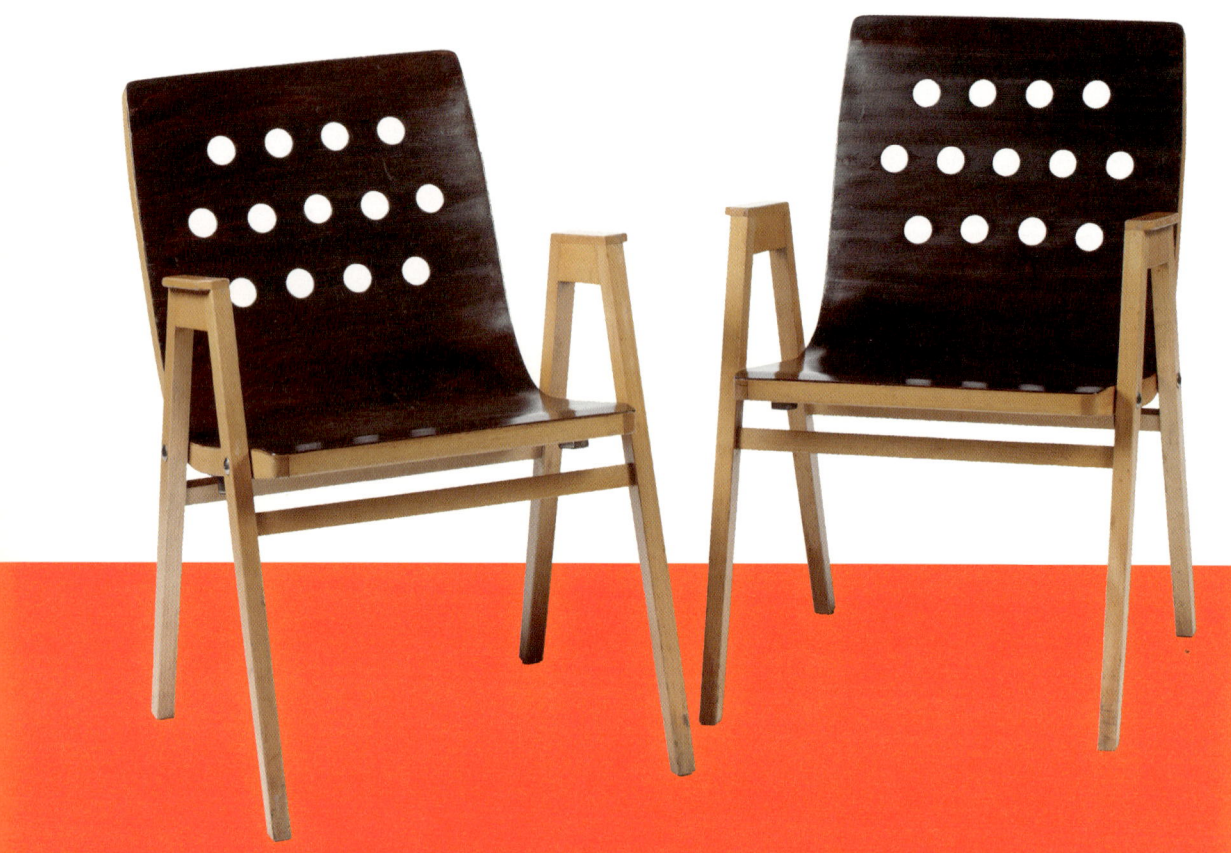

WR Stadthalle
WR 슈타트할레
81x51x56cm
Beech, plywood, bolt 너도밤나무, 합판, 볼트
Emil & Alfred Pollak, Austria 에밀&알프레드 폴락, 오스트리아
1956

Eero Saarinen 에로 사리넨

Having trained as an architect, Eero Saarinen approached the design of the *Tulip Chair* as if it was an element of a room. 'The undercarriage of chairs and tables in a typical interior creates an ugly, confusing and restless world,' he said. 'I wanted to clear up the sum of legs. I wanted to make the chair all one thing.'

건축가로 교육을 받은 에로 사리넨은 *튤립 의자*를 마치 방의 구성요소인 것처럼 디자인에 접근했다. '일반적인 실내에서 의자와 탁자들의 하부구조는 못생기고 혼란스럽고 불안한 세상을 만들죠. 나는 모든 다리를 없애고 싶었습니다. 나는 의자를 하나의 덩어리로 만들어보고 싶었어요.'

Tulip Chair
튤립 의자
80x50x41cm
Fibreglass-reinforced polyester, varnished cast aluminium, foam rubber and fabric
섬유유리-강화 폴리에스터, 알루미늄, 고무, 천
Knoll International, US 놀 인터내셔널, 미국
1955-6

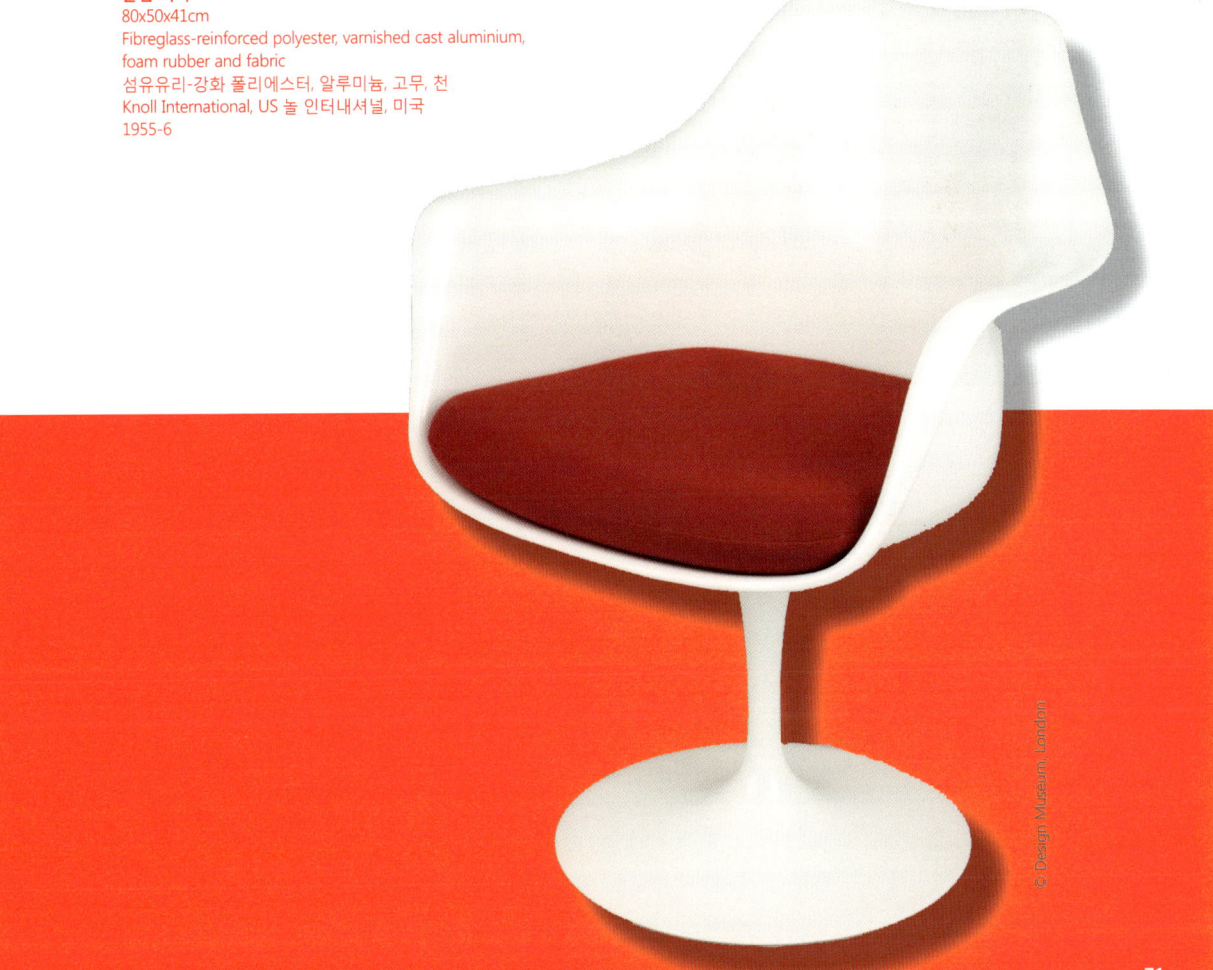

© Design Museum, London

Ib Kofod Larsen 입 코포드 라르슨

Furniture desginer Ib Kofod-Larsen's furniture from the 1950's and 60's are today more desirable than ever before. Danish Kofod-Larsen designed storage and seating for the Swedish market in the 60's but did not really reach any commercial success. Maybe his organic design was too extreme for the Swedish taste at the time. In Denmark, on the contrary, his sideboards produced by Faarup won immediate recognition. Today his creations are sold at higher and higher prices, as his clean designs, often in beautiful rosewood or palisander, have become highly appreciated by a global community of design enthusiasts.

가구 디자이너 입 코포드 라르슨의 1950, 60년대 가구는 그 어느 때보다 오늘날에 더 가치가 있다. 덴마크 디자이너 코포드 라르슨은 60년대에 스웨덴 시장을 위해 서랍장과 의자들을 디자인했지만, 상업적으로 큰 성공을 거두진 못했었다. 아마 그의 유기적인 디자인이 당시 스웨덴 시장에게는 너무 극단적이었던 것 같다. 반대로 덴마크에서는 파럽에 의해 생산된 그의 사이드보드(그릇장)가 바로 인정을 받았다. 그의 작품은 주로 장미나무나 자단나무로 만들어진 깔끔한 디자인으로, 오늘날 매우 높은 가격에 판매되는데 이는 디자인 애호가들이 코포드 라르슨의 진가를 인정하고 있는 것으로 보여진다.

Elizabeth Sofa
엘리자베스 소파
72x146x78cm
Rosewood, leather 장미나무, 가죽
Christensen& Larsen, Denmark 크아이스텐슨& 라르슨, 덴마크
1956

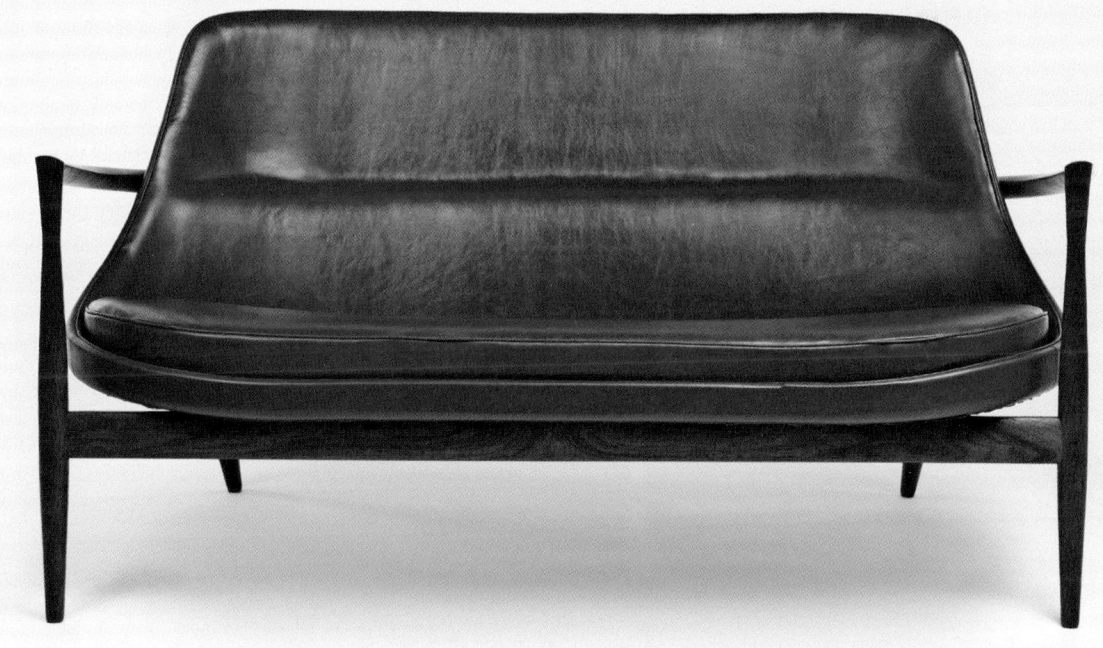

© _croft

George Nakashima 조지 나카시마

"Furniture is like a building. Its scale is only different. I find myself happy in making it small." Nakashima has been attached to a practical design which suits its space, so cherishes natural traces with human touches as time flows. "Wood is a medium that I can feel familiar the most." "Being touched by nature's generosity is one of marvelous experiences in life." The designer intended to admire nature through wood and learn true value of life.

Sources | Ahn, Bokrye, Crart, July 2006

"가구는 건물과 같다. 단지 그 스케일이 다를 뿐이다. 난 작게 만드는 것이 행복하다." 조지 나카시마는 공간과 잘 어우러지고 실용성이 있는 디자인에 애착을 가지고 있으며, 사람이 사용하면서 묻어나는 손때와 시간의 흐름에 의해 자연스레 생기는 흔적을 소중히 생각했다. "나무는 자연을 가장 친숙하게 느낄 수 있게 해주는 매체이다." "자연이 포용하고 있는 넉넉함에 감화되는 것은 인생에 있어 경이로운 경험 중 하나이다." 작가는 나무를 통해 자연에 대한 경외감을 가지고, 그것을 통해 인생의 참된 가치를 알고자 하였다.

출처 | 안복례, 크라트 2006년 7월호

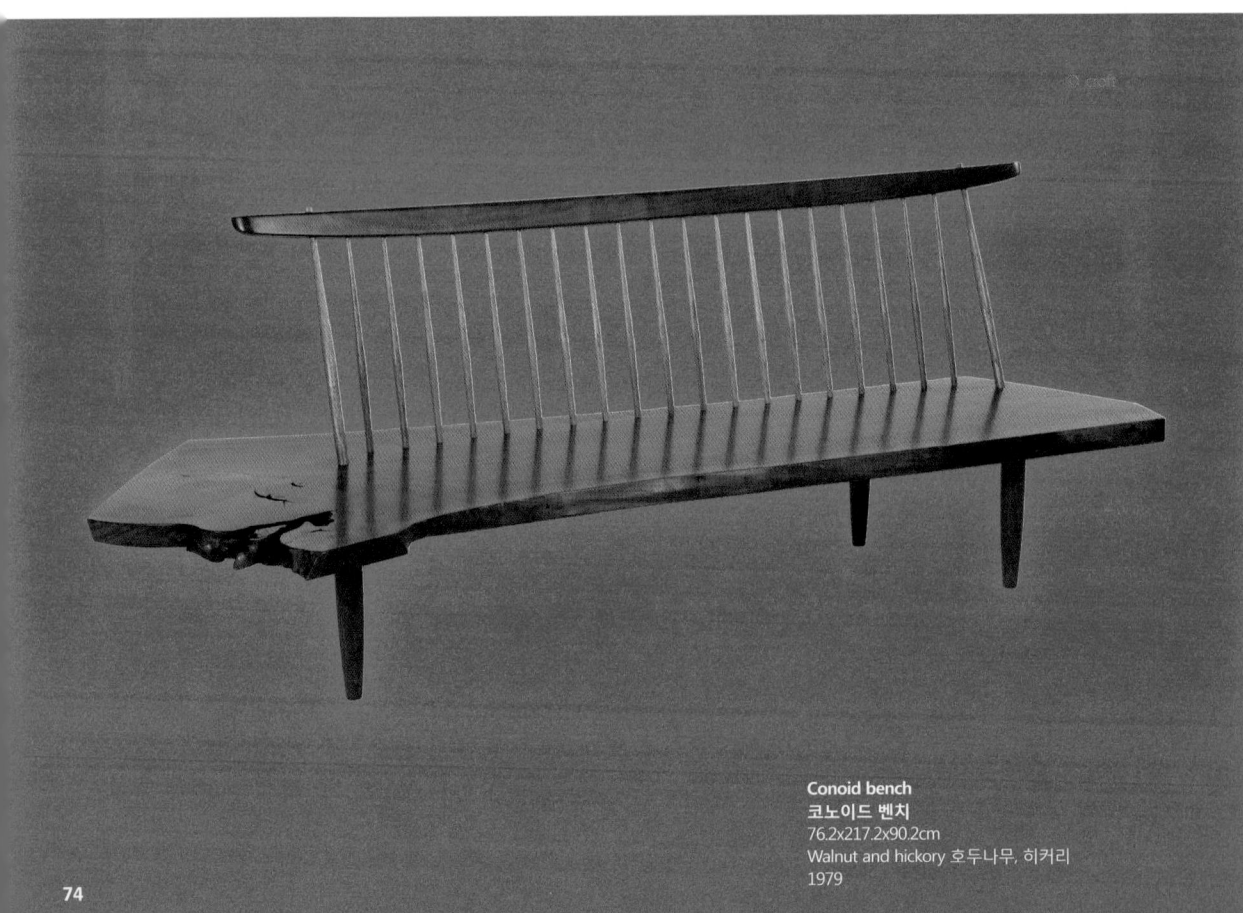

Conoid bench
코노이드 벤치
76.2x217.2x90.2cm
Walnut and hickory 호두나무, 히커리
1979

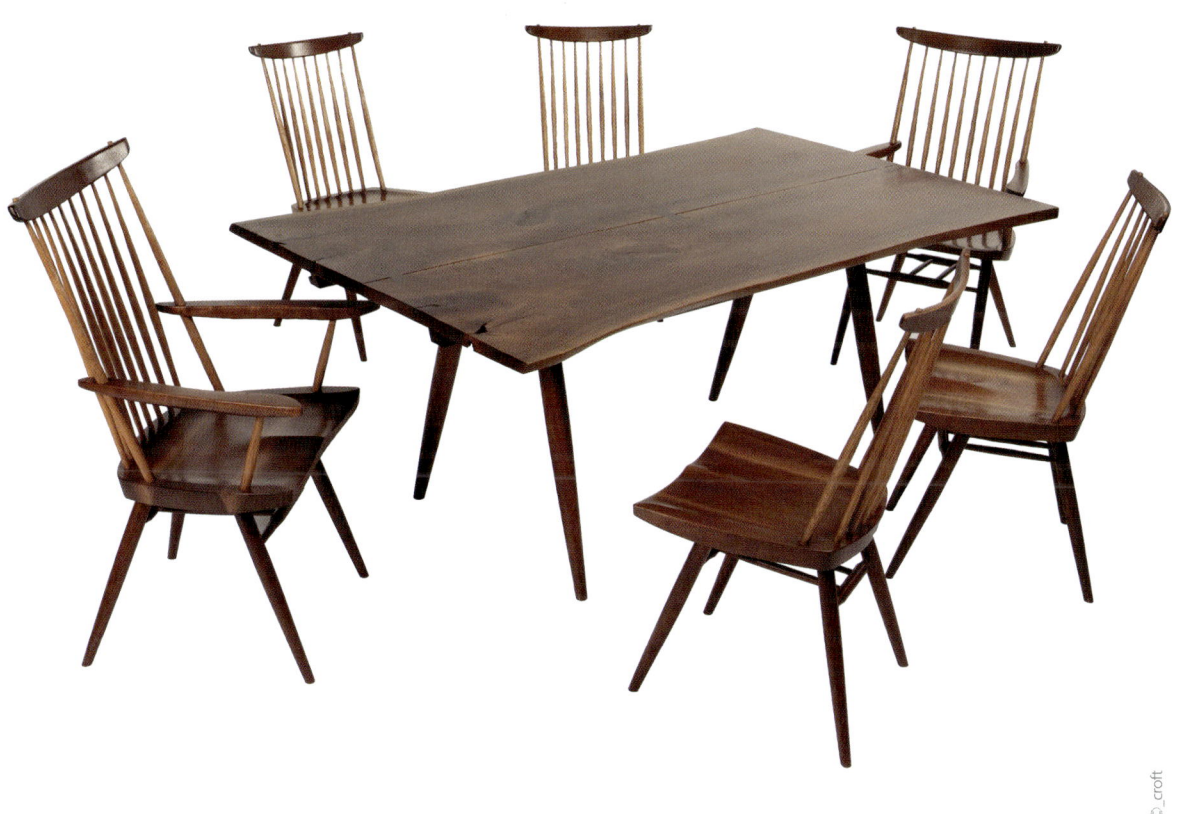

©_croft

Dining table, six new chairs, two extension leaves
다이닝 테이블, 여섯개의 의자와 두 개의 테이블 날개
73.2x181.6x114.8cm
Walnut, hickory and rosewood 호두나무, 히커리, 장미나무
1957

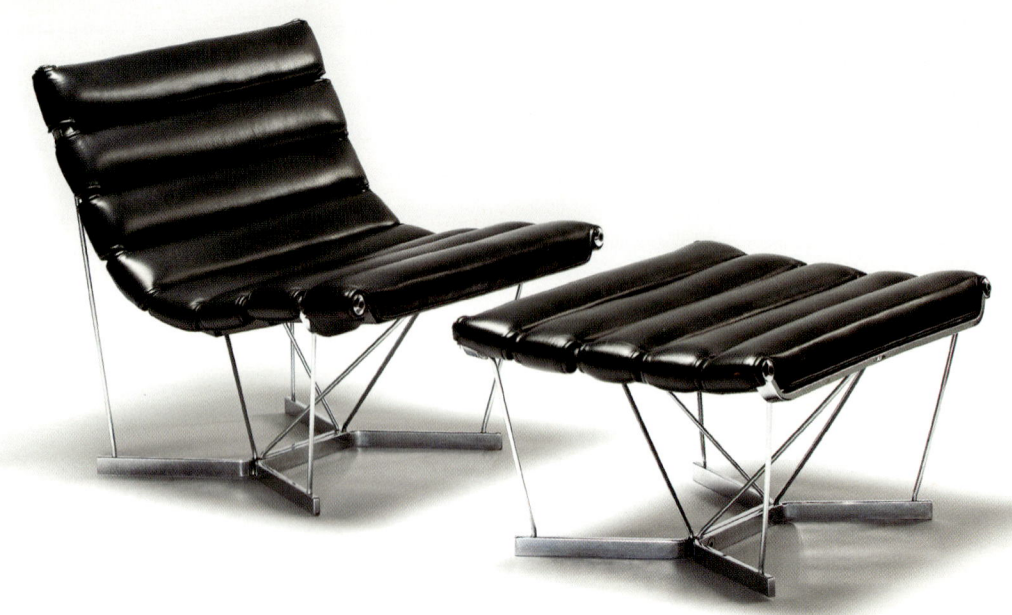

© _croft

Catenary Lounge Chair & Ottoman
캐터너리 라운지 체어& 오토만
chair 71x66x76cm
ottoman 39x56x76cm
Steel, leather 강철, 가죽
Herman Miller, US 허먼 밀러, 미국
1962

USA | 미국

George Nelson 조지 넬슨

About future furniture, this designer predicted that storage spaces will be expanded and finally a part of a house. Since the designer believes that wooden materials are inappropriate for mass production, he has avoided using wood in making furniture except decoration. He claimed that an easy design for production would be more economical and effective in the contemporary society.

Sources | Korean Institute of Interior Design, *Chair Design in the 20th Century*, Gimundang, 2003.

그는 미래의 가구에 관한 예언에서 수납공간은 확대될 것이고, 결국 가구는 주택의 일부가 될 것이라고 말했다. 그는 목재가 대량생산 기법에 적당하지 않다고 믿었기 때문에 장식을 제외하고는 가구에 목재를 사용하지 않았으며, 현대 사회에서는 생산이 용이한 디자인이 경제적이고, 효과적이라고 주장하였다.

출처 | 한국실내디자인학회, *20C 의자 디자인*, 기문당, 2003.

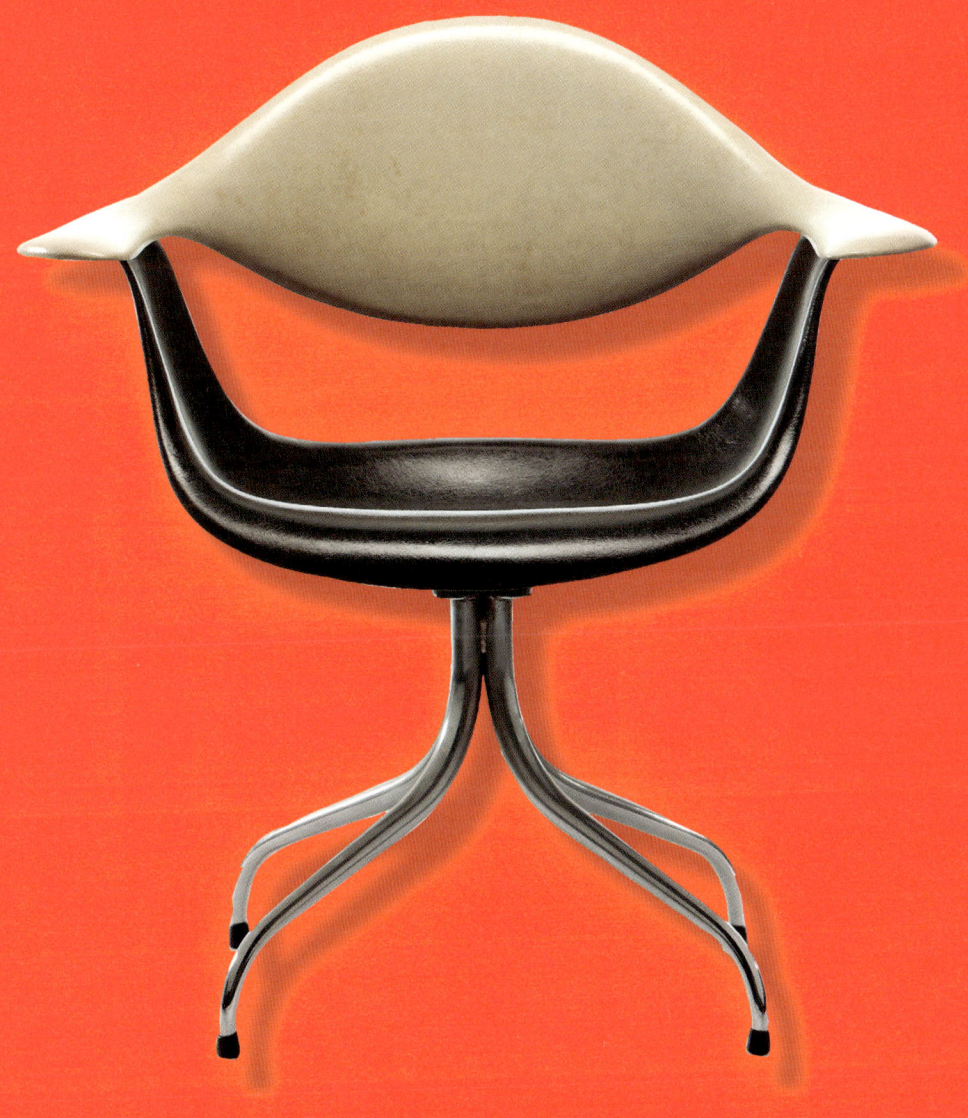

Daf Chair
다프 체어
72x73.5x54cm
Fiberglass, enameled steel 섬유유리, 에나멜 강철
Herman Miller, US 허먼 밀러, 미국
1958

Ejner Larsen & Aksel Bender Madsen
아이너 라르슨 & 악셀 벤더 매드슨

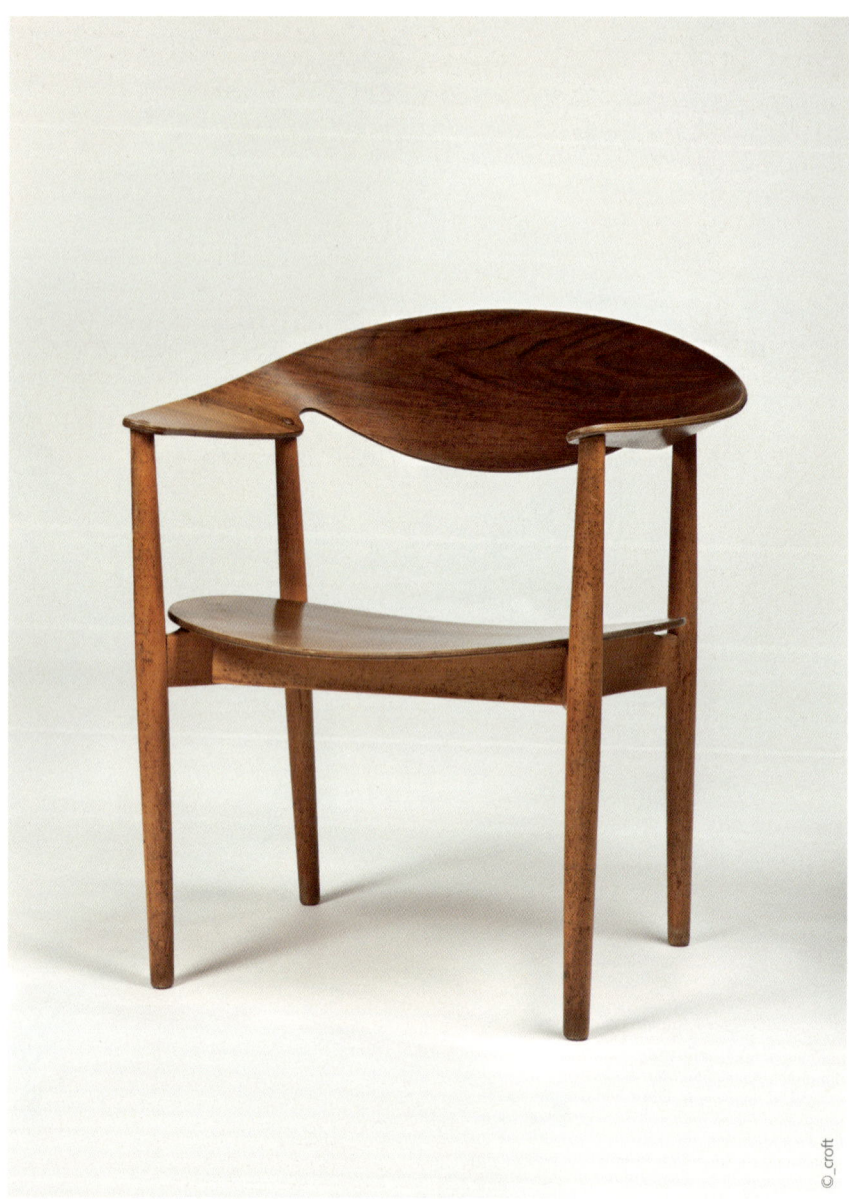

©_croft

Metropolitan Chair
메트로폴리탄 체어
77x72x51cm
Plywood, beech 합판, 너도밤나무
Willy Beck 윌리 벡
1959

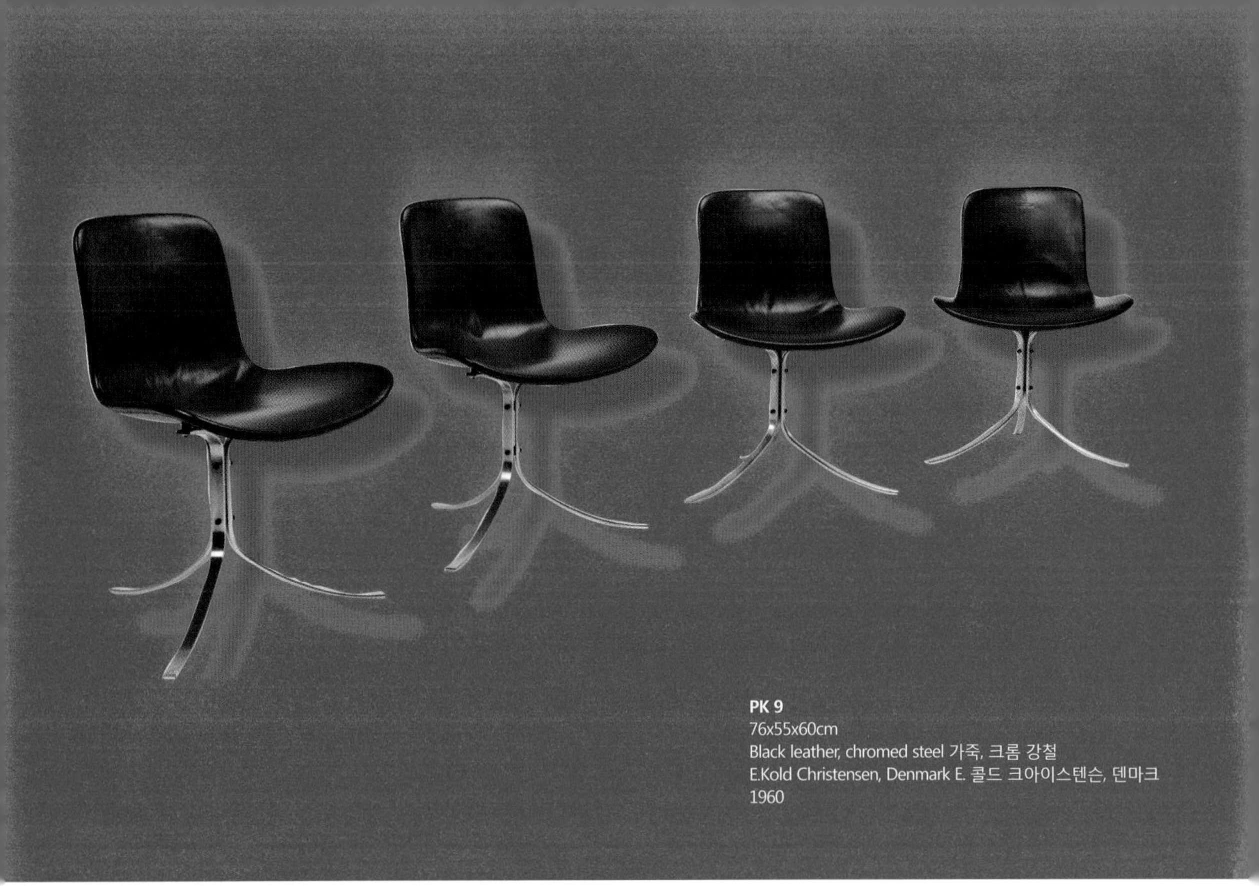

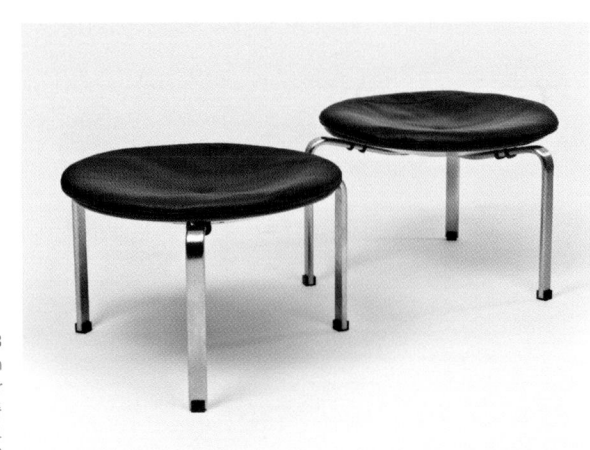

PK 9
76x55x60cm
Black leather, chromed steel 가죽, 크롬 강철
E.Kold Christensen, Denmark E. 콜드 크아이스텐슨, 덴마크
1960

Poul Kjaerholm 폴 키에홀름

PK 33
34.5xØ52.5cm
Stainless steel, leather
스테인레스 스틸, 가죽
E.Kold Chirstensen, Denmark E. 콜드 크아이스텐슨, 덴마크
1959

©_croft

Verner Panton 베르너 팬톤

It was designed in the late 1950s, the *Panton Chair* was not put into production until 1968 because of the difficulty of manufacturing such a light, strong stacking chair in plastic. Verner Panton was inspired by the freedom of designing in plastic. 'I try to forget existing examples even though they may be good, and concern myself with the material,' Panton once said. 'The result rarely has four legs.'

*팬톤 체어*는 1950년대 후반에 디자인되었지만, 가벼우면서 강하고, 동시에 쌓을 수 있는 의자를 플라스틱으로 제작하는 데에 따르는 어려움으로 1968년까지 생산에 들어가지 못했다. 베르너 팬톤은 플라스틱으로부터 설계의 자유에 대한 영감을 받았다고 한다. 팬톤은 이렇게 말했다.
'나는 아무리 좋은 것일지라도 기존의 사례들은 잊으려고 노력하고, 재료를 가지고 스스로 고민합니다. 그 결과 네 개의 다리를 가진 의자는 거의 없어졌답니다.'

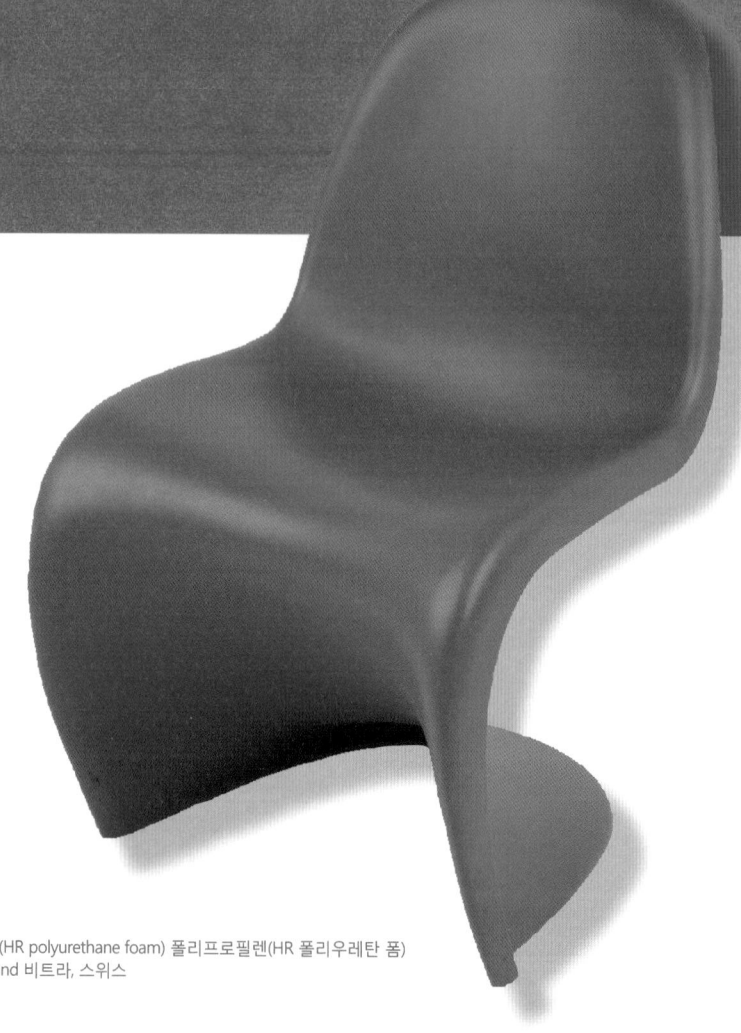

Panton Chair
팬톤 체어
83x50x62cm
Polypropylene(HR polyurethane foam) 폴리프로필렌(HR 폴리우레탄 폼)
Vitra, Switzerland 비트라, 스위스
1959-60

Carlo Mollino 카를로 몰리노

An architect, photographer, car designer and racing car driver, Mollino designed this chair for the Faculty of Architecture at Turin Polytechnic where he was professor from 1957. The bipartite organic design enhances the natural qualities of the oak. Although far from traditional in style, it was made using traditional furniture-making techniques.

건축가, 사진작가, 자동차 디자이너이자 자동차 레이싱 드라이버인 몰리노는 그가 교수로 있던 토리노 공과대학 건축학부를 위해 1957년 이 의자를 디자인했다. 두 부분으로 구성된 유기적인 디자인은 오크 나무의 자연적인 재질이 돋보인다. 스타일은 전통적인 것에서 벗어나 있지만, 제작은 전통적인 가구제조기술을 사용하여 만들어졌다.

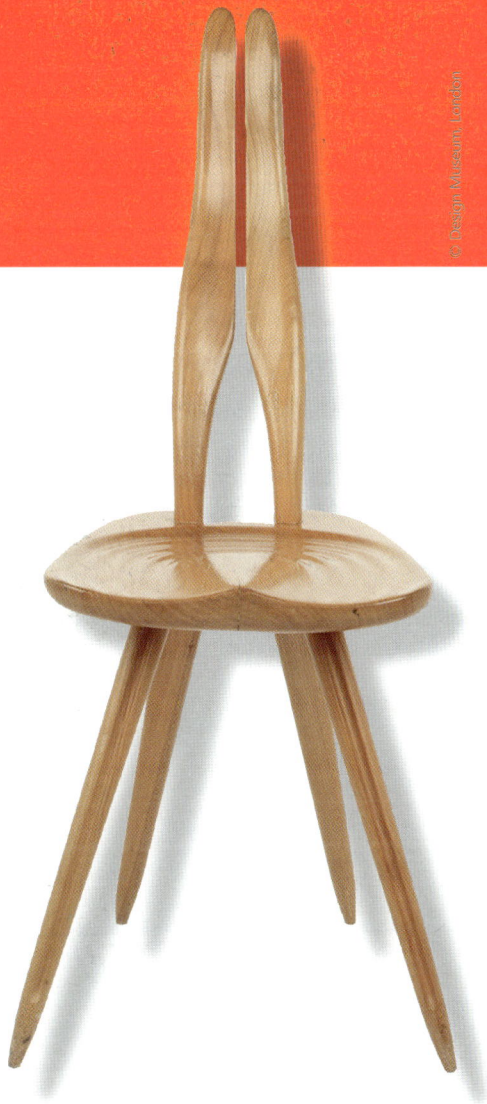

Chair for the Turin Faculty of Architecture
토리노대학 건축학부를 위한 의자
69x35x45cm
Solid Oak 오크 나무
Reissued by Zanotta, Italy 자노타, 이탈리아
1962

© Design Museum, London

Richard Young 리차드 영

The Scandinavian influenced works of Richard Young supplied post utility Britain with desirable modern furniture. Priced so that it could be bought one piece at a time, the series featured the three legged dining chair with a triangular upholstered seat. Although unfamiliar in design, research guarantees that the chairs are as robust and as comfortable as more familiar models, with its popularity confirming this.

스칸디나비아 반도로부터 영향을 받은 리차드 영의 작품들은 영국 사람들에게 매력적인 근대 가구들과 함께 받침대를 공급했다. 세 개의 다리 위에 착석 판이 삼각으로 놓인 이 시리즈 제품은 한번에 한 개의 의자를 살 수 있는 정도의 가격으로 책정되었다. 이러한 디자인 형태는 낯선 것이었지만, 이 작품에 대한 연구를 통해 기존의 친숙했던 모델들만큼 튼튼하고 편안하다고 보증했으며, 이 의자의 인기가 이러한 사실을 확인시켜주었다.

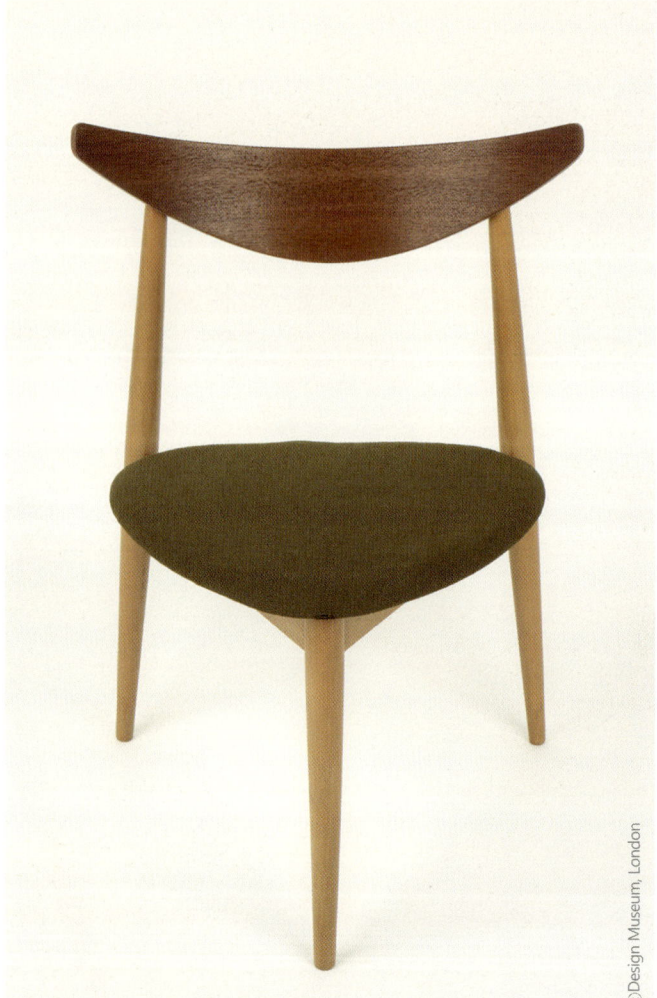

©Design Museum, London

G-Plan Dining Chair No. 4511
G-플랜 다이닝 체어 No. 4511
Wood and polyurethane shell, stainless steel, foam and wool
나무, 폴리우레탄, 스테인레스 스틸, 울
E. Gomme Ltd., UK E. 곰 Ltd., 영국
1962

Dutch design

Cowhorn Armchair
소뿔 팔걸이 의자
80x58x50cm
Rosewood, leather 장미나무, 가죽
Nijkerk, Netherlands 네이케르크, 네덜란드
1963

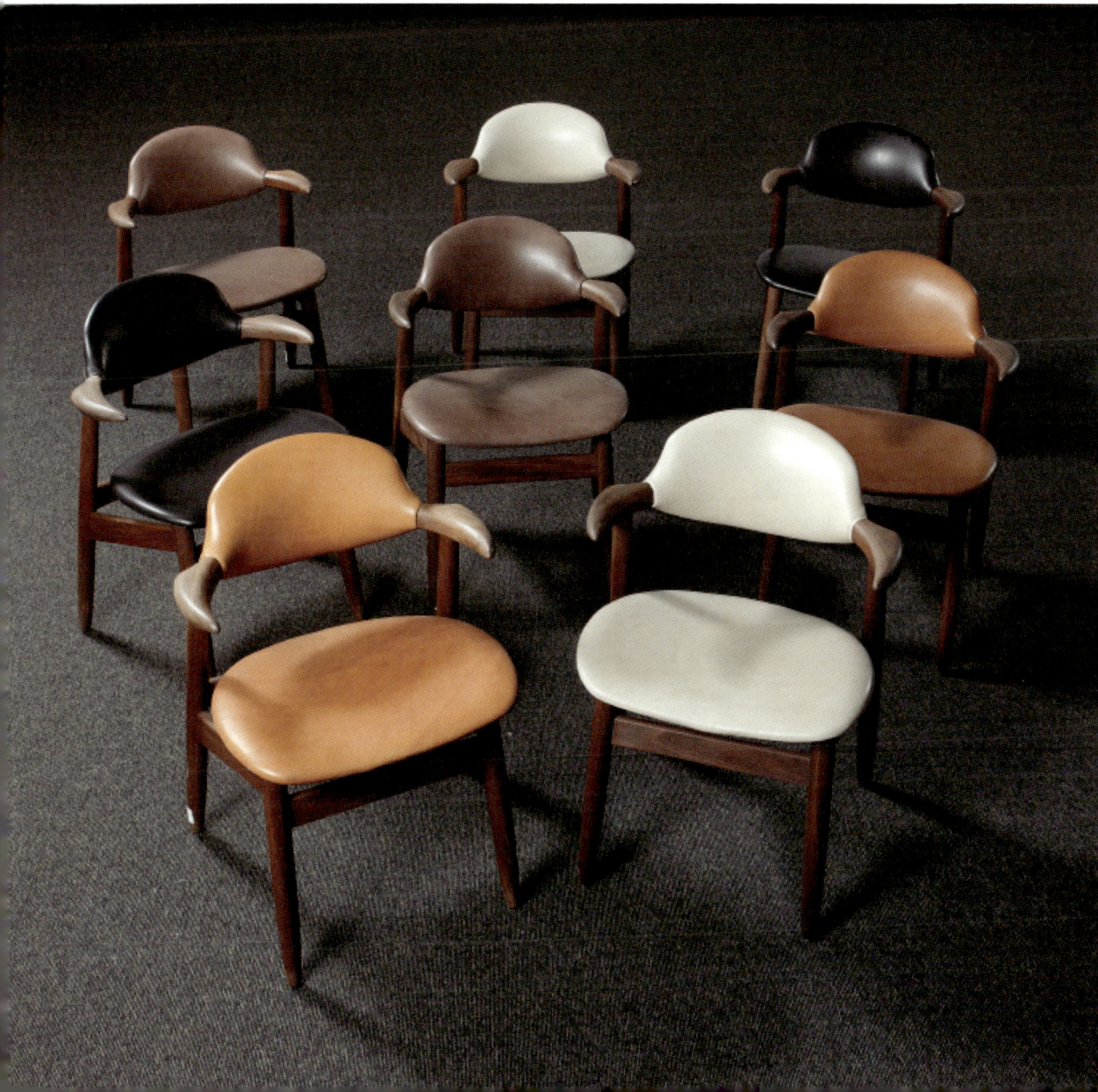

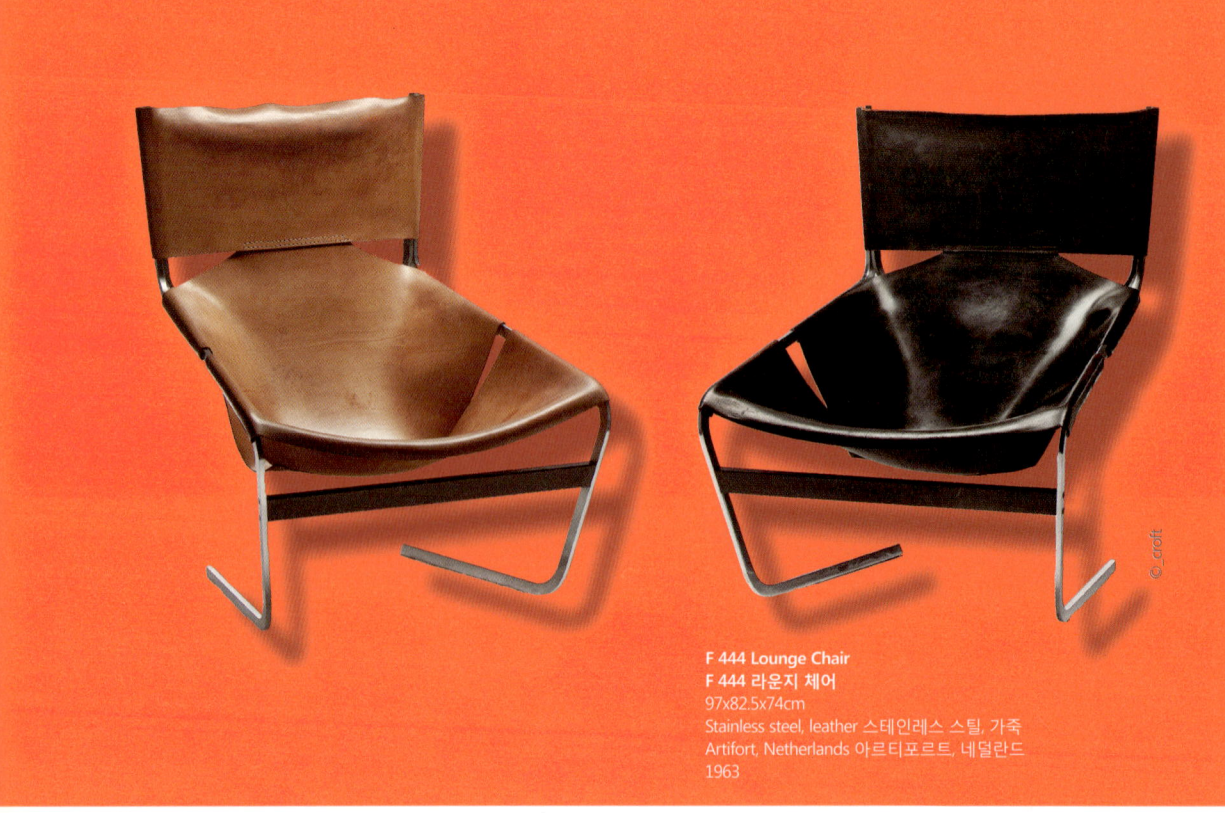

F 444 Lounge Chair
F 444 라운지 체어
97x82.5x74cm
Stainless steel, leather 스테인레스 스틸, 가죽
Artifort, Netherlands 아르티포르트, 네덜란드
1963

France | 프랑스

Pierre Paulin 피에르 폴랑

"In the process of creative works at the present viewpoints of mine, I have caused quite a number of scandals. Although modern science and techniques have achieved as many as miraculous, I don't feel myself to buy passions or talents from current designers or architects. It might be because, I observe, brainwashing by television and college education which brought the lack of communication have governed all parts of our life and changed even art. I am eager to let the young know, and to suggest, that such things cannot be used as their tools. There are still enough opportunities to revive their gifts and increase their imaginations. I believe that one of the two are required to create something truly new and finally to make it rare: severe struggles or great lucks. What I want to tell you lastly is that you should not behave like a sarcastic old man at your young ages, or not keep childish bad habits. Instead, try to experience and feel with your body, laying yourselves on the ground. When your body feels something, your soul feels it too."

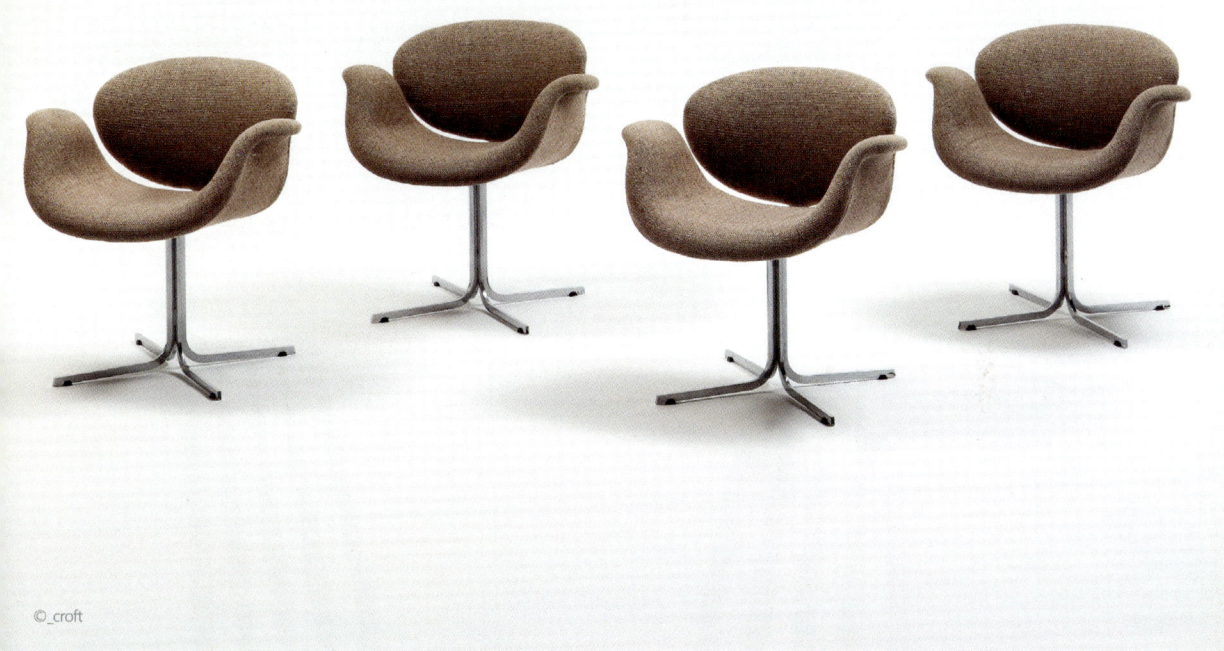

© _croft

© _croft

Tulip Chair
튤립 의자
73x72x62cm
Chromed brass, wood, fabric 크롬 황동, 나무, 천
1965

"나는 내가 바라보는 현 시점의 창조 작업 속에서 매우 많은 스캔들을 일으켜 왔지요, 현대의 과학과 기술은 거의 기적이라 할만큼 많은 업적을 남겼는데도 불구하고, 요즘의 디자이너들이나 건축가들에게서는 예전만큼의 뜨거운 열정이나 재능이 느껴지지가 않아요. 아마도 텔레비전과 대학의 세뇌교육 그리고 사람들과의 의사소통 부족이 모든 삶을 지배하고, 심지어는 예술까지 바꾸어 놓았기 때문이라고 생각합니다. 나는 젊은이들에게 그것이 모두가 아니라는 것을 알려주고, 또 제시하고 싶습니다.재능을 부활시키고 상상력을 증진시킬 수 있는 기회는 아직 충분히 있습니다. 정말로 새로운 것이 창조될 때에는. 그리고 그것이 진정 희귀한 결과물이 되려면 끔찍한 노력을 들이거나 엄청난 운이 따르는 두 가지 중 하나가 있어야 한다고 생각합니다. 마지막으로 여러분들에게 당부하고 싶은 것은. 젊은 나이에 냉소적인 영감처럼 굴거나 유치하기 짝이 없는, 나쁜 성질을 껴안고 있지 말라는 것입니다. 가끔씩은 땅에, 바닥에 드러누워 몸으로 느끼고 체험하세요. 몸이 느껴야 정신도 느끼는 것입니다."

Niels Kofoed 닐스 코포드

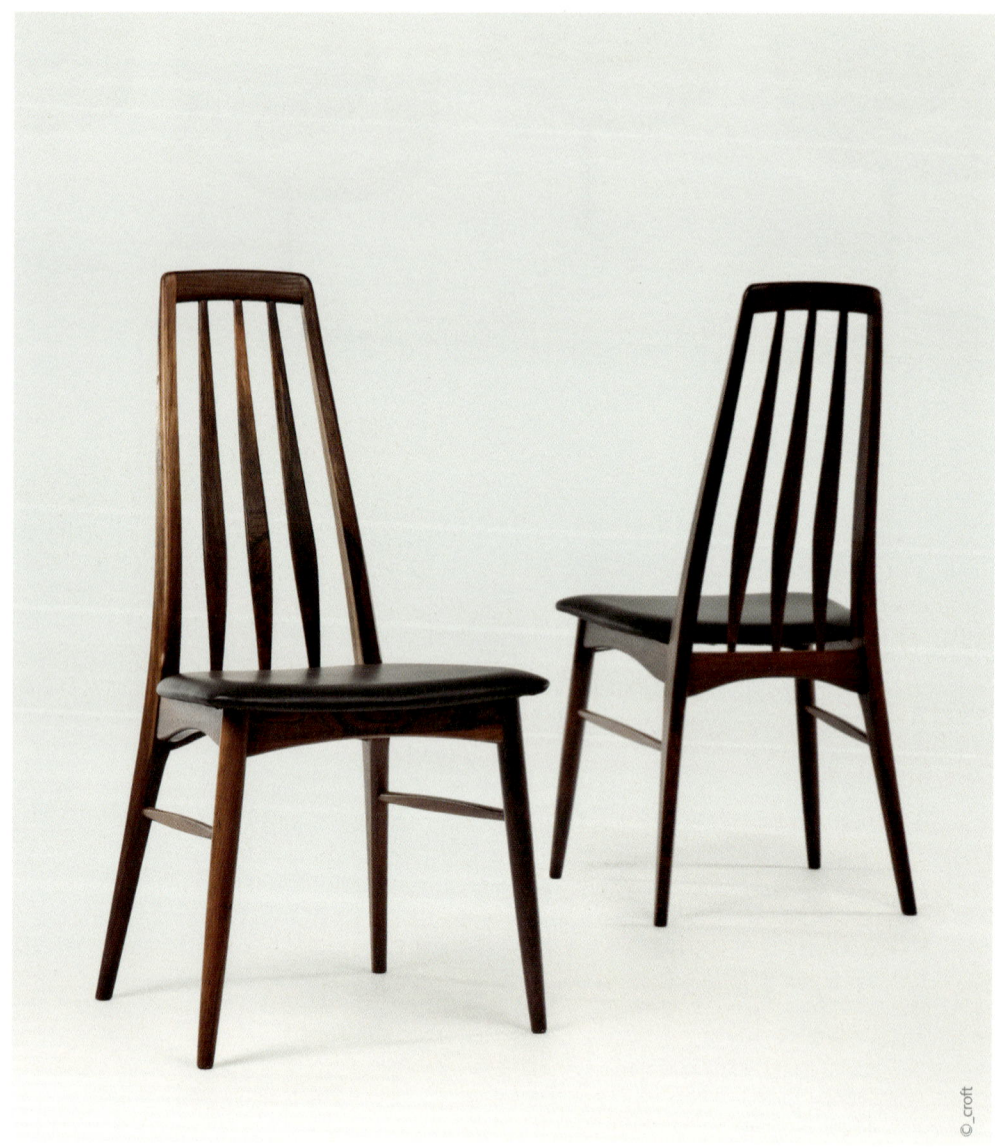

©_croft

Eva Dining Chair
에바 다이닝 체어
97x48x54cm
Rosewood, leather 장미나무, 가죽
Kofoed Møbelfabrik, Denmark 코포드 뫼벨파브릭, 덴마크
1964

David Rowland 데이빗 롤란드

One of the most commercially successful contract chairs ever produced, the *GF 40/4* was developed by the US designer David Rowland with practicality as the prime consideration. Determined to ensure that his chair would be as light and easy to stack, Rowland strove to reduce the structure to its barest elements. He succeeded in developing a comfortable chair for use in offices, conference rooms and other public buildings that could be stacked 40-high at a height of just 4 feet. Rowland named the chair – *40/4* – after this feat.

의자 중에 가장 상업적으로 성공한 계약 중 하나인 *GF 40/4*는 실용성을 가장 중요한 고려사항으로 하여 미국 디자이너인 데이빗 롤란드에 의해 개발되었다. 그의 의자는 가볍고 쌓기 쉽다는 것을 확실하게 하기 위해, 가장 기본적인 요소 중에 구조적인 부분을 최소화 했다. 그는 4피트 높이의 40개를 겹쳐 쌓을 수 있는, 사무실, 회의실, 공공 빌딩를 위한 편안한 의자를 개발하는데 성공했다. 롤란드는 이 같은 의자의 특징을 따서 이름을 *40/4* 이라고 지었다.

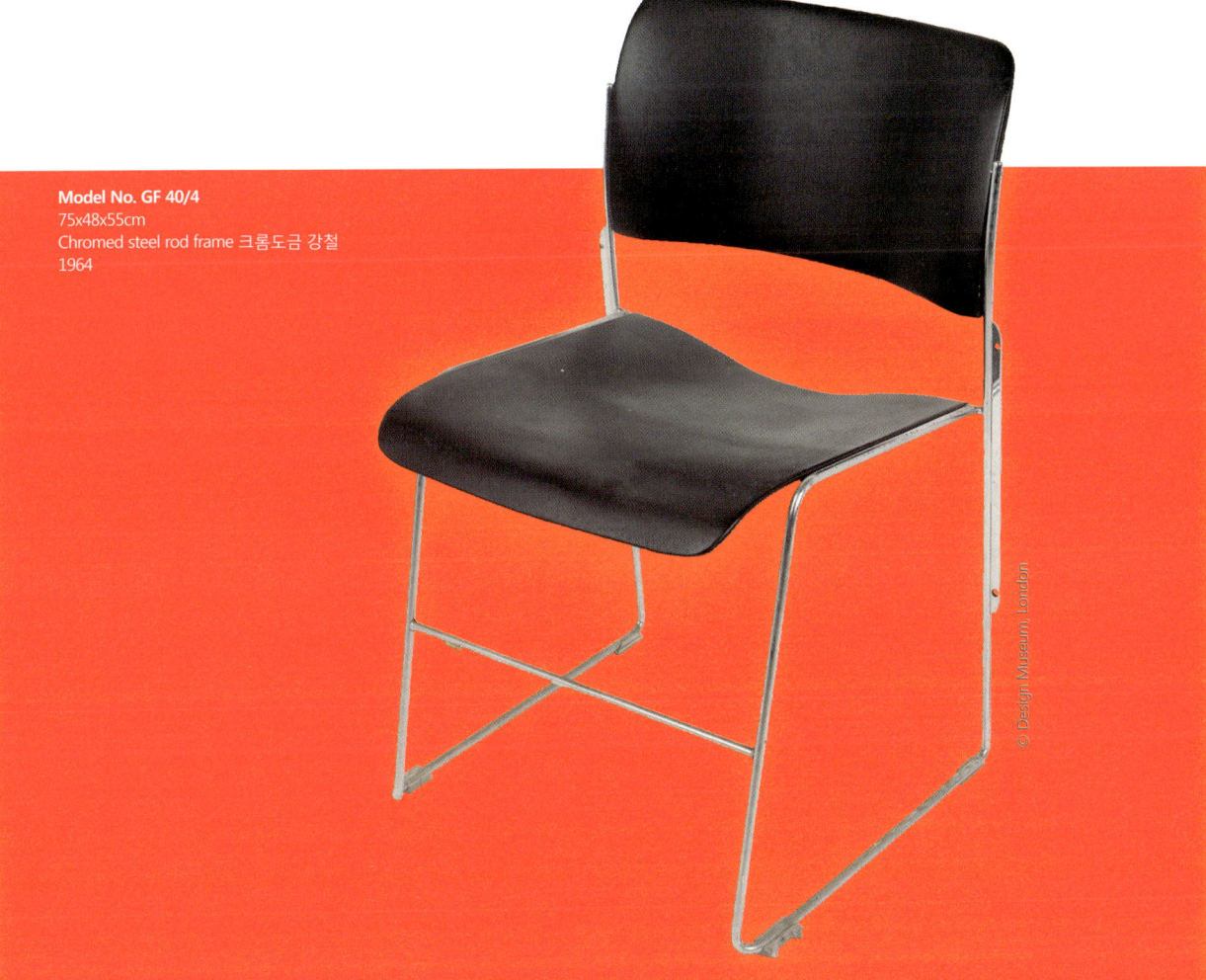

Model No. GF 40/4
75x48x55cm
Chromed steel rod frame 크롬도금 강철
1964

© Design Museum, London

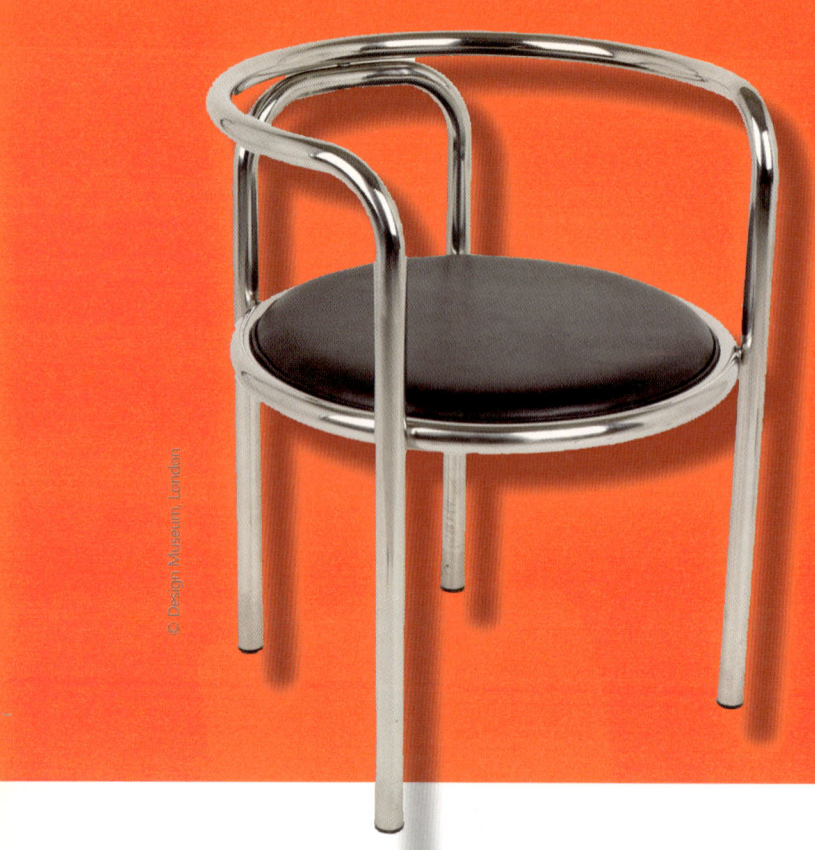

© Design Museum, London

Solus
솔루스
66.5x55.5x53cm
Tubular steel and leather 강철튜브, 가죽
Zanotta, Italy 자노타, 이탈리아
1965

Italy | 이탈리아

Gae Aulenti 가에 아울렌티

During the 1960s, furniture manufacturers reissued some of the modernist tubular steel pieces designed in the 1920s. Gavina reproduced Marcel Breuer's *Wassily chair* in 1962 and in 1965 Cassina started to manufacture furniture by Le Corbusier and Charlotte Perriand. These reproductions had a great influence over contemporary designers, like Gae Aulenti, who looked again at the principles and designs of modernist pioneers in pieces like the *Solus*.

1960년대에 가구 제조사들은 1920년대 디자인된 몇몇 모던 디자인의 강철튜브 제품들을 다시 만들기 시작했다. 가비나는 1962년 마르셀 브로이어의 *바실리* 의자를 재현했고 1965년 카시나는 르 코르뷔지에와 샬롯 페리앙의 가구를 생산하기 시작했다. 이러한 복제품들은 가에 아울렌티의 솔루스 같은 작품처럼 모더니스트 선구자들의 원칙과 디자인을 재고찰하고자 했던 당대의 디자이너들에게 커다란 영향을 미쳤다.

Charles Pollock 찰스 폴록

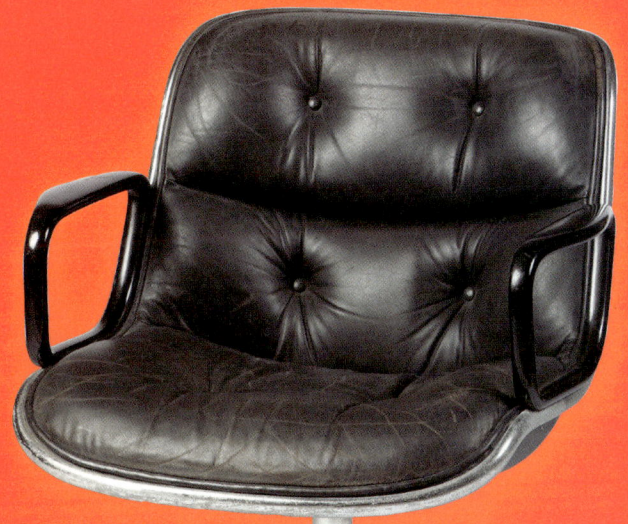

Executive Chair
이그제큐티브 체어
77.5x66x69cm
Aluminum frame, polypropylene shell, leather
upholstery 알루미늄, 폴리프로필렌
1965

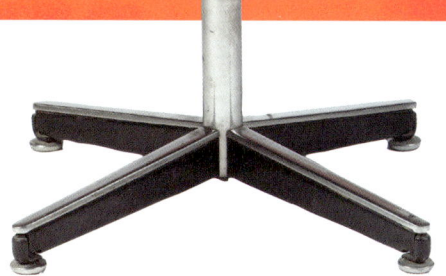

The Pollock chair continues to maintain its quintessential role with its timeless and contemporary elegance. Offered in a variety of luxurious fabrics, leathers and finishes, the versatile and extremely comfortable chair features a waterfall front, thick tufted upholstery and a signature aluminum rim. This is a perfect chair for conference rooms and private offices as well as many other environments.

폴록의 의자는 오늘날까지 의자의 본질적 역할과 변치 않는 현대적 감각의 우아함을 유지하고 있다. 다양한 고급 천과 가죽 등의 마감재를 이용해 다용도로 사용할 수 있는 극도로 편안한 이 의자는 폭포 같은 앞 모양과 두껍고 촘촘한 덮개, 독특한 알루미늄 테두리가 특징이다. 폴록의 의자는 회의실, 개인 사무실뿐만 아니라 다양한 환경에서 사용할 수 있는 완벽한 의자다.

Niels O. Møller 닐스 O. 묄러

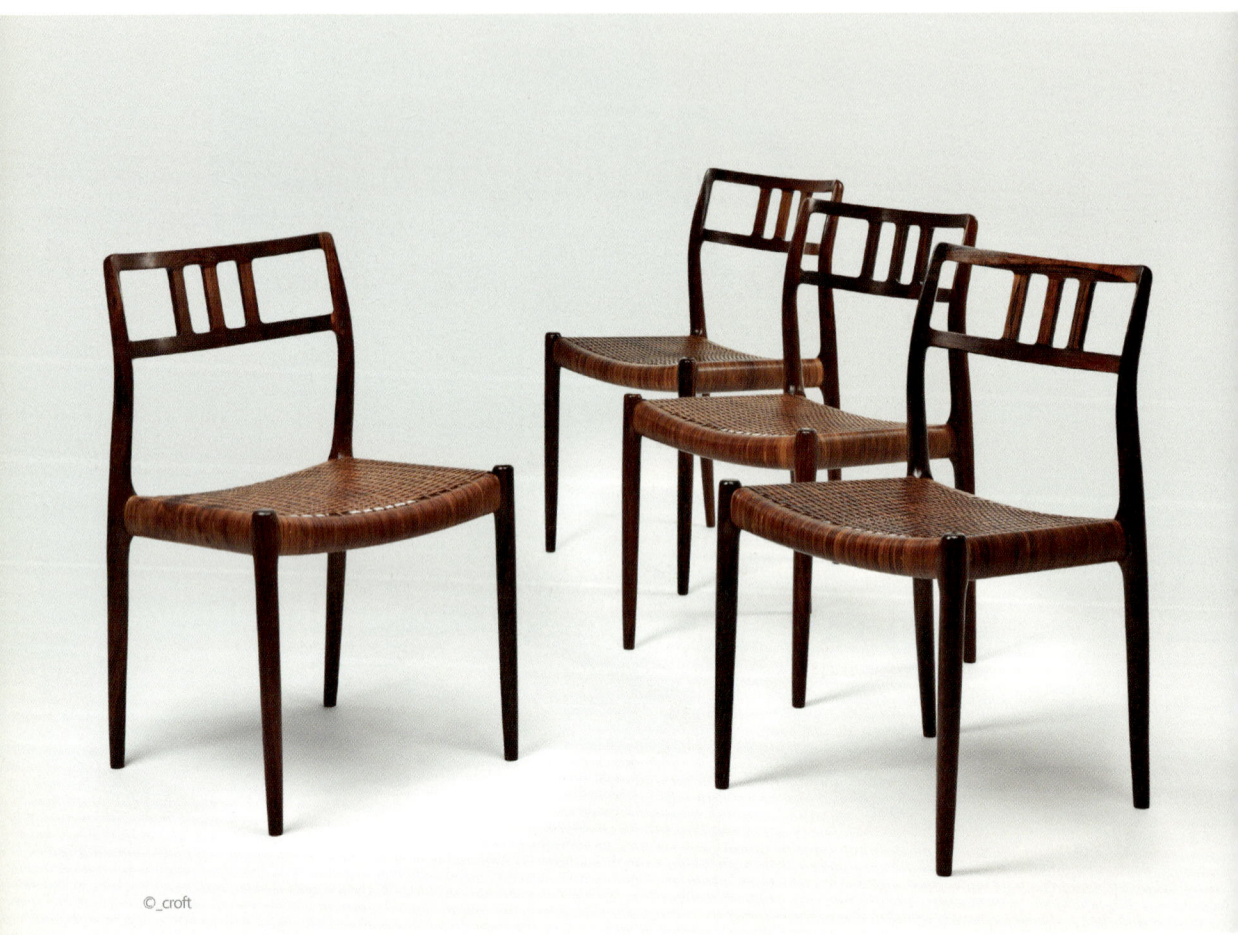

©_croft

Dining Chair No. 79
다이닝 체어 No. 79
76x50x48cm
Rosewood, woven leather 장미나무, 가
J.L.Møller, Denmark J.L.묄러, 덴마크
1966

Preben Fabricius & Jørgen Kastholm
프레벤 파브리시우스 & 요르겐 카스톨름

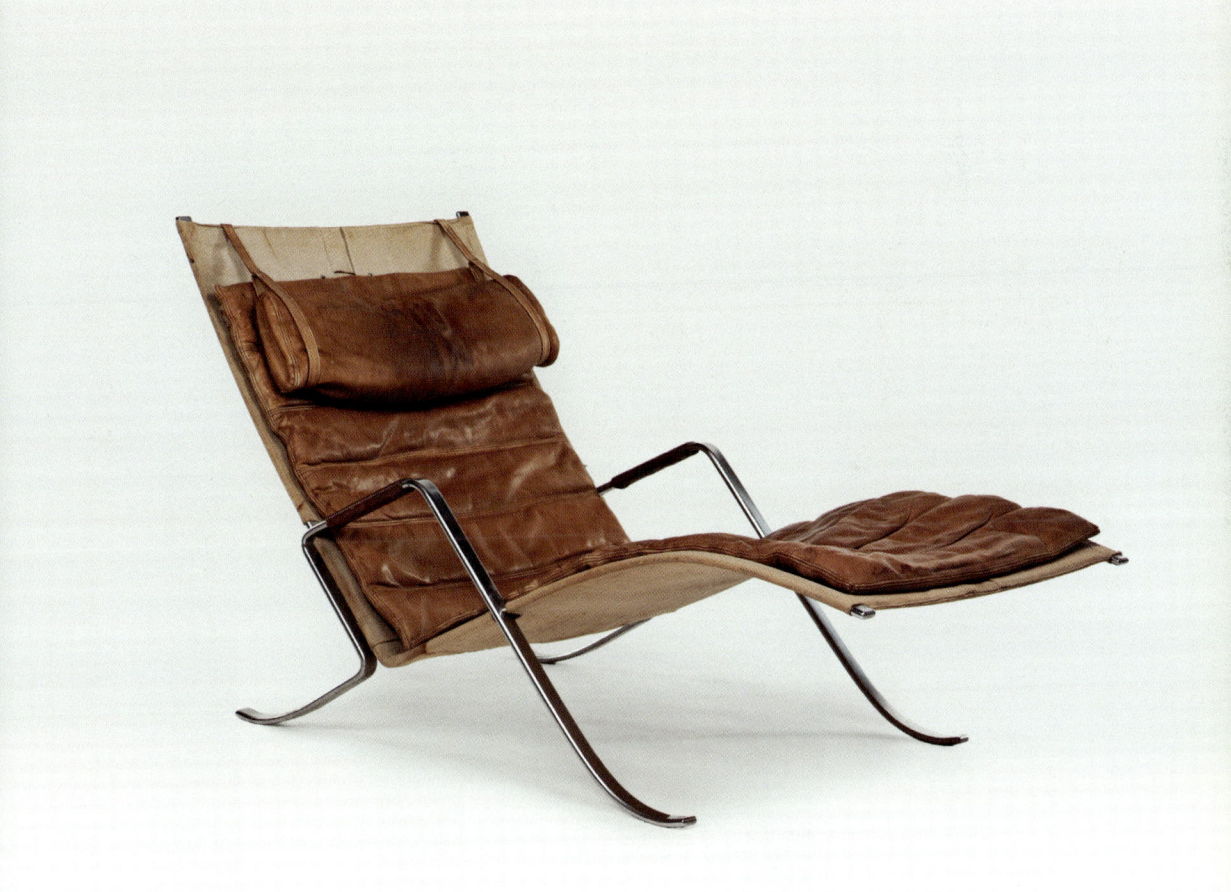

FK 87 – Grasshopper Chair
FK 87 - 메뚜기 의자
80x144X72cm
Chromed steel, leather 크롬도금 강철, 가죽
Alfred Kill, Germany 알프레드 킬, 독일
1967

Joe Colombo 조 콜롬보

A flamboyant force in 1960s Italian design, Joe Colombo made a major breakthrough with the Universale, which was the first adult-sized injection-moulded plastic stacking chair to go into commercial production. Quick and cheap, this method of production enabled manufacturers to respond to changes in fashion – in this case to Pop Art. The detachable legs are available in two heights: one for children and one for adults.

1960년대 이탈리아 디자인에 눈부신 영향력을 미친 조 콜롬보는 유니버셜 회사와 함께 최초로 성인이 사용할 수 있는 크기의 사출 성형 플라스틱 스태킹 체어(쌓을 수 있는 의자)의 생산에 큰 돌파구를 열었다. 생산이 빠르고 값싼 이 같은 방식은 가구회사들에게 팝아트와 같은 유행의 변화에 반응할 수 있게 했다. 분리 가능한 다리는 아이와 어른을 위해 각각 두 개의 높이로 조정 가능하다.

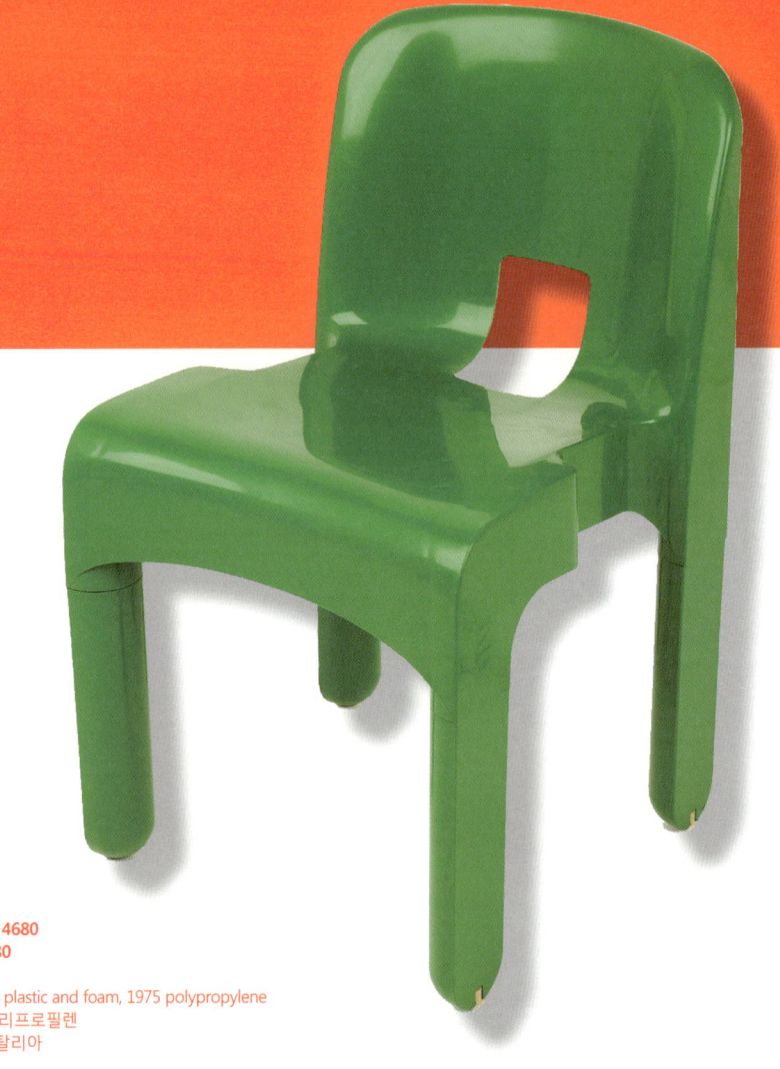

© Design Museum, London

Universale Model No. 4680
유니버셜 모델 No. 4680
72x42x43cm
Injection-moulded ABS plastic and foam, 1975 polypropylene
ABS 플라스틱, 1975 폴리프로필렌
Kartell, Italy 카르텔, 이탈리아
1965-67

Jorgen Hovelskov 요르겐 호벨스코브

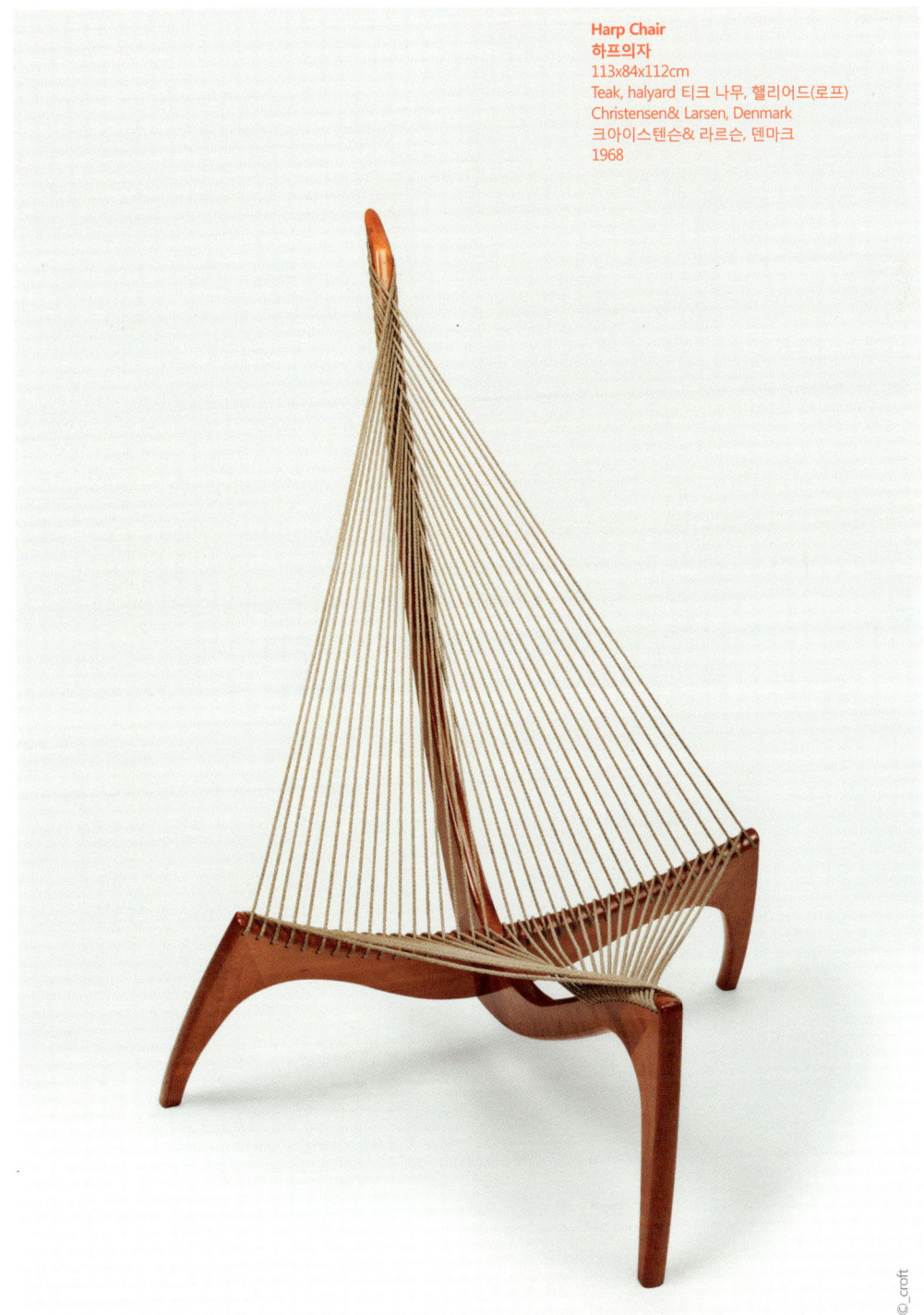

Harp Chair
하프의자
113x84x112cm
Teak, halyard 티크 나무, 핼리어드(로프)
Christensen& Larsen, Denmark
크아이스텐슨& 라르슨, 덴마크
1968

©_croft

Vico Magistretti
비코 마지스트레티

Beginning furniture design during the 1960's, Magistretti won a fame in 1967 by *Selene*, the world's first Monobloc Plastic Chair. The *Selene* was listed in a design company with its reasonable price for most people at that time, but was produced only until 1969 due to the company's situation. Long after that, the *Selene* has been produced with ABS plastic materials by an American company Heller since 2002. This chair consists with a single volume of tempered fiber glass polyester, with legs in distinctive S-shaped forms to solve a technical difficulty regarding the solidity of the parts to support sitter's weight. Using plastic seat, the chair expresses its uniqueness and elegance with a consideration of its stability.

마지스트레티는 60년대 가구 디자인을 시작하여 1967년에는 세계최초의 모노 블록 플라스틱의자와 *셀리니*로 우리에게 그 이름을 알렸다. 마지스트레티가 제작한 *셀리니*는 당시 대부분의 사람들이 적당한 가격에 구입할 수 있는 산업제품으로 디자인 사에 기록되어있지만 회사의 사정으로 인해 1969년까지밖에 생산되지 못했다. 그 이후 *셀리니*는 2002년부터 미국의 헬러 사에서 ABS 플라스틱 소재를 통해 현재까지 생산하고 있는 중이다. 이 의자는 3mm 두께의 강화 섬유유리 폴리에스테르 한 덩어리로 제작하였으며, 사람의 무게를 지탱하는 다리 부분의 강도와 관련된 기술적 어려움을 해결하기 위하여 'S'자 형태로 독특하게 디자인 되었다. 또한 플라스틱 시트를 재료로 한 의자는 안정성을 고려하여 독창적이고 우아하게 표현하였다.

New Selene Chair
뉴 셀리니 체어
75x47x47cm
Compression moulded "Reglar" fiberglass reinforced
polyester structure 강화 섬유유리 폴리에스테르
Heller, US 헬러, 미국
1969

CONTEMPORARY

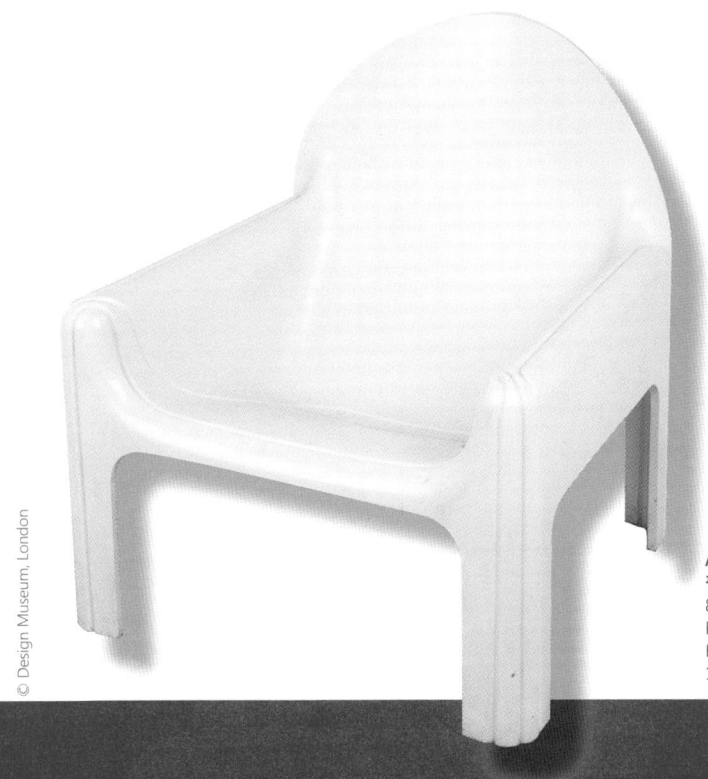

© Design Museum, London

Armchair 4794
팔걸이 의자 4794
80x70x68cm
Rigid expanded polyurethane 폴리우레탄
Kartell, Italy 카르텔, 이탈리아
1975

Italy | 이탈리아

Gae Aulenti 가에 아울렌티

Typical of the experimental designs developed by Gae Aulenti in the 1960s and 1970s, the *Armchair 4794* represents the successful integration of hard plastics into a living space. An architect as well as a furniture, lighting and interior designer, Gae Aulenti graduated in architecture from Milan Polytechnic in 1954 and swiftly made her name as an exhibition designer for Fiat and Olivetti.

1960년대와 1970년대 가에 아울렌티가 시도한 실험 디자인의 전형인 *팔걸이 의자 4794*는 일상생활공간에 딱딱한 플라스틱의 성공적인 도입을 보여주는 작품이다. 건축가이자 가구, 조명, 인테리어 디자이너인 가에 아울렌티는 1954년 밀라노 공과대학에서 건축학과를 졸업했고, 피아트와 올리베티에서 전시 디자이너로 급속히 유명해졌다.

Ron Arad 론 아라드

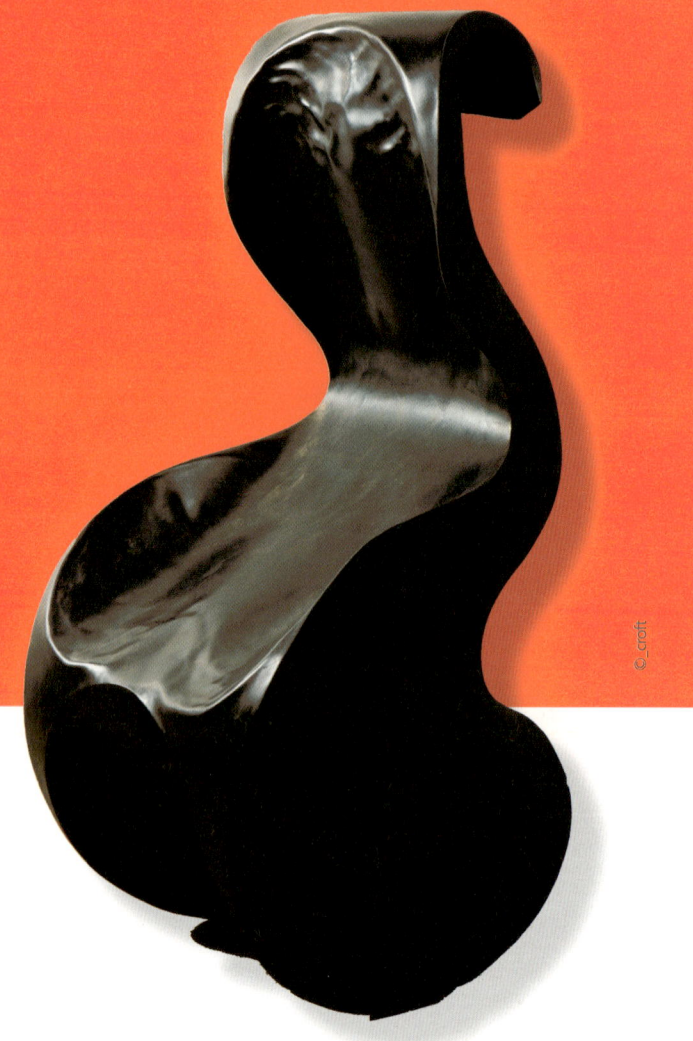

A.Y.O.R
100x49x46cm
Patinated steel AP 1(Unique) 강철
1991

©_croft

Soft Heart
One of a series of a dozen upholstered chairs designed by Ron Arad for the Italian manufacturer Moroso, the flamboyant form and vivid palette of the *Soft Heart* is typical of the designer's exuberant aesthetic. Both in his limited editions of sculptural furniture and his mass-produced pieces, Arad has played with similar forms to the *Soft Heart* again and again in a variety of materials from aluminium and steel to upholstery.

부드러운 심장
이탈리아 가구회사인 모로소에서 론 아라드가 디자인한 12개의 쿠션 의자 시리즈 중 하나인 *부드러운 심장*은 대담한 형태와 선명한 색깔로 론 아라드의 전형적인 생동감 넘치는 미감을 보여준다. 아라드는 알루미늄부터 강철까지 다양한 소재들로 *부드러운 심장*과 유사한 형태를 반복적으로 사용하여 한정판 조각적 가구와 대량생산 제품들을 제작하였다.

© Design Museum, London

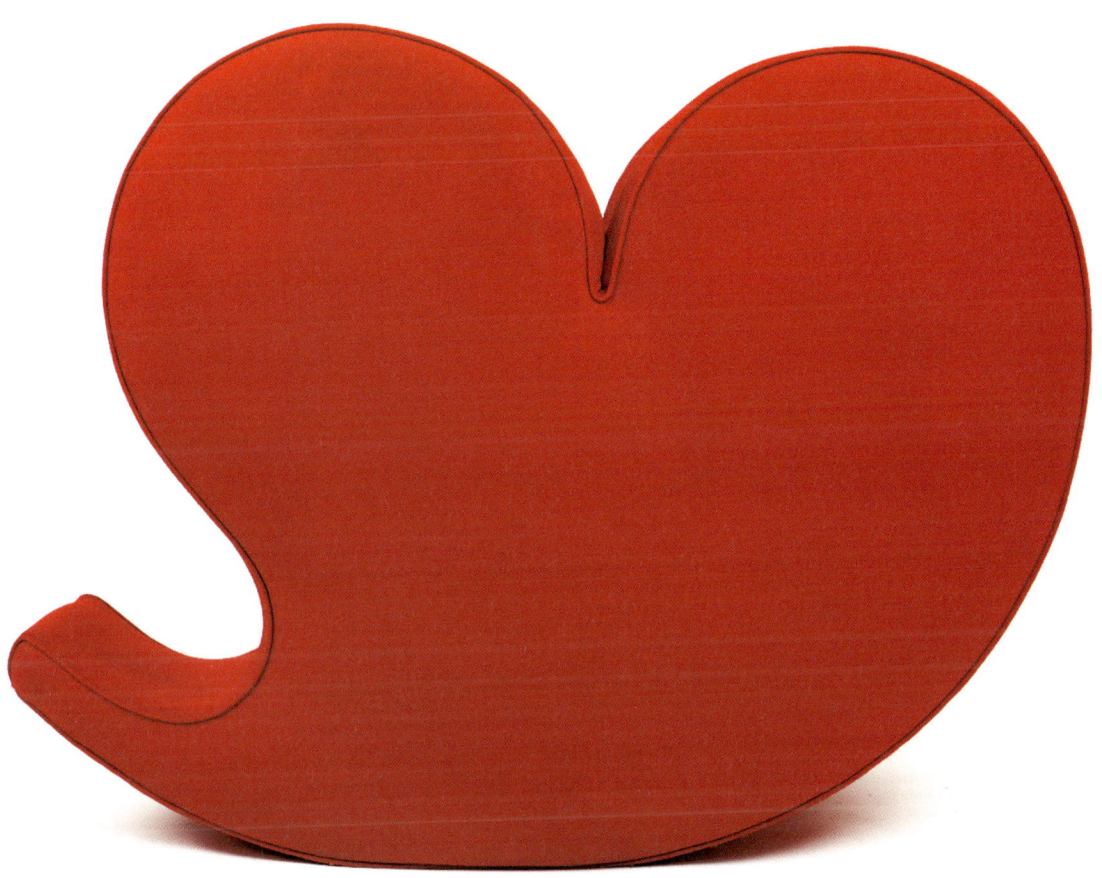

Soft Heart, Spring Collection
부드러운 심장, 봄 컬렉션
75x110x60cm
Steel frame covered with injected flame retardant polyurethane foam and fabric 강철, 방염 폴리우레탄, 천
Moroso, Italy 모로소, 이탈리아
1990

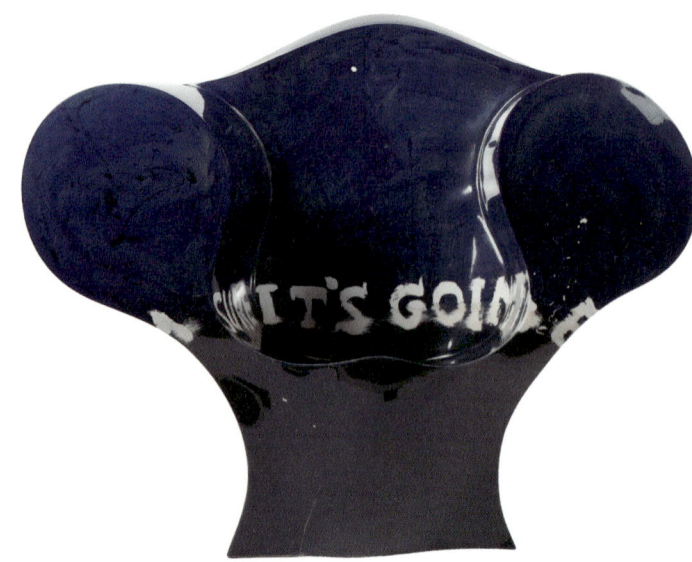

New Orleans A.P.
뉴올리언스 A.P.
90×60×80cm
Pigmented polyester reinforced with fiberglass
폴리에스터, 강화 유리섬유
2008

Afterthought
나중에 생각한 것
159×137×172cm
patinated unique cut(Unique)
2007

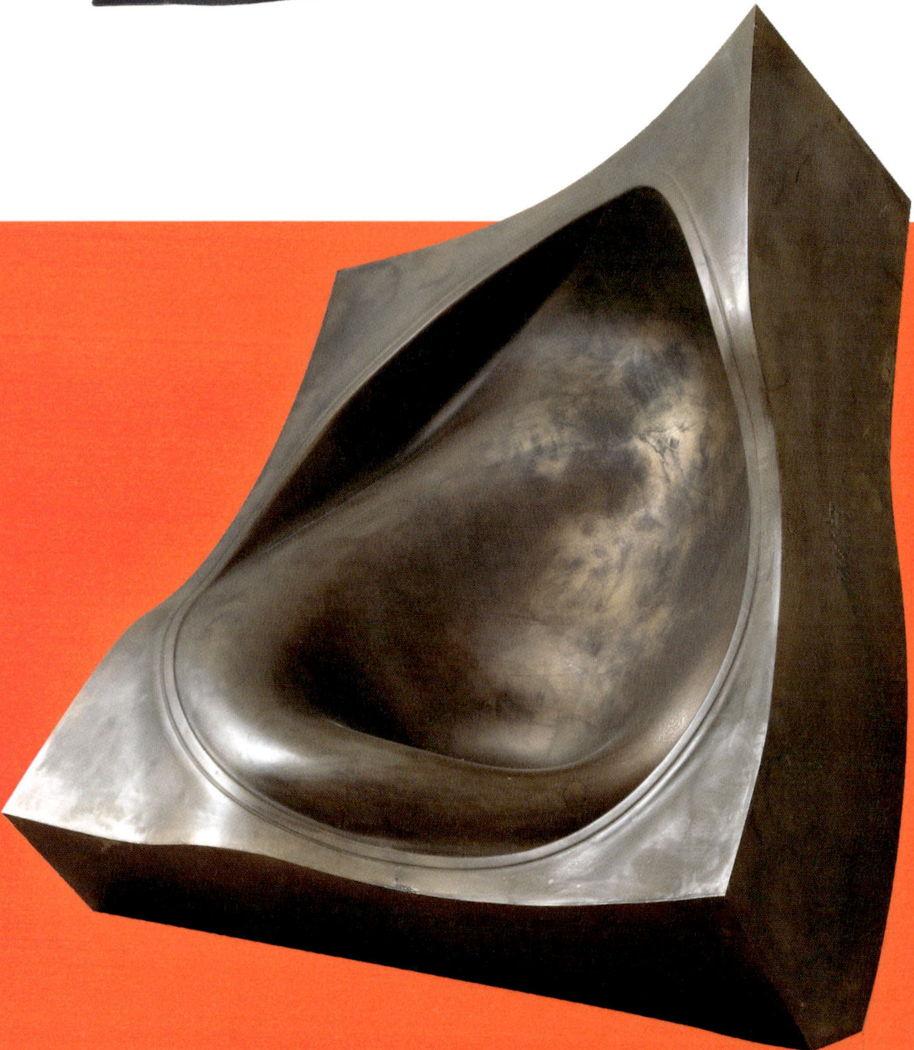

Jane Atfield 제인 앳필드

Earlier in her career Jane Atfield had developed a type of recycled plastic – Made of Waste – from discarded shampoo and bleach bottles collected from community recycling schemes. The board was made by heating and pressing the plastic chips so they bonded to form a single sheet of material. This chair for children is produced from the off-cuts of the adult's version of the *RCP2*.

제인 앳필드는 초창기에 재활용 커뮤니티 제도를 통해 수집한 버려진 샴푸 병, 표백제 병과 같은 쓰레기로 만든 재활용 플라스틱을 개발했다. 그녀는 이 플라스틱 조각들을 하나의 덩어리로 만들기 위해 열을 가하고 눌러서 판으로 만든다. 이 *RCP2 어린이 의자*는 성인용 의자인 *RCP2*를 만들고 남은 자투리 재료로 제작된 것이다.

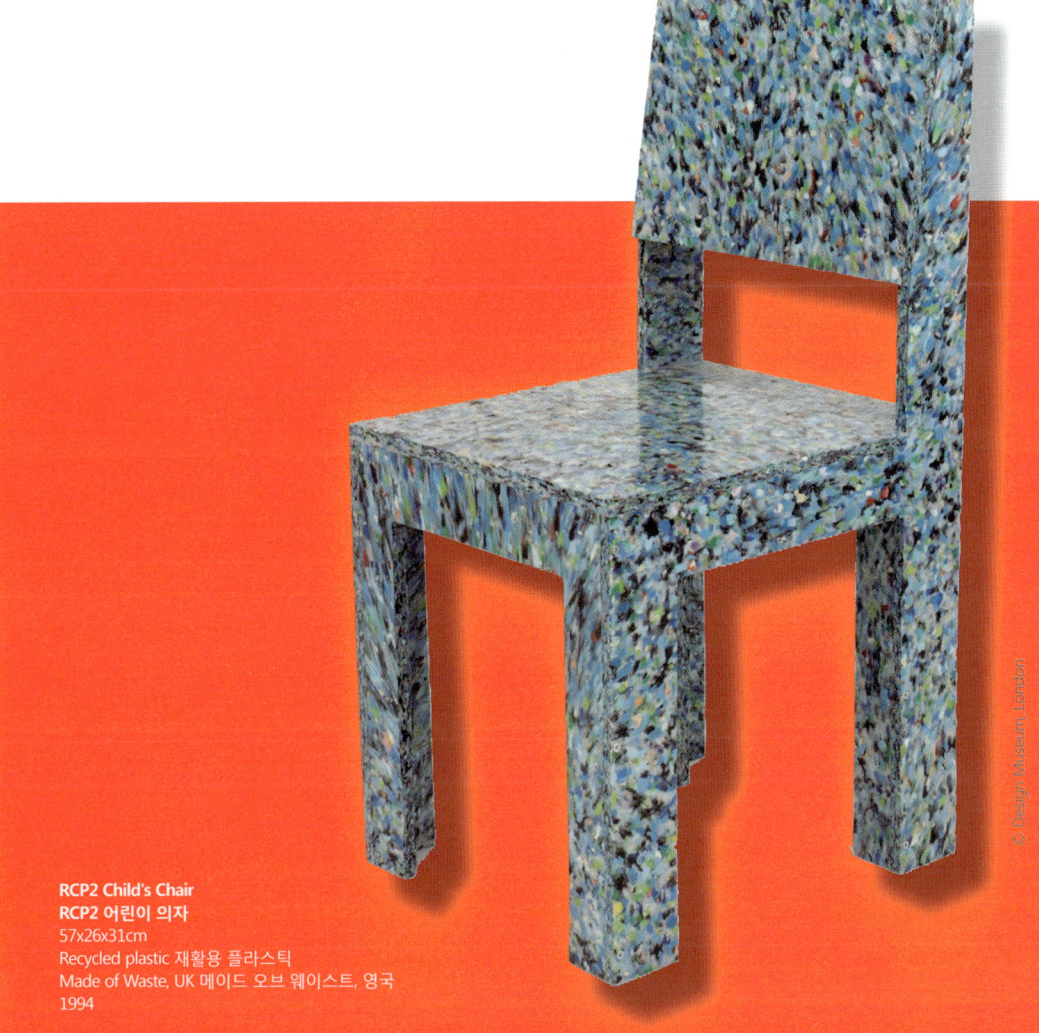

© Design Museum London

RCP2 Child's Chair
RCP2 어린이 의자
57x26x31cm
Recycled plastic 재활용 플라스틱
Made of Waste, UK 메이드 오브 웨이스트, 영국
1994

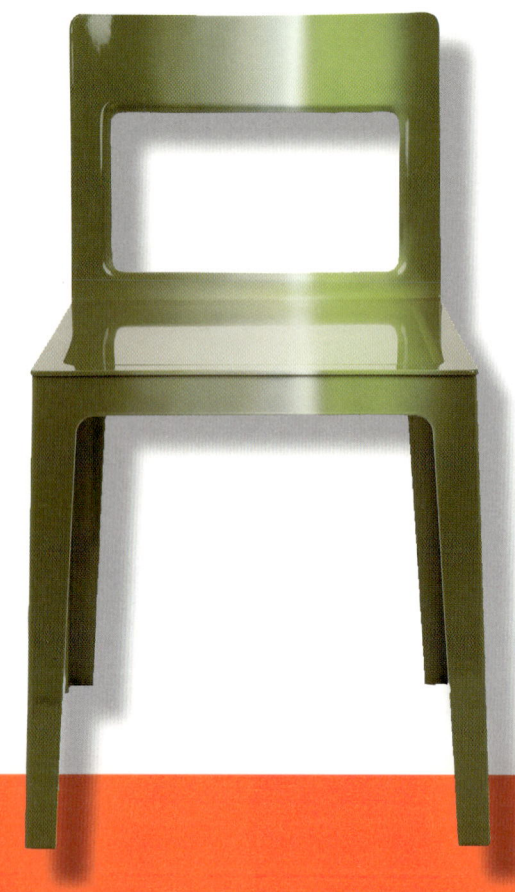

© Design Museum, London

Hole Chair
홀 체어
73x45x45cm
Aluminium, nylon 알루미늄, 나일론
Cappellini, Italy 카펠리니, 이탈리아
2000

France | 프랑스

Ronan Bouroullec & Erwan Bouroullec
로난 부훌렉 & 에르완 부훌렉

From a single sheet of aluminium, the *Hole chair* is created by cutting out several sections by laser, which are then stamped and folded offering reinforced structural qualities. The chair is then soldered together and finally lacquered with aerograph in decreasing tones in three different variances; pink, turquoise or green, leaving the surface ever changing depending on light and from which angle you look at it.

홀 체어는 레이저를 사용해 알루미늄판 한 장을 몇 개의 부분으로 자른 다음 도장을 하고 접어서 구조적인 품질을 강화하고자 했다. 그리고 그것을 접합한 후에 마지막으로 에어로그라프를 이용해서 톤을 감소시킨 핑크색, 터키색, 녹색으로 색을 입힘으로써 사람들이 의자를 보는 각도와 조명에 따라 표면의 색과는 상관없이 다양한 색으로 보이게 하였다.

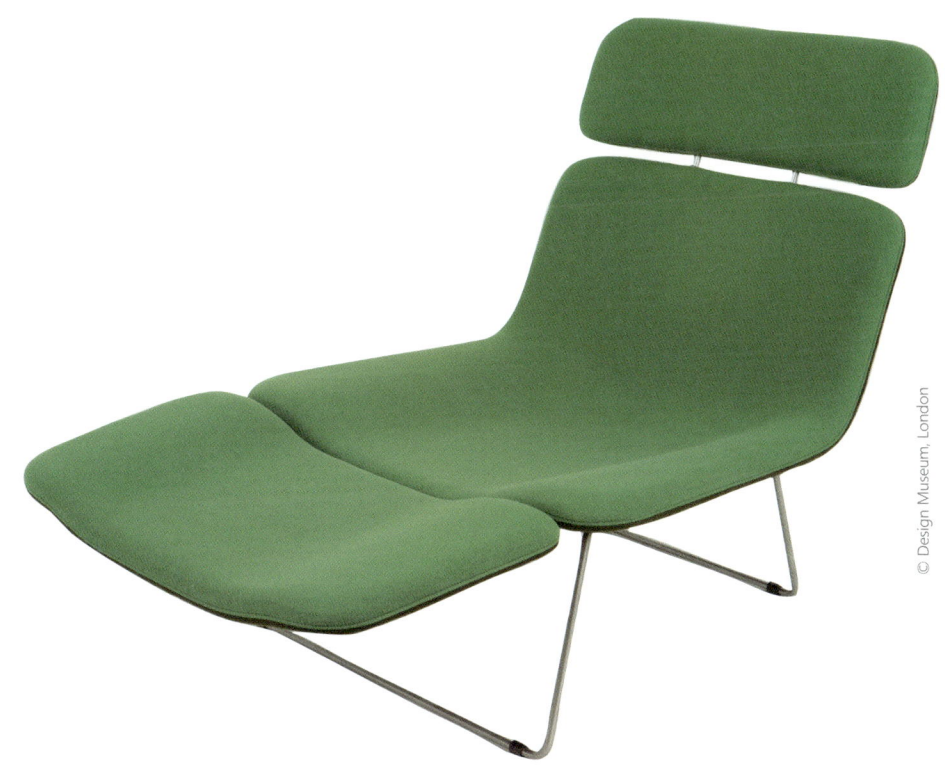

© Design Museum, London

Spring Chair
스프링 체어
90x78x130cm
Polyurethane shell, stainless steel, foam and wool
폴리우레탄, 스테인레스 스틸, 울
Cappellini, Italy 카펠리니, 이탈리아
1999

Like all the furniture designs of Erwan Bouroullec and his brother Ronan, the *Spring Chair* is light, compact, easily portable and intended to be adjusted by its user. During the design process, Erwan Bouroullec thought about what makes a chair comfortable and incorporated the essential elements – a removable headrest and footstool – into the finished piece. He also provided just enough padding for comfort without loosing the slender form of the chair.

에르완 부흘렉과 그의 형 로난의 모든 가구 디자인들과 마찬가지로, *스프링 체어*는 가볍고, 콤팩트하며, 쉽게 옮길 수 있고, 사용자가 의도하는 대로 조정된다. 에르완 부흘렉은 의자를 디자인하면서, 그것이 완성되었을 때 의자를 편안하게 만들기 위한 것으로 어떠한 필수적인 요소들-분리 가능한 헤드 레스트와 풋 스툴 같은-을 포함해야 하는지 고민했다. 그 결과 의자의 가느다란 형태를 유지하면서 동시에 편안함도 줄 수 있는 적당한 양의 충전재를 사용하게 되었다.

Anna Castelli-Ferrieri 안나 카스텔리 페리에리

The use of a blend of technolpolymers gives the surface of this light, portable chair a unique naturalistic quality. Like marble, no two pieces of the material are the same. Designed to be used indoors and outdoors, the *Lounge* was developed by Anna Castelli-Ferrieri in her ongoing experiments with plastics when she was artistic director of the Kartell furniture company during the 1980s.

혼합 테크노폴리머(플라스틱)는 가벼운 휴대용 의자의 표면에 독특한 자연스러움을 제공한다. 이는 대리석이 그러하듯 서로 같은 작품은 하나도 없다. 실내와 실외에서 모두 사용 가능한 *라운지 체어 4814*는 안나 카스텔리 페리에리가 카르텔의 아트디렉터로 있었던 1980년대에 플라스틱을 실험하는 과정에서 개발되었다.

Lounge Chair 4814
라운지 체어 4814
74x64.5x94cm
Technolpolymer blend and steel tubing 테크노폴리머, 강철튜브
Kartell, Italy 카르텔, 이탈리아
1987

© Design Museum, London

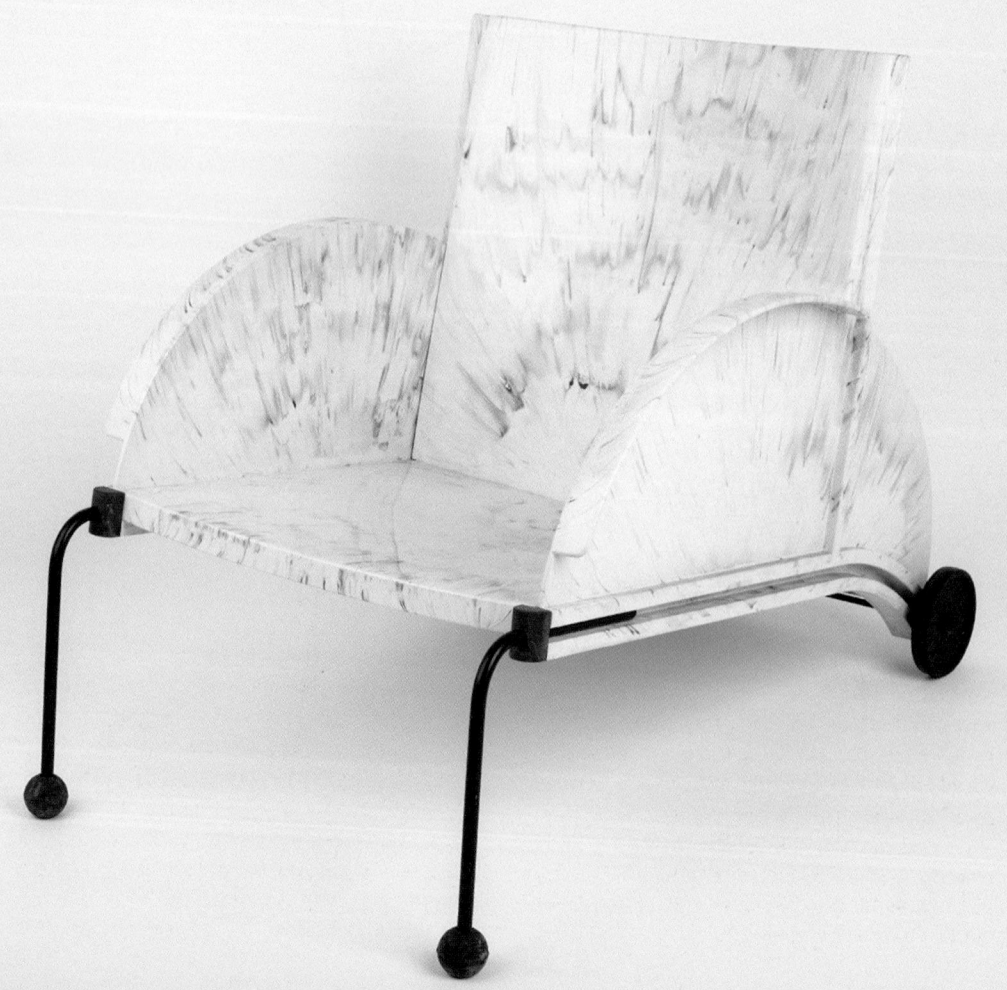

© Design Museum, London

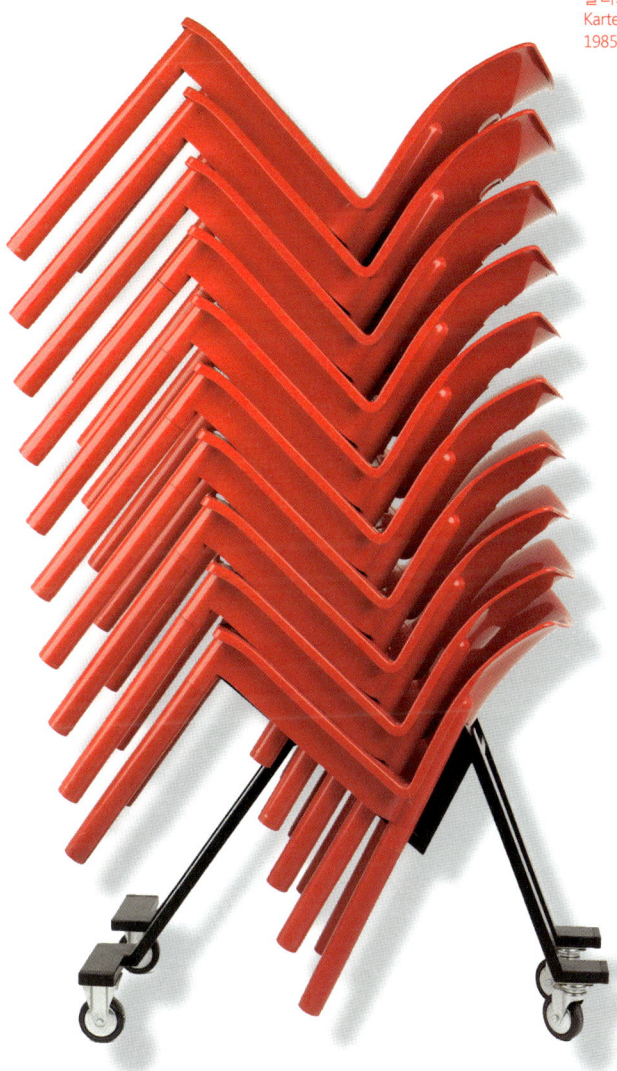

Stacking Chairs and Stack Cart
스태킹 체어(쌓을 수 있는 의자)와
적재 카트
Chair 75.5x46x46cm
Trolley 63x43x86cm
Polypropylene, Steel and rubber
폴리프로필렌, 강철, 고무
Kartell, Italy 카르텔, 이탈리아
1985

These *stacking chairs*, available with or without arms, were designed as all-purpose seating for use indoors and outdoors, in the home or public spaces. As many as a dozen chairs can be stacked on the stack cart at the same time. Kartell was founded in 1949 by Anna Castelli-Ferrieri's husband's family to explore the potential of plastics in consumer products.

팔걸이가 있는 의자와 없는 의자, 두 가지 타입의 이 *스태킹 체어(쌓을 수 있는 의자)*들은 집이나 공공장소, 실내와 실외에서 모든 용도의 좌석으로 사용할 수 있도록 디자인되었다. 무려 10개나 되는 의자를 동시에 카트 위에 쌓아 올릴 수 있다. 카르텔은 시판 제품으로서 플라스틱의 잠재력을 연구하기 위해 안나 카스텔리 페리에리의 남편과 그 가족들에 의해 1949년 설립되었다.

Joe Colombo 조 콜롬보

"The possibilities presented by the extraordinary development of audiovisual processes are enormous... Distance will no longer have much importance; no longer will there be any justification for the 'megalpolis'... Furnishing will disappear... the habitat will be everywhere... Now, if the elements necessary to human existence could be planned with the sole requirements of maneuverability and flexibility...,then we could create an inhabitable system that could be adapted to any situation in space and time..."

"시청각 프로세스들의 보기 드문 발전이 제시하는 가능성들은 엄청나다... 지역적 거리는 더 이상 크게 중요하지 않을 것이며, 따라서 '대도시'에 대한 정당성은 찾아볼 수 없게 될 것이다... 따라서 가구는 사라질 것이다... 주거지는 어디에든 존재하게 될 것이다... 인간 존재를 위해 필요한 요소들이 오로지 기동성과 적응성이라는 조건들로만 설계될 수 있다면, 이제 우리는 시간과 공간의 어떠한 상황에도 적응할 수 있는 주거 시스템을 창조해낼 수 있을 것이다..."

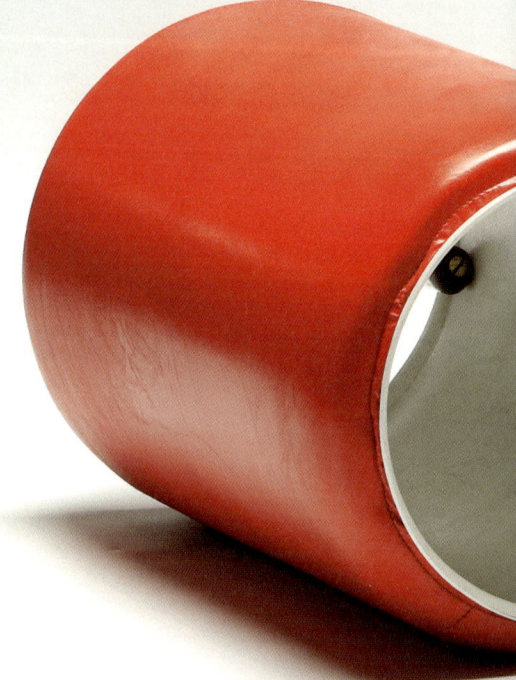

Tube Chair
튜브 의자
57x103x66cm
Plastic, vinyl, steel, rubber clips 플라스틱, 비닐, 강철, 고무 클립
Flexform, Italy 플렉스폼, 이탈리아
1970

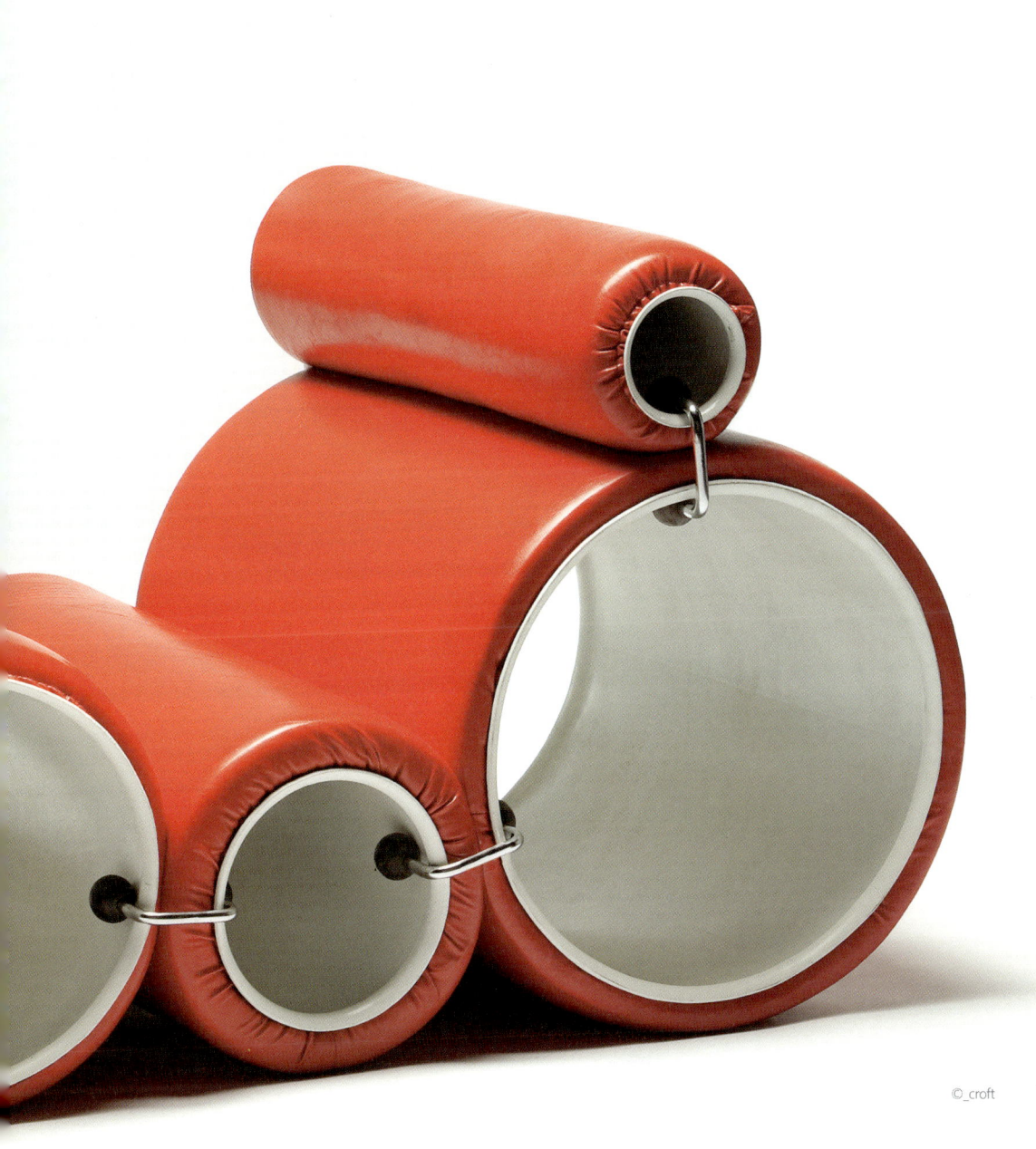

©_croft

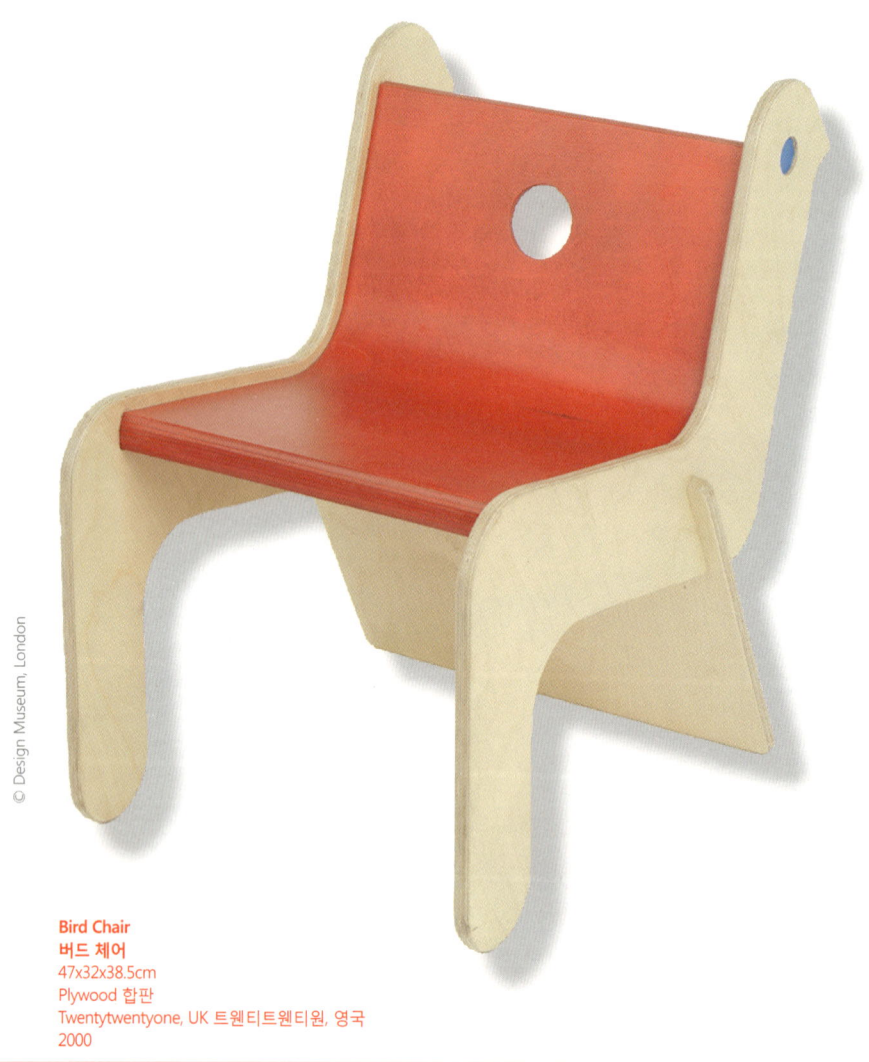

© Design Museum, London

Bird Chair
버드 체어
47x32x38.5cm
Plywood 합판
Twentytwentyone, UK 트웬티트웬티원, 영국
2000

Robin Day 로빈 데이

The decorative form of Robin Day's *plywood Bird chair* appeals to children and adults alike. However he also designed it with economy in mind: two of the chairs can be made from a single piece of 4' x 8' plywood. Thus *the Bird* combines the functionality, which is central to Day's designs, with a gentle wit.

합판으로 만든 로빈 데이의 *버드 체어*는 장식적인 형태로 아이와 어른 모두에게 어필했다. 또한 그는 4'x8'사이즈 합판 한 장으로 의자 두 개를 만들 수 있도록 경제적인 면을 생각하며 디자인했다. 그리하여 *버드 체어*는 데이 디자인의 주요한 요소인 기능성과 부드러운 위트를 모두 갖추고 있다.

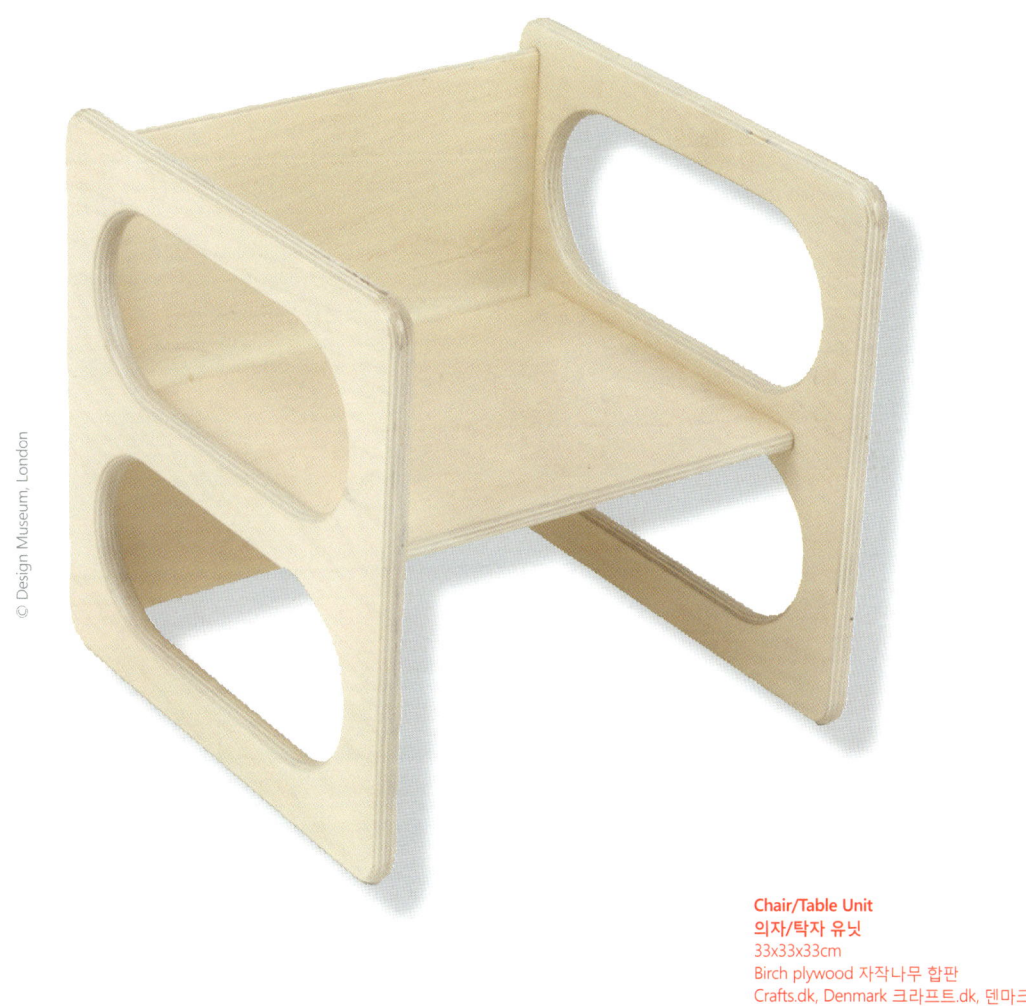

© Design Museum, London

Chair/Table Unit
의자/탁자 유닛
33x33x33cm
Birch plywood 자작나무 합판
Crafts.dk, Denmark 크라프트.dk, 덴마크
1998

Denmark | 덴마크

Nikolai de Gier 니콜라이 디 기어

This piece of furniture was designed by Nikolai De Gier, a young Danish designer, to function both as a chair and – when turned on its side – as a table.

의자가 되었다가 몸체를 뒤집으면 테이블이 되는, 두 가지 기능을 가진 이 작품은 니콜라이 디 기어라는 젊은 덴마크 디자이너에 의해 디자인되었다.

Paolo Deganello with Archizoom
파울로 데가넬로 & 아키줌 그룹

As a co-founder of Archizoom, the radical Italian architecture and design collective, Paolo Deganello was in the forefront of the post-1960s struggle to define a new approach to modernism. In the *A&O – or Alpha and Omega –* Deganello attempted to reinvent the armchair by developing a flat-packed piece in which the different parts are logically separated into the back, seat, base and frame: each of which is designed in a material suitable to its function.

급진적인 이탈리아 건축/디자인 단체인 아키줌의 공동창업자 파울로 데가넬로는 1960년대 이후의 모더니즘에 대한 새로운 접근 방식을 정의하는데 앞장섰다. 데가넬로는 *A&O(혹은 알파와 오메가)*의 각 부분별로 기능에 적합한 재료를 사용하여 등받이, 좌석, 기반 구조 그리고 프레임으로 구분되는 자가조립용 가구(플랫 팩)를 개발하여 팔걸이 의자의 재발견을 시도했다.

A&O
110x75x70cm
Plastic, varnished steel and cotton canvas 플라스틱, 강철, 캔버스 천
Cassina, Italy 카시나, 이탈리아
1973

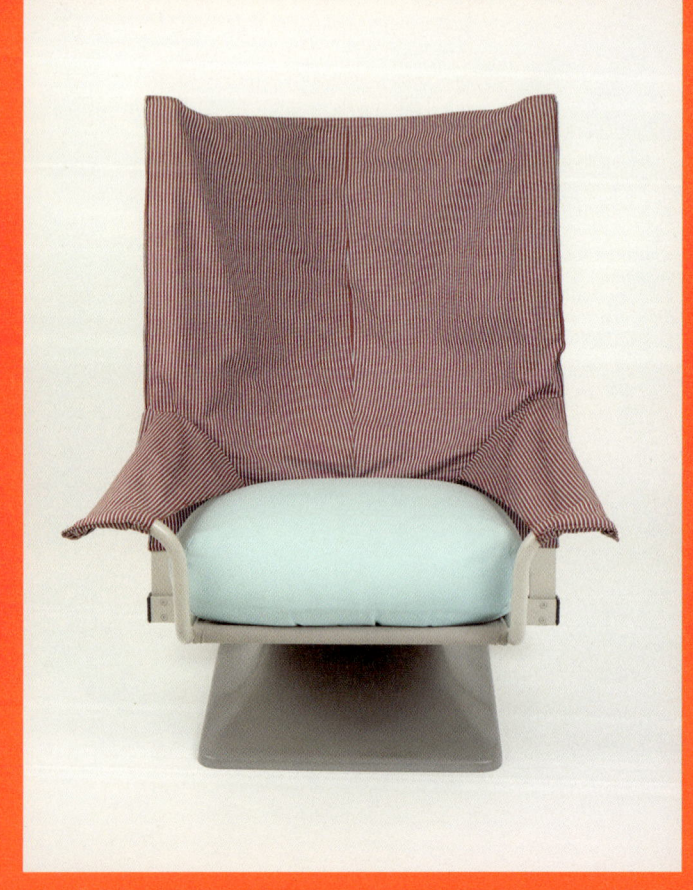

© Design Museum, London

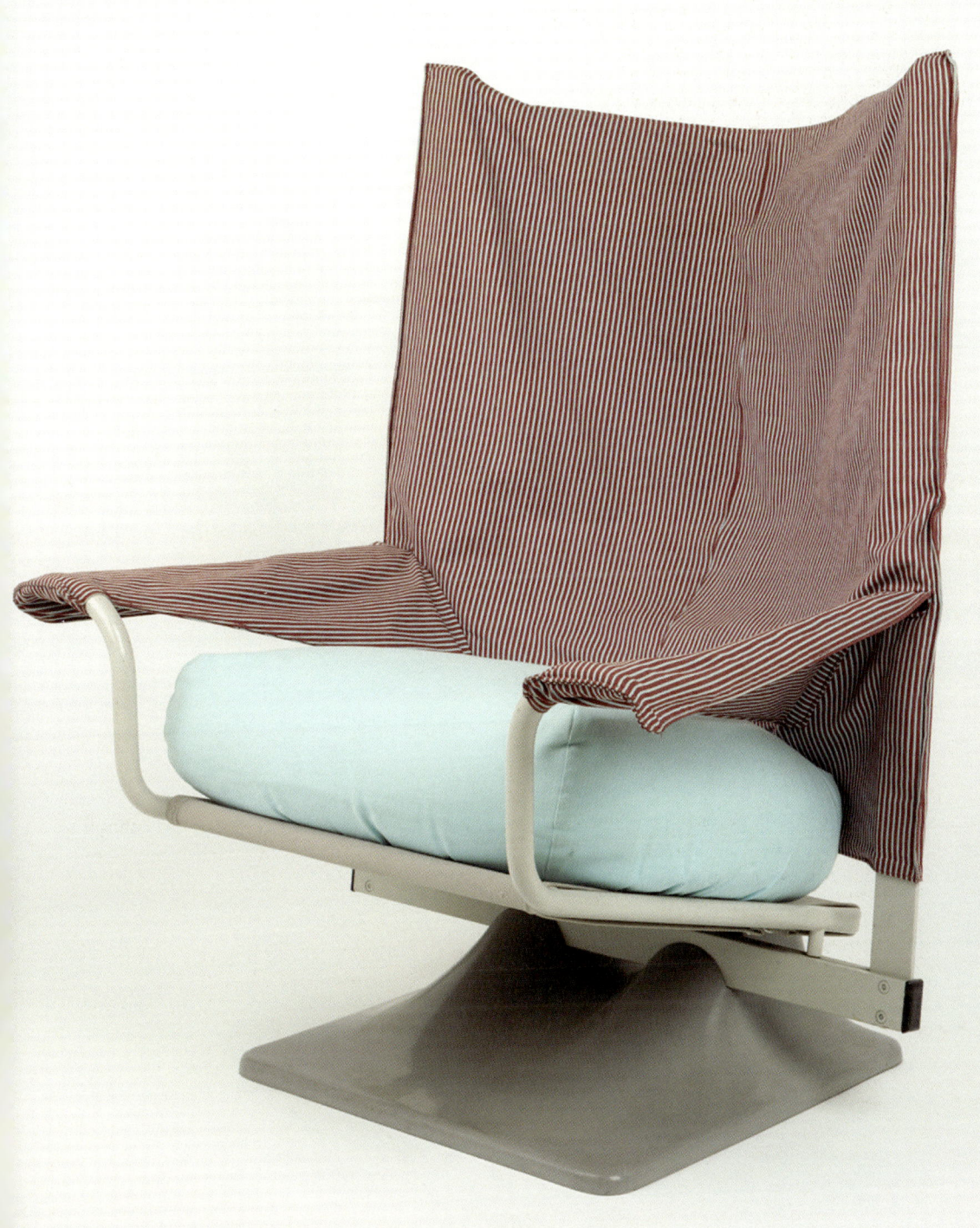

Tom Dixon 톰 딕슨

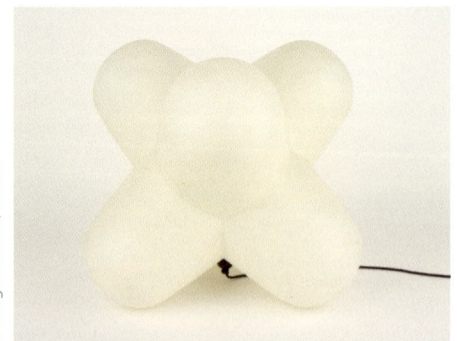

© Design Museum, London

Jack Light
잭 라이트
51x51x51cm
Plastic 플라스틱
Eurolounge 유로라운지
1996

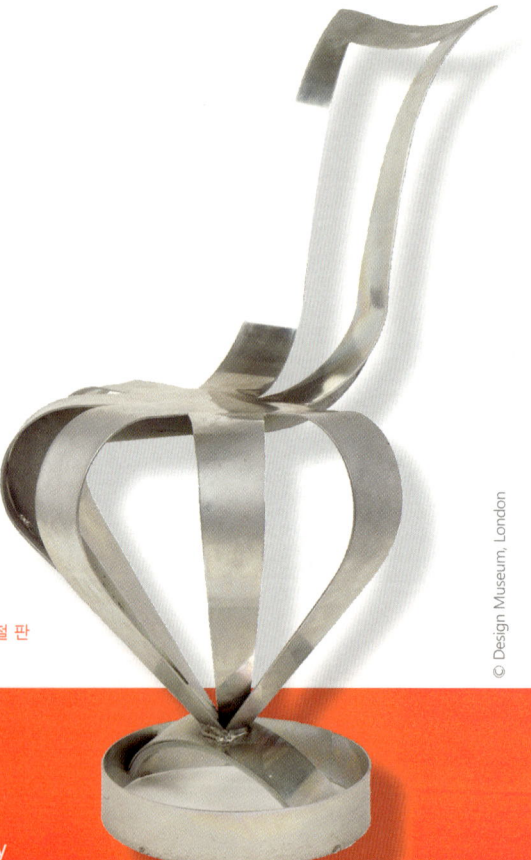

Crown Chair
왕관 의자
120x56x56cm
Sheared sheet steel 강철 판
1988

© Design Museum, London

Now the director of his own internationally successful furniture brand and former creative director of furniture retailer Habitat, Tom Dixon combined design with manufacturing and retailing in his earlier career as a freelance designer. Frustrated by the difficulty of funding UK manufacturers willing to put his work, and that of other London-based designers, into production he set up his own manufacturing company Eurolounge in 1996. Dixon's most successful design for Eurolounge is the *Jack light* which also functions as a seat.

현재 국제적으로 성공을 거둔 본인의 가구 브랜드 디렉터이자, 가구판매회사인 해비타트의 전 크리에이티브 디렉터였던 톰 딕슨은 일찍이 프리랜서 디자이너로서 제조 및 판매를 병행하며 디자인 작업을 진행해 왔다. 그의 작품과 런던에서 활동하는 디자이너들의 작품을 생산하기로 했던 영국 가구제작사들이 자금난에 시달리자 이에 좌절한 톰 딕슨은 1996년 스스로 자신의 가구제조회사 유로라운지를 설립했다. 유로라운지를 위한 딕슨의 가장 성공적인 디자인은 의자로써 기능하기도 하는 *잭 라이트*이다.

After dropping out of art school, Dixon taught himself how to make furniture by welding metal into pieces which trod the fine line between art and design. 'If it's a comfortable chair then I'm a designer,' he once said, 'but if it's an uncomfortable piece of scrap metal, then I'm an artist.' Judge for yourself whether this striking, throne-like chair is the 'comfortable' work of a designer or an artist's 'scrap metal'

딕슨은 예술학교 중퇴 후, 금속을 용접하면서 혼자 터득한 방법으로 예술과 디자인을 넘나드는 가구를 만들기 시작했다. '만약 그 의자가 편안하다면 나는 디자이너이고, 만약 그것이 고철로 된 불편한 작품이라면, 나는 예술가다.'라고 그는 말했다. 이 눈에 띄는 옥좌 같은 의자가 디자이너의 '편안한' 작품인지 예술가의 '고철'일 뿐인지는 여러분들 스스로 판단해 보라.

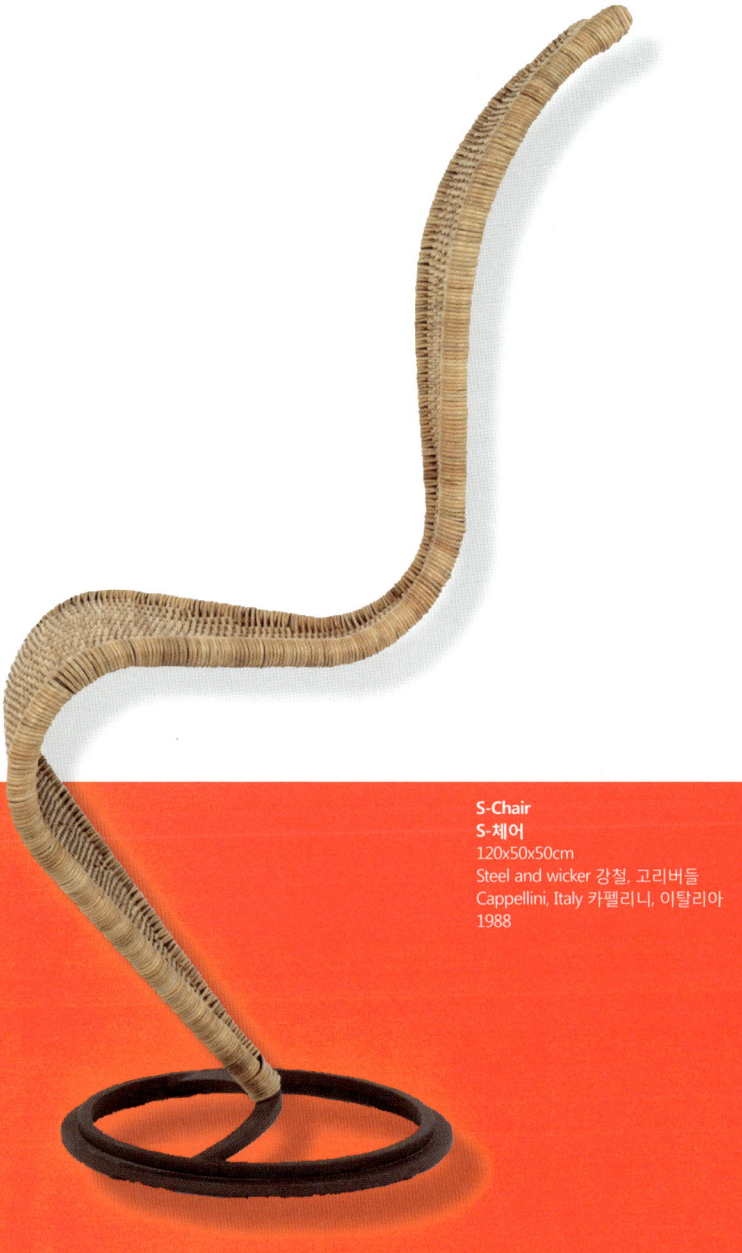

© Design Museum, London

S-Chair
S-체어
120x50x50cm
Steel and wicker 강철, 고리버들
Cappellini, Italy 카펠리니, 이탈리아
1988

Tom Dixon worked on more than fifty prototypes for the *S-Chair* using different materials including rush, wicker, old tire rubber, paper and copper. Its rough-hewn charm typifies the post-punk, do-it-yourself spirit of Dixon's 1980s designs. Originally made by Dixon himself, the *S-Chair* was later put into production by the Italian manufacturer Cappellini.

톰 딕슨은 *S-체어*를 위해 골풀(돗자리, 바구니 등을 만들 때 쓰는 풀), 고리버들(버드나무의 일종), 폐 타이어, 종이, 구리 등 다양한 소재들을 시험하여 50개가 넘는 프로토타입을 만들었다. 표면이 거친 *S-체어*의 매력은 1980년대 펑크운동의 DIY정신을 따른 딕슨 디자인의 전형적인 특징이다. 처음에 딕슨이 혼자서 만들었던 *S-체어*는 후에 이탈리아 가구회사인 카펠리니에 의해 생산에 들어갔다.

Naoto Fukasawa 나오토 후카사와

"Japanese people have traditionally had a deep love for the beauty that reveals itself through an almost obsessive concern with tools. Design is usually thought of in terms of decoration and ornamentation, but we are now returning to the concept of design based on functional beauty to which Japanese culture has traditionally aspired. It seems to me that the appropriate position (form) under the conditions in which this concept exists and an approach concerned to explore to the ultimate limit this sense of appropriateness stand at the basis of the Japanese aesthetic. I designed this chair while thinking about the iconic form of the chair that we all conjure up in our minds. Perhaps one might describe it as a "chair-like chair". I felt that I wanted to be concerned first and foremost with the "essence" of the chair. It seems to me also that the idea of simplicity and naturalness is an important aspect of the Japanese aesthetic. My design was based on my feeling that this idea, which contains within it the notion that the user should continue to feel attached to the object no matter how dirty, damaged and frayed at the edges it may have become in the course of years of use, is the equivalent of a blank sheet of paper on which the future history of the item will be written. I wanted this chair to become an object that would continue to exist for a long time in an unprepossessing and effortless manner. I feel that this is the essence of the Japanese aesthetic."

"전통적으로 일본인들은 도구에 대한 강박적인 집착을 통해 나타나는 아름다움에 깊은 애정을 가져왔다. 디자인은 일반적으로 장식과 치장의 견지에서 생각되곤 하지만, 현시점에서 우리는 일본문화가 전통 안에서 갈망해왔던 기능적 미에 근거하는 디자인의 개념으로 돌아가고 있다. 내가 보기에는, 이 개념이 존재하는 조건들과 절대적인 것을 탐구하려는 시도의 적절성을 제한하는 조건들은 그 적절한 위치의 근거를 일본 미학에 두고 있다. 나는 우리 모두가 상상 속에서 그려내는 의자의 이상적 형태를 생각하면서 이 의자를 디자인했다. 어떤 사람은 이 의자를 혹시 '의자 같은 의자'라고 묘사할지도 모르겠다. 나는 그 어떤 것보다 의자의 '본질'을 우선적으로 고려하고 싶었다. 또한 나는 단순성과 자연스러움에 대한 생각이 일본 미학에서 중요한 하나의 관점이라고 본다. 이러한 개념은 사물이 얼마나 더럽거나 손상되었든지, 그리고 그 가장자리들이 사용한 만큼 닳아 빠졌든 상관없이 사용자들은 그들의 물품에 대한 애착을 계속해서 가진다는 생각을 담고 있다. 내 디자인은 바로 이러한 개념이, 앞으로 사용할 물품의 미래가 기록될 빈 종이와 동일한 의미를 지닌다는 느낌에 기초하고 있다. 따라서 나는 이 의자가 외면적으로 보기에 좋거나 일부러 애쓴 흔적이 없는 방식으로 오랜 시간을 계속 존재하는 대상물이 되기를 바란다. 나는 이것이 바로 일본 미학의 정수라고 생각한다."

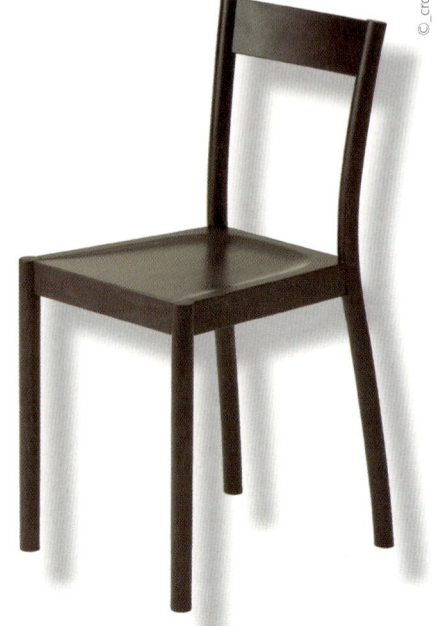

© _croft

Next Maruni by Naoto Fukasawa
넥스트 마루니 by 나오토 후카사와
81x38.2x46.2cm
Beech, urethane finish 너도밤나무, 우레탄
2005

"Next Maruni" was a project organized in 2005 by a Japanese furniture company Maruni, and had twelve international participants: Naoto Fukasawa, Harry Koskinen, Jasper Morrison, and Alberto Meda to list a few.

"넥스트 마루니"는 일본 가구회사 마루니에 의한 프로젝트로, 후카사와 나오토, 해리 코스키넨, 재스퍼 모리슨, 알베르토 메다 등 전세계 12인의 디자이너들이 참여하여 2005년에 진행됐다.

Frank O. Gehry 프랭크 O. 게리

In his furniture design as in his buildings, Frank Gehry – best known as the architect of the Guggenheim Museum, Bilbao – is noted for the complex curves of his fluid organic forms. In the Crosscheck chair Gehry succeeded in creating a basket-like woven piece which provides strength and stability without the need for a solid structure thereby giving the chair the appearance of transparency.

구겐하임 박물관 빌바오의 건축가로 잘 알려진 프랭크 게리는 그의 건축과 마찬가지로 가구디자인 역시 유동적 유기체 형태의 복잡한 곡선을 사용하는 것으로 잘 알려져 있다. 게리는 합판을 바구니처럼 엮어 단단한 구조물 없이도 강도와 안정성을 제공하는 작품을 만드는데 성공하여 의자에 투명성을 부여했다.

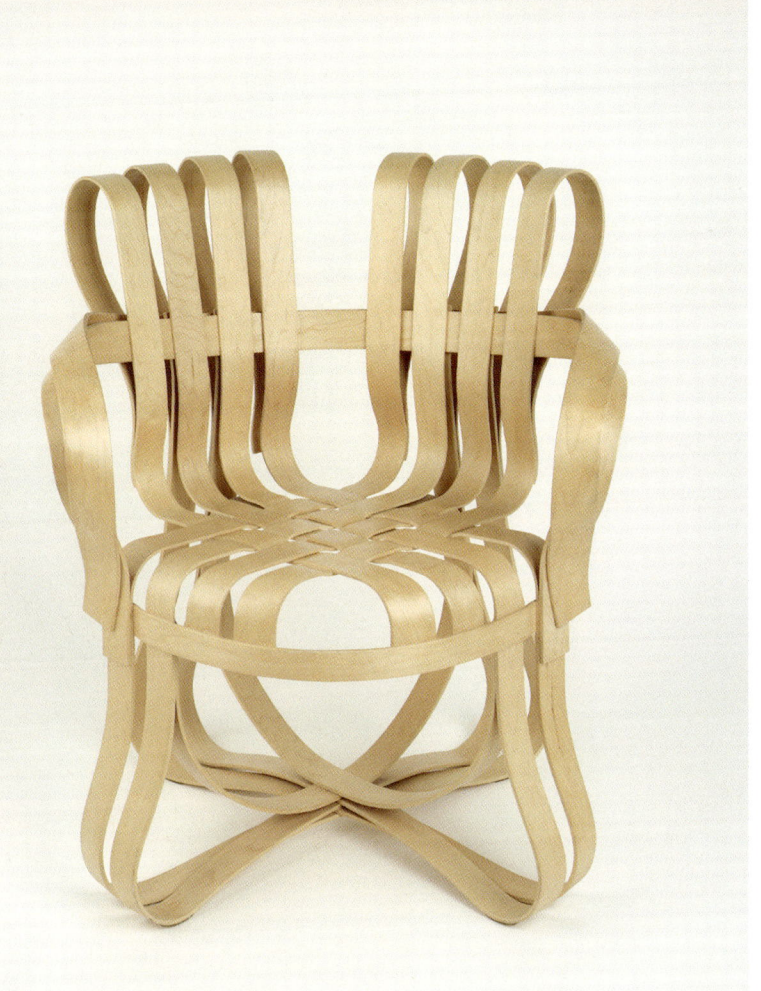

© Design Museum, London

Crosscheck
크로스체크
86x70x65cm
Bent and woven laminated wood
합판
Knoll International, US
놀 인터내셔널, 미국
1992

117

Konstantin Grcic
콘스탄틴 그리치치

Heralding a new development in the design style of Konstantin Grcic, the *One Chair* also marked a fresh departure for Magis as the first chair to be made by the company in metal rather than its traditional material, plastic. Magis asked Grcic to design a plastic chair, expecting one in the designer's rationalist style. Instead Grcic, who had recently begun to experiment with computers and was increasingly influenced by their frenzied, ambiguous aesthetic, suggested that they develop a die-cast aluminium weave to envelop the body in a single piece.

디자인 스타일의 새로운 발전을 예고하는 콘스탄틴 그리치치의 *체어_원*은 마지스에게 있어 처음으로 플라스틱이 아닌 금속으로 만든 의자로서, 마지스의 새로운 출발을 보여주었다. 마지스는 그리치치에게 디자이너들의 합리적인 소재 중 하나인 플라스틱으로 의자를 디자인하도록 요청했다. 하지만 최근에 컴퓨터로 실험을 시작한 그리치치는 점점 더 열광적이고 모호한 성격의 미학에 영향을 받아, 플라스틱이 아닌 알루미늄 그물을 주물로 만들어 의자의 몸체가 하나로 만들어진 작품을 개발할 것을 제안했다.

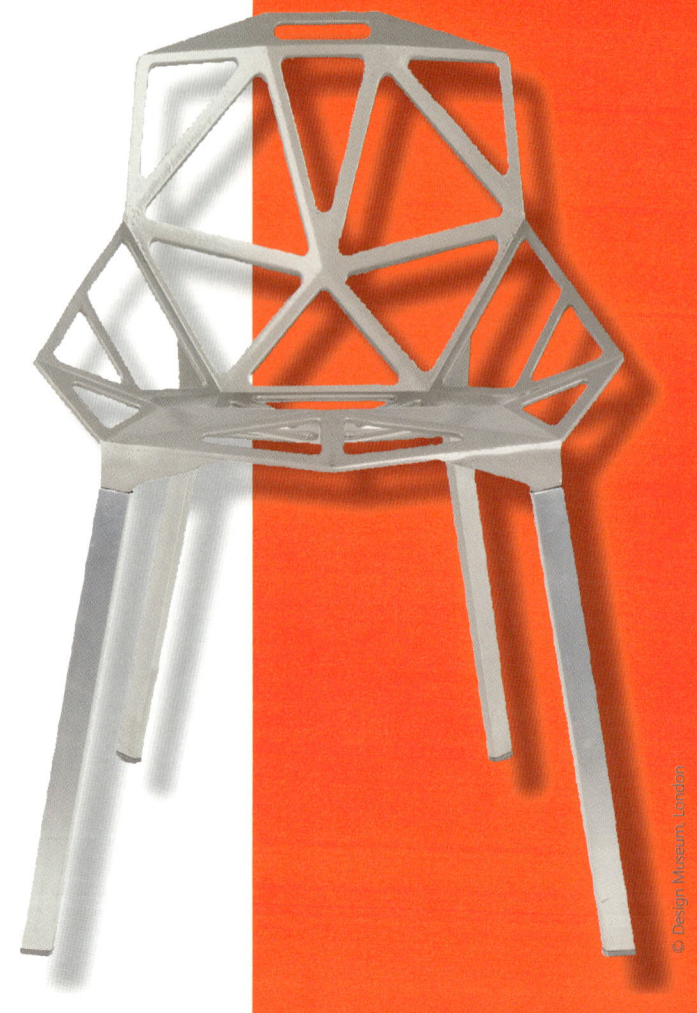

Chair_ONE
체어_ 원
81x55x60cm
Die-cast aluminium 알루미늄
Magis, Italy 마지스, 이탈리아
2002

© Design Museum, London

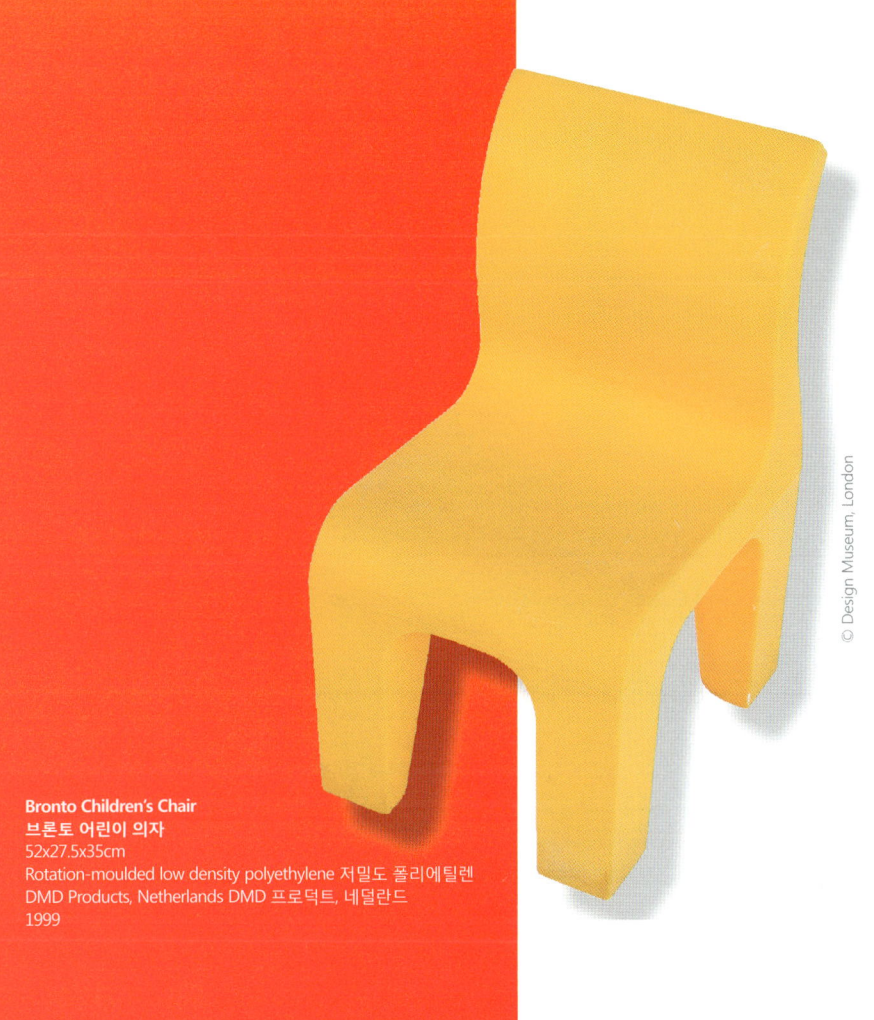

© Design Museum, London

Bronto Children's Chair
브론토 어린이 의자
52x27.5x35cm
Rotation-moulded low density polyethylene 저밀도 폴리에틸렌
DMD Products, Netherlands DMD 프로덕트, 네덜란드
1999

Netherlands | 네덜란드

Richard Hutten 리하르트 휘텐

Hutten is a Dutch designer who works independently and in collaboration with DMD Products, also known as the Droog design collective. For the *Bronto*, he used rotational moulding to produce a hollow, lightweight chair using a thin plastic surface. It is manufactured and distributed by DMD Products.

휘텐은 독립적으로 일하는 동시에 디자인 그룹 드훅으로 유명한 DMD 프로덕트와 협력하고 있는 네덜란드 디자이너이다. 그는 *브론토* 제작을 위해 회전 성형기법을 사용하여 속이 비고 가벼운 얇은 플라스틱 표면의 의자를 만들었다. 이 의자는 DMD 프로덕트에서 생산되고 판매되었다.

© JI, Suck Chul

Reaction· From the Image to the real space
반작용·이미지로부터 실재공간으로
12x6x6cm(100 mini chairs 미니의자 100점)
Wood 나무
1982

Korea | 한국

Ji, Seok Cheol 지석철

1982년에 이르러 지석철은 돌연 의식의 사물을 현실의 사물로서 번안시켜 볼 수는 없을까 하는 생각에 몰두 하였다. 반작용 • 이미지로부터 실제공간으로라는 다소 설명적인 작품의 명제가 탄생한 것이다. 수많은 미니의자를 만들어 이리저리 병렬해서 얻는 드라마는 물성의 또 다른 객체화, 정확히 말해 '사물화'하려는 데에 뜻이 있다. 따라서 미니의자에서 주목할 것은 그가 이것을 시각적 효과로서의 장식성이나 또는 어떤 주술적 목적을 위해서 만들고 있지 않다는 것이다. 오히려 그의 말대로 "의자가 아닌 또 다른 어떤 것이 되어도 좋을" 요컨데 실재하는 물성의 은유인 것이다. 그리고 배나무 가지로 만들어진 미니의자의 물성화가 어떻게 가시화 될 수 있는지를 실험하고 있는 것이기도 하다. 최근의 미니의자 시리즈는 종래의 쿠션작업의 역으로부터 시도한 것으로 풀이되는 만큼 이제 그는 또 다시 그 역의 역으로 되돌아가 또 다른 형상작업에 착수할 가능성을 인식하고 있다.

김복영, 미술평론가

In 1982, he turned in a sudden to another phase of study. It could be said how we translate the conscious thing into the actuality. A little long title such as *Reaction. From Image to Real Space* was from such idea. Instead of painted cushions, many mini chairs were displayed on the floor of gallery room. Here his special intention is alternatively to materialize thingness, correctly speaking, to actualize one thing into another. So what is paid attention to is that his mini chairs are not made for the visual decorations and magic for some special purpose. As his saying, it must be a kind of 'metaphor' of the real thingness. Only what the artist wants is to have "beholders to be plunged into his chair-objects." Wood, paper, white bronze, candle, and acrylic are his favorite materials for mini chairs. Displaying experiments is another method in order to visualize his mini chair's idea in the actual space. Recent mini chairs series are regarded as a counterpart of the painted cushions. Accordingly, he will come back again sooner or later to his image-making works on plane, I think.

Kim, Bok Yung, Art Critic

Donald Judd
도날드 저드

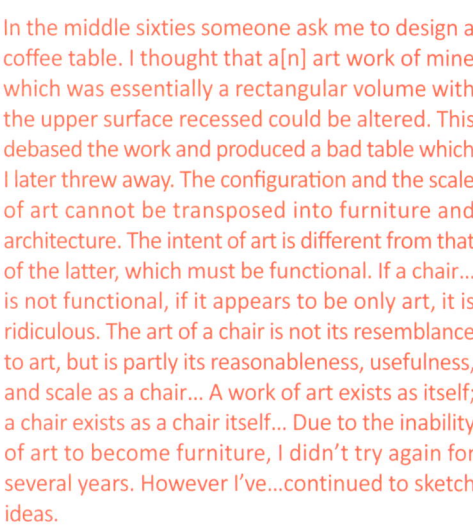

Chair, Style #10
의자, 스타일 #10
76.2x37.8x38.1cm
Black walnut 검은 호두나무
2002

In the middle sixties someone ask me to design a coffee table. I thought that a[n] art work of mine which was essentially a rectangular volume with the upper surface recessed could be altered. This debased the work and produced a bad table which I later threw away. The configuration and the scale of art cannot be transposed into furniture and architecture. The intent of art is different from that of the latter, which must be functional. If a chair... is not functional, if it appears to be only art, it is ridiculous. The art of a chair is not its resemblance to art, but is partly its reasonableness, usefulness, and scale as a chair... A work of art exists as itself; a chair exists as a chair itself... Due to the inability of art to become furniture, I didn't try again for several years. However I've...continued to sketch ideas.

1960년대 중반, 어떤 사람이 내게 커피 테이블을 디자인 해달라고 주문했었다. 나는 기본적인 직사각형의 형태를 띠고 윗부분의 표면이 오목한 내 작품을 변형하면 되겠다고 생각했다. 결국 그로 인해 내 작품은 질이 떨어진 형편 없는 테이블이 되어 버렸고, 나중에는 버려지고 말았다. 예술의 외형과 규모는 가구나 건축으로 변형될 수 없다. 예술의 목적은 반드시 기능적이어야만 하는 가구나 건축과는 다르다. 만일 의자가...기능적이지 않다면, 만일 그 의자가 단지 예술로서만 존재하게 된다면, 그것은 웃기는 일이다. 의자의 예술성은 예술작품과의 표면적 형태의 유사성으로부터 나오는 것이 아니라, 부분적으로 존재하는 적절함과 실용성, 그리고 의자로서의 규모에 있다. 예술작품은 예술 그 자체로서 존재하고, 의자는 의자 그 자체로서 존재한다. 예술이 가구가 될 수 없다는 그 불가능성 때문에 그 후로 몇 년간 다시는 그와 같은 시도를 하지 않았다. 하지만 나는...또 계속해서 아이디어들을 스케치하고 있었다.

Kim, Yik Yung 김익영

도예가 김익영의 작품세계를 이야기 할 때에 우선 문제가
되는 것은 형태감과 조형미를 현대적인 생활개념과 더불
어 그의 도예관에 잘 응용시킨 데 있다. 시각적인 감흥과
다양한 기형의 변모는 단순한 처리에도 불구하고 그의 작
품을 무게 있는 조형적 가치로 이끈다.
다음, 색채의 순도는 주로 백색을 주조로 하면서 형성되는
데, 그 백색 또한 깊은 곳에서 발하는 빛을 머금고 있는 청
백색의 세계이다. 해맑은 순도 높은 흰 유색은 겉으로부터
속까지 스며드는 맑은 감각의 승화를 경험케 한다. 방황하
는 한국 도예계에서 김익영 같은 도예가를 가졌다는 것은
그 개인을 위해서 보다도 우리들 모두를 위해서 지극히
다행스러운 일이다.

이경성, 미술평론가

The prior point in discussing Kim, Yik Yung's
ceramic works is his dexterous application of the
formative sense and aesthetic value of his pieces
to contemporary lifestyles and his own perspective
on ceramics. In spite of his management in a
simple way, their visual interest and various
transfigurations lead his works into grave values.
The purity of their colors is made up with mainly in
white tone, which is in fact a blue-white that has
light radiating deep inside of the color. The clean
and pure white provides viewers an experience of
a sublime of sensibility that permeates deeply into
the inner place. To have a ceramist like Kim, Yik
Yung for wandering Korean ceramics is a fortune
for all of us, a fortune not only for himself.

Lee, Kyung Sung, Art Critic

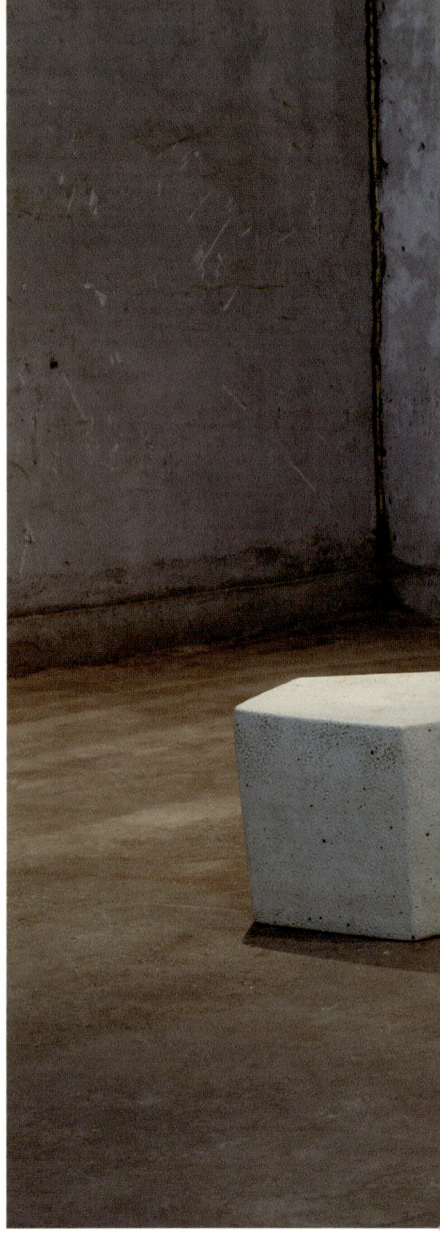

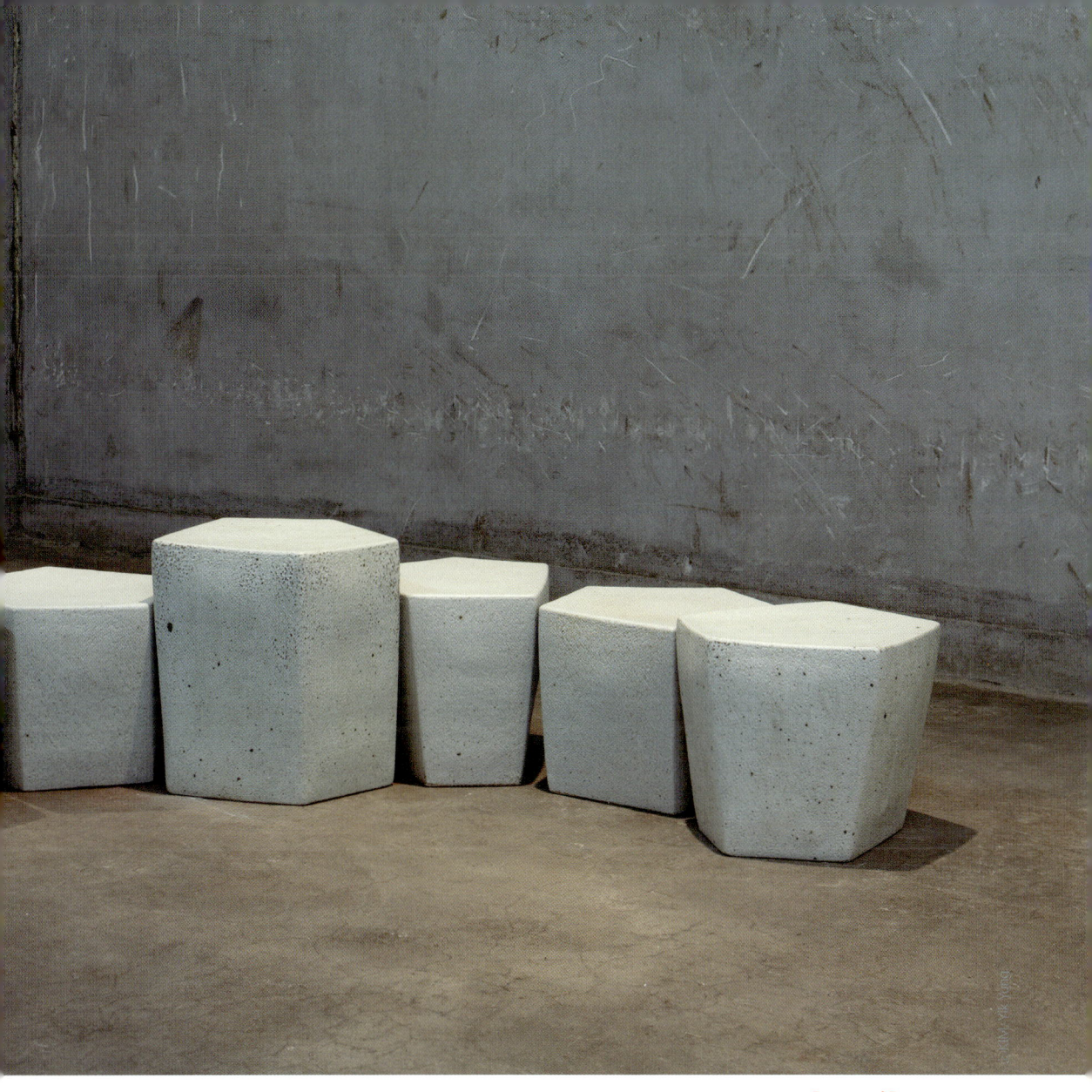

© KIM YIk Yong

Pentagonal Forms
오각형
53x46x36cm
Porcelain, clear glaze 백자, 투명유
(the tallest 높은 의자)
1998

Rodney Kinsman 로드니 킨스만

By combining characteristics of both Hans Coray's 1939 *Landi* chair and David Rowland's 1963 *40-in-4*, Rodney Kinsman created a best-seller in 1971 in his light, compact *Omkstak stacking chair*. Born in London, Kinsman studied furniture design at the city's Central School of Art and set up OMK Design in 1966 with two fellow graduates – Jurek Olejnik and Bryan Morrison.

로드니 킨스만은 한스 코레이의 1939년 *랜디*와 데이빗 롤란드의 1963년 *GF40/4*의 특징을 결합하여, 1971년 베스트셀러가 된 작고 가벼운 옴스탁 스태킹을 만들었다. 런던에서 태어난 킨스만은 런던중앙예술학교에서 가구 디자인을 공부했고, 1966년 두 명의 동료- 유렉 올레닉과 브라이언 모리슨 -와 함께 OMK 디자인회사를 설립했다.

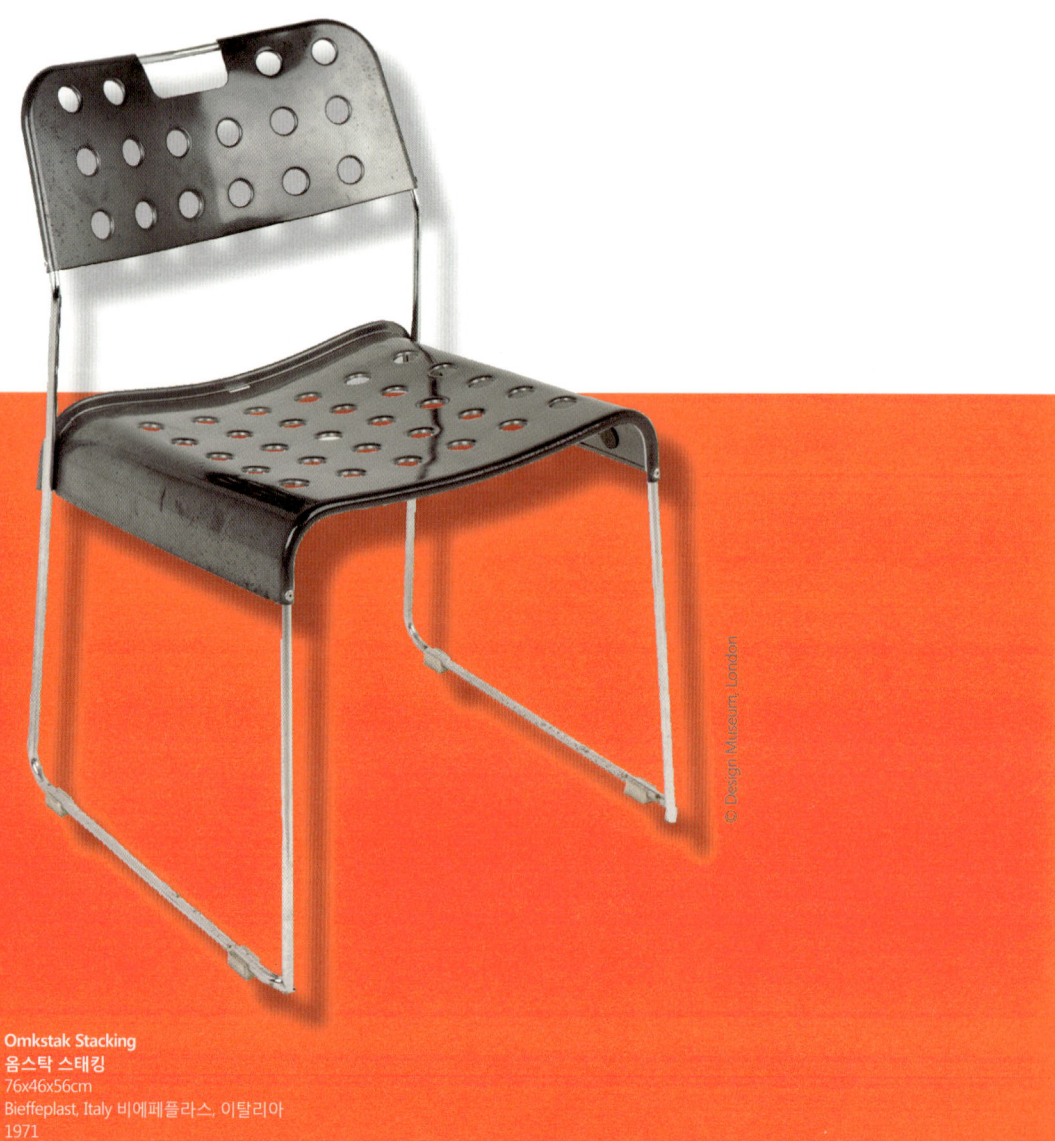

© Design Museum London

Omkstak Stacking
옴스탁 스태킹
76x46x56cm
Bieffeplast, Italy 비에페플라스, 이탈리아
1971

Harri Koskinen 해리 코스키넨

"Details makes the whole chair, whole chair is made of details. Wooden sticksused in structure creates logical and harmonious combination. Every stick supports the structure itself. You get touched some of them when sitting while all of them looks after the act. Wooden plane as a seating element is needed for convenient seating. It raises from the structure by the edges creating more air and lightness to the whole."

"각각의 디테일들이 하나의 완전한 의자를 만들어낸다. 다시 말하면, 하나의 완전한 의자는 디테일로부터 만들어진다. 의자의 구조를 위해 사용된 나무 막대들은 논리적이고 조화로운 조합을 창출해낸다. 각각의 막대가 구조 자체를 지탱한다. 사용자가 앉을 때는 그들 중의 일부하고만 닿게 되지만, 그것들 모두는 앉는 행위를 지탱하는 역할을 한다. 나무 판은 편리한 착석을 위해 필요한 요소로서, 그 모서리들로 인해 구조가 형성되고 전체적으로 더 많은 공간과 가벼움을 생성한다."

"Next Maruni" was a project organized in 2005 by a Japanese furniture company Maruni, and had twelve international participants: Naoto Fukasawa, Harry Koskinen, Jasper Morrison, and Alberto Meda to list a few.

"넥스트 마루니"는 일본 가구회사 마루니에 의한 프로젝트로, 후카사와 나오토, 해리 코스키넨, 재스퍼 모리슨, 알베르토 메다 등 전세계 12인의 디자이너들이 참여하여 2005년에 진행됐다.

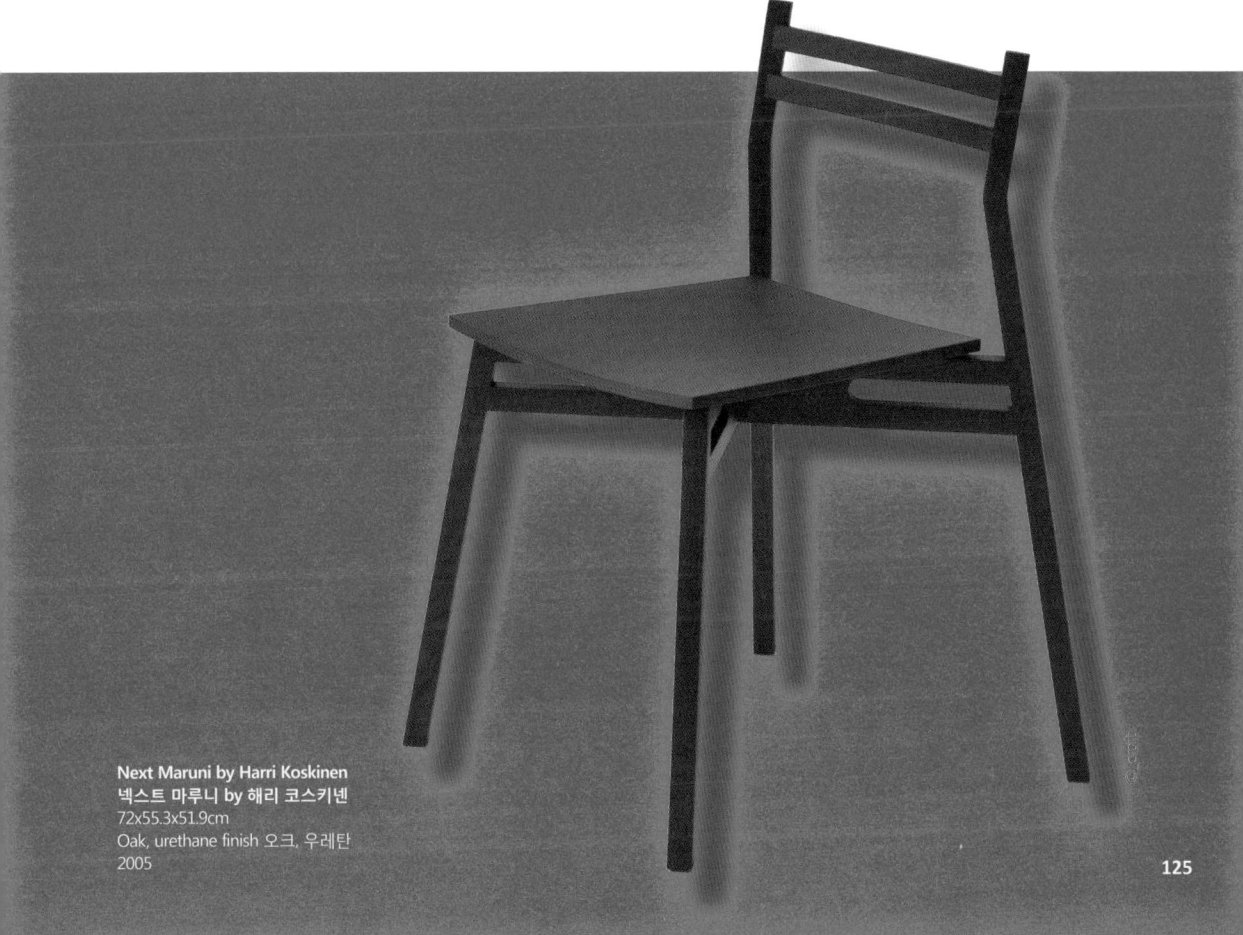

Next Maruni by Harri Koskinen
넥스트 마루니 by 해리 코스키넨
72x55.3x51.9cm
Oak, urethane finish 오크, 우레탄
2005

Shiro Kuramata 시로 쿠라마타

"Hard metal, transparent air, generous volume, light hue..." Shiro Kuramata's *How high is the Moon* was a succession of visual, structural contradiction. *How high is the Moon* is made of mesh iron plate coated with nickel and expresses the lightness of space and weight in a lyrical way. A Japanese designer Kuramata accomplished a poetic and dreamlike design with delicate and elegant proportion for a sense of the product's unique volume through which light rays and air can pass. This fantastic chair like silver moonlight is a piece which crosses over from practical design to poetic world. Achieving a combination of technical innovation and empty space with lyrical beauty, Kuramata's chair keeps distance from Western tradition and symbolizes Japanese design spirit during the 1980's when European and American modernism was a mainstream.

Sources | Design Museum, *50 chairs that have changed The world,* trans. Kwon, Eun Sun, Hong Design, 2010

"단단한 금속, 투명한 공기, 관대한 부피, 가벼운 빛, 시로 쿠라마타의 '*달은 얼마나 높나*'는 시각적 구조적 모순의 연속이었다. '*달은 얼마나 높나*'는 흔한 소재인 니켈이 코팅된 망사 철판을 이용해 공간과 무게의 가벼움을 서정적으로 표현했다. 일본 출신의 디자이너 쿠라마타는 어떤 면에서든지 빛과 공기가 의자를 통과하고 비치는 독특한 부피감을 위해 섬세하고 우아한 비례로 시적이면서 꿈꾸는 듯한 디자인을 완성했다. 마치 은색 달빛처럼 환상적인 이 의자는 그 이름처럼 실용디자인부터 시적 세계까지 넘나드는 작품이 됐다. 기술혁신과 서정적 미를 가진 여백이 조합을 이룬 쿠라마타의 의자는 서양의 전통을 경계하고, 유럽과 미국 모더니즘의 주류를 이야기하던 1980년대 일본의 디자인 정신을 상징한다.

출처 | 디자인 뮤지엄, 권은순 역
세상을 바꾼 50가지 의자, 홍디자인, 2010

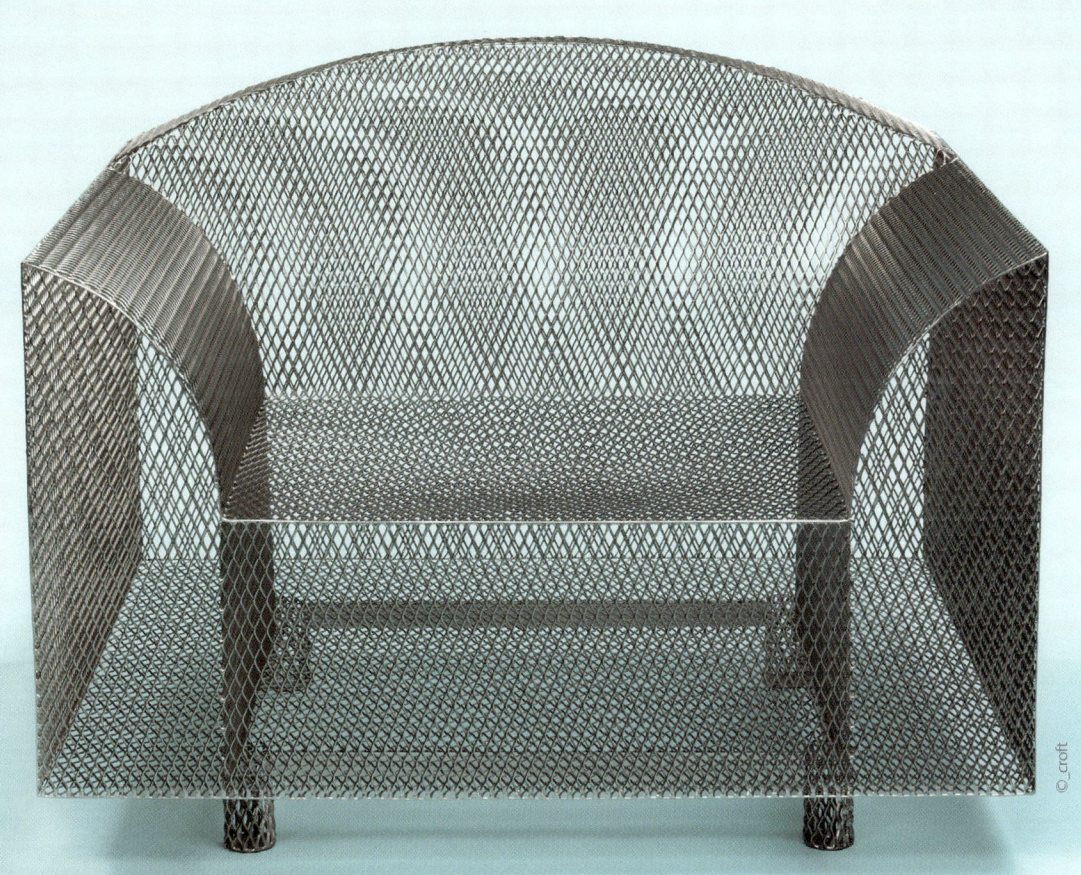

© _croft

How Hight the Moon
달은 얼마나 높나
71x93.7x82.5cm
Nickel-plated steel mesh 니켈도금 절망
1990

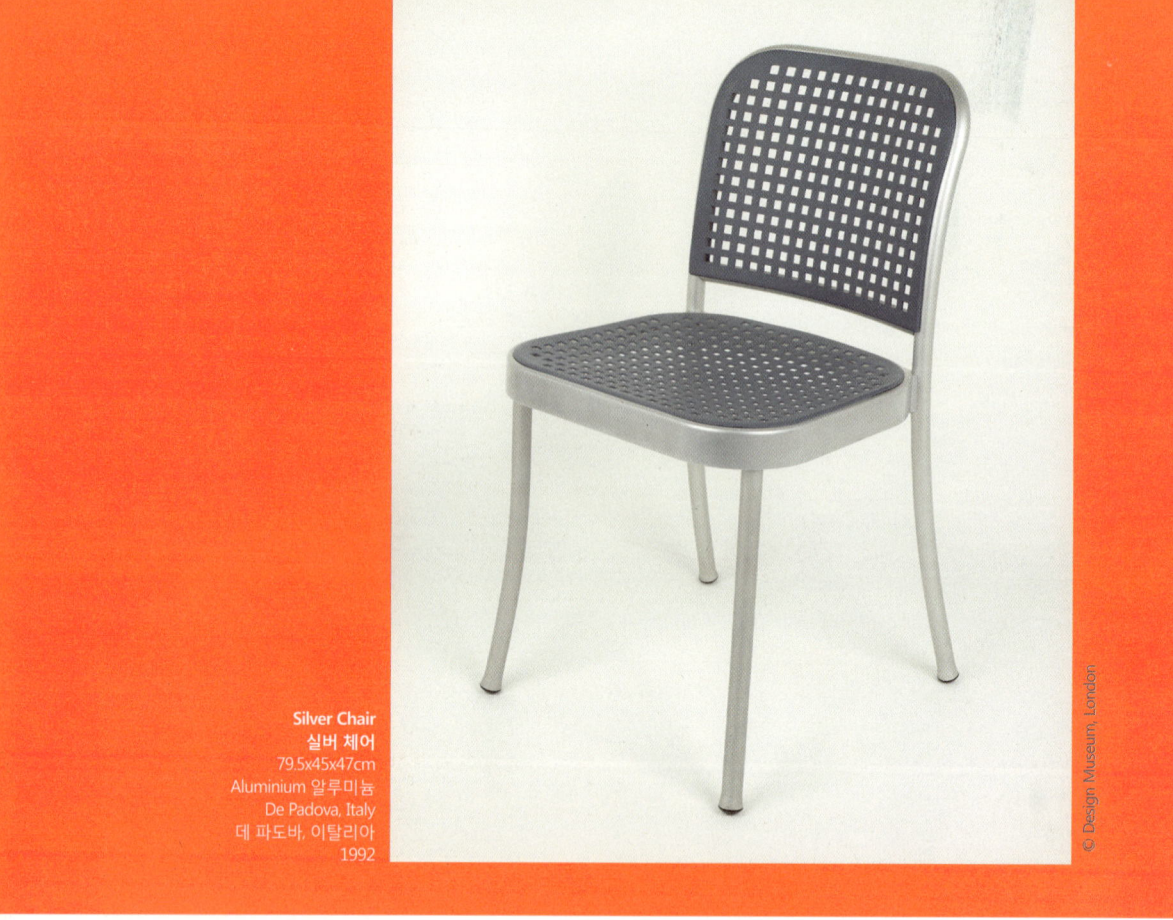

Silver Chair
실버 체어
79.5x45x47cm
Aluminium 알루미늄
De Padova, Italy
데 파도바, 이탈리아
1992

© Design Museum, London

Italy | 이탈리아

Vico Magistretti 비코 마지스트레티

This is an update of the classic *Thonet bentwood chair* which Vico Magistretti created by re-evaluating the original materials and adapting them for modern production. Once furniture designers like Magistretti developed chairs for specific functions – for outside or inside, or for the home, cafés or the office – but the *Silver* was part of the growing trend for chairs to be used in a variety of roles.

비코 마지스트레티는 토네트의 고전인 벤트우드(휜 목재) 의자의 재료를 재평가하고, 그것들을 현대적 생산에 적합하게 조정하여 업데이트된 버전의 의자를 만들었다. 그 동안 마지스트레티 같은 가구 디자이너들은 특정한 기능-실외, 실내, 집, 카페 혹은 사무실-을 위한 의자를 개발했었지만, 현재 다양한 용도로 사용할 수 있는 의자들을 만들어내는 추세이다. *실버 체어*는 그 변화를 보여주는 하나의 예이다.

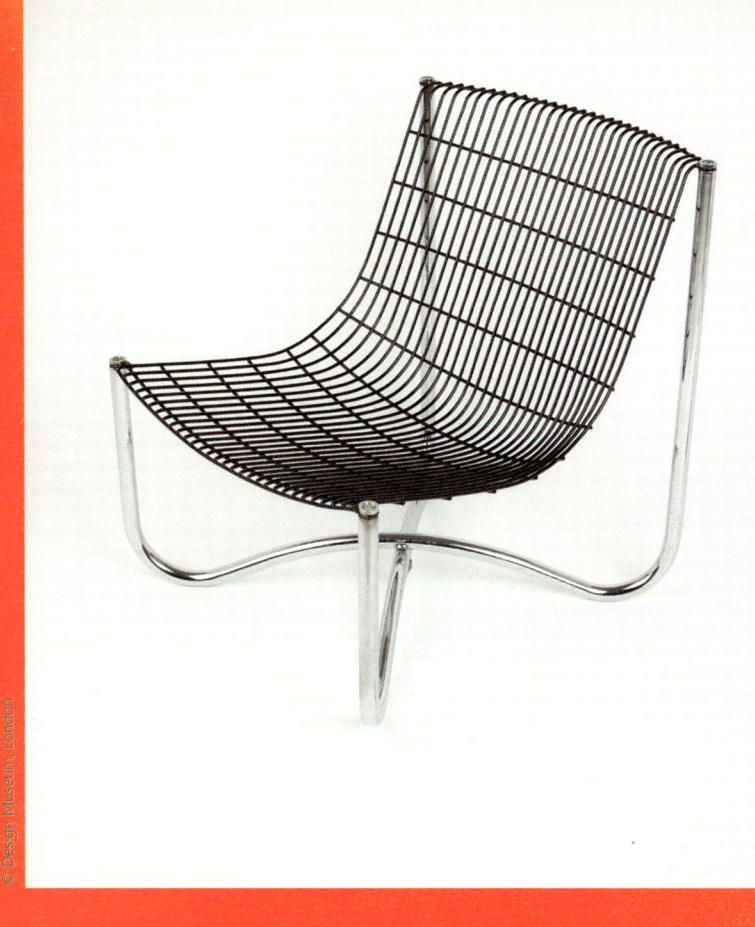

© Design Museum, London

Abacus 700
아바커스700
68x61x62cm
Tubular steel, wire mesh
강철튜브, 철망
Abacus, UK 아바커스, 영국
1973

UK | 영국

David Mellor 데이비드 멜러

David Mellor is best known for his cutlery design, but he has also applied his metalworking skills to other products, notably the *Abacus 700* series of outdoor seating. Born in Sheffield, the traditional heartland of the British steel industry, Mellor was educated at the local Junior Art School and then the Royal College of Art in London. Mellor designed this outdoor seating range in the fashionable 1970s high-tech style for Abacus, the Nottinghamshire-based manufacturer of furniture and lighting for public spaces.

식탁 기물(나이프, 포크 등) 디자인으로 유명한 데이비드 멜러는 그의 잘 알려진 작품 *아바커스 700* 시리즈와 같이 실외용 다른 의자 제품들에도 금속가공기술을 사용했다. 전통적인 영국의 철강산업 중심지인 쉐필드에서 태어난 멜러는 그 지역의 주니어 아트스쿨을 거쳐 런던의 왕립대학에서 교육을 받았다. 멜러는 공공장소를 위한 가구와 조명을 만드는 회사인 노팅엄셔의 아바커스를 위해 1970년대 유행했던 하이테크 스타일의 실외용 의자들을 디자인했다.

Jasper Morrison 재스퍼 모리슨

Originally designed by Jasper Morrison as part of *Some New Items For The Home*, an installation for an exhibition in Berlin, the *Ply Chair* had to be made very simply using the only tools he had at the time: an electric jigsaw and set of ship's curves. Despite these constraints Morrison produced a subtly sophisticated chair with a 'secret' plywood spring under the seat which bounces gently whenever it is sat upon.

재스퍼 모리슨의 *합판 의자*는 처음에 *집을 위한 몇 가지 새로운 물건들*이라는 주제로 열린 베를린 전시를 위해 디자인 된 것으로, 그 당시 그가 가지고 있던 유일한 도구인 전기 톱과 선도용 곡선자(배 그릴 때 쓰는 곡선 모양의 자)를 사용하여 아주 간단하게 만들어졌다. 이 같은 제약에도 불구하고 모리슨은 좌석 아래에 '비밀' 합판 스프링을 장착해 앉을 때마다 부드러운 반동이 일어나는 은근히 세련된 의자를 생산해냈다.

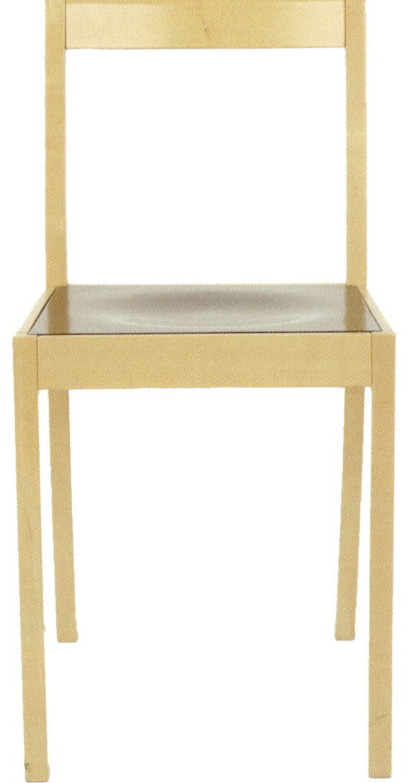

© Design Museum, London

Quattrogambe
콰트로감베
79x39x48cm
Solid maple and maple plywood veneer
단풍나무, 단풍나무 합판
Montina, Italy 몬티나, 이탈리아
1993

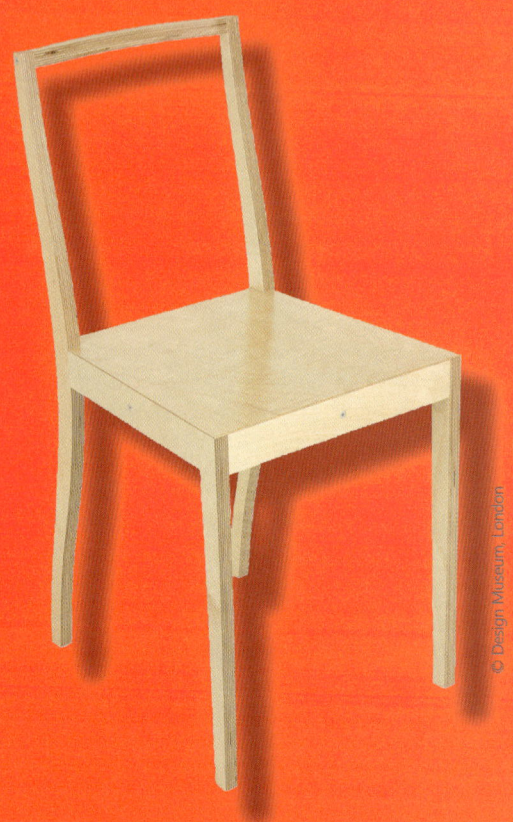

© Design Museum, London

Ply Chair
합판 의자
74x39.5x46cm
Plywood with birch veneer 자작나무 합판
Vitra, Switzerland 비트라, 스위스
1988

Quattrogambe

The *Quattrogambe*, which means 'four-legged' is a variation on the 1988 *Ply Chair*, one of Jasper Morrison's best-known designs. Unlike the uncompromisingly restrained *Ply Chair*, the *Quattrogambe* is made with a range of brightly coloured seats. 'The aim of this design was to arrive at a simple, modern wooden chair for the kitchen or for contract use, without resorting to nostalgic or decorative references,' explained Morrison.

'네발 달린'이라는 뜻의 *콰트로걈베*는 재스퍼 모리슨의 가장 잘 알려진 의자 디자인 중 하나인 *합판 의자*의 1988년도 버전이다. 단호히 절제된 *합판 의자*와는 달리, *콰트로걈베*는 좌석을 밝은 색으로 디자인했다. "이 디자인의 목적은 장식성 없이 주방 혹은 계약을 위한 단순하고 현대적인 나무의자를 만드는 것이었다." 라고 모리슨은 설명했다.

Cork stool

Morrison decided to work with cork after reading a newspaper article on the trend for winegrowers to seal bottles with plastic stoppers and twist-off metal caps instead of traditional corks. "With the cork industry in crisis, other uses for the material take on a new importance," observed Morrison. "It's a beautiful material with remarkable properties like being rot and insect proof." The Stool served as an inspiration for the *Cork Family* of furniture that Morrison later developed for the new Vitra at Home collection.

모리슨은 와인 제조자들이 병을 밀봉하기 위해 전통적인 코르크 마개 대신 플라스틱 마개와 돌려 따는 금속 마개를 사용하는 추세라는 신문기사를 읽고 코르크를 가지고 작업하기로 마음 먹었다. "코르크의 다른 활용방안들은 위기의 코르크 산업을 다시금 새로운 중심으로 이끌 것이다." 라고 전망하며 모리슨은 코르크에 주목했다. "이것은 썩기도 하고 곤충을 막기도 하는 훌륭한 특성을 가진 멋진 재료이다." 이 의자는 후에 모리슨이 비트라 앳 홈 컬렉션을 위한 가구, *코르크 패밀리*를 개발하는데 영감을 주었다.

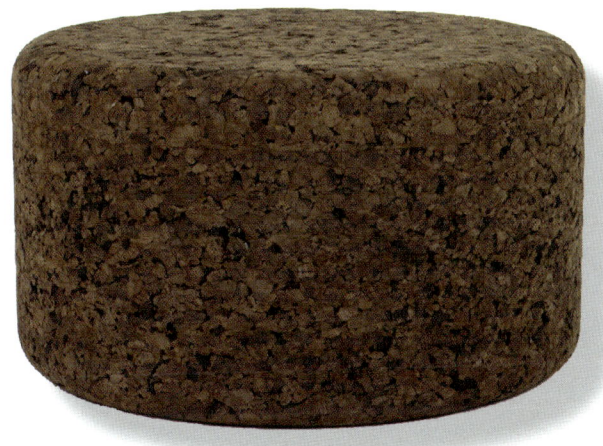

© Design Museum, London

Cork stool
코르크 스툴
24.5x44.5x44.5cm
Agglomerate cork 코르크 덩어리
Moooi, Netherlands 모오이, 네덜란드
2002

131

Jasper Morrison hit upon the idea of the *Air-Chair* when Magis, the Italian plastics manufacturer, showed him a tube made by the new plastic moulding technology of gas injection. This process enabled Magis to mould finer, lighter plastic products in hitherto impossible shapes. 'The design began from the leg up,' Morrison explained, 'describing the tubular structure of the chair.'

재스퍼 모리슨은 이탈리아 플라스틱 가구회사인 마지스가 가스를 주입하는 새로운 플라스틱 성형 기술로 만든 튜브를 보여줬을 때, *에어-체어*에 대한 아이디어를 생각해냈다. 이 방식으로 마지스는 지금까지 불가능했던 모양의 더 미세하고 가벼운 플라스틱 제품들을 주조할 수 있게 되었다. 의자의 관형 구조를 설명하면서 모리슨은 '디자인은 다리에서부터 시작했어요'라고 설명했다.

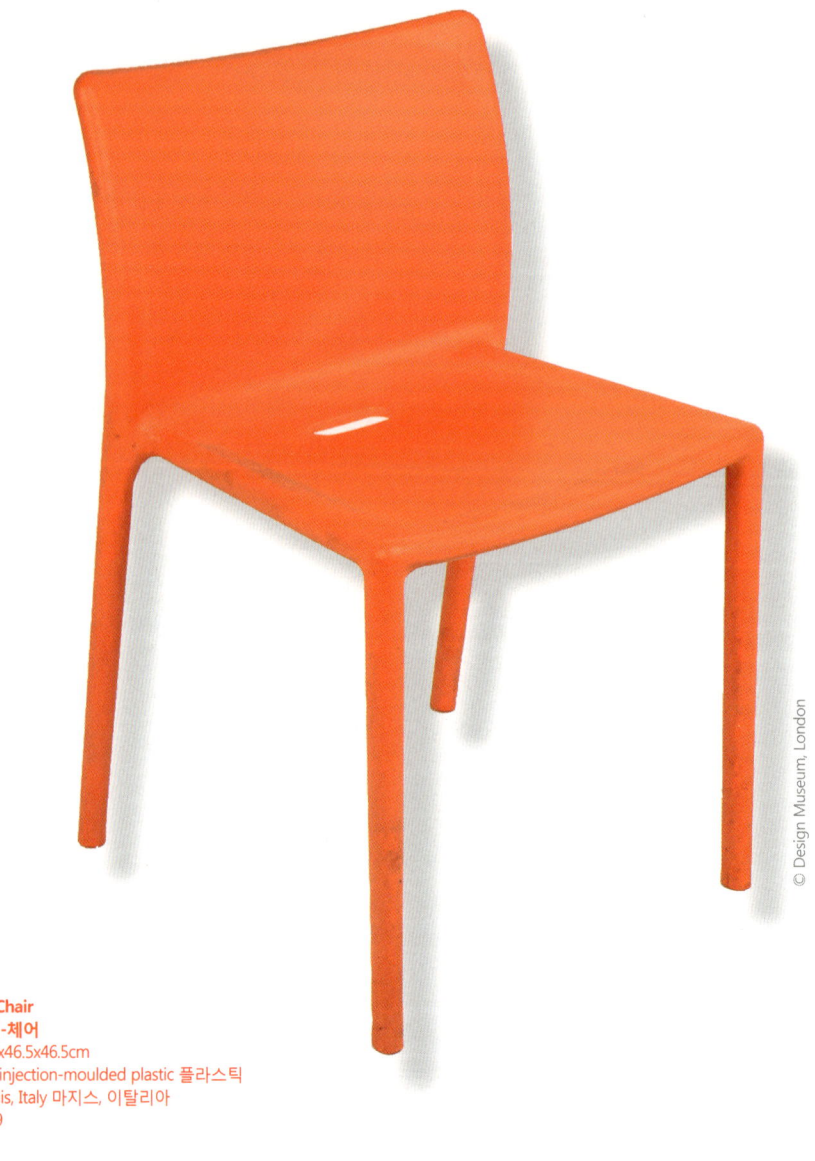

© Design Museum, London

Air-Chair
에어-체어
77.5x46.5x46.5cm
Gas injection-moulded plastic 플라스틱
Magis, Italy 마지스, 이탈리아
1999

Long an admirer of the compact day chairs designed by Poul Kjaerholm in the 1950s and 1960s, Jasper Morrison decided to create a contemporary version in his 1999 series of *Low-Pad* and *Hi-Pad* chairs. When he began the project Morrison was intent on developing a slimmer, but still comfortable variation on traditional upholstery. Inspiration struck when he spotted the dense sole of a training shoe while waiting in an airport departure lounge.

1950, 60년대에 폴 키에홀름에 의해 디자인된 컴팩트한 일상 의자의 오랜 팬이었던 재스퍼 모리슨은 1999년 그의 *로우 패드 체어*와 *하이 패드 체어*의 현대적 버전을 만들기로 결심했다. 이 프로젝트를 시작하면서 모리슨은 기존의 의자 커버를 얇으면서도 편안하게 발전시켜보고자 했다. 어느 날 그는 공항 라운지에서 기다리던 중에 운동화의 촘촘한 점박이 밑창을 보고 이 작품의 영감이 떠올랐다.

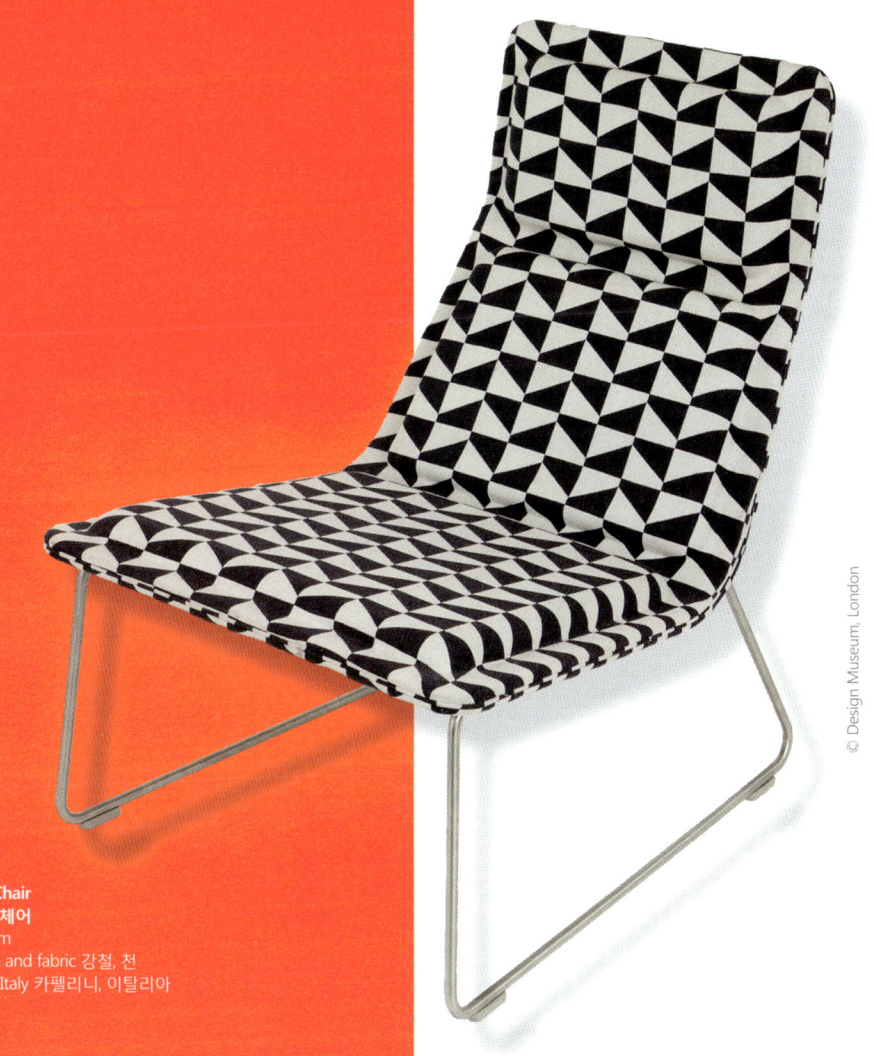

© Design Museum, London

Low-Pad Chair
로우-패드 체어
80x44x46cm
Steel, foam and fabric 강철, 천
Cappellini, Italy 카펠리니, 이탈리아
1999

Marc Newson 마크 뉴슨

An important inspiration for Marc Newson's early furniture designs was the D-I-Y culture of the surfing enthusiasts who made their own surfboards in the backyards of his native Sydney. Newson refined the fluid silhouette of the surfboard into the hourglass orgone form that appears in many of his late 1980s and early 1990s chairs and chaise longues including this fibreglass piece.

마크 뉴슨의 초기 가구 디자인에 중요한 영감이 되었던 것은 그의 고향인 시드니에서 자신들만의 서핑보드를 만들던 서핑 매니아들의 DIY문화였다. 그는 1980년대 후반부터 90년대 초반까지 유리섬유로 된 작품을 비롯해 많은 의자와 쉐즈롱(긴 안락의자)을 모래시계 형태로 만들면서 서핑보드의 부드러운 실루엣을 구현했다.

Felt Chair
펠트 의자
80x100x65cm
Fiberglass and steel 섬유유리, 강철
Cappellini, Italy 카펠리니, 이탈리아
1989

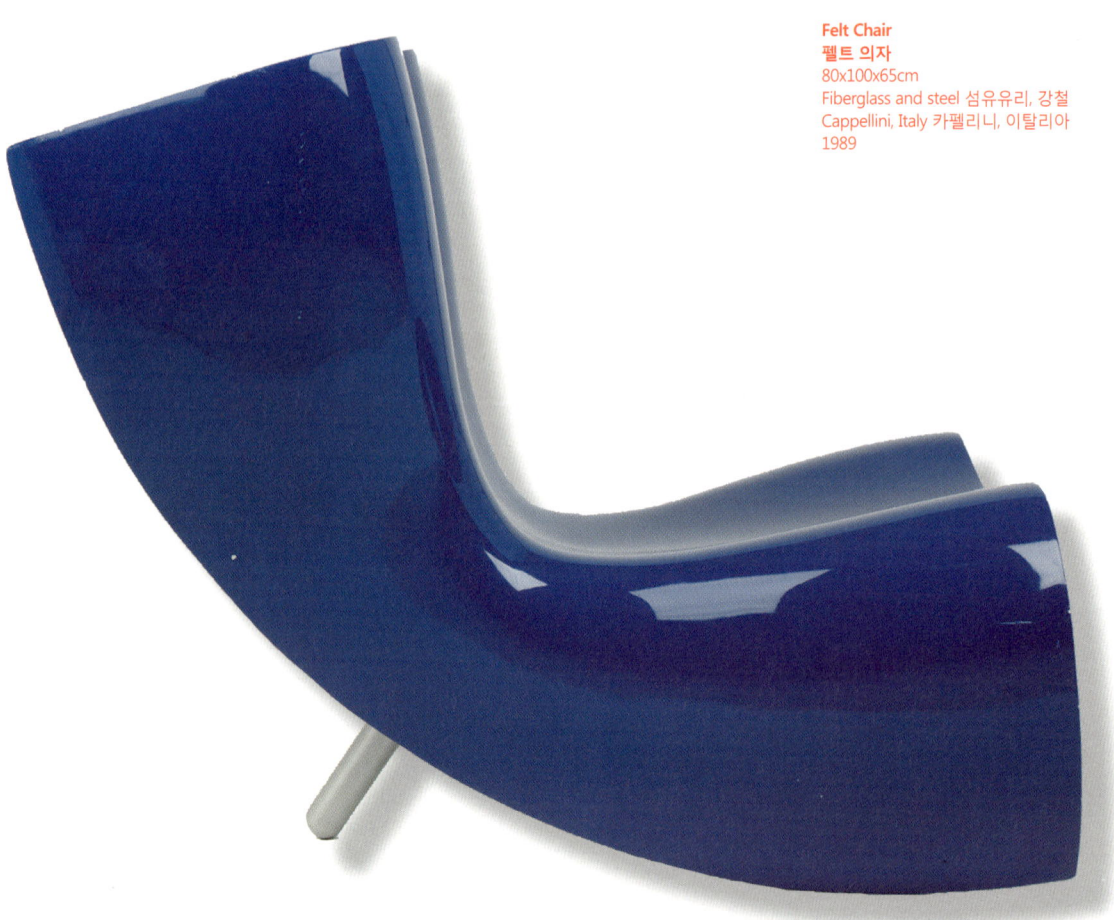

© Design Museum, London

134

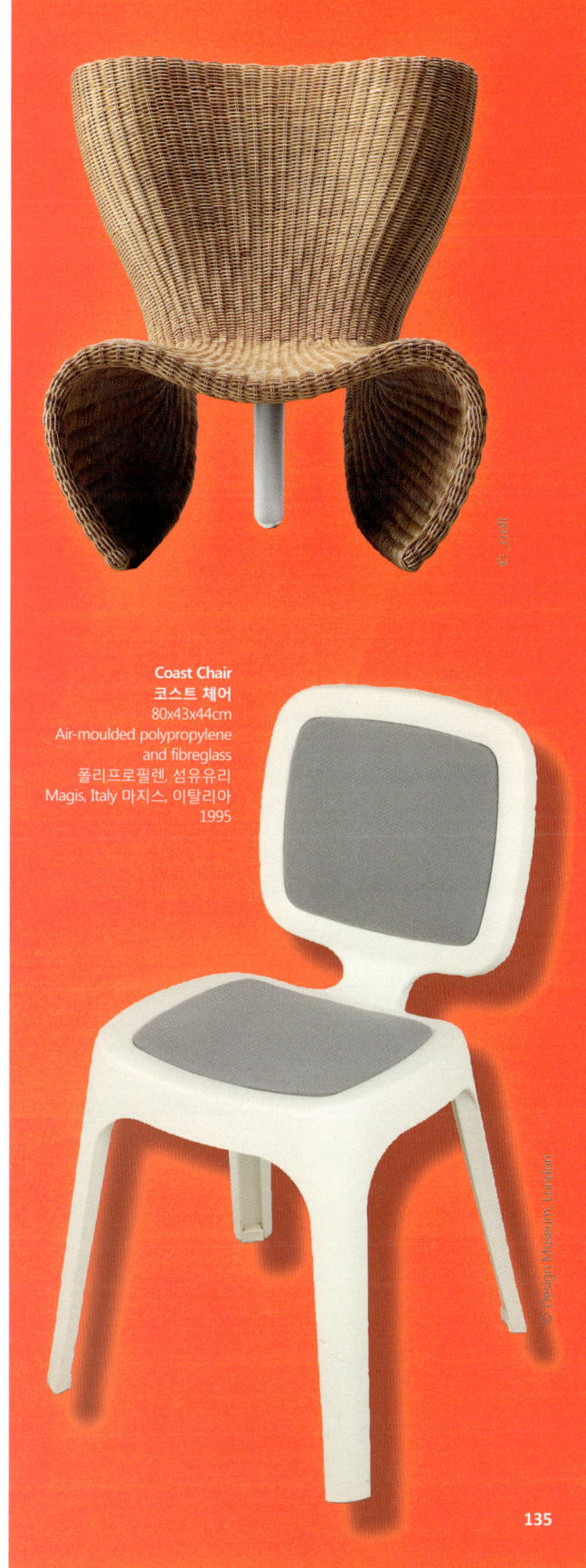

Wicker Chair
고리버들 의자
74x69x74cm
Aluminum, rattan 알루미늄, 등나무
Idée, Japan 이데, 일본
1990

Coast Chair
코스트 체어
80x43x44cm
Air-moulded polypropylene
and fibreglass
폴리프로필랜, 섬유유리
Magis, Italy 마지스, 이탈리아
1995

Marc Newson was commissioned by restaurant owner Oliver Peyton to design the interior of his new London restaurant, Coast. Like the rest of the interior, Newson's design of the dining chairs combined elements of the traditional and futuristic, evident in the manner in which Newson designed the seat and back of the chair transforming the traditional material, wood, and manipulating it to imitate the curve of a TV screen. This version of the *Coast chair* was later released in plastic by Magis at the Milan Furniture Fair in 2002.

마크 뉴슨은 레스토랑 오너인 올리버 페이톤으로부터 런던의 새로운 레스토랑인 코스트의 인테리어를 디자인 해 줄 것을 위임 받았다. 뉴슨의 식탁 의자 디자인은 다른 인테리어와 마찬가지로 전통과 미래적인 요소가 혼합되어 있는데, 전통적 소재인 나무를 TV 화면의 곡선모양으로 변형시켜 좌석과 등받이를 만든 것을 보면 잘 알 수 있다. *코스트 체어*는 후에 이탈리아 플라스틱 가구회사인 마지스가 플라스틱으로 제작하여 2002년 밀라노 가구박람회에 선보였다.

Jean Prouvé 쟝 푸르베

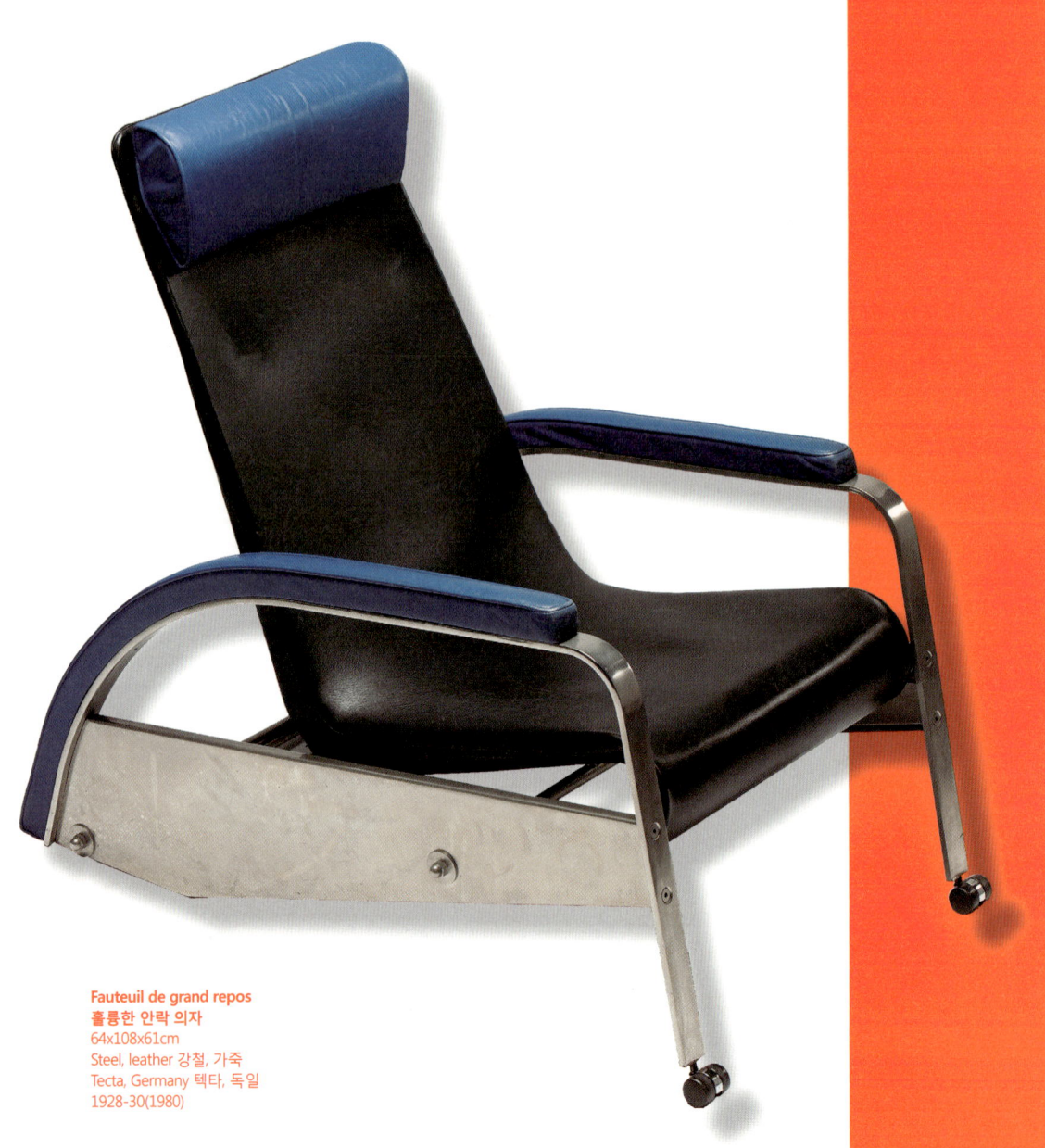

Fauteuil de grand repos
훌륭한 안락 의자
64x108x61cm
Steel, leather 강철, 가죽
Tecta, Germany 텍타, 독일
1928-30(1980)

"Cease attempting any design if you won't be able to produce in real." Jean Prouvé always pursued the function and simplicity of design. His simple but elegant furniture works are considered to have perfectly harmonized craftsmanship, techniques, and aesthetic sensibilities.

"만들어 낼 수 없는 디자인은 하지도 말라"고 말한 그는 항상 디자인의 기능성과 단순성을 추구했다. 그리고 그가 만든 단순하면서도 우아한 가구들은 장인 정신과 기술, 미적 감각을 완벽하게 조화시켰다고 여겨진다.

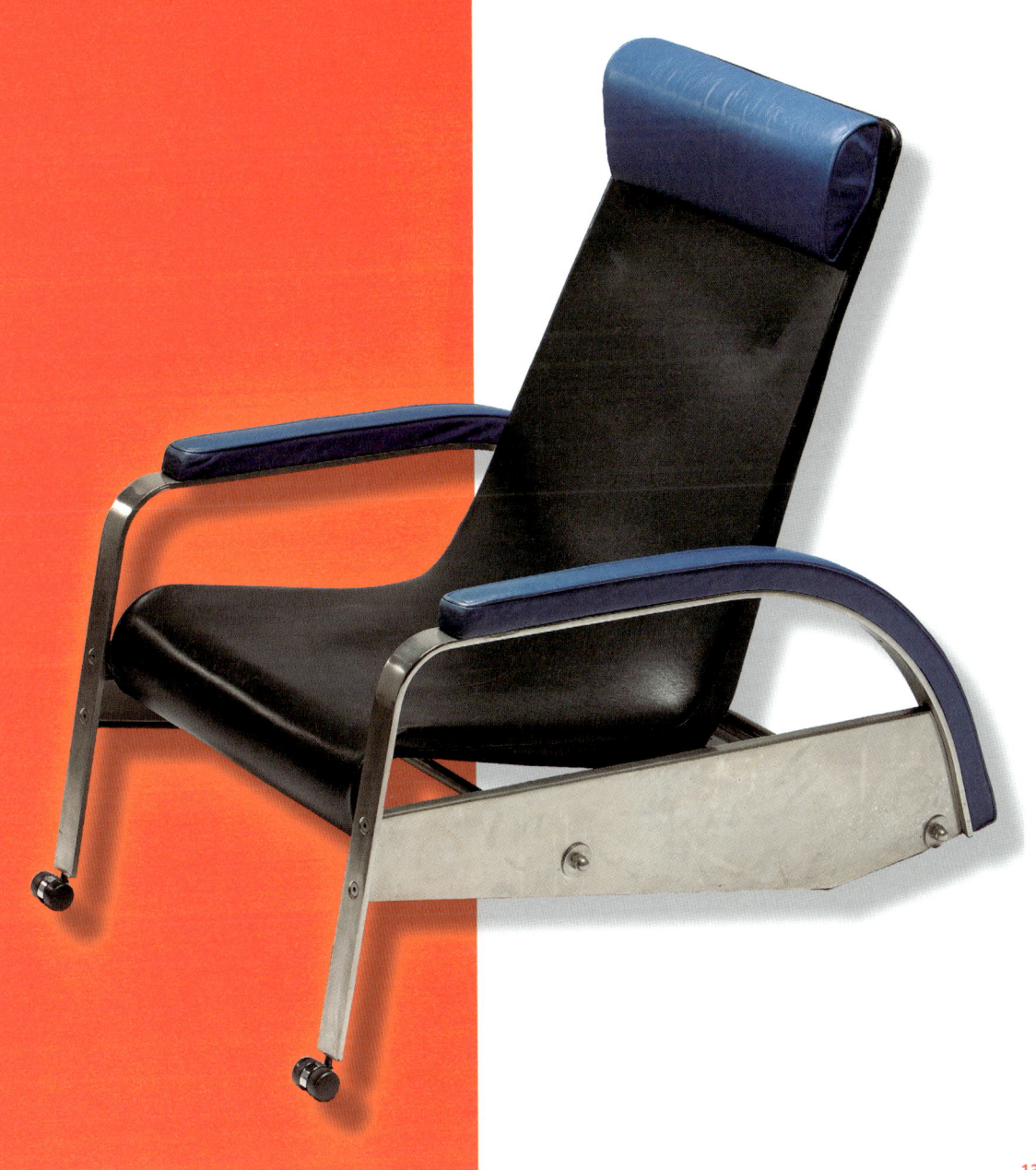

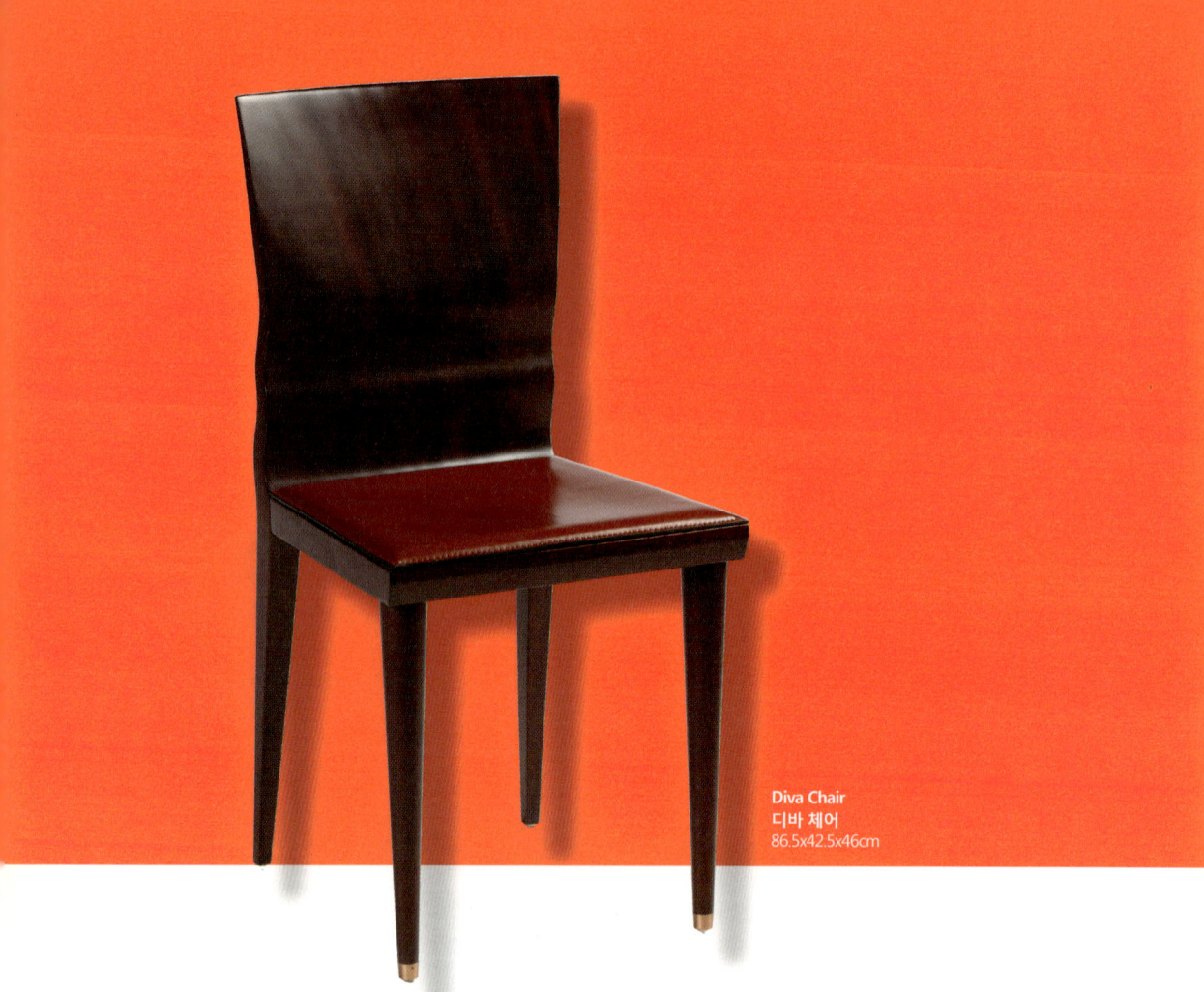

Diva Chair
디바 체어
86.5x42.5x46cm

Lebanon | 레바논

William Sawaya 윌리엄 사와야

The special point of William Sawaya's design is a freshness created by flowing lines, sensuous colors, and diversified materials. Particularly, he frequently has displayed organic forms with lines, and his design completed with his unique style exhibits a balanced sense of experimental spirit with reality and practicality. Meanwhile, his recent works in the series of Barock n' roll combine two disparate elements: aristocratic and feminine 'Baroque' with unconventionally rough 'Rock and roll.' This series provides the designers delicate but decisive sensibility which produces stylish and charming designs through the combination of tradition and exception.

윌리엄 사와야 디자인의 특별한 점은 흐르는 듯한 라인과 감각적인 컬러, 다채로운 소재의 활용을 통해 만들어 내는 신선함이다. 특히 곡선을 적용한 유기적인 형태의 디자인을 많이 선보였는데, 실험성과 현실성, 실용성이 균형을 이루고 있는 디자인은 다른 곳에서 찾을 수 없는 그만의 스타일로 완성되어 선보인다. 한편 비교적 최근 작업인 Barock n' roll의 제품들은 귀족적이고 여성적인 '바로크'와 파격적이고 거친 '로큰롤'이라는 이질적인 요소를 결합시키고 있다. 이는 전통과 파격을 믹스한 시도를 통해 스타일리쉬하고 매력적인 디자인을 자아내는 그의 섬세하면서도 과감한 감성을 느끼게 한다.

Afra &Tobia Scarpa
아프라 & 토비아 스카파

Libertà Chair
리바타 체어
77x50x49cm
Aluminium 알루미늄
1989

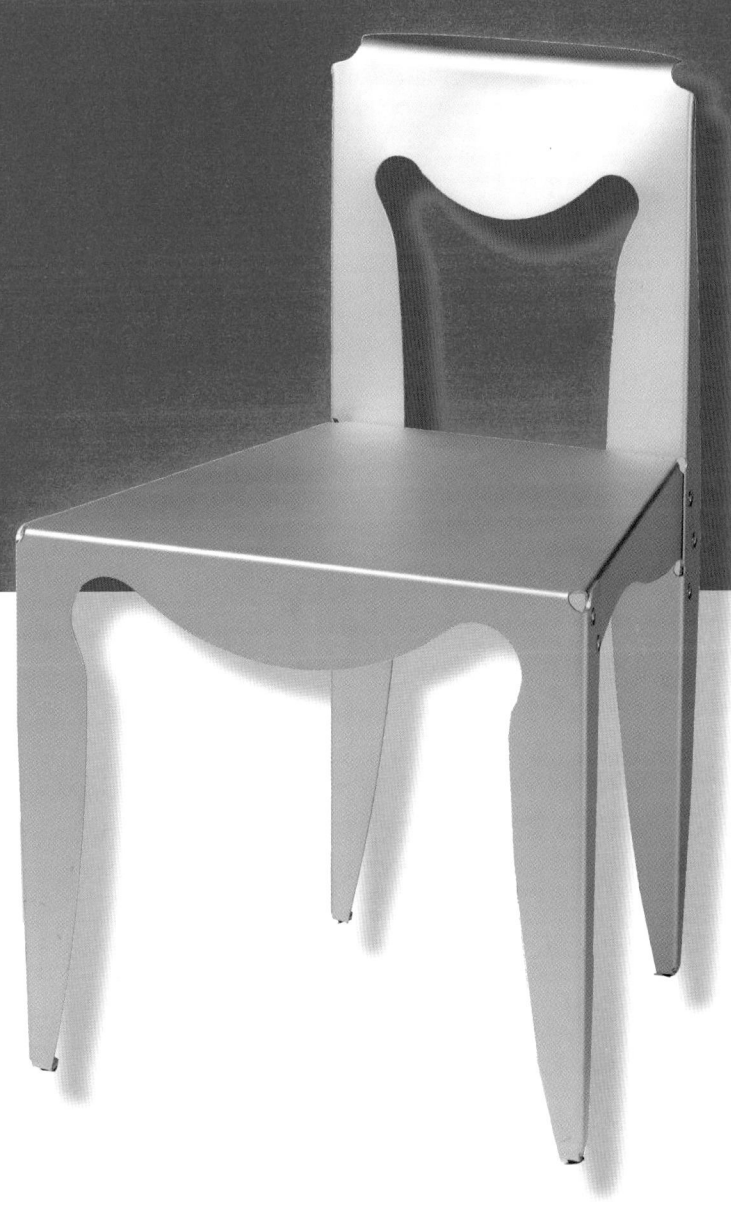

Jerszy Seymour 저지 시모어

Conceived by Jerszy Seymour as a comfortable armchair-cum-chaise longue, his *Play Station Chair* combines a soft, circular seat with a protruding leg-rest that can also be used to hold a Sony Play Station video game system or a TV dinner. As in many of Seymour's furniture and product designs, the chair's playful appearance belies its underlying practicality.

저지 시모어에 의해 탄생한 플레이 스테이션 의자는 편안한 안락의자 쉐즈 롱으로서 부드러운 원형좌석과 튀어나온 발 받침이 결합되어 있다. 이 의자는 소니 플레이 스테이션 비디오 게임 시스템 또는 TV디너(즉석식품)를 올려 놓는데 사용할 수 있다. 많은 시모어의 가구와 제품 디자인들과 마찬가지로, 이 의자의 우스꽝스러운 모습은 의자의 근원적인 실용성을 착각하게 만든다.

Play Station Chair
플레이 스테이션 의자
70x85x150cm
Polyurethane foam and vinyl upholstery 폴리우레탄, 비닐
BRF, Italy
2000

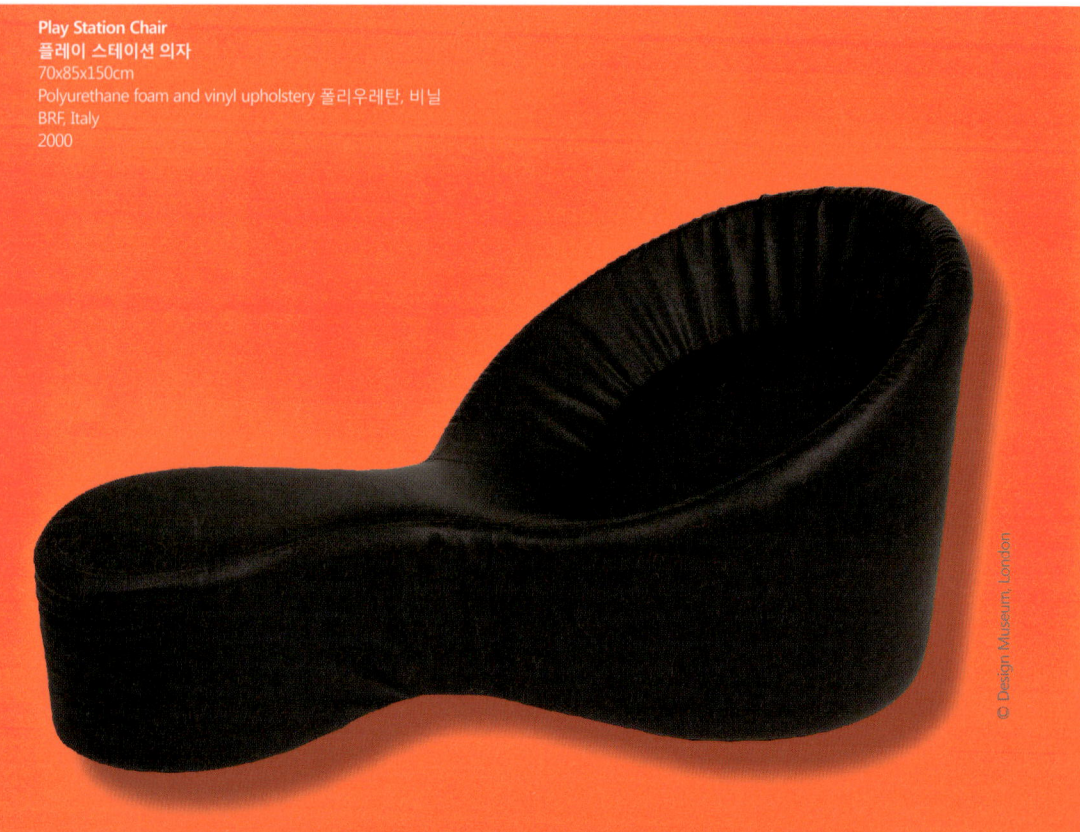

© Design Museum, London

Ettore Sottsass 에토레 소트사스

In 1958 Ettore Sottsass began a productive relationship as a design consultant to Olivetti, the Italian office equipment company. Among his classic designs for Olivetti was the playful *Valentine typewriter*. During the same period, Sottsass developed the *Synthesis 45* adjustable office chair which, like the *Valentine*, brought Pop design into the workplace.

에토레 소트사스는 1958년 디자인 컨설턴트로서 올리베티라는 이탈리아 사무기기 회사와 함께 일을 시작했다. 올리베티를 위해 만든 그의 대표적 디자인 중에는 장난기 가득한 *발렌타인 타자기*가 있다. 같은 시기 소트사스는 *발렌타인 타자기*가 그랬던 것처럼 팝 디자인을 업무공간 안으로 들여놓는, *신세시스 45*라는 조정 가능한 사무실 의자를 개발하였다.

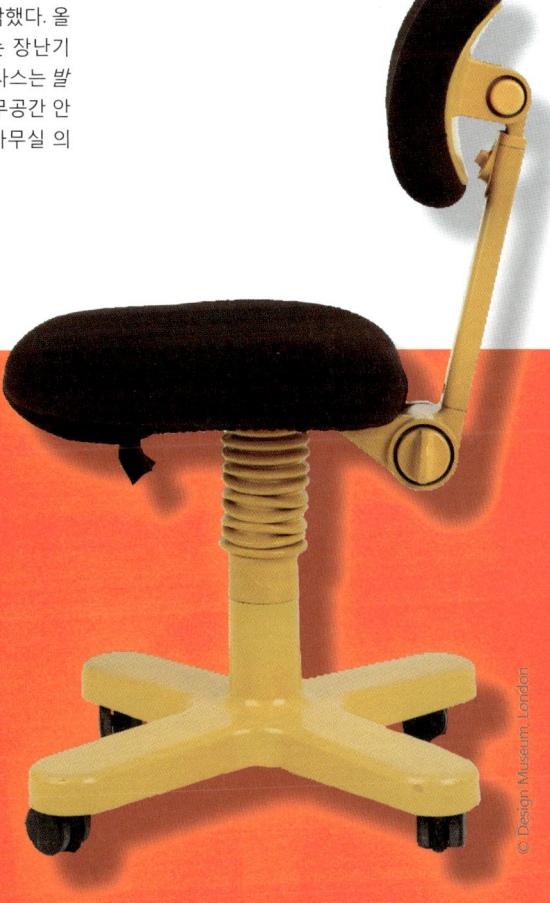

© Design Museum, London

Synthesis 45 office chair
신세시스(합성) 45 오피스 체어
80x56x56cm
Injection moulded ABS frame and fabric
ABS, 폴리우레탄, 천
Olivetti, Italy 올리베티, 이탈리아
1970-71

141

Philippe Starck 필립 스탁

At first glance the *Dr Glob stacking chair* is characteristic of the humorous spirit of so much of Philippe Starck's 1980s work, but it also reflects the designer's interest in sustainability. All the materials used in the *Dr Glob* are suitable for recycling.
'I dreamt about a small, sturdy, handy and considerate chair that would be plastic to avoid the killing of trees,' said Starck of its inception.

언뜻 *닥터 클로브 스태킹 체어*(쌓을 수 있는 의자)에는 필립 스탁의 1980년대 작품에 나타나는 유머러스한 정신의 특색이 지나치게 드러나 있는 듯 보이지만, 그것은 또한 환경파괴 없이 지속되는 것에 대한 디자이너의 관심을 반영한다. *닥터 글로브*에 사용된 모든 재료들은 재활용이 가능하다. 그와 같은 의자 디자인을 시도한 이유에 대해 스탁은 '나는 숲을 죽이지 않기 위해 플라스틱으로 된 작고, 견고한, 그리고 편리하고, 사려 깊은 의자를 생각했어요.'라고 말했다.

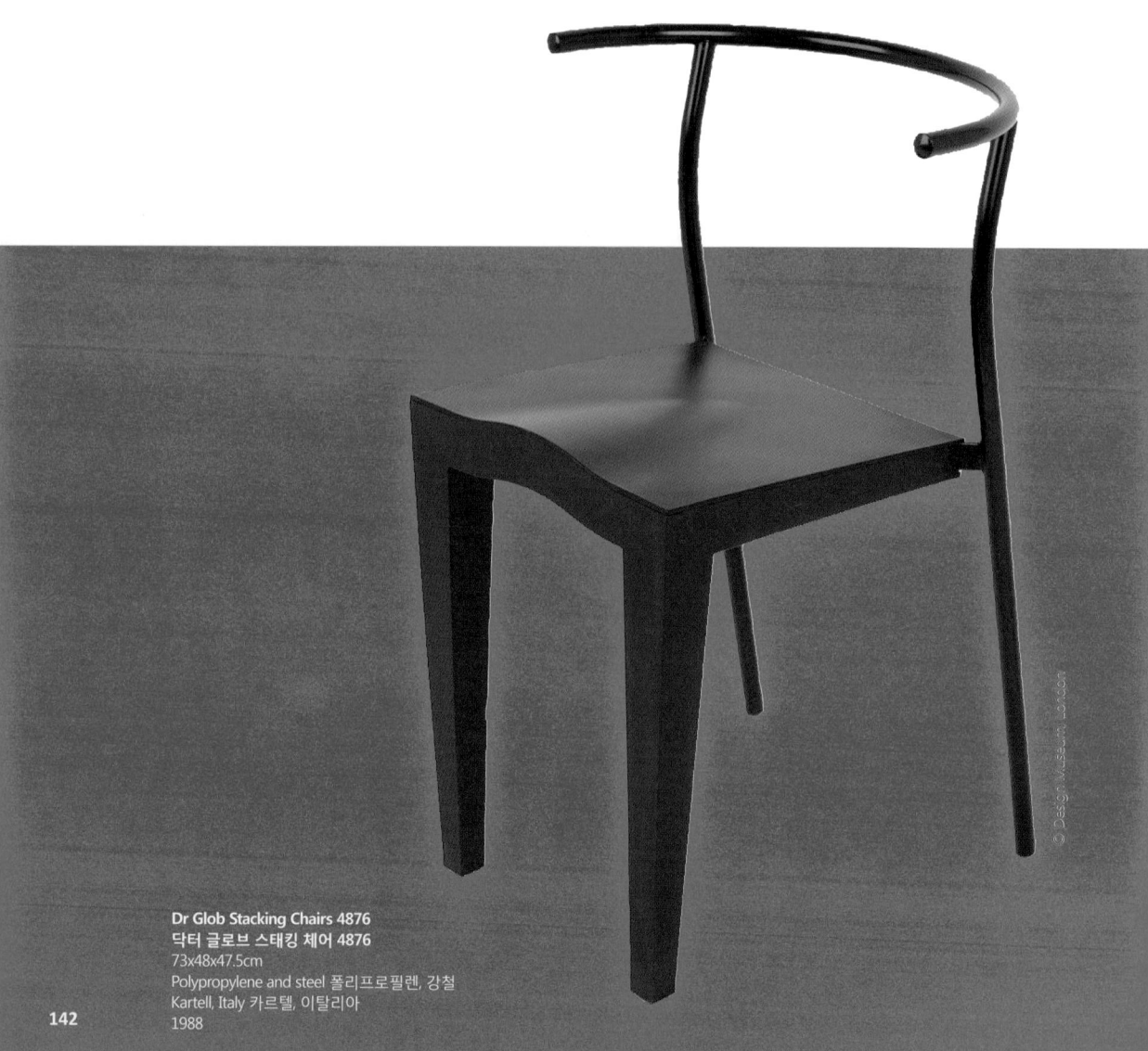

Dr Glob Stacking Chairs 4876
닥터 글로브 스태킹 체어 4876
73x48x47.5cm
Polypropylene and steel 폴리프로필렌, 강철
Kartell, Italy 카르텔, 이탈리아
1988

One of the 'surrealist or Dada objects' that Philippe Starck designed to liberate the user 'from the humdrum reality of everyday life,' the *W.W. stool* was originally designed as part of a fantasy workspace for the film director Wim Wenders. The only object in the room to go into production, this stool seems to ignore all functional constraints by barely providing a surface to be sat on and functions more as a piece of sculpture than furniture.

필립 스탁은 '일상생활의 평범한 현실로부터' 사용자들을 자유롭게 하기 위한 디자인을 했던 '초현실주의 혹은 다다이즘 작품'의 하나인, *W.W.* 스툴은 원래 영화감독인 빔 벤더스를 위한 것으로 판타지 영화 촬영지의 일부로 디자인되었다. 그 방 안에 있던 것들 중 유일하게 생산에 들어간 이 의자는 간신히 앉을 수 있는 자리만을 제공함으로써, 의자의 모든 기능적 조건들을 무시하고 있기에 가구라기 보다는 조각의 일부분으로 보인다.

Typical of the playful, self-parodic style which made Starck's work so popular in the 1980s and early 1990s, this stackable chair, manufactured by Vitra, combines plastic with metal. The plate attaching the back legs to the seat is over-sized to make it easier to dismantle for recycling. The name is a reference to the use of French kings' names in historic furniture such as the 18th century Louis XVI style.

1980년대와 1990년대 초 스탁을 아주 유명하게 만들었던 작품으로서 우스꽝스럽고, 자기 패러디적인 스타일의 쌓아 올리기 쉬운 모양의 이 의자는 플라스틱과 금속을 결합하여 비트라라는 회사에 의해 제작되었다. 뒷다리에 붙여서 좌석으로 이어지는 판은 재활용을 위해 더 쉽게 해체할 수 있도록 크게 만들었다. 작품의 제목은 18세기 루이 16세의 스타일처럼 역사적인 가구에 프랑스 왕의 이름을 붙이던 것에서 따왔다.

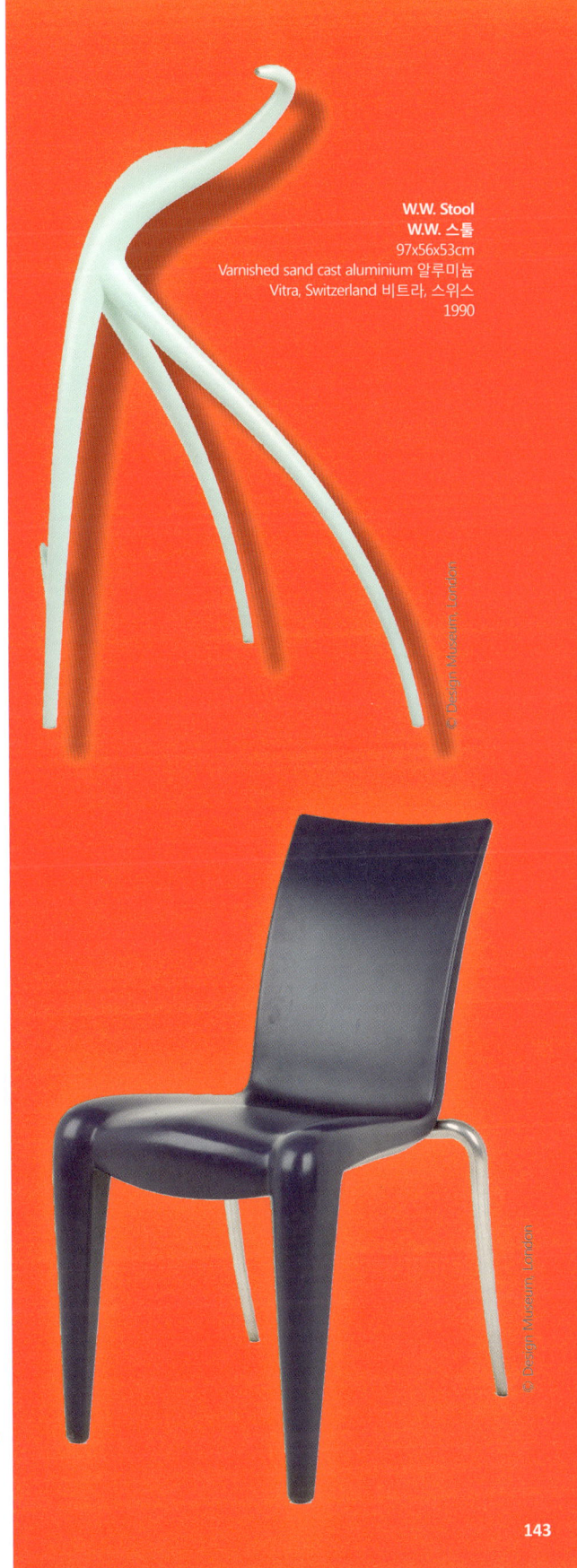

W.W. Stool
W.W. 스툴
97x56x53cm
Varnished sand cast aluminium 알루미늄
Vitra, Switzerland 비트라, 스위스
1990

© Design Museum, London

Louis 20
루이 20
85x41x55cm
Blown polypropylene and aluminium
폴리프로필렌, 알루미늄
Vitra, Switzerland 비트라, 스위스
1991

© Design Museum London

Hiroshi Tsunoda 히로시 츠노다

Like many of Hiroshi Tsunoda's designs, this low chair is functionally influenced by traditional Japanese rustic furniture and aesthetically by the intricate folds of origami. Born in Japan, but based in Spain, Tsunoda has combined these influences to create a light, portable piece of modern furniture that he describes as a chair-cushion. The Isu is also fun to use because the plywood seat springs playfully whenever it is sat upon.

히로시 츠노다의 다른 많은 디자인이 그러하듯 이 낮은 의자는 기능적으로는 일본의 전통적인 소박한 가구와, 예술적으로는 종이 접기의 복잡한 주름에서 영향을 받았다. 일본에서 태어났지만, 스페인에 기반을 둔 츠노다는 이와 같은 영향을 그가 의자방석이라고 설명한 가볍고 이동 가능한 현대적인 가구작품들에 적용했다. 이 *이스 체어*는 그 위에 앉을 때마다 합판 좌석 스프링 때문에 사용하는 재미가 있다.

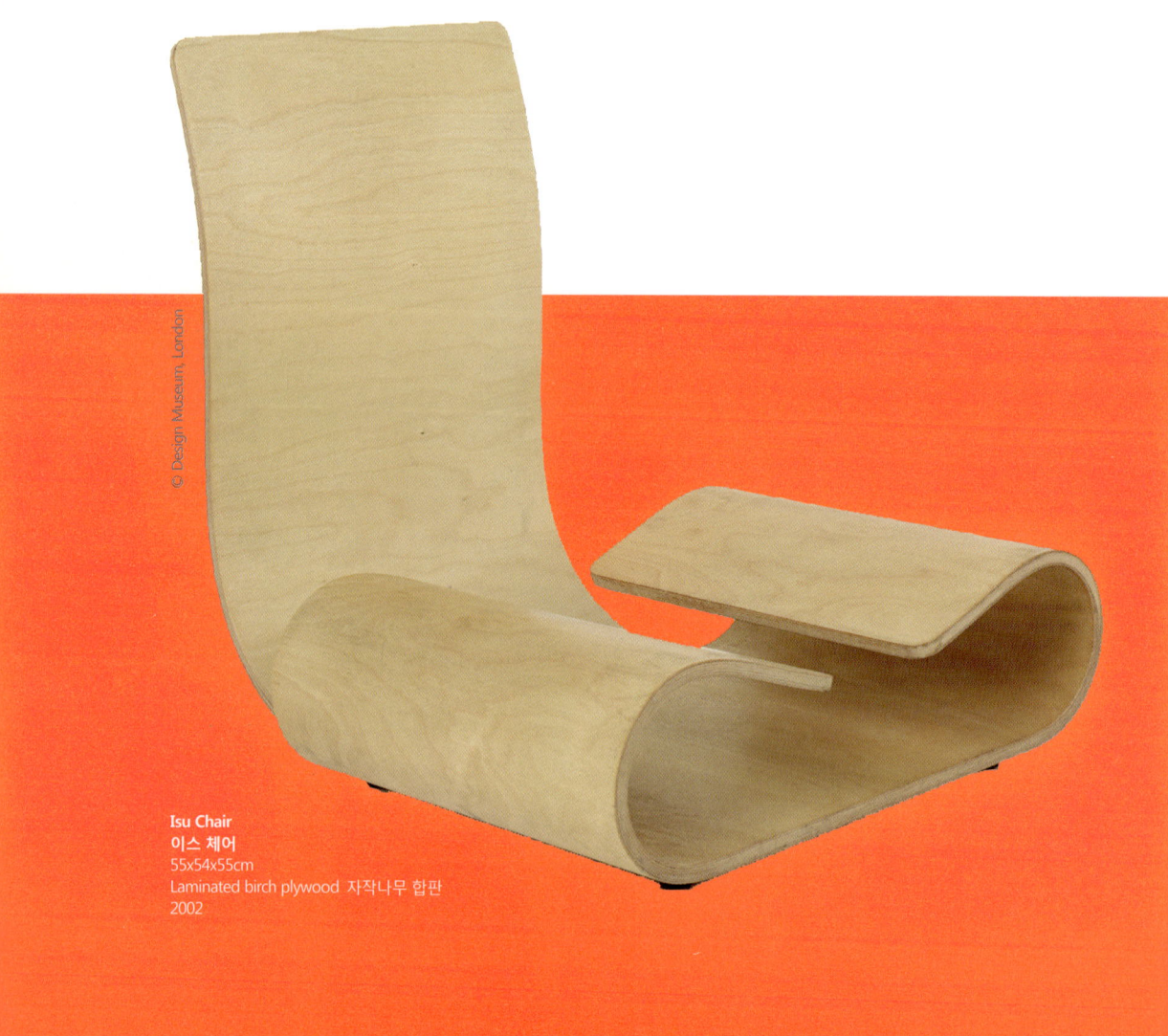

© Design Museum, London

Isu Chair
이스 체어
55x54x55cm
Laminated birch plywood 자작나무 합판
2002

Michael Young 마이클 영

Yogi forms parts of Michael Young's experiments with plastic rotation moulding for Magis, the Italian plastic products manufacturer. Invited to design a new collection of outdoor furniture *"with a smile on its face"*, Young created the engagingly cartoonish Yogi sofa, chair and table. Each Yogi piece is deliberately positioned low on the ground so that children can slip on comfortably, but adults feel incongruous as they sink down on to it. "Yogi places you in a vaguely humorous predicament and forces you to relax," said Young. "You can't take yourself too seriously."

*요기*의 형태는 이탈리아 플라스틱 제품 제조사인 마지스에서 이루어진 마이클 영의 플라스틱 회전 성형 실험에 의해 만들어졌다. 실외 가구의 새로운 컬렉션인 "*얼굴에 미소를 머금고*"의 디자인을 위해 초청된 마이클 영은 매력적인 동시에 우스꽝스러운 *요기* 소파, 의자 그리고 테이블을 만들었다. *요기* 각각의 작품은 아이들이 편안하게 미끄러져 내려올 수 있도록 의도적으로 낮게 만들어졌지만, 어른들은 의자 속으로 꺼져 들어가는 듯한 어색한 느낌을 받는다. "*요기* 작품이 당신을 약간은 유머러스한 상황에 빠져들게끔 하고 강제로 쉬도록 만들지만", 마이클 영은 말한다. "너무 심각하게 받아들이진 마세요."라고.

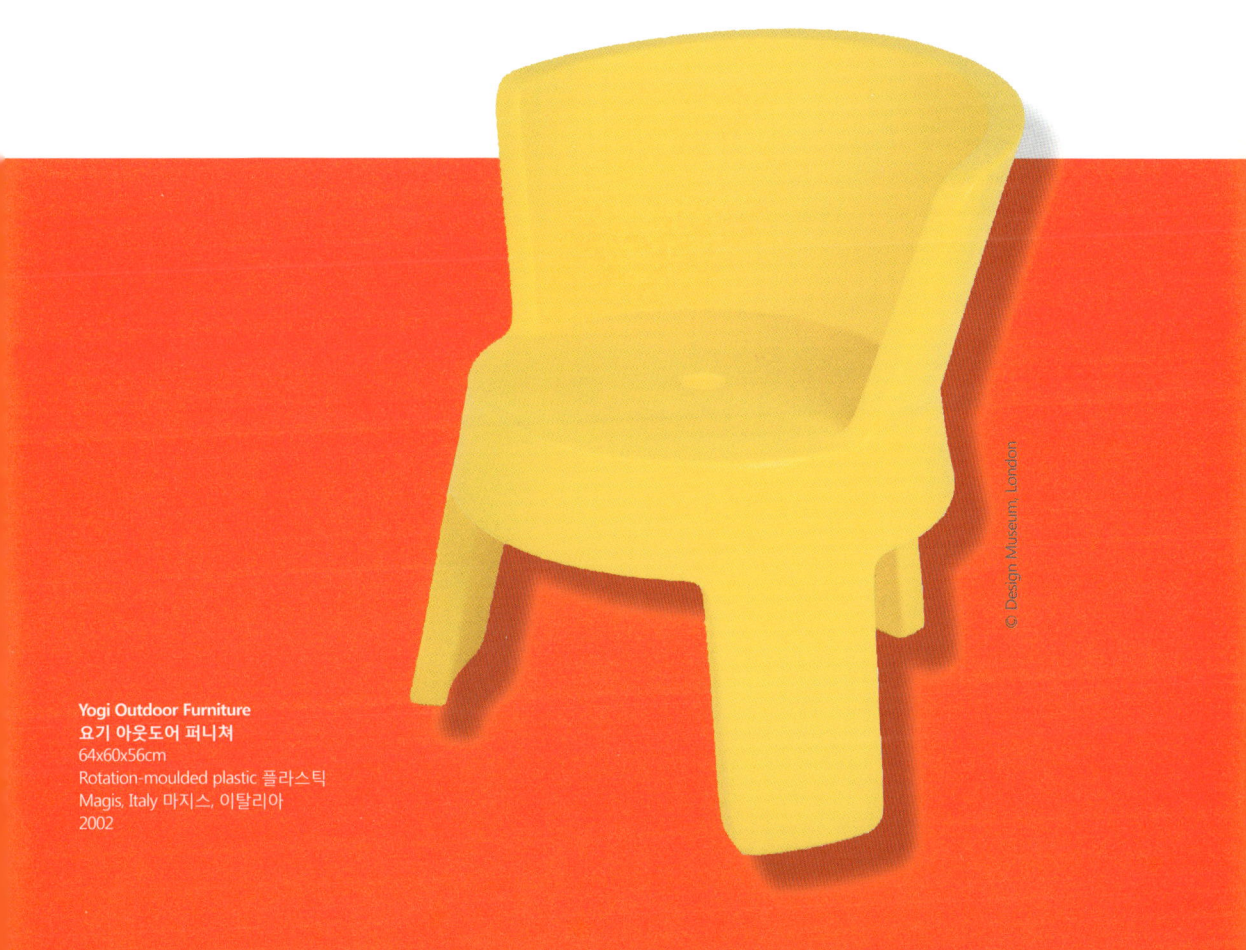

© Design Museum, London

Yogi Outdoor Furniture
요기 아웃도어 퍼니쳐
64x60x56cm
Rotation-moulded plastic 플라스틱
Magis, Italy 마지스, 이탈리아
2002

CONTEMPORARY
Leading Edge

My Own Super Studio_Rui Alves
마이 오운 슈퍼 스튜디오_후이 알비스

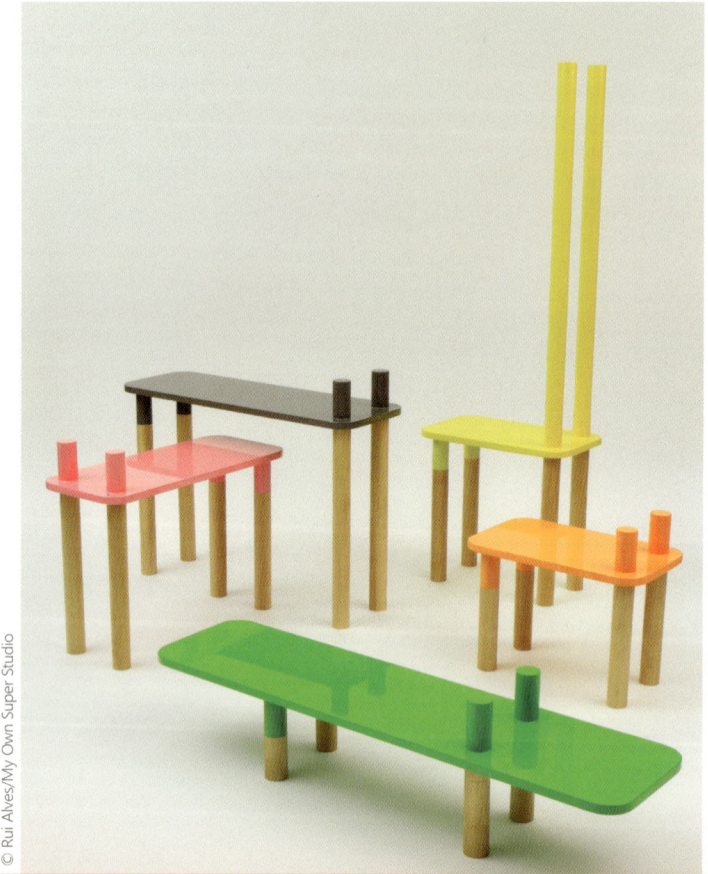

© Rui Alves/My Own Super Studio

Welcome to the jungle
정글에 오신 것을 환영합니다
150.7x30x50cm
(the tallest, 높은 의자)
31.9x120x30cm
(the widest, 넓은 의자)
Wood 나무
2009

Like many children, is age, my son loves to play with his ever growing collection of toy animals, and sharing this experience, with him, I came up with the idea of creating a group of special, small, pieces that might make children and adults feel the same about items of furniture. *Welcome to the jungle* is a group of 5 friends that you can use almost anyway that you want. They can be tables, stools, or even coat hangers. They can even jump over one another in order to make some shelves. Made of wood, and with a bright and glossy skin they've arrived and they have made the jungle their home.

또래의 많은 아이들처럼, 내 아들도 장난감 동물들을 모으는 것을 좋아했다. 그리고 이러한 경험을 아이와 공유하면서 나는, 어른과 아이들 모두가 가구의 아이템을 가지고 그와 같은 즐거움을 느낄 수 있는 특별한 작품을 만들어야겠다는 생각이 들었다. *정글에 오신 것을 환영합니다*라는 작품은 당신이 원하는 어떤 방식으로든지 사용할 수 있는 5개의 친구들로 구성되었다. 그들은 테이블도 되고, 스툴이 될 수도 있으며, 심지어 코트 걸이가 되기도 한다. 밝고 윤이 나는 표면을 가진 나무로 된 이 작품은, 집안을 정글로 만들어 줄 것이다.

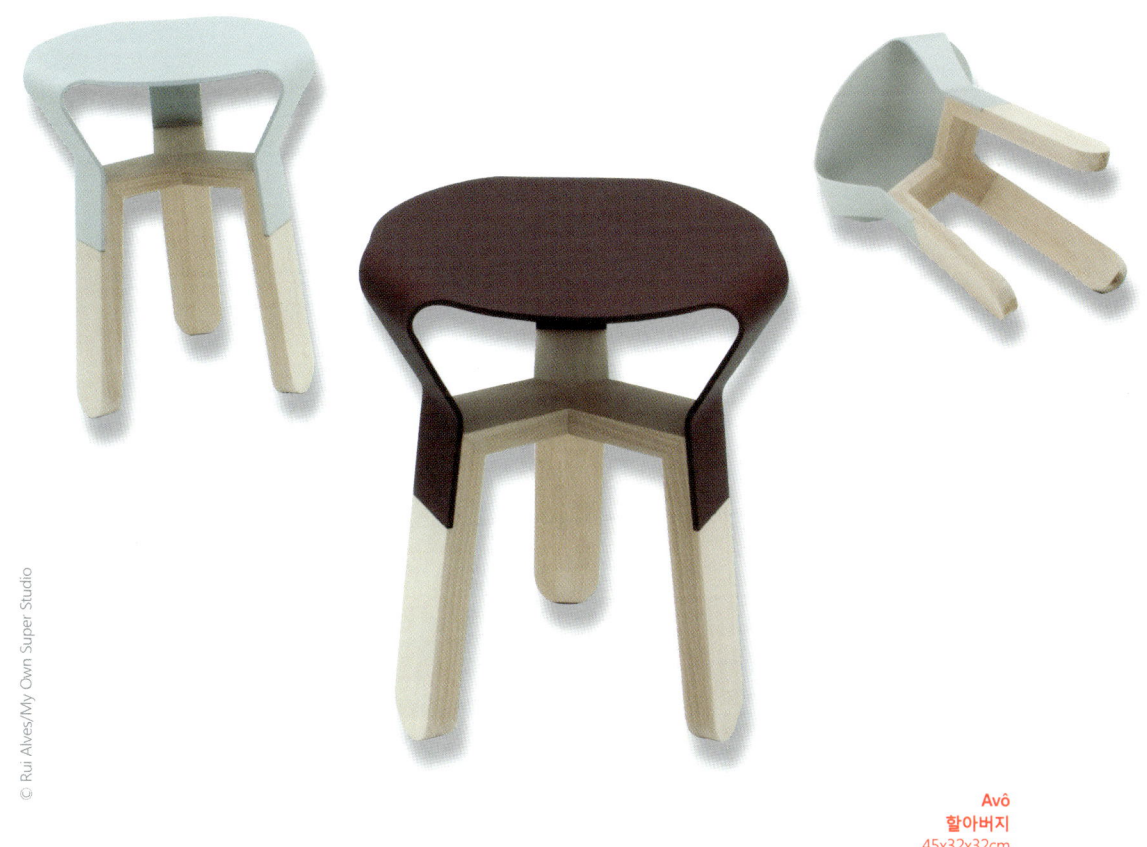

© Rui Alves/My Own Super Studio

Avô
할아버지
45x32x32cm
Wood and aluminium
나무, 알루미늄
2008

AVÔ is a stool and it's a small tribute to my grandfather who passed away a few months ago at the beautiful age of 97. He was the best carpenter and craftsman that I have ever known and a great "designer" in his own way. He used to have his favorite wooden stool. I remember it so well, because he would keep it handy for almost any occasion. He would use it when he sat in front of the fireplace and it would take it outside with him, when he wanted to sit quietly and read the newspaper. That small wooden stool was used anywhere and everywhere. AVÔ is made from anodized aluminium and solid wood and it's yours to use just as you please, just so long as you use it everyday and think of my grandfather whilst you enjoy it.

할아버지 스툴은 몇 달 전 97세라는 아름다운 나이에 돌아가신 나의 할아버지를 위한 작은 감사의 선물이다. 그는 내가 이제껏 보지 못한 최고의 목수이자 장인이었으며, 자신의 고유한 방식에 있어서 훌륭한 디자이너였다. 그는 자신이 가장 아끼는 나무로 된 스툴을 사용하곤 했다. 어떤 상황에도 그것을 지니고 있었기 때문에 나는 아주 잘 기억한다. 그는 벽난로 앞에 앉을 때에도 그것을 사용했고, 조용히 앉아 신문을 읽고 싶을 때, 밖에 나갈 때에도 가지고 다녔다. 그 작은 나무 스툴은 어느 장소에서나 사용되었다. *할아버지* 스툴은 양극 산화 처리된 알루미늄과 원목으로 만들어졌다. 당신이 그것을 매일 사용하는 한, 그리고 당신이 그것을 즐기며 나의 할아버지를 생각하는 한, 그것은 당신 것이 될 것이다.

Dror Bernshetrit 드롤 브른쉐트리트

I was fascinated by the growing dialogue between the digital world we work with and the physical world we live in. This mix is evident in every project we adapt, and with this chair I wanted to demonstrate a collision between forms - some made digitally and others made physically. I found that a simple physical collision is quite difficult to translate digitally, and that it is quite complex to physically represent a simple digital collision. The end result is the *Tron chair*: a physical translation of a digital collision.

나는 우리가 일하고 있는 디지털 세상과, 생활하고 있는 물질적 세상 사이의 대화를 촉진시키는 것을 좋아한다. 내가 선택한 모든 프로젝트에서 이러한 교류는 명백하게 드러난다. 이 의자를 통해 디지털 방식으로 만들어진 형태와 물질적인 방식으로 만들어진 형태 사이의 충돌을 실험해 보고 싶었다. 그럼으로써, 단순한 물질적 충돌을 디지털로 변환하는 것은 어렵고, 단순한 디지털 충돌을 물질적으로 표현하는 것이 매우 복잡하다는 것을 나는 깨달았다. 그 결과로 얻어진 것이 바로 디지털 충돌의 물질적 변환이라 할 수 있는 이 *트론 체어*이다.

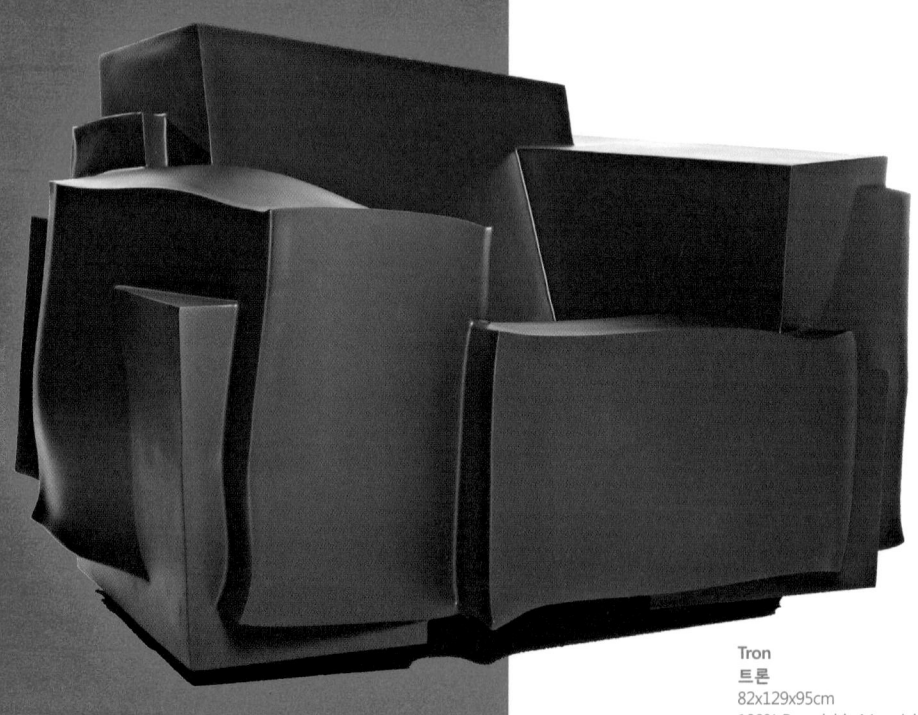

Tron
트론
82x129x95cm
100% Recyclable Material
100% 재활용 가능한 재료
Cappellini, Italy 카펠리니, 이탈리아
2011

The *Peacock Chair* started as a thought rooted in letting go, and the various ways one can. In dance, for example, you can fall forward, but you have to protect yourself. Or you can fall backwards and trust others to catch you. This duality also led me to think of the two opposing reasons a peacock opens its feathers – to attract a mate, or to defend itself from predators. I chose felt to represent this duality as it is a material that receives its integrity from the pressure of the folds, without which it would not have the structural integrity to hold a person. The chair has no glue, sewing, or any other traditional upholstery techniques.

Peacock
공작
90x110x90cm
Felt, metal 펠트, 금속
Cappellini, Italy 카펠리니, 이탈리아
2009

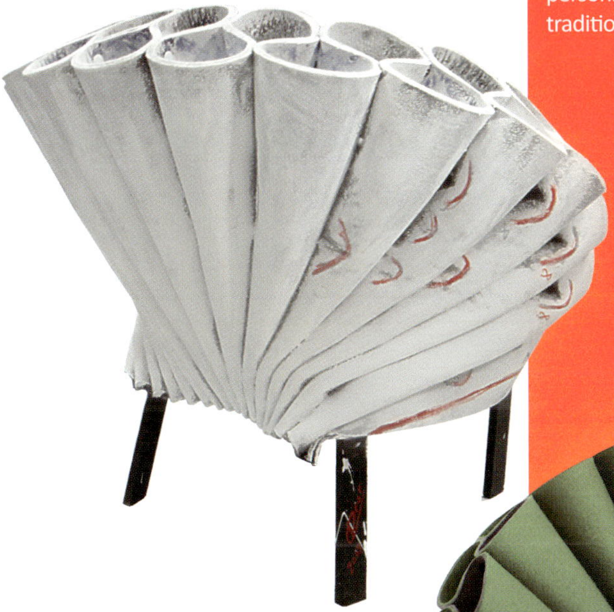

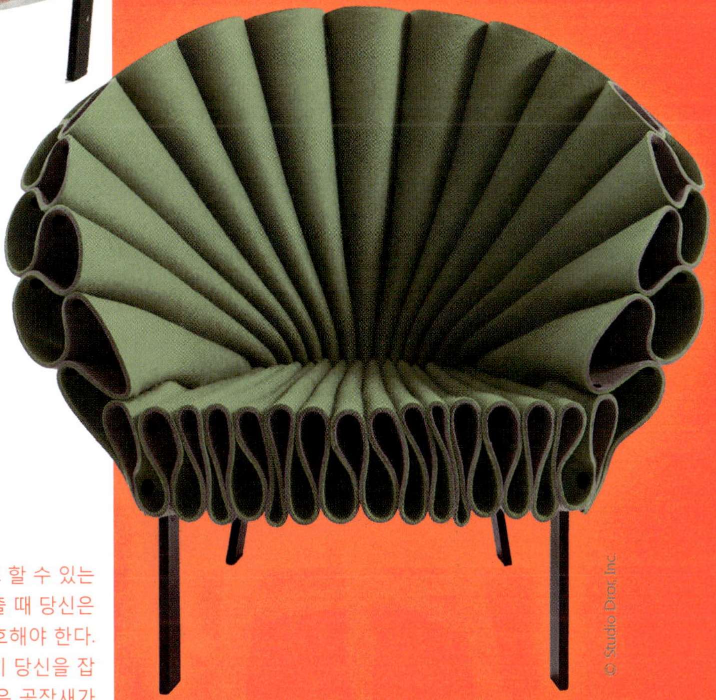

© Studio Diot Inc

공작 의자는 그저 내버려 두자는 생각, 그리고 할 수 있는 다양한 방법에서 시작했다. 예를 들어, 춤을 출 때 당신은 앞으로 넘어질 수도 있지만, 자기 자신을 보호해야 한다. 혹은 뒤로 넘어질 수도 있으며, 다른 사람들이 당신을 잡아줄 것이라 믿을 수도 있다. 이러한 이중성은 공작새가 깃털을 활짝 펼치는 두 가지의 대립적 이유-포식자로부터 자신을 보호하는 것, 그리고 짝짓기 상대를 유혹하기 위한 것-를 생각하게 한다. 나는 이러한 이중성을 표현하기 위해 펠트라는 재료를 선택했다. 이 의자를 제작하는 데에는 접착제, 재봉질, 혹은 다른 어떤 전통적인 업홀스터리 기법도 사용하지 않았다.

Guy Brown 가이 브라운

Constantly re-appropriating the everyday and found, Guy Brown works with known forms reinvestigating their function and materiality. Brown has a fascination with his national heritage through design, be it a lighthouse lamp, horse saddle stool or garden shed as garden furniture. Progressing from earlier work into creating hybrid, morphed forms with chairs, a new, on-going series of works take the familiar British plastic school chair as its point of departure.

매일의 일상을 끊임없이 다시 돌아보고 새롭게 발견하는 가이 브라운의 작업은 기능과 물질성을 재탐색하는 형태로 잘 알려져 있다. 브라운은 등대의 램프, 말의 안장, 혹은 정원 가구와 같은 디자인을 관통하는 조국의 문화유산에 깊이 매료되었다. 그는 초기 작업에서 발전하여, 혼종적이고 변형된 형태의 의자를 창작하게 되었으며, 현재 진행 중인 이 새로운 시리즈는 친근한 형태의 영국제 플라스틱 학교의자를 디자인의 출발점으로 삼는다.

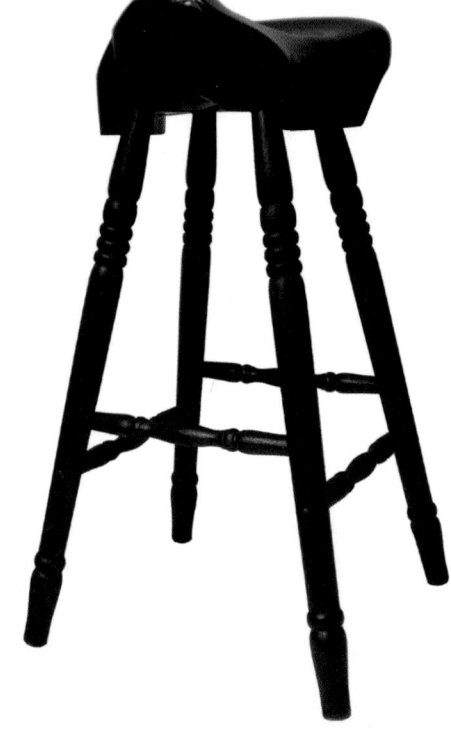

© Guy Brown

Horse Stool
말 스툴
59.5x35x35cm
Found wood and fiberglass 나무, 유리섬유
2009

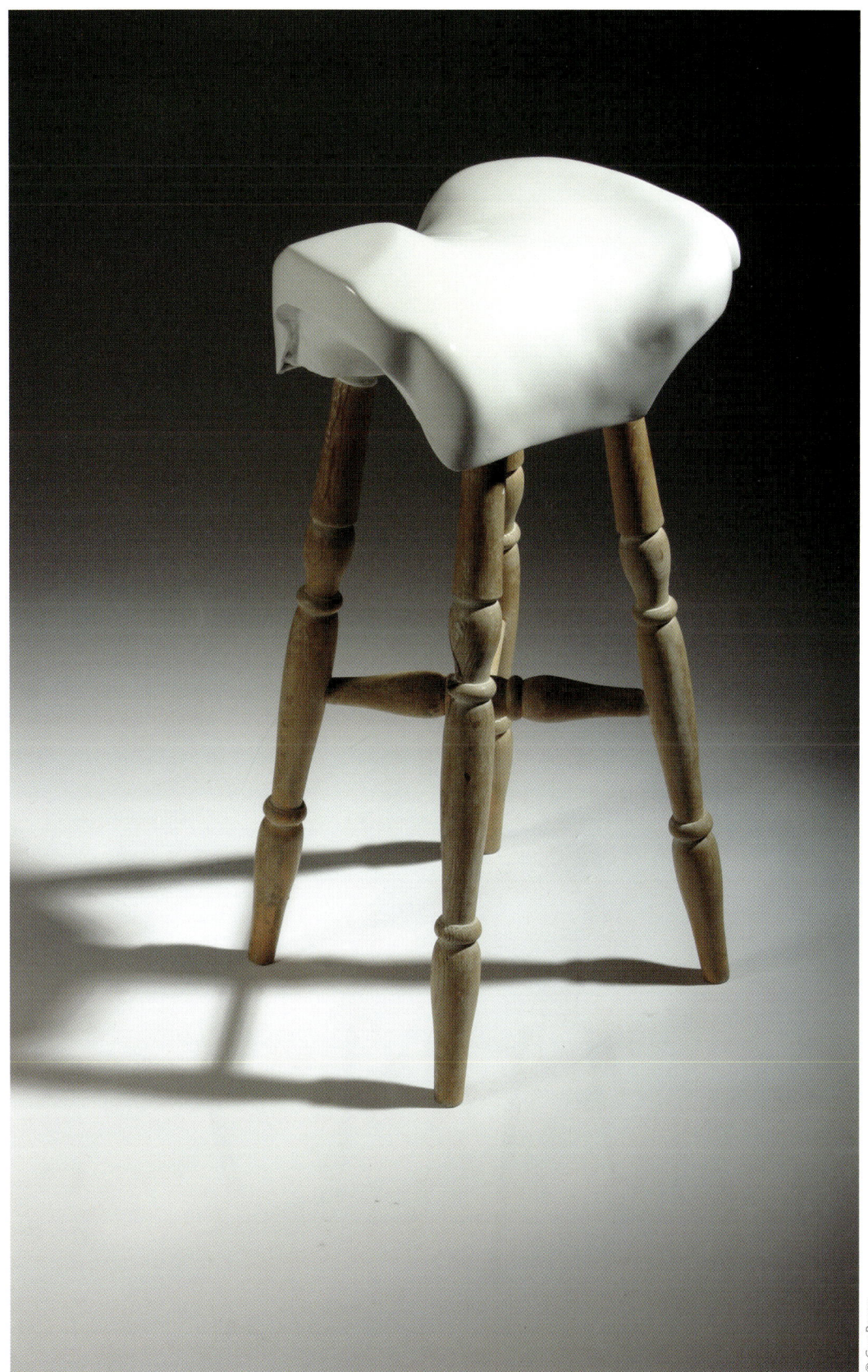

© Guy Brown

Beta Tank_Eyal Burstein
베타 탱크_아이알 벌스타인

The world of design fascinates me because it is so young and is simply waiting to be explored. As a designer I like to take regular, everyday objects and imbue them with a concept. My process for creating objects is always the same: I have a concept that excites and intrigues me, I research it, and then produce objects as a way to better understand the original idea, which results in further research. I have many reasons for using normal objects, such as chairs and tables. Firstly they have been with humans since early history and their presence is therefore ingrained in our minds. This means that I don't need to explain their use, which allows me to fully concentrate on the specific issue I'm concerned with - the idea that I am trying to get across to people. Secondly, when a well-known object like a chair is tweaked, the slightest alteration is instantly recognisable, making my idea very noticeable. Finally, an everyday object is reassuring to the viewer and ensures that the viewer will not be afraid of engaging with my objects. I want people to engage in my objects and have some kind of reaction to the concept.

디자인의 세계는 나를 매혹시킨다. 왜냐하면 그것은 젊디 젊으며, 탐구의 대상이 되기 때문이다. 나는 디자이너로서 평범한 일상의 사물들에 개념을 불어넣고 싶다. 오브제를 창작하는 나의 과정은 늘 같은 방식으로 이루어진다. 나는 흥미 있는 개념을 연구 하며, 원래의 아이디어를 더 잘 이해하기 위한 수단으로써 오브제를 제작한다. 이 오브제는 결국, 보다 발전된 연구가 된다.
내가 의자나 테이블 같은 일상의 사물들을 사용하는 데에는 많은 이유들이 있다. 첫째, 그들은 아주 오래 전부터 인류와 함께 해왔기 때문에 그것의 현존은 우리의 마음 속에도 존재한다. 이것은 내가 그것을 사용함에 있어 어떤 설명도 필요치 않다는 것을 의미하며, 내가 사람들을 통해 얻고자 하는 아이디어에 완전히 몰입하게 해준다. 둘째, 의자와 같이 익숙한 오브제는 약간이라도 변형된 경우, 그로 인한 미세한 변화가 즉각적이고 쉽게 인지된다. 나의 아이디어를 부각시키면서 말이다. 마지막으로, 일상의 사물들은 보는 이들을 안심시키고, 그들이 나의 오브제와 결부될 때 불안하지 않게 해준다. 나는 사람들이 나의 오브제에 몰입하고 그 개념에 반응하기를 원한다.

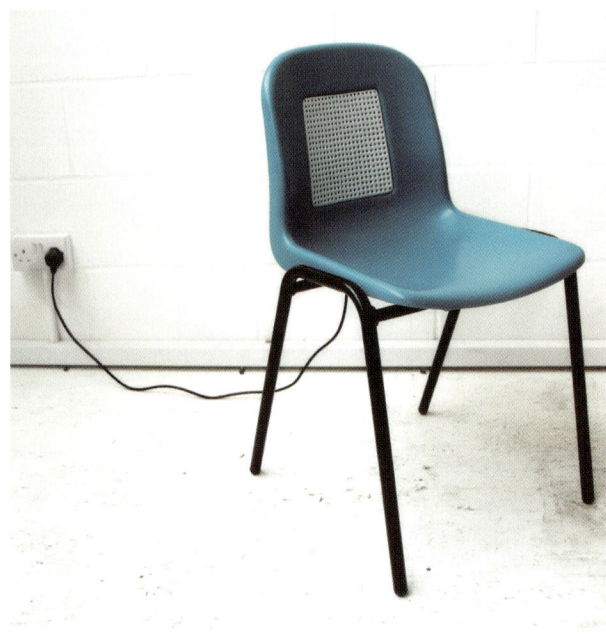

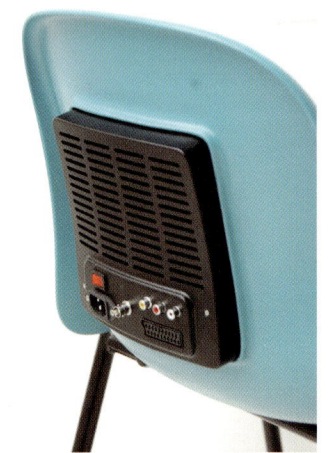

©Beta Tank

Mind Chair Polyprop(Beta Tank+Peter Marigold)
마인드 체어 폴리프롭(베타 탱크+피터 매리골드)
70x50x50cm
Fiberglass, steel and electronic components
섬유유리, 철, 전기부품
2007

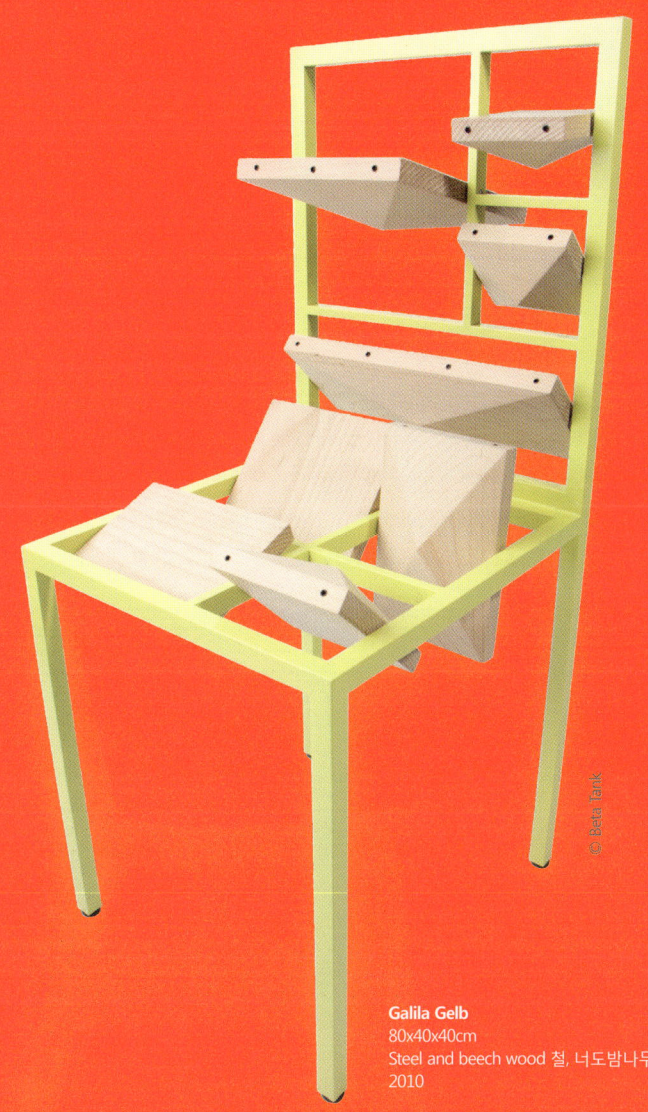

Galila Gelb
80x40x40cm
Steel and beech wood 철, 너도밤나무
2010

Choi, Joong Ho 최중호

2010년에 제작된 *바샤크*는 아이디얼그라피 프로젝트 일환으로서 서로 다른 느낌을 주는 대조적 이미지를 섞어 멋을 추구하는 믹스앤매치 스타일로 가구와 패션을 접목시킨 의자를 만들어내는 작업이었다. 가방의 구조와 사용성 그리고 가방이 가지고 있는 룩을 자연스럽게 느낄 수 있는 이 디자인은 사용자가 의자에 앉았을 때 가방을 맬 때와 같이 몸과 일체감을 주는 편안함을 느끼는데 중점을 두었다.

2010년에 제작된 *미려*는 인체공학을 반영해 사용자가 앉았을 때의 편안함을 느낄 수 있는 형태에 아름답고 고운 라인으로 최적화 시키는데 중점을 두고 디자인한 최중호의 첫 번째 의자이다. 미려는 한국고유어로 아름답고 고운이라는 뜻으로 형태에 있어 아름다운 라인의 연속성을 위해 피스별로 한 라인으로 이루어지게 제작하였고 두께와 무게를 줄여 형태의 섬세함을 느끼게 하였다.

유진영, 아이디얼그라피

The BACHAG produced in 2010 was a project of Idealgraphy to make chairs in which furniture and fashion were fused together in MIX & MATCH style; a style pursues a unique aesthetic effect by mixing elements in contrasting feelings. In this design users can naturally feel the bag's structure and usability. Not only for looks, the designer also focused on comfort from a sense of unity so that users can feel the same way, whether or not they have bags on them when they are seated on the chairs.

The Mi-Ryeoh in 2010 was the first chair that Choi, Joong Ho designed focusing on its optimization of beautiful lines and forms for user's comfort by adopting ergonomics. "Miryeoh", meaning "beautiful and lovely" in the Korean native tongue, was produced to keep a single line in its form through pieces for the continuity of beautiful lines and holds a formative delicacy by reducing thickness and weight.

Yoo, Jin Young, Idealgraphy

Mi-Ryeo
미려
90x60x66cm
Wood 나무
2010

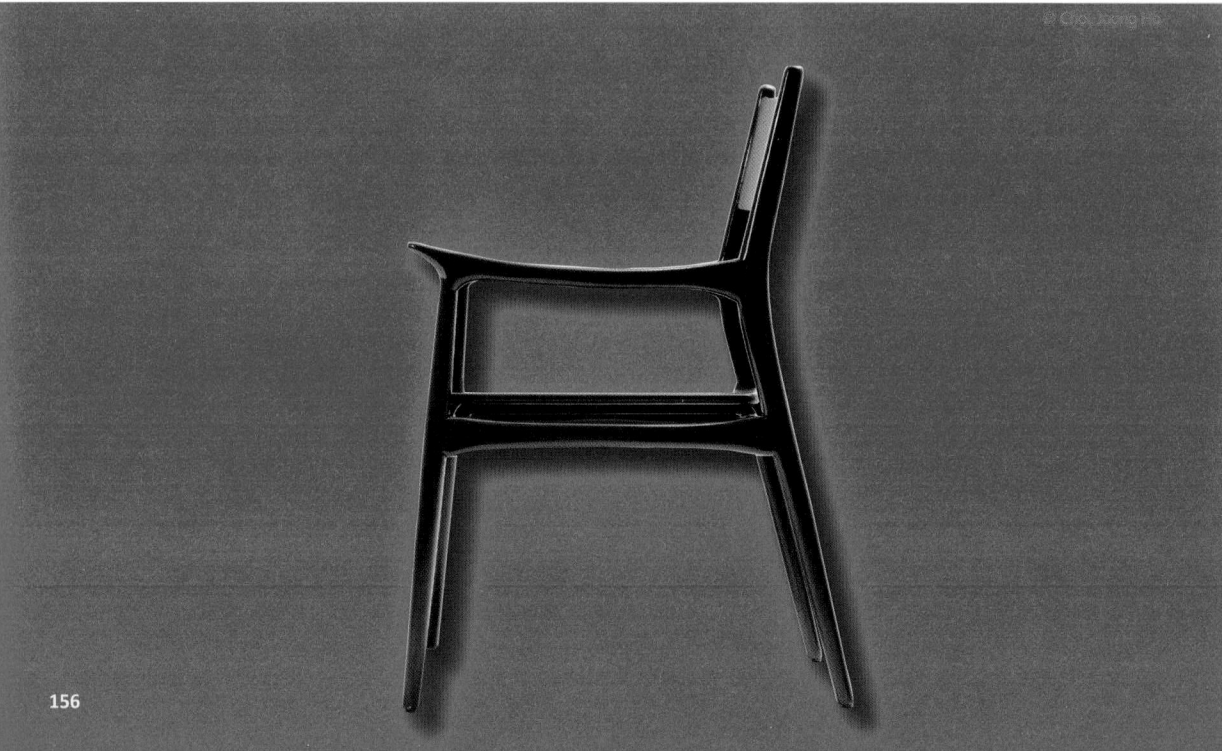

Bachag
바샤크
79x48x45cm
Wood, aluminium 나무, 알루미늄
2010

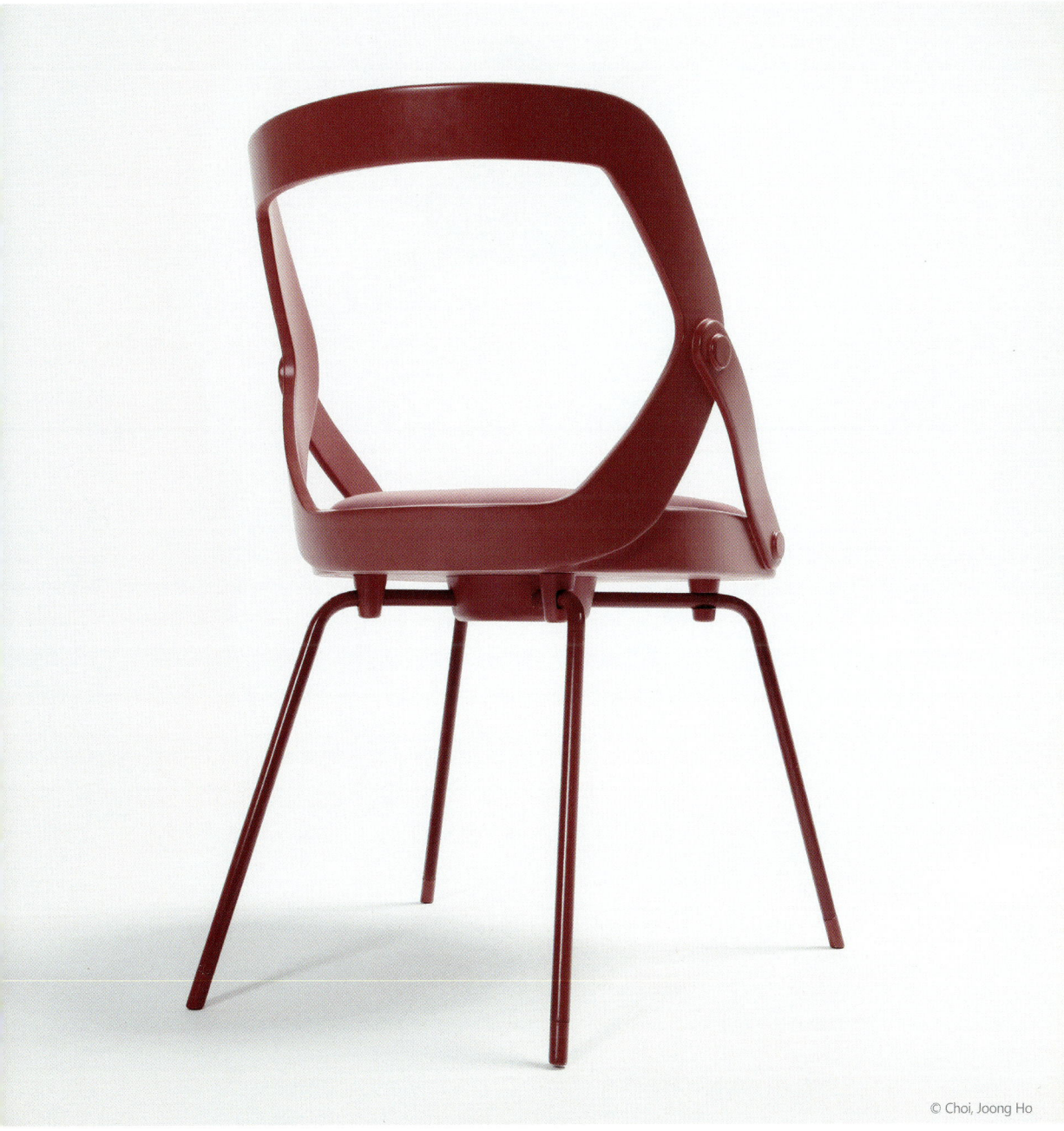

© Choi, Joong Ho

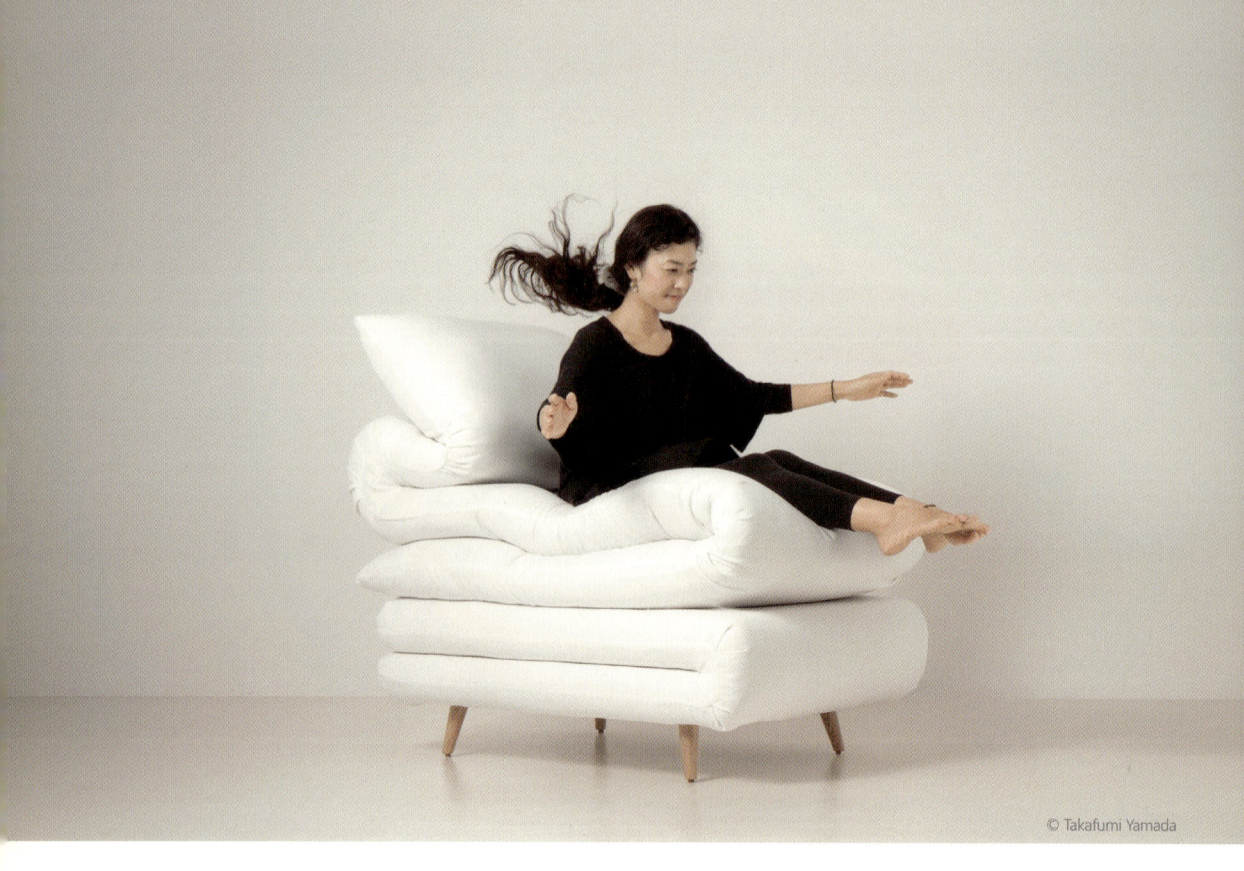

© Takafumi Yamada

Japan | 일본

Motogi Daisuke 모토기 다이스케

A chair as a FUTON (japanese kind of BED) which provides a space of warmth and happiness.
따뜻하고 행복한 공간을 선사하는 후통(일본식 잠자리)으로서의 의자

Sleepy chair
졸음이 오는 의자
95x110x70cm
Cover : Cotton, polyester 커버: 면, 폴리에스테르
Legs : Tamo Clear finish 다리: 들메나무
2011

Lost in Sofa
소파 속 분실물
70x90x70cm
Cover : Sweat shirts material 커버: 스웨터 소재
Inner side: AC100% 내부: AC100%
2010

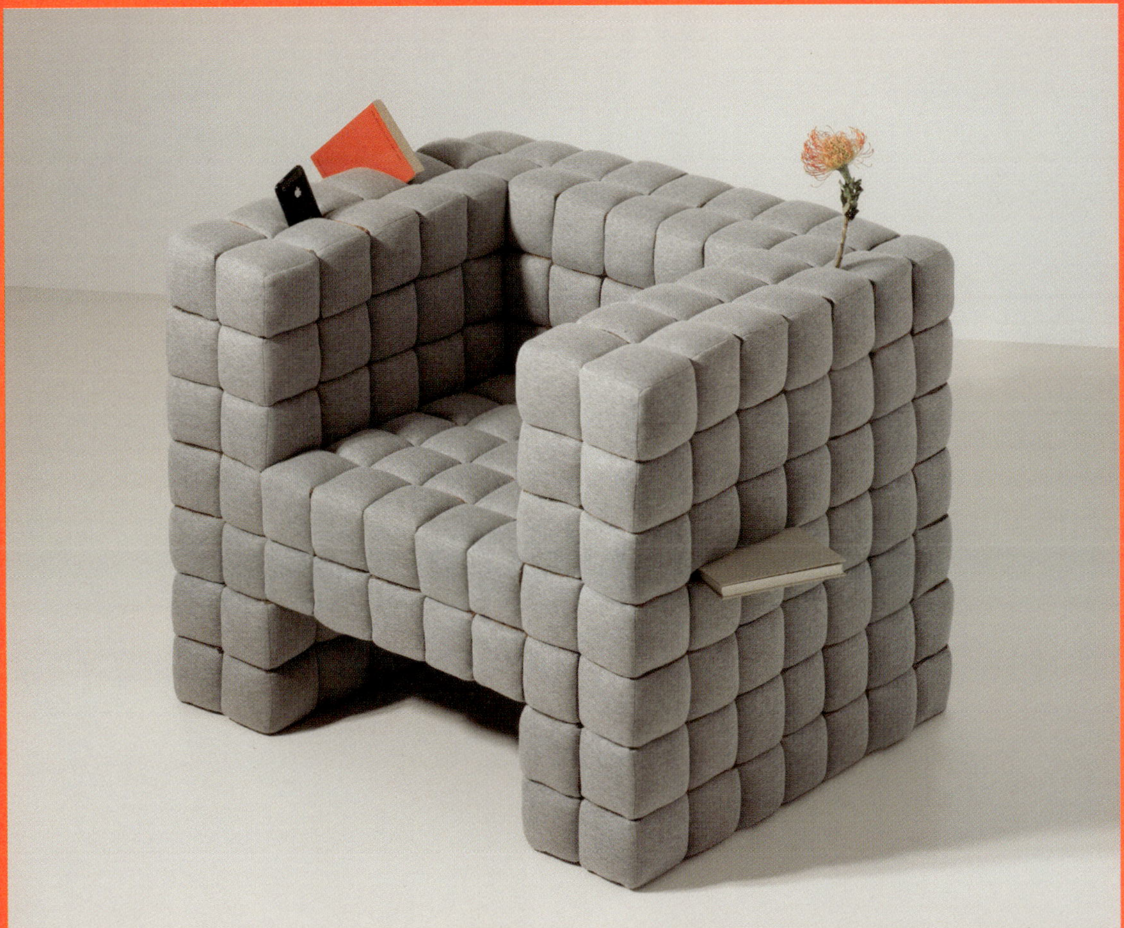

© Takafumi Yamada

Things often get lost under the sofa. It's ordinary for a coin which slipped out of your pocket, or a never-to-be-found remote to be accidentally found in between/underneath the sofa cushions.
Maybe you'll find a forgotten 10,000yen bill that you once hid there...

종종 물건들이 소파 밑으로 사라진다. 주머니에서 떨어진 동전이나, 절대로 찾을 수 없었던 리모콘이 소파의 쿠션 밑이나 그 사이에서 우연히 발견되곤 한다.
당신은 아마도 숨겨져 있던, 잃어버린 만엔짜리 지폐를 찾아낼지도 모른다...

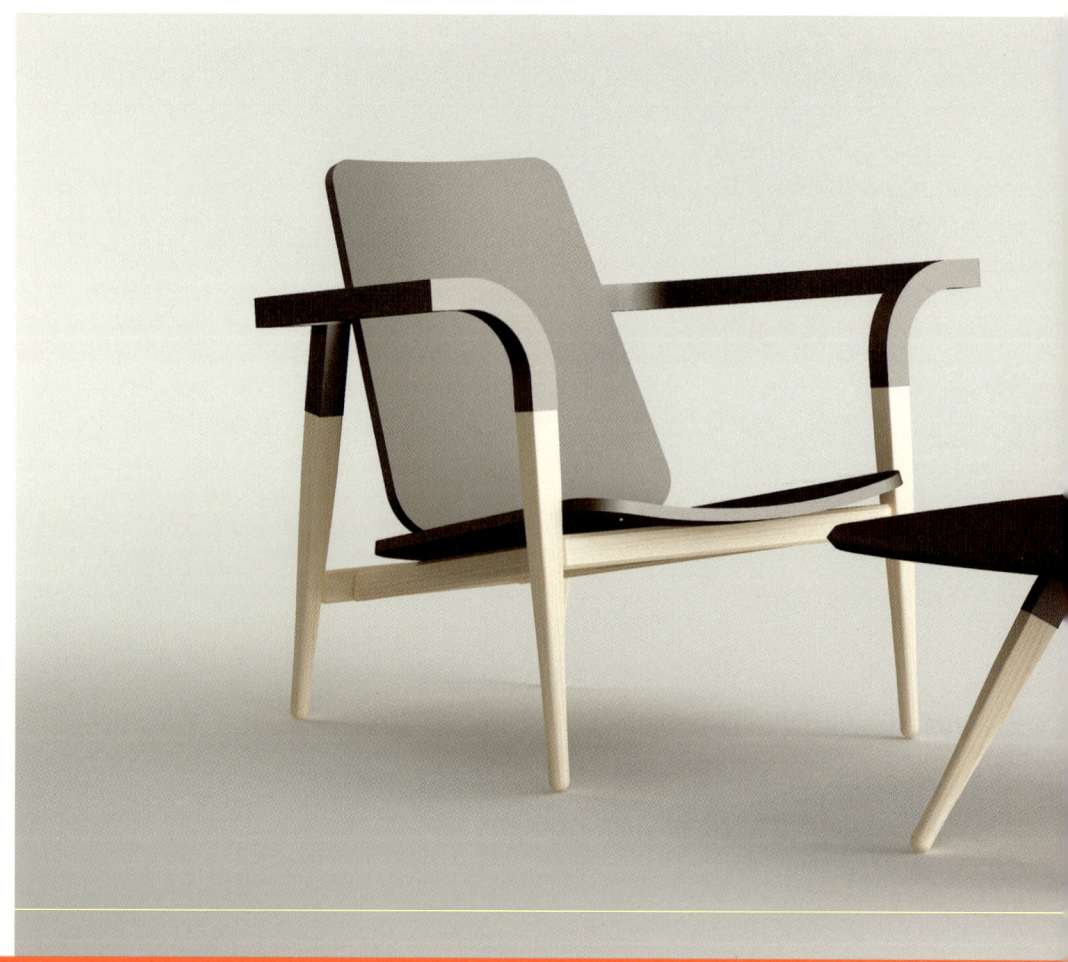

dialoguemethod 다이얼로그메스드

자신을 둘러싼 생활환경에서 영감과 아이디어를 얻는 디자이너 조형석은, 낯선 동네를 여행하고 지하철 플랫폼에서 사람들을 관찰하고 무작정 거리를 걸으며 서울에서 살아가는 이들의 다양한 삶을 경험한다. 가구와 제품 디자인을 하는 그는, 디자인이란 어렵고 대단한 것이 아니라 그것을 생활에서 사용하는 사람들과 '대화'하는 매체 혹은 매개로서의 언어라고 생각한다.

그렇다면 그의 디자인 제1원칙은 무엇일까. "실용성을 가장 기본으로 해요. 의자를 예로 들면, 외형보다 구조를 만드는 작업을 먼저 해요. 의자 디자인을 할 때 경험적인 요소를 담으려고 하는데, 돌아다니며 많은 의자에 앉아보고 뒤집어보고 뜯어도 보며 구조를 살펴요. 그리고 그 의자들과 아주 많이 다르지 않지만 무언가 악센트가 있는 정도의 변화를 시도해요."

"가구 디자인만큼은 그 누구보다 진지하게, 제품 디자인은 그 무엇보다 재미있게"를 모토로 디자인하는 조형석은 다이얼로그메스드 스튜디오 헤드 디자이너로 활동 중이고 국내외 디자인계와 매거진에서 주목해야 할 젊은 디자이너로 선정된 바 있다. 디자인이란 어렵고 대단한 일이 아니라 "무엇인가 느낄 수 있다면, 그 누구라도 디자이너가 될 수 있다."고 그는 생각한다. 그러므로 중요한 것은 세상과 사람과 만나는 일이다. 조형석이 묻는다. "당신의 대화 방식은 무엇인가?"

장남미, j.j. magazine, 서울, 2010

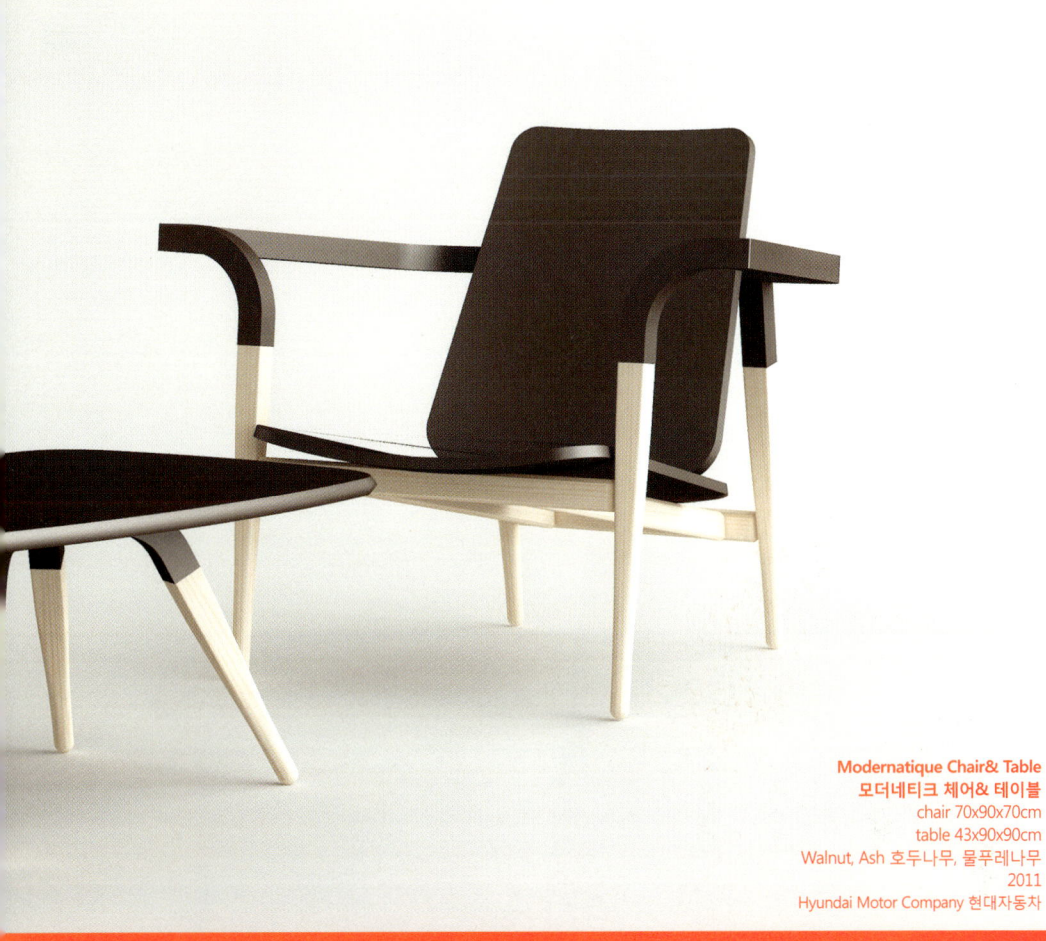

Modernatique Chair& Table
모더네티크 체어& 테이블
chair 70x90x70cm
table 43x90x90cm
Walnut, Ash 호두나무, 물푸레나무
2011
Hyundai Motor Company 현대자동차

The designer, Cho, Hyung Suk is inspired and acquires ideas from his own surroundings. He experiences the various lives of diverse people in Seoul when traveling in unfamiliar areas, like observing people on the subway platforms, and walking on the streets with no definite plans. As a designer of furniture and products, he believes that design is neither difficult nor great, but another language as a medium or a connector of conversation with those who use it in their daily lives.

If so, what is his foremost principle of design? He states, "I always give priority to the practicality of design. While making a chair, for example, I begin working on its structure rather than its appearance. Trying to use empirical elements, I get around sitting on as many chairs as possible and observing their structures in detail. Then I attempt a slight change with my own accent even though it would not be very different from other chairs."

With a motto that "more seriously than anyone else for furniture design, but more exciting than anyone else for product design," Cho, Hyung Suk is currently working as a head designer at Dialoguemethod studio in Korea, and once chosen as a designer to whom both domestic and international design magazines should pay attention. He believes that design is not a difficult and great thing, but "any individual can be a designer if he or she can feel something". Therefore, what is important for him is that the world and human beings meet each other. Cho, Hyung Suk asks, "What is your communication method?"

Chang, Nam Mi, j.j. magazine, Seoul, 2010

Netherlands | 네덜란드

Piet Hein Eek 피트 하인 이크

Dutch designer Piet Hein Eek is best known for his intricately composed scrap wood furniture—each piece a one-of-a-kind creation that merges artisan handcraft with skilled design processes.
But while his use of reclaimed materials has been widely recognized in the recent wave of sustainable design fandom, Eek has been working with scrap since well before the green boom, and his motivation arises as much from an obsession with time as a concern for resources.

네덜란드 디자이너 피트 하인 이크는 버려진 나무 조각들을 복잡하게 구성한 가구로 유명한데, 그의 작품 하나하나는 디자인의 과정이 잘 숙련된 장인이라고 할 수 있는 작가의 수작업으로 이루어진 창조물이다. 최근 지속 가능한 디자인에 관심이 있는 이들 사이에서 그가 버려진 나무 조각을 사용한다는 사실이 잘 알려져 있지만, 사실 그는 자연친화적 디자인이 유행하기 이전부터 나무조각들을 사용하여 작업을 하기 시작했고, 이는 자원에 대한 우려보다는 시간의 흐름이 녹아있는 것에 대한 그의 집착 때문이었다.

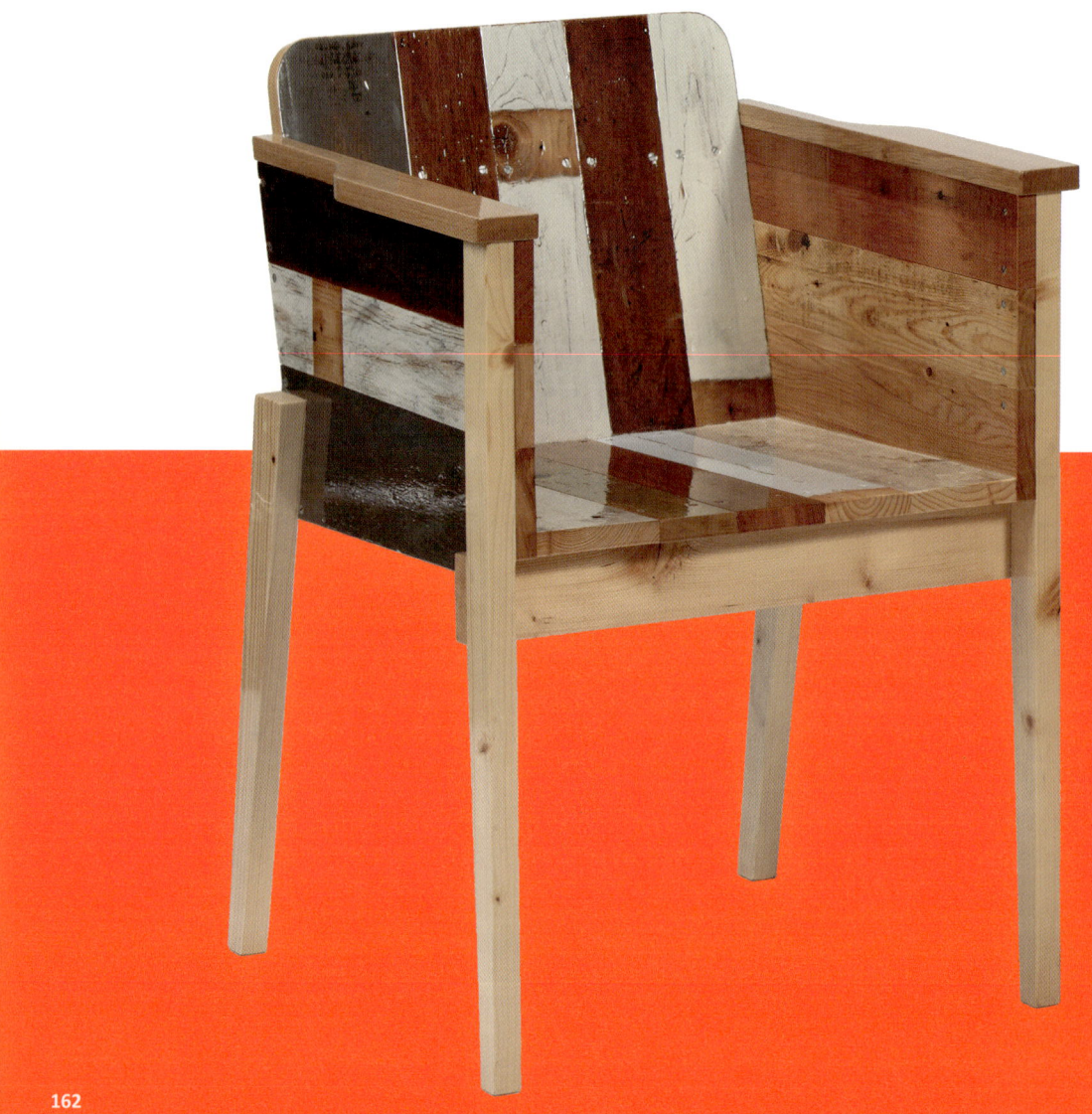

Oak Chair in Scrap Wood
나무 조각으로 만든 오크 체어
80x37x47cm
Scrap Wood 나무 조각
2011

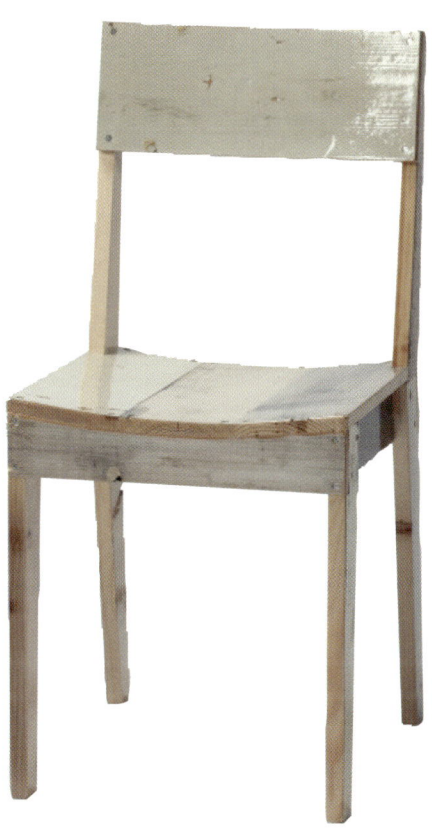

←
Bucket Seat in Scrap Wood
나무 조각으로 만든 일인용 의자
86x58x62cm
Scrap Wood 나무 조각
2011

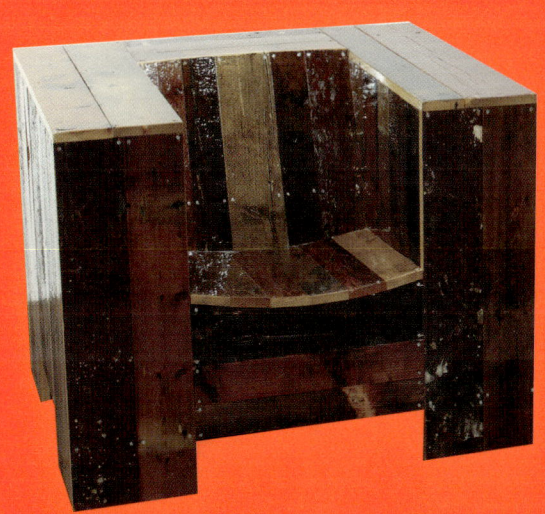
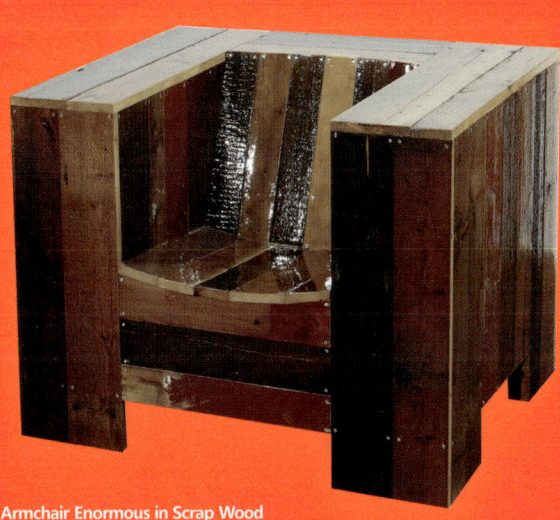

Armchair Enormous in Scrap Wood
나무 조각으로 만든 커다란 팔걸이 의자
76x98x90cm
Scrap Wood 나무 조각
2011

163

Guido Garotti from Life Given A Shape
귀도 가로티 From Life Given A Shape

My design activity is nurtured through the wish of creating environments in a direct relationship with the user and in balance with his/her daily existence. When I design I study shapes, materials and manufactures in order to encourage a psychological symbiosis between person and object; I take advantage of those principles found to be valid arguments for emotional durability. Due to this fundamental attention to their semantic properties, the objects I design have strong character and narrative potential. Most of my new ideas come from theoretical research and travels. On one hand I'm fascinated by cognitive sciences whose findings inform my narrative approach on design; on the other, traveling broadens my mind supplying new inputs and highlighting cultural diversity.

In addition, through my projects I like to feature highly skilled craftspeople and make use of high quality regional materials and local technologies. These values and principles form the foundation for all my projects and the brand 'Life Given A Shape' which houses my current and future work.

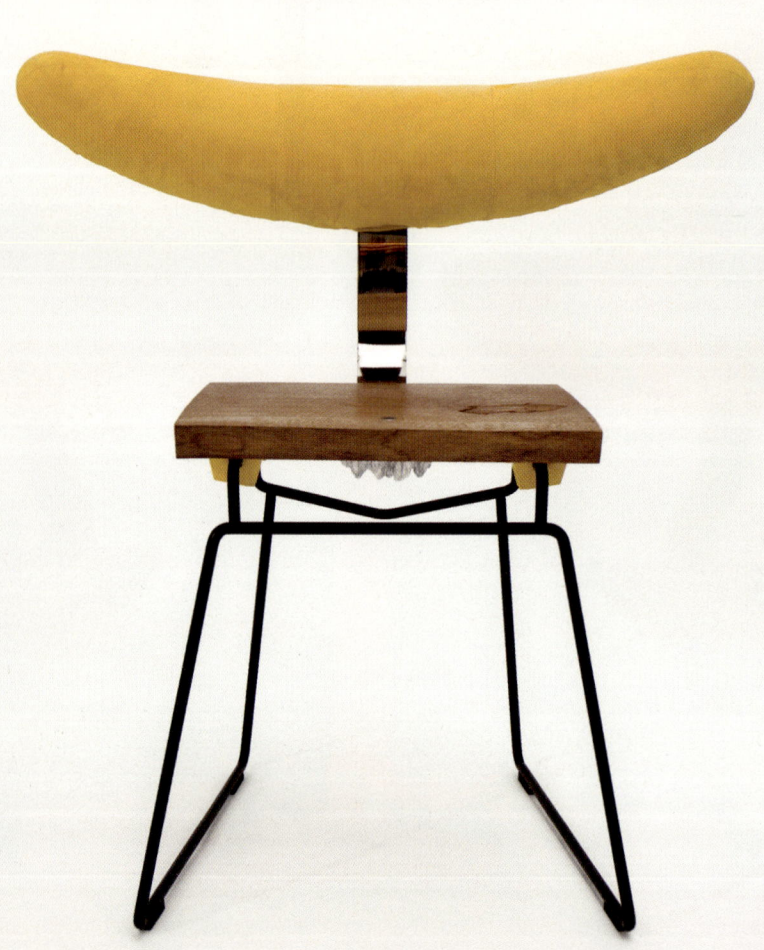

©Guido Garotti

나는 사용자와의 직접적인 관계를 맺는 환경을 창조하고자 하는 소망, 그리고 사용자의 매일의 실존과 균형을 맞추고자 하는 소망 속에 디자인 작업을 한다. 디자인할 때 나는 형태, 재료, 그리고 제품을 연구한다. 그것은 개인과 대상 사이의 심리학적 공생을 고무하기 위한 것이다. 이처럼 나는 정서적으로 지속적인 효과를 주는 원리들을 이용하곤 한다. 내가 디자인한 제품들은 의미론적 속성에 주로 집중했기 때문에 강한 특징과 서사적(narrative)잠재력을 갖는다. 나는 대부분의 새로운 아이디어들을 이론적 탐구나 여행을 하면서 얻는다. 한편으로 나는 인지 과학에 매료되어 있다. 그것은 디자인에 대한 나의 서사적 접근법에 도움을 준다. 다른 한편으로 여행은 내 마음을 넓혀주며, 새로운 것들을 알게 해주고, 문화적 다양성을 강조해준다.

또한 나는 내 프로젝트들을 통해 매우 숙련된 장인들을 다루고 싶다. 그리고 양질의 토산품들 및 지역의 기술들을 이용하고 싶다. 이러한 가치들 및 원리들은 나의 모든 프로젝트들 그리고 나의 현재 및 미래의 작품들에 거처를 제공하는 브랜드 <형태를 갖춘 인생(Life Given A Shape)>의 토대를 형성한다.

Individuale
각각의
88x88x67cm
Oak, suede leather, steel, aluminium, polyurethane foam
오크나무, 스웨이드 가죽, 철, 알루미늄, 폴리우레탄폼
2010

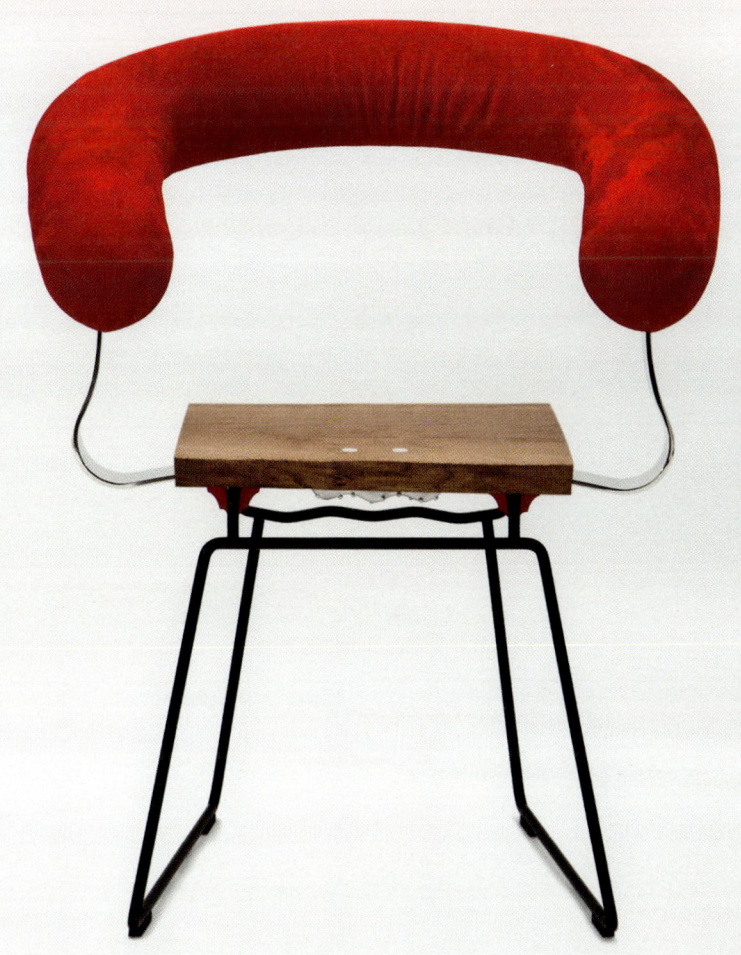

©Guido Garotti

Konstantin Grcic 콘스탄틴 그리치치

The team at Konstantin Grcic's studio collaborated with the Italian manufacturer Plank and chemical company BASF to create the *MYTO* chair. Reinterpreting the typology of the iconic cantilever chair, the *MYTO* was designed utilising BASF's engineered plastics and explored the potential of the material Untradur® High Speed (PBT - polybutylene terephtlate). Its extraordinary consistency, strength, viscosity and thermoforming abilities meant that the fluid plastic could be injected into a monoblock. *MYTO* represents an important breakthrough with regard to material utilised, manufacturing technique employed and the formal characteristics of the end product.

콘스탄틴 그리치치 스튜디오 팀은 *마이토 체어*를 만들기 위해, 이태리 제조업체인 플랭크 그리고 화학 회사 BASF 와 손을 잡았다. *마이토 체어*는 기존의 캔틸레버 의자들의 전형적 형태들을 재해석하여 BASF사에서 제조된 플라스틱을 이용하여 디자인되었고, 폴리부틀렌 테레프텔 염산 (Untradur® High Speed – PBT)의 재료적 가능성을 탐구하였다. 이 재료의 뛰어난 견고성, 단단함, 점성과 열성화의 능력들은 액화 플라스틱이 단일 주조 틀에 주입될 수 있다는 것을 의미했다. *마이토 체어*는 재료의 사용, 제조 기술의 채택, 그리고 최종 산물의 형태적 특징들과 관련해서 중요한 돌파구를 보여준다.

© Design Museum, London

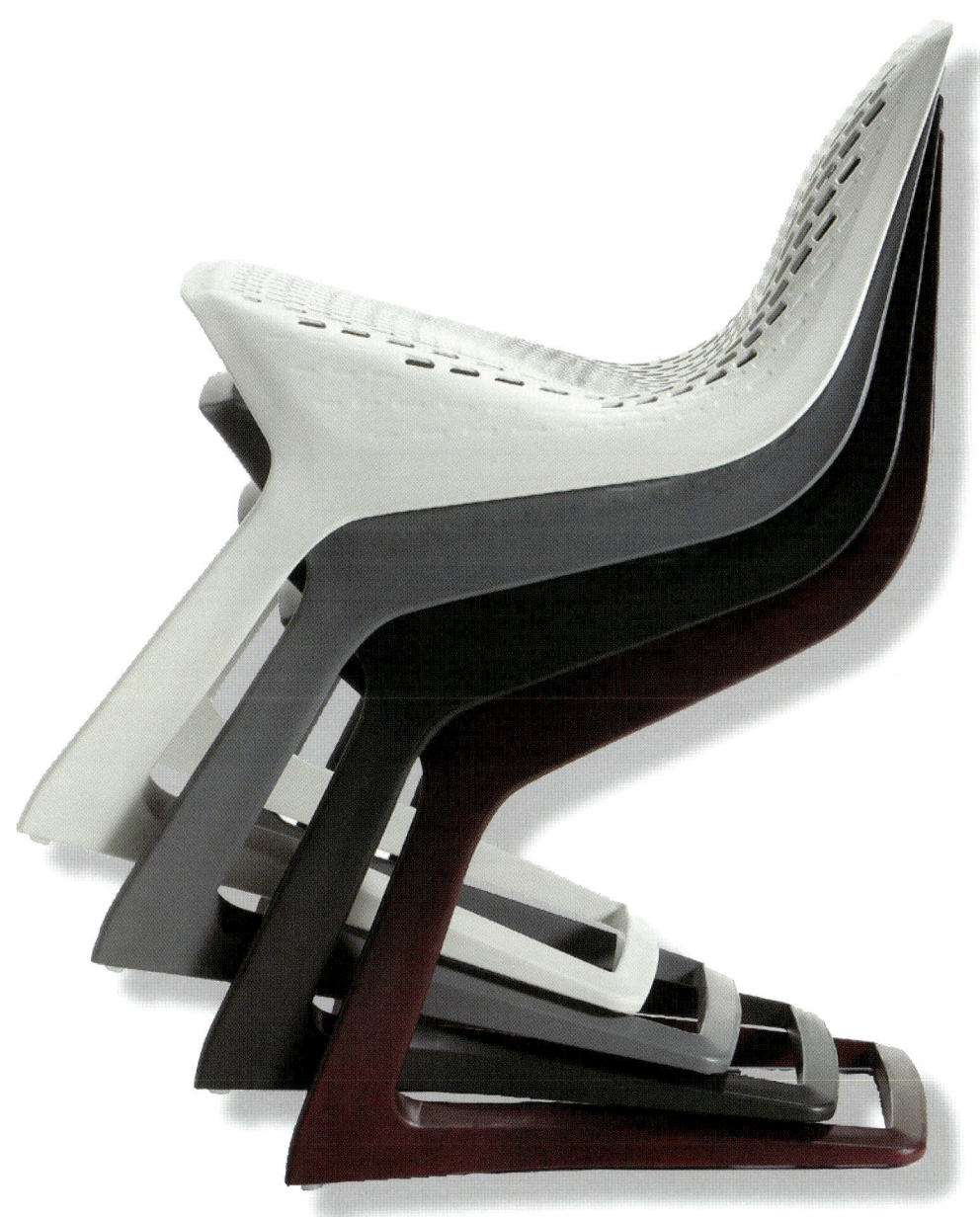

Myto Chair
마이토 체어
82x51x55cm
Untradur® High Speed (Polybutylene Terephtlate) 공업 플라스틱
Konstantin Grcic, Plank, and BASF, Germany
콘스탄틴 그리치치, 플랭크 & BASF, 독일
2009

h220430

We wanted to design not just primary shape of the things but secondary communication deriving from the messages in the things. We hope our works will produce communication and provide an "opportunity" for people to rethink and act against many difficult problems such as deterioration of the global environment and continuous conflicts all over the world.

우리는 단지 사물의 기본적인 형태를 디자인하는 것이 아니다. 그 사물들에 내재한 메시지에서 비롯되는 2차적인 커뮤니케이션을 디자인하고자 한다. 우리는 우리의 작업이 소통을 만들어내기를 원한다. 또한 작품을 통해 환경오염과 끊임없이 계속되는 전 지구적 분쟁과 같이 수많은 어려운 문제들에 대해 다시 생각하고 행동할 수 있는 "기회"를 제공하기를 원한다.

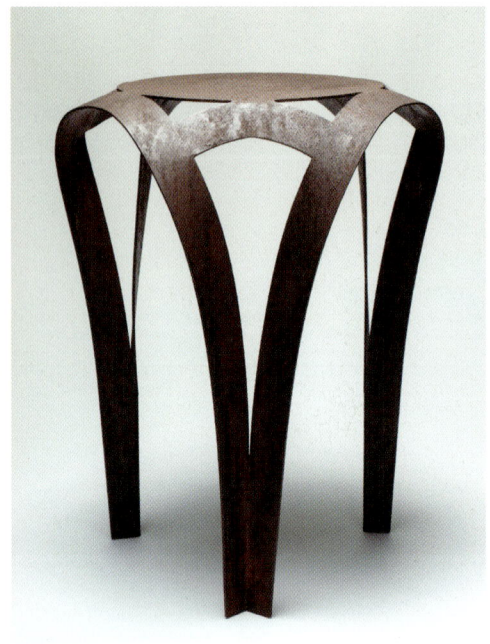

Schwarzwald Stool
검은 숲
42xØ 30cm
Steel 철
2010

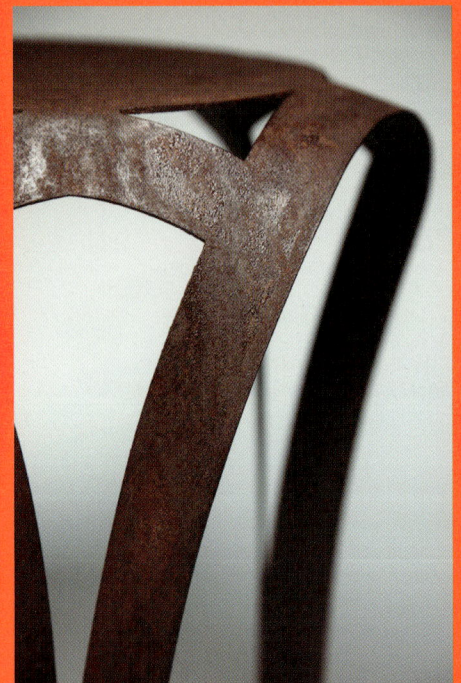

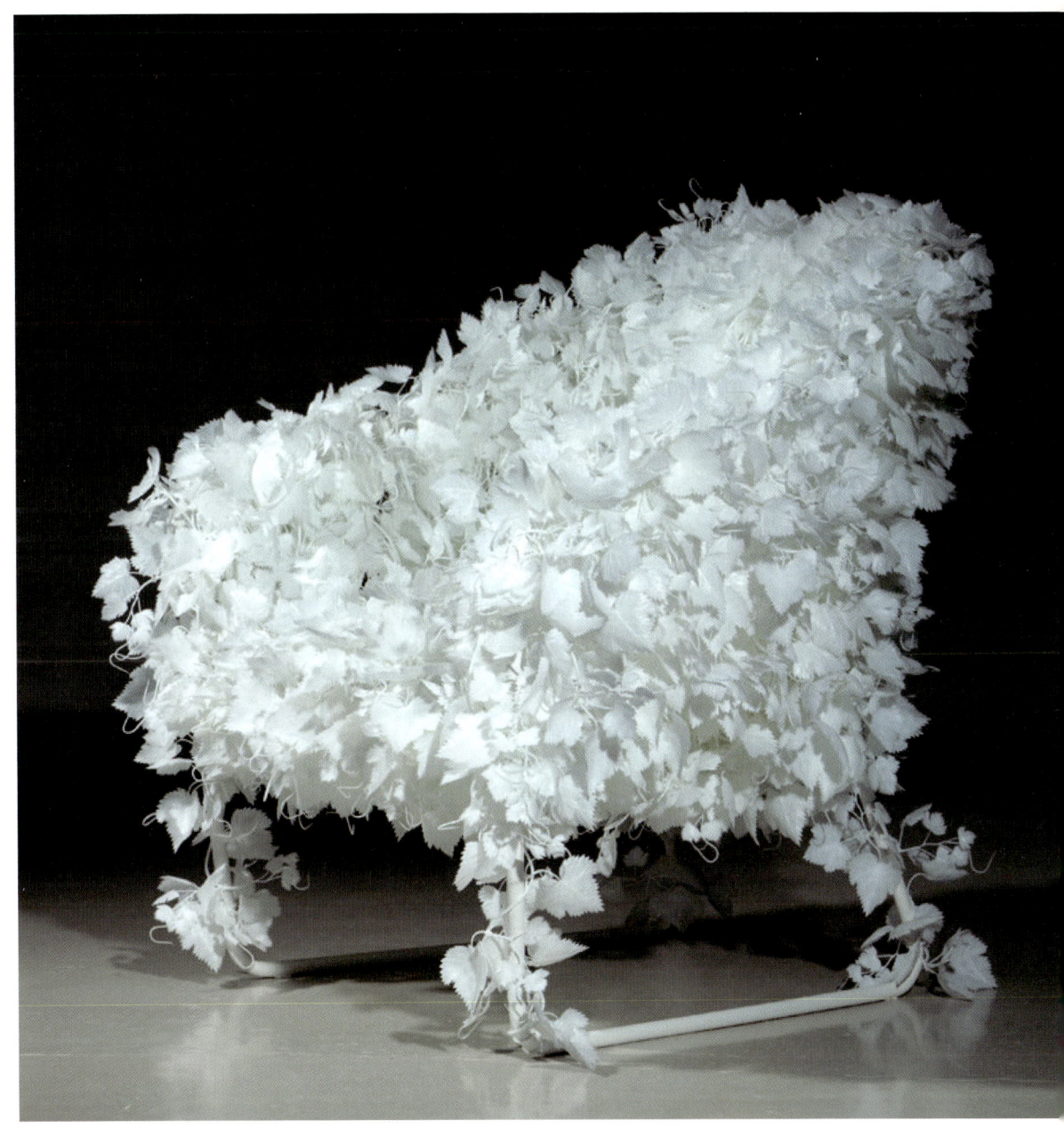

Ivy Chair
담쟁이덩굴 의자
75x63x67cm
Frame steel, polyethylene 철, 폴리에틸렌
2010
Gallery SOMEWHERE

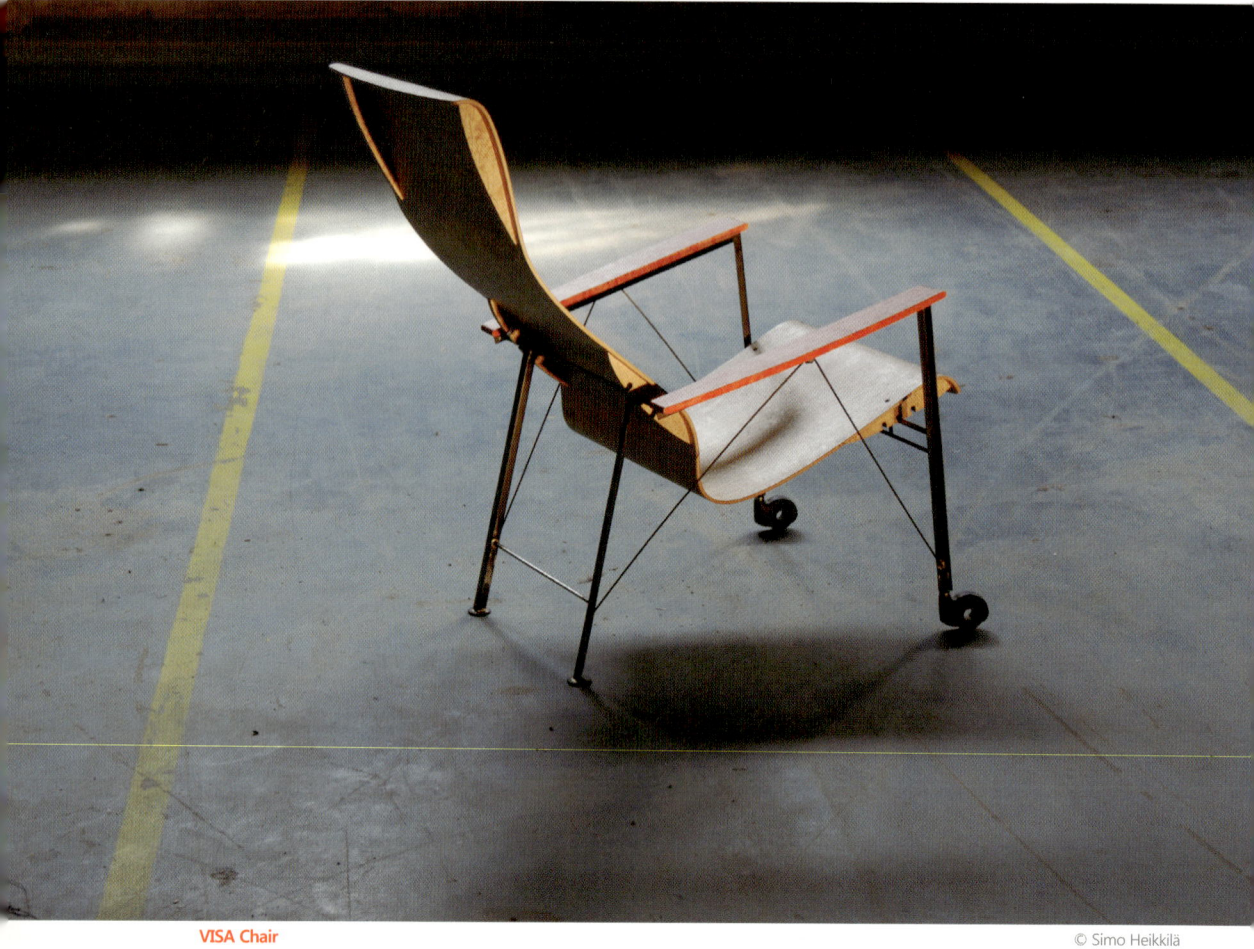

VISA Chair
80x50x90cm
Laminated birch and steel, red stain
자작나무합판, 철, 빨강색 스테인
1991

© Simo Heikkilä

Finland | 핀란드

Simo Heikkilä 시모 헤이낄라

In his design Simo Heikkilä concentrates on three parametres: the detail, the structure and the visible concept which collectively shape the totality. He often starts out with some small, modest detail, then advances to a larger scale, further dialogue with the structure and, as a result, the general form becomes clear. That detail "though it plays the main part, is not always a conspicuous one" as he says. Inconspicuous is the intriguing hallmark of higher caliber design.

Tapio Periäinen, tech.dr. former director of Finnish Design Forum

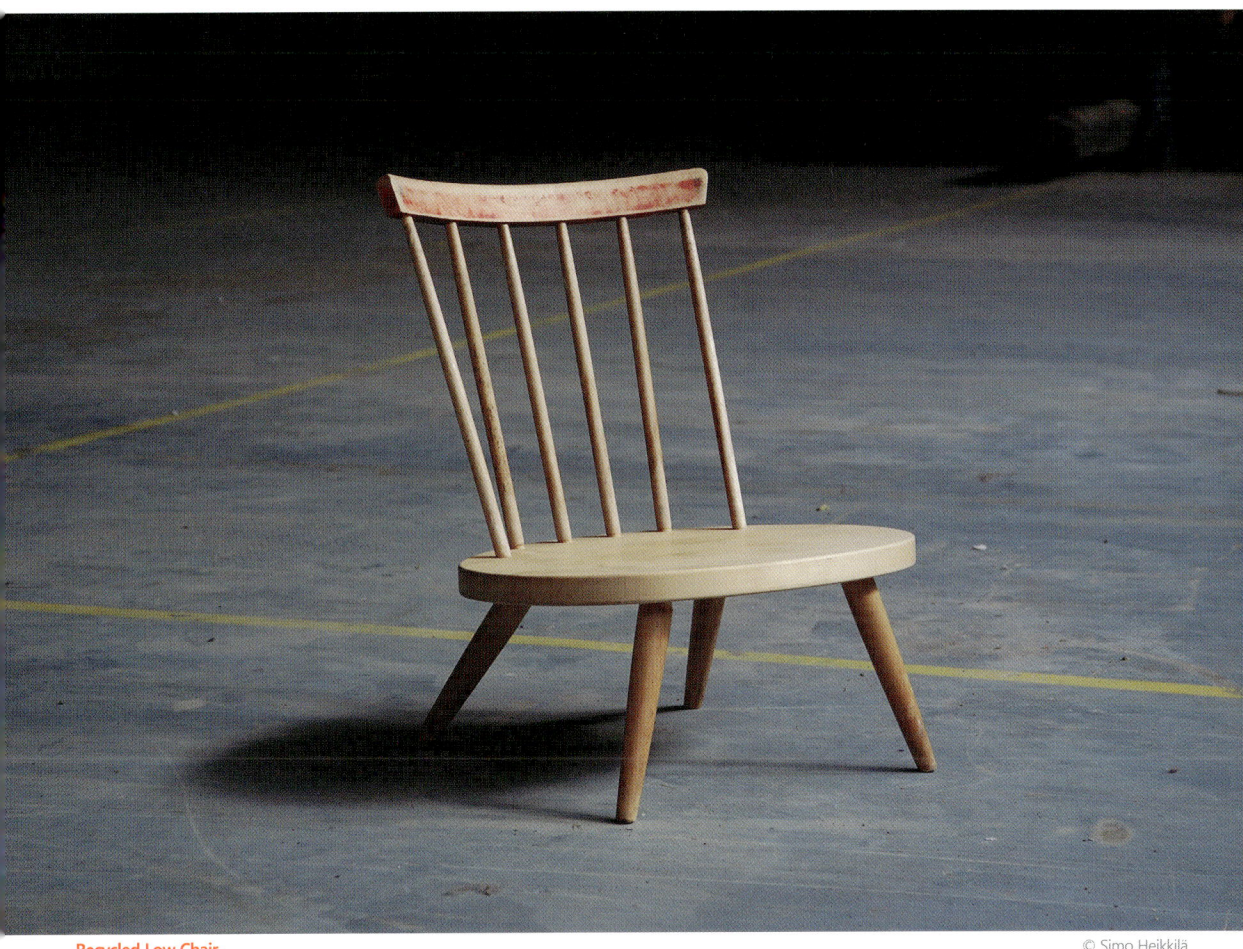

Recycled Low Chair
재활용 앉은뱅이 의자
60x40x50cm
Birch 자작나무
2006

© Simo Heikkilä

시모 헤이낄라는 디자인을 할 때 디테일, 구조, 그리고 가시적인 개념, 세 가지 요소에 집중하는데, 이들이 모여 전체적인 형태를 완성한다. 그는 주로 작고 사소한 디테일에서 시작하여 보다 커다란 스케일, 즉, 구조를 가진 담론으로 발전시키며, 그 결과 막연했던 형태는 명확하게 가시적으로 드러나게 된다. 그에 따르면 눈에 잘 띄는 것만이 중요한 역할을 하는 것은 아니다. 잘 드러나지 않는 것이 뛰어난 디자인의 흥미로운 특징이 될 수 있다.

타피오 페리아이넨, 전 핀란드 디자인 포럼 디렉터

Pepe Heykoop 페페 헤이콥

The *Brickchair* is a reaction on this drawing
I fell in love with the image immediately. The chair
up left in the corner caught my eye.
From now on I could only think of bricks when
looking at the picture.
I colored the image.
So the *Brickchair* is the interpretation of a drawing,
which was already an interpretation of an old
existing chair. It transformed twice and ended up
in bricks.
We see different things in the same image.

블록 *의자*는 다음 드로잉에 대한 하나의 반응이다.
나는 즉시 그 이미지에 빠져들었고, 그 의자는 나를 사로
잡았다.
이제부터 그림을 볼 때 나는 오직 블록만을 생각할 수밖
에 없었다.
나는 그 이미지에 색을 입혔다.
따라서 *블록 의자*는 드로잉에 대한 해석이며, 그 드로잉
은 이미 오래된 의자에 대한 해석이었다.
즉, 오래된 의자에서 드로잉으로, 드로잉에서 *블록 의자*
로, 두 차례에 걸쳐 변형되었고 마침내 블록이 되었다.
우리는 똑 같은 이미지에서 서로 다른 것들을 본다.

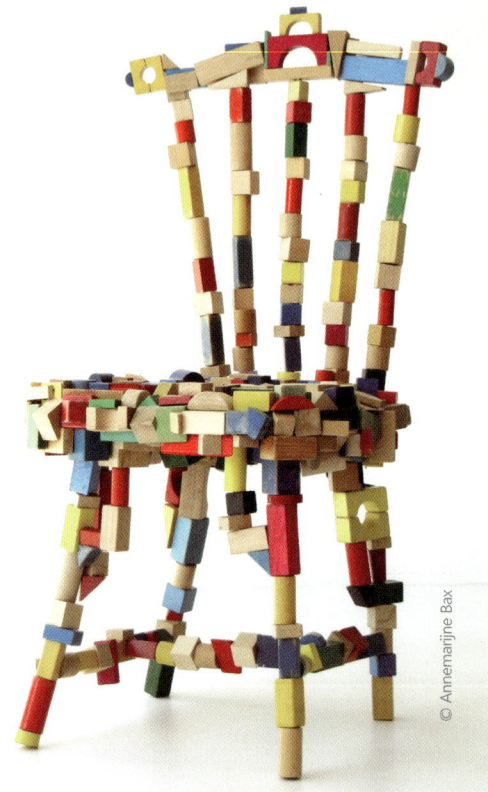

Brick Chair
블록 의자
80x45x45cm
Wood, metal 나무, 금속
2009

© Annemarijne Bax

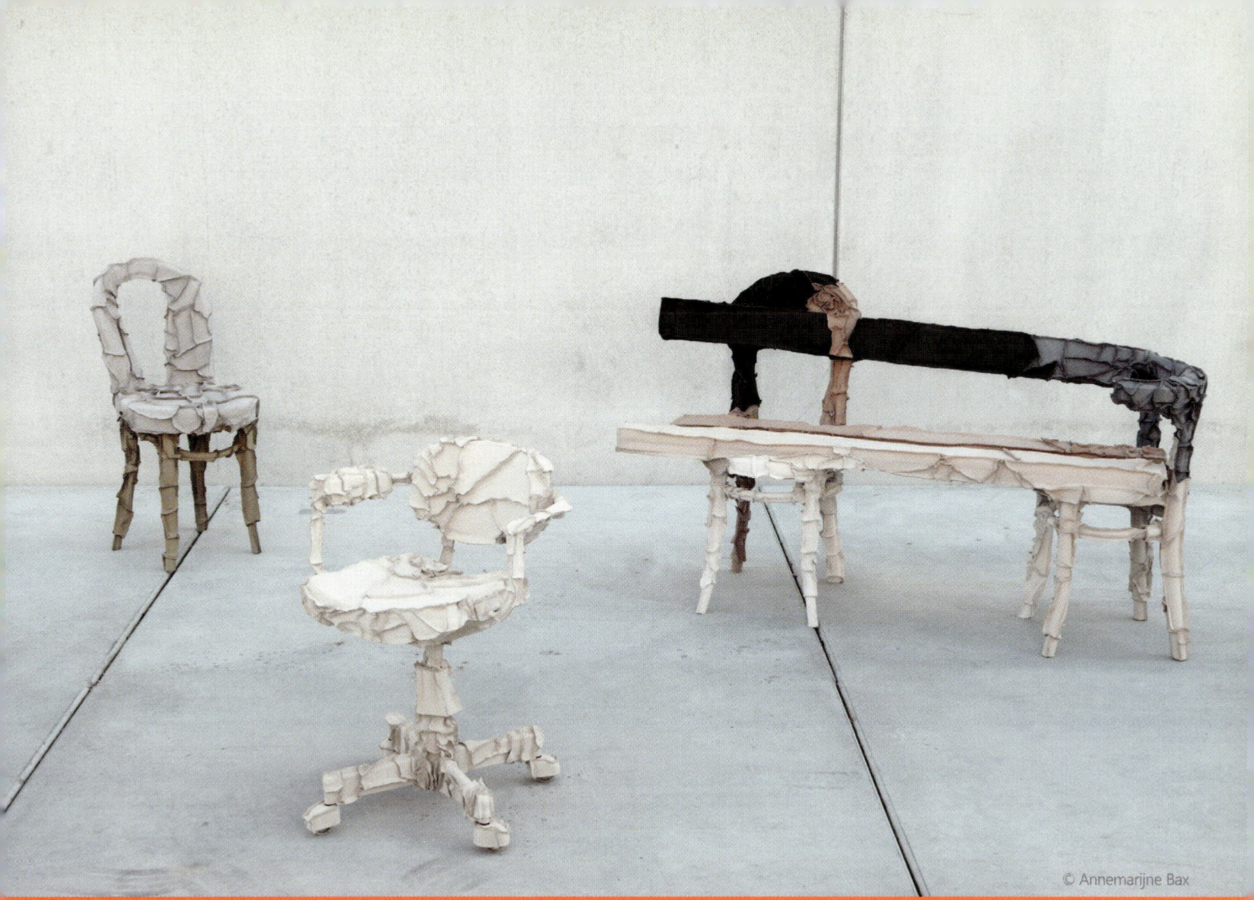

© Annemarijne Bax

Skin Collection
스킨 콜렉션
80x50x60cm
Found object modified, skinned in
leather 버려진 의자, 가죽
2011

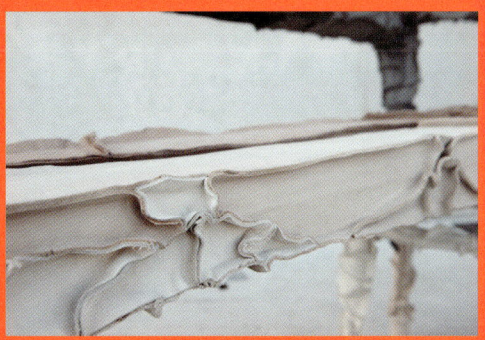

The skin collection is a reaction on the 25-30
percent excessive waste produced by the furniture
industry. The furniture used are existed, modified
and covered up in leather leftovers.
This project is fed by leather scrap, turning it into
random skin patterns, referring to cell structures
and growth in nature.

스킨 콜렉션은 가구산업에서 과도하게 버려지는 25~30
퍼센트의 자원에 대한 반발로 만들어진 작품이다. 이 프
로젝트는 기존에 사용된 가구를 재활용하여 그 위에 남은
가죽을 덮어 수선한 것으로, 세포구조와 생장을 연상시키
는 무작위적인 패턴의 가죽 조각으로 만들어졌다.

173

Hwang, Hyung-Shin 황형신

나는 어렸을 때부터 이사를 자주 다니는 편이었다. 내가 자라던 곳은 그 당시 도시개발이 한창 이루어 지고 있었기 때문에 어렸을 때의 추억이 있었던 장소가 금방 사라져 버리곤 했었다. 자고 일어나 보면 높아져 있는 새로운 건물들, 또 허물어지는 건물들의 모습을 보며 옛 기억들을 간직하려 건물의 잔해들 속에서 부서진 조각들을 다시 맞춰보며 놀던 기억이 있다.

수백 년 된 건물과 최첨단 건물이 공존하는 유럽의 도시와는 달리, 내가 살고 있는 대한민국의 수도 서울은 건물의 건축과 해체가 매우 자주, 짧은 주기로 일어난다. 원래 있던 건물을 허물고 새롭게 짓는 이 '재건축'이라는 행위에는 낡고 오래된 것에 대한 소중함과 아쉬움이라는 감정은 배제되고 단지 물질적인 가치만이 포함되어 있다. 너도 나도 재건축에 혈안이 되어 있는 지금, 점점 이 도시에서는 개발이라는 이름 아래 기억과 향수가 하나 둘 지워지고, 구석구석 밀어낸 자리에는 차가운 시멘트와 콘크리트가 반듯하게 채워진다. 이 서울 어디에서 영혼을 찾아낼 수 있을까. 우리는 영혼을 반납하고 물질에 굴복한 채 이 척박한 도시 안을 이리저리 유랑하고 있다.

이렇게 지어짐과 허물어짐의 과정에서 생겨나는 부산물들은 쓸모 있는 것이었다가 하루아침에 쓸모 없는 것으로 전락한 것이다. 불도저가 밀어버린 콘크리트의 파편 혹은 벽돌의 잔해처럼 버려지는 것들은 불과 얼마 전까지 벽의 일부분이었고 우리가 살던 삶터였다. 눈물과 웃음과 기쁨이 한데 모여 얼룩져있던 삶터에서 사람들은 재건축이라는 명목아래 자신의 의지와는 상관없이 물러나야 한다. 물질적인 가치에 따라 힘없는 사람들은 이리저리 옮겨지고 삶은 단편적으로 변하게 되는 것이다.

급변하는 사회 속에서 새롭게 만들어지기 위해 사라지는 사물들에서 연민과 아쉬움만이 아닌 새로운 의미를 찾아보려 한다. 새로운 것으로 대체되기 전의 기존 사물이 가지고 있던 또 다른 가치 혹은 사라져 가는 과정에서 나오는 부산물들에서 새로운 가치를 창조하는 것, 또는 새로운 것과 기존의 것의 관계에 대한 재정립과 같은 이야기다. 새로움과 대체에 대한 추구만이 아닌 기존 사물의 충분한 이해와 공감을 통한 작지만 따뜻한 변화를 만들고 싶다.

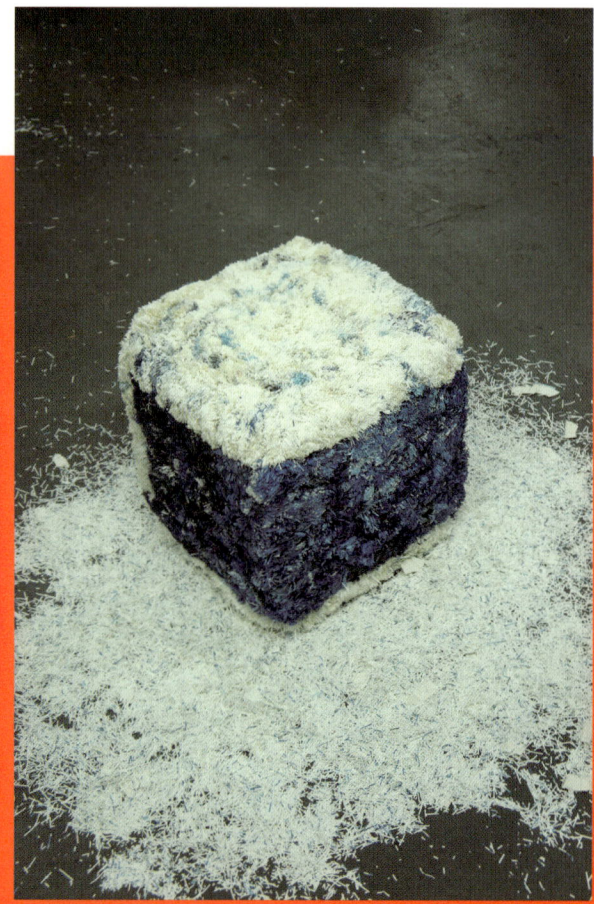

Left Over Paper Chair
폐지 의자
55x55x55cm
Left over paper 폐지
2011

As a child, my family and I moved very often. As a result of the new urban planning policy, we often had to move out of our home to let it be destroyed. As the walls crumbled back to stone, my childhood memories were left without evidence. Later, I would collect the debris of these buildings, in the hope to gather the pieces of the puzzle back into shape. And with this found dust I held not only lost evidences of my past memories but also the life cycle of the modern concrete jungle.

In my first travels to Europe I was stunned by the history that buildings held. I came from a land where the addiction to build and re-build seemed to grow dangerously and where the cold concrete was replacing our history, our traditions and our spiritual link to the land.

This is what brought me to work on the disappearing forms and ideas in the fast mutating society I live in. I attempt to create a new outlook on the present which can incorporate and not discard our history and values as I believe the future should be built with great respect for the past.

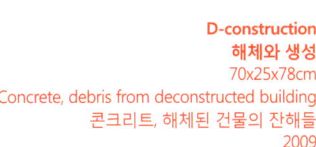

D-construction
해체와 생성
70x25x78cm
Concrete, debris from deconstructed building
콘크리트, 해체된 건물의 잔해들
2009

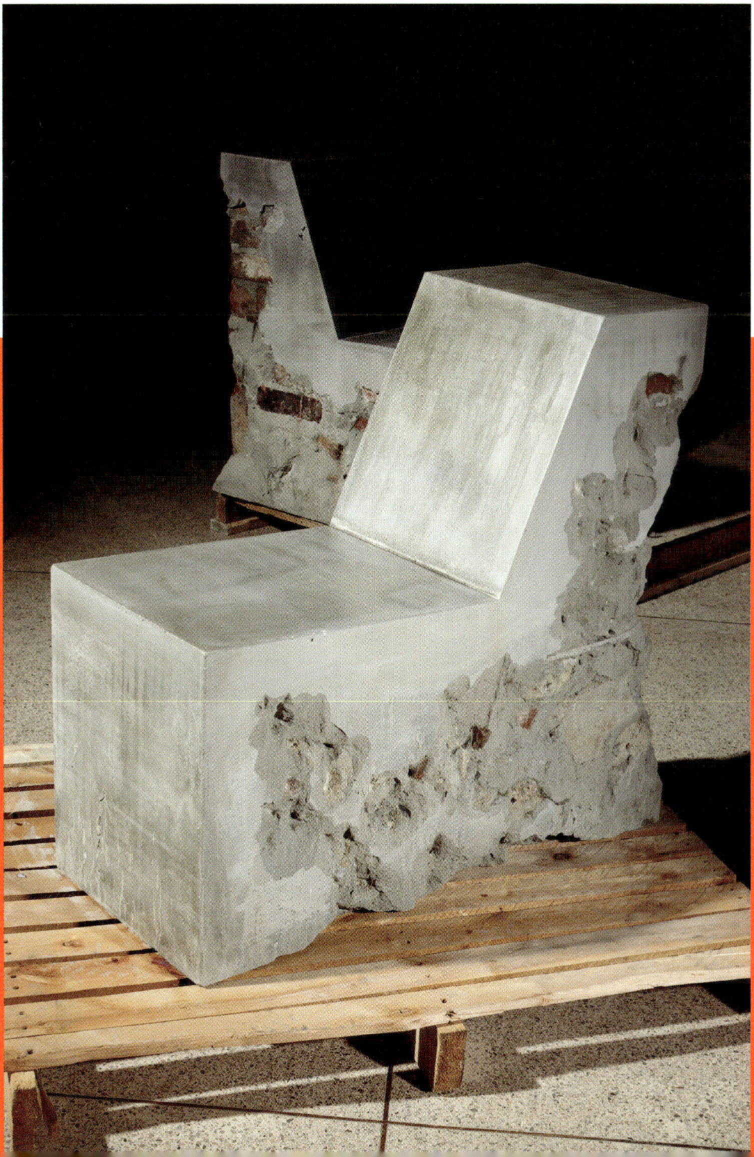

©HWANG, Hyung Shin

Jeong, Jae Beom 정재범

Graduated from metal craft and furniture design major in Hongik University, Jeong, Jae Beom then worked for a Korean chair manufacturer. Deeply attracted by the effective communication brought by chairs, Jeong decided to establish his own design studio. In 2009, he partnered with Lee, Gyeong Jin and the studio was officially named Stonenwater.

Stonenwater is named after the town Jeong spent his childhood, which has given him a zest for nature and creativity. Stone and water are origin of nature, therefore, Stonenwater Studio tries to explore the essence of all objects. An object's value of existence resides in its functionality. Subtracting the decorative part of an object while keeping the essence has been what they are going after. Like in *Grid Chair*, they combine traditional crafts with computer technique, leaving only the basic function of the chair. Except for the solid seat, other parts of the chair are welded by wires, giving viewers a transparent visual impact. There's always an artistic sense in their design, as JEONG said, they use furniture as a medium to share their thoughts with everyone, which is quite similar to art. On all accounts, what they are trying to do is to design a sincere product.

Sasha Lo, Design 360°_No.31, Sandu Publishing Co.,Ltd, Hong Kong, 2011

R60 (Reflex 60°)
90x176x176cm
Stainless steel, ash-black stain finished,
acryl 스테인레스 스틸, 물푸레나무,
아크릴
2008

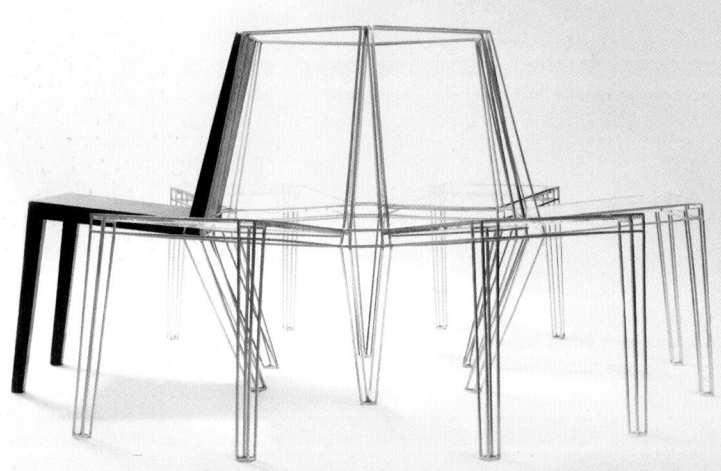

© Jeong, Jae Beom

정재범은 홍익대학교에서 금속공예디자인, 목조형가구디자인과를 졸업하고 한국에서 의자 회사를 위해 일했다. 의자를 통해 이루어지는 효과적 소통에 깊은 매력을 가진 그는 2009년 이경진과 함께 '스톤앤워터Stonenwater'라는 자신의 디자인 스튜디오를 설립하였다.

'스톤앤워터'는 그가 자연과 창조에 대한 열정을 키우며 어린 시절을 보낸 도시의 이름을 딴 것이다. 스톤(돌)과 워터(물)는 자연의 근원으로 '스톤앤워터' 스튜디오는 이름처럼 모든 사물의 본질을 탐구한다. 한 사물의 존재적 가치는 그 사물의 기능성에 있다. 사물의 본질을 유지하며 장식적인 부분을 제외함으로 그들은 자신의 소신을 추구해 왔다. *그리드체어*에서처럼 그들은 의자의 기본적 기능에 충실하면서도 전통적인 공예와 컴퓨터를 이용한 기술을 함께 사용하였다. 의자의 단단한 좌석부분을 제외하고, 다른 부분은 철사를 용접해 만들어 보는 이로 하여금 속을 들여다 보는 듯한 시각적 효과를 주기도 한다. 그들의 디자인에는 항상 예술적 감각이 존재한다고 정재범은 말한다. 그들은 가구를 모든 사람과 그들의 생각을 공유하는 매개체로 여긴다. 이는 예술작품과 많이 닮아있다. 어떤 일이 있어도 그들은 진실된 제품을 디자인하려 하는 것이다.

사샤 로, 디자인 360°_No.31, 산두출판사, 홍콩, 2011

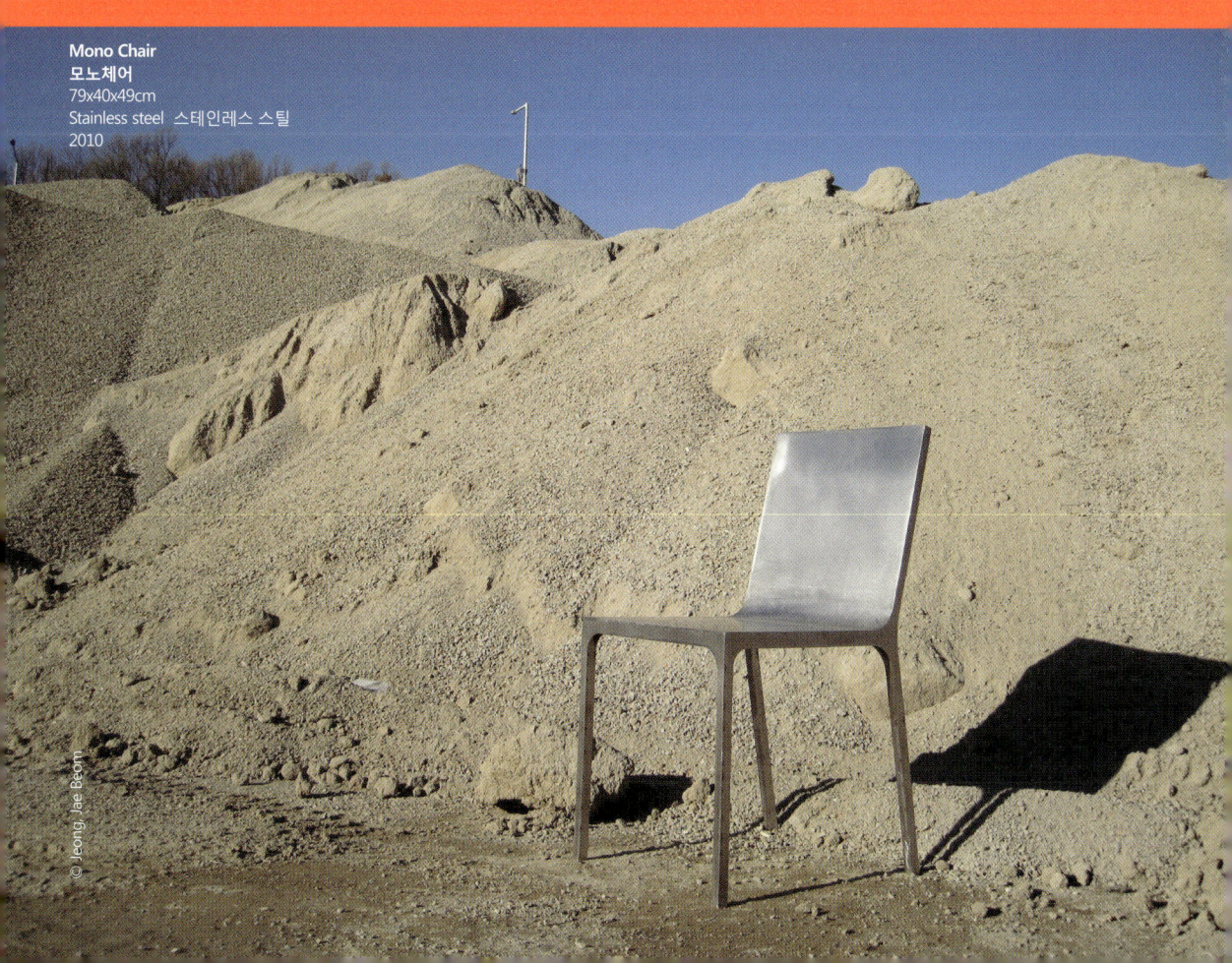

Mono Chair
모노체어
79x40x49cm
Stainless steel 스테인레스 스틸
2010

© Jeong, Jae Beom

Jo, Sook-Jin 조숙진

The 70 chairs JO has collected over the last 10 years are old-fashioned cast-offs. With elaborate and unapologetically decorative turned-wood backs and handsomely carved, form-fitting seats, they embody an era of hands-on craftsmanship and an ethos of artisanal integrity. Those days are long gone, replaced by the sleek, streamlined steel objects of industrial production and the cheap plastic knockoffs of the post-industrial present. But JO brings them back, rescuing some chairs from curbside rubbish heaps and others from friends and strangers who no longer had use for them. She soberly evokes the fact that each chair has been extracted or even forcefully removed from its counterparts and contexts by cutting off its legs. By arranging the mismatched set in a grid, facing a wall as if being punished, she creates an atmosphere of humble elegance and contemplative serenity. These simple gestures pay homage to what has been lost and what may never be known as they give visitors ample opportunity to recall some of the times and the places and the people we hold in our own memories.

David Pagel, Art Critic, L.A.Times

조숙진이 지난 10년 동안 모은 70개의 의자들은 유행이 지나 폐기된 것이다. 나무로 정교하게 장식된 의자 등받이와 그와 꼭 맞게 훌륭히 조각된 좌석부분은 수공제작의 시대와 장인정신의 기풍을 분명히 보여준다. 그 시대는 사라졌고, 산업품인 능률적이고 윤택 나는 강철 물건과 탈공업화 시대의 값싼 플라스틱 모조품으로 대체됐다. 그러나 조숙진은 의자를 길가의 폐물더미에서 구하거나 친구 또는 모르는 사람들로부터 더 이상 사용치 않는 의자들을 수집하였다. 그녀는 의자 다리를 절단함으로써 그 의자의 콘텍스트와 상응 부분을 축출하고 심지어 강력히 제거하면서 그러한 상실의 사실을 환기시킨다.
서로 어울리지 않는 조합을 격자로—마치 벌을 서고 있는 것처럼 —배치하여 겸손한 우아함과 명상적인 평온함의 분위기를 창조한다. 이 단순한 제스쳐는 지금까지 잃어버린 것과 어쩌면 알려지지 않은 것에 경의를 표하는 것이다. 그러면서 관객에게 그러한 사라진 시대와 우리기억에 담겨있는 장소들과 사람들을 상기할 수 있도록 풍부한 기회를 제공한다.

데이비드 패걸, 예술평론가, L.A.Times

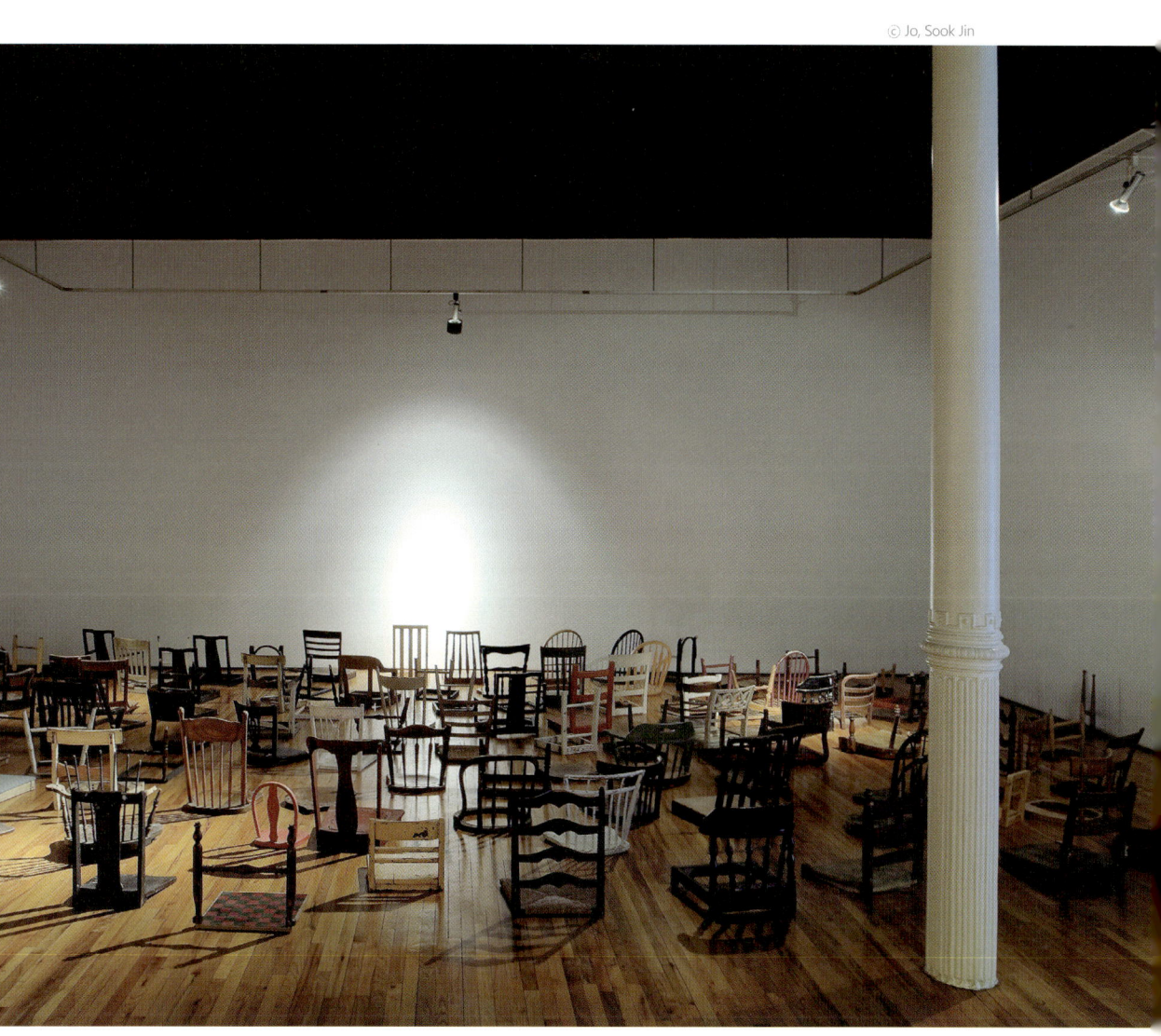

ⓒ Jo, Sook Jin

Chairs
의자들
45x100x80cm(dimensions vary 가변 크기)
2007-2009

Joo, Hong Kyu 주홍규

다이닝체어 전문회사인 악셀 한손은 1938년 악셀 L. 한손에 의해 노르웨이에서 설립되었다. 자연친화적인 자재의 사용과, 독특한 제작기법으로 70년 이상 생산되어온 *악셀 체어*는 현재까지 전세계에 고가의 명품의자로 대접을 받고 있으며, '차별성'을 최우선의 가치로 내세우는 디자이너 주홍규에 의한 *비젼 바이 악셀*은 북유럽의 장인정신과 대한민국의 디자인이 만나 악셀 한손사의 미래비젼을 제시한다.

Aksel Hansson, a company focusing on dining chairs, was established by Aksel L. Hansson in Norway in 1938. Having been produced with nature-friendly materials in its peculiar techniques over seventy years, the Aksel Chair has been highly praised for its brand-name in high prices. *'Vision by Aksel'* by a designer Joo, Hong Kyu who advocates 'differentiation' as its foremost value proposes a future vision of the Aksel Hansson Company, where Northern European craftsmanship and Korean design mingle together

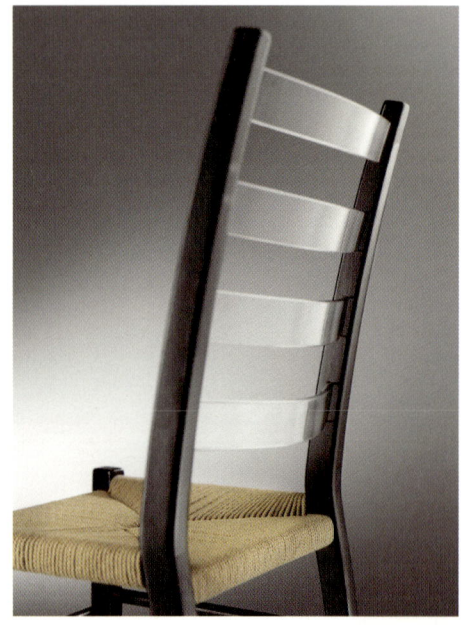

Vision by Aksel
비전 바이 악셀
97x45x42cm
Beech-wood, terylene, PVC, methyl methacrylate(PMMA)
너도밤나무, 테릴렌, PVC, PMMA
2011

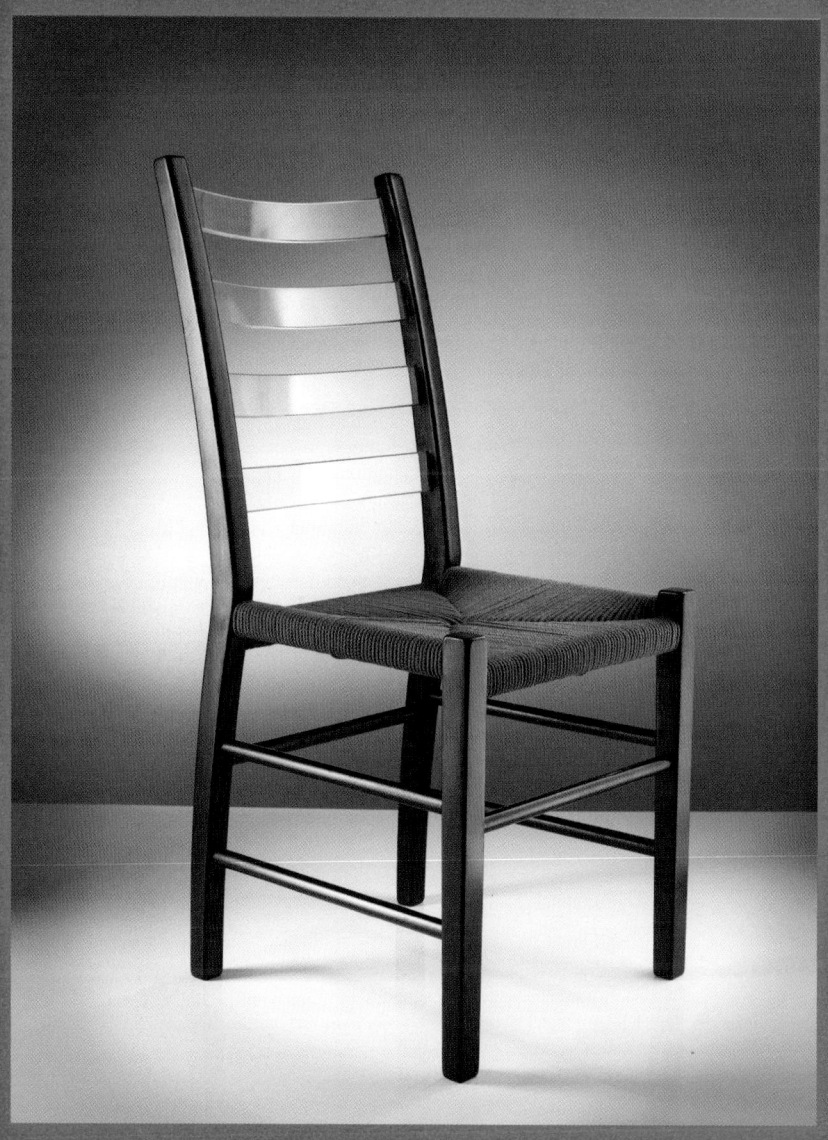

Jung, Hye Suk 정혜숙

Line Drawing I
라인 드로잉 I
72x45x45cm
Wodden chair, thread 부직포, 실
2010

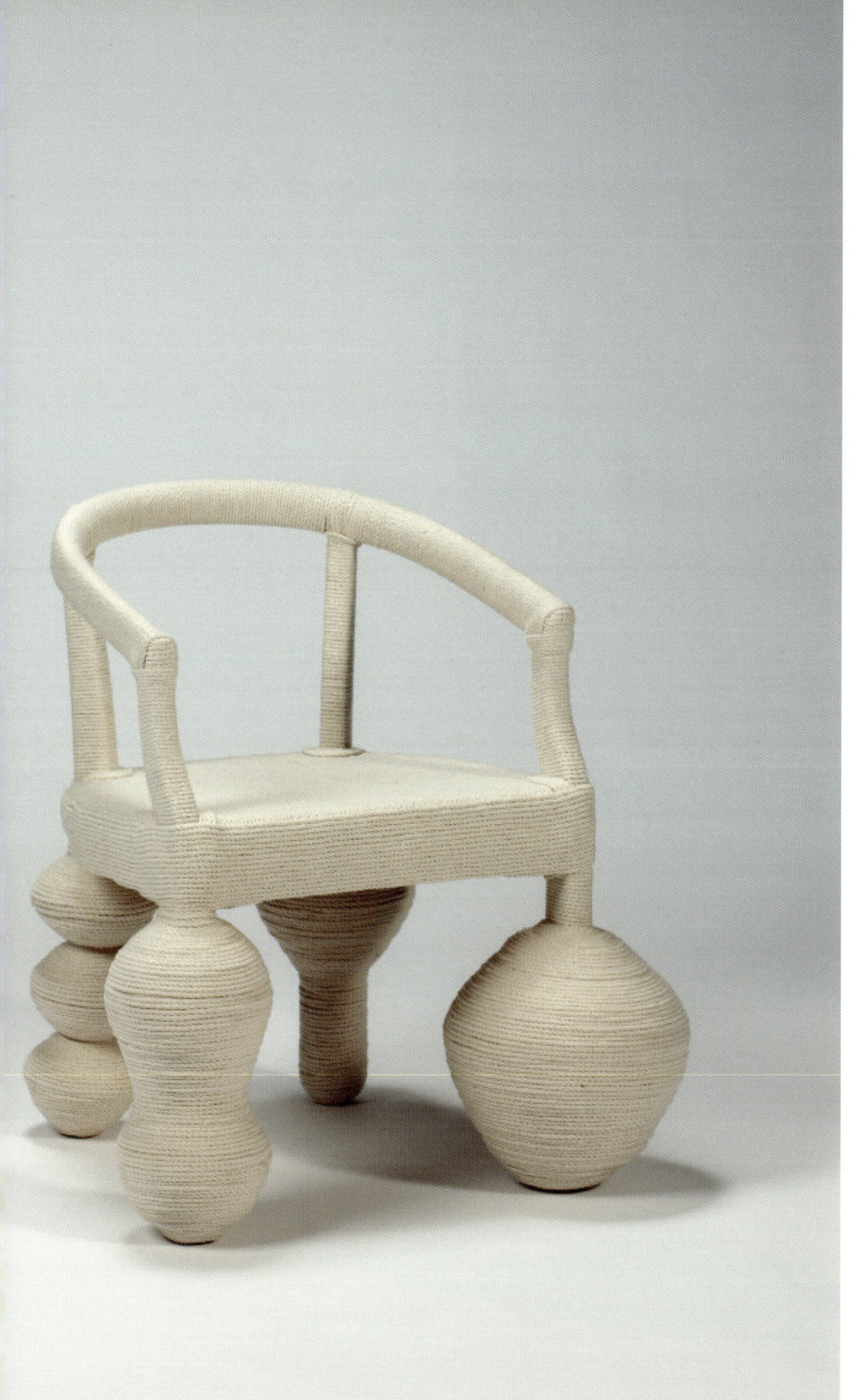

Jung, Myung Taek 정명택

정명택의 작품은 나무라는 물질을 이용, 물질 그 자체에서 그리고 그것을 어떻게 변화시키고, 변형시켜 예술적 작업으로 전환되었는가 하는 것이 문제이다. 물질이 가지고 있는 물성에 대한 탐구와 이용으로 물질에 대한 고정관념에 이의를 제기하는 것으로 해석한다.

물질이 가지고 있는 성격 혹은 성질을 완전히 숨기거나 은폐하지 않고, 적당히 드러내면서 자신의 성격을 보여준다. 그래서 작품은 물질이 가지고 있는 물성을 제약하거나 그것을 은폐하려는 의도, 혹은 물성의 한계를 찾아볼 수 없다.

작품을 단순하게 하나의 현상으로 파악하기는 불가능한 것이기는 하지만 주어진 물성에 적응하고 그것을 효과적으로 변형하여 창조적 정신이 깃든 산물로 변환한 것으로 해석한다면, 물질이 예술로 전환하는 가장 원초적 형태라고 할 수 있을 것이다.

임창섭, 부산시립미술관 학예연구실장, '물질에서 예술로의 전환' 전시도록, 부산시립미술관, 부산, 2010

By using wood, Jung, Myung-Taek's work exhibits the intricacies of how the designer transforms raw materials into his artistic pieces. It can be interpreted that he views an objection against stereotypes in materials through his experiences and utilization of the material's properties.

The designer does not entirely hide or conceal the properties of materials but eventually reveals and starts to show his own character. Therefore, neither an intention to conceal the properties of materials nor their limitation is found in his work.

Although it might not be possible to grasp a design work by a mere phenomenon, we can say that his design is that of the most primordial form. Materials transition into an art form when we interpret it as a transformation, the process where the work acclimates itself to the material's property then converts itself into a product with a creative spirit.

Im Chang Sup, Director of Busan Museum of Art
Exhibition Catalogue, *Transition from Materials into Art*, Busan Museum of Art, Busan, 2010

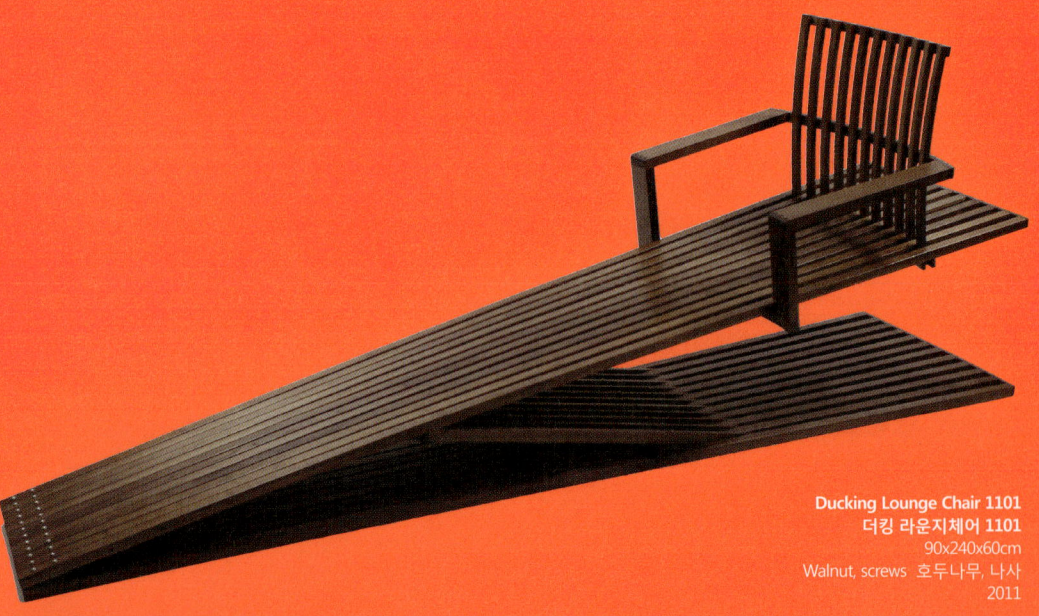

Ducking Lounge Chair 1101
더킹 라운지체어 1101
90x240x60cm
Walnut, screws 호두나무, 나사
2011

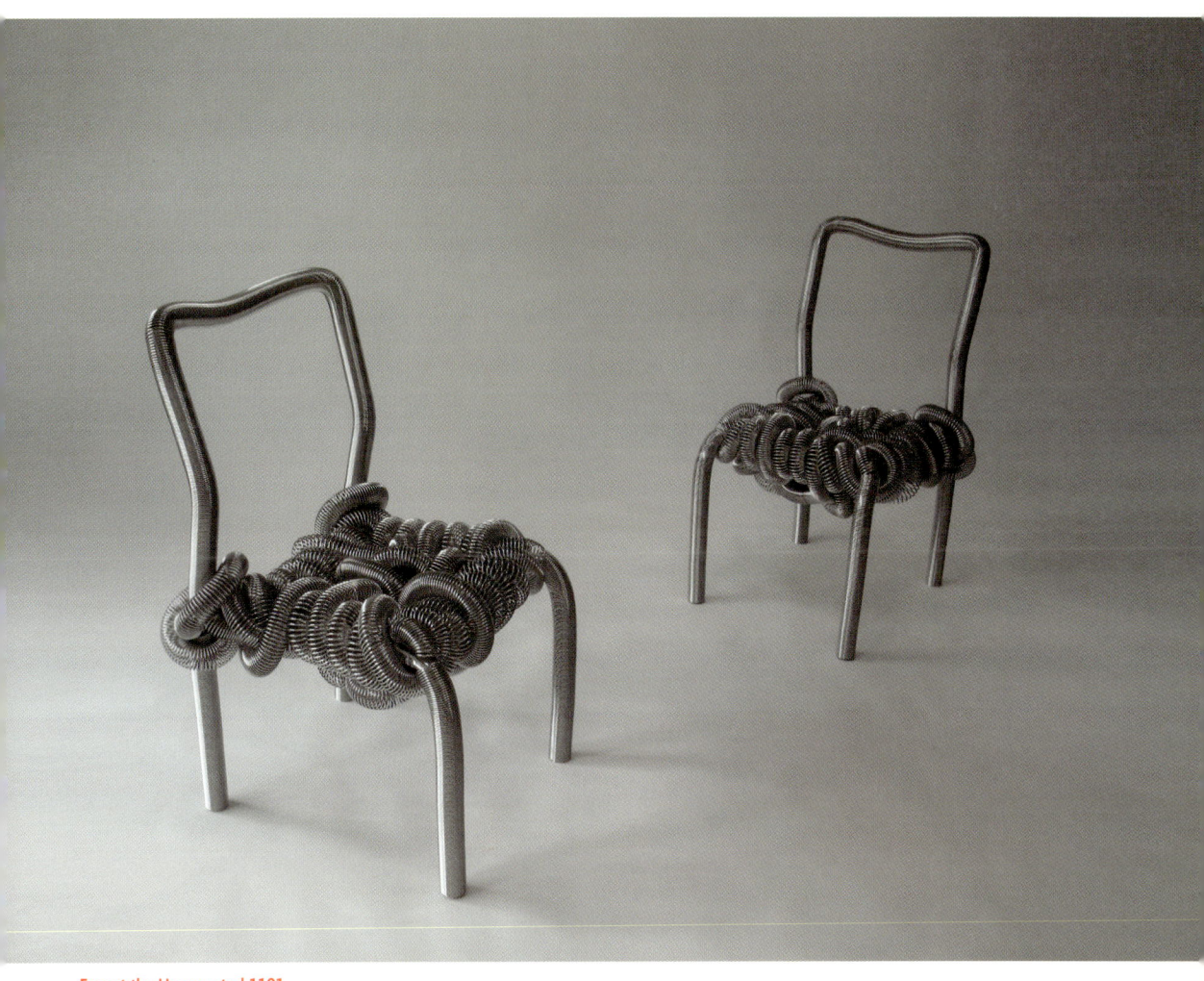

Expect the Unexpected 1101
예기치 못한 기대 1101
83x55x55cm
Nickel coated spring, steel tube, rubber
니켈 도금 스프링, 금속관, 고무
2011

Sami Kallio 사미 칼리오

THE FINNISH BLOOD IN ME

A Collection inspired, and interpreted of childhood memories from Finland.
The starting point in my design is often initially a detail.
One detail that I want to solve makes me start to work through experimentation, craftsmanship and problem solving brings me to my design. I want to combine craftsmanship with modern industry.

내 안의 핀란드 혈통

컬렉션을 통해 핀란드에서의 유년시절의 기억을 해석해 보았다.
나의 디자인은 종종 사소한 것에서 시작한다.
나는 실험, 장인정신, 그리고 문제 해결을 통해 작업을 시 작함으로써 디테일을 풀어내고자 한다. 나는 현대의 산업 과 장인정신을 결합하고 싶다.

Kallio`s collection of pieces falls under the umbrella moniker, The Finnish Blood in Me. An intimate story lies behind each piece – relating to his sense of home, memories of childhood and the moments in time which have influenced the designer along the way. A tender, well made and highly detailed triumvirate.

Richard Prime, Artist and Critic, Exhibit catalogue to *Swedish Love Story*, SuperStudio, Milan, 2011, Publish by Svensk Form

칼리오의 작품에는 집에 대한 그의 느낌이나 유년시절의 기억들, 그리고 디자이너의 길을 걸으며 영향을 받았던 순 간들과 같은 친밀한 이야기들이 숨어있다.

리차드 프라임, 작가, 평론가
2011년 밀라노 Swedish Love Story, SuperStudio 전시 도록 중에서.

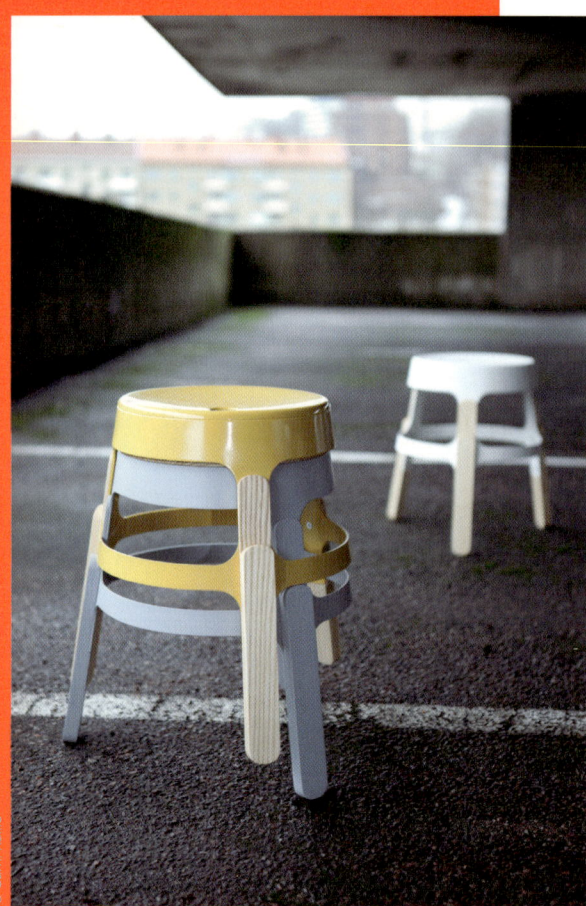

© Sami Kallio

Stool
스툴
41x44x44cm
Solid ash on the legs and metal frame
물푸레나무, 금속
2011

In the easy chair SLICED you can maybe see a glimpse that the inspiration is from Ilmari Tapiovaara. The STOOL from the department store that we visited. A collection where material and detail are in focus.
Nothing strange or conceptual, just memories and function.

슬라이스드라는 이름을 가진 이 안락의자에서 당신은 Ilmari Tapiovaara에서의 짧은 경험을 엿 볼 수 있을 것이다. 스툴은 우리가 방문했던 백화점에서 가져왔다. 이 컬렉션에서는 재료와 디테일에 초점을 맞추었으며, 낯설거나 개념적이라기 보다는 기억과 기능에 관한 이야기를 담았다.

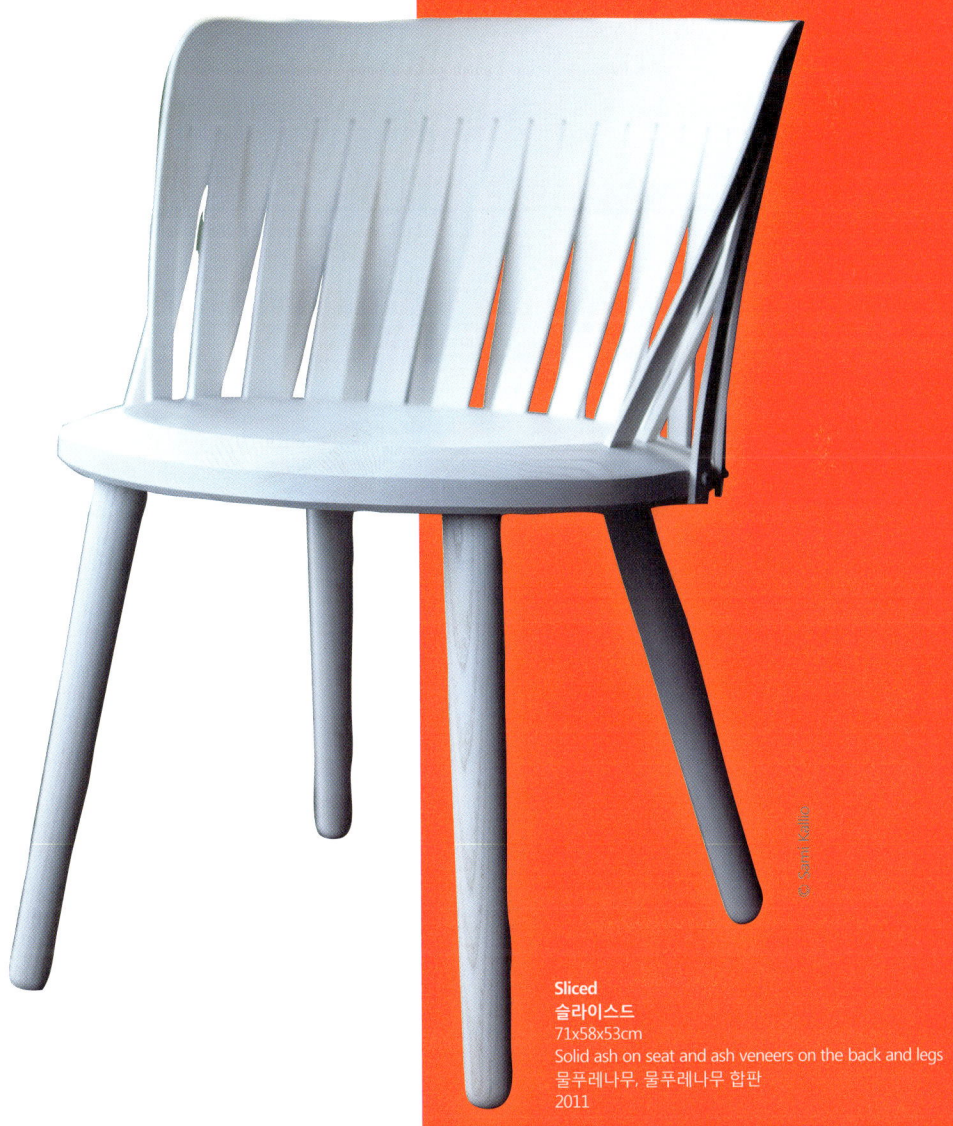

Sliced
슬라이스드
71x58x53cm
Solid ash on seat and ash veneers on the back and legs
물푸레나무, 물푸레나무 합판
2011

Kang, Soo Jin 강수진

Today's mass-production and the disposable fashion are deeply problematic. Current fast changing trends and low price that promote consumers to buy more than they need has pushed people to easily throw away their objects. I am fighting against this epidemic with needles and threads. *Dressed Furniture* is inspired by traditional crafts and antique raw materials, handmade by me, Obviously, the scarcity of the antique furniture used requires the total number of editions produced each piece is extremely limited. Each piece is therefore entirely unique and challenges a new aesthetic statement and it crosses the boundaries of art and design.

I believe that the lack of consciousness with which people easily throw their objects away will increase in the future even more. It is important now therefore that we need to consider our basic needs and what we already possess, and to use these materials wisely and beautifully. Using craft techniques and a combination of antique and raw materials is the logical means by which I work through these issues. The craft traditions convey a considered thought process and have always recognized the value in reusing and repurposing.

오늘날의 대량 생산과 일시적인 유행은 커다란 문제이다. 최근 빠르게 변하는 트렌드와 낮은 가격은 소비자들로 하여금 필요 이상으로 물건을 사게 만들고, 또 쉽게 버리게 한다. 나는 이러한 유행에 맞서 실과 바늘로 싸우고자 한다. 옷 입은 가구들은 전통 공예와 골동품의 원재료에 영감을 받아 수공으로 제작되었다. 누구나 알다시피, 골동품 가구의 희소성은 개개의 작품이 제작되는 양을 극도로 제한한다. 따라서 각각의 작품은 매우 독특하고 새로운 미학적 표현에 도전적이 며, 미술과 디자인의 경계를 가로지르게 된다.
사람들은 앞으로 더 많은 물건들을 쉽게 버리게 될 것이다. 따라서 오늘날 중요한 것은, 기본적으로 우리가 필요한 것과 이미 가지고 있는 것을 고려하여, 이러한 재료들을 현명하고 아름답게 사용해야 한다는 점이다. 공예적인 기법의 사용, 그리고 골동품과 가공되지 않은 재료의 결합은 이러한 문제들을 관통하는, 나의 논리적인 수단이다. 공예의 전통은 사 고의 과정을 전달하고 재활용의 가치를 깨닫게 한다.

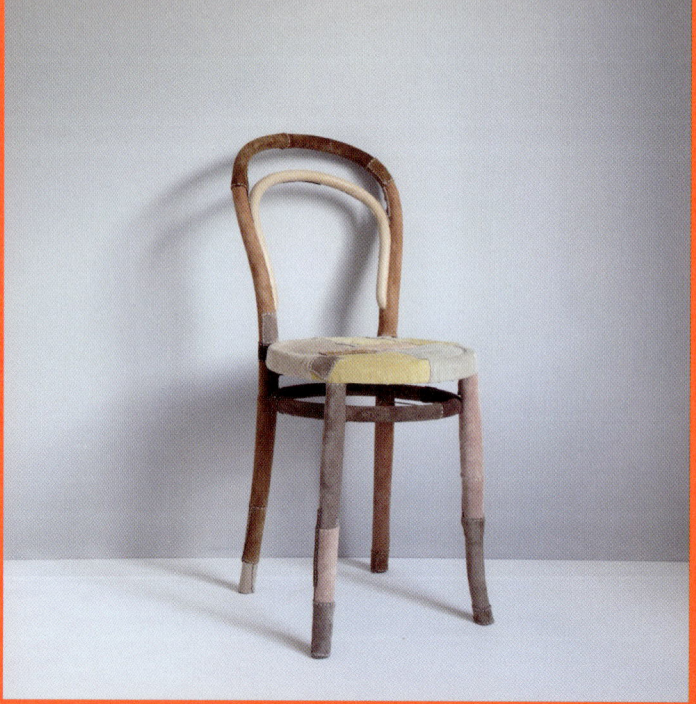

Dressed Dining Chair
옷 입은 다이닝 체어
82x39x32cm
Suede leather, wood
스웨이드 가죽, 나무
2010

Dressed Dining Chair
옷 입은 다이닝 체어
80x39x34cm
Suede leather, wood 스웨이드 가죽, 나무
2010

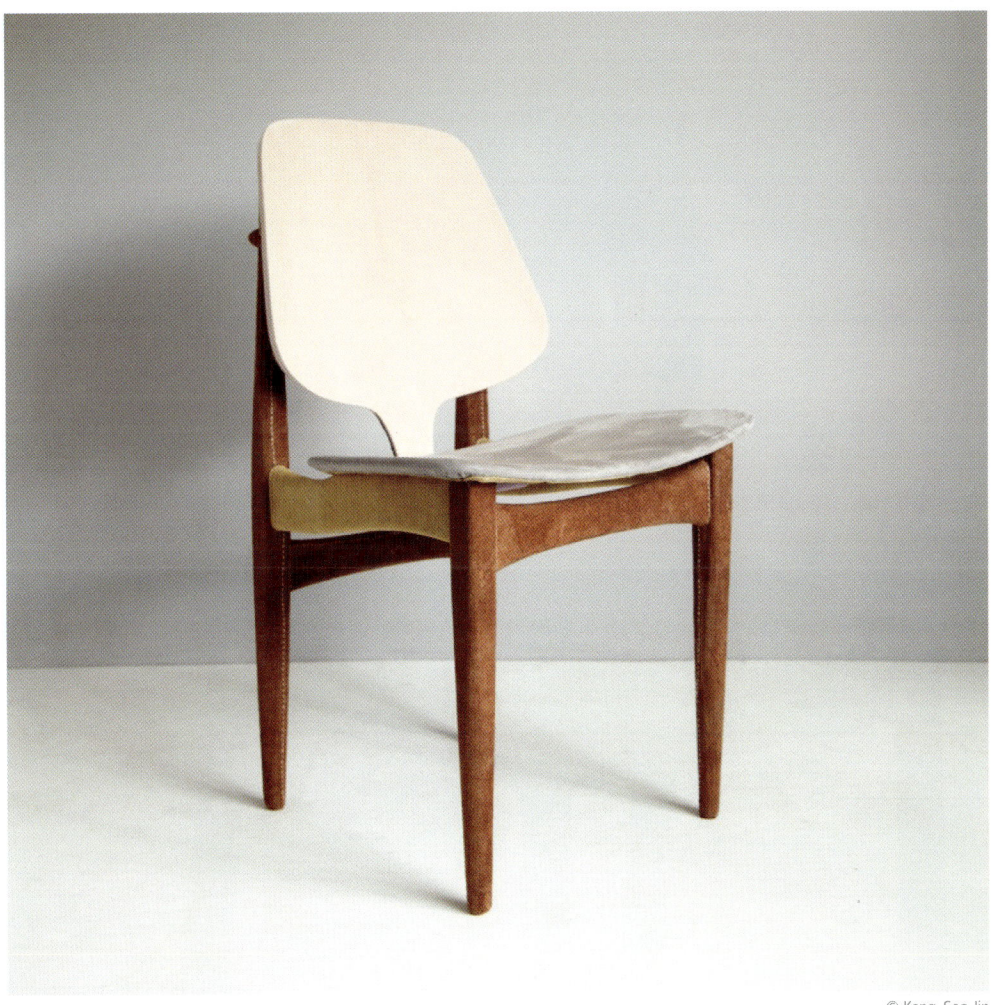

© Kang, Soo Jin

Keum, Ramei 금람해

Gorge Chair
협곡 의자
83x48x54cm
Wood(Glued Timber) 나무(집성목)
2011

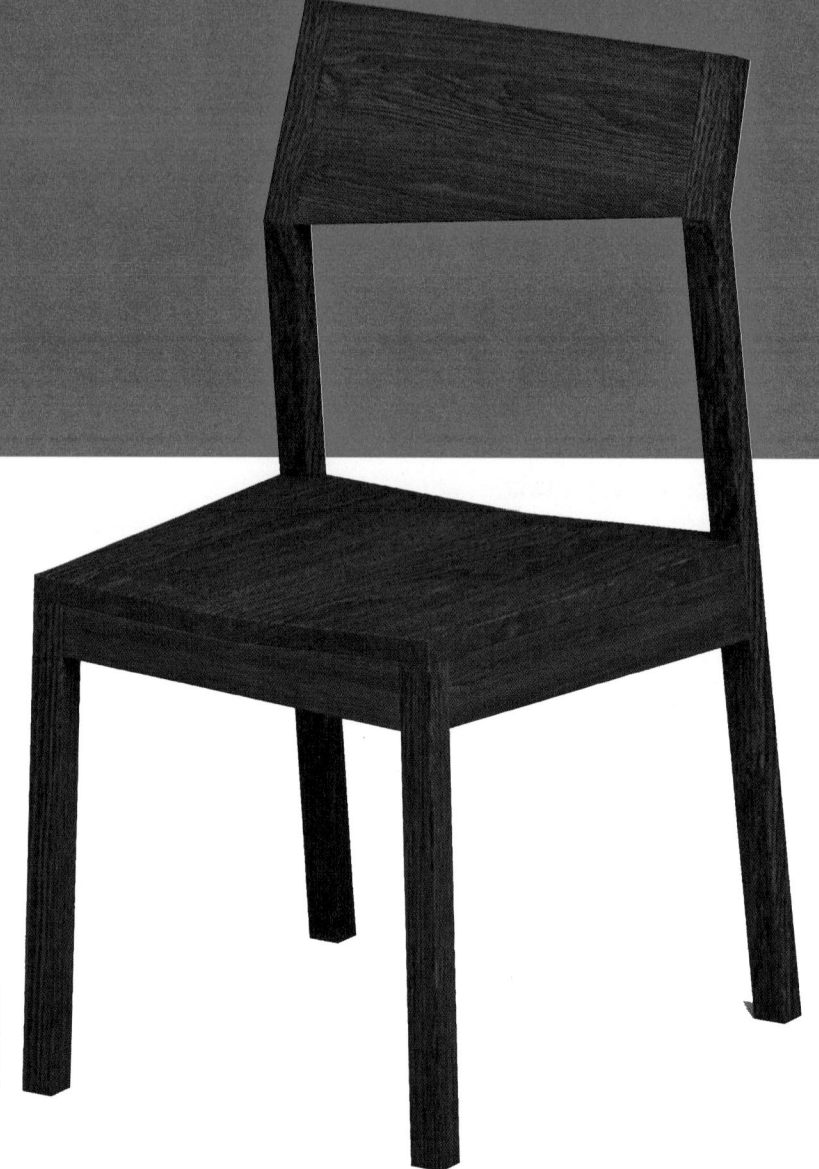

© Keum, Ramei

나의 경험과 주변환경은 내 작업에 있어 중요한 요소이다. 이는 내가 경험하지 못했고 알지 못하는 것들에 대해 이야기하는 것보다 내가 살아가며 경험하는 것들을 내 작업 속에서 이야기하는 것이 조금 더 나를 담아내는 작업이라는 생각에 기반한다.

나는 기능적으로 불필요하다고 느끼는 부분은 제거하고, 불편하다고 느끼는 부분은 보완하며 조형적으로 내 경험 속 시각적 데이터의 부분 혹은 전체를 적절하게 변화시켜 작업에 담아낸다. 이 과정에서 '작은 변화를 통한 새로움'을 구현하려 하는데 그 이유는 익숙함과 변화를 통한 새로움을 동시에 전달하기 위함이다.

*기와(TKF 체어 2011)*의 경우, 한국 전통 건축물 속 기와의 시각적 느낌을 의자의 장식요소로 적용시켰으며, *협곡 의자*는 협곡과 협곡에 존재하는 암벽의 시각적 느낌을 의자에 적용하였다.

TKF Chair1 2011
TKF 체어1 2011
80x52x55cm
Wood(Glued Timber) 나무(집성목)
2011

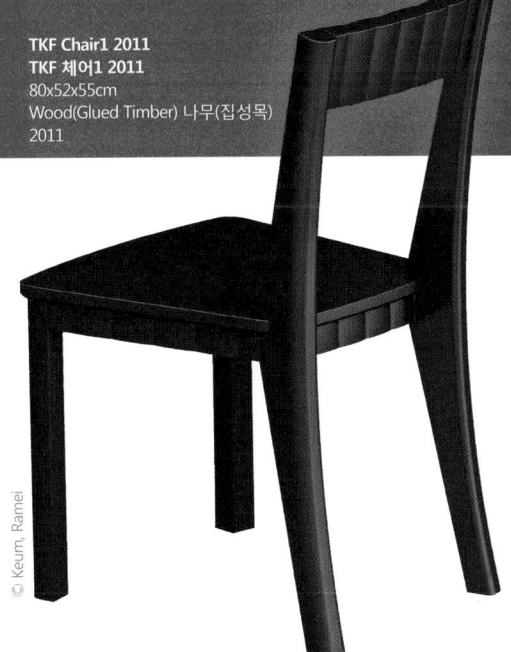

© Keum, Ramei

In my work, all my experiences and the surroundings around me are significant elements. These are based on my contemplations, in order to contain myself as much as possible; I should try to tell stories of my own experiences rather than seeking for what I do not know.

By eliminating unnecessary and inconvenient parts, I build up my work with the visual data from my experiences, from variations of many parts or a whole in formative balance. My artistic aim is to embody an 'innovation through slight changes' with this process; I want to convey the sense of familiarity and various novelties at the same time.

In the case of *Giwa (TKF Chair 2011)*, I applied a visual feeling of roof tiles used in Korean traditional architecture to chair's decorative elements, whereas the *Gorge chair* has visual senses of rock face among gorges in the mountains.

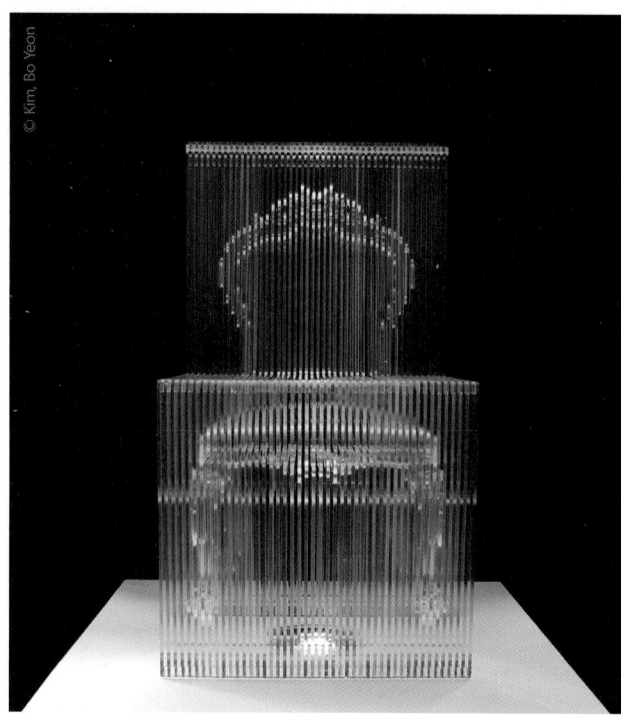

© Kim, Bo Yeon

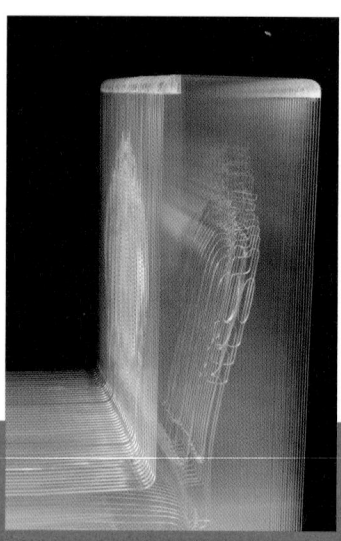

The Laser
레이저
91x59x60cm
Acrylic 아크릴
2010

Korea | 한국

Kim, Bo Yeon 김보연

투명 아크릴 속에 빛을 담다.
다양한 시각적 효과를 나타내기 위해 투명 아크릴을 레이저 컷팅하여 심플함과 클래식함을 동시에 표현하였다. 레이어 사이로 보여지는 컷팅 된 부분들은 각도와 위치에 따라 2D와 3D의 다양한 시각적 효과를 볼 수 있다. 이는 심플함 속의 클래식을 표현하고자 한 것이다.
또한 어떠한 각도에서는 홀로그램처럼 보여지며 투명아크릴에 빛을 쏘아주면 의자 안에서 빛을 담고있는 듯한 느낌이 표현된다. 이 빛의 효과를 통해 클래식의 의자형태는 더욱 선명하게 나타나게 된다. 이는 기존의 틀에서 벗어난 레이저 컷팅 작업으로써 시각적 효과를 극대화시킨 작품이다.

Reflected chair image in the clear acryl layer. Simplicity and classical aspect are simultaneously expressed to visualize various optical effects by laser cut of clear acryl. Chair image reflected through cut area expresses various optical effect in 2D or 3D style according to the viewer's position or angle. It intends to express classic feature despite its simplicity via effect reflected. Hologram also can be seen in different angle and you feel like chair holds light when light beams are projected into clear acryl. A classic chair image is clearly expressed by the effects of light. This work is significant because it escapes from traditional framework of furniture design and sheds light in maximizing optical effect by new technique using laser cut work.

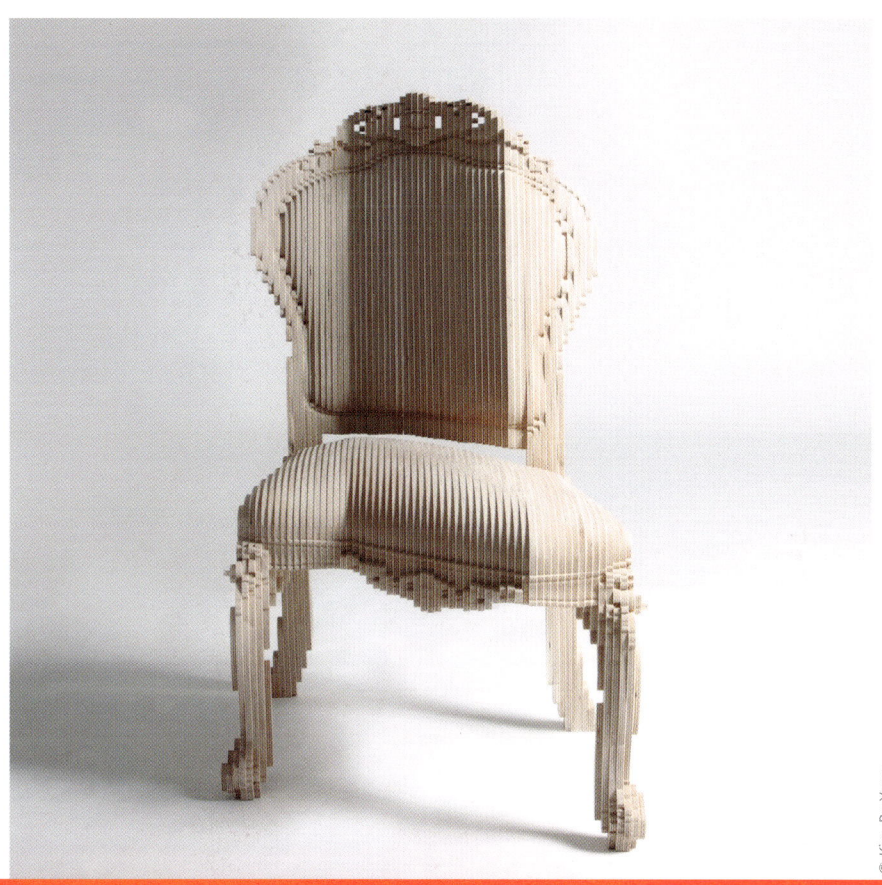

© Kim, Bo Yeon

Press Chair
찌그러진 의자
98x63x73cm
Birch plywood 자작나무합판
2010

의자의 형태는 똑바라야만 하는가?
기존의 알고 있는 형태에 약간의 변화만 준다면 어떠한
의자라도 새롭게 표현될 수 있다.
각기 다른 형태의 레이어를 통해 의자의 왜곡을 표현하였
으며 이를 위해 한쪽방향에서 압력을 주어 밀어내는 듯한
형상을 주었다. 이는 위치에 따른 다양한 시각적 변화와
재미를 준다.

Should a chair be straight?
Adding just a little bit of twist, any chair can turn
into a whole new one.
Different types of layers gave a distortion to the
chair. And for this pushing effect, pressure was
applied from one side. This provides both a various
visual variation and fun factor according to the
position.

Kim, Dai Sung 김대성

"사물은 존재이유를 인간에게 묻는다" 김대성은 컨셉디자인을 기반으로 사물과 인간과의 관계에 대한 사물이 가진 기호적 의미를 현 시대적 배경의 시각으로 다시 바라 봄으로써 사물이 의미하는 다각적 시각에서의 인간과의 관계를 표현함과 동시에 문화적 형성에 따른 사물을 디자인하고 현 시대에 의해 길들여진 자신의 모습을 디자인 한다. 디자인에는 반드시 이유가 존재해야 한다고 말하는 디자이너 김대성. 그에겐 디자인도 일종의 의미를 담고 있는 기호다. 김대성은 그 기호를 통해서 사람들과 의미 있는 소통을 이루길 원한다.

"Asking the reason of existence of objects to human beings." Kim, Dae Sung designs himself, a being domesticated in the present age, and objects produced during the cultural establishment of this period. It was possible on the basis of his conceptual design to observe semiotic meanings of objects toward the relationship between human beings and them. In other words, his observance in the contemporary viewpoint enabled him to express diverse perspectives of objects' meanings in their relationships with men.
Kim, Dae Sung is a designer who claims that design must be reasonable. Design is, for him, a sort of meaningful signs, through which he wishes to communicate significantly with others.

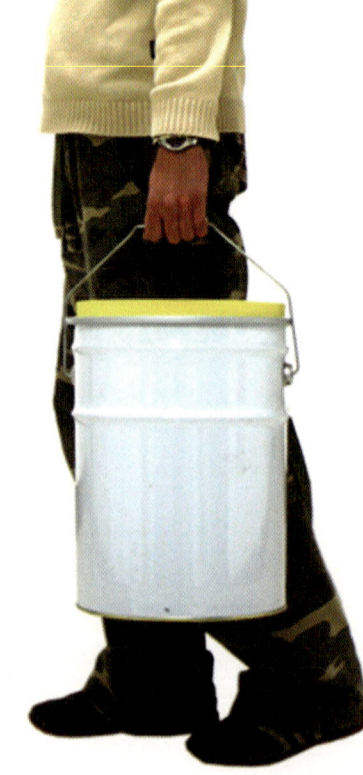

Can Chair
깡통 의자
40x30x30cm
Can, EVA 깡통, EVA 스폰지
2006

© Kim, Dai Sung

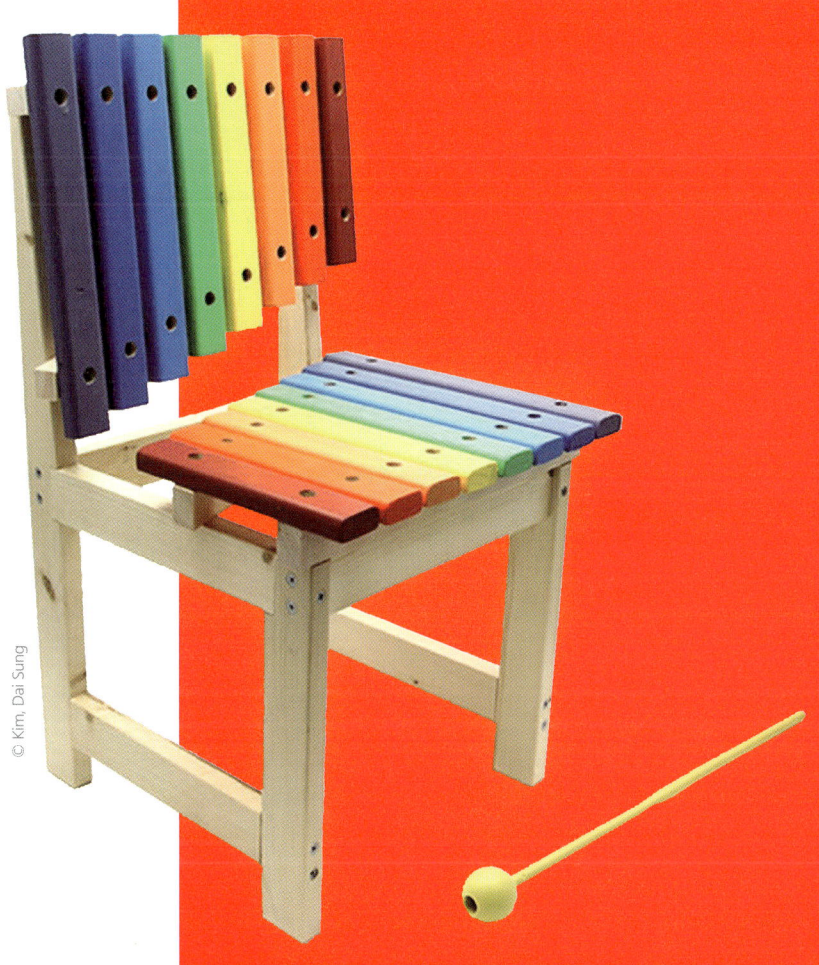

Xylophone Chair
실로폰 의자
42x26x26cm
Douglas fir wood and eco-friendly paint
미송 원목, 친환경 페인트
2007

© Kim, Dai Sung

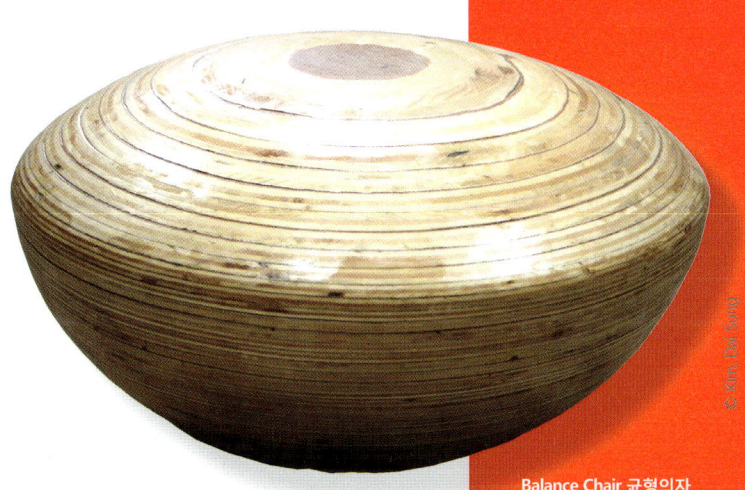

© Kim, Dai Sung

Balance Chair 균형의자
33x59x59cm
Overlaid plywood production wood
나무합판을 겹쳐 제작
2004

195

Kim, Do Yeon 김도연

김도연의 직업은 포토그래퍼이지만, 그는 2차원의 그래픽, 사진, 다큐멘터리영상의 영역을 뛰어넘어 가구와 같은 다양한 작업을 진행중이다. '작가가 직접 쓰고 싶은 제품은 모두가 원하는 제품'이라는 신념을 가지고 있다. 디자이너 자신의 라이프스타일이자, 오랫동안 직접 경험해온 스케이트보드 문화를 가구와 신개념의 일러스트에 적용했다. 스케이트보드를 이용한 의자로 시작한 가구작업은 테이블과 벤치 그래픽적인 요소를 가미한 스툴로까지 확장되었으며, 이제는 단순히 스케이트보드와 관련된 영역을 넘어선 작업을 시도 중이다. 스케이트보드의 개념을 소위 말하는 '하위문화'의 스타일에서 벗어나 실용주의에 기반을 둔 가구와 일러스트에 적용함으로 문화적 스타일의 확장을 시도한다.

Black Deck Stool
블랙 데크 스툴
45x80x25cm
Maple plywood, Aluminium 단풍나무 합판, 알루미늄
2011

Spider Deck Table
스파이더 데크 테이블
70x230x70cm
Tempered Glass, Aluminium 강화유리, 알루미늄
2009

© Kim, Do Yeon

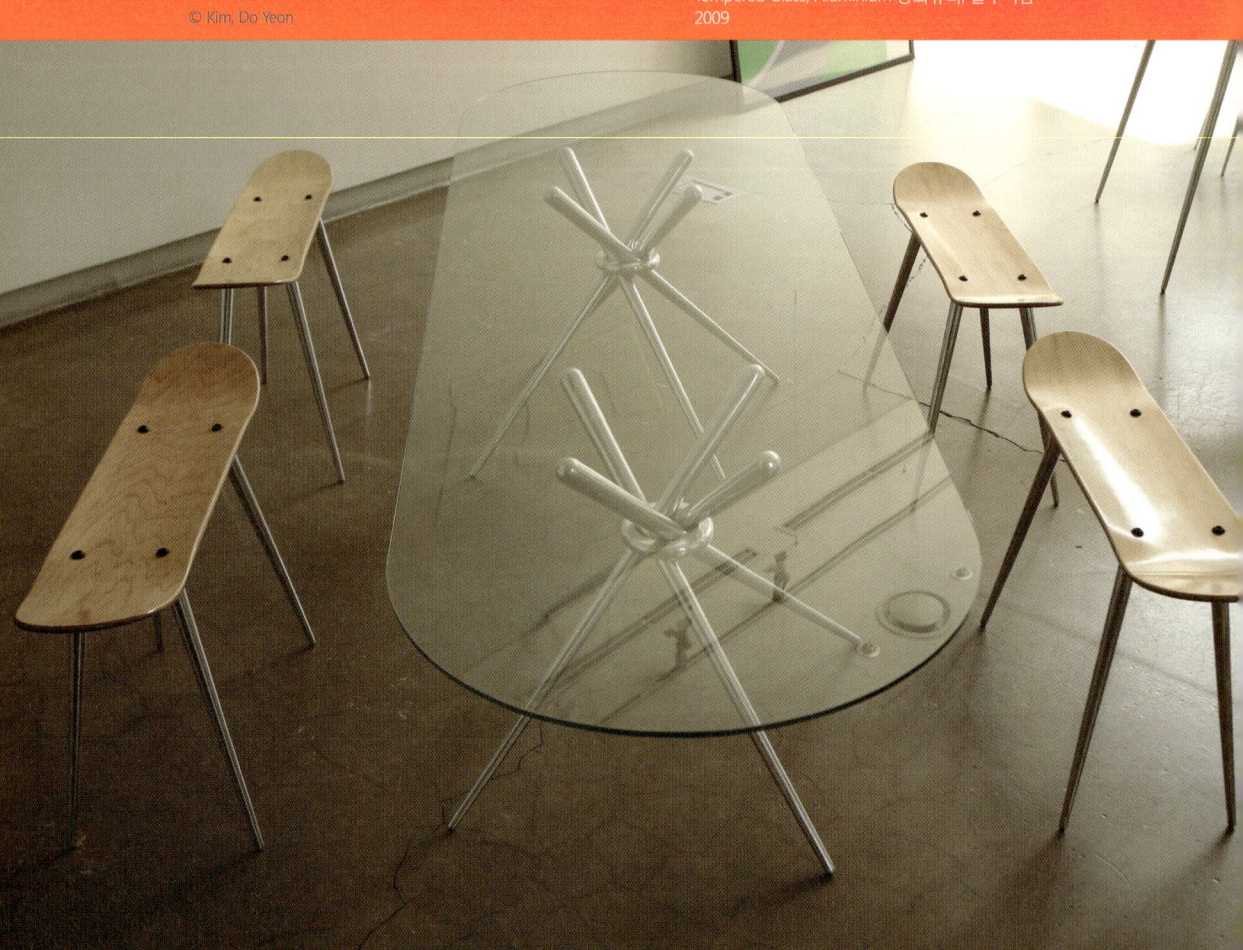

While Kim Do-Yeon's original profession is that of a photographer, he surpasses the two-dimensional domains of graphics, photography, and documentary pictures and now works on diverse pieces such as furniture works. He has a theory that a product which a designer wishes to utilize is what others tend to want. Therefore, the designer Kim, applied his own long-term skateboard lifestyle to furniture and new concept illustrations.

Initiated from the chairs used with skateboarding, his designs have been extended to tables, benches, and stools, combined with graphical elements and now is in experimental trial to overcome boundaries related merely to skateboards.
Kim attempts to expand on cultural styles by applying the concept of skateboards, out of the so-called style of 'low-culture,' to furniture and illustrations based on practicality.

Flag Deck Stool
플랙 데크 스툴
45x80x25cm
Maple plywood, aluminium 단풍나무 합판, 알루미늄
2010

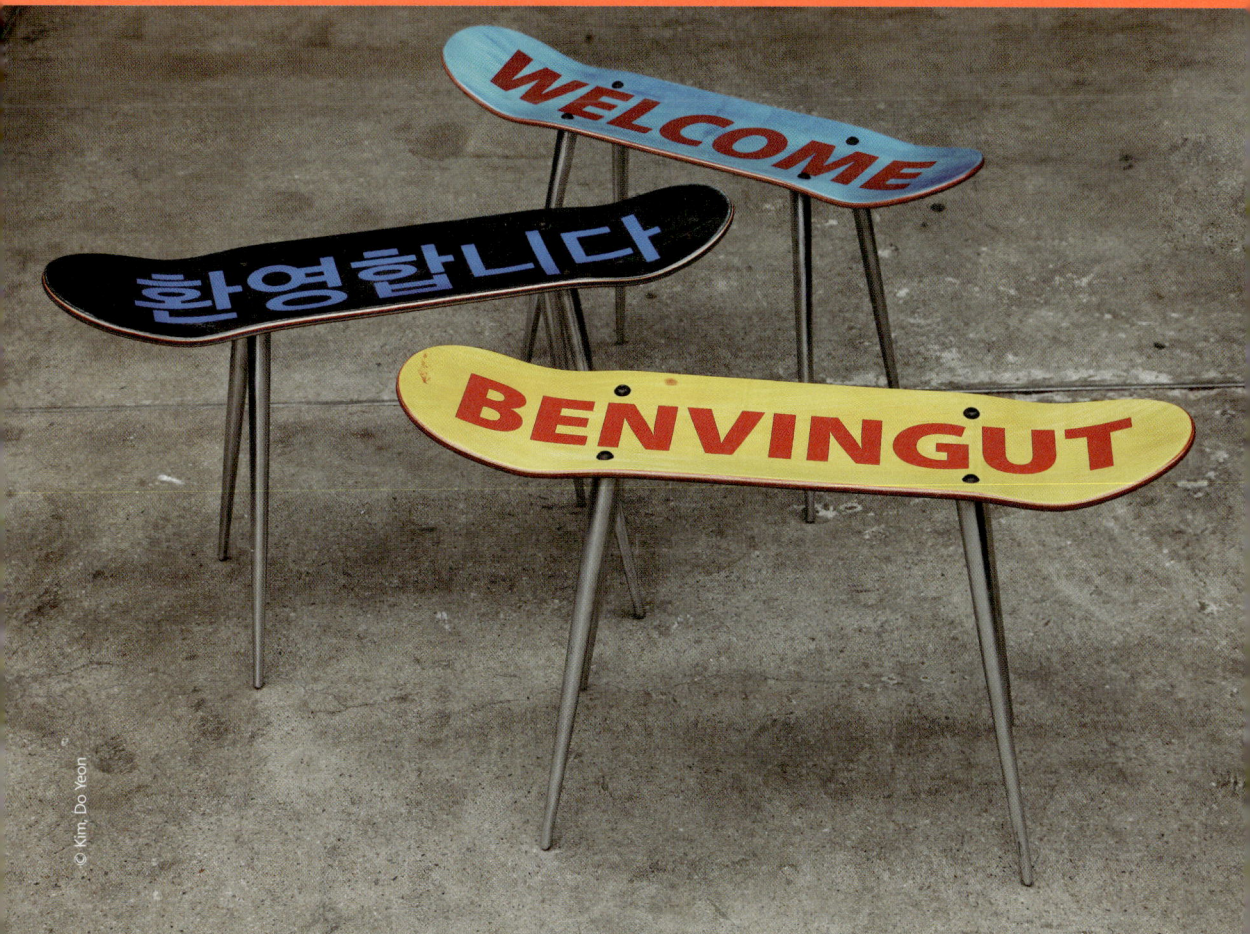

© Kim. Do Yeon

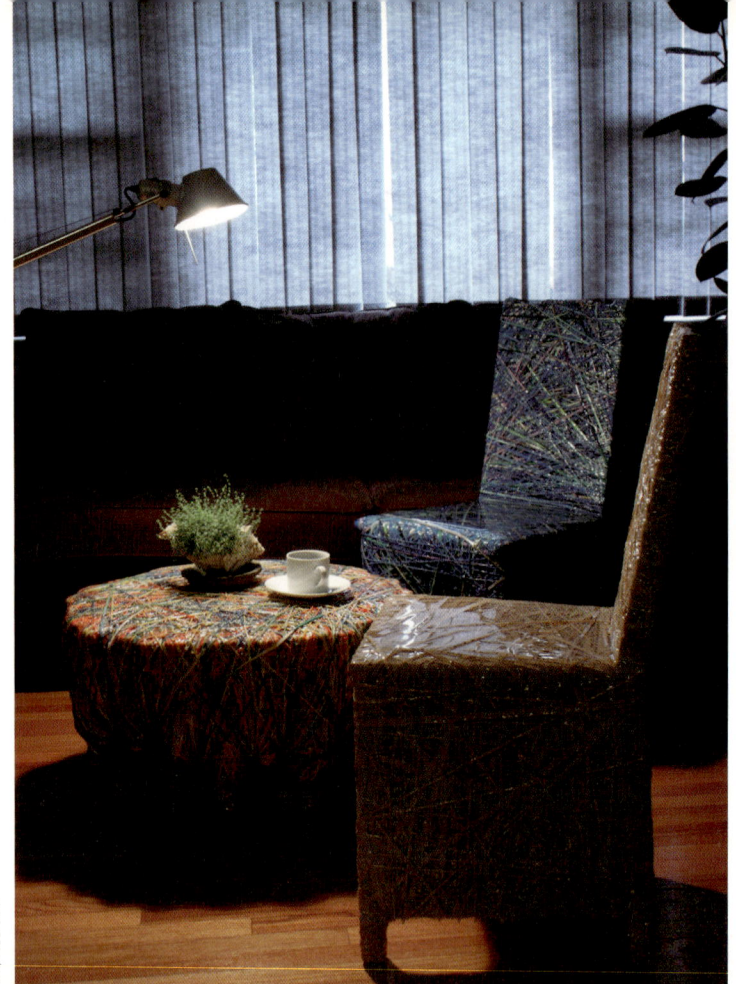

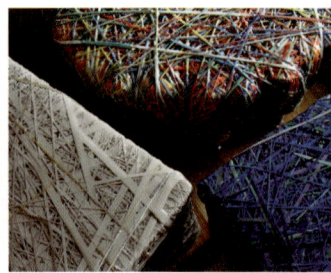

© Kim, Hee Soo

Meshed Chair #1, #2
85x45x45cm
Recycled chair, rubber bands, resin
재활용 의자, 고무줄, 레진
2009

Meshed Tea Table
50x70x70cm
Recycled glass bottles , rubber bands, resin
재활용 유리병, 고무줄, 레진
2009

Korea | 한국

Kim, Hee Soo 김희수

언제부터인가 나는 작업에서 사물의 부분이 전체를 이루는 과정에서 일어나는 이야기들에 관심을 기울이고 있었다. 내가 공상하는 것들은 무수한 별들의 집합체인 우주, 우리가 있는 지구, 지구를 구성하는 산과 물과 바람같이 작고 사소한 편린들이 모아져 하나의 거대한 유기체가 되어가는 과정과 이런 것들의 집합이 이루어내는 광경에 나는 매료되어 있었다. 특히 지난 8년여의 뉴욕생활에서 나는 내 주위의 사소한 물건들이 가진 가치를 발견하는 일에 몰두해왔다. 어느 날 작업실 책상에 무심히 놓여있던 플라스틱압정과 고무밴드 등이 주는 사소한 재미를 발견한 나는 사물들간의 상호적 결합으로 이루어지는 구조에 더욱 관심을 가지게 되었다. 우리가 일상에서 흔히 보는 재료를 이용한 조각과 설치작품들은 그러한 나의 개인적 관심을 아주 구체적으로 보여주고 있다. 또한 이러한 일련의 작업들은 그 동안 가져온 작업에 대한 탐미를 구체화시키는 일이었다. 아주 사소하고 작은 오브제들의 조화가 만들어내는 패턴과 형태, 색의 혼합은 나에게 재료가 주는 질료의 본래적 성질을 어떻게 이용하여 새로운 이미지를 가진 복합적 유기체를 만드느냐가 내가 작업을 통해서 하고 있는 이야기다.

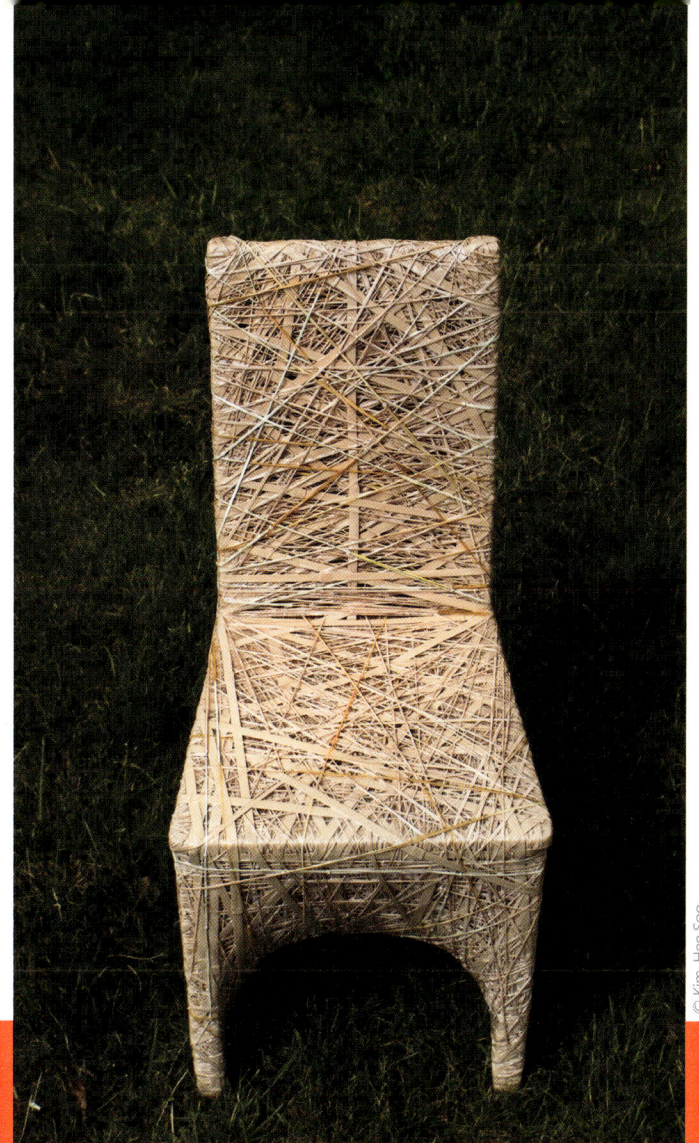

© Kim, Hee Soo

I do not remember exactly when, but I found myself paying attention to arousing stories, where parts of objects constitute the whole. I fantasize about the universe as an aggregation of countless stars, the earth, its mountains, water and wind; these have attracted me in the process of organizing scenery that small and tiny parts constitute a whole. In the past eight years of my life in New York, I was absorbed in finding the values of trivial objects around me. One day I found entertainment in a plastic thumbtack and elastic bands on my desk. I began to pay attention to the structure of the mutual combination among objects. My sculptures and installation works made from common materials from our daily lives exhibits that of my personal interest to detail. Such series of my work contain the embodiment of my aesthetic pursuit in design. It is my story shown through my pieces that illustrates how to utilize raw materials to make an organic body with new images mixing patterns, forms, and colors in harmony with tiny objects.

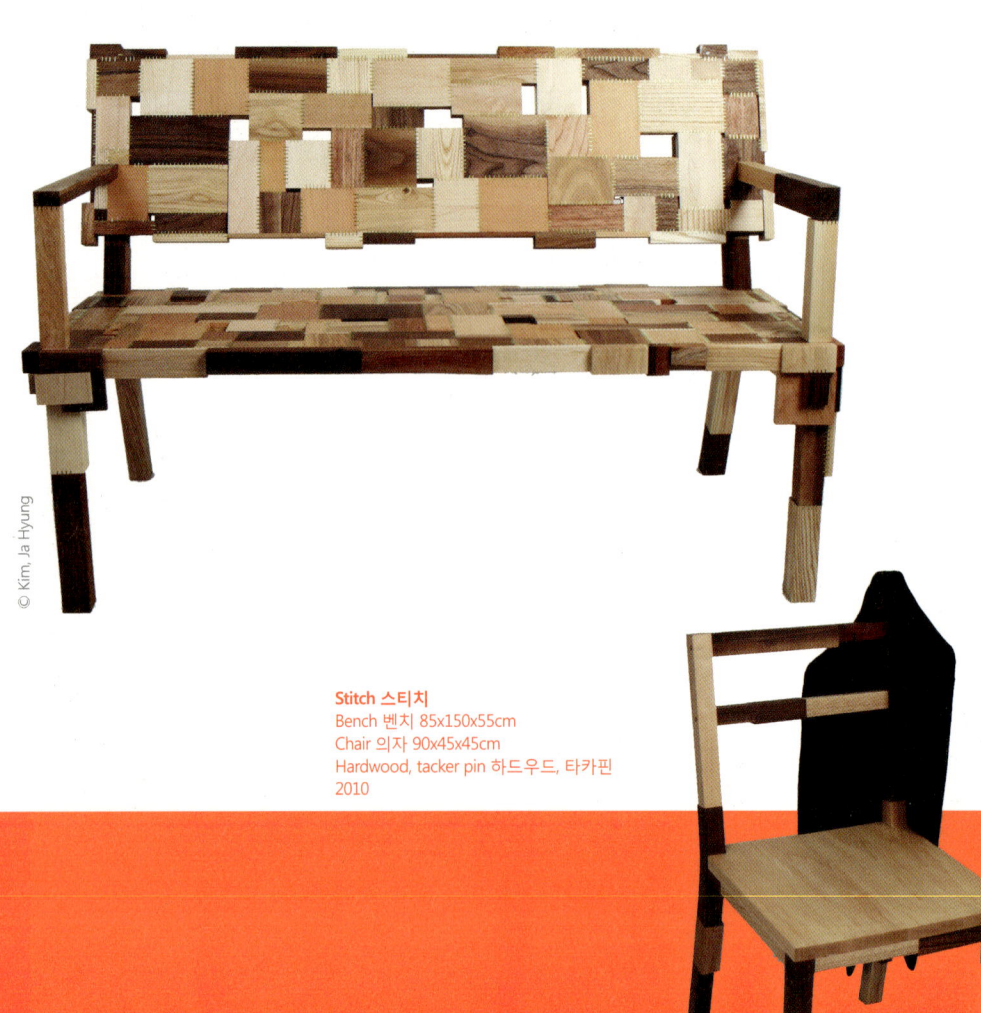

© Kim, Ja Hyung

Stitch 스티치
Bench 벤치 85x150x55cm
Chair 의자 90x45x45cm
Hardwood, tacker pin 하드우드, 타카핀
2010

Korea | 한국

Kim, Ja Hyung 김자형

친환경은 이제 디자인에 있어 떼어놓을 수 없는 개념이다. 이 시점에서 새로운 가치를 창조해내는 디자이너들에게 사회적 책임이 있다면 바로 "New worth from No worth", 즉 하나의 디자인을 위해 많은 환경문제를 일으키기 보다는 무가치의 재평가를 통해 새로운 가치를 창출해내는 마인드를 가질 필요가 있다.
스티치 시리즈는 이러한 의미에서 우리의 전통 규방공예에서 볼 수 있는 조각보에서 모티브를 얻어 수많은 조각천들을 한 땀 한 땀 바느질하듯이 제작한 가구이다.
또한, *브랜치* 시리즈에서는 자연의 이미지를 형상화하여 예술 가구(아트 퍼니쳐)로 표현하였으며, 자연에서 얻어지는 소재의 원형적 활용을 중심으로 디자인을 더 부각시키고자 하였다.
이처럼 나의 작업은 주로 원목을 이용한 작업과 로하스(LOHAS) 개념을 가지고 친환경적 디자인을 추구하고자 하였으며, 이로써 전통적인 작품의 재현뿐만 아니라 자연적인 색상의 여러 수종의 나무들의 접목을 통해 어느 나라 어느 사람이든 편안하고 은은한 미를 느낄 수 있다.

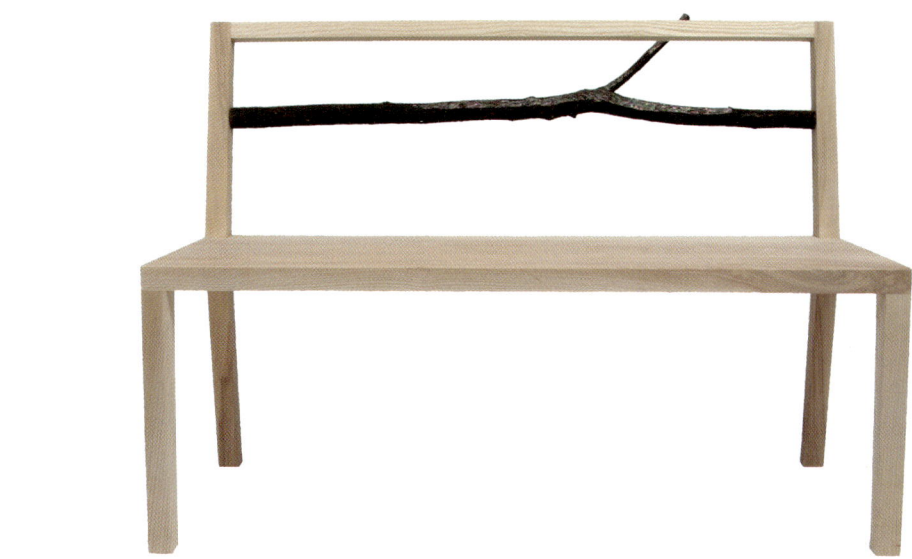

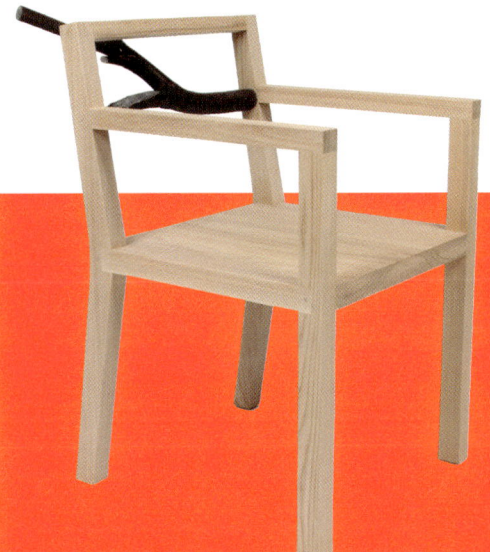

Branch 브랜치
Bench 벤치 90x120x50cm
Armchair 암체어 90x50x50cm
Chair 의자 90x50x50cm
Ash, Walnut, Branch, Mother of pearl 물푸레나무, 호두나무, 나뭇가지, 자개
2011

The concept of an eco-friendly environment is now barely separable from design. If any social responsibility at this point is endowed to designers who create new values, it is nothing else but "New worth from No worth". Namely, we should stop making environmental problems for design itself, but we need to have an innovative mind to create new values through the revaluation of worthlessness.

In this sense, *Stitch* Series is furniture designed as if one stitches numerous pieces of cloth together; motivated from patchwork quilts in Korean traditional boudoir crafts.

Branch Series embodies the image of nature as Art Furniture, which I intended to magnify its design by using the original forms of natural materials.

Like this, I tried to pursue environment-friendly design in hardwood with the LOHAS concept, which results not only in the representation of traditional works but it also has feelings through grafting various types of trees in natural colors and shows the delicate beauty of people of various nationalities.

Kim, Kyung Lae 김경래

'Fused-together(융합)'을 주제로 다양한 가구 작품을 표현하는 김경래 작가는 가구란 조형예술과 실용 예술의 중간 위치를 차지할 수 있는 가장 좋은 아이템이라고 여기며, 이를 위해 뿌옇게 날리는 먼지를 몸으로 받아내면서도 작업을 지속 해 나가고 있다. 주로 호두나무와 물푸레나무 원목을 사용하여 작업을 하는 김경래 작가는 '연리지' 라는 신비한 자연현상을 모티브로 하고 있으며, 작업을 통해 나무가 지닌 본연의 속성과 촉감을 잃지 않으면서도, 실제 나무에서 찾아보기 힘든 좀 더 자연스럽고 유기적인 곡선을 추가하여 작품을 통해 자연스러움과 안락함을 느끼도록 하고 있다.

With various expressions in a subject 'Fused-together' for his furniture works, the designer Kim, Kyung Lae believes that a furniture is one of the best item to occupy the middle section of fine arts and applied arts, so continues to pursue his work enduring to get covered with dust. Using the hardwood of walnut and ash tree, Kim works with the motive of 'yeolligi', a mysterious phenomenon of nature that two trees physically bond together. What this designer aims in his works is to achieve the feelings of naturalness and comfortability by adding unaffected organic curving lines which real trees lack while keeping their inborn property and tactile sensation.

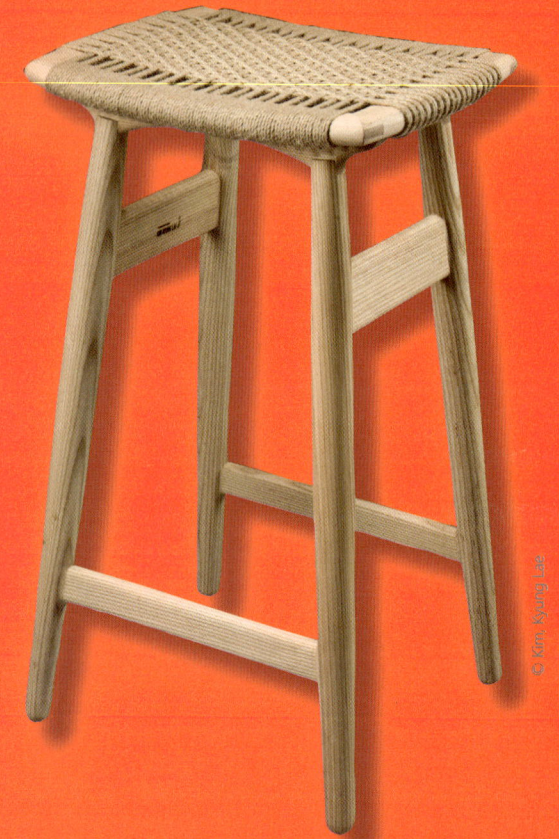

High Stool 2009-2
하이스툴 2009-2
70x40x33cm
Ash, Cord, Oil finishing
물푸레나무, 마닐라 끈, 천연오일
2009

© Kim, Kyung Lae

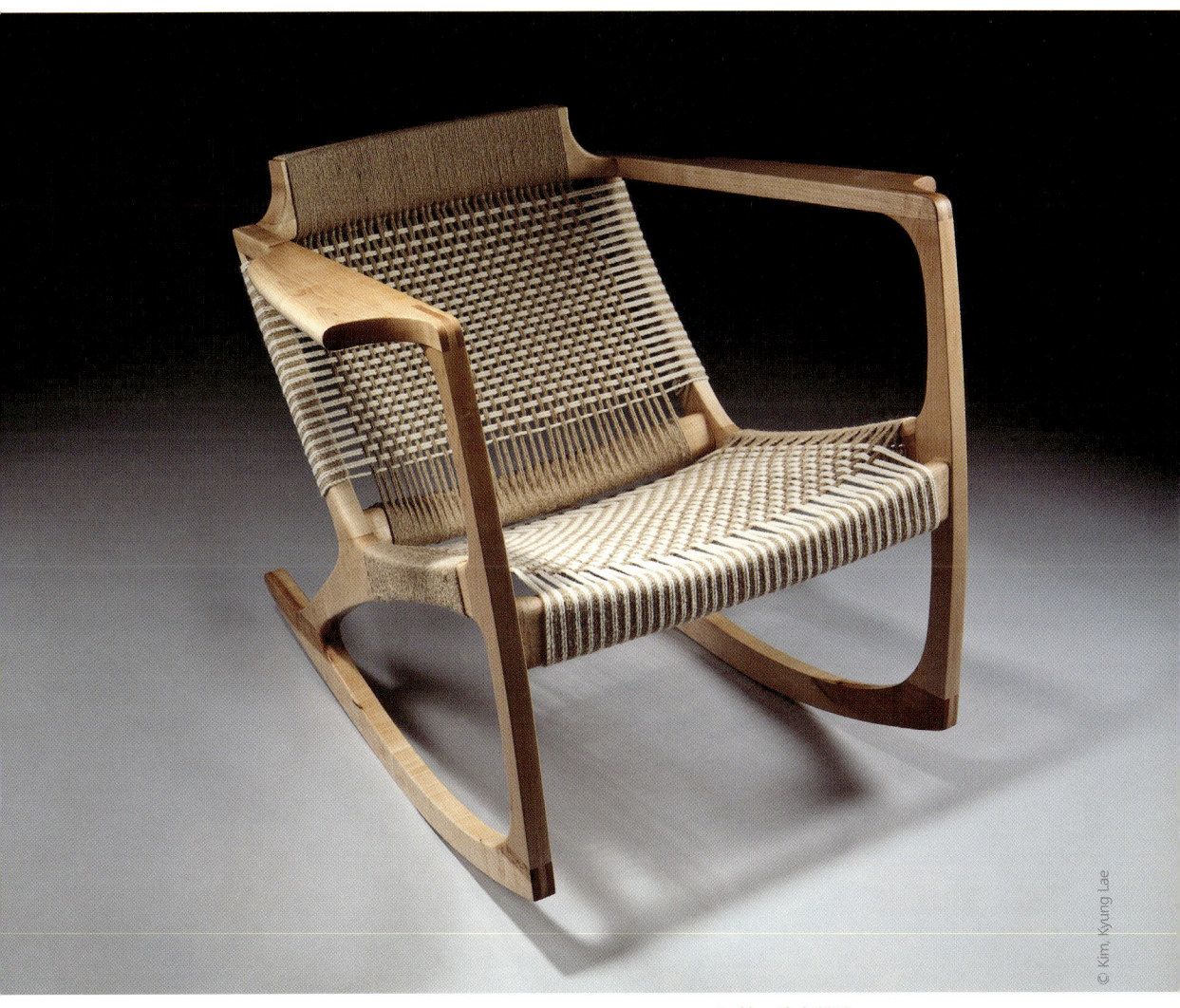

© Kim, Kyung Lae

Rocking Chair 2010
흔들의자 2010
60x74x65cm
Hard Maple, Cord, Oil finishing
경 단풍나무, 면사, 마닐라 끈, 천연오일
2010

Kim, Kyung Won 김경원

디자인은 경제적 가치 이외의 것을 실천해야만 한다. 그것은 단지 실용성이라고 속단하는 것도 단견이다. 일찍이 빅터 파파넥이 <인간을 위한 디자인>에서 말하지 않았던가. 우리가 살고 있는 현실(Real World)의 디자인은 윤리적 책임이 있다는 것을 말한다. 그에 따르면 디자이너는 항상 자신이 만든 제품의 재료와 제작방법은 물론 사후의 폐기문제나 재활용 가능성 등 모든 것을 심각하게 고려해야 한다. 디자이너의 사회적, 도덕적 책임감은 디자인을 시작하기 이전부터 머릿속에 각인되어야 한다는 것이다. 그의 주장이 현실적으로 이슈화 된 것은 1980년대 후반부터이다. 제품의 생산에 있어서 천연재료의 선택, 제작과정에서의 에너지 효율성, 제품의 수명 연장, 사용 후의 재사용 및 재생산, 폐기 시 자연분해 등 제품 기획의 순간에서부터 폐기에 이르는 전 과정에 있어서 디자이너와 소비자들은 점차 환경적인 요소를 고려하기 시작했다. 그리고 이러한 광의의 지속 가능한 발전을 위한 디자인을 우리는 '에코 디자인' 이라고 부른다.

Relish Bench와 Relish Stool은 에코 디자인의 관점으로 재생산 된 가구이다. four sides 제작 후 남은 재료들을 이용한 작품으로, 그것은 차기 작품의 원재료로서 활용가능성에 대한 제시였으며 작품제작 과정에서 발생하는 부산물(By-Product)을 재활용하려는 작가의 의도였다.오리지널 작품의 변형을 통해 바뀌어진 가구의 기능과 재형성된 공간을 그 과정의 중요성과 함께 선보이는 것이다. 단순히 배치를 바꿈으로써 이루어지는 것이 아니라 가구 그 자체의 변형으로 이루어진, 반복을 넘어선 재 공간화. 이것은 창의성을 바탕으로 만들어진 가구와 그 공간과의 관계에 대한 개념적 접근이자 에코디자인의 현실적 실천일 수 있다.

허태우, 안그라픽스

I have a belief that design should practice something more than merely an economical value. If someone might reach a hasty conclusion only with practicality from the statement, I might say that such an opinion is a narrow viewpoint. We can recall that Victor Papanek earlier advocated 'Design for the Real World'; it claims of a moral responsibility which design bears in our 'Real World.' According to Papanek, designers should seriously consider problems like disposal after use or recycling possibilities as well as the matters of using materials and productive methods. What he claims here is that the social and moral responsibilities of designers should precede their practice of design in real. It wan from the late 1980's when his claim first made an issue. At that time, both designers and consumers began to consider environmental effects in the whole process of design production from the very moment of production plans to the disposal: the choice of natural materials, energy efficacy during the production process, the life extension of products, recycling and reproduction after use, natural decomposition of the products when discarding, and etc. We now call such a design with the possibilities of continuous development in this wide term an 'Eco Design.'

The Relish Bench and the Relish Stool are furniture produced in eco design's perspectives. They were made from the spare materials after the production of four sides, and propose availability that raw materials still keep for next works. It certainly comes out of the designer's intention to recycle by-products in the production process. Namely, the designer exhibits the transmitted functions of furniture with reformed space and the significance of the working process itself through a modification of his original works. Re-spacing surpassing a mere repetition, not only from a change of arrangements but from the transformation of furniture itself; it can be a practical action of eco-design as well as a conceptual approach to a relationship between the furniture and its space in creativity, I believe.

HUR, Tae-Woo, ahn graphics

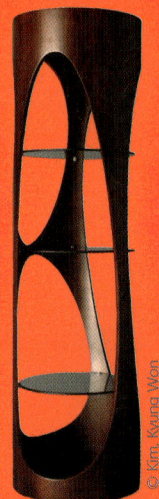

Four Sides
181x50x50cm
Plywood, Walnut
자작나무, 호두나무
2006

© Kim, Kyung Won

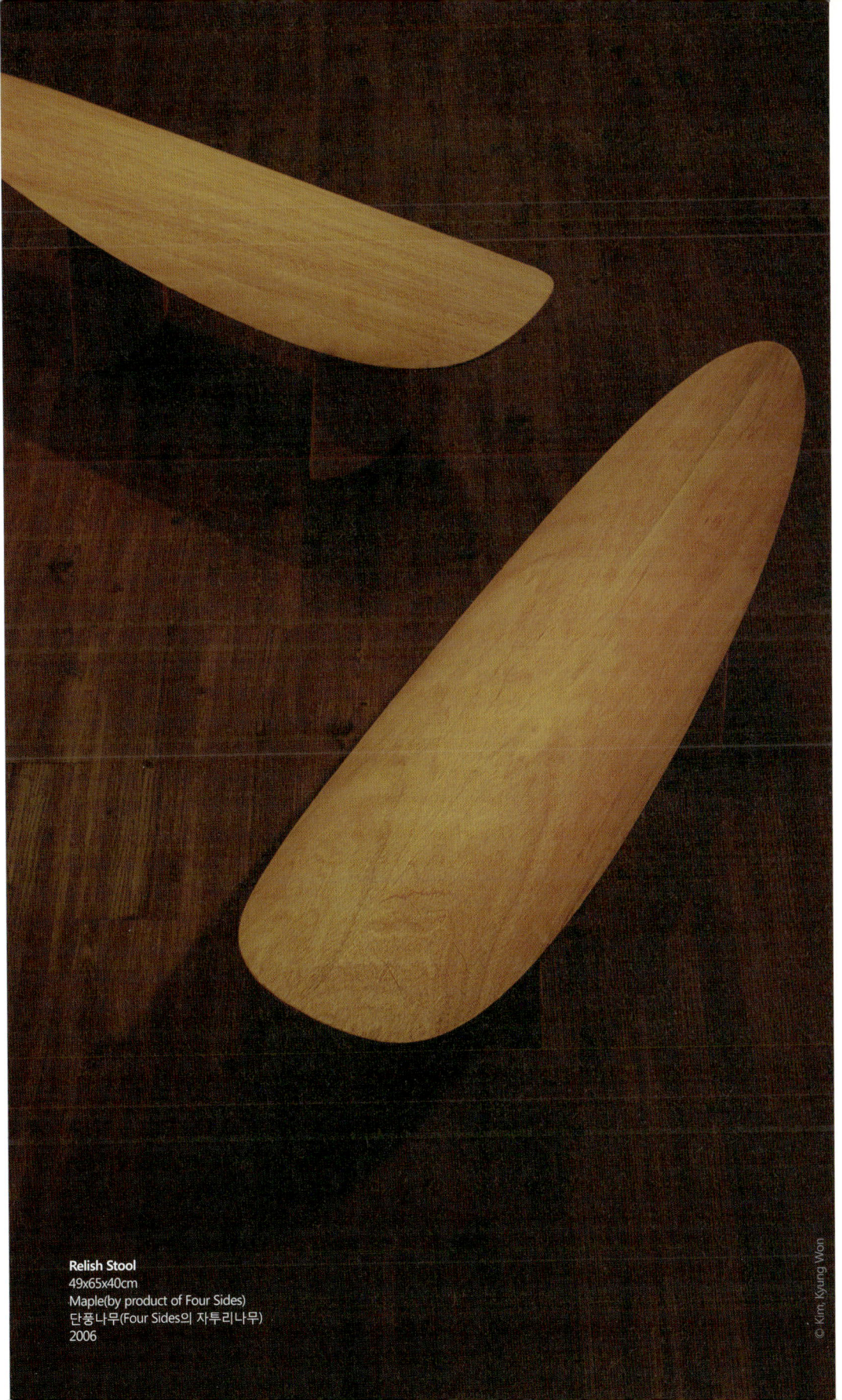

Relish Stool
49x65x40cm
Maple(by product of Four Sides)
단풍나무(Four Sides의 자투리나무)
2006

© Kim, Kyung Won

Arttu Kuisma, Janne Melajoki
아르뚜 쿠이스마, 얀 멜라요키

Just in Finland, 1,000,000 m^2 of exhibition carpet is thrown out as useless waste every year. There isn't much effort in trying to find new ways of re-using this carpet and most of it ends up in the garbage dump after one use. Ironically the idea for the *Rrround* chair came from a roll of exhibition carpet that we had used in an exhibition.

핀란드에서만 해도, 매해 백만 평방 제곱 미터의 전시회용 카펫이 쓰레기로 버려지고 있다. 이러한 카펫을 재활용하는 새로운 방법을 찾는 노력은 그다지 이루어지지 않고 있고, 대부분은 결국 한번 사용되고 나서 쓰레기 더미가 되는 것이다. 아이러니하게도 *Rrround*에 대한 아이디어는 우리가 전시회 때 사용했던 카펫에서 얻게 되었다.

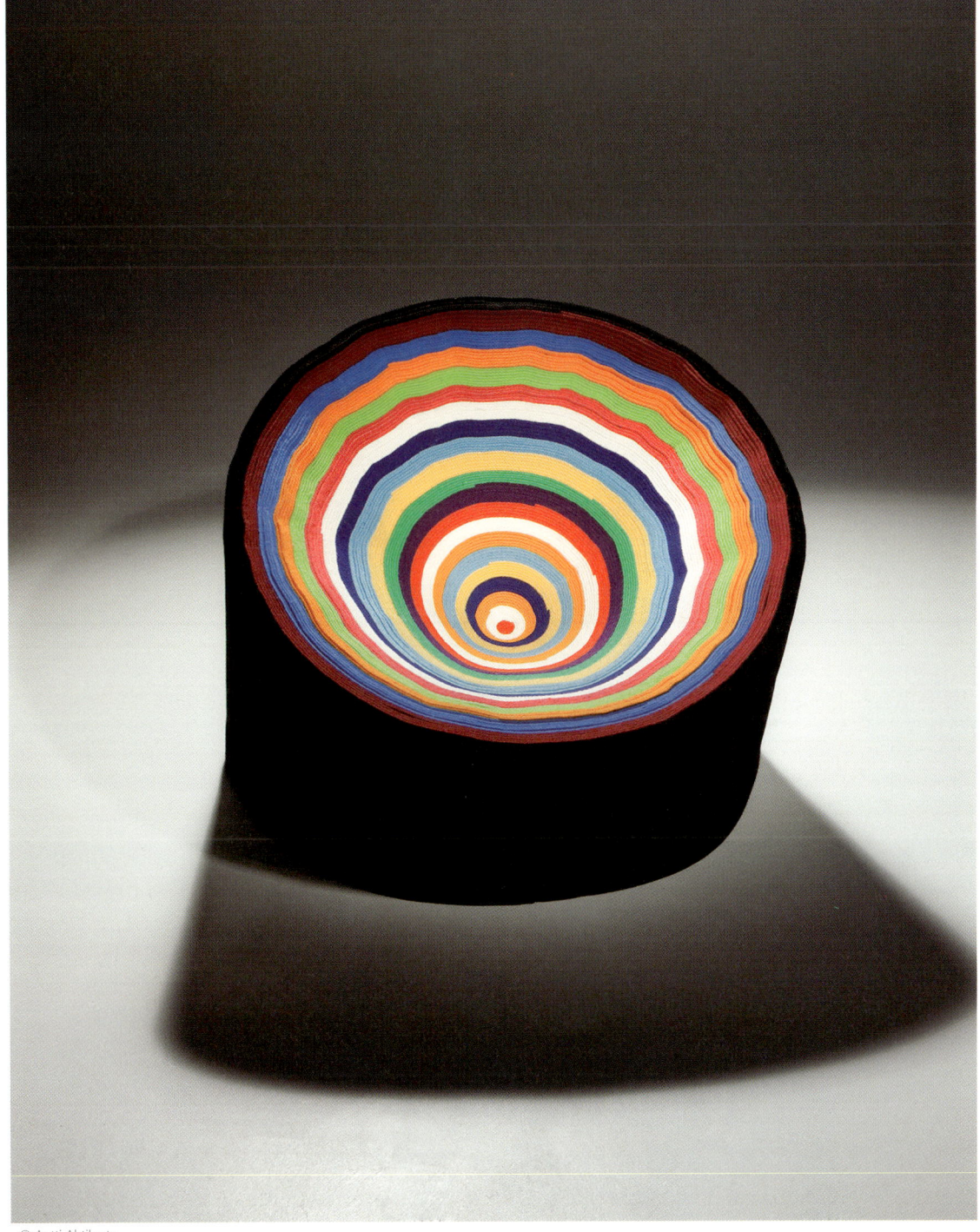

© Antti Ahtiluoto

Rrround
라운드
100x100x100cm
A roll of used exhibition carpet 전시장 폐 카펫 롤
2010

Carolien Laro 카롤리언 라로

Solid Wood that is flexible: that was my challenge in designing and developing Spring Wood. Just like in nature that surrounds us gently: branches of all trees are flexible otherwise they could not survive the wind and would break. And in nature every tree is Starting with 'the original' I invested 1200 Hours of testing and trying to create the first seat. After this we developed the range with The Paperclip and The Bridge. A step further was to incorporate the legs into the design so the Restless Legs version was born. All versions are 'made to weight' so every item is personal.
always 'in movement'. These were my starting points to develop Spring Wood.
The seating experience is unique: you expect a hard seat but it is soft...
After introduction we received worldwide interest; especially from the Asian and Scandinavian countries. Is this because the design is so 'less is more'?
In my designs for interiors and furniture I always try to rethink the basis.

유연한 춘재(春材 : 수목의 나이테의 부드러운 부분)를 이용한 디자인은 나에게 있어 하나의 도전이었다. 자연에서와 마찬가지로 그것은 우리를 부드럽게 둘러 싼다. 나무들이 바람 속에서 살아남지 못하고 부러지는 것과는 다르게 나무의 가지들은 유연하다. 자연 상태의 모든 나무들은 늘 '움직이고 있다.' 바로 이러한 점에서 나는 춘재를 이용해 작업하기 시작했다.
나는 첫 번째 의자를 만들기 위해 1200여 시간을 투자했다. 이후 페이퍼 클립과 Bridge로 그 범위를 넓혔다. 다음 단계는 이 디자인에 다리를 추가하는 것이었고, 움직이는 다리 버전이 탄생하게 되었다. 모든 버전들은 무게에 따라 만들어지며, 따라서 모든 작품들은 개인적이라고 할 수 있다.
부드럽지만 강한 이 의자에 앉는 경험은 특별하다.
이 작품을 처음 선보인 뒤, 우리는 세계적인 관심을 받게 되었는데, 특히 아시아와 스칸디나비아 국가로부터 많은 주목을 받았다. 이 디자인의 간결함 때문일까?
실내와 가구를 위한 디자인에 있어, 나는 늘 기본적인 것을 다시 생각해 보려 노력 한다.

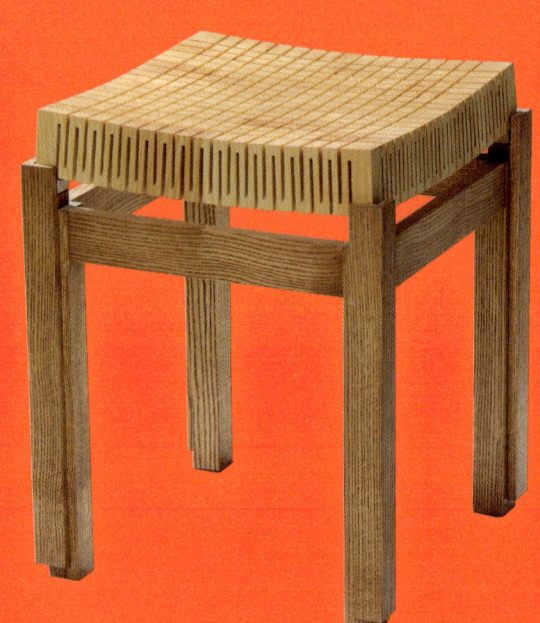

Spring Wood: Original
스프링 나무: 오리지널
45x36x36cm
Ash 물푸레나무
2009

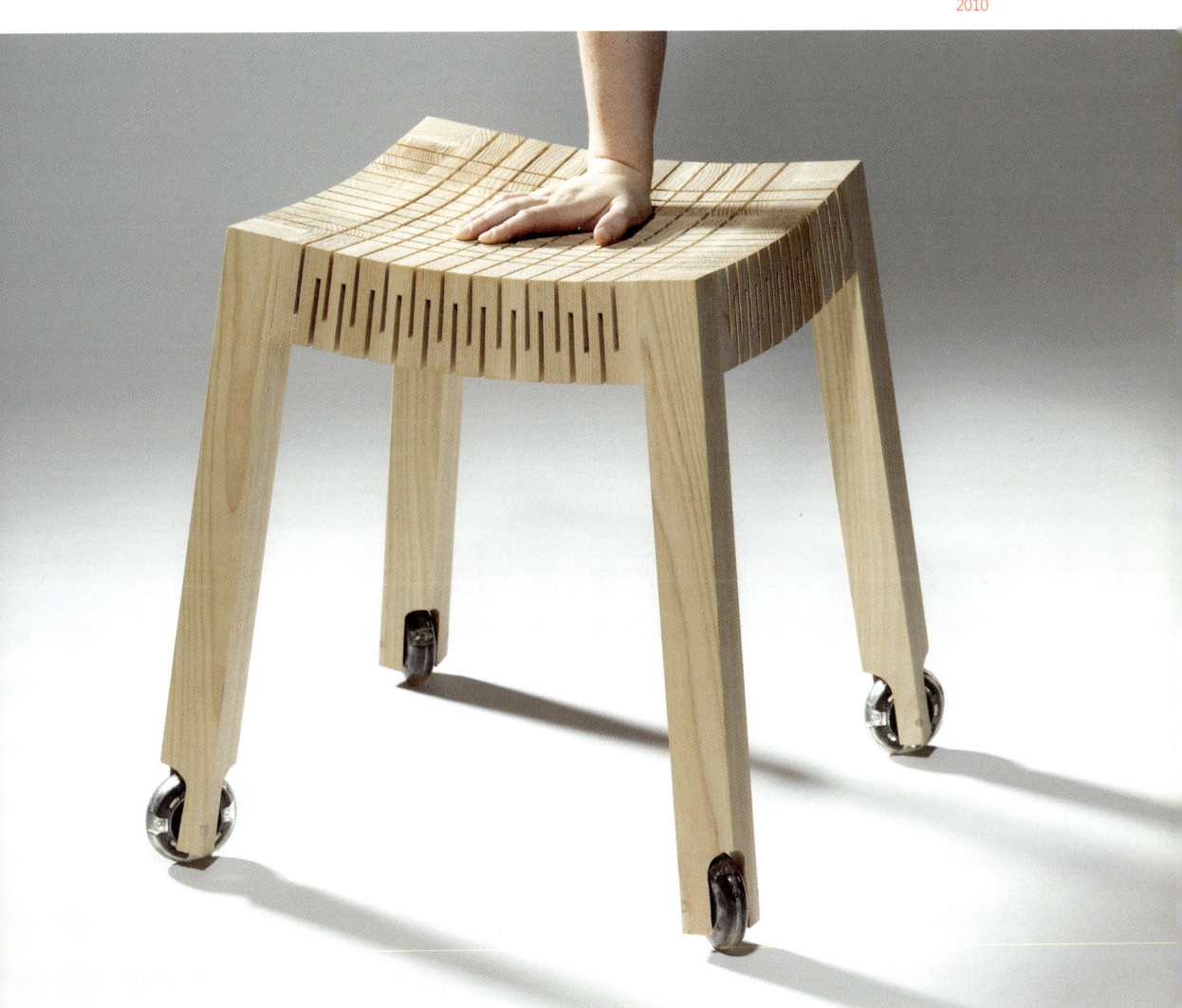

Lee, Sam Woong 이삼웅

이삼웅이 작업에 대해 근본을 두고 있는 철학은 사람과 환경, 사물간의 관계이다. 세상의 모든 존재는 고유한 의미와 정체성을 지니고 있으며, 조화와 혼돈 사이에서 상호보완의 관계를 형성하고 살아간다. 이러한 환경 안에서의 디자인의 역할에 대한 고민과 그 시대를 바라보는 디자이너로서의 역할을 실천하기 위한 해법을 찾아나가는 중이다.

하나의 아이디어에서 출발하여 물리적인 결과물로 만들어나가는 작업 과정 또한 그가 경험하는 세상과의 관계, 몰입을 통한 삶의 과정을 반영한다. 그가 추구하는 디자인은 인간의 삶에 중요한 하나의 부분을 차지하며 치유의 역할을 할 수 있는 감성적인 매개체로서, 가구를 통해 사람과 사물, 자연과의 소통을 위한 것이다.

표현 방법에 있어서도 제한을 두지 않고 리서치와 실험을 통해 한국의 전통적인 기법과 재료를 현대적으로 재해석하여 응용하거나, 신소재를 접목시켜 특유의 상상력으로 접근하여 독창적이고 새로운 형태에 감성을 담아내고 있다.

The basic philosophy that Lee, Sam Woong puts on his work revolves around the relationships between humans, the environment, and objects. Everything in the world has its own meaning and identity, and lives complementary between harmony and chaos. The designer persistently seeks for a solution so that he can practice his role as a designer. He thinks over the design for his contemporaries in such surroundings.

The designer's working process in which he develops an idea into a physical outgrowth also reflects his experiences, his relationships, and his life journey. The design he chases occupies an important part in one's life; like a sensuous medium which cures, his furniture aims to communicate among people, objects, and nature.

With no limitation in expressive methods, the designer applies Korean traditional techniques and materials to contemporary interpretations through various research and experiments or adopts new materials with his peculiar imagination to contain senses in novel and ingenious forms.

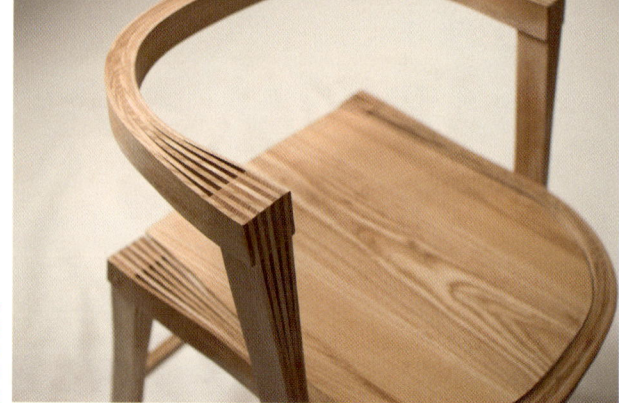

Finger Joint Chair
깍지 끼기 의자
65x58x53cm
Ash 물푸레나무
2010

© Lee, Sam Woong

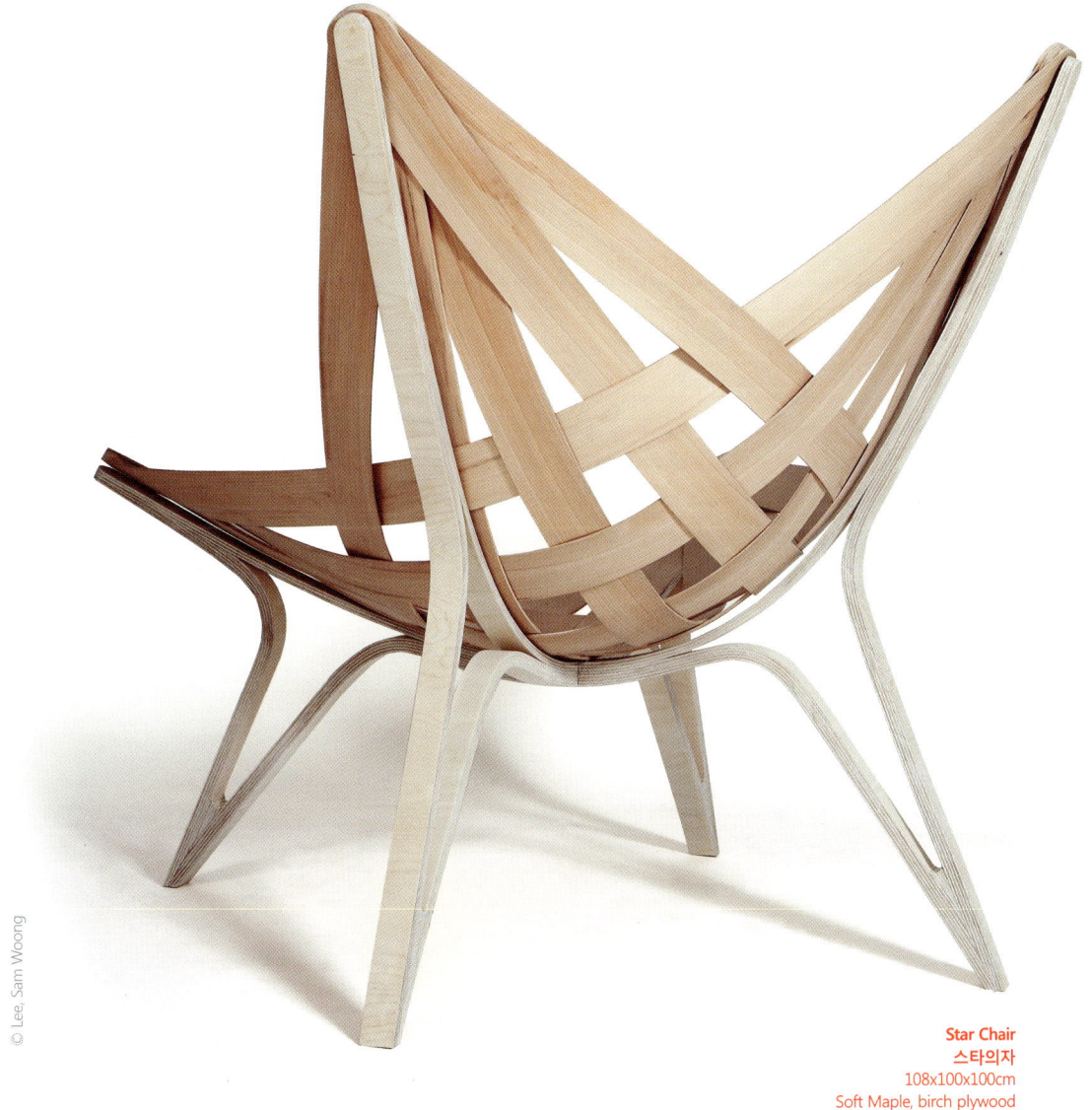

© Lee, Sam Woong

Star Chair
스타의자
108x100x100cm
Soft Maple, birch plywood
단풍, 자작나무합판
2007

Daniel Lorch 다니엘 로히

Daniel Lorch was born in 1980 in Baden-Baden, Germany. He studied communication-design at the HTWG-Konstanz under Michele Baviera. Before graduating from university in 2006, he did an internship at INTEGRAL RUEDI BAUR ET ASSOCIÉS in Paris.
In 2007, he founded DANIEL LORCH DESIGN in Berlin. Besides working in the field of communication-design, he began designing furniture, products and lighting. Conceptual clarity, simplicity and self-evidence, are significant for his designs.
In 2010 Daniel Lorch founded the furniture brand L&Z, together with Aidin Zimmermann. He is currently working on several commissions from furniture, products and lighting to corporate-design.
His works received the IF CONCEPT AWARD COMMUNICATION in 2006, the DESIGNPLUS AWARD in 2009 and the DESIGN REPORT AWARD 2011 / SPECIAL MENTION.

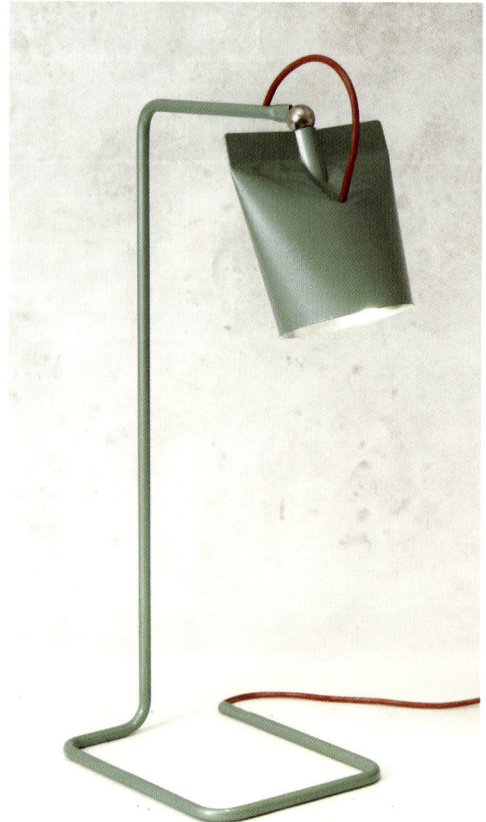

다니엘 로히는 1980년 독일의 바덴바덴에서 태어났다. 그는 HTWG-Konstanz under Michele Baviera에서 커뮤니케이션 디자인을 공부했다. 2006년 졸업 전, 파리에 있는 INTEGRAL RUEDI BAUR ET ASSOCIÉS에서 인턴쉽을 이수했고 2007년, 베를린에 다니엘 로히 스튜디오를 만들었다. 커뮤니케이션 디자인의 영역에서 활동하며 가구, 제품, 조명 디자인을 시작했다. 개념적인 명확성, 단순성, 자명성은 그의 디자인의 특징이다.
2010년 다니엘 로히는 Aidin Zimmermann와 함께 가구 브랜드인 L&Z를 설립했다. 최근 그는 가구, 제품, 조명디자인과 협업디자인을 아우르는 여러 업무를 맡고 있다.
그의 작품은 2006년 IF CONCEPT AWARD COMMUNICATION, 2009년 the DESIGNPLUS AWARD, 2011년 DESIGN REPORT AWARD/ SPECIAL MENTION 에서 수상한 바 있다.

X Y and Z, Table lamp
X Y Z 테이블 램프
60x25x18cm
Aluminum, steel tube 알루미늄, 철 튜브
2010

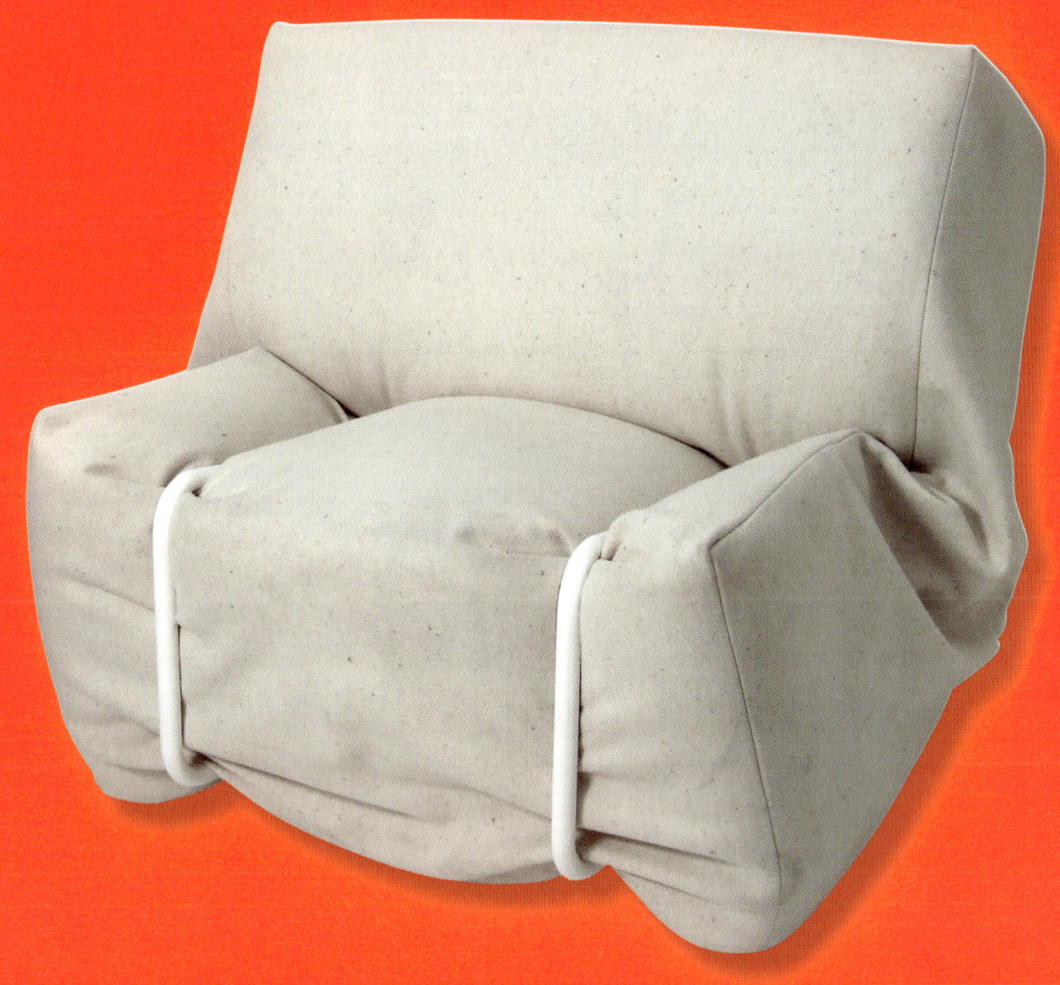

Marshmallow
마쉬멜로우
110x110x100cm
Linen, rubber foam, steel tube
린넨, 고무폼, 철 튜브
2008

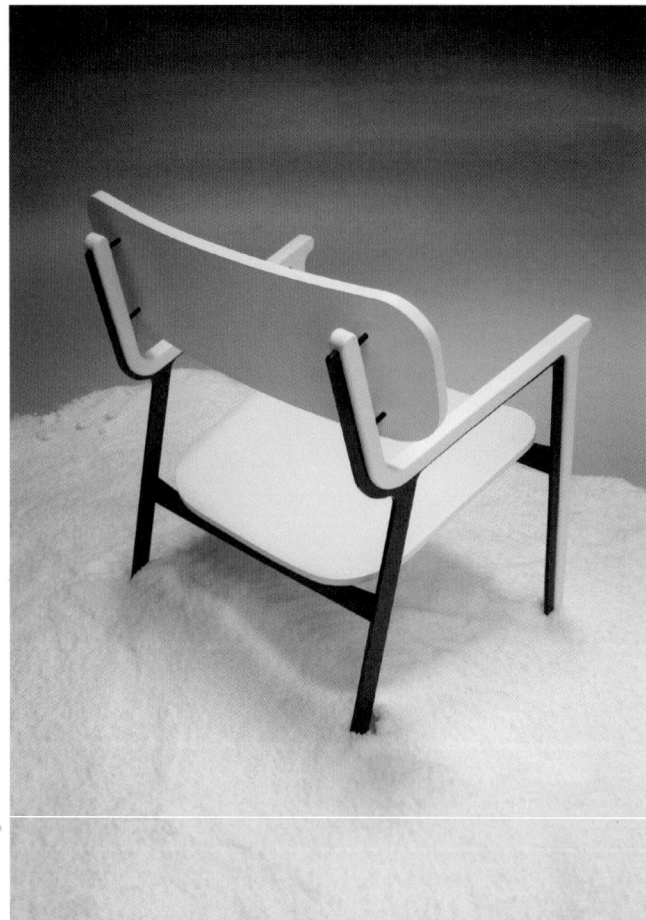

© Luff Design

Snow Chair
스노우체어
65x55x60cm
Birch wood, steel 자작나무, 철
2011

Korea | 한국

Luff Design_Lee, Jae Ha, Jung, Ji Ho
러프디자인_이재하, 정지호

이재하와 정지호 두 명의 디자이너로 이루어진 러프디자인은 2008년 gallery BMH에서 러프디자인 展을 시작으로, 다양한 전시와 프로젝트를 통해 꾸준히 활동하고 있다.
'혁신은 특별한 것이 아니다'
디자인이란 가장 현실적인 시선에서 가장 현명한 방법을 찾아나가는 것이라고 생각하는 러프디자인은 작업 초기 디자인 방향성을 만들어 나가는 과정에서 고전적인 가구들을 접하게 되었고, 오래된 디테일의 발견은 일종의 자극이 되었다. 그 후 지극히 회화적인 예술 가구(아트 퍼니쳐)가 아닌 현실을 반영한 디자인 가구를 지향하고 있다. 근래에 들어 예술 가구(아트 퍼니쳐)에 대한 관심이 늘어나면서 상대적으로 자극적인 형태의 가구들이 관심 받고 있다. 국내의 크고 작은 페어 에서도 이 같은 현상들을 쉽게 접할 수 있다. 러프디자인은 가구의 정도를 지키자는 소신을 가지고 있다.
앞서 언급한 예술 가구(아트 퍼니쳐)에 대한 비판이나 반감이 아닌 가구를 디자인 하는 입장으로서 균형을 이루고자 하는 것이 러프디자인의 바람이다.

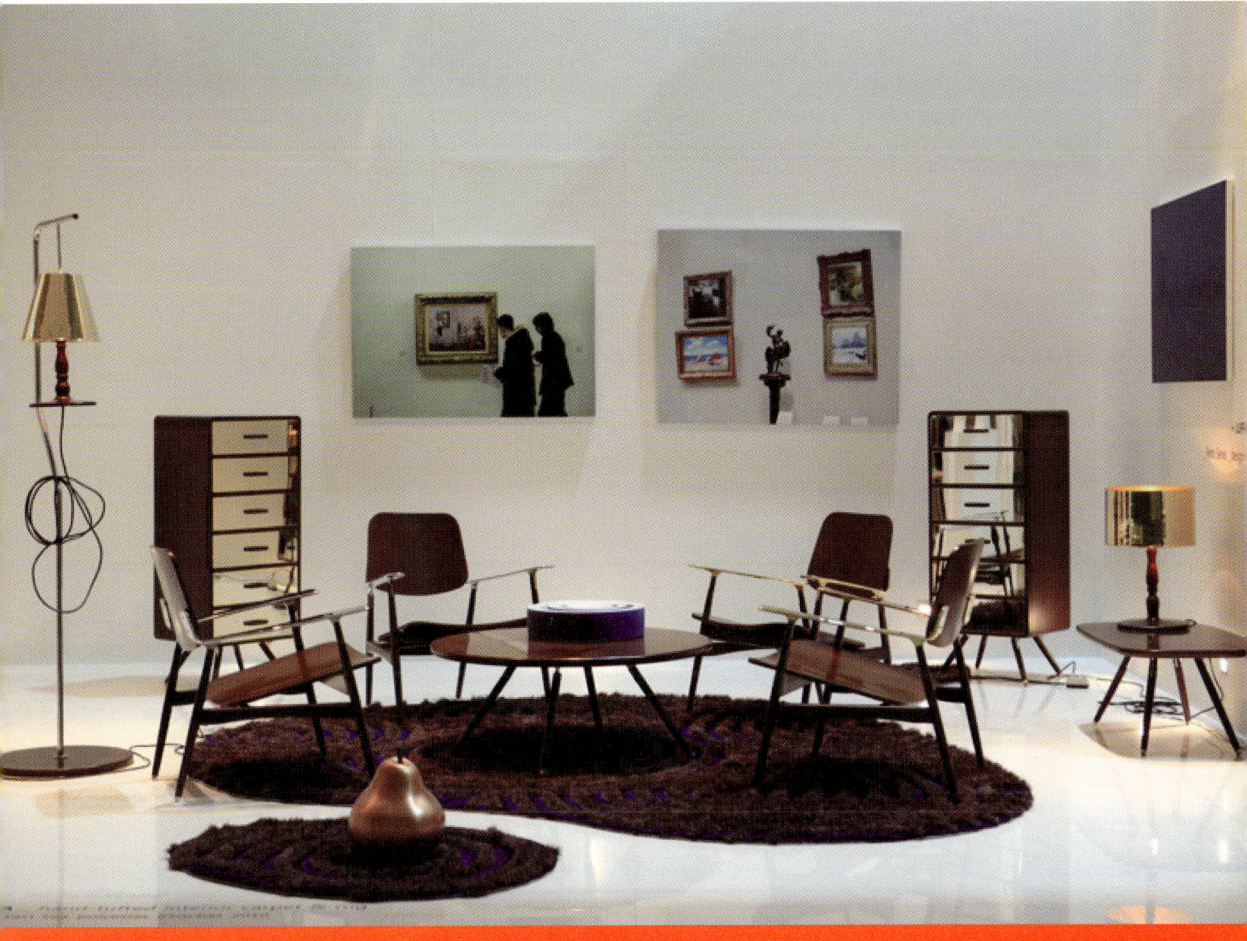

Retro Series
레트로시리즈
Chair 의자 75x60x70cm
Table 테이블 42x50x90cm
Cabinet 캐비닛 150x60x50cm
Rose wood, gold plating steel 로즈우드, 도금된 철
2009

The Luff Design, with two designer members, Lee Jaeha and Jung Jiho, has vigorously worked in various exhibitions and projects since their first design exhibition at the Gallery BMH in 2008.
'Innovation is nothing special.'
Believing that the design should seek for the wisest ways from the most practical viewpoints, the Luff Design encountered classical furniture which stimulated the designers with their antique details. From then on, they have aimed for design furniture which reflects the reality instead of pictorial 'art furniture.'
Furniture in excitative form recently has drawn more attention as the interest in art furniture grows. This phenomenon is easily found in domestic great and small design fairs.
Luff Design has a conviction to follow the straight path of furniture. It is not simply a criticism or antipathy toward art furniture as stated above, but the Luff Design wishes to keep balance in designing furniture.

Rainer Mutsch 라이나 무취

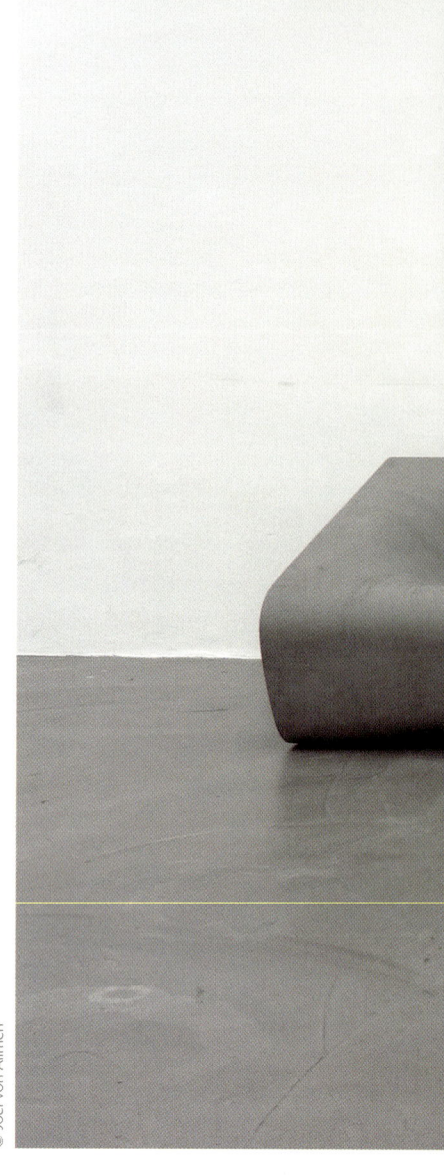

© Joel von Allmen

When I saw the very first ETERNIT – fiber cement - machine, I was amazed: 20 metres long, more than 100 years old and by now of course upgraded with high-tech computers, the very heart of the machine is still the cast-metal construction built back in 1905. This impressive device survived 2 world wars and is until today producing a very stable and sustainable material which is sold worldwide.

With DUNE I tried to visualize the present material-technical maximum parameters of this special fibercement material but furthermore I wanted to tell a story about the history of the company ETERNIT and the unique hand forming production process.

The design of DUNE was derived from the fiber cements technical characteristics in order to get the maximum stability out of 3d-deformed fiber cement; eventually, the geometry of the chair supports its stability through its controlled expansion and compression of the material which results in a load-capacity of around 900kg on the seating surface.

DUNE has been designed as highly modular and indefinitely expandable system for outdoor spaces to fit all spatial situations.

20미터의 길이에 100년도 더 된 –물론 현재는 고성능 컴퓨터로 업그레이드 되어 있다- 섬유 시멘트 기계인 ETERNIT를 처음 보았을 때 나는 깜짝 놀랐다. 기계의 심장부는 여전히 1905년에 주조된 구조물로 되어 있다. 이 멋진 기계는 두 차례의 세계 대전을 거치면서도 살아남았고 오늘날까지 매우 안정적이고 지속 가능한 재료를 만들어 내고 있으며, 이렇게 만들어진 재료는 전세계에 판매되고 있다.

나는 이 특별한 섬유시멘트 재료의 현존하는 재료기술의 최대 한계를 *모래 언덕*을 이용하여 시각화하고자 노력했고, 나아가 ETERNIT 사의 역사와 제조 과정에 대해 이야기하고자 한다.

*모래 언덕*의 디자인은 최대치의 안정성을 얻기 위한 섬유 시멘트 기술의 특징에서 유래한다; 마침내, 의자의 기하학적 구조는 제어된 확장과 재료의 압축을 통해 그것의 안정성을 지탱하며, 마침내 착석부분에 900kg 가량의 적재능력을 얻게 되었다.

*모래 언덕*은 고도로 모듈화되어 있으며, 모든 공간적 상황에 적합하도록 외부 공간으로 무한히 확장 가능한 시스템으로 디자인되었다.

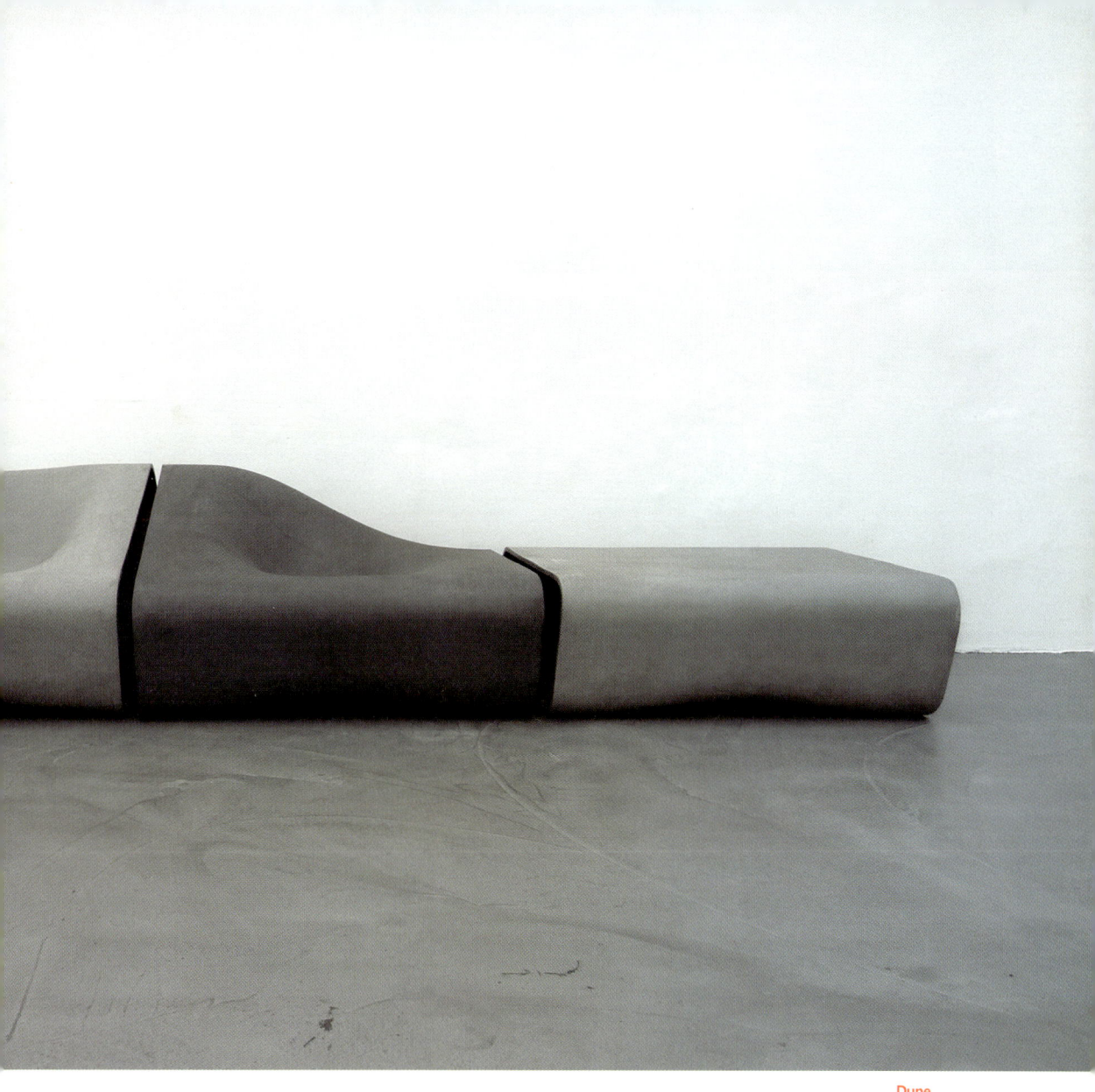

Dune
모래언덕
68x96x94cm
12mm fiber cement 12mm 섬유 시멘트
2010
Eternit(Schweiz) AG

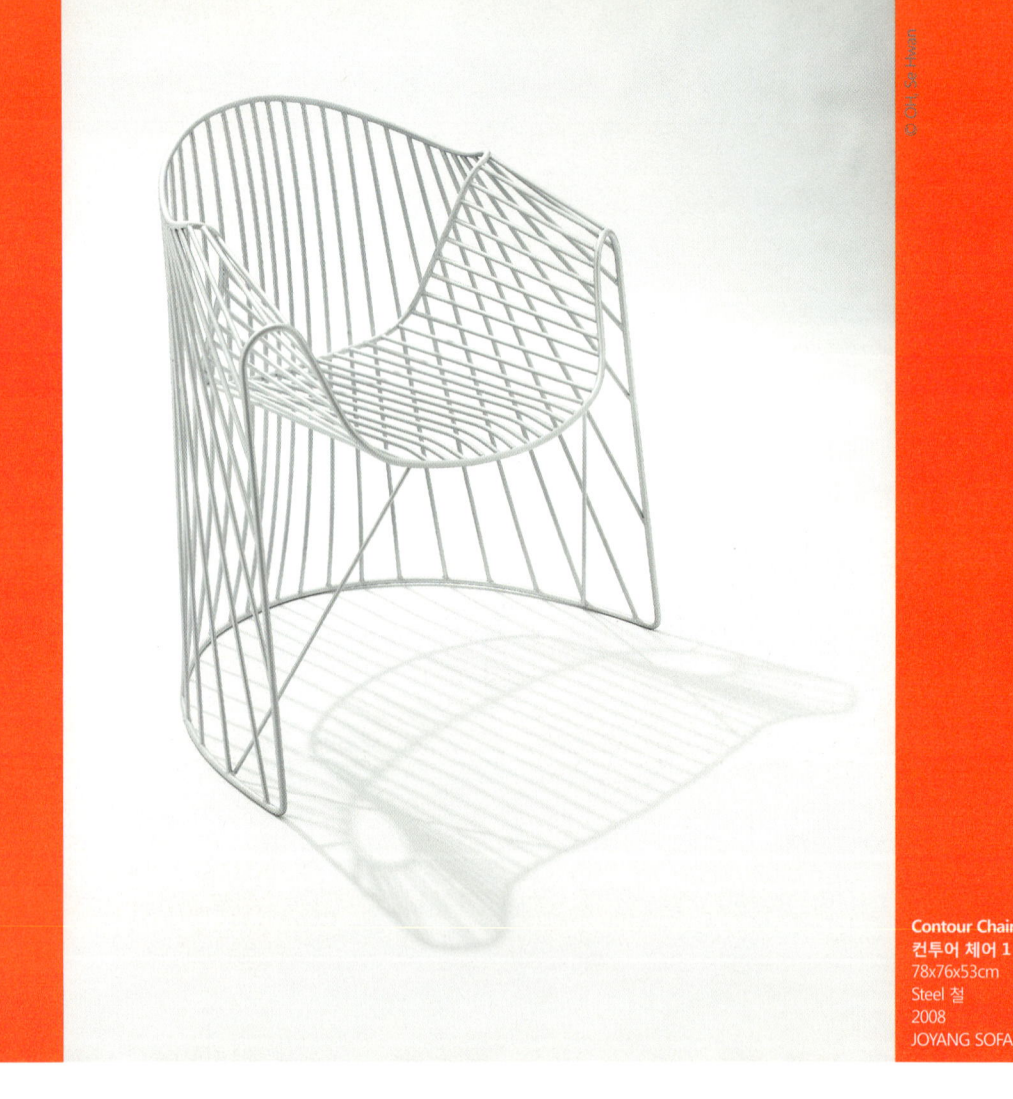

Contour Chair 1
컨투어 체어 1
78x76x53cm
Steel 철
2008
JOYANG SOFA 조양소파

Korea | 한국

Oh, Se Hwan 오세환

작가는 디자인 가구의 미학을 우리 생활 속의 소재들을 사용해, 익숙함과 편안함을 주는 동시에 아름다움으로 대중에게 전달하고 있다. 스틸을 구부린 심플한 형태와 곡선미를 강조하여 한복의 아름다운 곡선을 형상화 하여 디자인한 의자, 정수리 필터를 이용한 조명 등 다양한 물성의 소재들을 거침없이 사용한다. 다양한 소재에 대한 끊임없는 그의 고민이 보다 창조적인 디자인으로 이어지고 결국 대중에게 어필하는 가구 디자이너로 인정받게 하는 저력이 되고 있다. 반복되는 선의 아름다움은 새로운 실루엣을 만들어내고 이는 의자라는 오브제로 해석된다.

김신혜, 가양갤러리 대표

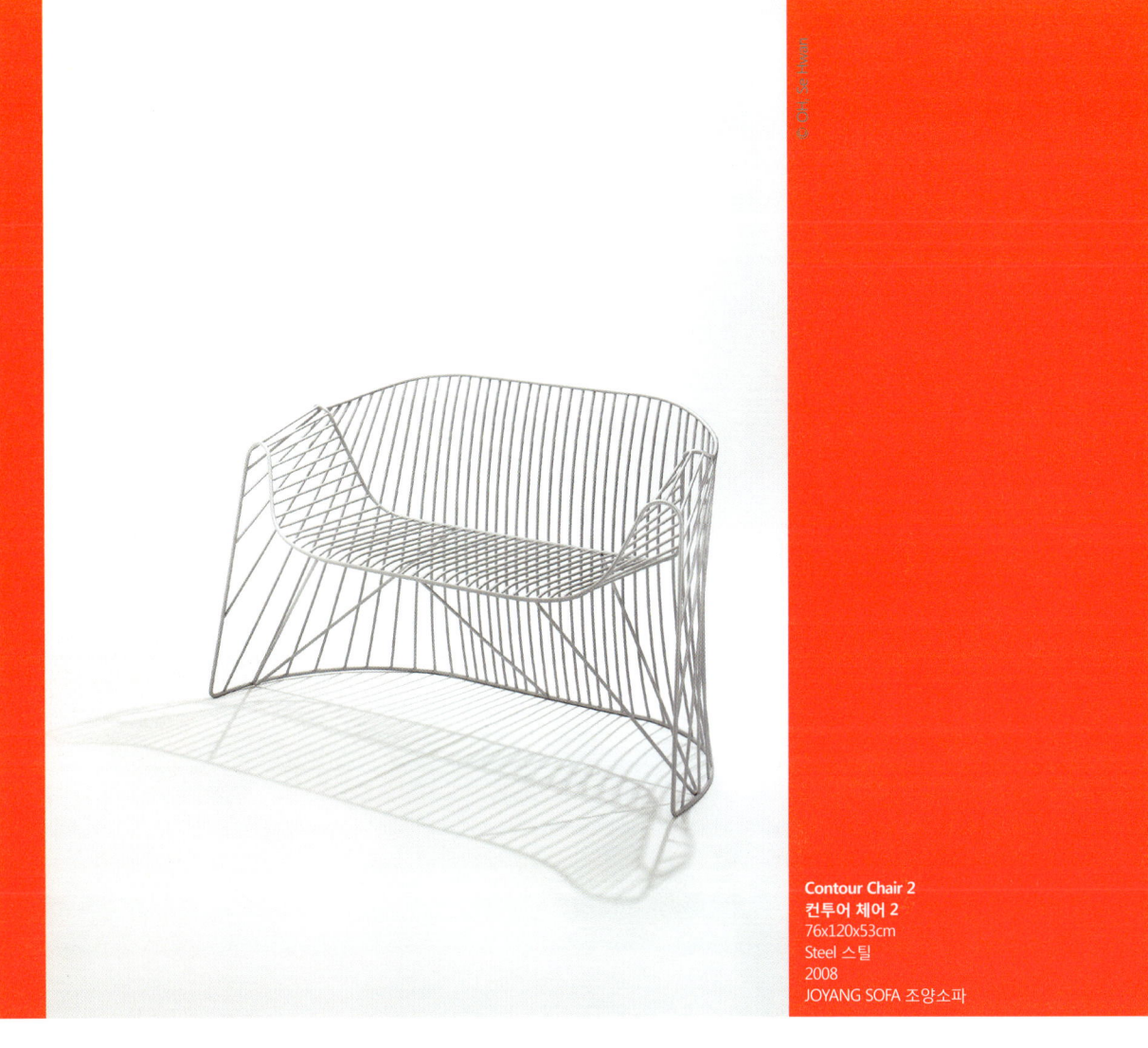

© Oh, Se Hwan

Contour Chair 2
컨투어 체어 2
76x120x53cm
Steel 스틸
2008
JOYANG SOFA 조양소파

The designer Oh, Se Hwan conveys familiarity and comfort as well as beauty to the public by using materials in our daily lives with the aesthetics of design furniture. He utilizes various properties of materials in his design such as chairs with simple forms of bent steel and beautiful curved lines of Hanbok (Korean traditional clothes), or electric lights utilized for filters of water purifiers. His incessant investigation on diverse materials has resulted in more creative designs, and has impacted his style to appeal more favorably to the public. The beauty of his repetitive lines creates new silhouettes, which we can interpret as a chair.

KIM, Shin Hye, Director of Gallery Kayang

Park + Yoo 박수우+유이화

Booboo Chair
부부체어
64x42x42cm
Brass, Fabric 놋쇠, 천
2008

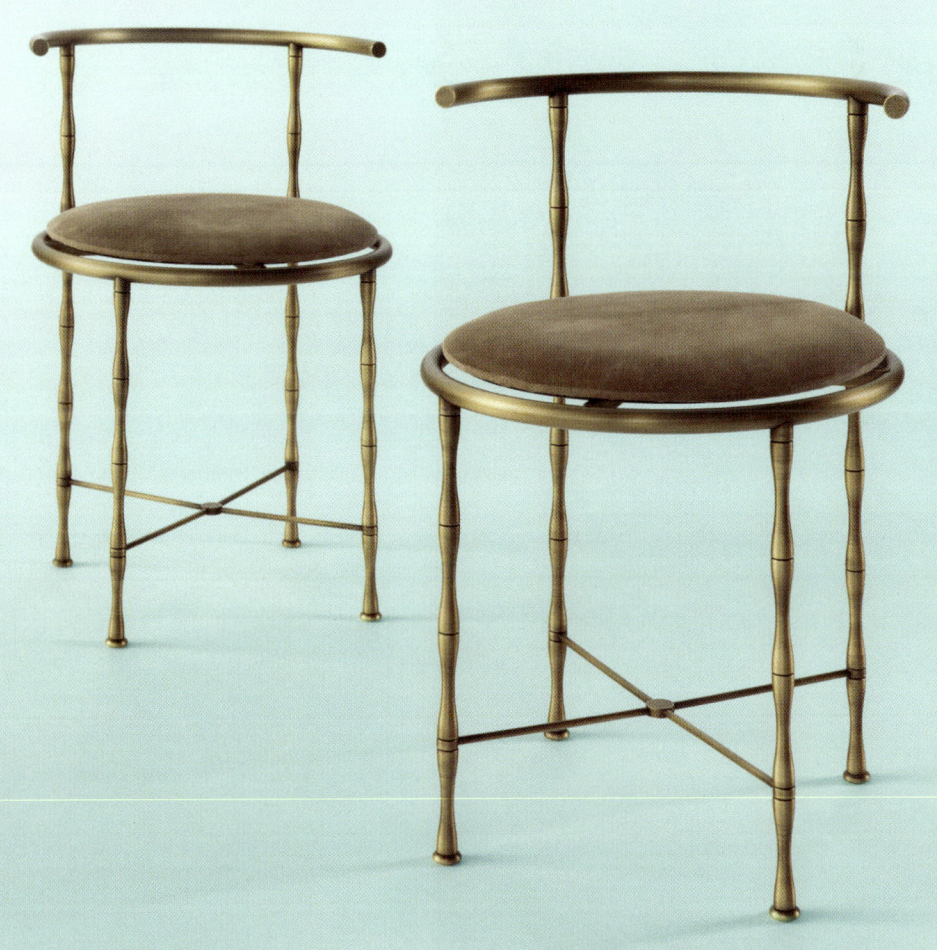

©_croft

Pyo, Yang Soo 표양수

*아프로 체어*는 실용적인 디자인 보다는 이야기와 느낌을 전달하는 과정을 중요시 한 디자인 작품이다. 헤어스타일 종류의 하나인 아프로 퍼머를 소재로 하여 부풀려진 형태에서 오는 푹신하고 따뜻한 느낌을 금속성의 스프링 소재로 전달하고자 한 작업이다. 금속성이 갖고 있는 차갑고 단단하고 무거운 느낌을 따뜻하고 부드럽게 표현하였다. 금속성으로 전달되는 푹신하고 부드러운 느낌을 통하여, 작품을 경험하는 모든 사람들이 작가의 생각과 해석방법을 느끼고 이해하며, 느낌이라는 메신저를 통하여 자연스럽게 소통하기를 바라는 의미가 포함되어 있는 디자인 작품이다. 디자인 작품이라는 점은 디자이너의 작업이기 때문이라기 보다는 작품에 앉게 되는 이의 배려가 작품의 제작과정에 표현 되었기 때문이다. 작품에 사용된 스프링이라는 소재를 보았을 때 일반적으로 스웨터나 짜임 구조의 직조물이 걸릴 것이라고 느끼겠지만 2링 스프링을 사용하여 스프링과 스프링의 결속력은 유지하면서 작품을 경험하고자 하는 모든 사람 에게 불편함을 주지 않도록 제작 되었기 때문이다. *아프로 체어*를 통하여 작가의 또 다른 작품들을 경험자들이 좀더 원활하게 이해하고 공감할 수 있는 소통의 통로가 열리기를 기대하며 만들어진 작품이다.

Afro Chair is a design work that stresses on the process of conveyance its story and feeling rather than design itself. It aims to have fleecy, warm feelings with metallic spring materials, like an inflated form of an Afro permanent; a kind of hairstyle. In this work, the designer transformed the metallic materials that had a sense of being cold, hard, and heavy natured into that of something warm and soft. Through the transmutation of metallic feelings into that of a fleecy and soft nature, the designer wishes that all people who experience the work could understand his own thoughts and interpretations and then communicate them back to nature through their own 'feelings' like a messenger. We call his piece a design work not because it is a work by a designer but because thoughtful consideration for the one sitting was expressed. One can assume that while seated, strands of one's sweater could easily get snagged by some parts of the structure due to its spring-like materials, but the two ring springs used for this work was produced to avoid any inconvenience for the sitter, while also keeping its firmness in act. The designer worked on this piece so that people can also apprehend other work and gain understanding through the *Afro Chair*.

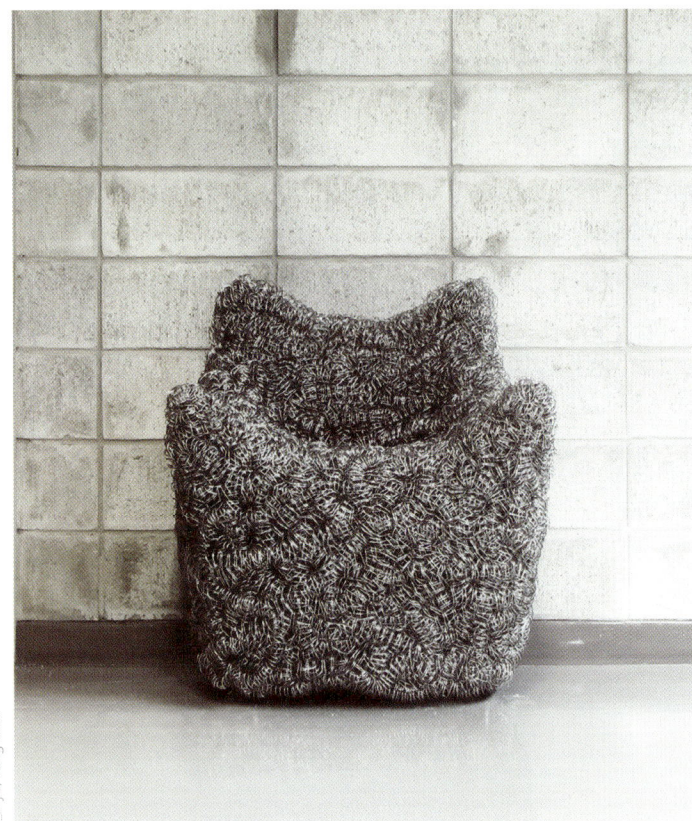

©Pyo, Yang Soo

Afro Chair Silver
아프로 체어 은색
100x83x95cm
2 Ring spring for note
2링 노트스프링
2009

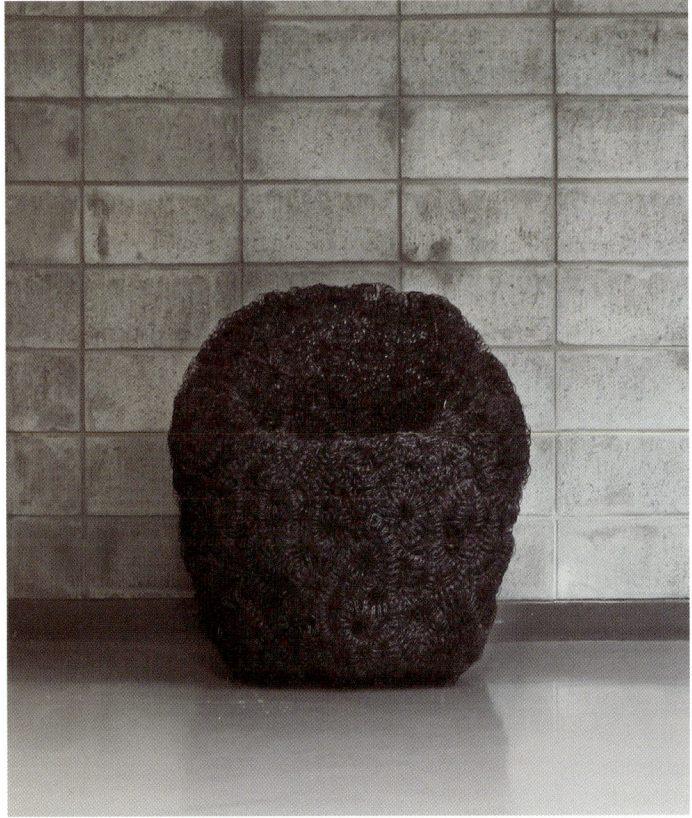

©Pyo, Yang Soo

Afro Chair Black
아프로 체어 검정
98x83x95cm
2 Ring spring for note
2링 노트스프링
2009

Shin, Ji Hun 신지훈

신지훈은 직관과 본능을 따른다. 그는 머리뿐만 아니라 마음에 달린 눈과 귀로 세상을 느낀다. 우연처럼 마주친 영감을 디자이너는 감각적으로 인지하고 감성적으로 접근할 수 있는 디자인 형태로 만들어낸다. 신지훈은 어떤 건축이나 오브제를 봤을 때 누가 만들었고 철학은 무엇이고 어떤 컨셉인지 따져 묻지 않아도 있는 그 자체에서 느낀 무언가로 또 다른 감각을 자극하는 디자인을 지향한다. 그가 말하는 감각이란 건축가 루이스칸이 <침묵과 빛>을 통해 이야기한 '만질 수 없는 성질'이다. 인간이라는 자연물이 본능에 따라 무언가를 인지하는 행위와 같은 것이다.

장남미, JJ magazine, no. 68

Shin, Ji Hun follows his intuition and instinct in design. He senses the world not solely with the intellectual work of his brain but also with the eyes and ears from deep inside his heart. This designer transforms his inspirations into design forms which are sensually perceptive and sentimentally accessible. Shin, Ji Hun pursues a design that stimulates another sense from itself; people can feel such a sense even if they are unaware of who produced it or what philosophy or concept it came from just by seeing the Art form. This kind of sense for him is what an architect Louis Kahn stated as a "property intangible" in *Silence and Light*. It is like a human being as a part of nature perceives something according to its instinct.

Chang, Nam Mi, J.J Magazine, no. 68

W1 Lounge Chair
더블류원 라운지 체어
54x160x49cm
Birch-veneered plywood 벤딩된 자작나무
2010

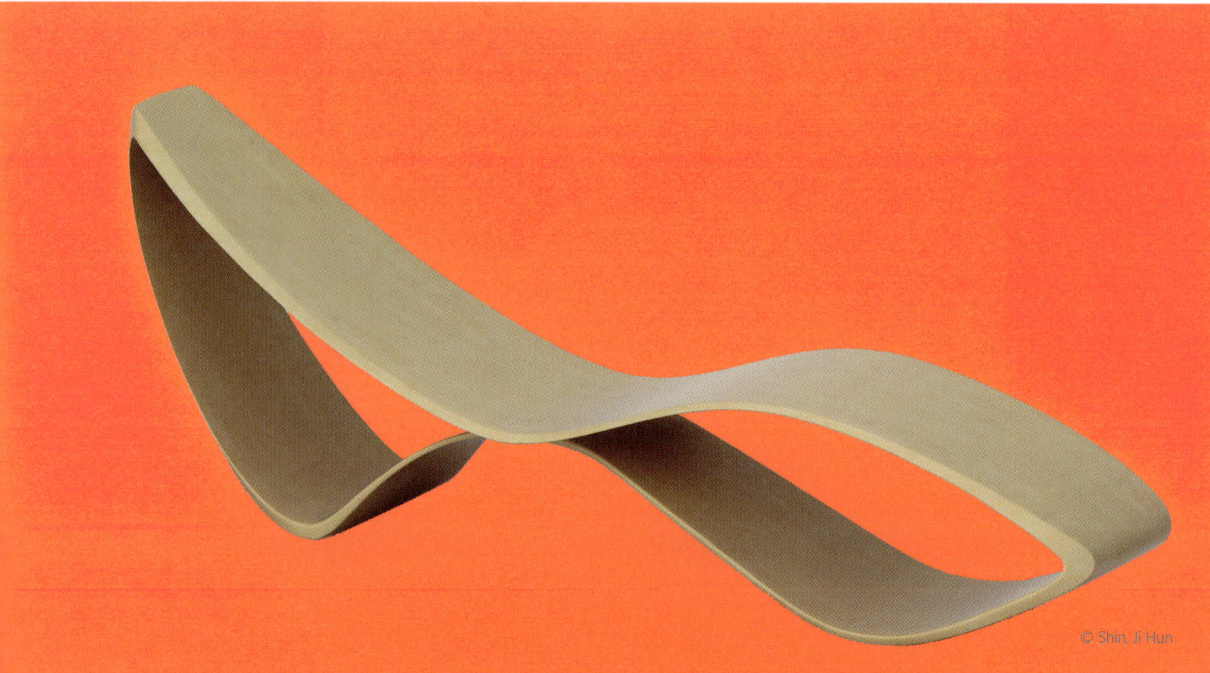

© Shin, Ji Hun

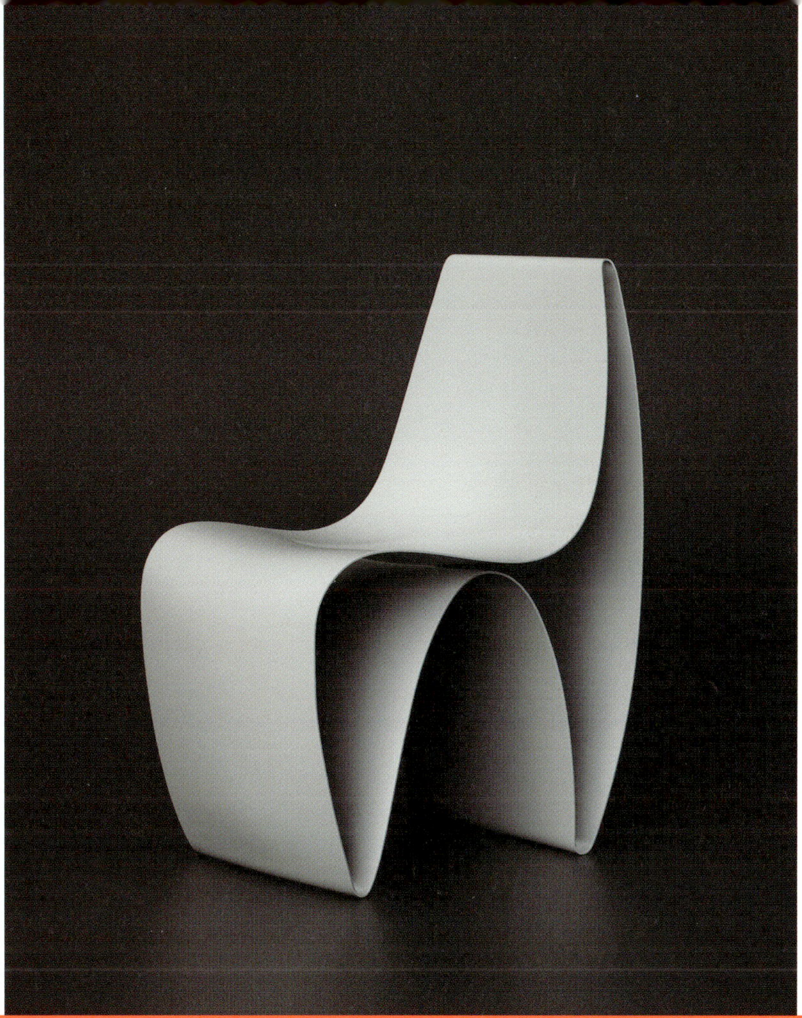

Tooth Chair
투스 체어
84x68x58cm
Fiberglass reinforced
강화섬유유리
2011

© Shin, Ji Hun

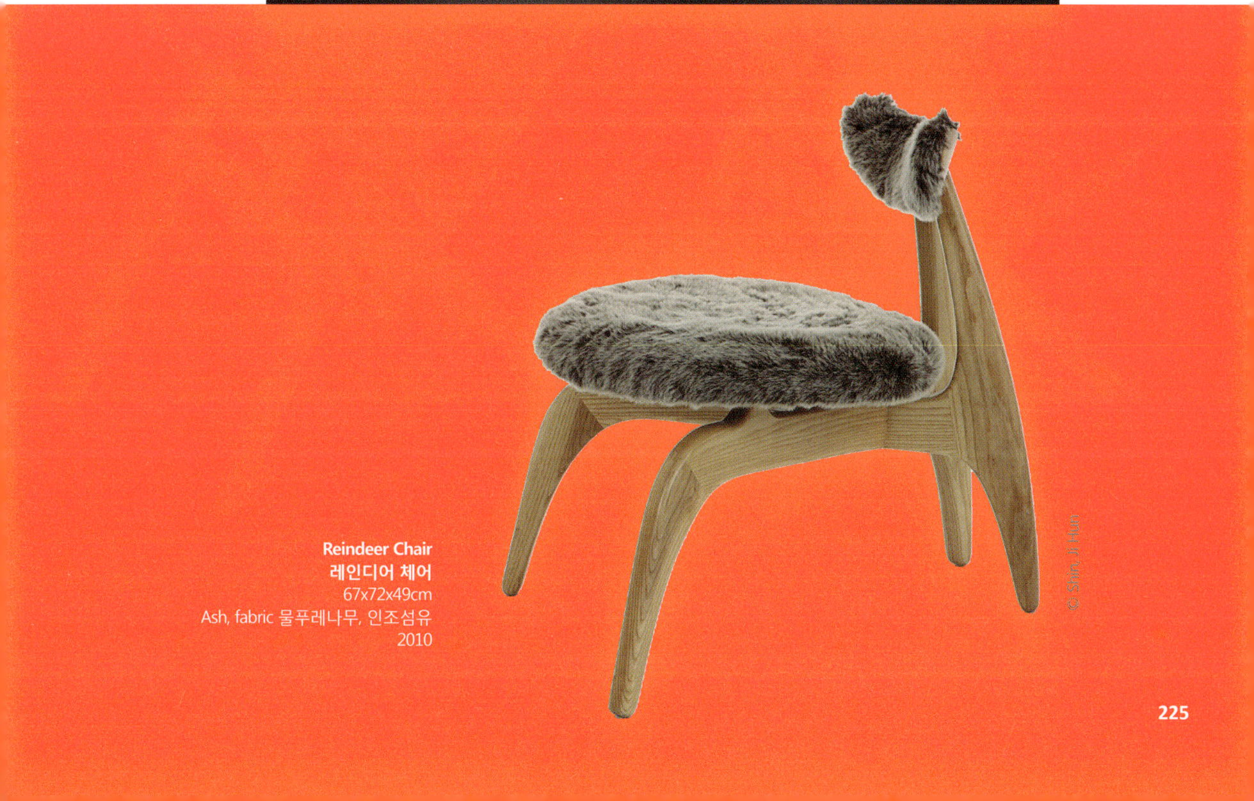

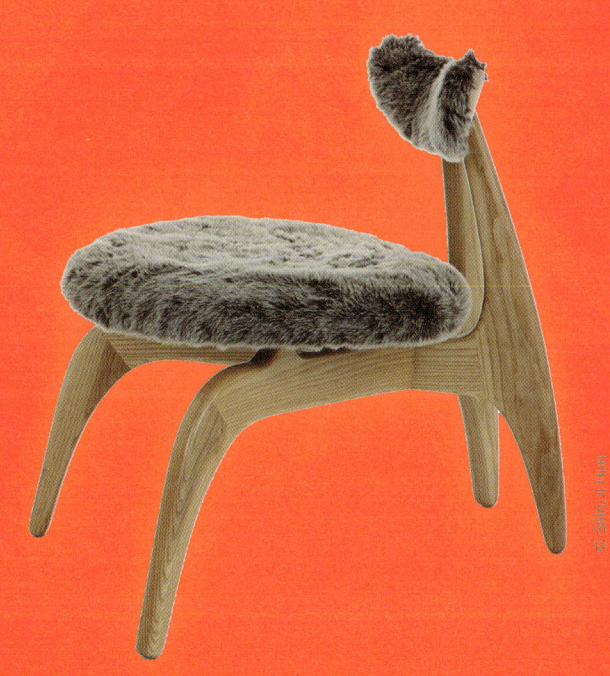

Reindeer Chair
레인디어 체어
67x72x49cm
Ash, fabric 물푸레나무, 인조섬유
2010

© Shin, Ji Hun

Jair Straschnow
야이르 스트라슈노브

Grassworks is a furniture collection of flat-pack, self-assembly structures using one single 'green' material - bamboo sheet laminates. Exploring the potential of the fastest growing plant on earth, Straschnow uses traditional woodworking techniques avoiding screws and glue. The work also considers physical space as a resource, aiming to use space economically resulting in multi-purpose objects. The *Grassworks* collection is an attempt to make maximum use of the structural and flexible qualities of a single material, as well as the physical space it occupies. Of equal importance, the product is also designed to leave a minimal footprint on the world around us.

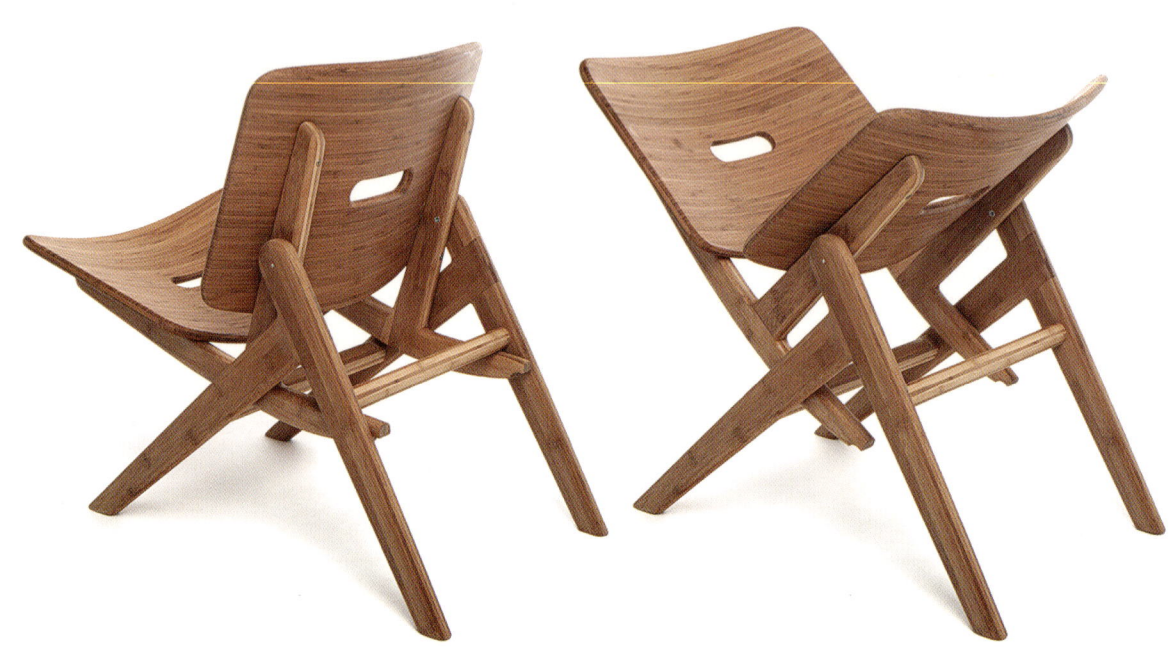

그래스웍스 체어는 대나무 껍질로 만든 합판이라는 친환경적 단일 소재를 사용하여 제작하고, 개폐 상자에 넣어 자체 조립할 수 있도록 만든 가구 컬렉션이다. 슈트라슈노브는 가장 빨리 자라는 식물의 잠재력을 연구하여 나사와 접착제의 사용 없이 전통적 목조 기술을 이용했다. 이 작품은 또한 다양한 용도를 지닌 제품으로 만들기 위해 공간을 효과적으로 사용할 수 있도록 물리적 공간성도 함께 고려했다. 그래스웍스 체어 컬렉션은 공간을 차지하는 물리적 특성과 함께, 단일한 재료의 구조적이고 유연한 특성을 최대한 끌어올릴 수 있게 하기 위한 하나의 시도이다. 이 제품은 이와 동일한 맥락에서 우리 주변 세계에 남겨지는 우리의 흔적을 최소화하기 위해 디자인되었다.

©Design Museum, London

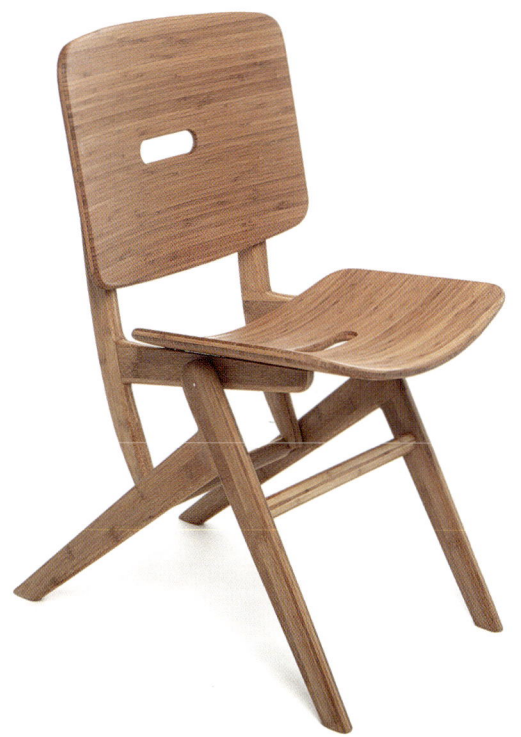

Grassworks
그래스워크
79x51x55cm
Bamboo 대나무
Jair Straschnow, Netherlands
야이르 스트라시나우, 네덜란드
2010

Marcel Wanders 마르셀 반더스

The world of design is rapidly changing, from a once-hermetic reality into a more human, accessible and versatile environment. Design is opening up and finding its way to a broader audience, as more and more people become interested in the way design contributes to their lives. Within the world of design, I can sense the will, power and potential to direct our creative talents toward areas and people our dreams have never touched before.

We should use this momentum to reach out and broaden the significance of our creative field. For too long now, we have kept the world of design small and secluded, shutting out many new friends in the process.

As a consequence of this horizontal growth in design over the last 10 years, I am starting to feel the need for vertical growth as well. There is an urge and commitment to grow toward greater depth, to touch people in a more profound, unique and personal way. Design can outgrow its traditional cultural value and aspire to work on a grander scale, giving more, moving the hearts of its audience in unknown, deeper and more individual directions. Tomorrow, we must be better creators, give more, touch others more deeply. Design is a wonderfully direct instrument, as it connects to daily life. It sits, in fact, right at its core.

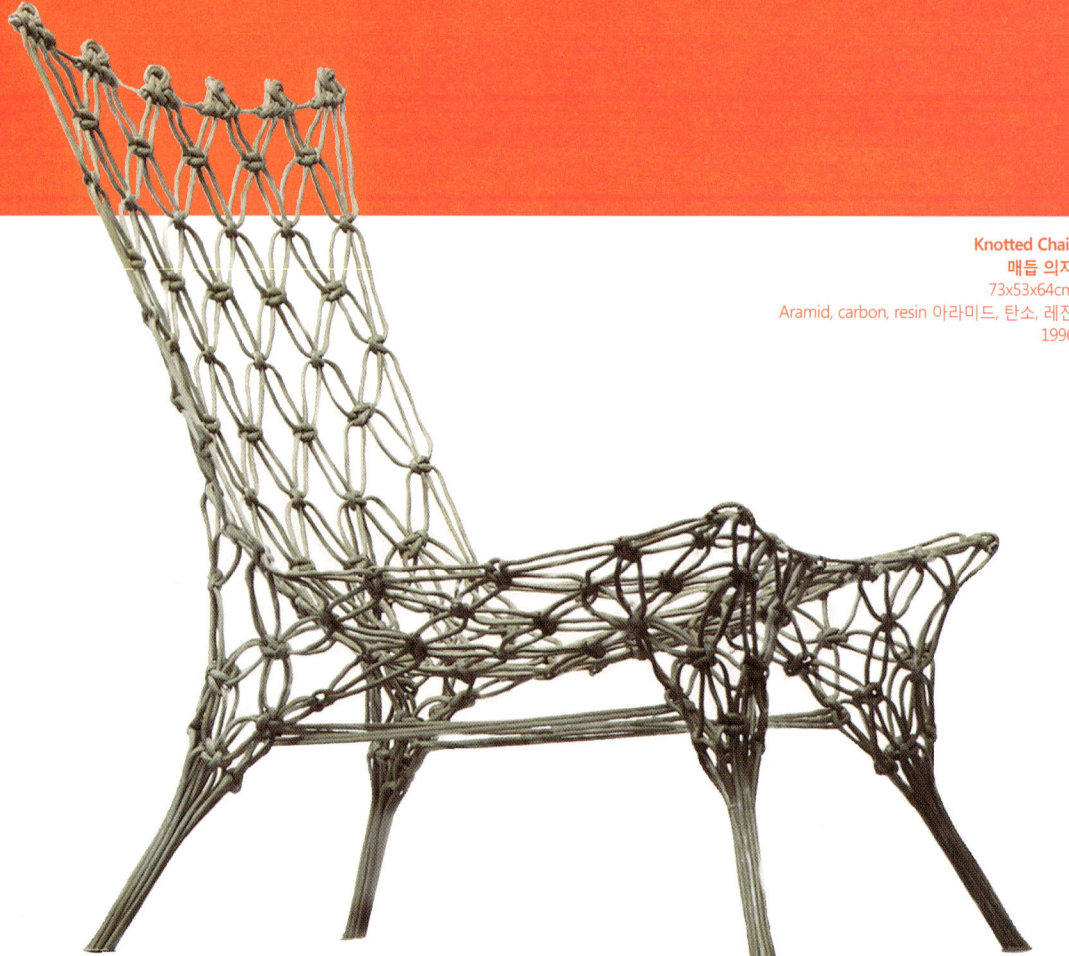

Knotted Chair
매듭 의자
73x53x64cm
Aramid, carbon, resin 아라미드, 탄소, 레진
1996

© Marcel Wanders

228

디자인의 세계는, 밀폐된 현실로부터 보다 인간적이고 접근가능하며 변덕스러운 환경으로 급속하게 변화하고 있다. 사람들이 점점 더 자신의 삶에 이바지하는 디자인 방식에 관심을 가지게 될수록, 디자인은 개방되고 있으며 보다 광범위한 관중들을 향한 방법을 찾고 있다. 디자인의 세계에서, 전에는 결코 감동을 주지 않았던 우리 꿈의 의지와 힘, 그리고 영역과 사람들을 향한 우리의 창조적 재능을 지휘하는 잠재력을 감지할 수 있다. 대중에게 다가가기 위한, 그리고 우리의 창조적 영역의 의미를 확장하기 위한 이러한 모멘텀을 잘 활용해야 한다. 아주 오랫동안, 그러한 과정에서 많은 새로운 친구들을 배제하며 우리는 디자인의 세계를 축소하고 격리시켜왔다.

지난 10여 년 간, 디자인에 있어서 이러한 수평적인 성장의 결과로, 나는 수직적 성장 역시 필요함을 느끼기 시작했다. 보다 깊이 있는 성장을 향한, 더 심오하고 독특하며 개성 있는 방식으로 사람들에게 감동을 전달하고자 하는 강한 욕구와 책임이 존재한다. 보다 깊고 더 개인적인 방향으로 익명의 관중들의 마음을 움직이면서, 디자인은 그것의 전통적이고 문화적인 가치보다 더 성장할 수 있고 더 원대한 규모에서 작업하기를 염원할 수도 있다. 미래에, 우리는 더 나은 창작자가 되어야 하고, 더 많이 주고, 다른 이들에게 더 큰 감동을 줄 수 있어야 한다. 디자인은 그것이 일상생활과 연관되기 때문에 놀라울만큼 직접적인 매체이다. 사실상, 디자인은 그것의 바로 그 핵심에 놓여있다.

Crochet Chair
뜨개질 의자
56x129.7x118cm
Fiber, resin 섬유, 레진
2006

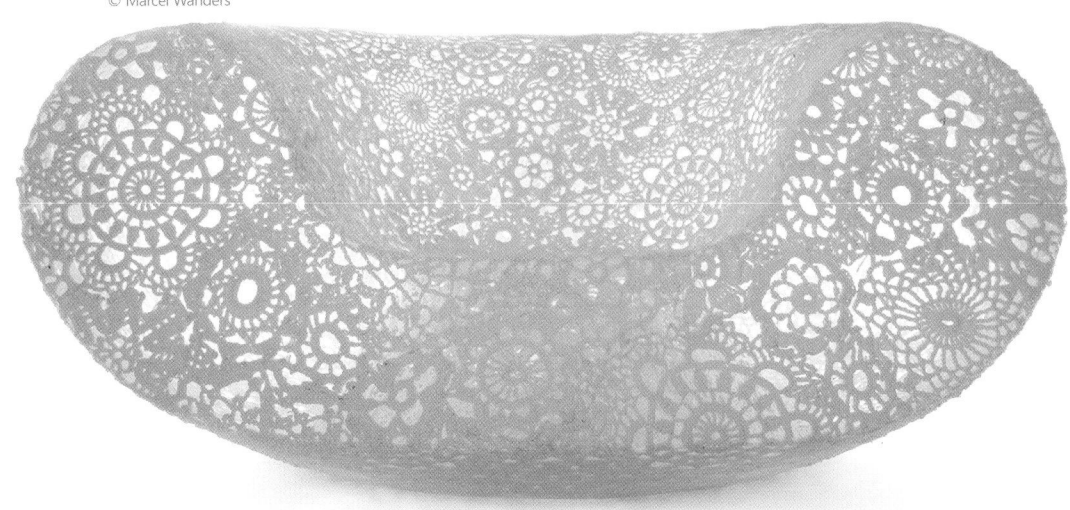

© Marcel Wanders

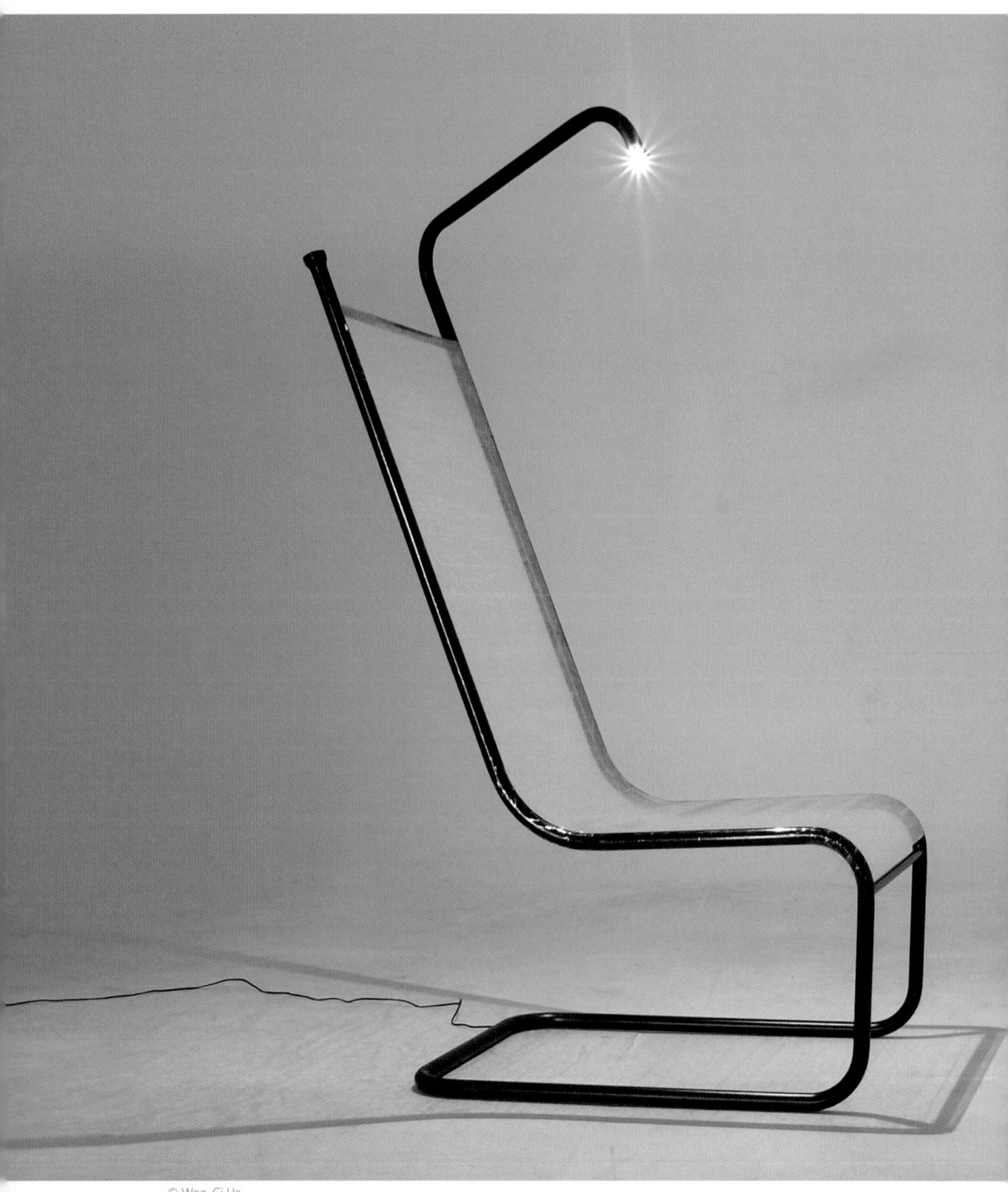

© Woo, Gi Ha

Woo, Gi Ha 우기하

제품디자이너 우기하의 작품은 사물에 대한 재해석을 통해 이루어지고 있다. 많은 사람들이 오랜 시간 동안 같은 이름으로 명명해왔던 사물 혹은 제품이, 그 이름 때문에 다른 쓰임 혹은 다른 가치에 대한 가능성이 닫혀질 수 있다고 그는 얘기한다.

예를 들어, 의자의 경우, 사전적 의미가 사람이 걸터 앉는 데 쓰는 기구라고 정의되어 있다. 의자라고 불려지는 제품들은 이 정의 안에서 규정되어 있고, 이것은 스스로 만든 생각의 철장이 되어 버리고 만다. 의자에서 조금 더 진보된 가치, 혹은 변형된 가치를 기대하기 위해선 의자에 대한 정의를 잊어버려야 한다. 그의 작품 *히든 라이트*는 인간의 앉는 행위와, 앉아서 하는 행위에 대한 고민이 담겨 있다. 의자와 조명이 그들의 사전적 정의에서 벗어났을 경우, 단순한 1대1의 물리적 결합이 아닌, 제품의 속성간에 섹스를 통한, 개념적 결합이 일어나게 된다. 그는 이번 작품 *히든 라이트*을 통해 그러한 하이브리드 디자인을 보여주고 있다.

The product designer, Woo, Gi Ha, has work that stems from reinterpretations of objects. He states that a product's possibility for another use or value due to its original name for purpose is limited. A chair, for example, is defined in the dictionary as a tool on which people sit. Provided that the product is named a chair in such a definition, this might predetermine our thoughts. To obtain more developed or transformed values from a chair, we should forget about the fixed definition of it. His work *Hidden Light* contains a thorough contemplation on the action of sitting and the action while seated. When chairs and electric lights break away from their literal definition, there happens to be a conceptual union through the so-called "sex among the properties" of products rather than a mere a physical combination. The designer exhibits such a hybrid design through his recent work, called *Hidden Light*.

Hidden Light
히든라이트
130x54x90cm
Stainless 스테인레스
2011

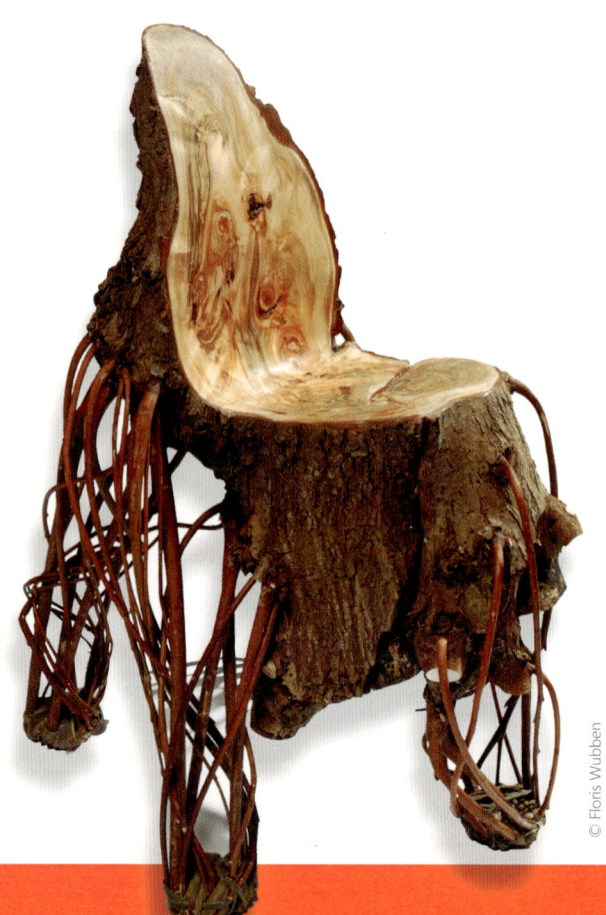

Upside down
거꾸로
80x50x50cm
Willow 버드나무
2010

© Floris Wubben

Netherlands | 네덜란드

Floris Wubben 플로리스 부븐

The Dutch Company "Studio Floris Wubben" tries to get the most out of the applied materials and craftsmanship within every design. They find it interesting that the result in designs will not directly be related to functional objects, but rather being viewed as sculptural objects.

In our work of designing we thus try to put a certain material into new perspectives. While transforming and combining materials, new purposes will arise naturally. By using uncommon materials, applications or combinations for a certain design, we focus on diminishing prejudices and on giving these materials a new face. An example of this is the use of decorative materials for constructive purposes.

The designs of "Studio Floris Wubben" enable products and nature to co-operate together into ultimate harmony. One uses the other, since they need each other to create the whole and final design. As a consequence, living qualities of nature will have a constant influence on our projects. We try to use human action as less as possible and to apply nature the way it is given. After creating a certain design, one can see that a part of nature is transformed into a sculpture, an utensil, without losing respect for nature.

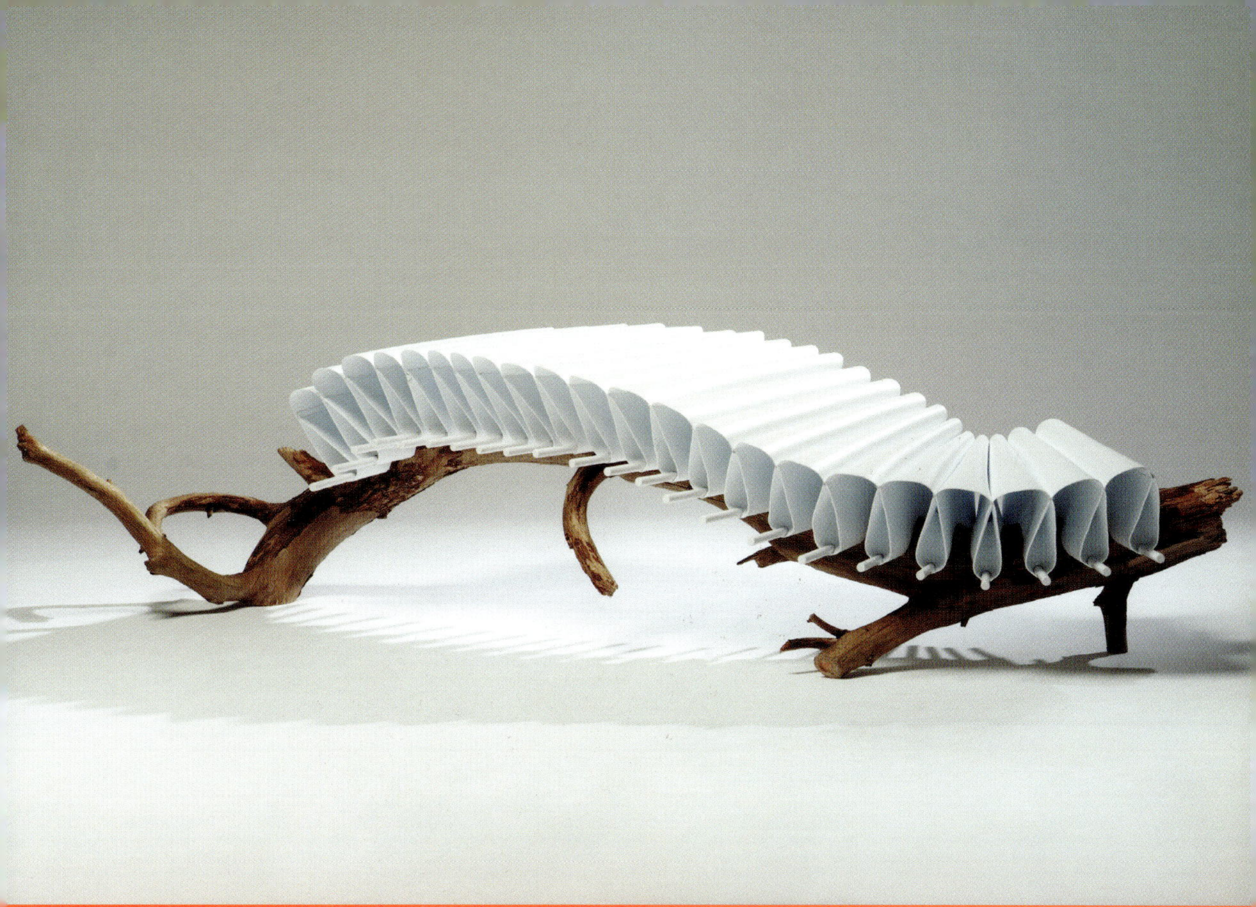

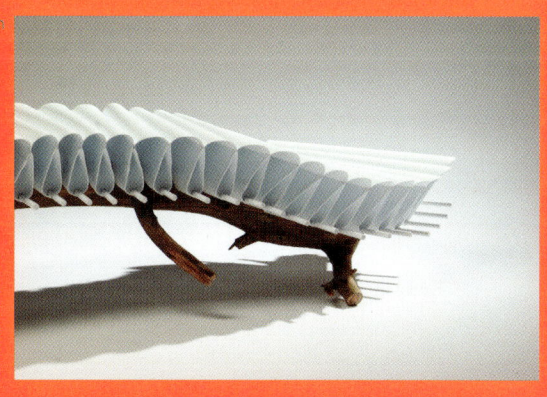

© Floris Wubben

No.3 Bench
No.3 벤치
50x190x65cm
Wooden, metal, polypropylene
나무, 금속, 폴리프로필렌
2010

네덜란드의 플로리스 부븐 스튜디오는, 응용 재료와 장인 정신을 모든 디자인에 최대한으로 활용하기 위해 노력한다. 사람들은 기능적인 오브제와 직접적으로 관련되는 디자인보다는, 오히려 조각적 오브제로 보여지는 디자인이 더 재미있다는 것을 깨닫게 되었다.

따라서 우리는 디자인 작품을 통해서, 새로운 시각에 특정 재료를 대입해보려 노력한다. 재료를 변형하고 결합하는 동안, 새로운 목표가 자연스럽게 떠오른다. 흔치 않은 재료를 사용함으로써, 또 특정 디자인을 위해 그것을 응용하거나 결합함으로써, 편견을 감소시키며 이들 재료에 새로운 얼굴을 부여한다. 이러한 사례는 구조적인 목적을 위한 장식적인 재료의 사용을 보여준다.

플로리스 부븐 스튜디오의 디자인은 제품과 자연이 완전한 조화를 위해 함께 협력할 수 있게 해준다. 자연 속에서의 삶의 질은 우리의 프로젝트에 끊임없는 영향을 줄 것이다. 우리는 가능하면 인위적인 행위를 지양할 것이고 자연적으로 주어진 자연의 방법을 적용하려 노력할 것이다. 어떤 디자인을 창조한 뒤에는, 자연에 대한 경외심을 잃지 않고도 자연의 일부가 변형되어 조각작품이 되고, 또 쓸모 있는 물건이 되는 것을 볼 수 있을 것이다.

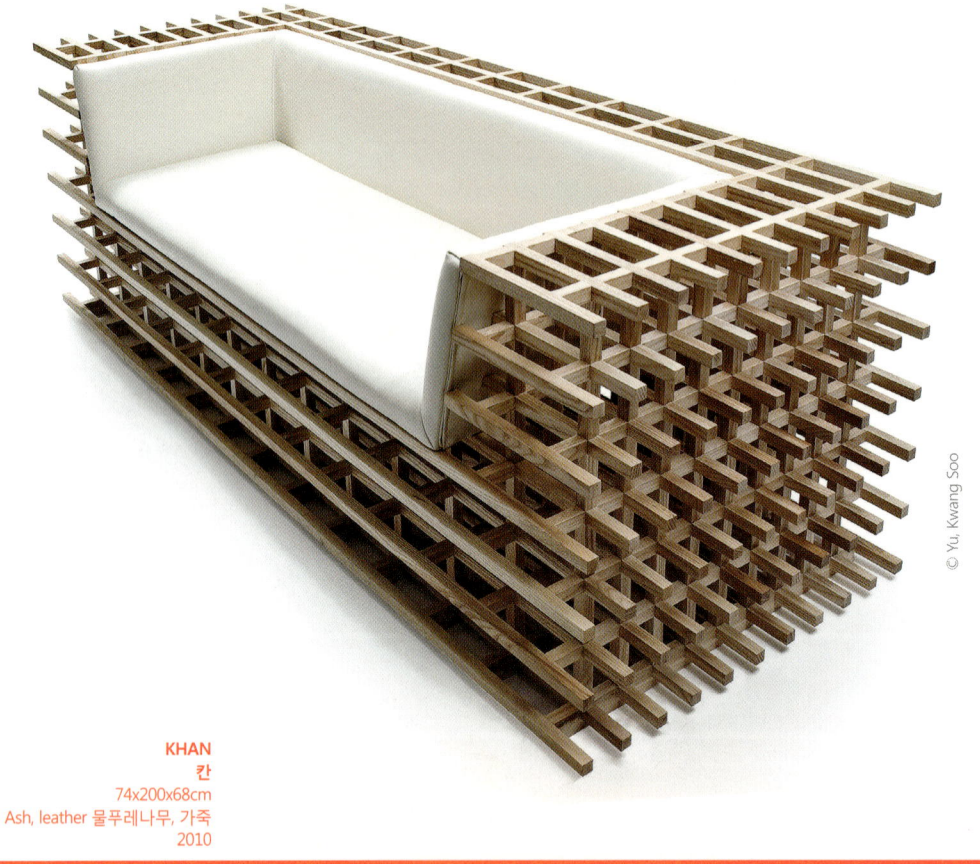

© Yu, Kwang Soo

KHAN
칸
74x200x68cm
Ash, leather 물푸레나무, 가죽
2010

Korea | 한국

Yu, Kwang Soo 유광수

상호간의 관계에서 모든 사물은 독립된 개체로 존재하지 않는다.
모든 사물의 상태는 상호간의 관계에 의해 구성되어 있으며 상호간의 관계에서 이루어지는 공간의 지속되는 깊이는 조형적 형태를 만들어 나간다.
세상 대부분의 사물은 전체의 부분이다. 각 부분은 전체로서 가시적인 가치를 수용하며 전체는 여러 가지 부분으로 가시적인 가치를 받아들인다. 본질적인 점과 선 그리고 한 대상에서 대상까지의 칸이 집합을 이루며 하나의 개체를 만들어 나간다 그리고 그것은 모든 것을 표현한다.

No object can exist independently in mutual relationships.
The status of all objects is composed by mutual relationships and thus the depth of the space between them builds up formative shapes together.
Most of the objects in the world are parts of a whole. Each part accepts visual values in a whole while the entity admits visual values in diverse parts. The fundamental points, lines, and spaces between one object and another compose a collective set to make an individual whole. And finally it expresses everything.

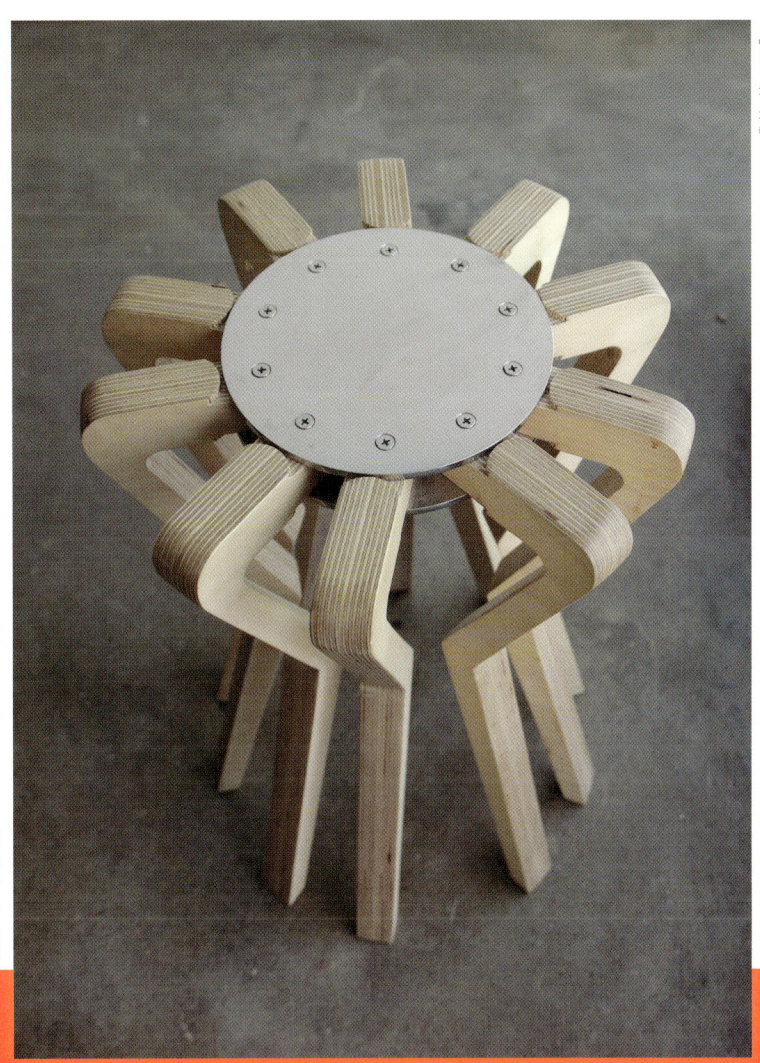

© Yu, Kwang Soo

Flower Stool
플라워 스툴
45x30x30cm
Birch plywood, steel
자작나무합판, 철
2010

꽃이 피다.
꽃이 활짝 피어나는 모습을 작은 의자에 형상화 하였다.
건조한 철학이 아닌 가구의 존재가 인간의 작은 미소를
머금게 하였으면 한다.
꽃이 피어난 의자의 공간은 서로서로 맞물려, 포개질 수
있다.

Flower is blooming.
I embodied the shape of flowers blooming into a
small chair.
What I wish in my design is that the existence of
furniture does not become a dull philosophy but
helps people smile.
The chair's place where flowers effloresce can
stack each other.

Biographies
작가약력

Alvar Aalto
알바 알토
Born in 1898, Finland
Died in 1976, Finland

1921 Completes an architecture diploma at Helsinki University of Technology. Work experience with Armas Lindgren in Helsinki and Arvid Berjke in Gothenberg, Sweden.
1923 Returns to Finland and opens the Alvar Aalto Office for Architecture and Monumental Art in Jyväskylä.
1924 Marries the architect Aino Marsio. They work together on small local projects such as housing and student clubs.
1927 Wins a competition to design an agricultural cooperative in Turku and moves there with his family.
1928 Starts work on the Viipuri Library, Turun Sanomat newspaper offices and the Paimio Sanaotorium.
1929 Attends his first Congrès Internationaux d'Architecture Moderne (CIAM) conference. He and Aino befriend Le Corbusier, Walter Gropius, Marcel Breuer and the critic Sigfried Giedion.
1933 Moves office to Helsinki. His Paimio moulded wood furniture is exhibited at Fortnum & Mason department store in London.
1934 Builds a new family home in a Helsinki suburb and founds the Artek furniture company with Aino and Maire Gullichsen.
1936 Aalto's Finnish Pavilion for the Paris International Exposition wins praise from Le Corbusier.
1937 The Savoy Restaurant opens in Helsinki with an interior and furniture designed by Aalto including the wavy glass Savoy Vase.
1938 Starts work on Villa Mairea for Maire Gullichsen and her industrialist husband, Harry. Exhibition of Aalto's work at the Museum of Modern Art, New York. Designs Finnish Pavilion for New York World's Fair.
1939 Travels extensively in the US and accepts a professorship at MIT until World War II forces him to return to Finland.
1946 After the War, Aalto returns to MIT and designs Baker House.
1949 Aino dies after a long illness.
1952 Marries the architect Elissa Mäkiniemi and builds a house for them in Muursalto. Begins work on the Helsinki House of Culture.
1955 Designs the Church of Three Crosses at Vuokenninska, Finland.
1959 Starts working on the Helsinki City Plan and Essen Opera House, which will eventually be completed after his death in 1988.
1969 Designs the Iran Museum of Modern Art in Shiraz.
© Design Museum 2002

My Own Super Studio_Rui Alves
마이 오운 슈퍼 스튜디오_후이 알브스
Born in 1977, Portugal

Education
2001 IADE Industrial Design, Lisbon, Portugal

Selected Group Exhibitions
2011 DMY, Berlin, Germany
Salone Satellite, Milan, Italy
Elipse da Duração, Porto, Portugal
2010 RedDot Design Award, Singapore, Singapore
DMY, Berlin, Germany
2009 DMY, Berlin, Germany
2004 DesignWise 2.0, Lisbon, Portugal

Ron Arad
론 아라드
Born in 1951, Israel

Education
1971 - 1973   Jerusalem Academy of Art

Selected Solo Exhibitions
2008 Guarded Thoughts. Friedman Benda, New York
Ron Arad, Centre Pompidou, Paris
Let's Play, Galerie Arums, P
2007 Restless, Friedman Benda, New York, NY
Bodyguards, Dolce & Gabbana, Milan, Italy
Paved with Good Intentions (2005), arums galerie, Paris
2006 THERE IS NO SOLUTION because there is no problem, Installation at 508 West 26th Street, NY. Barry Friedman Ltd., NY: September 14-30
Blo-Glo, Dolce & Gabbana, Milan, Italy
Blo-Jobs, Gallery Mourmans, Lanaken, Belgium

Selected Group Exhibitions
2010 European Design Since 1985. Shaping the New Century. High Museum of Art, Atlanta, GA Retrospective to be held at the Stedelijk Museum, Amsterdam, Netherlands
2009 Ron Arad: No Discipline retrospective at the Museum of Modern Art, New York, NY European Design Since 1985. Shaping the New Century. Indianapolis Museum of Art, Indianapolis, IN Ron Arad: New Work. Timothy Taylor Gallery, London, England Drunken Bodyguards. Gallery Mourmans, Lanaken, Belgium U.F.O.: Grenzgänge zwischen Kunst und Design, NRW Forum Düsseldorf, Germany Retrospective. Museum of Modern Art, New York, NY
2008 Ron Arad: No Discipline retrospective at the Centre Pompidou, Paris, France
2006 Exhibits in Designing Modern Britain at the Design Museum, London.
2003 Works on projects including the Maserati headquarters showroom in Modena, Italy and Y's fashion store for Yohji Yamamoto in Tokyo. Begins designing for the Upperworld Hotel at Battersea Power Station, London.

Collections
Musée des Arts Décoratifs, Paris
Vitra Design Museum, Weil am Rhein
Musée National d'Art Moderne/ Centre Georges Pompidou, Paris
Fond National d'Art Contemporain, Paris
Musée des Arts Décoratifs, Montreal
Metropolitan Museum of Art, New York

Jane Atfield
제인 앳필드

Jane Atfield studied architecture at the Polytechnic of Central London, later studied at the London College of Furniture and undertook postgraduate studies at the Royal College of Art.

제인 앳필드는 영국 런던 태생으로, 런던 중앙 공과대학에서 건축을 공부하고, London College of Furniture(런던 가구대학)와 Royal College of Art(왕립 예술대학)에서 각각 학사와 대학원 과정을 수료하였다.

Gae Aulenti
가에 아울렌티
Born in 1927, Italy

Gae Aulenti is an Italian architect, lighting and interior designer, and industrial designer. She is well known for several large-scale museum projects, including Musée d'Orsay in Paris(1980–86), the Contemporary Art Gallery at the Centre Pompidou in Paris, the Palazzo Grassi in Venice(1985–86), and the Asian Art Museum of San Francisco(2000–2003). A native of Palazzolo dello Stella(Friuli), she studied in Milan. She worked for the design magazine Casabella from 1955 until 1965 as an art director, and become part of a group of young professionals influenced by the philosophy of Ernesto Nathan Rogers. Aulenti has also occasionally worked as a stage designer for Luca Ronconi.

가에 아울렌티는 1954년 밀라노 공과대학 건축학부 졸업, 1955-65년까지 디자인 잡지 카사벨라의 아트 디렉터로 종사했다. 1964년 제13회 트리엔날레전 이탈리아관으로 국제대상을 수상. 1980년 파리 오르세 미술관 내장 디자인 설계 경기에서 우승함으로써 각광을 받기 시작 한다. 1986년 미술관의 완성과 동시에 높은 평가를 받았다. 1983년도 요제프 호프만상, 1992년 다카마츠궁전하기념 세계문화상 건축부문 수상. 1992년 세빌리아 세계박람회 이탈리아관, 바르셀로나 카탈로니아 미술관 개수 등, 세계 무대에서 건축활동을 전개한다.

Dror Benshetrit
드롤 브론쉐트리트
Born in 1977, Israel
Lives and Works in New York, USA

Education
Design Academy of Eindhoven, the Netherlands

Selected Exhibitions
2011 BrokenOff BrokenOff – An exhibition to celebrate the life and work of Tobias Wong – Gallery R'Pure, New York
2011 Salone Internazionale di Mobile, TRON designs CORIAN®
2011 Salone Internazionale di Mobile, INTERNI, Mutant Architecture and Design
2011 Salone Internazionale di Mobile, Handmade Exhibition by WallPaper @ Brioni
2011 New Museum - QuaDror: Exhibition to unveil the QuaDror system, a new way for building
2010 Contemplating the Void: Interventions in the Guggenheim Museum (Redlining the Guggenheim, watercolor, February
2009 Edition products from Cappellini's collection, 2005-2009
2008 Art Basel/Design Miami: Luminaire's Paperlove exhibition and auction
2008 Peel Gallery, Houston Texas: Solo exhibition
2008 Louis XIII Diner des Genies, featuring "Swept Under the Carpet" exhibition
2007 Art Basel Miami, Bentley Concept Debut
2007 "Radical Lace and Subversive Knitting Exhibit," Museum of Arts and Design, New York
2007 Clear Elevation, Top of the Rock, Pick Chair installation
2006 Urban Cast Away Exhibition, Marithé + François Girbaud boutique, SoHo, New York
2005 Bombay Sapphire Pop Up Store, curated by Surface Magazine
2003 Gallery 91, New York Tokyo Design Block

Harry Bertoia
해리 버토이아
Born in 1915, Italy
Died in 1978, USA

Harry Bertoia was an Italian-born artist, sculptor, and modern furniture designer. At the age of 15 he traveled from Italy to Detroit to visit his older brother, however he chose to stay and enrolled in Cass Technical High School, where he studied art and design and learned the art of handmade jewelry making. In 1938 he attended the Art School of the Detroit Society of Arts and Crafts, now known as the College for Creative Studies. The following year in 1937 he received a scholarship to study at the Cranbrook Academy of Art where he encountered Walter Gropius, Edmund N. Bacon and Ray and Charles Eames for the first time. In 1950, he moved to Pennsylvania, to establish a studio, and to work with Hans and Florence Knoll. (Florence was also a Cranbrook Graduate). During this period he designed five wire pieces that became known as the Bertoia Collection for Knoll. Among them the famous 'Diamond chair' a fluid, sculptural form made from a molded lattice work of welded steel.

조각가이자 가구 디자이너로, 이탈리아 우디네에서 태어나 1930년 미국으로 이주했다. 미시간 주 소재 크랜부룩 미술 아카데미에서 공부했고(1939-1939) 그후 그곳에서 금속공예를 가르쳤다.(1939-1943) 버토이아는 캘리포니아의 베네치아 소재 에반스 제조회사에서 전쟁물자로 성형 합판을 생산했으며(1939-1943) 이 회사에서 찰스 임스와 함께 의자를 디자인하기도 했다. 놀사의 후원으로 1950년 펜실베니아에 자신만의 사무소를 차렸고, 1951년 놀사를 위해 자신의 가장 유명한 작품 다이아몬드 의자를 출시했다.

Ronan & Erwan Bouroullec
로난 부훌렉 & 에르완 부훌렉
Ronan Bouroullec
Born in 1971, France
Erwan Bouroullec
Born in 1976, France

Ronan & Erwan Bouroullec is a design team formed by brothers from Brittany. In 2007 the firm's "North Tiles" design for Kvadrat in Denmark won the D - Design Forum AID Award and has been included in Cappellini's design collection. Their work has included a tree-house bedroom and a "table sprouting a bowl molded from a single piece of heat-welded Corian". The designs have been described as representing poetic practicality. "We don't want to make only functional pieces," Erwan Bouroullec noted. The Bouroullecs work in Paris for clients including Cappellini, Ligne Roset, Habitat, Domeau & Peres, Authentics, EandW, Magis, Vitra and Gallery Kreo. They received the grand prix du jury international at the Paris Furniture Fair in 1998 e de la ville de paris, the best new designer award in New York in 1999, a Compasso d'Oro nomination in 2001 in Milan, and designed the interior for Issey Miyake's APOC shop in Paris. In 2011, the Centre Pompidou-Metz hosts a major retrospective on the Bouroullec brothers.

로낭과 에르완 부훌렉 형제는 1990년대 말, 프랑스 산업 디자인의 기대주로 각광받으며 혜성과 같이 등장했다. 프랑스에서 디자인을 전공한 뒤 1999년에 공동으로 디자인 회사를 설립한 후 활발히 활동하고 있다.

Marcel Breuer
마르셀 브로이어
Born in 1920, Hungary
Died in 1981, USA

1920 Wins a scholarship to study painting and sculpture at Vienna Academy of Fine Arts. Leaves after a few weeks to work in an architect¡¦s office. Moves to Weimar, Germany to study at the Bauhaus.

1921 Becomes an apprentice in the Bauhaus furniture workshop where his first piece is the ornate African Chair.

1922 Designs the De Stijl-influenced Wood-slat chair.

1924 Leaves the Bauhaus for Paris, where he works for an architect.

1925 Accepts Walter Gropius¡¦ invitation to return to the new Bauhaus in Dessau as head of the furniture workshop. Starts to develop the innovative tubular steel Steel Club chair, later christened the Wassily Chair.

1927 Co-founds Standard-Möbel to manufacture and distribute his tubular steel furniture. Designs furniture for Erwin Piscator's apartment.

1928 Quits the Bauhaus when Gropius resigns as director and sets up an architectural office in Berlin, but struggles to find work.

1931 Still scratching for architectural commissions, Breuer takes several months off to travel in southern Europe.

1932 Dividing his time between Hungary and Switzerland, Breuer starts developing aluminium furniture with which he will win a competition in 1933.

1934 The first aluminium pieces go into production.

1935 Breuer joins Gropius in London, where he designs plywood furniture for Isokon, a company owned by Jack Pritchard, and opens an architectural office with F.R.S. Yorke. Together they design the Gane Pavilion in Bristol which combines local stones and woods with International Style glass and metal.

1937 When Gropius leaves London to become architecture professor at Harvard, Breuer follows. He is given a professorship there and opens an architectural office with Gropius which begins by designing their own homes.

1941 Closes practise with Gropius, but they remain friends and continue teaching at Harvard together.

1946 Completes his first post-war building, the Geller House on Long Island, and opens an office in New York with Eliot Noyes as his partner. This office will design some 70 houses mostly on the East Coast including Breuer's own.

1949 Having staged a touring exhibition of Breuer's work in 1948, the Museum of Modern Art, New York commissions him to design a house in the museum garden. This commission revitalises Breuer's career.

1953 Designs UNESCO's headquarters in Paris with Pier Luigi Nervi and Bernard Zehrfuss.

1957 Begins work on lecture halls and residences for New York University.

1963 Starts a three year project to design the Whitney Museum of American Art in New York.

1970 Designs Armstrong Rubber Company headquarters in West Haven, Connecticut with Robert F. Gatje and starts work on the Australian Embassy in Paris as consulting architect to former assistant Harry Seidler.

© Design Museum

Guy Brown
가이 브라운
Born in 1980, UK

Education
2006 loughbrough

Selected Solo Exhibitions
2009 tent, London, UK
2010 Nottingham open, Nottingham, UK

Selected Group Exhibitions
2010 Design museum, London, UK
2009 Salone Satellite, Milan, Italy
2008 tent, London, UK

Beta Tank_Eyal Burstein
베타 탱크_아이알 벌스타인
Born in 1977, Israel

Lives and Works in Berlin, Germany& London, UK

Education
2006 Royal College Of Art, MA , London, UK
2004 London College Of Printing, BA, Hons London, UK

Selected Solo Exhibitions
2011 Thoughts In Objects DMY Gallery Space, Berlin
Beta Tank June Gestalten Space Berlin

Selected Group Exhibitions
2011 Cheongju International Craft Biennale, KOREA
Victoria and Albert museum, London, UK
See Yourself Sensing, Work gallery, London, UK
Dilmos, Basel, SWITZERLAND
Unison exhibition, Dilmos, Milano, ITALY
2010 W Hotel, Istanbul Design Week, Turkey
Seeing Myself See, Wellcome Trust, London, UK
Ars Electronica, Linz, AUSTRIA
International Design Biennial, Saint-Etienne, FRANCE
Design Miami Basel (Designer Of The Future Award) Basel, SWITZERLAND
Design Vertigo, Milan ITALY
13,798 grams of design, Milan, ITALY
2008 Design And The Elastic Mind, MoMA, NY, USA
2005 Nordic Exceptional Design, Copenhagen, Denmark Collections
MoMA permanent collection, NY, USA

Anna Castelli – Ferrieri
안나 카스텔리 페리에리
Born in 1920, Italy

Italian architect and industrial designer Anna Castelli Ferrieri studied architecture at Milan Polytechnic. From 1946 to 1947 Anna Castelli Ferrieri was editor of the architecture magazine Casabella Costruzioni and at the same time founded her own architecture practice that collaborated with the architect Ignazio Gardella on projects in Milan, Turin, and Genoa. Other important projects include the Kartell company headquarters in Binasco and buildings for the car maker Alfa Romeo in Arese. From 1965 onwards, she was involved in designing objects for Kartell and other Italian manufacturers. At Kartell, experimenting with different kinds of plastic, she designed many innovative objects including the Componibili stackable container elements made of ABS plastic, and the Castelli Ferrieri 4822/44 stool that was the first successful combination of metal and polyurethane at Kartell.

안나 카스텔리 페리에리는 밀라노에서 태어나 밀라노 공과대학에서 건축을 공부하고 1943년 졸업했다. 건축 잡지 카사벨라 코스트루치오니의 편집 디자인에 종사한 후, 제품디자인을 시작 카르텔 사의 디자인 개발을 담당하여 1969년에는 명작 콤포니빌리를 발표한다. 이후 플라스틱의 미래적인 이미지를 살린 스툴과 재떨이 등을 발표해, 카르텔사의 브랜드 이미지를 격상시키는데 일조, 1976년에는 아트 디렉터로 취임했다. 밀라노 트리엔날레 골드 메달, 콘팟소 드로 상 등 수많은 디자인상을 수상하였고 많은 작품이 뉴욕 근대미술관이나 퐁피두 센터의 영구 컬렉션으로 소장되어 있다.

Achille Castiglioni
아킬레 카스틸리오니
Born in 1918, Italy
Died in 2002, Italy

1944 Graduates with a degree in architecture from Milan Polytechnic and joins his elder brothers – Livio (1911-1979) and Pier Giacomo (1913-1968) in their design studio.

1947 Joins the organising committee of the Milan Triennale in which he will play an active role for many years.

1950 Becomes creative consultant to RAI, the Italian public broadcasting network, for which he and Pier Giacomo will work designing pavilions and exhibitions until 1969.

1952 Livio ends his collaboration with his younger brothers to pursue his interest in designing lighting and sound installations. Achille and Pier Giacomo will continue working together until Pier Giacomo's death in 1968.

1955 Wins a Compasso d'Oro award, the prestigious Italian product design prize. Achille and Pier Giacomo will win the Compasso d'Oro four more times – in 1960, 1962, 1964 and 1967. After Pier Giacomo's death, Castiglioni will win the award three more times in 1979, 1984 and 1989.

1956 Co-founds the Association of Industrial Design to champion industrial design in Italy.

1957 Designs an exhibition at Villa Olmo, Lake Como for which he creates the first of his Wunderkammern, or ideal living environments. Achille and Pier Giacomo unveil the prototypes for their 'ready-made' seats, the Mezzadro tractor seat stool and Sella bicycle seat stool which will eventually be manufactured by Zanotta in 1971 and 1983 respectively.

1961 Starts a long collaboration with Flos, the lighting company, with the elegant domed Splügen Bräu hanging light.

1965 Brionvega launches the ingenious 126 stereo. With Pier Giacomo, Castiglioni creates the second Wunderkammern, The Home To Live In, for an exhibition at Palazzo Strozzi in Florence.

1968 Pier Giacomo dies leaving Achille to continue working on his own.

1970 Becomes a visiting lecturer in the architecture faculty at Turin Polytechnic, where he teaches until 1977.

1971 Ideal Standard launches Castiglioni's Aquatonda range of sanitaryware. Throughout the 1970s, Castiglioni continues to produce numerous products for longstanding clients such as Ideal Standard, Flos and Zanotta.

1979 Alessi, the metalware manufacturer, joins his list of loyal clients by reproducing archive designs and putting new ones into production.

1984 Curates and designs a retrospective exhibition of his work which tours to museums in Vienna, Berlin, Milan and Zurich. The third Wunderkammern is created for an exhibition of Italian design in Tokyo.

1986 Appointed a professor in the architecture department of Milan Polytechnic where he teaches industrial design.

1990 Now in his 70s, Castiglioni is still highly productive. Throughout the 1990s, he continues to work for Flos, Zanotta and other established clients and to accept commissions from new ones. Alessi continues to reproduce examples of his early work.

1995 Alla Castiglioni, a retrospective exhibition, opens at the Centre d'Art Santa Monica in Barcelona, and tours to international museums including the Museum of Modern Art, New York.

2002 Achille Castiglioni dies in Milan. He continued to work for old and new clients until the end of his life.

© Design Museum

Pierre Chareau
피에르 샤로
Born in 1883, France
Died in 1950, France

He was a French architect and designer, credited for building the first house in France made of steel and glass, the Maison de Verre. Chareau was born in Le Havre, France. He went to the École nationale supérieure des Beaux-Arts in Paris by the time he was 17. His designs were noted for their complex nature. He was member of Congrès International d'Architecture Moderne.

프랑스 태생 가구 디자이너이다. 1919년 「살롱 도똔느(Salond'Automne)와 「장식미술가 화랑」(Salon Des Artiste Decorateurs) 등에 기교적이고 엄격한 양식의 가구를 선보이면서 알려지게 되었다. 1930년에는 쥬르댕과 더불어「현대 예술인 연합(Union des Artistes Modernes)의 창립 멤버가 되었다. 풍부한 상상력으로 기본골격을 직선으로 조합시킨 그의 가구와 조명등, 금도금 유리잔 등은 완벽한 구조로서 현대적 양식의 전형을 이룬다.

Choi, Joong Ho
최중호
Born in 1982, Korea

학력
2010 건국대학교, 충주, 한국

개인전
2009 CASA 리빙디자인워크, 온프라이데이 카페, 서울
MIZY 패스트푸드 제너레이션 프로젝트, 서울디자인클러스터, 서울
KT&G 상상마당 '회색 옷을 입다',

상상마당

Education
2010 Konkuk University, Chungju,
  South Korea

Selected Solo Exhibitions
2009 CASA Living Design Walk, On
  Friday, Seoul
  MIZY Fast Food Generation
  Project, Seoul Design Cluster,
  Seoul
  KT&G Putting on Gray Clothes,
  Sangsangmadang

Selected Group Exhibitions
2010 Seoul Design Festival, Coex,
  Seoul
  16 Korean Young Designers,
  Masion
  Korea Design Week, Coex,
  Seoul
2009 Seoul Design Festival, Coex,
  Seoul
  Nefs 1000 Ornaments, Nefs
  Gallery, Seoul
  Seoul Design Olympic, Olympic
  Stadium, Seoul
  Living Design Fair, Coex, Seoul

Joe Colombo
조 콜롬보
Born in 1930, Italy
Died in 1971

1951 As an art student at the
  Accademia di Belle Arti in
  Brera, he joins Movimento
  Nucleare, an avant garde art
  movement founded by Enrico
  Baj and Sergio Dangelo.
1953 Designs the ceiling of Santa
  Tecla, a Milan jazz club.
1954 Creates three open-air spaces
  with benches and "television
  shrines" for the Milan
  Triennale exhibition. Enrols
  in the architecture faculty of
  Milan Polytechnic.
1958 When Mario Colombo fell ill,
  Colombo and his younger
  brother Gianni are left in
  charge of his factory. Sets up a

studio to experiment with
product design.
1961 The brothers withdraw from
  the family business to
  concentrate on design and art
  respectively.
1962 Opens a studio on via Piave
  next to Gianni's. Designs the
  Roll armchair and chair.
1963 Launch of the Elda, the first
  large fibreglass armchair,
  as well as the all-in-one Combi-
  Centre mobile storage unit and
  a miniaturised kitchen for Boffi.
1965 Completes the first two
  versions of the Universale
  stacking chair which, in ABS,
  will be the first chair made
  from a single material.
1966 Designs the Two-in-One
  drinking glass combined two
  goblets each of which can be
  used for drinking or as a base.
1967 Develops the Additional
  System self-assembly armchair
  which will form part of his
  Relaxation Area at the next
  year's Milan Trienniale.
1969 Launch of the self-assembly
  Tube Chair sold as a kit in
  drawstring bags, and of
  the Visiona series of mobile,
  customisable "habitats of the
  future".
1970 Co-writes New Form Furniture:
  Japan with fellow designers
  Pierre Paulin and Sori Yanagi.
  Unveils the Boby Trolley, an all-
  in-one ABS storage unit, the
  Linea 72 in-flight service tray
  for Alitalia and Birillo series of
  bar stools.
1971 Completes the design of the
  Total Furnishing Unit to be
  exhibited in the following
  year's Italy: The New Domestic
  Landscape show at MoMA,
  New York. Joe Colombo dies
  of heart failure on 30 July, his
  41st birthday.
© Design Museum

Hans Coray
한스 코레이
Born in 1906, Switzerland
Died in 1991, Switzerland

The creator of the legendary Landi
chair is the designer, sculptor and
painter Hans Coray. Born in Wald
(Zurich canton) in 1906, Coray
grew up in Zurich in an artistic
environment. His father, Han Coray,
founder of the local Pestalozzi school,
a patron of the arts and teacher,

introduced him to the intellectual
and artistic avant garde.

After completing a degree in
Romance languages, Coray initially
worked as a secondary-school
teacher. He received his doctorate
at age 23, with a dissertation on the
dialects of the Lipari(Aeolian) Islands.
In 1938 Hans Coray received the
commission to develop the model
for innovative display case supports.
That is the lightweight metal chair
that became a design legend of the
20th century: the "Landi Chair".

Hans Coray received accolades
around the world for the Landi chair.
He continued to design everything
from furniture to entire trade-fair
displays. In his later years, he took an
ever greater interest in his painting
and in plastics, often working
intensively with new materials.

Hans Coray's contemporaries
describe him as a charming, witty
and jovial character. He died in
Zurich in 1991. Coray is remembered
as a universalist – a thinker, artist,
designer and teacher.

Motogi Daisuke
모토기 다이스케
Born in 1981, Japan

Education
2004 Graduate from Musashino Art
  University, Tokyo, Japan

Selected Group Exhibitions
2011 Spaceourselves, 3331 Arts
  Chiyoda, Tokyo, Japan
2011 Spaceourselves, RAD , Kyoto,
  Japan
2010 Designtide Tokyo, Japan

Salvador Dalí
살바도르 달리
Born in 1904, Spain
Died in 1989, Spain

Education
1922 Studies in Madrid, at the Real
  Academia de Bellas Arte de San
  Fernando

Selected Group Exhibitions
2008 Monet to Dali, First center for
  the Visual Arts, Nashville, TN
2007 25 Years Brusberg Berlin,
  Galerie Brusberg Berlin, Berlin
2006 Spanish Painting, Solomon
  R.Guggenheim Museum, New
  York City, NY

Robin Day
로빈 데이
Born in 1915, UK
Died in 2010, UK

Robin Day was a British furniture designer. Day is best known for his injection moulded polypropylene stacking chair, of which over 20 million have been manufactured. It was one of the first pieces of furniture to fully use the mass-manufacturing opportunities of injection moulding. It is now so iconic, it was selected as one of eight designs in a 2009 series of British stamps of "British Design Classics." Day was a past winner of the Chartered Society of Designers's Minerva Medal, the highest accolade the Society can offer and is awarded for a lifetime achievement in the field of design, and is Patron of the South Coast Design Forum.

로빈데이는 1935년부터 1939년까지 왕립예술학교에서 수학하였고 그가 디자인한 의자는 1948년 뉴욕에서 열린 '저가형 가구를 위한 국제현상설계'에서 1등 상을 수상하였다. 여기에서 그의 작품은 힐레 (Hille)에 의해 주목 받았고, 힐레는 그를 디자인 고문으로 임명하였다. 그의 가구는 1951년에 밀라노 트리엔날레에서 금상을 차지했다. 1936년에 폴리프로필렌으로 만든 선구적인 의자는 영국에서 미니카 이래로 디자인계에 가장 중요한 기여 중의 하나가 되었다.

Paolo Deganello
파올로 데가넬로
Born in 1940, Italy

He is the Italian architect and designer Paolo Deganello studied architecture at Florence University from 1961 to 1966. In 1966 Paolo Deganello joined in founding Archizoom Associati in Florence. Archizoom was part of the radical design movement in Italy, designing anti-design furniture, such as the corner set "Safari" and the "San Remo" palm-frond lamp (both 1968 for Poltronova). Paolo Deganello showed work at numerous exhibitions, including, the 1972 exhibition mounted by the Museum of Modern Art in New York.

파울로 데가넬로는 이탈리아 건축가이자 디자이너로, 1961부터 1966까지 피렌체 대학에서 건축을 공부하고, 1966년 안드레아 브란치, 질베르토 코레티, 마시모 모로치와 함께 아르키줌 어소시아티를 창립하는데 참여했다. 아르키줌은 이탈리아의 급진적 디자인 운동의 하나로, 기능보다 감성에 중점을 둔 표현력을 내세운 반 디자인적인 디자인 움직임이었다. 그는 다양한 전시를 통해 자신의 작품을 선보였으며, 1972년 MOMA(뉴욕 현대 미술관) 에서도 소개되었다.

Dialoguemethod
다이얼로그메스드
Born in 1985, Korea

학력
2003 홍익대학교 목조형가구디자인학과, 서울, 대한민국

개인전
2010 What is your dialoguemethod, 서울, 대한민국
2009 MCDLX 개인전, 서울, 대한민국

단체전
2011 New Thinking New Possibilities, 서울, 대한민국
2010 디자인 페스티벌 2010, 서울, 대한민국
디자인코리아 2010, 서울, 대한민국
16 코리아 영 디자이너, 서울, 대한민국
Food design GUZZINI Made in ASIA 2010, 서울, 대한민국

소장
현대자동차, 서울, 대한민국

Education
2003 Hong-ik Univ. Wood working & Furniture design, Seoul, Korea

Selected Solo Exhibitions
2010 What is your dialoguemethod, Seoul, Korea
2009 MCDLX solo exhibition, Seoul, Korea

Selected Group Exhibition
2011 New Thinking New Possibilities, Seoul, Korea
2010 Design Festival 2010, Seoul, Korea
Design Korea 2010, Seoul, Korea
16 Korean Young Designers (by Maison), Seoul, Korea
Food design GUZZINI Made in ASIA 2010, Seoul, Korea

Collections
Hyundai Motor Company, Seoul, Korea

Tom Dixon
톰 딕슨
Born in 1959, Tunisia

He is a self-taught Tunisian designer specialised in welded salvage furniture. He moved to Great Britain at the age of 4. Dixon has been head of design for the Habitat chain of furniture stores (1997), and of the Finnish furniture manufacturer Artek. His artistic career began when he discovered pleasure in welding while repairing damaged motorcycle frames.Dixon became known as a designer when his S-Chair was manufactured by Giulio Cappellini. He holds an Honorary Doctorate from Birmingham City University (2004), and was awarded an OBE for services to British Design in 2000.

톰 딕슨은 4살이 되던 해 영국으로 이주, 그곳에서 줄곧 성장했다. 독학으로 디자인을 공부한 후, 갓 스무 살에 본격적으로 디자인 사업에 뛰어들었다. 영국에서 화려한 파티 기획으로 이름을 알리기 시작, 25살의 나이에 첫 오브제 제품을 발표하면서 동시에 놀라운 아방가르드 디자이너라는 평가를 받았다. 1991년 그는 자신의 스튜디오 '스페이스(Space)'를 설립하고 다기능 가구 시리즈 '유로라운지'의 생산에 돌입했다. 이 시기 딕슨은 '창조적 재활용'과 독특한 재료의 실험에 초점을 맞추었다. 주요 작업을 요약해 보면, 테렌스 콘란 경, 장-폴 고티에, 로메오 질리, 랄프 로렌, 비비안 웨스트우드 등의 브랜드에서의 오브제와 인테리어 디자인이 있다. 그보다 더 대중적으로는 카펠리니, 드리아데, 인플레이트 그리고 SCP와 같은 회사에서 작업한 제품들을 들 수 있다. 1998년에 영국의 가구 회사 해비타트는 톰 딕슨을 '최고의 디자이너'로 선정하였다.

Charles & Ray Eames
찰스 & 레이 임스
Charles Eames Born in 1907, USA
Died in 1978, USA
Ray Eames Born in 1912, USA
Died in 1988, USA

1912 Bernice Alexandra Kaiser, nicknamed Ray, is born in Sacramento California. Her father is an insurance salesman.
1915 While working in Virginia, Charles Eames Sr. is shot by train robbers. Injured, he ekes out a living as a journalist only to die in 1919.
1925 On graduating from high school, Charles wins an architecture scholarship at Washington University, St Louis.
1929 After marrying a fellow student, Catherine Woermann, Charles honeymoons in Europe

and discovers the buildings of Ludwig Mies Van Der Rohe and Le Corbusier.

1930 Back in St Louis, Charles opens an architectural office with Charles Gray. Ray and her widowed mother move to New York.

1933 She studies painting with Hans Hofmann and continues until 1939.

1936 With a new architectural partner, Robert Walsh, Charles designs the modern-style Meyer House in collaboration with Eliel Saarinen who becomes a friend and in 1938 offers him a fellowship at Cranbrook.

1940 Ray enrols at Cranbrook where Charles is teaching industrial design. Charles collaborates with Eero Saarinen on cabinets and chairs for an Organic Design competition at MoMA, New York.

1941 Having divorced Catherine, Charles marries Ray in Chicago and they drive to California. They turn a spare room into a plywood workshop.

1942 After winning an order from the US Navy for plywood leg splints, the Eames open a design studio on nearby Santa Monica Boulevard.

1945 The Plywood Chair goes into production.

1946 Charles is the subject of a "one man show" at MoMA, New York at which George Nelson persuades the Herman Miller company to hire him.

1948 Charles and Eero Saarinen win MoMA's Low Cost Furniture Competition with a design for a fibreglass chaise longue.

1949 Construction begins of the two Case Study Houses designed by the Eames in Pacific Palisades: one for themselves, the other designed with and as a home for the architect John Entenza.

1950 The Good Design exhibition series starts at MoMa featuring many of the Eames' designs. They design the (unbuilt) Billy Wilder House.

1952 Launch of the first version of the interlocking House of Cards. Henceforth, the Eames are increasingly preoccupied with films, games and puzzles.

1956 Lounge Chair goes on sale.

1958 The Eames complete an official report into design education in India. Launch of the Aluminium Series of office furniture.

1964 After years of making educational and promotional films for IBM, the Eames design the IBM Pavilion at the New York World's Fair.

1968 Power of Ten, one of the Eames' most influential films, is produced.

© Design Museum

Piet Hein Eek
피트 하인 이크
Born in 1967, Netherlands

Piet Hein Eek was born in Holland in 1967 and was graduated from the Academy for Industrial Design in Eindhoven in 1990. While at the Academy, he gained attention for his exam project Scrap Wood Cupboards. In 1993 he went into partnership with fellow designer Nob Ruijgrok, establishing Eek en Ruijgrok v.o.f. Eek first developed an interest in old materials; he thought the old wood looked nicer than the new. He has built his business around old materials, saving these discarded pieces of wood and working outside of the circuit of mass production.

피엣 하인 이크는 1967년 네덜란드에서 출생하였고, 그는 1990년 디자인 아카데미 아인트호벤에서 가구와 산업디자인을 공부했다. 학교에 다니는 동안 그는 그의 과제물이었던 '나무 조각 찬장(Scrap Wood Cupboards)' 으로 관심을 받았다. 1993년 그는 동료 디자이너인 Nob Ruijgrok과 함께 Eek& Ruijgrok v.o.f 를 설립하였다. 초기의 이크는 오래된 재료에 흥미를 느꼈다. 그는 오래된 나무가 새로운 나무보다 더 훌륭해 보인다고 생각했고 이후로 그는 오래된 재료들을 사용하며 작업해 오고 있다. 이는 버려진 나무 조각들을 활용하는 동시에 대량 생산의 틀 밖에서 작업하게 해준다.

Preben Fabricius & Jørgen Kastholm
프레벤 파브리시우스 & 요르겐 카스톨름
Preben Fabricius Born in 1931
Died in 2007
Jørgen Kastholm Born in 1931
Died in 1984

Inspired by functionalism and the resoluteness of Scandinavian design, which had a considerable influence on the aesthetics of the sixties, interior designers Preben Fabricius and Jørgen Kastholm devoted themselves to optimising shape, material and ergonomics. In 1961, they founded a studio together which became a birthplace of numerous classics in furnishing history. Their main concern was to clearly state the function of an aesthetic form. This principle resulted in lasting symbols of the modern age.

1960년대 미학에 상당한 영향력을 끼친 실용주의와 스칸디나비아 디자인의 간결함의 영향을 받은 인테리어 디자이너 프레벤 파브리시우스와 요르겐 카스톨름은 인체공학적으로 최적화된 재료와 형태를 만들어내는 데 집중했다. 1961년에 그들은 수많은 일류가구의 발생지가 된 스튜디오를 만든다. 그들은 가구의 명확한 기능을 조형적으로 아름답게 표현하는 데 주력하였고, 그 원칙은 현대까지 지표가 되고 있다.

Naoto Fukasawa
나오토 후카사와
Born in 1956, Japan

Naoto Fukasawa is a Japanese industrial designer, born in Yamanashi Prefecture in 1956. He graduated from Tama Art University in 1980. After having acted as the head of the American company IDEO's Tokyo office, he established Naoto Fukasawa Design in 2003. Representative works include MUJI'S CD player (part of the permanent collection, MoMA New York), the mobile phones "Infobar" and "neon" and the ±0 brand of household electrical appliances and sundries. In recent years, he has released a host of new works with Italian companies as well as in Germany and Northern Europe, and they have garnered a great deal of attention.

나오토 후카사와는 일본 야마니시 도에서 출생하여 타마 예술대학 디자인 학부를 졸업하였다. 세이코 엡슨 주식회사에서 디자이너로 근무한 후 미국 여행 중 IDEO의 조상격인 ID TWO에 합류한 후, 훗날 IDEO도쿄 사무실 개설하고 IDEO JAPNA의 대표로서 활약한다. 대표적인 그의 디자인은 IDEO JAPAN 의 인지도를 높였으며, 현재는 후카사와 나오토 디자인이라는 개인 사무실을 설립하였다. 마이니찌 디자인 상을 비롯하여 과거 유럽과 미국에서 40개가 넘는 디자인상을 수상한 나오토는 "Plus Minus Zero" 라는 가전제품의 새로운 브랜드를 창출하기도 하였다. 현재 나오토는 후카사와 나오토 디자인의 대표이며 타마예술대 제품디자인 부에서 강사로써도 활동 중이다.

Guido Garotti
귀도 가로티
Born in 1984, Italia

Education
2010 MA Furniture Design Sheffield, UK
2007 BA Industrial Design Florence, Italy

Frank O. Gehry
프랭크 O. 게리
Born in 1929, Canada
Lives and Works in Santa Monica, CA

1954 Received a degree in architecture from the University of Southern California(USC)
1962 Established his own firm, Gehry Associate, now known as Gehry Partners, LLP
1997 Frank O. Gehry since 1997, Triennale di Milano, Milan, Italy(solo)
2001 Frank Gehry, Architect: Retrospective Features Models, Plans, Drawings, Furniture, Photographs, and Video Footage, as well as Two Site-Specific Architectural Elements, Guggenheim Museum, New York, NY
2004-2005 Frank Gehry, Architect: Designs for Museums, Corocan Gallery of Art, Washington D.C.
2008 Frank Gehry, The Art Gallery Of Ontario, Toronto, Canada
2009 Frank O. Gehry: Design Process and the Lewis House, Philadelphia Museum of Art, Philadelphia, PA
2009 Living Architectures, Storefront for Art and Architecture, New York, NY
2009 From the Spoon to the City:Objects by Architects from LACMA's Collection, Los Angeles County Museum of Art(LACMA), Los Angeles, CA
2010 Fish Forms: Lamps by Frank Gehry, The Jewish Museum, New York, NY

1929년 캐나다 출생. 1947년 가족과 함께 로스앤젤레스로 이주, 남캘리포니아 대학 (USC)에서 건축을, 하버드 디자인대학원에서 도시계획을 전공. 프랭크 게리라는 이름은 오래잖아 체인 등 저렴한 재료를 사용한 조각 같은 건물의 대명사가 되었다. '건축은 예술'이라 믿으며, 작품으로 프라하 ING 사옥(1996), 빌바오 구겐하임 미술관(1997), 로스앤젤레스 월트디즈니 콘서트홀(2003)과 샌터모니카에 있는 자신의 저택 등이 있다. 1989년 프리츠커 상을 수상하고 2003

년 캐나다 기사단을 수작했다.

Nicolai de Gier
니콜라이 디 기어
Born in 1965, Denmark

Nicolai de Gier is an associate professor at the Institute of Design and Communication within the Royal Danish Academy of Fine Arts, School of Architecture. Nicolai de Gier graduated as an architect from Furniture and Room at the Royal Danish Academy of Fine Arts, School of Architecture in 1997. Prior to his architectural degree he completed his training as a cabinetmaker in 1988. In his research Nicolai de Gier focuses in particular on chairs from the modernist golden age of Danish furniture design in the middle of the 20th century and on why many of these designs remain as current as they do.

니콜라이 디 기어 덴마크 왕립 건축, 미술대학의 디자인, 커뮤니케이션 학과에 부교수로 있다. 그는 1997년 덴마크 왕립 건축, 미술대학에서 가구와 방 건축가로서 졸업하였다. 그 이전에도 그는 1988년 소목장으로써의 학위를 받았으며, 20세기 중반 덴마크 가구디자인 절정기의 의자에 주목하여 그 디자인이 지속되는 이유에 관한 논문을 냈다.

Konstantin Grcic
콘스탄틴 그리치치
Born in 1965, Germany

1985 Moves the the UK to study cabinet making at the John Makepeace School for Craftsmanship in Wood at Parnham College, Dorset
1988 Enrols on the masters' course in industrial design at the Royal College of Art, London
1990 Works in Jasper Morrison's design studio in London
1991 Returns to Germany to open his own studio in Munich
1992 Designs products for the Progetto Ogetto collection of objects commissioned for Cappellini by Jasper Morrison and James Irvine
1995 Produces a series of metal stands and tables for SCP.
1996 Begins a collaboration with Authentics, the German home products manufacturer, for which he designs a series of plastic products
1998 Completes the design of the MAYDAY-map for Flos
1999 Designs a collection of

porcelain objects for Nymphenburg and glassware for Iittala
2000 Develops the Hertz halogen light for Flos
2003 Designs the One series of die-cast aluminium furniture for Magis
2004 Unveils the first of his kitchen appliances for Krups as the start of a long term project for that brand
2005 Phaidon Press publishes a monograph on Konstantin Grcic
2005 Exhibited in The European Design Show 28 May 2005 – 4 September at the Design Museum. Exhibition tours.
2007 25/25 - Celebrating 25 Years of Design at the Design Museum
© Design Museum

h220430
Satoshi Itasaka
사토시 이타사카
Born in 1978, Japan

Education
2000 Department of Architecture, Faculty of Science and Technology, Meijo University in Japan

Selected Solo Exhibitions
2010 h220430 "opportunity" Design TIDE Tokyo 2010 Extension, Tokyo , Japan

Selected Group Exhibitions
2011 SHUSHU Opening Ceremony, Munich, Germany

Simo Heikkilä
시모 헤이킬라
Born in 1943, Finland

Education
1967 Graduates as an interior architect, University of Art and Design Helsinki

Selected Exhibitions
1982 Finnland Gestaltet, Museum för Kunst und Gewerbe, Hamburg
1984 New Chairs from Scandinavia, Artek, Helsinki
1988 New Form from Finland, the Royal Museum of Scotland, Edinburgh and the Museum of modern Art, Madrid
1995 Genealogy of Nordic Design 20th Century, the Yamagiwa Art Foundation,

Tokyo
1996 Private exhibition, Röhsska
Museet, Gothenburg
1997 Private exhibition, the Museum
of Central Finland, Jyväskylä
1997-98 Esthetics of Everyday,
Nagoya Design Center, Tokyo,
Helsinki
1998 SE -annual exhibition,
Kunstindustrimuseet,
Copenhagen
Finnish Modern Design
1930-97,
Brad Graduate Center,
New York
1999 Simo Heikkilä-Periferia design,
Design Forum, Helsinki
2000 100 (one hundred invited
designers), Makasiinit, Helsinki
2000-03 Finnish Design 125 years,
Design Forum, Helsinki,
Budapest, Berlin, St
Petersburg, Sydney,
Launceston,
Christchurch, Auckland, Lower
Hutt, Brisbane, Kuala Lumpur,
Hong Kong, Shenzheng
2003 Simo Heikkilä, Piccolo
Museum, Italy
Private exhibition, Local-Lukal-
Lukaali,
Design Museum, Helsinki
2004 Hapsu and Pietu, exhibition
together with Petteri Laiti
Rovaniemi Art museum
2005 'Feets on the ground'
exhibition together with Pentti
Hakala and
Jouko Järvisalo, Cabel factory,
Helsinki
2008 REMIX Fiskars Finland
2009 Budapest Design Museum

Collections
Design Museum, Helsinki
Kunstindustrimuseet, Oslo
Kunstindustrimuseet, Copenhagen
Röhsska Museet , Gothenburg
Museum för Kunst und Gewerbe,
Hamburg
Victoria and Albert Museum, London
The Cooper-Hewitt Museum, New
York

Pepe Heykoop
페페 헤이콥
Born in 1984, Netherlands

Education
2008 design academy Eindhoven,
netherlands

Selected Solo Exhibitions
Rad gallery, london

Selected Group Exhibitions
2011 Imm, Cologne
Dmy, Berlin
2010 cologne d3 contest
Salone del mobile cappelini
Dmy, Berlin
Designweek eindhoevn
2009 Cologne d3 contest
Designweek eindhoven
2008 Rosanna orlandi

Collections
Furnism brickseries

Josef Hoffmann
요제프 호프만
Born in 1870, Austria
Died in 1956, Austria

Austrian architect, interior designer
and applied artist
Josef Hoffmann studied architecture
at the Academy of Fine Arts in
Vienna, Austria, under Art Nouveau
architect Otto Wagner, whose
theories of functional, modern
architecture profoundly influenced
his works, and in 1896 he joined
his office. In 1898, he established
his own practice in Vienna. In
1897, inspired by Mackintosh and
the Glasgow School, he was one
of the founding members with
Gustav Klimt, of an association of
revolutionary artists and architects,
the Vienna Secession. In 1903, he
founded with architects Koloman
Moser and Joseph Maria Olbrich, the
Wiener Werkstätte for decorative
arts. In 1905, Hoffmann, Klimt and
the Wiener Werkstätte artists,
designed the Palais Stoclet, in
Brussels, the Capital of Art Nouveau
and city of Victor Horta.

오스트리아의 건축가이자 인테리어 디
자이너, 장식 예술가. 그는 아르누보 건축
가인 오토 바그너 밑에서 사사 받았으며,
1899년에 바그너는 그를 빈에 있는 응용미
술대학교 교수로 추천했다. 1903년에 프리
츠 바른도르퍼의 후원 아래 호프만은 콜로
만 모저, 요셉 마리아 올브리히와 함께 장
식 예술을 위한 바이너 베르크슈태테를 설
립했다. 호프만의 가장 유명한 건물은 1911
년에 계획된, 브뤼셀에 있는 스토클레궁
(Palais Stoclet)이다. 베르크슈태테 시절의
그의 작품은 매킨토시로부터 유래된 사각
형의 형태를 강조한 모습이었고, 또한 정교
한 홈파기로 네오 클래식한 형태를 수용하
였으며, 1920년대에 들어서는 네오 로코코
의 일면과 데카당트한 형태를 띠고 있었다.
그는 금세기에 있어 가장 절충적이며 다재
다능한 디자이너 중의 한 사람이다.

Richard Hutten

리하르트 휘텐
Born in 1967, Netherlands
1986 - 1991 Studies of industrial
design, Academy of Industrial
Design, Eindhoven, The
Netherlands

Selected Exhibitions
2010 Exhibition and Exhibition
design, Design Museum Gent,
The Netherlands
2009 Plusdesign, Venice Biennial,
Italy
European Design since 1985,
Shaping the New Century, IMA,
Indianapolis, USA
2008 Layers exhibition, Milan, Italy
Menagerie at The
Jones,London, Great Britain
Greenhouse, 100% Design
Shanghai/IHDD, China
2007 Homo Ludens, Retrospective,
Kunsthal, Rotterdam, The
Netherlands
Nature Design, Museum für
Gestaltung, Zurich, Switzerland
2006 Do Touch, Works in Use,
Museum Grand Hornu, Hornu,
Belgium
No Sign of Design, Sieboldhuis,
Leiden, The Netherlands
2005 Mastering Form and
Function, Felissimo Design
House, New York, USA
Love/Why? Design 21
Exhibition, UNESCO, New York,
USA

Hwang, Hyung Shin
황형신
Born in 1981, Korea

학력
2010 홍익대학교 일반대학원 목조형가구
학과 수료
2007 홍익대학교 미술대학 목조형가구학
과 졸업

단체전
2011 '쓰임' 갤러리 큐리오 묵
'Modern Haute Couture(Fashion
meets Furniture)' 부티크모나코
뮤지엄
2010 'Unique & Useful' 인터알리아
'16 Young Korean Designers' 가나
크로프트
'Living Collection(2010디자인한마
당)' 잠실종합운동장
'시대정신' 류화랑
'Translucency Art Square', 상상마당
'DMY International Design Festival
Berlin 2010 Flughafen' Berlin
Tempelhof, 독일
'Young Artist's New Leap' 관훈
갤러리

Education

2008 Master's course in Hongik University

2007 B.F.A. Hongik University

Selected Group Exhibitions

2011 'Usage' Gallery Curio Mook Seoul, Korea
'Modern Haute Couture(Fashion Meets Furniture)' Boutique Monaco Museum Seoul, Korea

2010 'Unique & Useful' Interalia Art Company Seoul, Korea
'16 Young Korean Designers' GANA croft Seoul, Korea
'Living Collection (Seoul Design Festival 2010)' Jamsil Olympic Stadium Seoul, Korea
'Zeitgeist' Gallery Ryu Seoul, Korea
'Translucency Art Square', Sangsangmadang Seoul, Korea
'DMY International Design Festival Berlin 2010 Tresor', M. Berlin, Germany
'New Leap 10 young artist' Kwanhoon gallery Seoul, Korea

Arne Jacobsen
아르네 야콥슨
Born in 1902, Denmark
Died in 1971, Denmark

1924 Enrols as an architecture student at the Royal Academy of the Arts in Copenhagen.

1925 Wins a silver medal for a chair design at the Exposition Internationale des Arts Décoratifs in Paris where he discovers Le Corbusier's work.

1927 Visits Berlin where he sees the architecture of Walter Gropius and Ludwig Mies Van Der Rohe. Wins a gold medal on graduating from the Royal Academy.

1930 After years of designing private houses as a young architect, Jacobsen wins his first public project to modernise the beach at Bellevue.

1935 Completes the groundbreaking Bellavista apartment blocks, now regarded as a classic of the Danish modern movement, in Klampenborg.

1935 Designs the controversial Stelling Hus building in Copenhagen.

1943 Begins two years of

wartime exile in Sweden where he concentrates on textile and wallpaper design and a summer house for two doctors.

1945 Returns to Denmark in peacetime to spend several years working on housing and schools.

1950 Starts a five year project to design the Søholm series of houses in Klampenborg, which mark the start of a looser, more experimental phase.

1951 Inspired by Charles and Ray Eames' furniture, Jacobsen designs the moulded plywood Ant Chair, later refined into

1955's best-selling Series 7.

1956 Designs two upholstered chairs - the Egg and Swan - for the SAS Royal Hotel in Copenhagen as well as the stainless steel cutlery later chosen by Stanley Kubrick as a prop in 2001: A Space Odyssey.

1957 Completes the circular Round House on the island of Sjaellands as the culmination of his experiments with the "houses of the future".

1960 Wins the commission to design St Catherine's College, Oxford. He insists on designing the fixtures, fittings and garden as well as the buildings.

1961 SAS Royal Hotel opens in Copenhagen as the apogee of Jacobsen's ambition to design a building in its entirety down to the smallest fixtures.

1964 The futuristic Belvedere Restaurant opens in Hannover above an early 18th century garden. Jacobsen begins a three year collaboration with Stelton, run by his foster son Peter Holmblad, on the Cylinda Line cocktail kit.

1966 Jacobsen wins the competition to design the new National Bank of Denmark headquarters in Copenhagen. Construction continues after his death with the building opening in 1978.

© Design Museum

Pierre Jeanneret
피에르 잔느레
Born in 1896
Died in 1965

Swiss architect and furniture designer. He was a cousin of Le Corbusier, with whom he twice went into partnership. He graduated from the Ecole des Beaux-Arts, Geneva, and in 1921-2 on Le Corbusier's recommendation he worked with Auguste Perret and Gustave Perret in Paris. In 1922 he went into partnership with his cousin, and in 1923 they built the Besnus Villa (now altered), Vaucresson, near Paris. This first partnership was marked by a number of major projects and works. Jeanneret's contribution to the partnership was considerable, not least in introducing a professionalism in following through projects and work on site, and he often stimulated and provoked his cousin's imagination or moderated it with his own realism. He often drew the first sketches for plans that he then gradually reworked and refined with Le Corbusier, and he also played an important part in ensuring the office's continuity, coordinating work and maintaining tight control over all the technical aspects. Moreover, his contribution in the use of metal and the industrialization and standardization of buildings, central to Corbusier's projects between the World Wars, was fundamental.

피에르 잔느레는 제네바의 에꼴 드 보자르를 졸업하고 1921-2년에 그의 사촌 르 코르 뷔지에의 제안에 따라 어거스트 페레, 구스타브 페레와 함께 파리에서 일을 하게 된다. 1922년에는 샬롯 잔느레와 그의 유명한 사촌인 르 코르뷔제와 함께 활동하기 시작하면서 그들은 실험적인 인테리어를 창조했으며 모던 디자인의 선구자로 평가 받게 된다. 장식 대신 질서와 조화를 강조한 새로운 형식의 건축을 주장하며 이 팀은 유리의 사용과 내부 벽의 제거를 통해 그들의 건축에 빛과 공기를 끌어들였다. 미니멀한 가구와 매끈한 디자인은 후에 공간과 형식의 순수성을 추구하는 감성에 기여했다.

Jeong, Jae Beom
정재범
Born in 1982, Korea

학력
2009 홍익대학교, 서울, 대한민국

개인전
2010 '디자인큐브', 쌈지길, 서울, 대한민국
'디자인큐브', N서울타워, 서울, 대한민국

단체전
2011 '핸드메이드코리아', 코엑스, 서울, 대한민국
'변신의자전', 갤러리맺음, 서울, 대한민국

245

SHOP BMM Season #1, Boutique Monaco Museum, 서울, 대한민국

2010 '디자인메이드2010', KCDF 갤러리, 서울, 대한민국
'서울디자인페스티벌2010', 코엑스, 서울, 대한민국
'Pacific Pedal Life Design', Tokyo Mid Town·Design Hub, 도쿄, 일본

2009 'Talent zone', Tent London, 런던, 영국

소장
Ikejiri Institute of Design, 도쿄, 일본
aA design museum, 서울, 대한민국

Education
2009 Hongik University, Seoul, Korea

Selected Solo Exhibition
2010 'Design Cube', SSamji-gil, Seoul, Korea
'Design Cube', N Seoul Tower, Seoul, Korea

Selected Group Exhibition
2011 'HANDMADE KOREA', COEX, Seoul, Korea
'Metamorphosis chair', gallery MAEZM, Seoul, Korea
'SHOP BMM Season #1', Boutique Monaco Museum, Seoul, Korea

2010 'Design Made 2010, KCDF gallery, Seoul, Korea
'Seoul Design Festival 2010', COEX, Seoul, Korea
'Pacific Pedal Life Design', Tokyo Mid Town·Design Hub, Tokyo, Japan

2009 'Talent zone', Tent London, London, UK

Collections
Ikejiri Institute of Design, Tokyo, Japan
aA design museum, Seoul, Korea

Ji, Seok cheol
지석철
Born in 1953, Seoul

학력
1982 홍익대학교 대학원 회화과 졸업, 서울
1978 홍익대학교 미술대학 회화과 졸업, 서울

개인전
2011 '리' 갤러리, 베를린, 독일
2003 도시 갤러리, 부산
2002 '인'화랑, 서울
1999 '노'화랑, 서울
1998 삼성플라자 갤러리, 분당
1997 조선호텔 나인스 게이트, 서울
1994 기림 갤러리, 대구
1992 나인 갤러리, 서울
1981 다무라 화랑, 동경, 일본

단체전
2011 대구미술관 개관 주제전, 대구
2010 젊은모색 30년전, 국립현대미술관, 과천
2007 이스탄불 아트페어, 터키
2004 시카고 아트페어, 페스티발 홀, 네이비 피어, 미국
2002 이것은 그림?, 포스코미술관, 서울
2001 사실과 환영<극사실회화의 세계전>, 삼성미술관, 서울
1995 의자, 계단 그리고 창, 환기미술관, 서울
1994 서울 국제 현대미술제, 국립현대미술관, 과천
1992 제24회 까뉴국제회화제, 프랑스
1991 '91 한국현대미술초대전, 선재 현대미술관, 경주
1989 한국의 현대미술전, 멕시코시티 현대미술관, 몬테레이 미술관, 멕시코
1983 한국현대미술전<70년대 후반 하나의 양상>, 일본 5개 지역 순회전
1982 제12회 파리비엔날레, 파리시립 대미술관, 프랑스

소장
삼성문화재단(호암미술관), 서울
와까야마 현립근대미술관, 일본
국립현대미술관, 과천

Education
1982 MFA Painting, Hongik University, Seoul, Korea
1978 BFA Painting, College of Fine Arts, Hongik University, Seoul, Korea

Selected Solo Exhibitions
2011 Lee Gallery, Berlin, Germany
2003 Dosi Gallery, Busan
2002 Inn Gallery, Seoul
1999 Roh Gallery, Seoul
1998 Samsung Plaza Gallery, Bundang
1997 The Ninth Gate, The Westin Chosun Hotel, Seoul
1994 Kilim Gallery, Daegu
1992 Nine Gallery, Seoul
1981 Tamura Gallery, Tokyo

Selected Group Exhibitions
2011 The Opening Exhibition of Daegu Art Museum, Daegu
2010 30th Anniversary of young Korean artists, The National Museum of Contemporary Art, Kwachon
2007 Istanbul Art Fair, Turkey
2004 Chicago Art Fair, U.S.A
2002 Is this painting?, Posco Art Museum, Seoul
2001 Hyper-realism Painting in Korea & America, Samsung Museum, Seoul

1995 Chair, Stair and Window, Whanki Museum, Seoul
1994 Seoul International Contemporary Art Festival, The National Museum of Contemporary Art, Kwachon
1992 The 24th Cagnes International Painting Festival, France
1989 Korean Contemporary Art Exhibition, Mexico City, Monterrey, Mexico
1982 The 12th Biennale de Paris, France

Collections
The Hoam Art Museum, Seoul
The Museum of Modern Art, Wakayama, Japan
The National Museum of Contemporary Art, Kwachon

Jo, Sook Jin
조숙진
Born in 1960, Korea
Lives and Works in New York, USA

학력
1991 프랫 인스티튜트 미술 대학원 졸업 (M.F.A.), 브루클린, 뉴욕
1985 홍익대학교 미술대학원 서양화과 졸업 (M.F.A.), 서울, 한국

개인전
2011 "월터 그로피우스 마스터 아티스트 시리즈", 헌팅턴 미술관, 헌팅턴, 웨스트 버지니아, 미국
2010 "사이에서", 존 스미스 갤러리, 바젤, 스위스
2009 "삶, 꿈, 죽음 그리고 삶", 라틴 아메리카 이민자들과 공동 작업, 테너먼트 미술관, 뉴욕, 미국
2007 "중진작가 초대전 2007: 조숙진", 아르코 미술관, 서울. 한국
2006 "뉴욕/파리", 존 첼시 아트 센터, 뉴욕;가나 부부흐 갤러리, 파리, 프랑스
2002 인디애나폴리스 아트 센터, 인디애나
1998 세인트 피터스 교회, 뉴욕
1990 오케이 해리스 웍스 오브 아트, 뉴욕, 미국
1986 "오늘의 서울", 아웅간 갤러리, 오사카, 일본
1985 관훈 갤러리, 서울. 한국

단체전
2011 "Land Art", 챠필리어리, 바젤/에쉬, 스위스
2010 "과정에서", 포름 스콜라플라쯔, 아라우, 스위스
2009 "카파상", 모아 미술관, 서울대학교, 서울, 한국
2007 "조각: 마틴 마길리즈 콜렉션의 선정 작품", 마길리즈 웨어하우스, 마이애미, 프로리다, 미국
"20 뉴욕 아티스트", 한가람 미술관, 서울

2004 "우쯔 비엔날레", 인터네셔널 아티스트 미술관, 우쯔, 폴란드
"광주 비엔날레", 광주 미술관, 광주, 한국
2000 "대지의 제단: 제식과 계시", 스톤 쿼리 힐 조각 공원, 카제노비아, 뉴욕
1999 "7,480,800cu ft.", 소크라테스 조각 공원, 롱아일랜드 시티, 뉴욕
1997 "호랑이의 눈", 엑싯 아트, 뉴욕;일민 미술관, 서울 순회전

소장
국립 현대 미술관, 과천, 한국
후사토닉 미술관, 웨스트포트, 커네티컷
아르코 미술관, 서울, 한국

Education
1991 Pratt Institute, Brooklyn, New York; M.F.A.
1985 Hong-Ik University, College of Fine Arts, Seoul, Korea; M.F.A.

Solo Exhibition
2011 "Walter Gropius Master Artists Project", Huntington Museum of Art, Huntington, West Virginia
2010 "The In Between", John Schmid Galerie, Basel, Switzerland
2009 "Life, Dreams, Death and Life", in collaboration with immigrants from Latin America, Tenement Museum, New York, New York
2007 "A Mid-Career Survey of the Work of Sook Jin Jo, Arko Art Center, Seoul, Korea
2006 "New York/ Paris", Zone Chelsea Center for the Arts, New York; Galerie Gana Beaubourg, Paris, France
2002 Indianapolis Art Center, Indianapolis, Indiana
1998 St. Peter's Church, New York, NY
1990 O.K. Harris Works of Art, New York, NY
1986 "Today in Seoul", Aunkan Gallery, Osaka, Japan
1985 Kwan - Hoon Gallery, Seoul, Korea

Selected Group Exhibitions
2011 Land Art, Tschäpperli, Basel/ Aesch, Switzerland
2010 In/Process, Forum Schloss Platz, Aarau, Switzerland
2009 For Excellence: KAFA Awards, Museum of Art, Seoul National University, Seoul
2007 Sculpture: Selections from the Collection of Martin Z. Margulies, Margulies Warehouse, Miami

20 New York Artists, Hangaram Art Museum, Seoul, Korea
2004 Lodz Biennale - Construction in Process, International Artists' Museum, Lodz, Poland Gwangju Biennale, Gwangju Art Museum, Gwangju, Korea
2000 Earth's Altars: Ritual and Revelation, Stone Quarry Hill Art Park, Cazenovia, New York
1999 7,480,800 cu ft., Socrates Sculpture Park, Long Island City, New York
1997 In The Eye of The Tiger: A Survey of Contemporary Korean Artists, Exit Art, New York, NY; Traveling to: Il Min Museum of Art, Seoul, Korea

Collections
National Museum of Contemporary Art in Korea, Gwacheon, Korea
Housatonic Museum of Art, Westport, Connecticut
Arko Art Center, Seoul, Korea

Joo, Hong Kyu
주홍규
Born in 1970, Korea
Lives and Works in Seoul, Korea& Jakarta, Indonesia

학력
2008 도무스 아카데미, 밀라노, 이탈리아
1996 국민대학교, 서울, 대한민국

개인전
2011 ICFF 국제 현대가구 박람회, 뉴욕, 미국
2010 ICFF 국제 현대가구 박람회, 뉴욕, 미국
슈퍼스튜디오, 밀라노, 이탈리아
쾰른 국제가구 박람회 D3탈런트, 쾰른, 독일
2009 슈퍼스튜디오, 밀라노, 이탈리아

단체전
2010 디자인코리아 '차세대디자인 리더', 서울, 대한민국
IFFT '인테리어 스타일 리빙' 도쿄, 일본

Education
2008 Domus Academy, Milan, Italy
1996 Kook Min Univ., Seoul, Korea

Selected Solo Exhibitions
2011 ICFF 'International Contemporary Furniture Fair', New York, U.S.A
2010 ICFF 'International Contemporary Furniture Fair', New York, U.S.A
Super Studio 'Innovation /

Imagination', Milan, Italy
D3 Talents in IMM, Cologne, Germany
2009 Super Studio 'Discovering / Other Worlds, Other Ideas', Milan, Italy

Selected Group Exhibitions
2010 Design Korea 'Next Generation Design Leader', Seoul, Korea
ICFF 'Interior Lifestyle Living' Tokyo Japan

Donald Judd
도널드 저드
Born in 1928, USA
Died in 1994, USA

American sculptor, designer, and writer on art, one of the leading exponents of Minimal art. He studied at Columbia University and the Art Students League. He had his first one-man exhibition in 1957. In 1959 he began writing reviews for Art News and Arts Magazine. In 1960 – 62 he made the transition from painting to sculpture and became a leading exponent of Minimalism. Much of his work consists of simple cubes or other geometric units that stand on the floor or are cantilevered from the wall, often in stacks or horizontal progressions. His materials included painted steel, Plexiglas, iron, wood, and concrete.

도널드 저드는1928년 미국 미주리주 엑슬시어 스프링스(Exelsior Springs)에서 태어났다. 1957년에 첫 개인전을 가졌고 1959년부터 아트 뉴스와 아트 매거진에 평론을 쓰기 시작했다. 1960년대 초에 회화에서 조각으로 작업 방향을 바꾸고 미니멀리즘을 이끄는 선구적 역할을 한다. 그는 회화와 조각의 경계를 넘나드는 '특수한 오브제'라는 개념을 만들고 이 오브제를 캔버스의 표면과 형태, 색채의 본질적인 단위로 간주하였다.

Finn Juhl
핀 율
Born in 1912, Denmark
Died in 1989

Finn Juhl (1912-1989) was first and foremost famous for his furniture. In the 1940s, he broke with the established furniture tradition and designed a number of creations that regenerated Danish furniture design. At the Milan Triennials in the 1950s, he was awarded no fewer than five gold medals and won international acclaim for his furniture. But Finn Juhl was not only an excellent furniture designer: he worked with all aspects of the architect´s profession. He gained international renown as an interior designer for his work on the Trusteeship Council Chamber at United Nations headquarters in New York. As an exhibition architect, he was the man behind the major showings of Danish applied art abroad which created the concept "Danish design" and paved the way for the Danish furniture industry´s export triumphs in the 1960s.

코펜하겐에서 건축을 수학했으나(1930-1934) 주로 독학을 통해 산업 디자인을 배웠다. 자신의 디자인 사무실을 열기 전까지 빌헬름 라우리첸의 건축사무실에서 일했다. 1950년대엔 에릭 헤를로프, 아르네 야콥센, 그리고 한스 베그너와 함께 덴마크 디자인을 국제적으로 영향력 있게 만든 장본인이었다. 그의 디자인은 특히 목재를 사용한 수준 높은 지역 공예기술에 의존했으나 코레 클린트의 선구적 작품에서 나타난 것보다 좀 더 사물에 풍부한 표현력을 부여했다. 그는 추상 예술가들의 작품뿐 만 아니라 아프리카 원시조각에서 영감을 받았다. 또한 덴마크의 프레데릭스베르 기술학교의 영향력 있는 강사였다.

Jung, Myung Taek
정명택
Born in 1971, Korea

학력
2007 석사, 로체스터 공과대학, 가구디자인 전공, 로체스터 미국
2001 석사, 홍익대학교 일반대학원, 목조형가구 전공, 서울 한국
1998 학사, 홍익대학교 미술대학, 목조형가구 전공, 서울 한국

개인전
2008 정명택 아트퍼니처전, 가나아트 포럼스페이스, 서울 한국
2006 정명택 아트퍼니처전, NTID 다이어 아츠 갤러리, 로체스터 미국

단체전
2011 패션과 가구의 만남, 부띠끄모나코 미술관, 서울 한국
2010 디자인 마이애미 바젤, 바젤 스위스 프리 스타일: 예술과 디자인의 소통 展, 홍익대학교 현대미술관, 서울 한국
텐트런던, 런던디자인페스티발, 런던 영국
물질에서 예술로의 전환, 부산시립미술관, 부산 한국
2009 공예트랜드페어, COEX, 서울 한국
Outdoor Furniture In The Circle, 리오갤러리, 파주 한국
디자인 코리아 2009, 송도 컨벤시아, 인천 한국

텐트런던,런던디자인페스티발, 런던 영국
소장
대양상선, 서울 한국

Education
2007 MFA, Woodworkign & Furniture Design, Rochester Institute of Technology, USA
2001 MFA, Woodworking & Furniture Design, Hong-ik University, Seoul, Korea
1998 BFA, Woodworking & Furniture Design, Hong-ik University, Seoul, Korea

Selected Solo Exhibitions
2008 Jung Myung Taek Art Furniture, Gana Art Forum Space, Seoul Korea
2006 Jung Myung Taek Art Furniture, NTID Dyer Arts Center, Rochester NY USA

Selected Group Exhibitions
2011 FMF(Fashion Meets Furniture),Boutique Monaco Museum, Seoul Korea
Design Miami Basel, Basel, Switzerland
Free Style: A Dialogue between Art and Design, Hongik Museum of Art, Seoul Korea
Tent London, Truman Brewery, London UK
2010 Change from Material into Art, Busan Museum of Art, Busan Korea
2009 Craft Trend Fair, COEX, Seoul Korea
Outdoor Furniture In The Circle, Gallery Lio, Paju Korea
Design Korea 2009, Songdo Convensia, Incheon Korea
Tent London, Truman Brewery, London UK

Collections
Dae Yang Shipping.,Co Ltd., Seoul Korea
Personal collection, Rochester NY USA
Personal collection, London UK
Personal collection, Seoul Korea

Sami Kallio
사미 칼리오
Born in 1975, Finland

Education
2003-2005 Master of Fine Arts in Design, HDK Gothenburg, Sweden
2000-2003 Bachelor of Fine Arts in Design, HDK University

Gothenburg, Sweden
1994 G.C.E. at A level as Joiner, Gothenburg, Sweden

Selected Solo Exhibitions
2011 The Finnish Blood in me, Greenhouse Stockholm Furniture Fair, Stockholm, Sweden
Swedish Love Stories, Superstudio, Milan, Italy
2007 Sitting on Green Gold, Vienna, Austria
2004, 2006 Promosedia International Chair exhibition, Udine, Italy
2004 International Furniture Fair of Valencia, Spain 2004

Selected Group Exhibitions
2011 2010, 2009 Brikolör, Salone Satellite, Milan, Italy
2011 20 Designers at Biologiska, Stockholm, Sweden
2011 2010, Röhsska Design Museum, Gothenburg, Sweden
2010 Special Needs, Art & Design Exhibition, Hotel Nhow, Milan, Italy

Collections
Chair Stitch, Museum for Arts and Crafts, Jyväskylä, Finland
Greenroom, Gothenburg Art Hall, Sweden

Kang, Soo Jin
강수진
Born in 1978, Korea
Lives and Works in London, UK

Education
2009 MA in Textile Futures at Central Saint Martins College of Art and Design, London, UK
2006 BA in Fashion Design and Prints at Central Saint Martins College of Art and Design, London, UK
2003 Foundation in Art and Design at Exeter College of Art and Design, Exeter, UK

Selected Group Exhibitions
2011 Talking Textiles, Spazio Gianfranco Ferré, Milan, Italy
Salone Satellite, Milan, Italy
2010 Homework, Mint, London, UK
Curiosity, Clerkenwell Road, London UK
Salone Satellite, Milan, Italy
Thirst, Beldam Gallery, London, UK
2009 Escapes, Mint, London, UK

Is This Textiles, Tent, London, UK
Textile Futures, Central Saint Martins, London, UK

Collections
Dressed Furniture, London, UK
A Continuous Chain, London, UK

Keum, Ramei
금람해
Born in 1981, Korea

학력
2006 계원디자인예술대학, 경기(의왕), 대한민국

개인전
2008 한국 전통 건축물의 구조와 형태, BMH, 서울, 대한민국

단체전
2010 에디션:확장된 장르, 인터알리아, 서울, 대한민국
2009 디자인페어 솔솔, 코엑스, 서울, 대한민국
New design generation, 동관, 중국
2008 Designer's Party, BMH, 서울, 대한민국
서울디자인올림픽 'Design is Air', 잠실종합운동장, 서울, 대한민국
Designer's Hand, 밀라노, 이탈리아
2007 서울디자인페스티벌, 코엑스, 서울, 대한민국
100%디자인 도쿄, 도쿄, 일본
디자인 메이드, 예술의 전당 한가람 미술관, 서울, 대한민국

Education
2006 Kaywon School of Art&Design, Uiwang, Korea

Selected Solo Exhibitions
2008 Frame and Shape of The Traditional Korean Style Structure, BMH, Seoul, Korea

Selected Group Exhibitions
2010 Edition:The Expended Genre, Interalia, Seoul, Korea
2009 Design fair 'Solsol', Coex, Seoul, Korea
New design generation, Dongguan, China
2008 Designer's Party, BMH, Seoul, Korea
Seoul Design Olympiad 'Design is Air', Jamsil sport complex, Seoul, Korea
Designer's Hand, Milan, Italy
2007 Seoul Design Festival, Coex, Seoul, Korea
100% Design Tokyo, Tokyo, Japan
Design made, Hangaram

design museum, Seoul, Korea

Kim, Bo Yeon
김보연
Born in 1987, Korea

학력
2010~ 홍익대학교 일반대학원 목조형 가구학과 석사과정
2008 계원조형예술대학 가구디자인과 전공

단체전
2011 하얀다락방전, 갤러리 스카이연, 서울
2010 16 Sense , 홍익대학교 현대미술관, Seoul
Korea Design Week 2010 , COEX, 서울
PRESS RELEASE , 류화랑, 서울
A to Z , Urban Loft, 서울
2007 Exhibition of Graduation, 계원조형예술대학, 경기
Outdoor(2007 KOFURN) , 킨텍스, 일산

Education
2010~ MA course in Woodworking & Furniture Design , Hongik University, Seoul, Korea
2008 B.F.A Kaywon School of Art & Design, Korea

Selected Group Exhibitions
2011 White Attic , Gallery Sky Yeon, Seoul
2010 16 Sense , Hongik University, Seoul
Korea Design Week 2010 , COEX, Seoul
PRESS RELEASE , RYU HWARANG, Seoul
A to Z , Urban LOFT, Seoul
2008 Furniture & Magic Carpets , Seoul
2007 Exhibition of Graduation, Kaywon School of Art & Design Outdoor (2007 KOFURN) , KINTEX

Kim, Dai Sung
김대성
Born in 1970, Kroea

학력
2001 프랑스 파리8 대학, 파리, 프랑스
1999 프랑스 리용II 대학 석사 – 리용, 프랑스

개인전
2011 국제 현대 가구 페어 (ICFF), 자빗컨벤션센터, 뉴욕, 미국
2010 뺄셈, 상상마당, 서울, 대한민국
2008 100% design London, 얼스코트, 런던, 영국

2007 100% design Tokyo, 요요기공원, 도쿄, 일본
2006 DESIGN CUBU, 예술의전당, 서울, 대한민국

단체전
2010 Asia design conference, 시조우카 아트센터, 시조우카, 일본
Design & Design, 두산 아트스퀘어, 서울, 대한민국
2008 100% design Tokyo, 요요기공원, 도쿄, 일본
2007 광주디자인비엔날레, 김대중컨벤션센터, 광주, 대한민국
ARCO - Korean new wave design, 스페인
2006 100% design Tokyo, 요요기공원, 도쿄, 일본
Kitchen X Kitchen, 예술의전당, 서울, 대한민국
밀나노 디자인 위크 « Global Edit », 조지알마니관, 밀라노, 이태리
2005 Design MADE, 예술의전당, 서울, 대한민국

소장
매일경제 아트센터, 서울, 대한민국
시조우카 아트센터, 시조우카, 일본
예술의전당, 서울, 대한민국

Education
2001 University Paris 8, Paris, France
1999 University Lyon II Master, Paris, France

Selected Solo Exhibitions
2011 International Contemporary Furniture Fair, Jacob Javits Convention Center, New York, USA
2010 Pelssem, SangSangMadang, Seoul, Korea
2008 100% design London, Earl's Court, London, UK
2007 100% design Tokyo, Yoyoki park, Tokyo, Japan
2006 DESIGN CUBU, Seoul art center, Seoul, Korea

Selected Group Exhibitions
2010 Asia design conference, Sijouka art center, Sijouka, Japan
Design & Design, Doosan art square, Seoul, Korea
2008 100% design Tokyo, Yoyoki park, Tokyo, Japan
2007 Kwangju design biennale, Kimdaejung convention center, Kwangju, Korea
ARCO - Korean new wave design, Span
2006 100% design Tokyo, Yoyoki park, Tokyo, Japan
Kitchen X Kitchen, Seoul art center, Seoul, Korea

Milan design week «Global Edit», George Armani hall, Milano, Italia
2005 Design MADE, Seoul art center, Seoul, Korea

Collections
MK TV art center, Seoul, Korea
Sijouka art center, Sijouka, Japan
Seoul art center, Seoul, Korea

Kim, Do Yeon
김도연
Born in 1981, Korea
Lives and Works in New York, USA

학력
2011 인터내셔널 센터 오브 포토그라피 뉴욕 미국
2008 국민대학교 시각디자인과 서울 한국

개인전
2010 Welcome to 4X1!, miel Seoul, Korea
CONS Launching Show, Kasina premium Seoul, Korea
2009 Deck project, Times Square Seoul, Korea
Aesthetic 4X1, On Friday Seoul, Korea
Supra Showcase, Daily Project Seoul, Korea
BlueDOT Asia, 예술의 전당 Seoul, Korea
2008 Buena Vista Foto, properfit Gallery Seoul, Korea
Relation, On Friday Seoul, Korea

단체전
2011 Capture and Release, ICP Gallery NewYork, USA
2009 Home & Table Deco Fair, COEX Seoul, Korea

Education
2011 International Center of Photography, NewYork, USA
2008 Kookmin Univ, Visual Communication Design Dept. Seoul, Korea

Selected Solo Exhibitions
2010 Welcome to 4X1, Miel Seoul, Korea
CONS Launching Show, Kasina premium Seoul, Korea
2009 Deck Project, Times Square Seoul, Korea
Aesthetics of 4X1, On Friday Seoul, Korea
Supra Showcase, Daily Project Seoul, Korea
2008 Buena Vista Foto, Properfit Gallery Seoul, Korea
Relation, On Friday Seoul, Korea

Selected Group Exhibitions
2011 Capture and Release, ICP Gallery NewYork, USA
2009 Home & Table Deco Fair, COEX Seoul, Korea
BlueDOT Asia, Seoul Art Center Seoul, Korea

Kim, Hee Soo
김희수
Born in 1977, Korea
Lives and Works in Seoul, Korea& New York, USA

학력
2007 School of Visual Arts, MFA, Fine art, 뉴욕, 미국
2003 홍익대학교 미술대학 조소과, 서울, 대한민국

개인전
2010 '빛나는 도시(La Ville Radieuse)', Loft H Gallery, 서울, 대한민국
2009 'Another Landscape', Amos Eno Gallery, 뉴욕, 미국
2008 'New Landscape', Art Space H, 서울, 대한민국

단체전
2010 'Selected of the Selected', Korean Cultural Center of Los Angeles, L.A, 미국
2009 'Mad for Furniture', Nefs , 서울, 대한민국
'2nd Annual Governors Island Art Fair ', Governors Island, 뉴욕, 미국
'Korea Tomorrow 2009', SETEC Seoul Convention Center, 서울, 대한민국
2008 '2008 National Juried Show', Studio Montclair, Montclair, New Jersey, 미국
'Origin', Fox Gallery at the University of Pennsylvania, Philadelphia, PA 미국
2007 '26th Annual Expo', b.j. spoke gallery, Huntington, New York, 미국
'15th Annual Juried Art Exhibition', Korean Cultural Center of Los Angeles, L.A, California, 미국
'MFA Road Show', Boots Contemporary Art Space, St.Louis, Missouri, 미국

소장
NRDC Residential Architect, 뉴욕, 미국
b.j. spoke gallery, 뉴욕, 미국
불교미술관, 서울, 대한민국
클럽모우, 서울, 대한민국

Education
2007 School of Visual Arts - New York, New York - M.F.A. Fine Arts.

2003 Hong-Ik University - Seoul, Korea - B.F.A. Sculpture

Selected Solo Exhibitions
2010 ' La Ville Radieuse ', Loft H Gallery, Seoul, Korea
2009 ' Another Landscape', Amos Eno Gallery, Brooklyn, New York
2008 'New Landscape', Art Space H , Seoul, Korea

Selected Group Exhibitions
2010 Korean Cultural Center of Los Angeles – Selected of the Selected - L.A, California.
2009 Nefs - 'Mad for Furniture' -Seoul, Korea
2nd Annual Governors Island Art Fair - Governors Island, New York, New York
Korea Tomorrow 2009 - SETEC Seoul Convention Center, Seoul, Korea
2008 Studio Montclair- '2008 National Juried Show'- Montclair, New Jersey
Fox Gallery at the University of Pennsylvania - 'Origin' - Philadephia, PA
2007 b.j. spoke gallery -26th Annual Expo - Huntington, New York
Korean Cultural Center of Los Angeles - 15th Annual Juried Art Exhibition - L.A, California.
Boots Contemporary Art Space- MFA Road Show- St.Louis, Missouri

Collections
NRDC Residential Architect, New York, USA
b.j. spoke gallery, New York, USA
Buddha Gallery, Seoul, Korea
Club Mow, Seoul, Korea

Kim, Ja Hyung
김자형
Born in 1985, Korea

학력
2011 홍익대학교 일반대학원 졸업, 서울, 한국
2008 동아대학교 졸업, 부산, 한국

단체전
2011 Rhythmic Chairs, 이도갤러리, 서울, 한국
서울리빙디자인페어, 코엑스 , 서울, 한국
2010 디자인페스티벌, 코엑스, 서울, 한국
메종 & 오브제, Paris-Nord Villepinte, Parc des Exposition, 파리, 프랑스
STITCH, TENSION, 갤러리 BMM, 서울, 한국

서울리빙디자인페어, 코엑스, 서울,
한국
2009 Indoor Design for Life, 클레이아크미
술관, 김해, 한국
12Prototypes, 덕원갤러리, 서울,
한국
Furniture Buffet – imm
cologne,cologne messe, 쾰른, 독일

Education
2011 Hongik University Graduate
School, Seoul, Korea
2008 Dong-a University, Busan,
Korea

Selected Group Exhibition
2011 Rhythmic Chairs, Yido gallery,
Seoul, Korea
Living design Fair, COEX, Seoul,
Korea
2010 Design Festival, COEX, Seoul,
Korea
Maison & Objet, Paris-Nord
Villepinte, Parc des Exposition,
Paris, France
STITCH, TENSION, BMM
gallery, Seoul, Korea
Living Design Fair, COEX, Seoul,
Korea
2009 Indoor Design for Life,
Crayarch Museum, Gimhae,
Korea
12Prototypes, Dukwon gallery,
Seoul, Korea
Furniture Buffet – imm
cologne,cologne messe,
Cologne, Germany

Kim, Kyung Lae
김경래
Born in 1979, Korea

학력
2008 홍익대학교 대학원 목조형가구학과
졸업
2006 홍익대학교 미술대학 목조형가구학
과 졸업

개인전
2009 'Feeling Tree'展, 서정욱 갤러리, 서울

단체전
2011 'Maison & Object Paris 2011', 파리,
프랑스
2010 'Unique & Useful', Gallery Interalia,
서울
'Craft Trend Fair 2010', COEX, 서울
서울디자인한마당 Living Collection
2010, 잠실 주경기장, 서울
'Mix up'展 Arts & Crafts
Collaboration, 한국도자재단, 이천
'Art of Craft'展, 벤쿠버 뮤지엄, 벤쿠
버, 캐나다
2009 공예트렌드 페어-기획 부스전, '의자'
초청전, 서울, COEX

Education
2008 M.F.A, Hongik University
Majored in Woodworking &
Furniture Design
2006 B.F.A, Hongik University
Majored in Woodworking &
Furniture Design

Selected Solo Exhibitions
2009 'Feeling Tree', Seojungwook
gallery, Seoul

Selected Group Exhibitions
2011 'Maison & Object Paris 2011',
Paris, France
2010 'Unique & Useful', Gallery
Interalia, Seoul
'Craft Trend Fair 2010', COEX,
Seoul
Seoul Design Fair 'Living
Collection 2010', Chamsil Sport
complex, Seoul
'Mix up' Arts & Crafts
Collaboration, Korea Ceramic
foundation, Ichon
'Art of Craft' (Vancouver
museum, Vancouver, Canada
2009 Craft trend fair, COEX, Seoul

Kim, Kyung Won
김경원
Born in 1972, Korea

학력
2011 홍익대학교 대학원 디자인공예학과
박사과정, 서울, 대한민국
2004 홍익대학교 대학원 목조형가구학과
석사, 서울, 대한민국
2001 홍익대학교 미술대학 목조형가구학
과 학사, 서울, 대한민국

개인전
2010 Betwixt in TENT LONDON, OLD
TRUMAN BREWERY, 런던, 영국
2007 CONTACTED, 덕원갤러리, 서울,
대한민국
2006 FURNITURE, Re-SPACE, 갤러리아이,
서울, 대한민국
FURNITURE to SPACE, 김진혜갤러
리, 서울, 대한민국

단체전
2010 KOREA_UAE 수교 30주년 기념 한국
현대미술초대전, 국립미술관, 아브
다비, 아랍에미리트
가구숲展, 더 갤러리, 서울, 대한민국
세계도자세라믹스, Mix up - 遊幸(유
행)展, 이천세계도자센터, 이천,
대한민국
Show Handarty Fair, HILLSTATE H,
서울, 대한민국
2009 공예트랜드페어, 코엑스, 서울,
대한민국

KOREA TOMORROW 展, 서울종합전
시장, 서울, 대한민국
신호탄展, 기무사(국립현대미술관
서울관 건립예정지), 서울, 대한민국
설화문화전, 크링, 서울, 대한민국
광주디자인비엔날레, 광주디자인센
터, 광주, 대한민국
2008 서울디자인올림픽, 잠실종합운동장,
서울, 대한민국
2007 서울디자인위크, 코엑스, 서울,
대한민국
2006 신세계 아트페어, 신세계갤러리,
서울, 대한민국

소장
현대백화점, 서울, 대한민국

Education
2011 The Doctor's Course in the
Hongik University, Seoul, Korea
2004 M.F.A Hongik University, Seoul,
Korea
2001 B.F.A Hongik University, Seoul,
Korea

Selected Solo Exhibitions
2010 Betwixt in TENT LONDON, OLD
TRUMAN BREWERY, London,
UK
2007 CONTACTED, Dukwon Gallery,
Seoul, Korea
2006 FURNITURE, Re-SPACE, Gallery
I, Seoul, Korea
FURNITURE to SPACE, Kim Jin
Hye Gallery, Seoul, Korea

Selected Group Exhibitions
2010 I Finding Beauty of Love and
Peace, the National Museum
of Arts, abu dhabi, UAE
Forest of Furniture, The
Gallery, Seoul, Korea
World Ceramix Exhibition-Mix
up, Icheon World Ceramic
Center, Icheon, Korea
Show Handarty Fair, HILLSTATE
H, Seoul, Korea
2009 CRAFT TREND FAIR , COEX,
Seoul, Korea
KOREA TOMORROW , SETEC,
Seoul, Korea
Beginning of New Era,
KIMUSA(KOREAN Old Defence
Security Command Site), Seoul,
Korea
Sulwha Culture Exhibition,
Kring, Seoul, Korea
GwangJu Design Biennale,
GwangJu Design Center,
GwangJu, Korea
2008 Seoul Design Olympiad, Seoul
Olympic Stadium, Seoul, Korea
2007 Seoul Design Week, COEX,
Seoul, Korea
2006 Shinsegae Art Fair, Shinsegae

Gallery, Seoul, Korea

Collections
Hyundai Department Store, Seoul, Korea

Kim, Yik Yung
김익영
Born in 1935, Korea

1965 1st Solo Exhibition, Salon
 Pagodon Gallery, Seoul
1978 Tongin Gallery, Seoul
1983 Tokyo Gallery and Gallery
 Ueda, Tokyo, Japan
1984 Gallery Odau, Tokyo, Japan
1985 Shinsegae Art Gallery, Seoul
1989 Hyundai Gallery, Seoul
1991 Meitetsu Art Gallery, Nagoya,
 Japan
1995 1st Gwangju Biennale as a
 Representative of, Gwangju,
 Korea

Major Activities
1999 Invitational Lecture, Detroit
 Institute of Arts, USA
 Jury for the Traditional Part
 of the Ceramic for Living,
 World Ceramic Exposition,
 Korea
2000 Invitational Lecture, Royal
 Museum, Edinburgh, UK
 Become a member of the
 International Ceramic
 Academy of IAC
2002 Participated in the General
 Assembly of IAC, Greece
2003 Commission Work, Bathroom
 as Ceramic House, Yeoju EXPO
 Gallery
 Commission Work, Design of
 Medalist Box for EXPO
 International Competition
 Prizes
2004 Incheon World Ceramic EXPO
 committee for 2004

1935 함경북도 청진 생
1957 서울대학교 공과대학 화공과 졸업
1958 서울대학교 대학원 요업공학전공
 수료
1959 홍익대학교 공예미술학과 학사편입
1961 미국 뉴욕주립 알프레드 요업대학원
 졸업(미술석사학위) 개인전
1965 살롱 파고돈 초대전
1978 통인화랑 초대전
1983 일본 동경화랑, 우에디화랑 초대전
1984 일본 동경 오다우화랑
1985 신세계 미술관 초대전
1989 현대화랑 초대전
1991 일본 나고야 메이테츠미술관 초대전
1995 광주 비엔날레 주전시 한국대표작가
 출품

경력
1999 디트로이트 인스티튜트 오브 아트
 초청강연
 세계 도자기 엑스포 생활 도자 전통
 부문 1인 심사
2000 로얄 미술관 초청강연, 에든버러,
 영국
 국제도예아카데미(IAC) 회원
2002 동서산업 타일 및 위생도기 디자인
 개발
 그리스 IAC 총회 회원
2003 세계 도자기 엑스포 세라믹 하우스
 욕실 디자인 및 설치
 세계 도자기 엑스포 국제 공모전
 상패 디자인 및 제작
2004 2004년도 인천 세계 도자 엑스포
 운영위원

Rodney Kinsman
로드니 킨스만
Born in 1943, UK

The British furniture designer Rodney Kinsman attended the Central School of Art there until 1965. In 1966 Rodney Kinsman joined Jurek Olejnik and Bryan Morrison in founding OMK Design to make the furniture they designed. Chairman and Managing Director of OMK Design Ltd. Visiting Professor at Central Saint Martins College of Art and Design.

영국인 가구 디자이너 로드니 킨스만은 1965년까지 중앙예술학교를 다녔다. 1966년 그는 쥬렉 올레닉, 브라이언 모리슨과 OMK 디자인 회사를 설립하며 그들이 디자인한 가구를 생산하기 시작한다. 현재 그는 OMK 디자인 Ltd.의 회장이자 경영 책임자이며 센트럴 세인트 마틴 예술&디자인 대학의 초빙 교수이다.

Poul Kjærholm
폴 키에홀름
Born in 1929, Denmark
Died in 1980

Born in Øster Vrå, Denmark, Kjærholm began as a cabinetmaker's apprentice with Gronbech in 1948, going on to the Danish School of Arts and Crafts in Copenhagen in 1952. He was very articulate and with his natural authority he started an outstanding career as an educator in the same year(1952) but continued to study with Prof. Erik Herløw and Prof. Palle Suenson.

덴마크의 제품 디자이너이다. 1950년부터 가구의 공업화와 수공작업과의 조화를 꾀해 작품을 설계하였다. 1957년 이후는 미술 아카데미에서 가구와 실내 디자인 강사를 역임했다. 그는 덴마크의 우아하고 섬세

한 전통을 표현하는 디자이너로서 목재에 대리석이나 강철등의 이질적인 재료를 결합시키는 독특한 스타일을 가졌다. 1957년 「밀라노 트리엔날레」에서 그랑프리, 1958년 스칸디나비아 라닝상을, 1960년에 에켈스베르상을 수상하였다.

Harri Koskinen
해리 코스키넨
Born in 1970, Finland

Harri Koskinen has studied at the Institute Of Art And Design in Helsinki. Koskinen is probably best known for his Block Lamp, a light bulb held inside two shaped pieces of clear glass, which is exhibited in MoMA in New York City. Also very well known for the two variants of his Fatty container (models 7150 and 7100) designed in 1998 for Schmidinger. He has designed for many different labels and companies, across many types of article; from furniture to cookware, as well as commercial packing.

젊은 핀란드 디자이너 코스키넨은 1970년 핀란드 카르스톨라에서 출생했으며 헬싱키 미술디자인대학에서 수학하였다. 그의 대표작인 블록램프는 두 개의 투명 유리 블럭 안에 전구가 들어간 형태로, 뉴욕 현대미술관에도 전시되어 있다. 1998년 슈미딩거 사의 의뢰로 제작한 두 종류의 패티 컨테이너(모델명7150, 7100) 역시 그의 유명한 작품으로 꼽을 수 있다. 그는 여러 회사 및 브랜드 사에서 가구는 물론이고 조리용품과 상업 포장재에 이르는 다양한 방면에서 활발한 디자인활동을 하고 있다.

Arttu Kuisma
아르뚜 쿠이스마
Born in 1988, Finland

Education
2008 Designer, Laht, Finland

SelectedGroupExhibitons
2010 UNI ON, Artek Store, Helsinki,
 Finland
2010 Olomuoto fair, Laht, Finland
2010 Habitare fair, Helsinki, Finland

Shiro Kuramata
시로 쿠라마타
Born in 1934, Japan
Died in 1991, Japan

Shiro Kuramata is one of Japan's most important designers of the 20th century. Kuramata was mainly known for his use of industrial materials such as wire steel mesh and lucite to create architectural interiors and furniture.

Revolutionary pieces such as the "How High the Moon" chair (1986) reflect the emerging dynamism and maturing creativity of postwar Japan, or his Ikabana, lead cristal free hand blown vase, realized by the Vilca from Colle Valdelsa (Siena) Italy, a unique example of fusion, between oriental and occidental cultures. In 1990 the French government awarded Kuramata the distinguished Ordre des Arts et des Lettres in recognition of his outstanding contribution to art and design.

구라마타는 동경 공업대학에서 건축을 공부한 후 동경 쿠와사의 디자인 연구소에서 캐비닛 제작 훈련을 받았다. 1957년에서 1964년까지 산 아이의 멤버였으며 1965년 동경에 구라마타 디자인 사무실을 설립했다. 그는 1969년에 동경에 있는 주드 클럽의 실내 디자인을 맡았고, 1981년 일본 디자인을 위한 문화상을 수상했다. 1981년부터 1984년까지 밀라노의 멤피스 그룹을 위해 디자인했고, 1987년에는 동경, 뉴욕, 파리에 있는 이세이 미야케 부티크의 실내를 디자인했다. 또한 비트라사의 비트라 에디션 콜렉션을 위해 철망으로 된 'How high the Moon' 암체어를 디자인 했다.

Carolien Laro
카롤리언 라로
Born in, 1982

Education
2005-2009 Wood- and Furniture College Amsterdam, Netherlands
2000-2004, Academy of Arts St. Joost, Breda, Netherlands
1995-2000, Havo, Roosendaal, Netherlands

Selected Group Exhibitions
2011 Design & Recycling; HVC-groep, Dordrecht, Netherlands
2010 Dutch Design Week, Klokgebouw, Eindhoven, Netherlands
DOEN-materiaalprijs, ICSE, Eindhoven, Netherlands
Houtbeurs, Ahoy, Rotterdam, Netherland
Jubileeu Exposition, Wood and Furniture College, Amsterdam, Netherlands
Design Bazaar; Designhouse, Eindhoven, Netherlands
2009 Living Fair Woonbeurs, RAI, Amsterdam, Netherlands
2007 Kunstroute Halderberge, Hoeve en Oudenbosch, Netherlands
2005 Kunstroute Halderberge, Hoeve en Oudenbosch,

Netherlands
2004 – 2005 Small town expo; Current designs a.d.h.v. Historical examples, Heemhuis, Baarle-Nassau, Netherlands
2004 Living Almelo; Exposition Dutch Designers, Almelo, Nethetlands

Collections
Spring Wood, Amsterdam, Wood- and Furniture College
Spring Wood, Rotterdam, Wood and Furniture College

Le Corbusier
르 코르뷔지에
Born in 1887, Switzerland
Died in 1965, France

Swiss-born French architect, designer, urbanist, writer and painter, famous for being one of the pioneers of what now is called modern architecture. He was born in Switzerland and became a French citizen in 1930. His career spanned five decades, with his buildings constructed throughout central Europe, India, Russia, one in North and several in South America. He was a pioneer in studies of modern high design and was dedicated to providing better living conditions for the residents of crowded cities. He was awarded the Frank P. Brown Medal in 1961.

르 코르뷔제는 20세기에 가장 영향력 있고 유명한 건축가이다. 그의 도시계획, 공공건물, 주택과 디자인 등에서의 근본적인 계획들은 어떻게 하면 만족스런 현대생활을 영위할 수 있는가 하는 문제에 완전히 새롭게 접근한 것이었다. 르 코르뷔지에의 가구는 그의 건축과 마찬가지로 새로운 생산 방법, 재료, 사회적인 추세가 디자인상의 문제들에 대한 새로운 접근을 가능케 한다는 그의 믿음을 실현시킨 것이다. 그는 기능적이고 아름다운 미학적 형태로 지난 인습을 완전히 뜯어고치려 했으며, 그가 만든 의자들은 디자인 역사상 획기적인 작품으로 평가되고 있다. 르 코르뷔지에의 것이라고 추정되는 디자인들은 사촌들인 피에르 잔느레과 샬롯 페리앙과 합작해서 작품활동을 하던 시기에 제작했던 것이다. 그것들은 처음에는 토네트 회사에 의해 제작되었으며, 1950년대 후반 이후로는 독일의 베버가 대량으로 생산했고, 최근에는 이탈리아의 카시나가 생산하고 있다.

Lee, Jae Ha
이재하
Born in Born in 1981, Korea

Education

2008 Kaywon Design& Art School, Gyeonggi, Korea

Solo Exhibition
2009 Design Group LUFF Launching Show, Gallery BMH, Seoul, Korea

Group Exhibition
2010.12 'tavillage', Sangsangmadang Design Sqare, Seoul
2010.12 Design Korea, in Hannam, Seoul
2010.06 Seoul design auction, Horim Art Center, Seoul
2010.04 Seoul Open Art Fair, COEX
2010.03 Seoul Living Design Fair, COEX
2009.12 Seoul Design Festival, COEX
2009.10 Olleh Art Exhibition, Keumho Gallery
2009.09 TENT LONDON, LONDON UK
2009.04 DESIGN CUBE 'Redevelopment', N Seoul Tower
2009.03 Furniture Fair 2009, Gallery BMH
2008.12 7th Designers Party, Gallery BMH
2008.12 Design Touch, Seoul Design Cluster
2008.11 100% 'hands-up' experience Furniture design team 'with' 1st exhibition, Gallery BMH
2008.10 Seoul Design Olympic, Jamsil Main Stadium
2008.03 Seoul Design Week 'F5', Design Cluster
2008.01 Furniture & Magic Carpets, KTF Gallery The Orange
2007.12 6th Designers Party, KT&G Art Square
2007.12 Seoul Design Week, COEX
2007.11 Design College Expo, COEX

Lee, Sam Woong
이삼웅
Born in 1981, Korea

학력
2011 홍익대학교 일반대학원 목조형가구학과 수료
2008 홍익대학교 목조형가구학과 졸업

단체전
2011 모던 오트쿠트르,부띠끄모나코 미술관, 서울
2010 16 KOREA YOUNG DESIGNERS, 스페이스크로프트, 서울
A TO Z, 어반로프트, 서울
디자인 마이에미, 바젤, 바젤
Site & Sight, 스톤엔 워터, 안양
2009 Korea Tomorrow, SETEC, 서울
서울 디자인 페스티벌, COEX, 서울

1000 Ornaments, Nefspace, 서울
홈엔 테이블데코 페어 2009, COEX,
서울
디자인 올림픽, 잠실 주 경기장, 서울
홍익 아트 앤 디자인 페스티벌,
HOMA, 서울
12 Prototypes, 덕원 겔러리, 서울
ON Off 전시, 라메르 겔러리, 서울
2008 12 Furniture Designers Fair, KT&G
상상마당, 서울
Living Goods Fair, BMH, 서울
2007 KOFURN, KINTEX, 일산

Education
2011 MA course in Woodworking &
Furniture Design, Hongik
University, Seoul, Korea
2008 BA in Woodworking &
Furniture Design, Hongik
University, Seoul, Korea

Selected Group Exhibitions
2011 Modern Haute Couture
Exhibition, Boutique Monaco
Museum, BMM, Seoul
2010 16 KOREAN YOUNG
DESIGNERS, Space Croft, Seoul
A TO Z, Urban LOFT, Seoul
Design Miami, Basel, Basel
Seoul Living Design Fair, COEX,
Seoul
Site n Sight, Stone & Water,
Anyang
Korea Tomorrow, SETEC, Seoul
2009 Seoul Design Festival, COEX,
Seoul
1000 Ornaments, Nefspace,
Seoul
Home & Table Deco Fair 2009,
COEX, Seoul
Seoul Design Olympiad, Jamsil
Olympic Stadium, Seoul
Hongik Art & Design Festival,
Hongik Univ., Seoul
12 Prototypes, Dukwon
Gallery, Seoul
ON Off Exhibition, Gallery
Lamer, Seoul
2008 12 Furniture Designers Fair,
KT&G Sangsangmadang, Seoul
Living Goods Fair, BMH, Seoul
2007 KOFURN, KINTEX, Ilsan

Daniel Lorch
다니엘 로히
Born in 1980, Germany

Education
2006 BA in Communication Design,
Konstanz, Germany

Selected Group Exhibitions
2011 Salone Satellite, Milan, Italy
2010 DMY Design Gallery, Berlin,
Germany

Interieur Design Biennale,
Kortrijk, Belgium
Sächsisches Industriemuseum,
Chemnitz, Germany
Tendence Talents, Frankfurt,
Germany
DMY International Design
Festival, Berlin, Gemany
Galerie im Regierungsviertel,
Forgotten Bar Project, Berlin,
Germany
Light+Building, Designplus
Award Show, Frankfurt,
Germany
2009 DMY Asia Tour, Tokyo/Seoul/
Singapore/Taiwan
DMY International Design
Festival, Berlin, Gemany
2008 DMY International Design
Festival, Berlin, Gemany

Collections
Privat Collection, Hannover,
Germany
Privat Collection, Brussels, Belgium
Privat Collection, Braunschweig,
Germany

Charles Rennie Mackintosh
찰스 레니 매킨토시
Born in 1868, Scotland
Died in 1928, England

1875 Attends Reid's Public School
and, in 1877, Allan Glen's
Institution
1883 Begins evening classes at
Glasgow School of Art, which
he attends until 1894 and
where he wins many prizes
1884 Trains with the Glasgow
architects John Hutchins
1889 On qualifying, Makcintosh joins
the renowned architects
Honeyman & Keppie, where
he befriends fellow
draughtsman Herbert MacNair
(1868-1955)
1894 Develops designs with
MacNair and their friends,
the sisters Margaret and
Frances Macdonald. Together
they are known as The Four.
Goes on the first of many
sketching holidays in England.
1896 Makintosh is the lead
designer on Honeyman &
Keppie's competition entry
for the new Glasgow School of
Art. The Four exhibits at the
Arts and Crafts Exhibition
Society in London. Designs and
produces stencil wall
decorations for the Buchanan
Street tea rooms, Glasgow for

Miss Cranston
1897 Designs Queen's Cross Church,
Glasgow. Construction begins
on Glasgow School of Art.
The Studio publishes an article
on Mackintosh
1898 Designs several buildings for
the 1901 Glasgow
International Exhibition.
Commissioned by Miss
Cranston to design the
furniture and decoration
for The Argyle Street tea
rooms. Produces designs for
Ruchill St. Church Halls,
Glasgow and two domestic
interiors: an all-white bedroom
at Westdel, Queen's Palace,
Glasgow for Robert Maclehose
and a dining-room for Hugo
Brückmann, editor of
Dekorative Kunst, in München
1899 The new Glasgow School of Art
opens, as does the Queen's
Cross Church, Glasgow
1900 Marries Margaret Macdonald.
Together they design the
decoration and furniture
for their flat at 120 Mains
Street, Glasgow. Miss Cranston
commissions Mackintosh to
design the interior and
furniture for The Ladies'
Luncheon Room, Ingram
Street tearooms. Completes
designs for Windyhill,
Kilmalcolm, his first detached
house, for his friend William
Davidson
1901 Becomes a partner in
Honeyman, Keppie &
Mackintosh. Designs interior
and furniture for Mrs Rowat at
14 Kingsborough Gardens,
Glasgow
1902 Designs a music room at Carl-
Ludwigstrasse, Vienna for
Fritz Warndorfer, a supporter
of the Secession Movement
and later of the Wiener
Werkstätte. Commissioned
to build Hill House,
Helensburgh for publisher
Walter Blackie
1903 Miss Cranston commissions
Mackintosh to design the
exterior and interiors of The
Willow tea rooms, Glasgow.
The Glasgow School Board
appoints Mackintosh to design
the Scotland Street School,
Glasgow
1904 Completes The Hill House,
Helensburgh. Designs the
decoration and furnishings of

the hall, dining room, drawing room and two bedrooms at Hous'hill Nitshill, Glasgow for Miss Cranston and her husband Major Cochrane

1905 Designs a shop at 233 Sauchiehall Street for Messrs Henry and Carruthers. Begins work on Auchinibert, a house at Killearn, Stirlingshire for F.J. Shand and on the Dutch Kitchen for the basement of the Argyle Street tea rooms, Glasgow

1906 Completes the designs for the boardroom at Glasgow School of Art. Moves with Margaret to 78 Southpark Avenue, where they create new interiors

1907 Produces designs for The Oak Room at the Ingram Street tea rooms for Miss Cranston and the west wing of Glasgow School of Art

1909 Designs the Card Room for Hous'hill as well as the Oval Room and ladies' rest room at the Ingram Street tea rooms. Opening of the west wing of Glasgow School of Art

1911 Creates the interiors of The Cloister Room and Chinese Room for the Ingram Street tea rooms, Glasgow

1914 Dissolves partnership in Honeyman, Keppie & Mackintosh and moves to Walberswick, Suffolk where he paints watercolours and is suspected by local people of being a spy

1916 Creates furniture and interiors for 78 Derngate, Northampton for W.J. Bassett-Lowke and produces fabric designs for Messrs. Foxton and Messrs. Sefton of London

1917 Designs the Dug-Out, a war-time café at the Willow tea rooms and clocks for W. J. Bassett-Lowke

1919 Completes designs for a guest bedroom at 8 Derngate, Nothampton and a cottage at East Grinstead for E.O. Hoppé

1923 Moves to Port Vendres in southern France where he paints a series of watercolours, mainly landscapes

© Design Museum

Vico Magistretti
비코 마지스트레티
Born in 1920, Italy

He was born in Milan and graduated Polytechnic in 1945. He then joined his father's studio and from 1948 onwards took part in various editions of the Milan triennial exhibition. He has won the gold medal at the 9th edition of the triennial (1951), the grand prix at the 10th edition of the triennial (1954), two compassi d'Oro (1967 and 1979), and the gold medal of S.I.A.D. society of industrial artists & designers (1986).

In the 60's he began designing furniture, and his works have been displayed in the major design exhibitions throughout Europe U.S.A. and Japan and are included in the permanent exhibitions of the world's most important museums.

비코 마지스트레티는 밀라노의 폴리테크닉에서 건축을 공부했고, 이후 디자인으로 전향했다. 1966년 아르테미데에서 만든 셀레네의자 같은 디자인으로 1960년대에 국제적인 명성을 얻었다. 마지스트레티는 이 의자를 디자인할 때 생산과 강도의 문제를 고려했으며, 굴곡진 형태는 플라스틱 제품을 위한 새로운 이탈리아 미학을 정립하는 데 도움을 주었다. 그는 20년 동안 특히 카시나를 위해서 기술적 • 예술적으로 혁신적인 가구 디자인을 생산했다. 1981년 작 신밧드 안락의자는 스프링 위에 느슨하게 던져져 있는 것 같은 말안장 이미지에서 착안한 것이며 휴게실 의자에 조각적 형태를 과감하게 시도한 작품이었다.

Bruno Mathsson
브루노 마트손
Born in 1907, Sweden
Died in 1988

Bruno Mathsson was a Swedish furniture designer and architect with ideas colored by functionalism/modernism, as well as old Swedish crafts tradition. Bruno Mathsson developed modernism in furniture and architecture, addressing both general and specific problems. His ideas of the "ultimate seating" was the basic concept of his furniture design, reflected in sitting curves and table heights. He also designed office furniture based on the thesis that people in office environments would work more comfortably and think more efficiently in a reposing position. The interest for Bruno Mathsson's design was renewed due to his success at the exhibition Interbau in Berlin 1957. In the 1960's he created the famous "Superelips" table together with and artist mathematician Piet Hein. This series

was produced both by Swedish manufacturer Karl Mathsson and in Denmark by Fritz Hansen. The most exclusive versions came with rosewood or teak tops.

브루노 마트손은 스웨덴의 선구적 현대가구 디자이너다. 베르나모에 있는 부친의 목조공장 카를 마트손(Karl Mathsson)에서 도제로 일했으며(1923-1931). 1930년대 초반 곡목(bent wood)을 연구하기 시작했다. 그는 나무의 비례와 하중을 견디는 내력을 분석했으며 산업공정을 통해 구부리고 표면을 처리하는 새로운 방식을 찾아냈다. 가구 제조업체 덕스 모에벨(Dux Möebel)이나 카를 마트손이 생산한 그의 디자인 대부분은 가벼움과 단순함이 특징이며 혁신적인 구조적 특성을 지니고 있는 경우가 많다.

Janne Melajoki
얀 멜라요키
Born in 1982, Finland

Education
2008 Designer, Laht, Finland
2011 Danish Design School, Copenhagen, Denmark

SelectedGroupExhibitons
2010 UNI ON, Artek Store, Helsinki, Finland
2010 Olomuoto fair, Laht, Finland
2010 Habitare fair, Helsinki, Finland

David Mellor
데이비드 멜러
Born in 1930, England
Died in 2009, England

1935 Attends Crookes Endowed School, Sheffield, later renamed Lydgate Lane School.

1942 Joins the Junior Art Department of Sheffield College of Art.

1945 Enrols at Sheffield College of Art.

1948 Wins a place at the Royal College of Art in London, but delays his entry for 18 months to complete National Service in the 8th Tank Regiment.

1950 Enrols in the RCA Silversmithing School under Robert Goodden. While still a student Mellor prototypes his silver plate Pride cutlery and writes his thesis on The Development of the Cutlery Industry.

1952 Wins a travel scholarship, and visits Sweden and Denmark.

1953 Chosen as one of two students to study at the British School in Rome.

1954 Graduates from the RCA with a

Silver Medal and returns to Sheffield to open a workshop on Eyre Street to work on one-off silverware commissions and for industry, notably as design consultant to Walker & Hall, which puts Pride into production.
Abacus Lighting manufactures the street lighting designed by Mellor at the RCA.

1957 Pride is given one of the first Design Centre Awards.

1960 Constructs a purpose-built studio-workshop at 1 Park Lane designed by the Sheffield architect Patric Guest of Gollins Melvin Ward.

1962 Designs the Symbol set of stainless steel cutlery for Walker & Hall's new factory.

1963 Commissioned to design the Embassy range of sterling silver tableware for use in Britain's embassies.

1965 Starts a five year consultancy for the Ministry of Transport on the design of a national traffic signal system and automatic half-barrier crossings.

1966 Launch of the Thrift stainless steel cutlery commissioned by the Ministry of Public Building and Works for use in government canteens in hospitals, schools and prisons.
Designs a controversial square pillar box for the Post Office.

1967 Collaborating with the sculptor Elizabeth Frink, Mellor designs a silver altar cross and candlesticks for new Roman Catholic cathedral in Liverpool.

1968 Exhibition of David Mellor's work at the Stedelijk Museum, Amsterdam

1969 Opens his first London shop on Sloane Square, selling kitchenware and tableware. This was followed by shops in Manchester and Covent Garden.

1973 Moves to Broom Hall, a historic building in Sheffield, where he constructs a cutlery production facility.
Launches Provençal as the first cutlery to be designed at Broom Hall.
Commissioned to make a silver bowl of 201 segments to mark the bicentenary of the Cutler's Company in Sheffield.

1975 Designs Black Provençal and Chinese Ivory cutlery.

1982 Becomes Chairman of the Crafts Council.
Develops Café as a new version of 1966's Thrift cutlery.

1984 Introduces the Classic range of stainless steel cutlery.

1986 Designs cutlery for people with disabilities in association with the Helen Hamlyn Foundation.

1990 The Round Building, designed by Michael Hopkins and Partners, opens at Hathersage in the Peak District. It receives many architectural prizes including an RIBA National Award and the Civic Trust Award.

1996 The Paris and English ranges of cutlery go into production.

1998 Designs the City range of cutlery and a trolley for Magis, the Italian plastics manufacturer.
A retrospective of David Mellor's work is organised by the Sheffield Galleries & Museums Trust for presentation at the Design Museum in London, Dean Clough Galleries in Halifax and the Mappin Art Gallery, Sheffield.

2003 Launch of the Minimal range of cutlery.

2007 Selector for 25/25 - Celebrating 25 Years of Design exhibition at the Design Museum 29 March - 22 June.

© Design Museum + British Council, 2007

Niels O. Møller
닐스 O. 뮐러
Born in 1920, Denmark
Died in 1982, Denmark

Danish designer and cabinetmaker Niels O. Møller is known for his elegant furniture in teak and rosewood. He is a strong representative for Danish post-war furniture design with high demands on materials and craft skills. Mr Møller founded the furniture factory J.L Møller Møbelfabrik in Århus, Denmark, in 1944. All of his designs were produced by J.L Møller. The company is still active and owned by the Møller family.

덴마크의 소목장이자 가구디자이너, 닐스 O. 뮐러는 우아한 티크와 장미목가구로 잘 알려져 있으며 재료에 대한 깊은 이해와 노련한 기술을 요하는 전 후 덴마크 가구 디자인에 있어 대표적인 위치에 있다. 그는 1944년 덴마크 오르후스에 J.L 뮐러 가구 공

장을 설립하고 모든 가구를 직접 디자인하였으며, 회사는 지금까지 뮐러 가문에 의해 활발히 운영되고 있다.

Carlo Mollino
카를로 몰리노
Born in 1905, Italy
Died in 1973

Architect Carlo Mollino was born in 1905 and trained at the Polytechnic in Turin, where he graduated in 1931. From 1933 to 1973, the year when he suddenly died, he made a total of only about ten architectural works. Equally important was his work as an interior designer. In 1949 he started teaching at the Faculty of Architecture at the Polytechnic of Turin, and the following year he was invited to take part in a travelling exhibition in eleven American museums. Mollino never worked for large industry. Most of his furniture were carried out as one-off items. In 1960 Mollino returned to his work as an architect and started redesigning the apartment in Via Napione in Turin, which is now Museo Casa Mollino.

이탈리아 토리노에서 태어나 건축을 공부하고 1931년 졸업했다. 1930년부터 1936년까지 엔지니어인 부친과 함께 일했고, 1936년 그가 독립해 일하게 되니 후에도 디자인 방법은 용인된 건축 방법을 사용하고 시장에서 구할 수 있는 건축, 장식재료 목록을 참조하는 등 아버지에게 물려받은 방법에 기초해 작업을 계속했다. 이에 따라 그의 건축, 인테리어 디자인 그리고 설비는 쉽게 구할 수 있는 사물의 콜라주가 되었다. 그의 건축과 디자인 프로젝트는 어느 정도 벨기에 아르누보와 안토니 가우디의 영향을 반영한 유동적이고 곡선적 느낌을 특징으로 한다. 몰리노의 작품은 1980년대 초반 1950년대 디자인에 대한 일반적인 관심이 늘어나면서 다시 부상했다. 결코 생산되지 못했던 정교한 부분은 대개 현대 가구 디자인에서 나무를 알루미늄으로 바꾸는 등의 개작을 통해 모방되었다.

Jasper Morrison
재스퍼 모리슨
Born in 1959, UK

1979 Studies furniture design at Kingston Polytechnic.

1982 After graduating from Kingston, Morrison enrols on the furniture design course at the Royal College of Art in London.

1986 Opens the Office for Design in London to design products and furniture which, initially, he manufactures himself using ready-made industrial materials and small workshops.

1987 Exhibits in the Documenta 8 exhibition at Kassel, Germany. Develops his furniture designs for production by SCP in the UK and Cappellini in Italy, as well as a door handle for FSB in Germany.

1988 Designs a room set entitled Some New Items For The Home to be exhibited in Berlin and presents a collection of images that have inspired him as the slide show, A World Without Words, in Milan. Vitra offers to manufacture the Ply Chair and other pieces from Some New Items For The Home.

1992 Collaborates with James Irvine to develop the Progetto Oggetto collection of home products for Cappellini from designers such as Marc Newson, Konstantin Grcic and Andreas Brandolini.

1994 Completes the design of Bottle, a plastic bottle rack, for Magis which, for many years, will be his best-selling product.

1995 Awarded a DM500m project, then the biggest light rail project in Europe, to design a new tram system for the German city of Hanover.

1997 Designs the Moon collection of porcelain dinnerware for Rosenthal.

1998 Launches the Op-lá Tray Table and Tin Family for Alessi and the Sim stacking chair for Vitra.

1999 Completes the protoype of the Air Chair, a one piece gas injection-moulded plastic chair for Magis, the Globe lights for Flos and densely upholstered Low Pad and Hi-Pad range of chairs for Vitra.

2000 Tate Modern Museum opens in London with public spaces furnished by Morrison.

2002 Lars Müller publishes a monograph of Morrison's work, Everything But The Walls. Opens a design studio in Paris.

2003 Completes the development of the ATM desk system for Vitra.

2004 Designs kitchen appliances for Rowenta and cutlery for Alessi.

2005 Completes the development of

a collection of furniture for the Vitra At Home and develops products for Muji. Nominated for the Design Museum's Designer of the Year prize.

© Design Museum, 2006

Koloman Moser
콜로만 모저
Born in 1868, Austria
Died in 1918

Koloman Moser was an Austrian artist who exerted considerable influence on twentieth-century graphic art and one of the foremost artists of the Vienna Secession movement and a co-founder of Wiener Werkstätte. During his life, Moser designed a wide array of art works - books and graphic works from postage stamps to magazine vignettes; fashion; stained glass windows, porcelains and ceramics, blown glass, tableware, silver, jewelry, and furniture - to name a few of his interests.

빈 아카데미(1886-1892)와 미술공예학교 (School of Arts and Crafts, 1892-1895)에서 공부했으며 1899년부터 이곳에서 강의했다. 그의 그래픽 디자인은 유기적인 양식으로부터 분리파의 전형적인 기하학적 양식으로 점진적으로 변화했다. 그는 분리파의 창시자이기도 했다. 요제프 호프만과 함께 1903년 빈 공방을 설립했으며, 이 공방을 위한 그의 가구 디자인은 직선적이며 정교했다.

Rainer Mutsch
라이너 무취
Born in 1977, Austria

Education
2002 UDK Berlin, Product Design, Berlin, Germany
1998-2003 Univ. of Applied Arts, Industrial Design, Prof. Paolo Piva, Vienna, Austria
2001 Denmarks Design Skole, Furniture Design, Copenhagen, Denmark

Selected Solo Exhibitions
2011 Sofia Design Week 2011, Sofia, Bulgaria
2007 Rainer Mutsch "Fragmented Spaces", Landesgalerie, Eisenstadt, Austria

Selected Group Exhibitions
2011 Design Vision Austria exhibition, Zona Tortona, Milano, Italy

Furniture Designs of the Year, Design Museum London, England
Sofia Design Week 2011, Sofia, Bulgara
2010 22nd Biennial of Industrial Design, Ljubljana, Slowenia
Vienna Design Week, Dune, Verdarium, Vienna, Austria
2009 PAD, Gallery O, Milano, Italy
Tokyo Design Week, Tokyo, Japan
2008 Wien Products, ICFF, New York, USA
21st international Biennale for Interior Design, Kortrijk, Belgium
100% Design, Tokyo Design Week, Tokyo, Japan
2007 Pure Austrian Design, ICFF, New York, USA
Installation, Museum of Applied Arts, Vienna, Austria

George Nakashima
조지 나카시마
Born in 1905, USA
Died in 1990

George received his BA in architecture from the University of Washington and his MA in architecture from MIT. Nakashima spent about a year at the École Américaine des Beaux-Arts before going to MIT. Nakashima's work emphasizes wood's textural lines and forms that are naturally acquired through aging. His works, such as Conoid and Mira series among others, embrace all types of household items from chairs, tables, sofas to lighting. He had a likeness towards the functionality of furniture that was designed in harmony with architecture. He also enjoyed working with aging marks of trees and patinas that were naturally formed by human touch and use. Nakashima produced beautiful and elegant Zen style pieces while at the same time underscoring their practicality until his death in 1990.

1905년 미국에서 일본인 부모 아래 태어난 나카시마는 1929년 워싱턴 대학교 (University of Washington)에서 건축학 학위를 딴 후 파리의 에콜데보자르 (École Américaine des Beaux-Arts)에서 수학했으며 1930년 M.I.T.에서 건축석사학위를 받았다. 나카시마의 가구작품은 나무에서 자연적으로 생겨나는 결과 선을 그대로 살리면서 심플하지만 한층 격이 높은 실용성이 겸비된 것들이었다. 코노이드 시리즈, 미라 시리즈 등 여러 종류의 의자, 테이블, 소파 및 전등까지 그의 작업은 집안의 구석 구석에 안착되는 모든 것들을 포용했다. 건축물과 가구가 함께 어우러지는 실용성을 따지는 디자인에 애착을 가졌던 작가는 사람의 사용으로 인해 묻어나는 손때와 시간의 흐름에 의해 자연스레 생기는 흔적을 소중히 생각했다. 또한 그는 동양적인 절제된 선 스타일의 미감이 가미된 실용적이고 아름다운 작품들을 50여 년 동안 선보였다.

George Nelson
조지 넬슨
Born in 1908, USA
Died 1986

George Nelson studied architecture at Yale University. A fellowship enabled him to study at the American Academy in Rome from 1932-34. In Europe he became acquainted with the protagonists and major architectural works of modernism. A programmatic article on residential building and furniture design, published in Architectural Forum by Nelson in 1944, attracted the attention of D.J. DePree, head of the furniture company Herman Miller. Shortly after this, George Nelson assumed the position of design director at Herman Miller. Remaining there until 1972, he became a key figure of American design, also convincing the likes of Charles and Ray Eames, Isamu Noguchi and Alexander Girard to work for Herman Miller.

미국의 건축가이자 산업디자이너. 예일대학에서 건축을 공부하며, 1931년 건축학 학위를 받았다. 다음 해 워싱턴의 아메리칸 카톨릭 대학과 로마의 아메리칸 아카데미에서 수학한다. 1936년부터 1941년까지 윌리엄 햄비와 함께 뉴욕에 건축사무소를 열고 감독을 맡는다. 1944년 헨리 라이트와 함께 분리된 상태의 부속으로서도 기능을 갖는 조립식 정리대를 구상해 냈다. 아키텍츄얼 포럼지에서 묘사되는 이 연구의 적절성은 그에게 허먼 밀러 가구회사의 가구 제작부의 미술책임자 자리를 제공하게 되었다.

Marc Newson
마크 뉴슨
Born in 1963, Australia

1982 Enrols at Sydney College of the Arts to study jewellery and sculpture.
1986 Exhibits Lockheed Lounge at Roslyn Oxley Gallery in Sydney.
1987 Lives in London. Makes Pod of Drawers from materials stolen from the model making workshop where he works part-time.

1988 Designs Embryo Chair and Andoni fashion store back in Sydney.
1989 Moves to Tokyo to work for Teruo Kurosaki's company, Idée, which produces Orgone Chair, 1987 Super Guppy Light,
1988 Black Hole Table and 1990 Wicker Chair and Lounge. Kurosaki exhibits Newson's work in Milan.
1992 Opens studio in Paris rag trade district. Cappellini puts old pieces, including 1989 Orgone Lounge and 1989 Felt Chair, into production.
1993 Designs Helice Lamp for Flos, and Gluon and TV Chairs for Moroso. Develops Seaslug watch for Ikepod, a company co-founded with Oliver Ike.
1995 Coast restaurant opens in London with interior and furniture by Newson.
1996 Komed restaurant opens in Cologne. Newson develops retail concept for fashion designer, Walter Von Beirendonck. Meets Benjamin De Haan.
1997 Moves to London. Designs Rock and Dish Doctor for Magis, Apollo Torch for Flos and Alessi bathroom and kitchen products.
1998 Starts work on MN1 bicycle for Biomega and Falcon 900B jet.
1999 Spends most of the year in Turin developing the 021C concept car for Ford at Ghia carrozzeria. 021C unveiled at Tokyo Motor Show.
2002 Designs new business class seats for Qantas airline and sanitaryware for Ideal Standard.
2003 Develops a range of cookware for Tefal, mobile phones for KDDI and completes work on a bar at Lever House in New York. Participates in Somewhere Totally Else - The European Design Show at the Design Museum.
2004 Creates Kelvin 40, a concept jet, commissioned and presented at Fondation Cartier, Paris. Unveils a range of sports footwear for Nike, Stages a major survey exhibition of his work at the Design Museum.
© Design Museum

Oh, Se Hwan
오세환
Born in 1971, Korea

학력
2009 연세대학교 생활디자인학과 디자인 석사, 서울, 대한민국
1998 홍익대학교 목조형 가구학과 학사, 서울, 대한민국

개인전
2008 밀라노 국제 가구 전시 (살로네 사테리테), 로 피에라, 밀라노, 이태리
2007 밀라노 국제 가구 전시 (살로네 사테리테), 로 피에라, 밀라노, 이태리

단체전
2010 디자인 코리아, 코엑스, 서울, 대한민국
     서울디자인 한마당, 잠실 올림픽주경기장, 서울, 대한민국
     디자인 & 디자인, 두산 아트스퀘어, 서울, 대한민국
2009 디자인 코리아, 인천 송도 컨벤시아, 인천, 대한민국
     움직이는 갤러리, 연세대학교, 서울, 대한민국
2008 메종, 스타일 페어, 크링, 서울, 대한민국
     서울디자인 올림픽, 잠실올림픽주경기장, 서울, 대한민국
     100%디자인, 얼스코트, 런던, 영국
2007 서울 디자인 위크, 코엑스, 서울, 대한민국
     광주 디자인 비엔날레, 김대중 컨벤션 센터, 광주, 대한민국
     상상으로 거듭난 13개의 의자 전, 상상마당, 서울, 대한민국
     디자인 마이 페스티벌 전, 독일 한국 대사관, 베를린, 독일
2006 서울 디자인 페스티벌, 코엑스, 서울, 대한민국
     테이블 데코 앤 플라워 페어, 코엑스, 서울, 대한민국
     내방에 빛을 비추다, KT광화문지사, 서울, 대한민국
     포스트-밀란 전, 한가람 디자인 미술관, 서울, 대한민국
     밀라노 국제 가구 전시 (살로네 사테리테), 로 피에라, 밀라노, 이태리

소장
안양 예술 공원, 안양시, 대한민국

Education
2009 Yonsei University: M.F.A in Department of Human Environment & Design, Seoul, Korea
1998 Hong-ik University: B.F.A in Woodworking & Furniture Design, Seoul, Korea

Selected Solo Exhibitions
2008 Salone Internazionale del Mobile(Salone Satellite), Rho-Fierra, Milano, Italy

Verner Panton
베르너 팬톤
Born in 1926, Denmark
Died in 1998, Denmark

He is considered one of Denmark's
most influential 20th-century
furniture and interior designers.
During his career, he created
innovative and futuristic designs
in a variety of materials, especially
plastics, and in vibrant and exotic
colors. His style was very "1960s" but
regained popularity at the end of the
20th century; as of 2004, Panton's
most well-known furniture models
are still in production.

베르너 팬톤은 덴마크 건축가이자 디자이
너로 플라스틱 제품분야에서 가장 선구적
인 디자이너다. 팬톤은 코펜하겐의 아르네
야콥센 밑에서 근무하던 1955년, 플라스틱
으로 만든 쌓기형 의자를 최초로 디자인했
다. 그리고 1960년대의 고전적인 플라스틱
디자인에 대한 사회적 관심이 다시 생기면
서, 1990년에 비트라 사가 <팬톤 의자>를
재생산할 판권을 갖게 되고 그 의자는 가장
유명한 의자 모델로 유명하다.

Pierre Paulin
피에르 폴랑
Born in 1927, France
Died in 2009, France

Pierre Paulin, one of the most
important French designers, is
famous for the sensuous curves
and impeccable proportions
of his seating designs. In 1952,
Pierre Paulin's first designs caught
the attention at the Thonet firm
through which he discovered and
mastered new materials in the
manner of the American designers
Eames, Saarinen and Bertoia. In
1956, after responding to Harry
Wagemans' invitation to join Artifort,
Paulin found the means and the
support he needed to realize the
production of his designs. In his
concern for simplicity and refusal
of any lyrical effect, his designs
were given numbers. His innovate
productions anticipated social
revolutions through the lifestyles
they encouraged.

피에르 폴랭은 프랑스의 디자인 겸 실내디
자이너로 파리의 카몽도학교에서 수학한
폴랭은 특히 원형제작 기술에 중점을 두면
서 조각을 배웠다. 1950년대 초, 그는 가구
의 제작에 흥미를 느끼면서 그의 최초의 의
자들이 1954년 토네트사에 의해 제작되었
다. 그리고 1958년에는 네덜란드의 아티포
트사의 주요 디자이너들 중 하나가 되었다.
그는 당시 베르너 팬톤과 함께 생생하게 채
색되는 유연한 형태들의 뛰어난 제작자로
각광을 받았다. 그는 의자의 무스 자식을
만들어 낼 수 있는 받침 구조들을 제작하기
위해 유리 섬유가 보강된 폴리에스테르의
주조 가능성들에 관심을 가졌다. 이에 따라
그는 1960년 안락의자 F560을 구상하며 이
모델은 아티포트에 의해 제작된다. 이러한
원칙을 바탕으로 그는 프랑스의 국립가구
협회와 함께 여러 가구들을 만들어 냈다.

Charlotte Perriand
샬롯 페리앙
Born in 1903, France
Died in 1999, France

Charlotte Perriand became known
for her sleek furniture created with
innovative materials such as copper
and steel. Since the 1930s, she
worked frequently with Jean Prouve,
developing a series of innovative
modular storage units and low-cost
residential furnishings. Many of
these pieces are still seen as icons of
the new machine age.

샤를로트 페리앙은 가구 디자인, 산업디
자인, 건축 등 여러 분야를 넘나들며 다양
한 활동을 했다. 무엇보다도 유명한 것은
1920년대 말과 1930년대에 르 꼬르뷔지에
(Le Corbusier)의 스튜디오에서 스틸과 알
루미늄, 그리고 유리로 만들어낸 가구들이
다. 이 가구들을 통해 그녀는 '기계화 시대'
의 미학을 인테리어에 도입한 선구적인 인
물로 평가를 받게 되었다. 그녀는 진보적
인 사고와 적극적인 활동으로 가구디자인
및 건축계에 많은 업적을 남겼으며 일본의
산업디자인에도 큰 영향을 주었다. '생활의
예술(L'art de vivre)'을 통해 일상의 환경을
개선하려 했던 그녀의 디자인 철학은 오늘
날에도 많은 이들에게 영감을 주고 있다.

Charles Pollock
찰스 폴록
Born in 1930, USA

He studied at the Cass Technical High
School in Detroit before winning a
stipend to attend Pratt Institute of
Design, which helped him secure a
place working with George Nelson
after college. Later, Florence Knoll's
recognition of his talent helped
secure his reputation as one of
the world's preeminent furniture
designers. His Pollock-Chair is the
best-selling executive chair in the
history of office furniture design,
and now has a place in the Louvre in
Paris. Pratt Institute's 1991 tribute
honored Pollock with its Excellence
by Design Award.

폴록은 디트로이트의 카스기술고등학교에
서 수학 후 장학금을 받아 이후 프랫 인스
티튜트에서 학사과정을 마쳤으며 졸업한
이후에는 조지 넬슨의 작업실에 들어갔다.
폴록의 재능은 플로렌스 놀의 주목을 받았
는데 이는 세계 유명 가구 디자이너로서
의 명성을 얻게 된 원동력이 되었다. 그의
폴록의자는 사무가구디자인의 역사를 통
틀어 가장 많이 팔린 사무용 의자이며, 현
재 파리 루브르박물관에도 소장되어 있다.
1991년 프랫 인스티튜트 디자인 어워드에
서 수상하였다.

Jean Prouve
장 푸르베
Born in 1901, France
Died in 1984, France

2He was a French metal worker, self-taught architect and designer. His main achievement was transferring manufacturing technology from industry to architecture, without losing aesthetic qualities. His design skills were not limited to one discipline. During his career Jean Prouvé was involved in architectural design, industrial design, structural design and furniture design.

장 프루베는 1916년 낭시에서 금속세공인으로 처음 일을 시작하여 1924년 자신의 공방을 열면서 금속에 대한 지식을 점차 넓혀나갔다. 이어 당시 혁신적인 건축가들과 함께 작업하다 1930년부터 장 프루베는 현대미술가연합의 설립회원으로 활동하면서 가구디자인을 시작하였으며 그룹전에 참여하였다. 그는 세계 대전 이전부터 공방의 규모를 조금씩 확장하기 시작하였는데, 1947년 마침내 낭시 외곽의 맥세빌이라는 도시에 '장 프루베 아뜰리에'를 열어 새롭고 전문화된 제품을 제작하였다. 르 크르뷔지에, 캉딜리 등과 같은 유명한 건축가들과 함께 일을 할 때도 장 프루베는 언제나 그들의 계획을 충족시키는 동시에 미적 수준을 향상시키는데도 커다란 공헌을 했다.

Ernest Race
어니스트 레이스
Born in 1913, UK
Died in 1964, UK

1932 Bartlett School of Architecture, London
1934 Troughton & Young, London
1937 India
1937-39 Interiors & furnishings retail, London
1939-45 War service with Auxiliary Fire Service, London
1946 BA Aluminium furniture designed
1946 Britain Can Make It exhibition, Victoria & Albert Museum, London
1948 Low-Cost Furniture Competition, Museum of Modern Art, New York
1950-51 Antelope and Springbok steel rod furniture for Festival of Britain, London
1953 Plywood furniture for Peninsular & Orient shipping line
1955 Heron upholstered lounge chair
1957 Flamingo upholstered lounge chair, Design Centre award 1959
1958 Furnishings for the British Pavillion, World's Fair, Brussels
1962 Race Furniture Ltd relocates from Clapham to Sheerness, to concentrate upon furniture for the contract market
1962 Ernest Race resigns from Board of Ernest Race Ltd to operate as a consultant designer
1964 Dies, London

Roland Rainer
롤란트 라이너
Born in 1910, Austria
Died in 2004, Austria

Roland Rainer was an Austrian architect. Born in Klagenfurt, he studied at the Vienna University of Technology. After World War II, he returned to Austria. He then wrote his first theoretical works, including his most famous one Urban design prose. In 1953, Rainer became professor for housing, urban design, and land use planning at the University of Hanover. In 1954, he became professor for structural engineering at the Graz University of Technology, which forced him to commute between Graz and Hanover. From 1956 to 1962, one of his most significant works, the Wiener Stadthalle in Vienna, was built. In 1958, Rainer was commissioned with the development of the zoning plan by the town council of Vienna.

롤란드 라이너는 오스트리아의 건축가로 클라겐푸르트에서 태어나 비엔나 기술 대학에서 공부하였다. 제2차 세계대전 이후 그는 떠났던 조국 오스트리아로 다시 돌아와 그의 가장 유명한 '도시 디자인 산문'을 포함한 여러 이론들을 발표한다. 라이너는 1953년 하노버 대학의 교수가 되었고 1954년에는 그라즈 기술대학의 교수가 되었다. 이는 그로 하여금 그라즈와 하노버 사이를 통근하게 만들었다. 1956년부터 1962년까지 그의 가장 중요한 작업 중 하나인 뷔너 스타드트할레가 비엔나에 건축되었다. 1958년에 라이너는 비엔나 시의회에 의해 도시 구획 계획 사업의 책임자가 되었다.

Jens Risom
옌스 리솜
Born in 1916, Denmark

Jens Risom is an exemplar of Mid-Century modern design, Risom was one of the first designers to introduce Scandinavian design in the United States. Risom's furniture is in numerous collections including the Museum of Modern Art, New York; and The RISD Museum, Providence, Rhode Island. In 1970 Risom was appointed a trustee of The Rhode Island School of Design where in 2004 he received an Honorary Doctorate of Fine Arts. In 1996 Risom received the Danish Knight's Cross. Risom continues to live and work in New Canaan, Connecticut.

옌스 리솜은 근 현대 중엽 가구디자인의 표본이자 미국에 스칸디나비아의 디자인을 최초로 소개한 인물 중 하나이다. 그의 가구는 뉴욕 현대미술관(MOMA)과 로드아일랜드 디자인학교 미술관(RISD Museum)을 포함하여 수많은 곳에 소장되어 있다. 1970년에는 그가 2004년에 명예 박사학위를 받은 로드아일랜드에 이사로 임명되었으며, 1996년에는 덴마크 기사 십자상을 수여 받았다. 그는 현재 미국 뉴 캐년에 거주하며 작품활동을 이어나가고 있다.

David Lincoln Rowland
데이빗 링컨 롤란드
Born in 1924, USA
Died in 1924, USA

He was an American industrial designer. Rowland earned his undergraduate degree in 1949 from Principia College and was awarded a master's degree from Cranbrook Academy of Art. He is best known for the 40/4 chair he created in the late 1950s, a stacking chair so named because 40 chairs can be stored in a stack 4 feet (120 cm) high, with sales in the millions. The chair took off, earning critical recognition in winning the grand prize at the Milan Triennale and was included in the Museum of Modern Art's permanent collection. It was recognized by the American Institute of Interior Designers in 1965.

데이빗 링컨 롤랜드는 미국 산업 디자이너로, 1949년 프린시피아 대학에서 공부한 후, 크랜브룩 아케데미에서 석사 학위를 받았다. 그는 1950년 후반에 만든 40/4 의자로 유명해졌는데, 밀리언셀러가 된 이 의자의 이름은 그의 스태킹 의자 40개를 포개어 고작 120cm의 높이로 만들 수 있는 데에서 기인하였다. 의자는 급속히 인기를 얻었고 밀라노 트리엔날레에서 그랑프리를 수상하였으며 뉴욕현대미술관MoMA의 영구 컬렉션에도 소장되어 있다. 1965년 미국 인테리어 디자이너 협회에서도 높은 평가를 받은 바 있다.

Eero Saarinen
에로 사리넨
Born in 1910, Finland
Died in 1961

Born in Helsinki, he emigrated with his family to the United States in 1923. Initially studied sculpture at the Académiе de la Grande Chaumiére in Paris (1929/30) and later architecture at Yale University in New Haven, Connecticut, graduating in 1934. He received a scholarship there which enabled him to travel to Europe (1934/35). On his return, he taught at the Cranbrook Academy of Art. In 1937, he began a collaboration with Charles Eames which culminated in a series of highly progressive and prize-winning furniture designs for The Museum of Modern Art's 1940 "Organic Design in Home Furnishings" competition. He later produced several highly successful furniture designs for Knoll International. His greatest architectural project was the remarkable TWA terminal at John F. Kennedy Airport, New York.

핀란드 태생의 미국 건축가이자 디자이너로 1923년에 부모와 함께 미국으로 이주하였다. 1929년 그의 부친이 있던 킹스우드(Kingswood) 여학교를 위해 가구디자인을 했으며, 1930년~31년 파리로 건너가 Academie de la grande Chaumiere에서 조각을 공부하였다. 1931~34년 예일대학에서 건축을 공부했다. 1940년에 찰스 임스와의 공동 작업으로 MOMA가 주최한 '유기적 가구' 공모전에서 수상하였다. 사리넨의 전후 작품으로는 유명한 플라스틱 의자 '웜(Womb, 1946)'과 플라스틱 좌석과 알루미늄 촛대 받침을 지닌, '튤립(Tulip, 1957)'이라는 의자가 있다.

William Sawaya
윌리엄 사와야
Born in 1948, Lebanon

He graduated in 1973 from the national academy of fine arts of Beirut. Particularly interested to the definition of internal spaces, he extends his professional activity to France, Italy, Greece, Japan and the USA. In Paris and Milan he studied and experienced in the field of furniture design which he considers an important part of a coherent project in living culture. He joins various personal and collective art and design exhibitions. Occasionally he also designs for other companies like Swissair, the FIFA, the Museo Bagatti Valsecchi, Heller.

윌리엄 사와야는 1973년 베이룻 국립 아카데미에서 순수 미술을 전공으로 졸업하였다. 그는 특히 내부 공간에 관심을 가졌으며, 프랑스, 이탈리아, 그리스, 일본, 그리고 미국에 이르기까지 활동의 폭을 넓혔다. 파리와 밀라노에서 공부하며 가구 디자인이 생활에서 중요한 부분임을 느꼈으며 이후

다양한 디자인 전시에 참여한다. 그는 '스위스항공', '헬러' 등과 같은 회사를 위해 디자인을 하기도 한다.

Afra & Tobia Scrapa
아프라 & 토비아 스카파
Afra Scarpa Born in 1937, Italy
Tobia Scarpa Born in 1935, Italy

Afra Bianchin was born in Montebelluna in 1937 and Tobia Scarpa in Venice in 1935. Both were influenced by Tobia's father Carlo Scarpa, particularly his interest in the technical properties and aesthetic possibilities of materials. After graduating in architecture in 1958 they began working together with Venini in Murano. In 1960 they collaborated with Cassina where they designed furniture exclusively for the home including the Soriana armchair which won the Compasso d'Oro award in 1970, and the 925 armchair which is part of the permanent collection at MoMA in New York. In 1960 they joined Flos and worked as designers with the Castiglioni's. Their best known pieces for B&B Italia are the Coronado and the Erasmo, and for Maxalto they designed a whole collection of very fine furniture including the Torcello system which is still available today.

토비아 스카파는 카를로 스카파의 아들로 고향 베네치아에서 건축을 공부했고 그 후 1961년까지 베니니 유리공장에서 디자이너로 일 했다. 부인 아프라와 동업한 이래 B&B 이탈리아, 카시나, 놀, 그리고 플로스를 클라이언트로 둔 프리랜서 디자이너로 일하였고, 스카르파 부부는 카시나를 위해 만든 시라나(Sirana,1968) 의자처럼 부드러운 형태의 가구로 잘 알려져 있다.

Jerszy Seymour
저지 시모어
Born in 1968, Berlin

Jerszy Seymour grew up in London, where he studied engineering at South Bank Polytechnic 1987 -1990 and industrial design at the Royal College of Art 1991 – 1993. His work has been exhibited in the Design Museum in London, the Vitra Design Museum in Basel and Berlin, the Palais De Tokyo in Paris and Gallery Kreo in Paris. His work is held in the permanent collections of the Museum of Modern Art, New York, the 'Fonds National de Art Contemporain' France and the 'Musee d'Art Grand-Duc Jean' Luxembourg. In 2005 he was guest

of honour at Design Brussels where he created the Brussels Brain installation. In 2007 the project Living Systems was part of the "My Home" exhibition at the Vitra Design Museum in Weil am Rhein. In 2008 he realized the installation "First Supper" for the MAK in Vienna.

저지 시모어는 베를린에서 태어나 런던에서 자라난, 캐나다인 디자이너로, 사우스뱅크 폴리텍 대학에서 엔지니어링을, 왕립예술대학에서 산업디자인을 공부했다. 그는 런던 디자인 박물관, 베를린과 바젤의 가구 디자인 박물관, 파리의 팔레 드 도쿄, 크레오 갤러리에서 작품전을 하였고, 뉴욕 현대 미술관과 '프랑스 현대 미술관, 룩셈부르크 국립 역사미술박물관에 영구 소장되어 있다.

Shin, Ji Hun
신지훈
Born in 1985, Korea

학력
국민대학교 실내디자인과

단체전
2011 SHOP BMM season2, Bmm 갤러리, 서울, 한국
2010 서울디자인페스티발, 코엑스전시관, 서울, 한국
이때다, 이앙갤러리, 서울, 한국
1%프로젝트, BMH 갤러리, 서울, 한국

Education
Kookmin University Interior Design

Selected Group Exhibitions
2011 SHOP BMM season2, Bmm Gallery, Seoul, Korea
2010 Seoul Design Festival, COEX, Seoul, Korea
Etteda, Iang Gallery, Seoul, Korea
1% Project, BMHGallery, Seoul, Korea

Ettore Sottsass
에토레 소트사스
Born in 1917, Austria
Died in 2007, Italy

1929 Family moves to Turin so Ettore Jr. can study architecture there.
1936 Travels to Paris on his own with very little money. Stays in a flophouse near Gare du Lyon and survives on two cans of preserved fruit in three days.
1939 Graduates in architecture from Turin University only to be called up into the Italian army. Spends most of World War II in

a concentration camp.

1945 Returns home to work for his father. Moves to Milan in 1946 to curate a craft exhibition at the Triennale and starts contributing to Domus magazine. Sets up his own architectural and industrial design practice.

1956 Travels to New York to work in George Nelson's studio for a month. Back in Italy, he is invited to design furniture for Polotronova, near Florence.

1958 Appointed as design consultant to Olivetti's new electronics division.

1959 Launch of Elea 9003 calculator. Works on Tekne electronic typewriter.

1961 Travels to India for three months, but is hospitalised in Milan with a mystery ailment. Roberto Olivetti sends him for treatment in the US.

1965 Designs pop-influenced "totem" ceramics and the first "superbox" closets coated in stripey plastic laminate. Sottsass describes them as "crazy things".

1967 Co-founds the Planeta Fresco literary magazine with Allen Ginsberg.

1970 Valentine typewriter wins the Compasso d'Oro. Sottsass art directs an ad campaign featuring the Valentine being held by people all over the world.

1972 Participates in Italy: The New Domestic Landscape at MoMA, New York.

1973 Founds Global Tools design school with Archizoom and Superstudio.

1978 Collaborates with Alessandro Mendini and Andrea Branzi on Studio Alchymia's exhibition of 'new design' furniture at Milan Furniture Fair.

1980 Having left Alchymia, he forms a new design collective, Memphis.

1981 Over 2,000 people flood into the opening party for the first Memphis exhibition in Milan. Sottsass Associati is also founded that year.

1985 Announces that he has left Memphis. Returns to architecture at Sottsass Associati where he completes numerous industrial design projects too.

2000 Sottsass Associati designs new Milan airport, Malpensa 2000.

2001 The Memphis revival begins with the opening of Memphis Remembered at the Design Museum.

2007 Ettore Sottsass: Work in Progress exhibits at the Design Museum

2007 Ettore Sottsass dies in Milan
© Design Museum

Philippe Starck
필립 스탁
Born in 1949, France

Philippe Patrick Starck is a French product designer and probably the best known designer in the New Design style. His designs range from interior designs to mass produced consumer goods such as toothbrushes, chairs, and even houses. He was educated in Paris at the École Camondo and in 1968, he founded his first design firm, which specialized in inflatable objects. In 1969, he became art director of his firm along with Pierre Cardin. Starck's career started to climb in earnest in 1982 when he designed the interior for the private apartments of the French President François Mitterrand. Starck has worked both independently as an interior designer and as a product designer since 1975. Most notably, in 2002, he created a number of what are considered relatively inexpensive product designs for the large American retailer Target Stores.

필립 스탁은 항공기 엔지니어인 아버지의 영향을 받아 어린 시절부터 물건을 분해하고 조립하여 새로운 것으로 만들어내는 일을 즐겼다. 스탁은 1960년대 중반 파리의 에콜 니심 드 카몽도(École Nissim de Camondo)에서 공부하였다. 1968년 19세라는 젊은 나이에 회사를 차려 공기를 넣어 부풀릴 수 있는 제품들을 생산하였고, 1969년에는 피에르 가르댕사의 아트디렉터가 되었다. 1976년 파리의 '라 맹 블뢰(La Main Bleu)' 나이트클럽과 1978년 '레 뱅 두슈(Les Bains Douches)' 나이트클럽의 실내를 장식해주면서 명성을 얻었다. 스탁은 1980년 독립전문회사인 '스탁 프로덕트(Starck Product)'를 설립하고 초기 디자인을 상품화하였다. 이후 1982년, 엘리제 궁 안에 있는 미테랑 대통령의 개인 사저의 인테리어 디자인을 맡게 되는데, 이를 계기로 그는 국제적인 명성을 얻게 된다. 그 뒤 그는 인테리어를 비롯한 건축, 가구, 생활 소품 등 모든 영역에 걸쳐 전 방위로 활동하면서 세계 최고의 디자이너 자리를 차지하게 된다. 레스토랑에서 오징어 요리를 먹다가 아이디어를 얻은 문제작 레몬즙 짜는 기구, '주시 살리프(Jucy Salif)'는 그의 대표작일 뿐 아니라 1990년대를 대표하는 디자인의 아이콘이 된다.

Gustav Stickley
구스타브 스티클리
Born in 1958, USA
Died in 1942, USA

Gustav Stickley was an American furniture maker, architect and publisher. Through his designs and articles, he became a leading advocate of the Arts and Crafts movement, which flourished in the United States around the turn of the 20th century. Stickley's company manufactured furniture, metalwork and textiles from 1900 to 1916. Although Stickley called his style Craftsman, it's also often referred to as Mission or Mission Oak. The word "mission" refers to the California Spanish missions - one of Stickley's design influences - but it also reflects one of Stickley's core values: that all furniture fulfill a purpose, or mission.

구스타브 스티클리는 미국의 가구제작자이자 건축가이며 출판업자이다. 그는 디자인을 통해 19세기 말 20세기 초 미국에 성행한 미술공예운동(또는 장인운동)에 앞장섰다. 스티클리가 설립한 회사는 1900년부터 1916년까지 가구, 금속공예, 섬유제품을 만들어왔다. 스티클리 스스로 본인의 작업 방식을 장인스타일로 명명하였지만, 그의 작업 방법은 미션스타일 또는 미션오크 스타일로도 불린다. "미션"이라는 단어는 스티클리가 많은 영향을 받았던 캘리포니아의 스페인 선교단체를 의미하는 한편 스티클리의 핵심 가치를 반영한다. 모든 가구는 고유의 목적 또는 임무를 충족시켜야 한다는 것이 그의 주된 생각이다.

Michael Thonet
미하엘 토네트
Born in 1796, Germany
Died in 1871, Austria

Austrian furniture-maker of German birth. Around 1830 he began to develop the bentwood technique (long, narrow veneers glued together) to make Biedermeier chairs in Boppard; his new technique made it easier and cheaper to produce bold designs. In 1842 Thonet presented his furniture to the Niederösterreichische Kunstgewerbeverein and received a licence authorizing him to practise in Vienna. From that time he and his sons, Franz(1820–98), Michael(1824–1902),

August(1829–1910), Josef(1830–87) and Jakob(1841–1929), began to produce cheap furniture in the workshop of the Viennese master joiner Clemens List.

독일 출신의 오스트리아의 목재 기술자로 가구 디자이너. 보스파르트에서 출생, 빈에서 사망하였다. 오랜 연구 결과 나무에 증기를 가해 구부리는 기술을 개발, 단순 명쾌한 의자를 만들었다. 1841년 프랑스, 독일에서, 42년 빈에서 특허를 받고, 1856년 오스트리아의 시민권을 받았다. 파리 박람회(1855), 런던 박람회(1862)에서 최고상을 수상하였으며 근대 디자인 운동은 토네트의 의자에서 유래된 부분이 있으니, 그 정도로 영향력 있는 디자이너였다.

Hiroshi Tsunoda
히로시 츠노다
Born in 1974, Japan

Barcelona-based Japanese designer Hiroshi Tsunoda, a graduate of the Rhode Island School of Design, heads Hiroshi Tsunoda Design Studio, a studio focused on bringing practical, functional and memorable designs within the reach of everyday customers. His recent works have been showcased at the Salone Satellite in Milan and at design festival, Designersblock in London. Hiroshi specializes in developing projects with a focus on aesthetics, practicality and ecology. Hiroshi Tsunoda Design Studio is known for exploring the possibilities of geometric figures, reflected in Hiroshi's work with The Fire Company, and for its aim to bring sensational new designs to the general public.

히로시 츠노다는 미국 로드아일랜드디자인스쿨을 졸업하였으며, 본인의 이름을 딴 히로시 츠노다 디자인 스튜디오의 대표이기도 하다. 그의 디자인 스튜디오는 일상 속에 널리 쓰일 수 있는 실용적이고 기능적이며 인상적인 디자인에 주안점을 두고 있다. 그의 최근작은 밀라노 가구박람회의 살롱 사텔리테 신인상전, 디자인페스티벌, 런던 디자이너스 블록에서 선보인바 있다. 히로시는 특히 심미성, 실용성, 친환경성을 충족시키는 작업으로 높은 평가를 받는다. 히로시 츠노다 디자인스튜디오는 기하학적 구조의 가능성을 탐색하며, 일반 대중들에게 감각적으로 소구할 수 있는 새로운 디자인을 만들어내고자 한다.

Marcel Wanders
마르셀 반더스
Born in 1963, Netherlands

Education
1988 Hogeschool voor de Kunsten, Arnhem, the Netherlands
1985 Academie voor Schone kunsten, Hasselt ,Belgium
1982 Academie voor Industriele Vormgeving, Eindhoven, Netherlands

Selected Solo Exhibitions
2010 'Daydreams, Philadelphia Museum of Art USA, Pennsylvania, USA
2007 'Personal Editions', Salone del Mobile, Milan, Italy
1999 'Wanders Wonders: Design for a New Age', Stedelijk Museum sHertogenbosch, NL

Selected Group Exhibitions
2009 Telling Tales: Fantasy and Fear in Contemporary Design,V&A Museum, London, UK
European Design Since 1985:Shaping the New Century,Indianapolis Museum of Art, Indianapolis, USA
2008 Figuration in Contemporary Design, The Art Institute of Chicago, Chicago, USA

Collections
MOMA, New York, USA
SFMOMA, California, USA
V&A, London, UK
The Art Institute of Chicago, Illinois,USA
Stedelijk Museum, Amsterdam, NL

Hans J. Wegner
한스 J. 베그너
Born in 1914, Denmark
Died in 2007

Hans J Wegner trained as a cabinet-maker before attending the Copenhagen School of Arts and Crafts, where he later lectured from 1946 to 1953. From 1938 to 1942, he worked as a furniture designer in Arne Jacobsen and Erik Møller's architectural practice. In 1943, he set up his own office in Gentofte and collaborated with Borge Mogensen in the design of an apartment shown at Copenhagen in 1946. Throughout his long career, he has designed furniture extensively for Johannes Hansen and Fritz Hansen. The Royal Society of Arts, London made him an Honorary Royal Designers for Industry in 1959.

코펜하겐에서 가구 제작자로 훈련을 받았고(1927-1931) 그곳의 미술공예학교에서 1936년부터 38까지 가구 디자인을 공부

했다. 그 후 아르네 야콥센의 사무실에서 근무했다. 1940년대 말부터 전후 덴마크의 국제적 명성을 세우는 데 기여한 가구 제조업자 요하네스 한센을 위해 의자 시리즈를 디자인했다. 그의 디자인의 특징은 세부에 대한 주목, 구조적 복잡성, 물리적 • 시각적 가벼움, 우아함, 그리고 주로 자연 재료를 사용하여 만들어졌다는 사실에 있다.

Woo, Gi Ha
우기하
Born in 1979, Korea
Lives and Works in Seoul, Korea, Germany, UK

학력
2005 한양대학교 산업디자인과 졸업, 안산, 한국

개인전
2011 <Ugly Duckling-the wrong objects project 2>, 상상마당 디자인스퀘어, 서울, 한국

단체전
2011 <Front & Back>, <Bent Hands> SHOP BMM Season1, 부띠끄 모나코, 서울, 한국
2010 <The Wrong Objects>, DMY Berlin 2010, 베를린, 독일
2007 <Maven SORA>대덕 연구프로젝트 성과보고 전시, 대전, 한국
2005 <Giorgio Armani Coupe> 한양대학교 졸업작품 전시회, 서울, 한국
2004 <Nari> 서울 브랜드 캐릭터쇼, 서울, 한국
<Vehicle> Industrial Design Membership 정기전, 안산, 한국

Education
2005 Hanyang University Industrial Design, BA,, Ansan, Korea

Selected Solo Exhibitions
2011 <Ugly Duckling> Sangsang madang Design square, Seoul, Korea

Selected Group Exhibitions
2011 <Front&Back>, <Bent Hands>Shop BMM Season1, Seoul, Korea
2010 <The Wrong Objects>DMY International Design Festival, Berlin, Germany
2005 <Armani Luxury Coupe > Hanyang Univ. Graduated Exhibition, Seoul, Korea
2004 <Nari> Seoul Brand Character Show, Seoul, Korea
<Vehicle> Industrial Design Membership Regular Exhibition, Ansan, Korea

Frank Lloyd Wright

프랭크 로이드 라이트

Born in 1867, USA
Died in 1959, USA

1886 Enters the School of Civil Engineering at University of Wisconsin at Madison.

1887 Abandons his studies in Madison for Chicago and finds employment at the architectural office of Joseph Lyman Silsbee.

1888 Wright finds works with the progressive architects' Adler and Sullivan.

1889 After marrying Catherine Lee Tobin and Wright starts building work on their home at Oak Park, Illinois.

1891 The first of Wright's seven children, Frank Lloyd Wright, Jr is born.

1893 Opens his own architectural practice.

1897 Moves his office to Steinway Hall, Chicago and builds drafting studio connected to his Oak Park home.

1900 Designs the Hillside Home School, Spring Green, Wisconsin for his two aunts.

1902 Completes the design of the Susan Lawrence Dana House in Springfield, Illinois and Larking Company headquarters in Buffalo, New York.

1905 Travels to Japan with his wife, Catherine and clients Mr and Mrs Ward W. Willits. Designs the Unity Temple in Oak Park.

1908 Construction begins on Frederick C. Robie house, Chicago Illinois

1909 After falling in love with Mamah Borthwich Cheney, Wright travels to Europe with her after signed architectural practice over to Herman von Holst.

1911 Returns to US and draws plans for a cottage for his mother near Spring Green, Wisconsin. She transfers the property and building over to Wright and he renames it Taliesin.

1913 Sails for Japan with Mamah Cheney in pursuit of the Imperial Hotel commission in Tokyo.

1914 Mamah Cheney, her two children and four others are murdered by a servant Julian Charleton at Taliesin who then sets fire to the property.

1915 Wright rebuilds Taliesin and Miriam Noel moves in.

1916 Sails for Japan to work on the Imperial Hotel with Miriam Noel and his son John.

1917 Returns to Taliesin. Designs the Hollyhock House for Aline Barnsdall in Los Angeles.

1919 Construction begins on the Imperial Hotel.

1923 Death of Anna Lloyd Jones Wright. The Great Kanto Earthequake, demolishes most of Tokyo but the Imperial Hotel survives with minor damage. Wright marries Miriam Noel. Completes the design of the Charles Ennis House in Los Angeles.

1924 Miriam Noel leaves Wright and he meets Olgivanna Lazovich Hinzenberg.

1925 Olgivanna Hinzenberg moves to Taliesin with her daughter Svetlana. A fire destroys the residential block of Taliesin but the adjacent studio, vault and workrooms are spared. Reconstruction begins immediately. Miriam Noel files for divorce. Birth of Iovanna Lloyd Wright.

1926 Moves to Minnesota. Wright and Oligivanna arrested under the Mann Act charges, which are dropped in 1927. Wright starts to write his autobiography.

1928 Wright marries Olgivanna Lazovich Hinzenberg at Rancho Sante Fe, California

1932 Publication of Wright's An Autobiography. He and Olgivanna found the Taliesin Fellowship architectural schools.

1935 Builds the Fallingwater Bear Run house in Pennsylvania.

1936 Commissioned to design the offices of S.C. Johnson & Son Company at Racine, Wisconsin

1938 Purchases property on Maricopa Mesa, Phoenix and with the Taliesin Fellowship begins construction of winter home, Taliesin West.

1940 Exhibition of Wright's work at the Museum of Modern Art, New York

1943 Commissioned to design the Solomon R. Guggenheim Museum in New York and a Research Tower for the S.C. Johnson & Son Company

1950 Designs the David Wright House in Phoenix, Arizona and the Woodside, Richard Davis house in Marion, Indianna

1953 Completes the design of the Beth Sholom Synagogue at Elkins Park, Pennsylvania

1958 Builds the Pilgrim Congregational Church at Redding California

1959 Design the Norman Lykes House, Phoenix, Arizona. Frank Lloyd Wright dies in Phoenix, Arizona.

© Design Museum

Floris Wubben
플로리스 부븐

Born in 1983, Netherlands

Education

2007-2008 Bachelor degree, department furniture design, KHM Mechelen, Belgium

2004-2007 Bachelor degree, department interior design, KHM Mechelen, Belgium

Selected Solo Exhibitions

2011 Van segeren gallery, Breda, Netherlands

2010 Dutch Design Week, Eindhoven, Netherlands Route Window, Eindhoven, Netherlands

2009 Dutch Design Week, Eindhoven, Netherlands

Selected Group Exhibitions

2011 Designsalon, Amsterdam, Netherlands Tutto Bene, Milan, Italy

2010 Liberation of light, Eindhoven, Netherlands Dutch Design Week, Eindhoven, Netherlands Interieur08, Kortrijk, Belgium Hidden Heroes, Milan, Italy Designbazaar, Eindhoven, Netherlands EAH shop, Amsterdam, Netherlands

2009 Dutch Design Week, Eindhoven, Netherlands

2008 Portfolio, Kortrijk, Belgium Interieur08, Kortrijk, Belgium Design Brussels, Table talks, Brussels, Belgium

Collections

Anthropologie, New York, USA
Outdoorz, Paris, France
Gallery Tallulah, Milan, Italy

Utopia now!, Köln, Germany

Richard Young
리차드 영
Born in UK

Richard Young is a former Royal College of Art student who later studied at the Royal Art Academy Copenhagen under Professor Ole Wanscher. He founded the British high-end furniture manufacture Merrow Associates. Young trained as a cabinet maker and materials listed high in his design priorities. Young combined his own, British, design with a strong respect for materials as influenced by the Scandinavians.

리차드 영은 영국왕립예술학교에서 수학한 후 코펜하겐의 왕립예술학교 들어가 올벤셔교수 밑에서 공부하였다. 그는 영국 고급 가구 제조사인 메로우 어소시에이트(Merrow Associates)을 설립하였다. 영은 캐비닛 제작자로서 교육을 받았고 그의 디자인에 있어 재료는 매우 중요한 부분을 차지한다. 영은 스칸디나비아 디자인이 갖는 강한 재료성에 영향을 받았으며 이를 바탕으로 자신만의 디자인 양식을 만들어냈다.

Yu, Kwang Soo
유광수
Born in 1980, Korea

학력
2011 홍익대학교 일반대학원 목조형가구 전공, 서울, 한국
2009 홍익대학교 미술다학 목조형가구학과 졸업, 서울, 한국

단체전
2011 부띠크 모나코 뮤지엄, COEX, 서울, 한국
서울 리빙 디자인페어, COEX, 서울, 한국
2010 DMY Berlin, Tempelhofer airport, 베를린, 독일
서울 리빙 디자인페어, COEX, 서울, 한국
2009 서울 디자인페스티벌, COEX, 서울, 한국
12 Prototypes, 덕원 갤러리, 서울, 한국
2008 Art at Home "Wonderful Life", 두산 아트센터, 서울, 한국
Seoul living design fair, COEX, SEOUL, KOREA

Education
2011 Master's Course in Hongik University, Seoul, Korea
2009 Hongik UNIV woodworking & furniture Design, B.F.A

Selected Solo Exhibitions

2010 PAIK HAEYOUMG GALLY, SEOUL, KOREA

Selected Group Exhibitions
2011 Boutique Monaco Museum, COEX, Seoul, Korea
Seoul living design fair, COEX, Seoul, Korea
2010 DMY Berlin, Tempelhofer airport, Berlin, Germany
Seoul living design fair, COEX, Seoul, Korea
2009 Seoul design festival, COEX, Seoul, Korea
12 Prototypes, Dukwon Gallery, Seoul, Korea
2008 Art at Home "Wonderful Life", Doosan Atr Center, Seoul, Korea
Seoul living design fair, COEX, SEOUL, KOREA

Index
찾아보기

Organization
조직

2011 청주국제공예비엔날레조직위원회 2011 Cheongju International Craft Biennale Organizing Committee

조직위원장	한범덕	Chairman	Han, Beum Deuk
부위원장	곽임근	Vice Chairman	Kwak, Im Guen
사무총장	김동관	Secretary General	Kim, Dong Gwan
총감독	정준모	Director	Chung, Joon Mo

운영위원회 Operation Committee

위원장	곽태영	Chairman	Kwak, Tae Young
운영위원	김내수	Members	Kim, Nae Soo
	김달진		Kim, Dal Jin
	김두영		Kim, Doo Young
	김정희		Kim, Jung Hee
	김현태		Kim, Hyun Tae
고	남상재		The Late Nam, Sang Jae
	노준의		No, Joon Eui
	박경순		Park, Keung Soon
	박제덕		Park, Jae Duek
	백 은		Back, Eun
	서진환		Seo, Jin Hwan
	손순옥		Son, Soon Ock
	신랑호		Shin, Rang Ho
	이규남		Lee, Gyu Nam
	차영순		Cha, Young Soon
	최영근		Choi, Young Keun
	편종필		Pyeon, Chong Pil

전시부 Exhibition Department

전시/학술총괄	박남희	Chief Curator	Park, Nam Hee
본전시	김윤애	Associate Curator	Kim, Youn Ae
	이성용	Associate Curator	Yi, Sung Yong
	정득순	Associate Curator	Chung, Duk Soon
특별전	윤효진	Associate Curator	Yoon, Hyo Jin
초대국가전	도화진	Coordinator	Do, Hwa Jin
공모전	남지선	Coodinator	Nam, Ji Sun
	이재선	Assistant Coodinator	Lee, Jae Sun
페어	안승현	Coordinator	An, Seung Hyun
	김유경	Assistant Coodinator	Kim, Yu Kyeong

기획홍보부 Planning & PR Department

부장	변광섭	General Manager	Byeun, Gwang Sub
기획/시설팀장	박원규	Planning/Facilities Manager	Park, Won Kyu
기획	곽노현	Planning	Kwak, No Hyun
	정민용		Jung, Min Young
시설	심동섭	Facilities	Sim, Dong Seop
디렉터	장백순	Director	Jang, Back Soon
	손순옥		Son, Soon Ock
	이영송		Lee, Young Song
홍보팀장	박지은	PR Manager	Park, Ji Eun
	한기선	PR	Han, Ki Sun
	김지윤		Kim, Ji Yun
	황은아		Hwang, Eun A

관리운영부 Administration Operating Department

부장	유향걸	General Manager	Yoo, Hyang Keol
총무/운영팀장	윤기영	Affairs/Administer Manager	Yoon, Ki Young
총무	송화옥	Affairs	Song, Hwa Ok
	심소영		Sim, So Young
운영	박건주	Administer	Park, Gun Joo
	조필성		Cho, Pil Sung
	김시은		Kim, Si Eun
사업팀장	백인석	Business Manager	Baek, In Seok
사업	윤민석	Business	Yun, Min Seok
	김규식		Kim, Kyu Sik
의전팀장	김인환	Protocol Manager	Kim, In Hwan
의전	김수연	Protocol	Kim, Soo Yeun
	김현미		Kim, Hyun Mee
	김보경		Kim, Bo Kyung
	강앙미		Kang, Ang Mi
	강안나		Kang, Ang Na